Supply Chain Transformation Through Generative AI and Machine Learning

Ehap Sabri
University of Texas at Dallas, USA

IGI Global
Scientific Publishing
Publishing Tomorrow's Research Today

Vice President of Editorial Melissa Wagner
Managing Editor of Acquisitions Mikaela Felty
Managing Editor of Book Development Jocelynn Hessler
Production Manager Mike Brehm
Cover Design Phillip Shickler

Published in the United States of America by
IGI Global Scientific Publishing
701 East Chocolate Avenue
Hershey, PA, 17033, USA
Tel: 717-533-8845
Fax: 717-533-8661
Website: https://www.igi-global.com E-mail: cust@igi-global.com

Library of Congress Cataloging-in-Publication Data

Names: Sabri, Ehap H., 1967- editor.
Title: Supply chain transformation through generative AI and machine learning / edited by Ehap Sabri.
Description: Hershey, PA : IGI Global Scientific Publishing, [2025] | Includes bibliographical references and index. | Summary: "This book is meticulously crafted to serve as a pivotal resource in the rapidly evolving domain of digital supply chain management. It synthesizes the latest best practices and cutting-edge research in digital supply chain enablement, offering business professionals an indispensable guide to navigate and excel in supply chain business transformation initiatives"-- Provided by publisher.
Identifiers: LCCN 2024053567 (print) | LCCN 2024053568 (ebook) | ISBN 9798369344330 (hardcover) | ISBN 9798369344378 (paperback) | ISBN 9798369344347 (ebook)
Subjects: LCSH: Supply chain management--Data processing. | Supply chain management--Technological innovations.
Classification: LCC HD38.6 .S88 2025 (print) | LCC HD38.6 (ebook) | DDC 658.500285--dc23/eng/20250115
LC record available at https://lccn.loc.gov/2024053567
LC ebook record available at https://lccn.loc.gov/2024053568

British Cataloguing in Publication Data
A Cataloguing in Publication record for this book is available from the British Library.

Editorial Advisory Board

Table of Contents

Detailed Table of Contents

data to pinpoint vulnerabilities, assess risks, and craft strategies to make fashion's supply chains more adaptable and recovery-swift in the face of surprises. This data-driven approach involves gathering and monitoring data, meticulously assessing risks, using predictive analytics to anticipate future challenges, and crafting both scenario planning and contingency plans. Additionally, it optimizes supply chain networks for efficiency. By proactively identifying and mitigating risks, fashion companies can ensure smooth production, distribution, and customer satisfaction. This translates to better operational efficiency, responsiveness to customer demands, and the ability to consistently deliver high-quality products. Ultimately, supply chain resilience analytics empowers fashion companies to navigate uncertainties with greater ease and build a robust and resilient supply chain ecosystem.

Section 2
Key Strategies for Successful Gen AI/ML-Driven Supply Chain Transformations

Transforming the supply chain using best practices and the latest digital technologies is no longer optional; it is a strategic mandate for staying relevant. However, 70% of all transformation initiatives fail. The low success rates of transformation make firms reconsider moving forward with transformation journeys. These firms have doubts about integrating digital technologies like ML and Gen AI into supply chain operations and often postpone efforts until experts address their challenges. This chapter provides the top seven challenges and explains how to address them during supply chain digital transformation programs. Additionally, it offers a practical change management framework to ensure smooth digital supply chain transformations. This framework includes eight steps (phases) needed to implement change in the organizational culture and five success factors to maintain throughout the change lifecycle. These five factors can serve as a checklist to evaluate an organization's readiness for change and its chances of a successful digital transformation.

In response to the dramatic changes in the business landscape over the past few years, companies are assessing whether they have the right supply chains to support their dynamic and digital business and exploring supply chain segmentation to reduce complexity and increase profit. Today's supply chains have become increasingly complex due to globalization, outsourcing, complicated networks, logistics capacity uncertainty and volatility, and the rapid proliferation of stocking keeping units (SKUs) and product configurations. However, many companies continue to use an outdated approach to supply chain segmentation This chapter explains the concept of segmentation, its historical background, its importance for today's business, and challenges to implementation. The chapter also provides an end-to-end supply chain practical segmentation framework. Companies can utilize this to ensure a smooth and successful implementation journey leveraging digital technologies like ML and Gen AI. Several client examples will be discussed to illustrate the "fast track to success" framework.

In today's rapidly evolving business landscape, organizations must embrace digital-driven supply chain planning transformations leveraging GEN AI/ML technologies to maintain their competitive edge. This chapter explores the potential value embedded in these transformations and provides insights into achieving and maximizing this value. It offers a proven, comprehensive performance measurement and value realization framework, illustrated by a case study and two success stories. Firms can leverage this framework to achieve value from their digital transformation efforts.

One of the important sectors that need to keep up with digital transformation quickly is healthcare. Given its direct impact on human lives, it is crucial to conduct studies to improve service quality in this sector. Considering the effects of the lean management approach in the healthcare sector on digital transformation in the supply chain is the first important research question for this study. Another research question is the contribution of artificial intelligence (AI) and machine learning (ML) approaches developed in recent years to digital transformation in the healthcare sector. The necessity of digital transformation tools, including artificial intelligence and machine learning, in healthcare services and the challenges faced during their implementation were identified as criteria and a weighting analysis was conducted with the help of multi-criteria decision-making (MCDM) analysis. Step-Wise Weight Assessment Ratio Analysis (SWARA) was used to determine the importance weights of the

in large enterprises, we also discuss the opportunities and benefits for small and medium-sized enterprises (SMEs), including practical strategies for incremental AI adoption and subscription-based tools. The chapter analyzes the key challenges and opportunities associated with AI/ML adoption, delves into ethical considerations and sustainability implications, and provides practical strategies for logistics and supply chain leaders to successfully integrate these technologies into their operations, ultimately boosting their bottom line.

The application of AI in the demand-driven supply chain is changing significantly the way businesses forecast their demand and manage their inventory. In the same context of the book, which emphasizes the transformative potential of generative AI and ML in supply chains, this chapter explores how these technologies revolutionize supply chain management and presents the impacts of these technologies in DDSC.The aim of this chapter is to explore, through a literature review, how AI is transforming supply chain management by using particularly ML, and to analyze the current state of their applications in demand driven supply chain, highlighting the key algorithms used, their practical implementations, and the benefits and challenges associated with their adoption. This chapter reveals that AI and ML significantly enhance forecasting accuracy, optimize inventory management, improve decision-making and operational efficiency. It also emphasizes key ML algorithms such as regression approaches and time series in predicting more accurate forecasts from historical data analysis.

Personalization, Customization, increased transparency, sustainability, last mile tracking of shipments, etc. are some of the many features which customers are demanding, which is increasing the competition in global supply chains considerably. Additionally, the increase all product categories and the increase in product categories are also significantly to costs and risks. To meet today's supply chain challenges, businesses are embarking on digital transformation to these challenges. These chapter aims at embarking on deployment of Smart factory technologies which combine capabilities in industrial internet of things (IIoT), cloud and edge computing, robotic process automation (RPA), artificial intelligence (AI), machine learning and computer vision systems. Hence there is a huge opportunity where these technologies can potentially reinvent supply chains as customer centric, service oriented, self-learning, intelligent and agile, and, in so doing, improve customer experiences and increase margins. For organizations, providing a compelling customer experience is paramount to ensure market leadership across sectors.

Businesses use AI to manage and optimize supply chain activities—such as monitoring product quality, balancing inventory levels, and identifying fuel-efficient delivery routes—with more efficiency than traditional software. Artificial intelligence(AI) is a general term for applications that simulate human intelligence and perform complex tasks. Its subfields include machine learning(ML), in which systems learn from consuming vast amounts of data rather than being programmed with step-by-step instructions. These learning process, AI systems can outperform traditional software in functions such as deciphering information from video feeds, interpreting spoken and written text, predicting future market behavior, making decisions in complex scenarios, and surfacing insights buried in large data sets. These kinds of capabilities are proving extremely useful in managing and optimizing workflows across almost every leg of the supply chain. These Chapters aims to Objectified the supply chain systems powered by AI/ML algorithms can discover patterns and relationships within data sets.

This chapter examines the paradigm shift in supply chain forecasting brought about by generative AI and machine learning technologies. Through real-world examples and case studies, the proposed chapter explores how these technologies enhance forecast accuracy, streamline operations, and drive cost efficiency. The

Preface

BACKGROUND

In the wake of dramatic shifts in the global business landscape, beginning with the COVID-19 pandemic and continuing through the Ukraine war, global inflation and the position of the new US administration on tariffs, companies across industries are undertaking business transformation programs to stabilize and enhance their supply chain processes. The complexity of supply chain management has been a hot topic for years, but the pandemic exposed vulnerabilities that reinforced the need for lean and agile systems. Today, the integration of digital technologies such as Generative AI, Machine Learning (ML) offers businesses the tools to navigate disruptions, improve operational efficiency, and gain a competitive edge.

Supply chains have traditionally been composed of discreet, siloed steps, from marketing to product development, planning, procurement, production and customer fulfillment. Digitization removes these barriers, creating an integrated ecosystem that is transparent to all stakeholders—suppliers, manufacturers, and customers alike. A fully digital supply chain integrates planning, execution systems, intelligent logistics, visibility tools, and advanced analytics, enabling companies to anticipate and mitigate disruptions in real-time. Leveraging technologies such as Generative AI, ML tools, businesses can achieve leaner, more agile operations that deliver superior service and outcomes.

However, adopting a digital supply chain ecosystem requires more than just gathering technologies. Success depends on a comprehensive strategy encompassing process redesign, technological deployment, governance, talent development, and cultural transformation. A flexible roadmap aligned with corporate goals, quick-win initiatives, and measurable performance indicators are essential for creating and maintaining momentum. Equally critical is a robust change management strategy to address organizational resistance, data governance issues, and skills gaps. Collaboration with stakeholders across the supply chain is key to building an integrated and efficient network.

The transformative power of AI and ML in supply chain management is undeniable. According to the "2024 Gartner Digital Business Impact on Supply Chain" study, AI has emerged as the top technology priority for 2024 by a significant margin. Furthermore, the "2023 Gartner Supply Chain Technology User Wants and Needs" survey revealed that over 75% of participants stated that AI, advanced analytics, and simulations are either being deployed or undergoing proof-of-concept (POC) implementation.

Industry statistics highlight rapid adoption, with the AI supply chain market projected to reach $21.8 billion by 2027, growing at a compound annual rate of 45.3%. Early adopters of these technologies report significant benefits, including increase forecast accuracy, reduced logistics costs and improved service levels. Despite these gains, digital transformation remains challenging: 70% of initiatives fail to meet their objectives due to integration complexities, organizational resistance, and insufficient skills and governance frameworks. To implement a successful digital supply chain ecosystem and avoid failure, companies must develop capabilities in the following areas:

- Processes: Redesign end-to-end supply chain processes, eliminating non-value-added activities.
- Technology: Develop a value-driven roadmap for deploying Gen AI/ML systems and analytics
- Governance: Establish frameworks for new business models and performance metrics and ensure strong executive engagement in addition to leverage effective change methodologies
- Organization and Culture: Shift from reactive problem-solving to proactive organization. Also, Foster collaboration internally and externally with suppliers and distributors.
- Talent Development: Build skills and partnerships to support new technologies.
- KPIs: Define metrics to measure progress and drive desired behaviors.

This book aims to bridge the gap between theory and practice in digital supply chain transformation. By synthesizing best practices, cutting-edge research, and industry insights, it provides actionable strategies for leveraging Generative AI, ML, and other digital technologies. Through case studies and practical frameworks, it equips readers to address challenges, optimize processes, and achieve measurable outcomes. This book is not just a guide but an inspiration for professionals to rethink supply chain processes, embrace innovation, and drive sustainable business growth.

Objectives of the Book

The primary objectives of this book are:

- To Educate: Provide a deep understanding of digital supply chain principles, focusing on the transformative roles of Generative AI and ML.
- To Guide: Offer actionable strategies for implementing effective digital transformation initiatives.
- To Innovate: Highlight emerging trends and showcase successful case studies to inspire creative approaches.
- To Address Challenges: Identify common obstacles and propose solutions to overcome them.
- To Inspire: Motivate decision-makers to reimagine traditional supply chain processes for greater efficiency and sustainability.

By achieving the above objectives, this book serves as an important resource for professionals navigating the complexities of business transformation in supply chains through Gen AI/ML.

Target Audience

The book caters to a diverse audience, including:

- Executives and Business Leaders: Insights into strategic aspects of AI and ML integration.
- Supply Chain and AI/ML Managers: Best practices for process optimization and change management.
- Graduate and MPA Students: Bridging academic research with real-world applications.
- AI/ML Developers and Data Scientists: Practical challenges and opportunities in applying technologies.
- Industry Analysts and Consultants: Trends and strategies for advising clients.
- Technology Enthusiasts and Innovators: Latest developments in AI and ML for supply chain management.

Structure of the Book

The chapters stand alone in covering their individual topics, but also form a cohesive overview of library-related professional development as it stands now along with future trends in the field. The book is divided into three sections:

- Overview and Impact of Generative AI and Machine Learning on Supply Chain (Chapters 1-6): Common understanding of Gen AI/ML and how it can improve supply chain management
- Key Strategies for Successful Gen AI/ML-Driven Supply Chain Transformations (Chapters 7-11): Enablers for digital transformation and building capabilities for sustainable change.
- Optimizing Supply Chain Planning Processes Leveraging Gen AI/ML Technologies (Chapters 12-18): Improving efficiency and effectiveness of supply chain processes

Each chapter combines practical insights with future trends, offering a comprehensive guide for supply chain professionals and researchers. The authors of each chapter followed the adage of "write what you know," having been personally involved in every topic they covered. After writing what they knew, the authors went beyond their experience to focus on future trends, assessments, and applicability to Gen AI/ML supply chain optimization and transformation. The result is a book that provides useful guidance to supply chain practitioners and researchers in the digital business world.

The book serves as a comprehensive guide to supply chain transformation through Generative AI and Machine Learning, addressing the challenges and opportunities of the modern business environment. Through practical strategies, case studies, and expert insights, it empowers readers to drive successful transformations and stay ahead in an increasingly dynamic industry.

ACKNOWLEDGMENTS

Gratitude is extended to the chapter authors, who contributed their expertise and perspectives. Thanks also to the Editorial Advisory Board for their invaluable support in reviewing and refining the content. This book would not have been possible without their efforts.

Acknowledgment

I would like to express my heartfelt gratitude to all the individuals who contributed to the success of this unique and timely project. A special thank you goes to the authors and reviewers who devoted their time and expertise to the review process. Without your dedication and collaborative spirit, this book would not have come to fruition.

To the authors, thank you for sharing your knowledge and insights. Your hard work and contributions have greatly enriched the depth and quality of this book. To the reviewers, your thoughtful feedback and meticulous attention to detail have significantly elevated the clarity, coherence, and presentation of each chapter, ensuring the highest standard for the final product.

On a personal note, I extend my deepest gratitude to my father, Hisham, whose unwavering support has been a cornerstone throughout my life's journey. To my wife, Sawsan, your boundless encouragement, patience, and love have been my anchor throughout all of my endeavors. To my two beloved daughters, Jana and Jude, you are my constant source of inspiration and joy, and I am endlessly grateful for your light in my life.

My sincere gratitude goes out to all of you.

Ehap Sabri
University of Texas at Dallas, USA

Section 1
Overview and Impact of Generative AI and Machine Learning on Supply Chain

Chapter 1
How Machine Learning and Generative AI Are Enabling the Autonomous Supply Chain

Hemant Chickermane
https://orcid.org/0009-0000-7961-9452
Blue Yonder Inc., USA

ABSTRACT

To achieve Resilience in their Value Chains, organizations are looking to drive greater speed in decision making, agility in responding to changes and cross-functional collaboration and move away from the siloed and linear processes that are common today. As organizations strive towards driving digitalization of their operations and processes, what started as exploration of ML and Gen AI in Supply Chain management, is now a reality and gaining adoption. As companies experience manpower and talent shortages, they are looking at ML and AI to drive greater automation and productivity improvements.This chapter will cover three primary areas in-depth with examples from the supply chain area: 1) What are Autonomous Supply Chains and why they are important 2) Applications of ML and Gen AI in Supply Chain Management, and how this is a key enabler to Autonomous Supply Chains 3) The Evolution of AI and ML powered by the rapid advancements in computing technology, and its supply chain and its geo-political implications

DOI: 10.4018/979-8-3693-4433-0.ch001

INTRODUCTION

If there is one key lesson businesses have learned over the past few years, it is that supply chains need to be much more resilient. But the answer doesn't lie in simply holding more inventory and building redundant capacity—both of which increase costs. To achieve Resilience in their Value Chains, organizations are looking to drive greater speed in decision making, agility in responding to changes and cross-functional collaboration and move away from the siloed, manual and sequential processes that are common today. Over the past two decades Supply chain management processes and systems have increased in sophistication to support all the Supply chain functions from order management, demand and supply planning, procurement, production scheduling, logistics and warehouse management. As organizations strive towards driving digitalization of their operations and processes, what started as exploration of ML and Gen AI in Supply Chain management, is now a reality and gaining adoption.

Advanced mathematical techniques such as time-series statistical forecasting, multi-echelon inventory optimization, heuristic and linear programming solvers for Master Production scheduling, genetic algorithms and simulated annealing for finite scheduling have been widely adopted by supply chain solution providers and corporations. As Supply chains have become increasingly globally dispersed and complex, placing greater demands on organizations to react to changes quickly, traditional mathematical techniques are no longer adequate. AI (Artificial Intelligence) and ML (Machine Learning) offer several advantages over traditional mathematical methods in supply chain management. Here are some key aspects where AI and ML can be considered superior or more advantageous:

Table 1. Comparing AI and ML applications to traditional methods of meeting Supply Chain management needs

Supply Chain Management Needs	Traditional Methods	AI and ML
Data Handling and Processing	Often rely on structured data and may not efficiently process large datasets or integrate multiple data types.	Capable of processing and analyzing large volumes of data from multiple sources, including structured and unstructured data. They can handle diverse datasets such as text, images, and sensor data, which traditional methods may struggle with
Adaptability and Learning	Typically static and require manual updates or re-modeling to adapt to changes, which can be time-consuming and less responsive to real-time changes	These systems can learn from historical data and continuously improve over time. They adapt to new patterns and changes in the supply chain environment, making them suitable for dynamic and evolving scenarios.
Complexity and Non-Linearity	Often rely on linear or simplified models, which may not fully capture the complexities of real-world supply chains	Excel at modeling complex, non-linear relationships in data, which are common in supply chain networks. They can capture intricate dependencies and interactions that traditional methods may oversimplify.
Predictive and Prescriptive Capabilities	Primarily focused on optimization within a defined set of constraints, with less emphasis on prediction	Offer strong predictive analytics capabilities, forecasting future trends, demands, and risks. They can also provide prescriptive insights by suggesting optimal actions based on predictions.
Real-Time Decision Making	May require significant computation time, making real-time decision-making challenging.	Can process data in real-time, enabling timely decision-making and rapid response to supply chain disruptions or changes
Pattern Recognition and Anomaly Detection	May not be as effective in identifying subtle patterns or anomalies without explicit modeling.	Particularly effective at recognizing patterns and detecting anomalies in data, which can help in identifying potential issues or opportunities in the supply chain.
Scalability and Flexibility	Scaling can be challenging, especially for complex problems, and may require significant computational resources	Easily scalable to accommodate growing data and business needs. They are flexible and can be customized to specific supply chain requirements
Integration with Emerging Technologies	While integration is possible, it may not be as seamless or dynamic as with AI/ML solutions.	Can seamlessly integrate with other advanced technologies like IoT, blockchain, and robotics, enhancing the overall efficiency and intelligence of supply chain operations.

While AI and ML offer these advantages, it's important to recognize that traditional mathematical methods still play a crucial role in supply chain management, particularly for well-defined problems with clear constraints. A hybrid approach that combines the strengths of AI/ML with traditional methods can often provide the most robust solutions. A big factor in the adoption on AI/ML has been the evolution of supporting technologies such as specialized ML processors, Cloud services providers providing libraries of ML models and Gen AI services, and Data warehouses capable of storing and moving vast amounts of data.

People, Process and Technology have always been the mantra behind business transformations. The human element has been crucial in Supply Chain management, where years of knowledge and experience have effectively integrated new technologies to improve processes. According to a survey from the Council of Supply Chain Management Professionals, 64% of companies are experiencing a supply chain talent gap. As companies experience manpower and talent shortages, they are looking at ML and AI to drive greater automation and productivity improvements.

This chapter will cover three primary areas in-depth with examples from today's Supply Chain management world:

1) What are Autonomous Supply Chains and why they are important
2) Applications of ML and Gen AI in Supply Chain Management, which will be the primary focus of this chapter
3) The Evolution of AI and ML powered by the rapid advancements in computing technology, and its supply chain and its geo-political implications

Autonomous Supply Chains

Before we discuss what constitutes an Autonomous Supply Chain, it is important to distinguish between definitions of Autonomous vs Automated systems. An autonomous system or machine can perform tasks or make decisions on its own, without human intervention. It can adapt to new situations, learn from experiences, and make decisions based on a wide range of inputs. The key feature of an Autonomous system is independence in decision-making and the ability to adapt to changing environments often using Artificial Intelligence.

An **autonomous Mobile robot** acts without recourse to human control. Examples include self-driving vacuums and self-driving cars.

An Automated system or machine performs tasks according to a set of predefined rules or programming. It does not make independent decisions but follows the instructions it has been given. The key feature of an Automated system is reliance on pre-programmed instructions, with limited or no ability to adapt to new situations.

To take an example, an **automated guided vehicle (AGV)** is a portable robot that follows along marked long lines or wires on the floor, or uses radio waves, vision cameras, magnets, or lasers for navigation. They are most often used in manufacturing applications to transport heavy materials or containers with components around a large factory or warehouse.

Recent global disruptions from the pandemic and geopolitical conflicts have explored vulnerabilities in global supply chains, companies are exploring ways to be more resilient. This requires a supply chain that can overcome volatility in demand and supply, reduce latency in information through improved visibility, and eliminate inefficiency in operations while responding to changes in an automated manner, in other words an Autonomous Supply Chain. It has also been defined more as a *self-governing supply chain built upon intelligence and automation, in which key structural entities are capable of making and enforcing their decisions with little or no human intervention (Xu et al., 2024).*

Table 2. Potential changes in process due to automation (McKinsey & Co., 2020)

Characteristics of Autonomous Supply Chains	*From*	*To*
Efficiency	*Manual processes and sequential steps*	*Automation of inputs and planning; Streamlined and automated decisions based on an exceptions framework*
Powered by advanced Analytics	*ERP, best of breed solutions with data warehouses and reporting infrastructure that is functionally siloed*	*Advanced planning tools with embedded Artificial intelligence and Machine learning – predictive, prescriptive and descriptive*
Speed	*Typically, daily, weekly, and monthly cadence; with time consuming data review and discussions across the enterprise*	*Shorter, tactical, cross-functional collaboration driven by real-time information from within the enterprise or from the edge combined with advanced analytics*
Cross-functional alignment and hard-wiring to business	*Owned by Supply Chain/ Operations and not integrated with companywide operations*	*KPIs aligned across functions and integrated with all business processes*
Self-Transforming	*Projects that replace one black box with another*	*Teams with data scientists embedded constantly piloting new use cases*

Studies on supply chain resilience have highlighted a significant gap between the time it takes for companies to become aware of a disruption and the time it takes to react to it. A study by Accenture found that, on average, companies take about 30 days to learn about a supply chain disruption. However, once they are aware of the disruption, they can typically respond within a week. This disparity underscores the importance of improving visibility and early detection capabilities within supply chains. The lag in awareness can be attributed to several factors, including siloed data, lack of real-time monitoring, and insufficient integration of supply chain systems. By leveraging advanced technologies such as AI, ML, and IoT, companies can enhance their ability to detect disruptions earlier and reduce the time it takes to respond effectively, ultimately improving supply chain resilience and minimizing the impact of disruptions.

The paper by the Supply Chain AI lab at Cambridge University (Xu et al., 2024) has proposed a seven-level maturity model for Supply Chain autonomy. This makes a distinction between automation and autonomisation at the highest level of maturity.

Figure 1. 7-level maturity model for Supply Chain autonomy

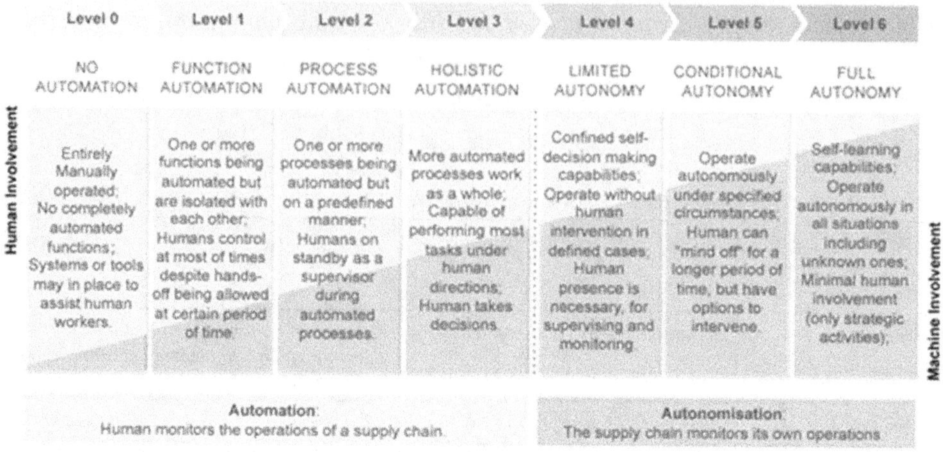

Intelligence and Automation are the two key requirements for Autonomous Supply Chains, and in this chapter the technology enablers for these will be described in detail. We will now look at the different types of AI and ML which are being deployed to support Intelligence and Automation.

Applications of AI and ML in Supply Chain Management

AI/ML techniques that have been adopted and under development broadly fall into three categories: Descriptive, Predictive and Prescriptive. Generative AI which has emerged recently could be considered a separate category by itself based on the large-scale investments and applications it is finding.

Descriptive - provides insights on what has happened in the past or is happening currently in a business environment.

Descriptive models use data aggregation and data mining to summarize and understand the key characteristics of a dataset, essentially describing the patterns and trends within the data without attempting to predict future outcomes. Descriptive ML techniques are often used in combination with data visualization tools to present the findings in an easily interpretable and actionable format.

Common Supply chain applications of Descriptive ML include:

- **Demand Analysis**: By analyzing historical sales data and the order book, descriptive ML can help identify patterns and trends in customer demand, provide insights into the performance of the product portfolio, performance of regions, key accounts, channels and promotion performance

- **Inventory Management**: Descriptive ML can be used to analyze past inventory levels and turnover rates, helping businesses understand which products move quickly and which do not. This can inform decisions about stock levels and reorder points.
- **Supplier Performance Evaluation**: By examining historical data on supplier deliveries, quality, and costs, descriptive ML can help assess supplier reliability and performance. This information can be used to optimize supplier selection and negotiation strategies.
- **Anomaly Detection**: Identifying unusual patterns or outliers in the data that may indicate potential issues or opportunities.
- **Cost Analysis**: Analyzing historical cost data across the supply chain can help identify major cost drivers and areas where savings can be achieved. This includes evaluating costs related to production, transportation, storage, and labor. Understanding customers for whom it costs more than the average to deliver goods can also help shape sales and fulfillment strategies.

Descriptive ML helps organizations gain valuable insights into their historical data, enabling them to make data-driven decisions, improve processes, and better understand their business environment. These insights often serve as a crucial first step in the machine learning pipeline before building predictive models.

Predictive - enables us to predict what will happen in the future

Predictive ML is the predominant analytics tool deployed today. It is capable of processing massive amounts of historical data and future looking data streams or causals (e.g. historical sales, GDP growth, population growth, product pricing) to automatically identify patterns, learn from the past and make predictions about the future.

Predictive ML involves the following key components and processes:

1. Data Collection: Gathering historical data that is relevant to the prediction task. This data serves as the foundation for training predictive models.
2. Feature Engineering: Selecting and transforming variables (features) from the data that are most relevant to the prediction task. This step is crucial for improving model accuracy.
3. Model Selection: Choosing appropriate algorithms to build the predictive model. Common algorithms include linear regression, decision trees, random forests, support vector machines, and neural networks.
4. Training and Testing: Splitting the data into training and testing sets. The model is trained on the training set and evaluated on the testing set to assess its predictive accuracy.

5. Evaluation Metrics: Using metrics such as accuracy, precision, recall, F1-score, and mean squared error to evaluate the model's performance.
6. Deployment: Implementing the model in a real-world setting where it can make predictions on new, unseen data.

Some examples of Predictive ML include:

- **Demand Forecasting**: Predictive ML models analyze historical sales data, market trends, and external factors to forecast future product demand. Accurate demand forecasting helps in optimizing inventory levels, reducing stockouts, and minimizing excess inventory.
- **Predictive Maintenance**: In manufacturing, predictive ML is used to anticipate equipment failures by analyzing data from sensors and historical maintenance records. This helps in scheduling maintenance activities before failures occur, reducing downtime and maintenance costs.
- **Logistics and Transportation Optimization**: Predictive ML can forecast expected delivery times and identify potential disruptions in the logistics network. This enables better route planning, efficient resource allocation, and improved delivery performance.

Prescriptive - helps decide what should be done in order to meet business goals

Prescriptive ML refers to the use of machine learning techniques to recommend actions or strategies that can help achieve desired outcomes. Unlike descriptive ML, which provides insights into what has happened, or predictive ML, which forecasts what might happen, prescriptive ML goes a step further by suggesting specific actions to take based on the predictions.

Prescriptive ML involves the following key components and processes:

1. Data Collection and Preparation: Gathering and preprocessing data to ensure it is suitable for analysis.
2. Predictive Modeling: Using machine learning algorithms to predict future outcomes based on historical data.
3. Optimization Algorithms: Applying optimization techniques to determine the best course of action to achieve the desired objectives.
4. Simulation and Scenario Analysis: Testing various scenarios and strategies to understand their potential impact and effectiveness.
5. Decision Support: Providing actionable recommendations and insights to decision-makers.

Of these components, Mathematical optimization has been the leading prescriptive analytics tool available to corporations for a few decades. Mathematical optimization applications are based on a detailed mathematical model (which functions as a digital twin of the operating environment), run on the most up-to-date data and generate a prescriptive solution while meeting specified business objectives such as maximizing sales based on a demand prediction while reducing inventory pre-build and considering supply chain constraints like production, supplier and logistical constraints. The robustness of mathematical optimization models comes at a cost, as these models typically require a greater investment of time and effort to build upfront than their machine learning counterparts. Essentially, prescriptive ML uses mathematical optimization algorithms as a core component to provide actionable insights and decision support

While predictive models provide insights into what might happen in the future, prescriptive models offer recommendations on what actions to take to achieve a specific outcome or goal. Example of Predictive ML are:

- **Supply Chain Network Design**: AI can analyze various scenarios and suggest the best configuration for a supply chain network, including the location of warehouses and distribution centers, to minimize costs and improve service levels.
- **Dynamic Pricing Strategies**: By analyzing market conditions, competitor pricing, and customer behavior, prescriptive AI can recommend dynamic pricing strategies that maximize revenue and market share while maintaining competitiveness.
- **Transportation Optimization**: Prescriptive AI can suggest optimal transportation routes and modes by considering factors such as fuel costs, delivery times, and capacity constraints. This helps in reducing transportation costs and improving delivery reliability.
- **Delivery logistics:** A predictive algorithm would inform a Transportation planner how long it will take drivers on each route to complete their deliveries. A prescriptive algorithm will determine the most efficient route that each driver should take to complete their deliveries quickly and safely.

Generative AI

Generative AI (Gen AI) diverges from both Descriptive and Predictive AI in that it is not bound by past data alone. Instead, it crafts new data or content, based on learned patterns. While descriptive and predictive models can tell you what happened or what might happen, Gen AI can create something entirely new, pushing the boundaries of machine creativity. Gen AI leverages Large Language Models

(LLMs) such as GPT-3 and GPT-4, Llama and Claude that are designed to understand, generate, and manipulate human language. They are used for tasks related to natural language processing (NLP), such as text generation, translation, summarization, and question answering. LLMs are trained on vast amounts of proprietary textual and historical business data to learn language patterns and context. Applications of Gen AI include chatbots, copilots, virtual assistants, automated content creation, and language translation services. Copilots allows users to query in natural language, then pulls data from all relevant and permissible sources, determines correlations, and serves up in an easy-to-consume format all relevant data along with insights that can help guide the next steps and decision making (Microsoft, 2024).

Some examples of Gen AI copilots in Supply Chain Management are:

- Generation of role-based summaries or daily briefs for demand, inventory, logistics planner and warehouse managers on what had changed in the last few days or what to expect in the next few days
- Root cause analysis that provides insights into changes in the forecast or supply plan since the last plan was generated

Intelligent AI Agents

The next frontier of Artificial Intelligence is Agentic AI which uses sophisticated, goal-oriented reasoning and iterative planning to autonomously solve complex, multistep problems. Intelligent AI agents are autonomous entities that leverage AI techniques to interact with real-world data, automate tasks, and make decisions to achieve specific goals. These agents are designed to operate independently, adapt to changing conditions, and learn from their experiences to improve their performance over time. They can also use external tools to obtain up-to-date information and optimize workflows. They are sometimes called LLM agents because of the central role LLMs play. While AI agents are autonomous, they still require humans to define goals and environments for them. Intelligent AI Agents are set to reshape how businesses operate, potentially redefining roles, workflows and human-AI collaboration models across supply chains.

Applications of intelligent AI agents span various domains, including:

- **Robotics**: Autonomous robots that can navigate and perform tasks in dynamic environments, such as self-driving cars, drones, and industrial robots.
- **Virtual Assistants**: AI-powered virtual assistants like Siri, Alexa, and Google Assistant that can understand and respond to user queries, provide recommendations and perform tasks such as controlling connected devices, and provide recommendations.

- **Customer Service**: Chatbots and virtual agents that can handle customer inquiries, provide support, and assist with transactions.

Overall, intelligent AI agents are a crucial component of modern AI systems, enabling automation, enhancing decision-making, and providing valuable assistance across a wide range of applications. Some applications AI agents in Supply Chain management include:

- **Inventory Management Agents**: can monitor inventory levels in real-time, predict future inventory needs, and automatically reorder products when stock levels fall below a certain threshold. These agents can also optimize warehouse space and manage stock rotation.
- **Predictive Maintenance Agents**: can analyze data from machinery and equipment to predict when maintenance is needed. By identifying potential issues before they become critical, these agents help prevent equipment failures and minimize downtime. When coupled with an inventory management agent, this could place automatically place orders for replenishing parts based on certain guardrails before requiring a planner review and approval.
- **Supplier Relationship Management Agents**: evaluate supplier performance, manage supplier contracts, identify potential risks in the supply chain and suggest alternative suppliers if needed.

We will now review how AI and ML techniques are being deployed in end-to-end Supply chain management processes. Explainability for the inferences provided by AI/ML are key to driving user adoption, which we will examine in detail with specific use-cases in supply chain process areas such as:

Supply Chain Network Design

Supply Chain Network Design involves pulling together data the supply chain's configuration and operations to create a digital twin or model to represent it. With this model, you can test changes and measure key metrics: cost, service, sustainability, risk, and more. Supply chain design can explore every type of decision regarding the structure and policies of the supply chain, such as:

- How many facilities – manufacturing or warehouses do you need, and where should they be located?
- Which items should be stocked, and where?
- How can you better plan and deploy inventory?
- What modes of transportation should you use in each lane?

- What should you do about our suppliers?
- How, where, and when should we invest in our supply chain?
- How should we adjust course if our demand assumptions are off, or a major disruption impacts our network like war or closure of the Suez Canal, or trade tensions between countries lead to new tariffs are added to imports from your supplier base?

Network design tools utilize mixed integer linear programming (MILP) to optimize network configurations by formulating the supply chain network design problem as a mathematical model where some variables are constrained to be integers (representing discrete choices like selecting a specific link capacity), allowing for the simultaneous consideration of both continuous variables (like flow on a link) and discrete decisions (like which equipment to install), ultimately finding the most efficient network design that minimizes cost or maximizes performance while adhering to constraints like capacity limits and connectivity requirements. The goal of the optimization is typically to minimize the total cost of building and operating the network, which is formulated as an objective function in the MILP model. Commercial solvers like CPLEX or Gurobi are used to solve the MILP problem, which efficiently explores the solution space to find the optimal network design that satisfies all constraints.

One of the common applications of Network optimization is deciding where to locate warehouses and distribution centers, and how to allocate inventory to minimize transportation costs. The process of evaluating the best network design requires multiple scenarios or multiple simulations to be run to determine the impact on the key business metrics for specific What-Ifs. These What-ifs could involve changing variables in the model such as increasing demand on certain product lines or decreasing supplier capacity for certain raw materials. The stakeholders may also have questions about the outputs such as the top 10% of the products with the highest manufacturing or transportation costs. While Supply chain analysts know what they need to do to answer them, they may lack the technical knowledge and/or the time to get it done at the speed of business. Network design tools now leverage the use of AI to run textual queries and provide descriptive responses. LLM based AI can help create the queries in SQL and run them against the underlying data model or analytical engine. These help any analyst level up and become an expert in data handling and SQL so they can do more in less time. These can also automate repetitive tasks for skilled modelers to speed up the design process and enable teams to answer more questions across the enterprise.

Supply Chain Segmentation

In this strategic process that sets up the overall supply chain policy, best-in-class organizations establish a policy framework using attributes such as customer, sales channel, product type, margin or region/location attributes for processes from demand planning, inventory policies, fulfillment including allocation and order promising, transportation and warehousing. While defining a segmented planning strategy for different products, customers and locations is not a new idea, market dynamics often change faster than the ability of organizations to change strategies. Companies struggle with the definition of segments based on ever changing attributes, and hence this process is tedious and performed infrequently. This results in excess inventory, high cost to serve and loss of market share.

Clustering models: are a type of unsupervised learning technique used to group similar data points into clusters or segments. These models are particularly useful in segmentation tasks where the goal is to partition a dataset into distinct groups based on the inherent structure of the data. K-Means Clustering is one of the widely used models for segmentation. After the data has been cleansed to normalize or standardize attribute values, it can partition the data into K clusters by minimizing the variance within each cluster. The number of clusters can be specified beforehand or determined by the algorithm.

For developing an effective segmentation strategy, it is necessary to consider attributes such as order lead time, price, variability and countless other factors that affect the service profitability equation. If humans manage the segmentation process manually and attempt to combine all these factors into a matrix, it can be a very time-consuming process and the suboptimal segment populations will result. The challenges companies run into with this process are:

- Determining which attributes to use to define segments and how important these attributes are
- How many segments should be defined
- What are the segments, what are their definitions and how frequently should they be revisited?

Machine learning offers a solution for the complex mathematical problems that underlie dynamic segmentation. Clustering models for segmentation can choose the right segmentation attributes automatically and build up the segments and feed the policies back into the planning systems to act on. Another advantage of using machine learning for segmentation is that these fast-moving and ever-changing segments are continuously updated. Supply chain solutions that provide this ML powered Dynamic Segmentation capability, enable supply chain experts the ability to simulate segments and add their own intelligence. The ability to define not only segments, but to allocate segment-specific policies such as customer service levels, allocation and promising policies, and short-term resolution rules can drive significant business value as the supply chain strategy is translated into supply plans and customer order commits. Some examples of how the attributes used for segmentation can drive business strategy in supply chain processes are:

- Integrated Business Planning: Corporate objectives for segments drive business parameters – Revenue targets, growth, investment
- Demand planning: Demand related attributes such as volumes (high, low, intermittent), New vs mature product, number of customers it is sold to etc. can be used to determine the most appropriate demand planning approach taken for a set of customers and items i.e. us statistical or ML forecasting, POS based, primarily based on customer order collaboration, and more
- Multi-echelon Inventory Optimization: Utilize recommended segments and service levels to create multi-echelon FG and part safety stock targets
- Master Planning / Supply Planning: Segment priorities can be treated as prioritized demand layers in an optimization solve to create an optimal Supply Plan
- Distribution planning: Segments determine use of replenishment or fulfillment strategies such as Direct Ship, Vendor Managed Inventory, Less Than Truckload (LTL), Full Truckload (FTL) and Expedite
- Allocations and Order Promising: Channel hierarchy for allocations and promising policies used for order promising
- Logistics and Warehousing: Here segmentation can drive shipping, storage and handling policies

Demand Planning

Demand forecasting has the most mature deployments of Predictive ML techniques. By selecting and applying the appropriate ML techniques, organizations can achieve more accurate and reliable demand forecasts, leading to better decision-making and optimized operations. Predictive algorithms such as Time-series analysis, Regression models, Neural Networks, Bayesian methods and Ensemble methods continue to be enhanced and widely available for use. While a detailed examination of these methods is beyond the scope of this chapter, we will discuss some specific topics and the implications they have in driving greater automation and intelligence with the Demand planning function in an enterprise.

- Hybrid models: combining different ML techniques to leverage their strengths and improve forecasting accuracy. For example,
  - o Combining Bayesian models for short term demand sensing with time series models for longer term forecasting
  - o Combining ARIMA with neural networks to capture both linear and non-linear patterns in the data.

Leading supply chain providers such as Blue Yonder have brought to market the Autonomous Mix-and-match capability that leverages the best combination of statistical methods, market-leading AI, and ML algorithms to generate high accuracy forecast.

- Extensible Machine Learning: These refer to supplementing available out-of-the-box ML based demand forecasting methods with customer in-house developed algorithms that use widely available ML libraries.
- Explainability and Real time causal simulation: Evaluating the impact of change to a causal variable to the forecast in near real time also helps understand downstream implications on potential supply shortfalls or explore demand shaping actions such as price increases
- Probabilistic forecasts provide a range of possible outcomes and the likelihood of each outcome occurring, rather than a single deterministic prediction. Probabilistic forecasts can help optimize inventory levels by predicting demand variability. This reduces the risk of overstocking or stockouts, leading to cost savings and improved customer satisfaction.

Demand Planning is also an area which is currently seeing the exploration of Gen AI and LLMs to provide analyses and insights from the underlying data.

Master Planning/ Supply Planning/ Distribution Planning

In this area that drives the heartbeat of every manufacturing and distribution-oriented business, the use of mathematical techniques referred to as solvers for demand and supply matching while considering material, capacity, labor and logistical constraints, in ERP or APS solutions has been in existence for several decades. With increasing variability in demand and supply, and the pendulum shifting from demand-constraints to supply-constraints depending on the business conditions, companies rely on scenario planning to evaluate the best possible outcomes after they have an initial production, procurement and distribution plan provided by the solver. This can be a manual and time-consuming process with many differing objectives and levers. The role of ML here is key in automating scenarios based on predetermined risks and opportunities along with levers that the stakeholders can agree on. In this use case of Prescriptive ML there is ongoing to leverage Polytopes for scenario automation. Polytope analysis is a mathematical technique used to study the properties and relationships of polytopes, which are geometric objects with flat sides in any number of dimensions. In supply chain management, "polytopes" are used as a mathematical tool to represent feasible regions within optimization problems, allowing analysts to model complex constraints related to inventory levels, production rates, transportation capacities, and other factors within a supply chain network, ultimately helping to find the most efficient and cost-effective solutions by identifying optimal points within these feasible regions.

Polytope analysis can be used to study how changes in the constraints or parameters of the demand-supply planning matching problem affect the feasible region. This is valuable for scenario automation as it narrows the search space and allows for the generation of fewer scenarios that reflect different conditions and constraints, helping in robust and speedier decision-making.

Self-Healing or Automated Plan parameter tuning: Another use case for Prescriptive ML in Supply Planning which is increasingly data parameter (lead times, yields etc) driven, is to recommend changes to parameters also referred to as self-healing processes. Often these the values for these used for planning purposes may not match what has been occurring in reality. E.g. using a lead time of 3 weeks for a shipping container to come across the Atlantic from Europe to the US, while in reality this may be taking close to 4 weeks as ships are avoiding the Suez Canal and taking routes that go past the Cape of Africa.

Self-healing ML processes compare key planning parameters modeled to the actual data and recommended parameter values based on the data patterns of actual observed values

Integrated Business Planning

The IBP or Sales and Operations Planning process brings together various key stakeholder teams and leaders within a company such as Product groups, Sales, Marketing, SC Planning, Operations (Mfg, Logistics & warehousing) & Finance at a set cadence to align on an operating plan. The underlying sub-processes for Demand review, Supply review, reconciliation and management review that are today driven by supply and demand planning can leverage the ML techniques referred to in the previous sections for Demand and Supply Planning. One area that is increasingly seen key to driving collaboration is how technologies used for remote collaboration such as Microsoft Teams using Gen AI can help during S&OP/IBP meetings with recording attendees, capturing real-time summaries, contextual notes, Tasks assigned, Pros and cons of the decisions made and Next steps for the future meeting.

IBP also relies heavily on running multiple scenarios to explore potential strategic long-term decision. The use of polytopes for scenario automation is also applicable to IBP.

Supplier Collaboration and Supply Chain Visibility

With increasingly diversified supply globally, risks from supplier constraints in a multi-tier network, geopolitical events, trade, weather, macroeconomics etc. need to be considered as part of the strategic and tactical planning process. Research has shown that in a multi-enterprise value chain, the "Informational Lead Time"- the time it takes for relevant operational information to be transmitted among all affected trading partners throughout any supply chain ecosystem, is a key driver of excessive low inventory turns and high safety stocks. Visibility and collaboration platforms aim to bring these parties together to share information and proactively resolve issues and reduce the impact of disruptions from cascading down to the end customer.

End-to-End Supply Chain Visibility: By integrating data from various sources, prescriptive AI can provide a comprehensive view of the supply chain, enabling proactive decision-making and real-time adjustments.

Risk Mitigation Strategies: By analyzing potential risks and disruptions, prescriptive AI can recommend contingency plans and risk mitigation strategies, helping businesses maintain continuity and resilience in their supply chains.

Transportation Management

Application of ML in the transportation process can support better decision making based on insights from the networks data. Potential deviations are visible early, and this helps identify and address risks early, for example, predicting carrier capacity shortfalls. This improves and automates planning and optimization.

Expected Time of Arrrival (ETA) and Delay predictions

In the Supply Chain process most susceptible to disruptions, Realtime GPS tracking information from Logistics Visibility Providers combined with data such as port congestion, weather etc. can be used by predictive ML model to provide more accurate ETAs for shipments. This is the most commonly deployed ML

Carrier Performance Risk scoring

Predictive carrier On Time Performance (OTP) scores can be generated by using ML on executed load information. The carrier performance score can be used by the TMS during future optimization runs and considered during carrier selection.

Load Lifecycle optimization

The lifecycle of a load starts with load planning 24-48 hours prior to execution, with review and adjustments done 4-8 hours prior to execution. ML can help with continuous learning and improvement

Near-term Forecasting: the expected Loads for the next week along with potential delays can be forecasted. A predictive carrier score can be used in optimizing loads and in predictive fleet sizing. This leads to improved resource utilization and improved service levels.

Failure risk Prediction: can provide for each load both its probability to arrive late, and the probabilistic root-causes for the lateness. Planners can identify attributes contributing to risk and update load configuration to reduce the risk. Risk predictions can be independently established at load, DC and carrier level. This would be typically done 24-72 hours prior to load execution.

At the time of execution, the Carrier Performance score can be used to provide carrier selection recommendations.

ML based Distance and Transit Time

A ML based time and distance engine to more accurately estimate journey times by considering actual journey times. It considers multi factors: origin, destination, equipment type, time of day, day of week, day of year, vehicle, driver, commodity, etc.

Warehouse Management

While the demand for Supply Chain Professionals outweighs supply and the gap continues to grow, the Gig Economy workforce is growing at 2x the rate of the traditional workforce. Warehouses typically rely on employees on hourly wages and turn to part time workers during peak seasons or buys periods to address shortfalls. Increasing Wage Rates and Lower pieces per lines shipped are driving up distribution costs. Companies are looking for opportunities to drive productivity improvements and lower distribution cost through better utilization of manpower, inventory, space and equipment in the warehouse. Many of the ML applications in

Warehouse Management Systems (WMS) and Yard Management Systems (YMS) address these areas.

Time of Arrival Forecasting

ML based ETA forecasts can help determine impact on Warehouse labor. In warehousing, early arrivals of trailers are as bad as late trailers. Expected arrival times can be based on data in the WMS such as the Carrier, ASNs and planned Arrival times. If that trailer was planned in a TMS, the route taken by the trailer is known, the weather and traffic along the way can be factored in to predict more accurately when that trailer will arrive.

Task Completion Forecasting

Machine learning can be used to determine when tasks will actually complete, not based on averages but based on a discrete understanding of individual users and tasks without requiring engineered standards to be setup. The WMS has the data to learn an user's pick rate in different areas of the warehouse, based on actual items or types of item. It can also differentiate between a "team lift SKU" that indicates a heavy item that requires multiple people to lift it safely versus a simple case pick. It also learn travel speeds on different machines, and the travel distance between locations,. With this data ML can determine how long it would take a specific user to complete a specific task in the warehouse. This results in accurate predictions of task completion times, SLAs and labor forecasts.

Autonomous Task Prioritization

Autonomous task prioritization automatically determines the order in which tasks should be executed, without manual intervention. This combines ML and real-time data to optimize the sequence of warehouse activities, such as replenishment and pick-pack-ship. By prioritizing tasks based on criteria such as order deadlines, resource availability, and workload balancing, the WMS ensures that warehouse operations are carried out in the most efficient manner possible. This reduces the likelihood of human error, ensuring that critical tasks are not overlooked and that orders are fulfilled accurately and on time. Task priorities can be dynamically adjusted in response to changing conditions, such as unexpected delays, inventory shortages, or urgent orders, ensuring that the most critical tasks are always addressed promptly. By considering factors like worker skill levels, equipment availability, and travel distances within the warehouse, the WMS can allocate resources more effectively, reducing idle time and maximizing productivity. Autonomous task prioritization provides warehouse managers with actionable insights and data-driven recommendations, enabling better decision-making and strategic planning.

Warehouse Execution System

A Warehouse Execution Systems (WES) need to orchestrate tasks between human resources and warehouse automation and devices such as Conveyors and sorters, Pick and put to Light, Autonomous Mobile Robots, Robotics and Goods-to-person such as AS/RS and shuttles. Mix and Match technologies as operation sees fit. With standard technologies (APIs) that enable communication with the Warehouse Contol System (WCS), Machine Learning helps utilize greater intelligence within the four walls of the warehouse by breaking down siloed information and intelligence. Task interleaving enables the most efficient task assignments to either robots or human resources based on proximity, priority and permissions to maximize efficiency and service.

Overall, these ML use cases in a warehouse enabled by a WMS help streamline warehouse operations, improve service levels, and reduce operational costs, contributing to a more agile and responsive supply chain.

Technology Advances Powering the Evolution of AI and ML

The widespread adoption and exploration of AI and ML applications in Supply Chain Management has been enabled by the easy availability of AI and ML commercial software, open-source libraries and computing power. The manufacturing of computing hardware including CPUs and memory technology has its own supply chain implications. Semiconductor companies are striving for diversification of supply so that the chip shortages that had widespread economic impact during the pandemic do not recur. Global trade and geo-political tensions have led to governments in Europe and the US supporting investments in ensuring the manufacturing of advanced chips that may have national security implications are not concentrated only in one region or country. According to research firm International Data Corp, the market for AI semiconductors was an estimated $117.5 billion in 2024, and will reach an estimated $193.3 billion by the end of 2027. Nvidia has an estimated 95% of the market for AI chips.

The computational requirements for Artificial Intelligence have evolved over several decades and there has always been a symbiotic relationship. Innovations in computational hardware (HW) has allowed newer AI techniques to flourish and conversely the intense computational requirements of AI have compelled computer scientists and engineers to seek newer computer architectures and pushed the frontiers of the underlying electronics circuitry, microelectronics and solid-state physics. In this section we will examine the HW foundations of AI and how that has driven the semiconductor industry.

The three major generations of AI

The early AI systems were often known as expert systems codifying and automating the existing body of knowledge. For example, the methods of partitioning a large shipment of packages into smaller consignments were based on rules, best practices and heuristics synthesized from the wide experience and deep knowledge of logistics experts. Mainframe computing systems could process data in batch mode and provide recommendations in minutes or hours specifying the optimal assignment of packages to containers under a set of constraints such as delivery deadlines, fuel costs, toll fees, excise duties, distances traveled, labor constraints etc. The heuristics were combined with algorithms and mathematical techniques from the field of Operations Research that had matured during 40s and 50s to optimize the logistics and supply chain management for conducting large scale military operations and manufacturing of automotives. Also in play were algorithms borrowed from the world of games such as chess, Go and backgammon that could analyze large "game trees" of possible scenarios to seek the optimal solutions under the constraints. Mainframe computers were later supplanted by general purpose computer servers built with microprocessors by Intel and AMD and CPU hardware built by IBM, HP, Sun and others. As DRAM sizes soared from kilobytes to Gigabytes, and secondary storage from megabytes to terabytes and storage costs fell exponentially, it was possible to process vast quantities of data This generation was largely prescriptive focusing on providing answers to a limited set of well-understood problems and scenarios, that pooled the wisdom of multiple experts but provided solutions vastly beyond their computational reach or capacity to absorb data.

The next generation AI brought in the world of advanced statistics and probability and dubbed as statistical learning or machine learning (ML). As opposed to relying on expert knowledge and calculations, the key driver was data. Statistical methods were used to analyze large bodies of data and extract recurring patterns or anomalies. This field of statistical learning enabled predictions or inferences to be made based on the identified patterns, essentially "learning" from data by identifying systematic regularities or unexpected outliers within it. Key points about statistical learning. Computational resources shifted to primarily focusing on extracting meaningful information from data to make informed decisions. The primary driver was data and rules, and expert knowledge played only a supporting role. One benefit of using statistics was the ability to move beyond the determinism of the first generation and use probability to deal with uncertainty and risk. ML could be used to extrapolate into the future and build models that could more accurately predict future outcomes based on observed and recurring data patterns.

Higher CPU speeds combined with cheaper, faster and larger memories and secondary storage made it possible to process complex data sets and make complex statistical predictions. Some applications such as handwriting recognition, image identification and classification rapidly evolved in parallel adding ancillary capabilities in the field of supply chain management.

The era of ML also enabled the movement from supervised learning that required large teams of experts to train and fine tune the ML to find optimal solutions to unsupervised or self-supervised learning where the ML technology is trained with a small subset of data from past history and known outcomes to fine tune the model. In the words of AI guru Yann LeCun- "In self-supervised learning, a portion of the input is used as a supervisory signal to predict the remaining portion of the input....more knowledge about the structure of the world can be learned through self-supervised learning than from [other AI paradigms], because the data is unlimited and the amount of feedback provided by each example is huge."

The third and more recent generation AI has accelerated the progress of self-supervised learning to levels that were unimaginable only a few years ago. Advances in the underlying technology such as neural networks and dedicated computational hardware to process AI models has completely changed the focus from expert knowledge, and data analytics to natural language processing. OpenAI's GPT-3 awed the world in when it was unveiled in 2022, but it is the culmination of a long line of technology starting with artificial neural networks that started showing great promise in the 1980s for pattern recognition and handwriting recognition and the early natural language processing (NLP). Neural networks of different types proved to be excellent at processing data of different types such as words, images, audio clips and classifying them but required a lot of computational power beyond what was possible with traditional CPUs that could process instructions and data serially.

Foundational AI technology

A major breakthrough was when Graphical Processing Units (GPUs) such as those built by nVidia and AMD for advanced graphics, visualization and gaming turned out to be excellent computational foundations for neural networks. GPUs can rapidly process data in parallel computation streams such as needed to decide the color and intensity if each pixel in an Ultra HD display and refresh the data at extremely high speeds. Another breakthrough in NLP was the introduction of a major innovation called "Transformers" which parallelized the stream of input data- words, or small portions of images and audio clips and concurrently analyzed entire sentences, images and audio clips. Transformers are combined with an AI mechanism called "attention" which can analyze the relationships and between words for example regardless of how far apart they occur in the input sentence and to determine which words and phrases in a passage are most important to "pay attention to" and get the context or meaning of the sentence. This parallelization makes the usage of GPUs even more efficient allowing massive datasets of 500 billion words or more to be processed in a matter of days rather than years or decades.

While AI hardware mainly relies on off-the-shelf GPUs built by companies such as AMD and Nvidia, other specialized AI accelerator HW are used for more narrowly focused tasks such as matrix operations and vector processing, image processing, speech processing, compressing large images or soundtracks etc. Some of these AI accelerators are used in data centers for identifying, classifying images or in automotive applications for identifying obstacles, traffic signals, highway markings, etc.

Companies that operate massive data sets are increasingly building their own AI hardware and pushing the boundaries of semiconductor design and manufacturing. They use a mix of in-house talent and third-party silicon design vendors such as Broadcom and Marvell to design the chips with electronic design automation (EDA) software from Cadence, Siemens and Synopsys. The taped-out designs are then sent off to silicon foundries such as TSMC and Samsung who are pushing the envelope of semiconductor physics with transistor and wire dimensions in the single digit nanometer (one millionth of a meter) range. The latest generation of AI chips is at 3 NM which allows almost twice as many transistors and wires to be placed in a chip as the previous generation of technology which is 2-3 years older. In addition to the custom AI silicon engineering newcomers like Google, Microsoft, Amazon, Qualcomm and Meta, the general purpose and off-the-shelf AI HW specialists such as Nvidia and AMD also manufacture their chips overseas at TSMC or Samsung, though they are actively looking at Intel's latest semiconductor plans for nearshoring.

In addition to CPUs, GPUs and custom AI accelerators, AI systems also require massive amounts of high-bandwidth memory (HBM) which provide high-speed access intermediate computational results and secondary storage such as disk-drives for storing Petabytes of datasets. All the computational elements have to communicate with HBM and storage with high-speed networks and I/Os such as PCIe, SerDes, gigabit ethernet, and other solutions. All of these devices take up a lot of space and consume vast amounts of power and produce a lot of heat. One solution is to place all these resources in a highly efficient and scalable data center, variously known as warehouse scale computing or cloud computing centers with dedicated power sources and cooling/venting systems. A typical facility houses racks of physical servers, cutting-edge networking equipment, and massive storage devices—all supported by a highly redundant power and cooling infrastructure designed to ensure near-perfect uptime. While the Public Clouds/ Hyperscalers such as Microsoft Azure, Amazon Web Services and Google Cloud were the earliest to invest in AI computing, more recently there have been multibillion dollar investments by companies such as CoreWeave, Meta and xAI in building AI Data Centers. Built specifically to meet the demanding computational requirements of AI workloads with clusters of AI chips, these facilities require high efficiency and substantial power infrastructure. The high costs of AI computing are also leading to AI Data centers subdividing into training AI data centers, which handle intensive data processing and machine learning training, and inference AI data centers, which focus on deploying trained models in real-world applications and delivering AI-driven insights in real-time.

Now that we have explored the applications of AI and ML in enabling greater automation and productivity in end-to-end supply chain processes, we will conclude by reviewing other elements that are needed to operate a supply chain with minimal human intervention (Blue Yonder, 2020 and 2023). An autonomous supply chain requires:

1. **The Edge and Data Clouds**:
    - o **IoT Devices**: Sensors and IoT devices collect real-time data from various points in the supply chain, such as production lines, warehouses, and transportation vehicles.
    - o **Data Platforms**: Centralized platforms such as Data Clouds can aggregate and integrate data from multiple sources, enabling seamless data flow and real-time visibility across the supply chain.
2. **End-to-End Supply Chain Management microservices with embedded Machine Learning**:
    - o **Predictive Analytics**: Machine learning models analyze historical and real-time data to predict future demand, inventory needs, maintenance requirements, and potential disruptions.
    - o **Prescriptive Analytics**: Advanced algorithms recommend optimal actions and strategies to achieve desired outcomes, such as inventory replenishment, production scheduling, and route optimization.
3. **Automation and Robotics**:
    - o **Automated Warehousing**: Robotics and automation systems manage warehouse operations, including picking, packing, sorting, and inventory management, with high efficiency and accuracy.
    - o **Autonomous Vehicles**: Self-driving trucks, drones, and delivery robots transport goods within and between facilities, reducing the need for human drivers and increasing delivery speed.
4. **Artificial Intelligence and Intelligent Agents**:
    - o **AI Agents**: Autonomous AI agents make real-time decisions based on data analysis, optimizing various aspects of the supply chain, such as procurement, inventory management, and logistics.

- **Virtual Assistants**: AI-powered chatbots and virtual assistants handle customer inquiries, order processing, and support tasks, enhancing customer service and operational efficiency.

5. **Blockchain and Distributed Ledger Technology**:
    - **Transparency and Traceability**: Blockchain technology ensures secure, transparent, and immutable records of transactions and product movements, enhancing traceability and trust in the supply chain.
    - **Smart Contracts**: Automated, self-executing contracts on the blockchain streamline and enforce agreements between supply chain partners, reducing the need for intermediaries and manual intervention.
6. **Real-Time Monitoring and Control**:
    - **Supply Chain Control Towers**: Centralized control towers provide real-time visibility and monitoring of the entire supply chain, enabling proactive management and rapid response to issues.
    - **Dynamic Adjustments**: Dynamically adjust operations based on real-time data, such as rerouting shipments, reallocating inventory, or rescheduling production to address changing conditions.
7. **Collaborative Ecosystems**:
    - **Partner Integration**: Seamless integration with suppliers, manufacturers, logistics providers, and customers fosters collaboration and information sharing, enhancing overall supply chain efficiency.
    - **Shared Platforms**: Collaborative platforms enable multiple stakeholders to access and contribute to a unified view of the supply chain, facilitating coordinated decision-making.
8. **Cybersecurity and Data Privacy**:
    - **Robust Security Measures**: Advanced cybersecurity protocols protect sensitive data and systems from cyber threats, ensuring the integrity and confidentiality of supply chain operations.
    - **Compliance and Governance**: Adherence to regulatory requirements and data privacy standards, maintaining compliance and building trust with stakeholders.
9. **Sustainability and Environmental Impact**:
    - **Sustainable Practices**: Incorporating sustainable practices such as optimizing resource usage, reducing waste, and minimizing carbon emissions.
    - **Environmental Monitoring**: IoT sensors and AI analytics monitor environmental impact and ensure compliance with sustainability goals and regulations.

By integrating these key elements, an autonomous supply chain can operate with high efficiency, agility, and resilience, while reducing costs, enhancing customer satisfaction, and supporting sustainability initiatives. Leveraging machine learning along with the expertise of their human planners, organizations can achieve a unique combination of artificial intelligence and human intelligence and a high level of automation.

REFERENCES

Blue Yonder Inc. (2020). The autonomous supply chain: seven steps to get there. https://blueyonder.com/ knowledge-center/collateral/7-steps-to-an-autonomous-supply-chain-white-paper

Blue Yonder Inc. (2023). The Next Evolution of Technology Innovations Transforming Supply Chain Planning. https://blog.blueyonder.com/the-next-evolution-of-technology-innovations-transforming-supply-chain-planning/

McKinsey & Company. (2020). Launching the journey to autonomous supply chain planning. Kuntze, C., Lal, S., & Seibert, K. https://www.mckinsey.com/capabilities/operations/our-insights/launching-the-journey-to-autonomous-supply-chain-planning

Microsoft Inc. (2024). Optimize supply chain resiliency by integrating diverse AI-powered solutions. Raval, R. https://www.microsoft.com/en-us/industry/blog/manufacturing-and-mobility/2024/08/29/optimize-supply-chain-resiliency-by-integrating-diverse-ai-powered-solutions/

Xu, L., Mak, S., Proselkov, Y., & Brintrup, A. (2024). Towards Autonomous Supply Chains: Definition, Characteristics, Conceptual Framework, and Autonomy Levels. *Journal of Industrial Information Integration.*

Chapter 2
Journey to the Autonomous Supply Chain

Ayoub Abielmona
https://orcid.org/0009-0004-3737-904X
Ernst & Young LLP, USA

ABSTRACT

This chapter presents an in-depth analysis of the evolution of supply chains in response to the increasing frequency and severity of market disruptions. The author envisions a future where supply chains transcend their reactive nature to become autonomous, self-driving networks that are not only efficient but also capable of learning, adapting, and operating with minimal human intervention. GenAI is presented as a game-changing technology that can help supply chains shift from rigid, linear systems to resilient ecosystems. The author cites several real-world implementations of GenAI in supply chains, including the automation of supplier negotiations, AI-driven drug discovery, and the streamlining of logistics operations. These examples demonstrate the transformative potential of GenAI, paving the way for a future where adaptability and resilience are embedded into the very fabric of supply chains.

DOI: 10.4018/979-8-3693-4433-0.ch002

INTRODUCTION

A World of Constant Change

It's no secret the world is in a constant state of volatility. From economic uncertainty to regional wars, from natural disasters to pandemics, these disruptive events are wreaking havoc on supply chains around the world and forcing companies to scramble for solutions that keep products on shelves and consumers happy. According to the 2021 Global Board Risk study, a survey of 935 global business executives conducted by EY organization and the University of Oxford's Saïd Business School, found that 82% of board members and CEOs believe market disruptions are becoming more frequent and more impactful.

Figure 1.

McKesson Health Systems Editorial Team, 2022; Dzinkowski, 2024; Berger, 2024; Segal, 2024; Tett, 2023

Economic disruptions, such as the 2008 financial crisis or the more recent trade wars between major economies, have profound effects on supply chains. For instance, the imposition of tariffs can suddenly increase the cost of raw materials, forcing companies to either absorb the cost or pass it on to consumers. Currency fluctuations also play a critical role; a weaker currency can make imports more expensive and exports cheaper, thereby affecting global trade patterns and supply chain strategies.

Geopolitical tensions and regional conflicts can lead to sanctions, embargoes and the disruption of trade routes. The war in Ukraine, for example, has not only caused tragic human suffering but also significant supply chain disruptions. Ukraine and Russia are major exporters of commodities like wheat and natural gas, and the conflict has led to a spike in global prices and shortages in these essential resources (Hamilton, 2023).

Climate change is another disrupter, leading to more frequent and severe weather events. Hurricanes, floods, and wildfires can shut down production facilities, damage infrastructure, and disrupt transportation routes. The 2011 Thailand floods, which inundated major industrial centers, disrupted global supply chains for automakers and electronics companies, as Thailand was a key hub for automotive parts production and assembly (O'Toole, 2011). More recently in 2023, the Panama Canal, one of the world's most important waterways, faced extreme water shortages that caused severe shipping delays and cost increases for shippers and consumers.

Health-related disruptions, such as the COVID-19 pandemic, have underscored the fragility of global supply chains. Lockdowns and social distancing measures led to factory closures, labor shortages, and a dramatic shift in consumer behavior. The pandemic also exposed the risks of over-reliance on just-in-time inventory systems and single sourcing, as companies struggled to adapt to the sudden changes in supply and demand (Department of Homeland Security [DHS], 2020).

Adding to the chaos, the economic world order has changed significantly in recent years. After the fall of the Soviet Union, the world economy was dominated by the United States and the American dollar. This unipolar system brought about stability and enabled supply chains to reach far and wide to optimize cost. For example, an American company could go all the way to China to save a dollar and they often did simply because they could — no significant barriers prevented them. Today's economic world order is a multi-polar system dominated by heavyweights like China and India in addition to the US. In fact, India is projected to overtake the US economy by 2075 according to Goldman Sachs (Shan, 2023). The increase in economic polarity brings a surge in competition and unpredictability as supply chains become more vulnerable to regional alliances and geopolitical tensions.

What was Once Important, is now Urgent

To alleviate these pressures, companies are re-evaluating their supply chain strategies. They are diversifying their supplier base to avoid overreliance on a single source, investing in predictive analytics to better forecast demand, and increasing inventory buffers to cushion against shocks. Some are reshoring or nearshoring production to reduce the distance goods must travel to mitigate the risk of cross-border supply chain disruptions. These strategies are a good start, but they don't go far enough in helping supply chains become more resilient and autonomous.

Against a backdrop of steady disruption and global volatility, the need for self-driving supply chains is not just a futuristic ideal but a necessary evolution whose time is way overdue. It's not enough to leverage technology to facilitate work. We must take it a step further and use the latest advancements to execute work on our behalf. Leveraging advanced technologies such as artificial intelligence (AI), internet-of-things (IoT) and cloud computing, supply chains of the future will operate with unprecedented levels of agility and resilience, autonomously coordinating and executing end-to-end activities to optimize and automate performance with little to no human intervention.

Automatic Supply Chain Control System

Just as modern-day airliners rely on an Automatic Flight Control System (AFCS) to counteract the effects of atmospheric challenges, supply chains need a similar technology to navigate through turbulent times and maintain steady operations. An airplane's AFCS uses input from various sensors, such as gyroscopes, accelerometers and air data instruments to detect gusts and deviations from the set flight parameters (altitude, heading, speed, etc.). When turbulence causes the aircraft to deviate from these parameters, the AFCS sends commands to the engine and control surfaces (ailerons, elevators, rudders) to adjust the aircraft's systems accordingly. Supply chains need their own AFCS equivalent, leveraging real-time input from across the entire network to ensure uninterrupted operations despite the economic and market fluctuations they encounter. The journey toward this level of supply chain automation is a complex one, requiring the integration of intricate systems and the reimagining of traditional processes across the entire ecosystem.

The increasing frequency and impact of disruptions from economic, geopolitical, climate and health-related events are challenging companies to build more resilient supply chains. By leveraging the latest advancements in digital technologies, such as AI for decision intelligence, blockchain for greater transparency, and IoT for real-time tracking of goods, businesses are striving to adapt to the new normal of persistent change and uncertainty. The ability to navigate these turbulent times will separate the leaders from the laggards in the quest for supply chain excellence and brand superiority.

From Linear to Networked Supply Chain Ecosystems

Once a rigid and linear sequence of events, the supply chain has undergone a remarkable transformation. Historically, supply chains were characterized by a unidirectional flow of goods from suppliers to manufacturers, wholesalers, retailers, and finally to consumers. This model was often inflexible, with each link in the chain operating in silos, leading to inefficiencies such as overstocking, understocking and a lack of responsiveness to market changes.

As globalization expanded, the need for more adaptable supply chains became evident. The advent of cloud technology marked a significant turning point. Cloud computing enabled the centralization of data and the facilitation of real-time communication across external stakeholders within the supply chain (Kurkina, 2023). This shift from isolated operations to a more integrated approach led to the development of Multi-Enterprise Collaborations (MEC) systems. These systems are characterized by their dynamic and interconnected nature, where each participant in the supply chain can access and share information seamlessly. The cloud platform became the common link for collaboration, enabling better visibility, coordination and optimization of resources.

From Networked to Autonomous Supply Chains

Today, we stand on the brink of the next evolutionary leap, the self-driving autonomous supply chain. This new paradigm leverages the next generation of AI technologies to create systems that can operate independently, learn from their environment, and make decisions without human intervention. Autonomous supply chains will go beyond predicting demand fluctuations and making recommendations; they will execute tasks on our behalf, for example, by adjusting production schedules, rerouting logistics in response to disruptions, and even negotiating with suppliers and customers. They are self-optimizing, constantly seeking the most efficient and cost-effective methods to meet consumer needs. This evolution of supply chains from rigid linear structures to self-driving autonomous ecosystems represents a transformation in how we produce, distribute and consume goods. It is a testament to human ingenuity and our relentless pursuit of resilience in the face of an ever-changing world. As we continue to innovate and reimagine traditional processes, the supply chain of the future will be more connected, intelligent and autonomous than ever before, and the pivotal force propelling this transformation is artificial intelligence.

Autonomous Requires Next-Generation AI

This new vision of a self-driving supply chain cannot be fulfilled without the power of advanced technologies such as artificial intelligence and the transformative capabilities that have been unlocked through generative AI (GenAI), in particular. Traditional AI has played a significant role in supply chain management for decades, with its ability to automate repetitive tasks, detect patterns and make predictions based on historical data. It has been utilized in various areas of supply chain, such as inventory management, route planning, scheduling, forecasting supply and demand, warehouse management through robotics, and customer service with chatbots. However, despite the longstanding use of AI in supply chain, and the existence of GenAI models such as recurrent neural networks (RNNs), generative adversarial networks (GANs) and variational autoencoders (VAEs), it's only recently that supply chain practitioners have begun to truly uncover the potential for leveraging this technology to bring about more autonomous and resilient supply chain systems. There are several factors contributing to this delayed discovery and the ensuing excitement around these technologies. First, advances in computational power and data storage have made it feasible to deploy complex AI models at a scale that was not previously possible. The advent of cloud computing and the decrease in the cost of processing have allowed businesses of all sizes to utilize and experiment with sophisticated algorithms that can learn and adapt autonomously. Second, the proliferation of data across the supply chain has also played a crucial role. With IoT devices, radio-frequency identification (RFID), and other forms of digital tracking, there is a wealth of data available that can feed GenAI systems, enabling them to predict demand more accurately, optimize inventory, or simulate various supply chain scenarios.

Generative AI Comes of Age

But the most significant driver for the recent excitement about AI has been the tremendous capability leap in the generative algorithms themselves, facilitating more natural and coherent content generation than ever before. Generative artificial intelligence (GenAI) refers to a class of AI that is capable of creating new data, hence the name "generative." Whereas traditional AI is adept at finding patterns and uncovering relationships in the data, generative AI can go much further to create new content that is a novel combination or extrapolation of the existing patterns found in the training data. GenAI stands out in its ability to support self-driving supply chains through its advanced capabilities to not only analyze and interpret vast amounts of data but also simulate scenarios, devise strategies and create plans that adapt to changing conditions in real-time with unprecedented speed and accuracy. For example, GenAI can optimize delivery routes, not just based on current traffic conditions, but also by simulating future scenarios to avoid potential disruptions. It can assist in designing warehouse layouts that maximize space utilization and efficiency or create new supply chain models that balance cost, speed and environmental impact. Unlike traditional AI, which primarily focuses on data-driven insights and automation, GenAI can design new processes, forecast future demands with greater accuracy, and dynamically adapt to changing market conditions. This capability will be instrumental in navigating the uncertainties of the global market, allowing supply chains to become more resilient, responsive and able to operate autonomously with limited human intervention. While generative AI technology isn't new, it's the maturation of the technology coupled with advancements in hardware, the abundance of data, improved algorithms and the broader disruptive trends that have recently made its application in supply chains both practical and attractive to practitioners.

To truly appreciate the groundbreaking power of today's GenAI technology, we must first understand the basic makeup of AI solutions, their inherent limitations and how today's GenAI models transcend those boundaries by offering new capabilities that were previously unattainable with traditional machine learning methods.

Artificial Intelligence at its Most Basic Level

At its core, a typical AI solution begins with the development of a statistical model — a mathematical representation of a real-world challenge or domain that we want to understand better, such as climate patterns, disease spread, economic trends or traffic flow. These models help us understand which variables or features in the domain are important, how those features are related to the outcomes we want to understand, and how we can use those relationships to make predictions or informed decisions. For example, a model of a retail domain might reveal that sales are strongly correlated with certain times of the year and that this relationship can be used to forecast future sales. Essentially, an AI solution is embodied in a mathematical model that represents a particular domain by formalizing assumptions about the relationships between its data features and outcomes. While the specifics of an AI project will dictate the type of model required, nonetheless, the cornerstone of any AI development will always rely on the application of an existing model or the creation of a new one.

Machine Learning Methods

Statistical models developed for AI solutions are built using a variety of machine learning (ML) methods. These methods range from simple algorithms like linear regressions to highly complex models such as deep neural networks that are inspired by the function of the human brain. Neural networks feature interconnected nodes that behave like neurons in the brain to learn complex patterns and make sophisticated decisions by adjusting the strength of connections among the nodes, much as our own neural pathways strengthen with experience. This brain-inspired approach allows neural networks to effectively handle and make sense of large and complex data sets by learning from examples, without explicit programming.

Early Generative Models

Prior to 2017, the leading generative AI models for language processing included a class of neural networks known as recurrent neural networks (RNNs). These models work by processing data sequentially — that is one data element at a time, in the order in which the elements appear in the input. When the input is relatively short in length, RNNs are able to effectively maintain context between the sequential elements to perform tasks like language processing or speech recognition. However, as the sequence length grows, RNNs can struggle to maintain relationships between elements that are far apart from each other. For example, in a complex sentence where the subject is introduced at the beginning and the main verb or action appears much later, an RNN may lose track of the subject's association with the verb, leading to an inaccurate interpretation of the sentence structure and meaning. Additionally, the inherent sequential nature of RNNs limits their speed, making it time-consuming to train and run on long sequences of data. As datasets grow and the demand for real-time processing increases, RNNs' one-at-a-time approach can become a significant bottleneck.

The Rise of Transformers and the Birth of Modern Generative AI

In 2017, Google researchers published a paper titled "Attention is All You Need," in which they introduced a new, groundbreaking neural network architecture, known as the Transformer, that can overcome the inherent limitations of RNNs. This model pivots away from the sequential processing of data and, instead, relies on a mechanism called "attention" to weigh the significance of different parts of the input data relative to one another. Unlike RNNs, the Transformer processes all elements of the input data in parallel, enabling it to maintain context between distant elements effectively, regardless of their position in the sequence. This attention mechanism allows the model to focus on the most relevant parts of the input when making predictions or generating text, vastly improving its ability to understand complex sentence structures and relationships between distant elements. Additionally, because the Transformer processes data elements in parallel rather than sequentially, it significantly speeds up training and inference times, making it much more efficient and scalable for handling large datasets and complex tasks. This innovation has set a new standard for performance in various natural language processing tasks and has paved the way for the development of advanced GenAI models.

Figure 2. What AI Does

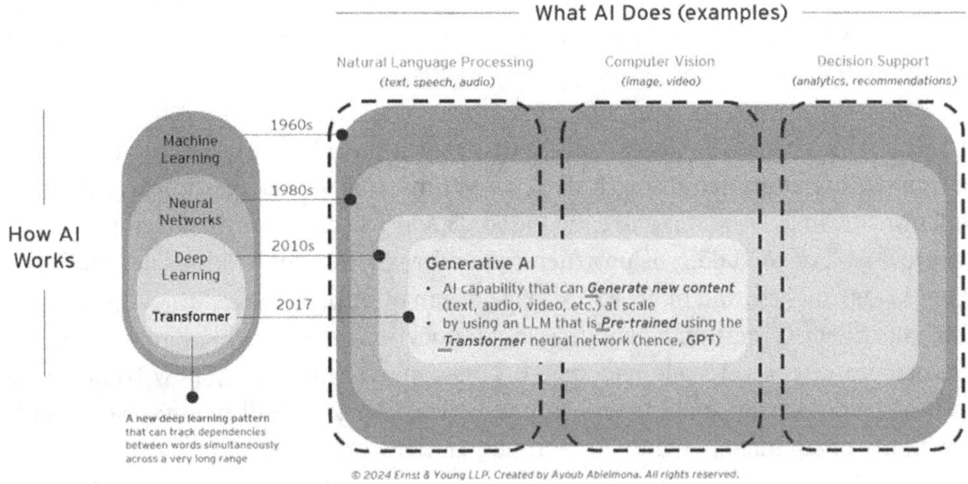

What Makes GenAI Different

Emerging from the solid foundation established by traditional AI, GenAI represents a new frontier in artificial intelligence, differentiating itself from classical AI in several key ways. While traditional AI is often rule-based and focused on analyzing data and automating tasks, GenAI goes a step further by creating new content and ideas. It can generate text, images, plans and other content by learning from existing data sets, enabling it to simulate scenarios, design products, and even innovate processes.

For the first time, AI is significantly more accessible. Through the power of large language models (LLMs), GenAI unlocks benefits and capabilities previously deemed unfeasible. It brings the sophistication of AI to everyday workers doing everyday work, whether it's composing an email, analyzing a contract, or drafting a new RFP. AI is no longer the exclusive domain of data scientists and engineers working on "special" data projects. Now, anyone in the organization can access an AI chatbot, such as ChatGPT, which allows users to query data sources without needing to master specialized tools or languages like SQL. GenAI democratizes access to data and information, empowering nontechnical staff to explore any data source by simply asking questions in their natural language.

For the first time, AI is significantly more creative. Not only is it able to recognize patterns in the data, but it is able to create new patterns that didn't exist before — a new image, new recipe or new song. You can train the LLM on all of Billy Joel's greatest hits and then ask it to write a brand-new song in that same style. There's no guarantee the song will be a hit, but it will certainly sound like a Billy Joel song. If you can train a model to write a new song in the style of a particular artist, then there is no reason why you can't train it to write a new contract or project plan in the style of historical documents.

For the first time, AI is significantly more context aware. Through the power of LLMs, AI can do with words and letters what it has always been able to do with numbers. It can crunch through massive volumes of unstructured data, like word documents, images, audio and even video. When you consider that over 80% of the world's data created daily is unstructured in format, the implications are profound. GenAI can analyze and interpret this vast ocean of information, extracting valuable insights, identifying trends, and making connections that would be impossible for humans to discern at scale and speed. This capability opens up new frontiers for data-driven decision-making and strategic planning across all sectors, particularly in supply chain management where timely and informed decisions are critical.

For the first time, AI is significantly more scalable. GenAI models have demonstrated significantly greater scalability and power compared to traditional AI approaches, mainly due to their ability to effectively leverage extremely large unlabeled datasets and learn complex relationships from them. The notion of "labeled" vs. "unlabeled" data is the key to understanding this concept. Imagine you want to learn Spanish. There are two ways you can approach it. The "labeled" or supervised way would be like having a dictionary where every word is translated for you. Each word or phrase in the dictionary has a "label" telling you exactly what it means. Using the "unlabeled" or unsupervised learning approach would be like being dropped into a country where everyone speaks Spanish. You don't have a dictionary or any direct translations (labels), but you figure things out by listening to conversations, watching TV, and seeing how words are used in different contexts. Using the unsupervised learning method, the AI algorithm is given huge amounts of raw information — like millions of web pages, books or images — without explicit labels or explanations. It then uses neural network algorithms to find patterns, make connections and understand context on its own. This approach is powerful because it doesn't require humans to manually annotate or label every piece of data, which further enhances scalability. It can uncover patterns and relationships that humans might not have thought to label.

While the concept of unsupervised machine learning existed prior to generative models, it wasn't until the transformer architecture came along that AI models were able to leverage massive amounts of unlabeled data with significant scale and speed. Additionally, the attention mechanisms in the transformer architecture enables extensive amounts of data to be processed simultaneously while maintaining long-range relationships in the data. These factors combine to produce models with remarkable performance on diverse tasks like language understanding, image generation, and multi-modal reasoning, far surpassing the capabilities of most traditional AI systems. The ability of generative AI to understand context, learn from new data, and generate creative solutions makes it particularly suited for the complex and dynamic nature of modern supply chains. As organizations face an increasingly uncertain world, the ability to quickly adapt and innovate is crucial. GenAI provides the tools to not just respond to change but to anticipate and shape it, heralding a new era of supply chain management that is proactive, resilient and forward-thinking.

Figure 3. Classical vs Generative AI

	Classical AI	Generative AI	
1 From single-use to **broad application**	• **Model creation** - starts with creating new model from scratch • **Fit for purpose** - single-use model to address specific topics with specific KPIs (churn, fraud, risk, etc.)	• **Model adaptation** - starts with existing model, already trained and ready to be adapted with domain specific data • **Multi-purpose** - one large generative model can address variety of tasks	• Versatile • Ready to use • Adaptive • Easier/cheaper
2 From complex interface to natural **human language**	• **Computer language** - requires technical expertise to build model and interpret results	• **Natural human language** - understands commands in human language	• Accessible • Conversational • Speed to insight
3 From pattern recognition to **pattern creation**	• **Discriminative** - ideal for making predictions and recommendations • Repeatable and deterministic results	• **Generative** - answer questions, summarize text and generate original content • Leads to innovative/unexpected solutions	• Creative • First draft • Probabilistic
Example:	• Analyze user behavior data to identify attributes of most engaging content	• Use that same data to create entirely new personalized content that is likely to increase engagement and drive sales	
Key Enablers:	• Machine learning, neural networks, deep learning	• Massive computing power (GPUs), advanced deep learning (transformer architecture with attention mechanism), natural language interface	

Adoption of Generative AI in Supply Chain (HFS Study Findings)

A recent study conducted by HFS Research in collaboration with the EY organization (Steinberg et al., 2024), aiming to understand the adoption and impact of GenAI in supply chain management, finds the appetite for GenAI is gaining momentum, with 73% of organizations already adopting it and 80% viewing it as a high priority for reinventing their supply chains. This enthusiasm stems from GenAI's unique capabilities that go beyond traditional AI analytics and rule-based automation. The research, carried out in February and March 2024, surveyed 460 senior supply chain and operations leaders across 19 countries and various industries. The study focused on organizations with annual revenues exceeding $1 billion that were at least in the planning stages of deploying GenAI in their supply chains.

Figure 4. GenAI statistics

The research reveals that companies are deploying GenAI across various supply chain functions, with certain use cases showing strong potential. Current focus areas include product design in manufacturing, logistics network design, global trade optimization and demand forecasting. Other applications being considered include supplier management, production yield optimization, risk management and customer service chatbots. These areas offer clear commercial returns and address significant pain points in supply chain operations. Leveraging GenAI's ability to handle unstructured data and provide natural language interfaces, these applications democratize access to powerful analytical tools previously limited to data scientists. For instance, GenAI-powered chatbots can rapidly expand query resolution capabilities by learning from past customer interactions, while production yield optimization can significantly reduce costs.

Adoption Does not Come Without its Challenges

Despite the positive momentum, the path to realizing the full benefits of GenAI in supply chains is hampered with multifaceted challenges, ranging from strategic alignment to technical and operational hurdles. The three most cited challenges reported by the HFS survey respondents were data quality and access, skill gaps among employees, and security risks, offering valuable insights into the critical areas where organizations must focus their efforts.

Figure 5. Challenges and risks of GenAI

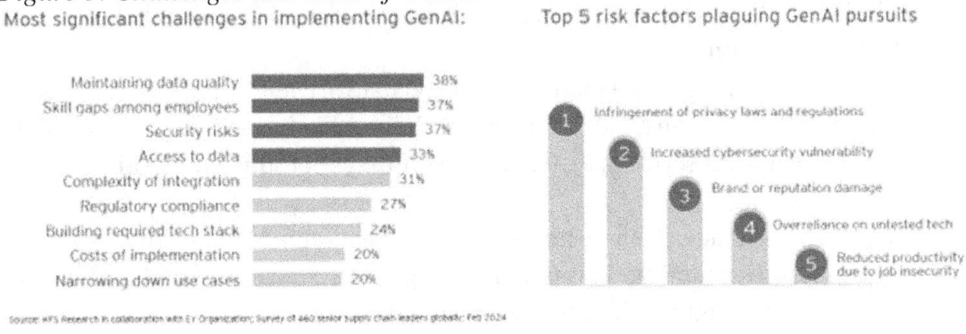

Data Readiness

Chief among the barriers in implementing GenAI is data quality and access. According to the HFS study, maintaining data quality (38%) and ensuring data access (33%) are the top implementation challenges reported by respondents. This should come as no surprise, as data readiness has long been a critical challenge in software development. Traditionally, software applications have struggled with data quality issues such as inconsistency, incompleteness and inaccuracy. These problems arise from various sources including human error during data entry, legacy systems with outdated or incompatible data formats, siloed information across different departments or systems, and lack of standardization in data collection and storage practices. For example, a supply chain management system might encounter discrepancies in product codes between the warehouse inventory and the ordering system, leading to incorrect stock levels and potential fulfillment issues. These issues, which have historically plagued data-driven applications, are now amplified in the context of AI and present even greater obstacles, especially in the supply chain domain, which often struggles with fragmented data across a multitude of systems and external parties, massive data volumes and data privacy regulations.

Data access has also been a persistent challenge. This is often driven by data privacy and security concerns, technical limitations in integrating disparate systems, organizational silos reluctant to share information, and regulatory compliance requirements. In a typical scenario, a company might struggle to combine customer data from its CRM system with transaction data from its e-commerce platform due to differences in data structures and access restrictions. While these issues have always impacted software applications, they become even more critical and complex for GenAI solutions. Here's why:

1. Scale and complexity: GenAI models, especially LLMs, require vast amounts of high-quality data to train effectively. The sheer volume of data needed amplifies any existing quality issues.
2. Bias and representation: AI models can perpetuate or even amplify biases present in training data. For instance, if a supply chain AI is trained on historical data that reflects past discriminatory practices, it may reproduce those biases in its generated solutions.
3. Context and nuance: GenAI needs to understand subtle contextual cues and domain-specific nuances. This requires not just large quantities of data, but data that accurately captures the complexities of the problem space.
4. Real-time adaptation: Many GenAI applications in supply chains need to adapt to rapidly changing conditions. This requires continuous access to fresh, high-quality data streams.
5. Explainability and traceability: For AI-generated solutions to be trustworthy and actionable, there needs to be a clear understanding of the data sources and reasoning behind the outputs. Poor data quality or limited access can make this challenging.

Consider a GenAI system designed to optimize routing in a global supply chain. To function effectively, it would need access to real-time traffic and weather data, up-to-date information on port congestion and customs delays, accurate inventory levels across multiple warehouses, historical performance data on various routes and carriers, and contractual terms with different logistics providers. Any gaps or inaccuracies in this data could lead to suboptimal or even harmful recommendations. Moreover, ensuring consistent, high-quality access to all these data sources — some of which may be owned by different entities or subject to varying privacy regulations — presents a significant challenge. Another example is a GenAI system for demand forecasting. It might struggle if historical sales data is incomplete or inconsistent across different regions or if it lacks access to external factors like competitor actions or macroeconomic indicators that influence demand patterns.

While data quality and access have always been important for software applications, they become even more critical for GenAI solutions. The increased complexity, scale and potential impact of AI-generated outputs make robust data management practices not just a technical necessity, but a strategic imperative for organizations looking to leverage GenAI in their supply chains.

Skills Gap

Generative AI technologies are evolving at an unprecedented pace, outstripping the ability of many organizations to adapt. As a result, employees often find themselves unprepared to utilize these tools effectively. Addressing the workforce reskilling challenge created by the rise of GenAI is another key hurdle facing organizations. This was the second highest obstacle to implementing GenAI identified by 37% of respondents in the HFS study. These gaps are primarily rooted in the lack of awareness regarding the specific skills needed to effectively leverage GenAI and the insufficient training resources available. Addressing these gaps is critical for supply chain organizations to enhance operational efficiency, improve decision-making, and ultimately drive competitive advantage.

One of the most pressing skill gaps is the lack of technical proficiency in AI and ML. Many employees in supply chain roles may not have a foundational understanding of how GenAI algorithms work or how to apply them to optimize processes such as inventory management, demand forecasting, or logistics planning. Another critical gap is data literacy. Supply chain professionals must be adept at interpreting and analyzing data generated by GenAI tools to make informed decisions. However, many lack the skills to work with large datasets or utilize advanced analytics tools, which can hinder their ability to derive actionable insights from AI-generated outputs. As GenAI becomes integrated into supply chain operations, understanding the ethical implications of AI usage is also essential. Employees need training on how to use GenAI responsibly, including recognizing biases in AI outputs and ensuring compliance with data privacy regulations.

A 2023 international survey by the Boston Consulting Group found that while 86% of workers believe they need training in AI, only a small fraction received any formal education on these critical topics (Boston Consulting Group [BCG], 2023). To address these gaps, supply chain organizations can implement comprehensive training programs tailored to the specific needs of their workforce. These programs should provide a tiered training initiative that covers both foundational and advanced GenAI skills, ensuring that employees across various roles are equipped to use these technologies effectively. Such programs can include hands-on training with AI tools, simulations and real-world case studies to enhance learning and retention.

Interestingly, organizations can utilize AI itself to help bridge the skills gap. GenAI tools can analyze employee performance data to identify specific skill deficiencies and recommend personalized training paths. For example, AI-driven platforms can create customized learning modules that adapt to individual learning styles and paces, making training more effective and engaging. Another option is for supply chain organizations to partner with educational institutions to develop targeted training programs that align with industry needs. By collaborating on curriculum development, companies can ensure that the next generation of supply chain professionals is equipped with the necessary skills in AI and data analytics. This proactive approach not only helps address current skill gaps but also builds a pipeline of talent for the future. Ultimately, upskilling and reskilling the organization should be part of an ongoing effort to create a culture of continuous learning that is vital for keeping pace with all technology advancements, not just in GenAI. Organizations should encourage employees to pursue ongoing education and professional development opportunities, such as certifications in AI and data analytics. This could involve providing access to online courses, workshops or industry conferences, which can help employees stay updated on the latest trends and best practices in GenAI.

The skill gaps in supply chain organizations present a formidable challenge in the implementation of generative AI solutions. By recognizing the common deficiencies in technical proficiency, data literacy and ethical AI use, organizations can take proactive steps to bridge these gaps. Through comprehensive training programs, leveraging AI for skill development, collaborating with educational institutions and fostering a culture of continuous learning, supply chain organizations can equip their workforce to harness the transformative power of GenAI, ultimately driving efficiency and innovation in their operations.

Security Risks

Just as data quality and access have been a persistent challenge for software applications, so too has data security. Unsurprisingly, data security was the second highest obstacle to implementing GenAI identified by 37% of respondents in the HFS study. In supply chain applications, data security has traditionally faced several key challenges. First, supply chains typically involve multiple partners, suppliers and customers, each with their own systems and security standards. This large and interconnected footprint creates a vast attack surface, rich with highly sensitive information, including pricing strategies, supplier relationships and proprietary logistics processes. Expanding the attack surface even further is the proliferation of connected devices and cloud-based services which dramatically increase the number of potential entry points for attackers. Additionally, supply chains typically span multiple countries or regions, subjecting them to stringent data protection regulations and increasing the complexity of securing data across borders.

While these traditional security challenges persist, generative AI introduces new dimensions to the cybersecurity landscape. GenAI models used for demand forecasting or route optimization are trained on vast datasets. If an attacker can introduce malicious data into the training set, they could potentially manipulate the model's outputs causing the compromised AI system to recommend inefficient routes or inaccurate inventory levels, disrupting operations and causing financial losses.

Privacy leakage is another potential issue. LLMs used for supplier communication or contract generation might inadvertently memorize and reproduce sensitive information from their training data. This could lead to unintentional disclosure of proprietary sourcing strategies or confidential supplier agreements. As technology evolves, so does the sophistication of the methods and tools used by malicious actors to breach systems and steal data, and the need for stronger cybersecurity becomes even more critical. For example, sophisticated attackers could craft prompt inputs designed to trick GenAI systems into producing harmful or biased outputs. In a supply chain context, this could lead to the AI recommending unreliable suppliers or suggesting dangerous shipping routes. Over time, GenAI models can grow to become a treasure trove of intellectual property, making them valuable targets for theft or reverse engineering. Competitors might attempt to steal or recreate proprietary models that give a company its competitive edge in areas like demand forecasting or dynamic pricing. GenAI systems in supply chains add another layer of complexity, often requiring real-time access to large volumes of data from various sources, including IoT devices, ERP systems and external data providers. Securing these complex data flows presents significant challenges.

While data security has always been a critical concern for supply chain applications, GenAI introduces new and complex challenges, necessitating a comprehensive and proactive approach to cybersecurity. It begins with robust data governance, establishing strict controls on data used for training AI models to protect sensitive information and proprietary processes. To counteract emerging threats, continuous monitoring with AI-powered security tools provides real-time detection and response capabilities. Upholding ethical AI frameworks ensures that the development and deployment of these technologies are conducted with fairness and integrity, considering the impact on all partners and stakeholders. Regular audits and penetration testing are equally indispensable, rigorously evaluating the security of AI systems and their infrastructure. Finally, a collaborative security approach with information sharing among industry peers, suppliers and cybersecurity experts ensures the collective resilience against the ever-evolving landscape of cyber threats.

Strategies for Success

The HFS study underscores that generative AI represents a powerful tool in the quest for autonomous supply chains. GenAI's ability to process vast amounts of data, generate creative solutions and adapt in real-time to changing conditions makes it a game-changer for supply chain management. However, the journey from enthusiasm to full-scale implementation reveals a landscape fraught with challenges. The study indicates that a mere 7% of organizations have fully deployed GenAI solutions, while only 28% have made significant strides toward achieving a low-human-touch supply chain. This gap underscores the complexity of integrating GenAI into the intricate web of supply chain operations, necessitating a strategic and holistic approach to overcome the barriers to adoption.

According to the study, those organizations who have demonstrated success in implementing GenAI have done so by employing a multifaceted approach: securing unwavering leadership support (67% prioritize this), forging strategic third-party partnerships (65%), ensuring a deep bench of technical talent (64%), and by strategically prioritizing GenAI initiatives that align with their overarching business objectives.

Central to their success is an unwavering commitment to data readiness — a cornerstone often overlooked by their peers. This encompasses rigorous standards for data quality, availability, security and governance practices, coupled with enhanced metadata management and the implementation of real-time data collection systems. This data-centric approach significantly bolsters the accuracy and efficacy of GenAI outcomes, addressing the most common implementation challenges — data quality and access.

Equally critical is their proactive approach to risk management. Front-runners collaborate intimately with cybersecurity teams from the outset, navigating the complex landscape of potential inaccuracies, legal liabilities and cybersecurity vulnerabilities that 40% of organizations struggle to fully comprehend. Perhaps most notably, the research reveals a growing trend among successful organizations to foster a culture of innovation as another key differentiator. Front-runners are 1.5 times more likely than their counterparts to empower their workforce by providing controlled access to GenAI tools (51% vs. 33%), thereby accelerating adoption and promoting innovation.

Industry Success Stories

DHL Embraces Generative AI to Revolutionize Logistics Operations (Stöppler, 2024)

As one of the largest logistics and delivery service providers in the world, DHL operates in more than 200 countries globally and offers a portfolio of logistics services ranging from parcel delivery, e-commerce solutions, road, air and ocean transport to industrial supply chain management. In a press release dated May 16, 2024, DHL announced the integration of GenAI into its customer portal, myDHLi, aimed at helping customers navigate the challenges in their logistics operations to combat the increasing frequency and impact of supply chain disruptions and global volatility. With over 20,000 customers already relying on the myDHLi platform to track over 400,000 shipments per month, DHL sought to leverage GenAI to further streamline these processes and improve the user experience.

To tackle this challenge, DHL introduced a GenAI-powered virtual assistant to the myDHLi customer portal designed to enhance the efficiency and usability of the platform by providing customers with faster access to critical information through a 24/7 chatbot. The chatbot acts as copilot in the tactical management of logistics, helping customers to inquire about shipment statuses, find contact details and receive support on various topics. The implementation of GenAI in myDHLi goes beyond just the virtual assistant. To improve resilience in the face of supply chain disruptions, DHL also leveraged AI to enhance the shipment tracking features in the portal, allowing users to quickly identify unforeseen changes in their shipments, providing them more time for informed decision-making. Additionally, the portal's reporting feature was enhanced with configurable and schedulable reports, with options for proactive updates through customizable notification settings.

The combined benefits of these AI-driven enhancements allow DHL customers to have greater visibility and control over their logistics operations, leading to improved efficiency and productivity. The GenAI-powered virtual assistant serves as a reliable partner in day-to-day supply chain management, offering instant support and guidance, providing quicker access to critical information and enabling faster response times to potential issues. Tim Scharwath, CEO of DHL Global Forwarding, said it best when describing the benefits of these AI-driven tools for customers. He stated, "The integration of GenAI into myDHLi allows us to further enhance their logistics experience, offering innovative solutions that drive usability, resilience and sustainability. Together, we are shaping the future of logistics, providing our customers with the tools they need to navigate the ever-changing landscape with confidence."

Exscientia Pioneers Generative AI for Rapid Drug Discovery (Keown, 2024)

Exscientia is an AI-driven PharmaTech company focused on the rapid discovery and development of effective medicines at faster speed and lower cost. They are pioneers in using artificial intelligence for drug discovery. In 2020, Exscientia, in partnership with Sumitomo Dainippon Pharma of Japan, was the first to advance an AI-designed drug candidate to go into human clinical trials — a potential treatment for obsessive-compulsive disorder (OCD). In July 2024, the company leveraged cloud computing and GenAI technologies to enhance their drug discovery process even further. They launched a state-of-the-art platform that further expanded their AI capabilities by integrating GenAI models for drug design with robotic lab automation, aiming to accelerate the discovery of high-quality drug candidates at lower costs.

The typical industry pace of the drug discovery process is hindered by conventional methods, which involve outsourcing large-scale chemical processing and biological testing to contract research organizations. This process is typically slow, expensive and sometimes yields suboptimal results. To solve this problem, Exscientia developed a novel approach that combines GenAI-driven design with automated experimentation, that consists of two main components. The first component, DesignStudio, uses GenAI models to "learn" rather than "screen" for discoveries in vast chemical spaces, enabling faster discovery of drug candidates that better target specific diseases and patients. The second component, AutomationStudio, uses state-of-the-art robotics to synthesize and test the drug candidates identified by the DesignStudio. It automates the molecular synthesis process, increasing efficiency in the physical experimentation phase. The key innovation in Exscientia's approach is the creation of a closed-loop system between these two components. Data from the testing completed at the AutomationStudio is fed back to the DesignStudio, continually improving its GenAI algorithms.

This innovative approach represents a significant shift in the drug discovery paradigm, offering multiple advantages. By integrating GenAI design workflows into the process, Exscientia was able to accelerate drug development, reduce costs, improve drug candidate quality and enable more precise targeting of specific diseases and patient populations, thus delivering higher-quality therapies to patients faster and at a lower cost than traditional methods allow. This revolutionary approach not only streamlines the drug discovery process but also holds the promise of more effective, tailored treatments for a wide range of medical conditions.

Walmart Automates Supplier Negotiations (Van Hoek et al., 2022)

Organizations that can effectively harness the power of GenAI, in combination with traditional AI and other technologies, will be well-positioned to build more resilient, efficient and autonomous supply chains. While full end-to-end autonomy may remain an aspirational goal, the journey toward it has already begun. One of the earliest examples of a successful GenAI solution in supply chain management was Walmart's implementation of AI-powered automated negotiations with suppliers.

As one of the world's largest retailers, Walmart faced a common challenge in procurement; the inability to conduct focused negotiations with all of its 100,000+ suppliers due to time and resource constraints. This resulted in about 20% of their tail spend suppliers having agreements with standard, non-negotiated terms, leaving untapped value on the table for both sides. To address this issue, Walmart worked with Pactum, a Canadian AI solution provider, to implement an innovative solution to automate negotiations using AI-powered technology.

The system included a GenAI-powered chatbot that autonomously negotiated with human suppliers on Walmart's behalf. Internal Walmart buyers selected target suppliers and created training scenarios for the machine learning algorithm, which were used to develop structured scripts guiding suppliers through negotiations. Suppliers could respond to scenarios at their own pace, providing flexibility in the negotiation process.

To minimize risk during testing, Walmart initially focused on a preapproved list of indirect spend suppliers, which included goods that are not resold to Walmart customers, such as fleet services, carts, and other equipment used in the stores. Walmart was extremely prescriptive regarding the outcomes it wanted to achieve in the negotiations, clearly defining acceptable trade-offs for the AI chatbot to negotiate effectively. The company targeted payment schedules, aiming to negotiate early payment discounts or extended payment terms without discounts. In exchange, Walmart offered suppliers options like changing termination provisions and opportunities for growth in assortment and sales volume. The pilot lasted three months and involved 89 suppliers, five buyers, and representatives from various departments. The results achieved exceeded expectations, with the chatbot running 2,000 negotiations simultaneously and successfully reaching agreements with 64% of participating suppliers, well above the initial 20% target.

Following the successful pilot, Walmart improved the scenarios and scripts based on supplier feedback and extended the solution to suppliers in other geographies. The expanded implementation resulted in deals with 68% of approached suppliers and generated an average savings of 3%. As the system continues to learn from each negotiation, setup time for new categories decreases, further improving efficiency. This shift toward algorithmic sourcing management allows procurement professionals to focus more on strategic relationships, exceptions, and continuous improvement, rather than routine negotiations. Walmart's successful implementation of AI-powered negotiations demonstrates how GenAI can be effectively applied to solve real-world business challenges, offering benefits to both buyers and suppliers while increasing the flexibility and resiliency of the supply chain.

THE ROAD AHEAD

In the tangled web of global commerce, supply chains are the orchestrators of organized chaos, setting the pace for the elaborate flow of goods and services among suppliers, producers, distributors and consumers. Along the way, these intricate networks navigate a myriad of challenges and uncertainties, from geopolitical tensions and regulatory changes to natural disasters and shifting consumer demands. As organizations face an increasingly volatile world, the ability to quickly adjust and innovate is crucial. They must adapt to unforeseen disruptions, optimize operations for efficiency, and strike a delicate balance between just-in-time delivery and robust risk mitigation strategies.

The emergence of generative AI ushers in a new era of possibilities for supply chain practitioners, promising a future where supply chains are not just responsive, but preemptive; not just efficient, but resilient. It enables systems that can learn from the past, adapt to the present, and anticipate the future, crafting strategies that are dynamic and risk-aware. The journey toward autonomous supply chains is paved with data — data that GenAI can interpret with insight that borders on intuition. This is not the cold calculation of traditional algorithms but a more nuanced, almost human-like understanding of the complex patterns that govern the global exchange of goods and services.

As we embrace this technology, we must do so with a sense of responsibility, a commitment to ethical principles and a recognition that the role of GenAI in supply chains is not to replace human ingenuity but to augment it — freeing us from the mundane and unleashing our creative potential. The road ahead is filled with both promise and challenges. It demands bold leadership, continuous innovation and a commitment to responsible AI practices, data preparedness, and the human element that remains at the heart of all we do. As practitioners and educators, our role is to guide this transition, equipping the next generation of supply chain professionals with the knowledge and the tools they need to navigate this new landscape.

REFERENCES

Berger, P. (2024). New disruptions geopolitics hang over 2024 supply chains. The Wall Street Journal.

Dzinkowski, R. (2024). "The Latest Supply Chain Crisis," Global Finance, https://gfmag.com/economics-policy-regulation/houthis-gaza-supply-chain-crisis,

Hamilton, E. (2023). The global supply chain consequences of the Russia-Ukraine war. University of Florida News, 21.

Keown, D. (2024). "Exscientia Launches AWS AI-powered Platform to Advance Drug Discovery," *Exscientia.com*, https://investors.exscientia.ai/press-releases/press-release-details/2024/Exscientia-Launches-AWS-AI-powered-Platform-to-Advance-Drug-Discovery/default.aspx.

Kurkina, I. (2023). "Leveraging of Cloud Computing in Supply Chain Management," *Academy Smart*, academysmart.com/insights/ leveraging-of-cloud-computing-in-supply-chain-management.

McKesson Health Systems Editorial Team. "Challenges Affecting Supply Chain to Continue Beyond Pandemic," McKesson, https://www.mckesson.com/pharmacy-management/health-systems/prescribed-perspectives/challenges-affecting-supply-chain-to-continue-beyond-pandemic, 2022

O'Toole, J. (2011). "Thailand floods stall automakers," *CNNMoney*, www.money.cnn.com/2011/10/28/news/international/ thailand_floods_automakers/index.htm.

Segal, E. (2024). "Most Surveyed Companies Are Vulnerable To Another Supply Chain Crisis," Forbes, https://www.forbes.com/sites/edwardsegal/2024/01/28/most-surveyed-companies-are-vulnerable-to-another-supply-chain-crisis,

Steinberg, G., ... (2024). "How will GenAI prompt a step change toward autonomous supply chains?" EY, www.ey.com/en_gl/insights/consulting/how-will-genai-prompt-a-step-change-toward-autonomous-supply-chains.

Stöppler, D. (2024). "For increased usability and efficiency: myDHLi meets GenAI," *DHL.com*, www.group.dhl.com/en/media-relations/press-releases/2024/for-increased-usability-and-efficiency-mydhli-meets-genai.html.

Tett, G. (2023). "How rising conflict is reshuffling global supply chains," Financial Times, https://www.ft.com/content/98766d3f-65ad-41c0-84cc-9b6e2757a17c,

Van Hoek, R., DeWitt, M., Lacity, M., & Johnson, T. (2022). “How Walmart Automated Supplier Negotiations,” *HBR.org*, www.hbr.org/2022/11/how-walmart-automated-supplier-negotiations.

Chapter 3
Generative Artificial Intelligence and Its Transformative Power in Supply Chain Operations Management

Kamalendu Pal
https://orcid.org/0000-0001-7158-6481
University of London, UK

ABSTRACT

Globalization and digitization have significantly influenced supply chain operation management in recent decades. This chapter outlines the critical challenges in supply chain management (SCM) and underscores the need to enhance operational resilience and visibility. It advocates for the integration of generative artificial intelligence (GenAI) applications to address these challenges. The chapter's primary focus is on the transformative potential of GenAI in promoting efficiency, agility, and strategic decision-making in supply chain operation management. It also highlights how cutting-edge GenAI technologies are reshaping the landscape of demand forecasting, operations, inventory management, and logistic resilience. A systematic review of GenAI technologies available for supply chain operations management is presented. The chapter underscores the transformative power of GenAI, suggesting a shift towards more intelligent, sustainable, and responsive supply chain ecosystems.

DOI: 10.4018/979-8-3693-4433-0.ch003

INTRODUCTION

Interconnected trade networks, a cornerstone of supply chain operations, have played a significant role in the awe-inspiring evolution of human civilization. These networks span social, economic, and environmental issues and have facilitated cross-border trade since ancient times. The early days of civilization saw the exchange of goods such as rice, wheat, spices, textiles, metals, petroleum products, and other essential commodities. The Silk Road, the Spice Route, and other interconnected trade transportation networks are evidence of these evolving trade patterns, which have only intensified with industrialization (Bardhan, 2003) and globalization (Stiglitz, 2017).

While the central perception of global trade is simple and unchanged to move goods and services from point A in one country to point B in another, the reality is much more complex (Pal, 2017) (Pal, 2018). This business operational practice includes tracking and tracing goods and related services along supply chains and verifying the source and the quality of those goods through provenance and product pedigree. As global trade has grown in scale, operational business processes have become more numerous and complex (Pal, 2020). In addition, these business practices strain to accommodate the demand of increased trade volume among more participants – business financiers, partners as importers and exporters servicing different market segments, freight forwarders, customs and port authorities, regulatory governing bodies, and insurance providers. It is important to recognize that the business communities genuinely understand and appreciate the concept of global supply chain operations, their values, and their management practices, and their role is crucial in the success of these operations (Pal & Ul-Haque, 2020) (Pal & Karakostas, 2014).

These management practices, combined with business process automation, operational data collection at different points of operations, and data-driven decision support systems (DSS), have dramatically reshaped operations management in supply chains. Moreover, applications of Generative Artificial Intelligence (GenAI) techniques have attracted significant interest from academics and practitioners in recent years. It supports big data analytics (Pal, 2023), enhances supply chain integration, and develops unprecedented capabilities by generating unusual, innovative, and creative content. The potential of Generative AI (GenAI) to create innovative solutions to supply chain challenges, such as developing new product designs or optimizing distribution routes, is not just promising but truly exciting, offering a glimpse into the future of supply chain management.

In the rapidly evolving digital transformation landscape, supply chains—the backbone of our global technological infrastructure—face unique and significant challenges. The advent of artificial intelligence applications represents a game-changing opportunity for modern industries and their supply chains. By harnessing manufacturing systems that can emulate human reasoning and engage in self-learning, organizations can unlock vast operational advantages and drive innovative solutions across various sectors, including marketing, procurement, logistics, and customer service.

AI applications in supply chain management can be effectively categorized into two distinct sections. The first encompasses tools designed to support managers and personnel without fully automating tasks, providing critical decision-making and process modelling assistance. GenAI empowers organizations to leverage big data analytics, fosters greater supply chain integration, and stimulates creativity by producing innovative content. This technology presents an opportunity to address complex supply chain challenges, such as generating novel product designs and optimizing distribution networks.

A wealth of literature reinforces the essential role of GenAI applications like ChatGPT and ChatBots in facilitating innovative work methodologies. These tools are crucial for organizations striving to enhance their digital supply chains, allowing them to capitalize on AI-powered predictive analytics for demand forecasting and inventory optimization. Furthermore, AI-driven automation can streamline production workflows and minimize lead times. This chapter seeks to elucidate the core capabilities of AI—learning, perception, prediction, interaction, adaptation, and reasoning, as shown diagrammatically in Figure 1 while emphasizing their interdependent nature in fostering a collaborative ecosystem that maximizes AI's potential within the supply chain operations.

- Learning allows AI systems to draw insights from data to make informed predictions and decisions, employing techniques like supervised, unsupervised, semi-supervised, and transfer learning.
- Perception exemplifies AI's ability to interpret and understand the environment through methods akin to human senses, encompassing computer vision, audio processing, and natural language processing.
- Prediction enables AI to foresee future outcomes based on historical data, utilizing approaches such as regression analysis, classification, time series forecasting, and anomaly detection.
- Interaction pertains to AI's capability to engage and make decisions within environments, including direct interactions with humans, employing reinforcement learning and human-AI collaborative approaches.
- Adaptation reflects AI's capacity to evolve and improve through continuous learning, utilizing mechanisms like continuous learning strategies and evolutionary algorithms.

- Reasoning encapsulates AI's ability to effectively plan and make decisions within complex scenarios, incorporating elements of symbolic reasoning, strategic planning, and informed decision-making.

Figure 1. Diagrammatic representation of artificial intelligence capabilities

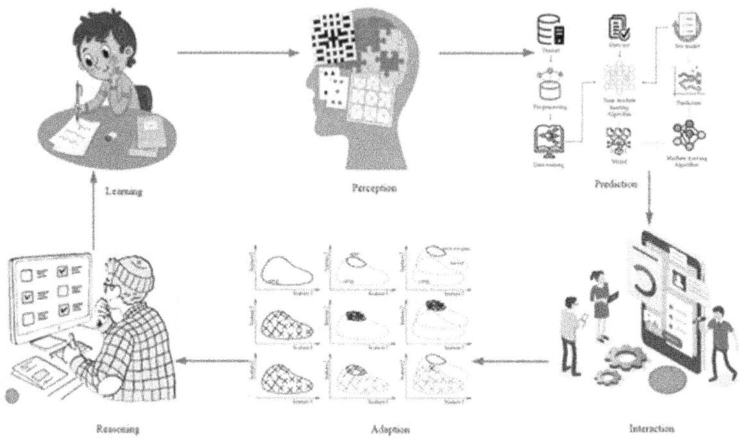

Additionally, the taxonomy of AI capabilities aligns with established frameworks within supply chain operations, underscoring the need for these capabilities to function cohesively to harness their full potential effectively. Following ambidexterity theory, innovation can be divided into exploratory (novel and radical) and exploitative (enhancing existing capabilities). Generative AI not only uncovers new opportunities but also optimizes the utilization of resources, leading to cost-effective innovations that ultimately improve supply chain performance.

BACKGROUND AND PROPOSED SOLUTION

The rapid advancement of AI, specifically the blossoming of generative models, has ushered in a new era for diverse fields, fundamentally altering the way we perceive, interact, and innovate with technology. Tools like ChatGPT (OpenAI, 2023) and DALL-E (Reddy et al., 2021) show the world their incredible power of generating content such as text or images. The impressive capability to generate human-like text, understand context, and even create artistic content was revolutionary and brought people's attention to the science beneath these AI tools — Deep Generative Models (DGMs).

Generative AI (GenAI) is at the forefront of a transformative wave in artificial intelligence (AI), driving a monumental shift in the capabilities of AI systems. This cutting-edge technology, enhanced by breakthroughs in machine learning algorithms and intensive data processing, empowers the creation of entirely new and original content—from text and images to intricate simulations (McKinsey, 2023). This transformative wave is characterized by the shift from AI Systems that primarily analyze and interpret data to those that can actively generate innovative outputs.

This exhilarating period in AI evolution signifies a decisive departure from simply analyzing and classifying existing data to actively generating innovative outputs. The potential applications across various sectors are vast, particularly in supply chain management, where generative AI can dramatically enhance efficiency and inform strategic decision-making, sparking excitement about its real-world impact.

LLMs showcase a groundbreaking advance in natural language processing, leveraging deep learning while being trained on enormous datasets. Their remarkable ability to create context-sensitive text closely emulates human communication, and this capability extends beyond text to encompass the generation of images and videos, significantly broadening the horizons of generative AI. Unlike traditional AI models, which primarily focus on pattern recognition and make predictions from existing data, generative AI stands apart with its unique talent for producing original content, sparking intrigue about its creative potential.

Business world is witnessing a revolutionary shift in artificial intelligence that offers a generative glimpse into a future where AI systems can not only understand but also create. To truly grasp the essence of Generative AI, it is essential to explore its core definition, pivotal concepts, and the innovative technologies driving its capabilities, such as Generative Adversarial Networks (GANs) and Variational Autoencoders (VAEs). This transformation represents a significant transition from traditional AI's data analytical focus towards a future where AI thrives as a creator and innovator, reshaping the technological landscape. The inspiring potential of generative AI invites us to imagine the future of technology we are on the brink of realizing (Tanielian, 2021).

At its core, GenAI refers to a class of artificial intelligence systems that possess the remarkable ability to generate new, original content. This content can take various forms, including text, images, music, and videos. Unlike traditional AI models that focus on data analysis and interpretation, GenAI emphasizes creativity and innovation, allowing machines to comprehend existing information and produce entirely new and creative outputs.

GenAI stands at the forefront of artificial intelligence and is powered by several key concepts and technologies, serving as the building blocks that enable its creative capabilities. Understanding these fundamental concepts can provide deeper insights into how generative AI operates.

Generative Adversarial Networks (GANs): GANs are the driving force behind Generative AI. They consist of two neural networks—the generator and the discriminator—engaged in a continuous duel. The generator's objective is to produce content that is indistinguishable from real data, while the discriminator aims to differentiate between real and generated data. This adversarial process ultimately leads to the creation of highly realistic content (El-Sayed et al., 2023)

Variational Autoencoders (VAEs): VAEs are probabilistic models skilled at learning the underlying structure of data. They encode input data into a lower-dimensional space and then decode it back to its original form. VAEs facilitate the generation of data that adheres to the learned distribution, making them particularly useful for creative endeavours (El-Sayed et al., 2023).

Recurrent Neural Networks (RNNs): RNNs are a type of neural network designed for processing sequences of data. They are essential for generating sequential content, such as text and music, by maintaining a hidden state that retains contextual information about the sequence, thereby generating coherent and contextually relevant outputs (El-Sayed et al., 2023)

Transformer Architecture: The Transformer architecture, exemplified by models like GPT (Generative Pre-trained Transformer), has fundamentally transformed natural language processing. This architecture serves as the powerhouse behind text generation and understanding, enabling AI systems to produce human-like text on a large scale (El-Sayed et al., 2023).

The development of the research database is methodically outlined, detailing the steps involved in selecting appropriate data sources, extracting pertinent data, and filtering this information to retain only the most relevant content for analysis. The process encompasses the integration and categorization of data, culminating in a robust framework for analyzing the impact of GenAI on procurement strategies, supplier selection, demand planning, manufacturing, operations, warehousing, and overall supply chain efficiency.

Figure 2. Generative artificial intelligence applications in supply chain market

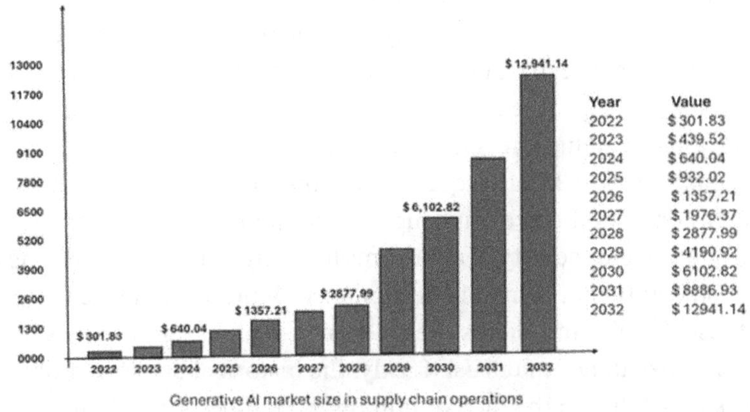

Based on the comprehensive market analysis, the global generative AI in the supply chain market, valued at USD 301.83 million in 2022, is projected to surge to approximately USD 12,941.14 million by 2032, with a CAGR of 45.62%, as shown in Figure 2 This significant growth is driven by the demand for efficient, cost-effective solutions facilitated by real-time data analytics. However, the challenge of inadequate data quality poses a restraint, potentially leading to erroneous algorithmic outputs. Despite this, opportunities abound in the increasing need for automated operations, particularly in global labour shortages, with cloud-based deployment modes dominating due to their data management capabilities. This analysis underscores the evolving landscape of GenAI applications in supply chain management, highlighting the critical balance between leveraging advanced AI capabilities and addressing inherent data quality challenges to optimize supply chain operations.

The demand for advanced GenAI solutions in supply chains is driven by their ability to utilize real-time data, enhancing efficiency and cost-effectiveness. However, the integration of GenAI faces challenges, particularly with the quality of data, which can lead to inaccurate predictions. This highlights a research gap in developing methods to ensure data integrity, which is crucial for the practical application of GenAI in supply chain management. Additionally, there is an opportunity to expand automated operations, further optimizing supply chains in response to labour shortages and market demands.

This methodological framework is instrumental in unravelling the advanced capabilities of Generative AI, enabling a nuanced analysis of its role in revolutionizing traditional supply chain practices through predictive analytics, scenario simulation, and data-driven decision-making processes. Each methodology phase is explicated, offering a clear roadmap of the research journey and constructing the foundational database that supports the ensuing analysis.

In delving into the nuanced interplay of generative AI within the supply chain milieu, we confront a tapestry of constraints that temper the exuberance of our findings. Paramount among these is the alchemy of data—the lifeblood of AI—where its abundance and fidelity are indispensable yet often elusive. The labyrinthine complexity and the fiscal heft required to summon GenAI into the supply chain arena further compound these challenges, erecting barriers to entry and mastery. Ethical quandaries and security conundrums loom significant, whispering questions of privacy and equity that demand our vigilance. Moreover, the arcane "black box" nature of these AI systems cloaks their decision-making in obscurity, challenging our quest for transparency and trust. Lastly, the historical anchoring of AI's predictive prowess may falter in the face of unforeseen tempests, reminding us of supply chains' inherent dynamism and caprice.

GENERATIVE AI TOOLS AND CAPABILITIES

The magic of Generative AI lies in its ability to synthesize content that is remarkably close to what a human might create. It can generate realistic images, write compelling stories, compose music, and even simulate scenarios. This opens a world of possibilities across various domains.

Generative AI represents a significant advancement in the field of artificial intelligence, defined by its ability to create original content. It leverages complex algorithms and deep learning techniques, learning from large datasets to produce novel outputs like text, images, audio, and even code. This contrasts with traditional AI, which primarily focuses on data analysis and interpretation. (Singh Gill & Kaur, 2023).

The applications of generative AI are diverse, impacting industries ranging from digital content creation to scientific research. For example, in content creation, it can generate realistic images or write coherent and contextually relevant text, offering significant opportunities for creative industries. It is also simulating complex scenarios or generating hypotheses, thereby accelerating innovation. (Roger Roberts, et al., 2023)

As technology continues to evolve, the fidelity and creativity of its outputs improve, presenting new possibilities and raising important considerations about ethics, authenticity, and the potential impact on various sectors. (Noorden, et al., 2023).

The ascent of generative AI is a testament to remarkable advancements in computational power and algorithmic innovation. This progress is not merely a linear extension of existing technologies but represents a paradigm shift in AI capabilities.

Generative AI's evolution is intricately linked to the surge in data availability and the increasing sophistication of neural networks. These networks, trained on diverse and massive datasets, have acquired an ability to understand and mimic complex patterns, whether in language, images, or even behavioural predictions. (McKinsey, 2023).

The integration of techniques like transfer learning and reinforcement learning has further propelled the potential of these models, enabling them to learn efficiently and adapt to new tasks with minimal human intervention. This development phase of generative AI reflects a broader trend in technology: a move towards systems that are not just reactive or analytical but are inherently creative and generative. This shift is poised to redefine the boundaries of machine intelligence, opening possibilities for AI to contribute not only to analytical capacities but also as drivers of innovation and creativity. (Tanielian, 2021).

The implications of this are profound, particularly in fields like supply chain management, where the ability to generate predictive models and creative solutions can lead to significant enhancements in efficiency and strategic planning.

The evolution of GenAI is not only a narrative of technological advancement but also a story of its growing economic and societal impact. The emergence of GenAI has ushered in new dimensions in the digital economy, fundamentally altering how businesses interact with data and technology. These AI models, particularly in the context of supply chain management, are reshaping traditional methodologies, introducing unprecedented levels of efficiency and predictive accuracy. The economic potential of generative AI extends beyond mere automation, fostering a new era of digital creativity and innovation. This transformative power of GenAI is underscored by its ability to generate realistic simulations and forecasts, which are invaluable in strategic planning and decision-making. As businesses and industries adapt to this new technological landscape, GenAI is poised to become a cornerstone in the digital transformation journey, offering both challenges and opportunities for organizations aiming to stay at the forefront of innovation. (by Michael Chui, 2023).

GenAI has demonstrated remarkable capabilities, fundamentally transforming various domains through its wide-ranging applications. One of its key strengths lies in the realm of natural language processing, where models like GPT and BERT have shown exceptional proficiency in generating human-like text, revolutionizing communication, and content creation. Beyond text, generative AI's capabilities extend to creating realistic images and simulations, significantly impacting fields such as design, media, and entertainment. In the business world, especially in supply chain management, these AI models are being employed for predictive analytics, decision support, and optimization, offering new levels of efficiency and insight. The application of generative AI in these domains underscores its versatility and transformative potential, positioning it as a critical tool in the advancement of digital strategies and innovation across various sectors. (Härlin et al., 2023).

The potential of generative AI extends into more specialized applications, illustrating its transformative impact across various industries. In healthcare, for instance, these AI systems are being explored for drug discovery and personalized medicine, leveraging their ability to analyze complex biological data. In finance, generative AI aids in risk assessment and fraud detection, offering new ways to handle large-scale financial data. The technology's adaptability is further evident in its use for environmental modeling, aiding in climate change research and sustainable development initiatives. These applications highlight not only the versatility of GenAI but also its potential to contribute to critical global challenges, offering innovative solutions that were previously unattainable.

GenAI's influence is particularly notable in creative industries, where it is revolutionizing content creation. This technology enables the generation of novel artworks, music, and literary works, challenging traditional notions of creativity. Its application in customizing user experiences, from personalized marketing to dynamic web content, showcases its capacity to understand and adapt to human preferences. Additionally, in logistics and supply chain management, generative AI plays a pivotal role in scenario planning and demand forecasting, greatly enhancing operational efficiencies. These diverse applications demonstrate generative AI's unique ability to not only process information but also to create and innovate, making it an asset across various sectors. (Härlin et al., 2023).

GENERATIVE AI AND SUPPLY CHAIN

In the dynamic landscape of supply chain management, Generative AI has emerged as a transformative force, as recent studies have quantified. Customer Service and Operations have seen the most significant improvement, with a remarkable 78% enhancement in their processes. This leap in performance can be attributed to AI's real-time data processing, allowing for rapid decision-making and heightened efficiency.

Operational Process and Optimization follow closely, with a 66% improvement. Generative AI has played a pivotal role in refining these processes, cutting down waste, and enhancing productivity across the board. Planning and Scheduling also benefit from

USE CASE 1: Predictive Maintenance

Supply chain resilience, the power of a company's end-to-end supply chain to proactively sense, absorb, adapt to, and recover from disruptions, is a field where predictive maintenance offering by integrating GenAI. Siemens has elevated its predictive maintenance offering by integrating GenAI. This novel feature transforms the maintenance process into a conversational and intuitive experience, enhancing the synergy between machine learning and GenAI. Such an integration ensures a robust solution that leverages the best of both technologies, offering a comprehensive approach to predictive maintenance (Siemens, 2024).

USE CASE 2: Smart Manufacturing

In the realm of smart manufacturing, parallel manufacturing emerges as a transformative approach, exemplified by the case of SANBODY technology company's FlexVega production line. The 3D computer vision-based unmanned line epitomizes the integration of parallel manufacturing within the industrial metaverse, showcasing a significant leap in production efficiency and automation (Yang J., et al., 2023).

USE CASE 3: Autonomous Delivery Service

Robots and autonomous vehicles are increasingly impacting last-mile delivery, transforming the logistics landscape with innovative solutions to traditional challenges. In this way, autonomous delivery robots and vehicles streamline the delivery process by navigating complex urban environments and delivering packages directly to customers' doorsteps. These robots operate autonomously, reducing the need for human intervention and enabling round-the-clock delivery services, significantly enhancing operational efficiency (Thyattchristopher, 2024).

FUTURE RESEARCH DIRECTIONS

Building on the transformative role of GenAI in supply chain operations, briefly described in this chapter, future research directions present a rich landscape of opportunities. Business organizations can significantly bolster their resilience and trust among the supply chain stakeholders by leveraging cutting-edge technologies like GenAI. In this way, GenAI approaches facilitate process automation, comprehensive analysis, and actionable insights that align perfectly with practical strategies for resolving critical cyber supply chain management issues and decision-making processes with real-time data. With the exponential growth of supply chain operational data, the role of AI and big data in SCM has become increasingly significant. Modern supply chain professionals leverage big data analytics, including data science, to enhance processes and performance. The importance of data quality for effective SCM decision-making cannot be overstated, emphasizing the need for functional capabilities, information sharing, and data proficiency. Successful SCM now hinges on a data-centric approach, having evolved from traditional reporting to advanced analytics encompassing statistical analysis and real-time optimization. However, there remains considerable scope for research in integrating big data analytics into supply chain operations.

Despite advancements in computing, supply chain operations still involve complex decision-making. While optimization tools have enhanced efficiency, they often necessitate input from individuals lacking expertise, leading to prolonged interactions with program managers and data experts. The emergence of large language models (LLMs) like ChatGPT has sparked interest in the potential of AI within supply chains, promising to revolutionize decision-making processes. LLMs, with their advanced capabilities, play a crucial role in deciphering intricate probability distributions. In the retail sector, ChatGPT is enhancing inventory management and trends in customer inquiries, seamlessly integrating with supply chain software and warehouse management systems. In the military domain, AI is revolutionizing equipment acquisition, predicting demand, optimizing transport routes, and automating inventory management to improve supply chain efficiency.

Security breaches are a critical aspect of the supply chain that cannot be overlooked. Relying on software systems increases vulnerability, leading to significant financial and data losses. This underscores the essentiality of prioritizing cybersecurity. Traditional methods for analyzing past failures involve manual report reading. However, automated support through natural language processing (NLP) and LLMs can reduce costs and enhance incident analysis.

Many industries are using NLP and AI to enhance supply chain efficiency. For example, IBM Watson offers supply chain management solutions that use NLP to analyze unstructured data, providing insights into supply chain risks and opportunities. SAP Ariba leverages AI and NLP for procurement and supplier management, aiding supplier discovery and risk assessment. Llamasoft's supply chain design software utilizes AI and machine learning to optimize networks, processing textual data for improved decision-making. Additionally, platforms such as GEP SMART employ AI for spend analysis and contract management, enhancing understanding of procurement data. Some companies also develop text analysis tools that integrate LLMs like GPT-3 to process unstructured data from various sources, extracting insights relevant to supply chain management. In addition, big data handling ethical issues is essential for developing new-generation SCM applications.

CONCLUSION

The exploration of GenAI in supply chain operations unveils a transformative landscape where traditional processes are redefined through advanced predictive capabilities and automation. This thesis has meticulously examined the multifaceted applications of GenAI, revealing its profound influence on the efficiency and dynamism of supply chain management. By analyzing data from specific types of sensors and IoT devices, such as temperature sensors in refrigerated trucks and RFID tags on shipping containers, GenAI predicts equipment failures before they occur, scheduling timely maintenance that minimizes downtime and enhances operational efficiency. This predictive maintenance approach extends the lifespan of critical equipment and ensures uninterrupted supply chain operations, fostering a more resilient and efficient system.

GenAI introduces a new era of precision and consistency in quality assurance. Through advanced analytics and machine learning, it continuously monitors production processes and identifies deviations from quality standards in real time. This continuous monitoring capability provides a constant reassurance of quality, enabling immediate corrective actions and ensuring the final product meets the desired quality criteria. Integrating Generative AI in quality assurance processes elevates product standards and significantly reduces waste and rework, contributing to overall supply chain sustainability.

As encapsulated in this thesis, the exploration of GenAI in supply chain operations serves as a beacon for future research. The potential avenues for further investigation are as diverse as they are critical, from delving deeper into the long-term effects of GenAI integration to unravelling its implications for sustainability and ethical supply chain practices. Other potential areas for research include the development of more advanced predictive models, the exploration of GenAI's role in supply chain decision-making, and the investigation of its impact on workforce dynamics. The quest for knowledge in this domain is far from over; it is an ever-expanding horizon, urging us to push the boundaries of what we know and venture into the realms of what we can imagine. The potential for future research in this area is vast and inspiring, offering numerous opportunities for further exploration and discovery.

In conclusion, the journey through the landscapes of GenAI and supply chain operations is a testament to the transformative power of technology. It is a narrative of innovation, challenges, and the relentless pursuit of efficiency and agility. As we stand on the brink of this new era, the final thoughts resonate with optimism and a call to action. The future of supply chain management, underpinned by GenAI, is not just about adapting to change; it is about leading it, shaping it, and, in doing so, redefining the very essence of how we conceive, manage, and evolve the supply chains that underpin our global economy. In this way, GenAI is a future, and it has the power to shape and the responsibility to lead a future where the potential of GenAI is fully realized in the transformation of supply chain management.

REFERENCES

Ageron, B., Bentahar, O., & Gunasekaran, A. (2020, July). Digital supply chain: Challenges and future directions. In Supply chain forum [). Taylor & Francis.]. *International Journal (Toronto, Ont.)*, 21(3), 133–138.

Bardhan, P. (2003). *International Trade Growth and Development: Essays*. Wiley-Backwell. DOI: 10.1002/9780470752777

Bengesi, S., El-Sayed, H., Sarker, M. K., Houkpati, Y., Irungu, J., & Oladunni, T. (2024). Advancements in Generative AI: A Comprehensive Review of GANs, GPT, Autoencoders, Diffusion Model, and Transformers. *IEEE Access : Practical Innovations, Open Solutions*.

Deloitte. (2023). *How Generative AI will transform Sourcing and Procurement Operations.*

Gill, S. K., & Kaur, R. (2023). ChapGPT: Vision and challenges.

Harlin, T., Rova, G. B., Singla, A., Sokolov, O., & Sukharevsky, A. (2023). Exploring opportunities in the generative AI value chain.

Hyunjin, C. (2020). A study on application of generative design system in manufacturing process. [). IOP Publishing.]. *IOP Conference Series. Materials Science and Engineering*, 727(1), 012011.

McKinsey (2023). What is generative AI?

Noorden, C., Stokel, W., & Van, R. (2023). The Promise and Peril of generative AI.

Pal, K. (2017). Supply Chain Coordination Based on Web Services. In Chan, H. K., Subramanian, N., & Abdulrahman, M. D. (Eds.), *Supply Chain Management in the Big Data Era* (pp. 137–171). IGI Global Publication. DOI: 10.4018/978-1-5225-0956-1.ch009

Pal, K. (2018). "A Big Data Framework for Decision Making in Supply Chain", In M. V Kumar, G. D. Putnik, J. Javakrishna, V. M. Pillai, L. Varela (Edited); IGI Publication, September 2018, USA, Chapter 1, IGI Global Publication, Hershey PA, USA.

Pal, K. (2020). "Information Sharing for Manufacturing Supply Chain Management Based on Blockchain Technology", in Dr Idongesit Williams (Eds.), Cross-Industry Use of Blockchain Technology and Opportunities for the Future, Chapter 1, May, IGI Global Publication, Hershey PA, USA. DOI: 10.4018/978-1-7998-3632-2.ch001

Pal, K., & Karakostas, B. (2014). A Multi Agent-Based Service Framework for Supply Chain Management, In the proceeding of International Conference on Ambient Systems, Networks and Technology. *Procedia Computer Science*, 32, 53–60. DOI: 10.1016/j.procs.2014.05.397

Pal, K., & Ul-Haque, A. (2000). "Internet of Things and Blockchain Technology in Apparel Manufacturing Supply Chain Data Management", In the proceeding of 11th International Conference on Ambient Systems, Networks and Technologies (ANT-2020), Procedia Computer Science, pp. 450- 457, April 6-9, Warsaw, Poland.

Siemens (2024). https://www.siemens.com/global/en/products/services/gbs/our-insights/newsroom/generative-ai.html

Stiglitz, J. (2017). *Globalization and its Discontents Revisited: Anti-Globalization in the Era of Trump*. Penguin.

Thyattchristopher (2024). https://digitaltechnologysolutions.tech.blog/2024/03/16.

Yang, J., Wang, Y., Miao, Q., Wang, F. Y., Zhao, A., Deng, J. L., & Liubo, V. L. (2023). Steps towards Industry 5.0 [parallel industries with cyber-physical-social intelligence]. *Building (London)*, •••, 6S.

Chapter 4
The Convergence of Artificial Intelligence and Graphical User Interface

Swetha Chenchu
Sreenidhi Institute of Science and Technology, India

Vignesh Kandem
https://orcid.org/0009-0007-6956-1163
Sreenidhi Institute of Science and Technology, India

T. Dattaram
https://orcid.org/0009-0005-4206-0874
Sreenidhi Institute of Science and Technology, India

T. Venkat Narayana Rao
https://orcid.org/0000-0002-1996-1819
Sreenidhi Institute of Science and Technology, India

ABSTRACT

AI (Artificial Intelligence) and GUI (Graphical User Interface) are the two most cutting-edge technologies. These technologies individually can make a comprehensive change in industries and alter economic and social interactions and connections. In general, Now-a-days AI is integrated with human technology and used in some wide range of sectors like healthcare, finance to education, banking, manufacturing, transportation, etc. GUI is used in gaming, designing, AR (Augmented reality) and VR (Virtual reality), media, smart home devices, etc., Integration of Artificial Intelligence and Graphical User Interface is beneficial for both users and app developers. The convergence of AI and GUI gives dynamic applications like Data Visualization, Insights, Smart assistants, Adaptions, Navigations, and Predictive

DOI: 10.4018/979-8-3693-4433-0.ch004

analytics. This integration will increase the ease of access for new information to users. Now we are facing some general problems based on these technologies like Adaptive User Interfaces, Automated user interface testing, AI-Enhanced data visualization, Intelligent GUI Design Assistance, Real-Time Emotion Recognition for GUI Adaptation, etc., User interfaces are often designed with a one-size-fits-all approach, which does not account for individual user preferences and abilities. Designing perceptive and attractive GUIs requires significant space and time. This chapter focus on how can we develop a UI (User Interface) with base of AI which can be capable of solving the above obstacles and gives the simple objectives and technical solutions. By this integration we can execute some future projects like AI-Enhanced Customer Support Portals, Adaptive Gaming Interfaces, Interactive Financial Management Systems, and more.

INTRODUCTION

In this chapter of "convergence of AI and GUI" we are addressing some problems on AI and GUI on how it will help in modern technologies of the world. What can be trends in the coming future, what can we master so we can work on them and what are the different objectives in the GUI. GUIs (graphical user interface) are types of user interfaces which allows users to interact with digital devices and software applications by some sort of graphical designs.

As we all know that NEED is the word which sounds simple but that is the thing which makes people to discover, invent or develop great things like GUI.(D. B., N. Bicocchi,2020) This was made to make technology accessible by everyone. GUIs are designed to make operations on the technologies more easily accessible. GUIs are user friendly, easily accessible to even non- technical users. It allows users to do multitasking by allowing multiple windows and applications to be used simultaneously. Icons and graphics can provide an intuitive understanding of their use which makes navigation easier.

A GUI is a type of user interface through which users interact with electronic devices via visual indicator representations (L.c. Briland, 2012). Any UI that can interact with end users in an intelligent way AI techniques is termed an intelligent user interface. GUIs have revolutionized how we interact with computers, making complex tasks more intuitive and accessible to a wide range of users. With advent of AI and GUI, it makes easier, creating a seamless and efficient user experience. One of their abilities is to understand the natural language. AI can enhance GUIs with features like computer vision, enabling them to recognize and interpret visual inputs from users, such as gestures or facial expressions. Eventually this can lead to hand free gestures. AI'S can enhance GUIS by automating repetitive tasks and providing very good suggestions based on data analysis. This will help the user to complete his task more effectively and efficiently. The some of the future trends and problem facing technologies in GUIS are Adaptive User Interfaces, (D. Ferrucci et al.,2013), Automated user interface testing, AI-Enhanced data visualization, Intelligent GUI Design Assistance, Real-Time Emotion Recognition for GUI Adaptation. AI developers typically command salaries ranging from $100,000 to $150,000 annually, with individuals in senior roles or specialized domains like computer vision frequently enjoying higher compensation packages. Proficiency in coding is indispensable for various professions within the realm of artificial intelligence, such as:

- Python
- Java
- Apache Spark
- Python 3
- Pandas

The Evolution and Convergence of AI and GUI Technology

1. Graphical User Interface (GUI)

Definition

A Graphical User Interface (GUI) is a type of interface that allows users to interact with computers and devices through visual elements, such as icons, buttons, windows, and menus. Unlike command-line interfaces (CLI), which require users to type textual commands, GUIs rely on graphical representations to make interaction more intuitive and user-friendly.

Historical Context

The concept of a GUI was first introduced in the 1970s by researchers at Xerox PARC (Palo Alto Research Center), notably with the Xerox Alto computer, which featured the first graphical desktop interface. This approach was revolutionary because it allowed users to interact with the computer in a more visual, accessible manner, rather than requiring them to remember complex commands. In the 1980s, Apple's Macintosh and Microsoft's Windows operating systems popularized the GUI, making it the standard for personal computers. Today, GUIs are used in almost all consumer electronics, including smartphones, tablets, and smart TVs, and are a central component of user experience (UX) design.

The Evolution of Graphical User Interfaces (GUIs)

The concept of the graphical user interface emerged in the early 1970s, largely thanks to the research done at Xerox PARC (Palo Alto Research Center). The Xerox Alto, introduced in 1973, is considered one of the first computers to feature a graphical interface, using windows, icons, and a mouse to facilitate user interaction. This was a groundbreaking development, as it shifted away from command-line interfaces (CLI) where users had to type text commands to interact with a computer.

The 1980s marked the rise of GUIs in personal computing. Apple's Macintosh (1984) and Microsoft Windows (released in 1985) brought graphical interfaces to the mass market, making them standard on personal computers. These GUIs featured icons, buttons, and windows that represented tasks and applications visually, significantly improving usability for non-technical users. During this time, GUIs evolved to include more sophisticated user interface (UI) design principles, focusing on user-centered design to create more intuitive experiences.

The advent of smartphones in the late 2000s, notably with Apple's iPhone (2007), revolutionized GUI design once again. The introduction of multi-touch screens allowed users to interact with devices through gestures like tapping, swiping, and pinching. The flat design trend also became popular in the 2010s, focusing on simplicity and clarity in visual elements. As GUIs continued to evolve, responsive design became crucial, ensuring that interfaces ad**ones and tablets.**

GUI Design's Influence on Other Disciplines

1. Human-ComputerInteraction (HCI)

One of the most significant fields influenced by GUI design is Human-Computer Interaction (HCI), which studies how humans interact with computers and how to design systems that are easy and intuitive to use. The evolution of GUIs from text-based interfaces to graphic-based ones in the 1980s and 1990s drastically improved accessibility, making technology available to a wider audience.

o Impact on Cognitive Psychology: GUI design has informed cognitive psychology by revealing how people process visual information and interact with digital environments. For example, research into cognitive load—the amount of mental effort required to process information—has led to principles like minimalism in GUI design, where interfaces aim to present only essential information in a clear, uncluttered way. This helps reduce the cognitive load on users, making tasks easier to complete.

- Impact on Accessibility: GUI design also intersects with accessibility and inclusive design. It has influenced how users with disabilities interact with technology, resulting in the development of features like screen readers, voice commands, and high-contrast visual themes to ensure that GUIs are usable by people with visual, auditory, or motor impairments.

2. Design and Aesthetics

The visual and aesthetic principles underlying GUI design have been influenced by various art and design disciplines, including graphic design, industrial design, and visual communication. These fields have shaped how GUIs present information to users in an engaging and intuitive manner, using principles such as balance, contrast, typography, and color theory.

- Impact on Product Design: GUIs have influenced the broader field of product design, particularly in consumer electronics. The development of smartphones and wearable devices relies heavily on effective GUI design to create intuitive and aesthetically pleasing user interfaces. The Apple iPhone, for instance, revolutionized mobile design by integrating both functional and aesthetic GUI elements, which were influenced by industrial design principles.

3. Sociology and Anthropology

GUI design has been shaped by how different cultures interact with technology. Sociology and anthropology contribute to understanding how social norms, cultural expectations, and technological habits influence the way people use and perceive computer interfaces. As technology spreads globally, understanding cultural differences in visual representation, language, and user behavior becomes increasingly important.

- Impact on Globalization: GUIs must be adapted to different languages and cultural contexts to reach global audiences. For example, right-to-left (RTL) reading systems are incorporated in GUIs for languages like Arabic and Hebrew, influencing how designers approach interface layout and text direction. Similarly, color symbolism varies across cultures, requiring thoughtful decisions in design choices to avoid misunderstandings or offense.

Definition: Artificial Intelligence (AI) refers to the simulation of human intelligence in machines, enabling them to perform tasks that would normally require human cognition, such as learning, reasoning, problem-solving, and decision-making.

Machine Learning (ML) is a subset of AI that focuses on teaching computers to recognize patterns in data and improve their performance over time without being explicitly programmed.

Historical Context

The field of AI was formally established in 1955 by computer scientist John McCarthy, who coined the term and organized the Dartmouth Conference, which is considered the birth of AI as an academic discipline. Early AI research focused on creating symbolic systems that could solve problems through logical reasoning. In the 1980s, machine learning began to gain traction, particularly through neural networks, which are designed to mimic the way the human brain processes information. However, it was not until the 2010s, with advances in deep learning (a more sophisticated form of neural networks), that AI and ML achieved widespread success in areas such as image recognition, natural language processing, and emotion detection. Today, ML and deep learning techniques are the backbone of emotion recognition systems, helping them analyze complex data sets to detect emotional cues accurately.

The Evolution of Artificial Intelligence (AI)

AI as a formal field began in the mid-20th century. In 1956, John McCarthy coined the term "Artificial Intelligence" at the Dartmouth Conference, which is considered the birth of AI as an academic discipline. Early AI research focused on symbolic systems, where computers followed explicit rules to solve problems. One of the most influential figures during this period was Alan Turing, who introduced the Turing Test in 1950, aiming to measure a machine's ability to exhibit intelligent behavior indistinguishable from that of a human.

In the 1970s, AI research shifted towards expert systems, which aimed to mimic the decision-making abilities of a human expert in specific fields. These systems, such as MYCIN (developed in 1972), could diagnose bacterial infections based on user input, demonstrating the potential of AI to support decision-making in real-world applications. This period also saw advancements in natural language processing (NLP), allowing computers to understand and respond to human language.

Machine Learning and Neural Networks (1990s-2000s)

By the 1990s, AI research had evolved to focus on machine learning (ML), where algorithms could learn from data without being explicitly programmed. The introduction of neural networks—models inspired by the structure of the human brain—revolutionized the field of AI. The 2000s saw the rise of deep learning, a subset of ML, which enabled more complex and accurate tasks, including image recognition, speech recognition, and emotion detection.

In the last decade, deep learning and large datasets have driven AI's rapid advancement, leading to breakthroughs in a wide range of applications, including computer vision, speech recognition, and emotion recognition. With tools like TensorFlow and PyTorch, researchers and developers can now create AI models that analyze vast amounts of data to detect complex patterns, such as identifying human emotions based on facial expressions, voice tones, and other biometric signals.

AI's Influence on Other Disciplines

1. Cognitive Science and Psychology

AI has long drawn inspiration from cognitive science and psychology, particularly in its early stages. The concept of mimicking human intelligence, as proposed by pioneers like Alan Turing, is rooted in cognitive psychology, which seeks to understand the mental processes involved in perception, learning, reasoning, and decision-making. Early AI systems, such as expert systems and neural networks, were designed based on how humans solve problems and process information.

- Impact on Emotion Recognition: In AI's more recent advancements, affective computing—a field focused on emotion recognition and emotional AI—has emerged from the intersection of AI and psychology. Research in emotion theory, such as Paul Ekman's six basic emotions, directly informs AI systems that analyze facial expressions, voice tones, and other emotional cues to detect users' emotional states.
- Impact on Machine Learning: Cognitive science has also influenced the development of machine learning (ML) algorithms. For example, reinforcement learning—where AI agents learn through trial and error, mimicking how humans learn through feedback—has its roots in psychology, specifically in behaviorist theories of learning (e.g., B.F. Skinner's operant conditioning).

2. Neuroscience

AI's neural networks are explicitly inspired by the biological neural networks in the human brain. In particular, deep learning algorithms, which have become central to modern AI, simulate the way neurons in the brain work by processing information through layers of interconnected nodes (artificial neurons). The more complex the network, the "deeper" the learning process, which is why this technique is called deep learning.

- o Impact on AI Algorithms: Insights from neuroscience helped shape how AI systems process sensory data and recognize patterns. Convolutional neural networks (CNNs), for instance, are widely used for image recognition and are based on the visual processing mechanisms of the human brain, specifically mimicking how the visual cortex processes images.

3. Ethics and Philosophy

AI has raised significant ethical concerns, particularly in areas such as bias in algorithms, privacy, and the potential impact on jobs. The development of AI systems, especially in areas like facial recognition, has led to discussions about the moral implications of using AI in everyday life. The field of AI ethics is now a growing interdisciplinary area that includes contributions from philosophers, ethicists, and technologists.

- o Impact on AI Policies: Philosophical discussions around free will, autonomy, and the nature of intelligence influence how AI is framed in society. Ethical concerns also lead to the creation of guidelines and regulations such as the General Data Protection Regulation (GDPR) in Europe and calls for greater transparency in AI systems. The principles of fairness and accountability also guide the development of AI algorithms to ensure they are unbiased and respect user rights.

3. Natural Language Processing (NLP)

Definition: Natural Language Processing (NLP) is a branch of AI that deals with the interaction between computers and human (natural) languages. It involves enabling machines to understand, interpret, and generate human language, allowing systems to process textual or spoken input to discern meaning, sentiment, or intent.

Historical Context

NLP has its roots in the 1950s, when early computer scientists like Alan Turing began to explore how machines could understand and mimic human language. One early milestone was the development of the ELIZA program (1966), which simulated conversation using pattern-matching techniques. Over time, NLP progressed from simple rule-based systems to more complex statistical models and machine learning approaches. The rise of deep learning in the 2010s revolutionized NLP, with techniques like transformers (used in models such as GPT-3) significantly improving the accuracy of text-based emotion recognition and sentiment analysis.

Convergence of AI and GUI Technology

In the 1990s, as AI technology became more advanced, some early applications began to integrate AI with GUI design. One example was Clippy, the Microsoft Office assistant launched in 1997, which used basic AI to interact with users through a GUI, offering help based on the user's behavior. Though Clippy's execution was often criticized, it represented one of the first instances of AI being integrated into GUIs to enhance user experience.

The real convergence of AI and GUIs came in the 2000s with the development of virtual personal assistants like Siri (2011), Google Assistant (2016), and Amazon Alexa (2014). These AI-driven systems used natural language processing and machine learning to interpret voice commands and respond with contextually relevant actions, all within a user-friendly graphical interface. In this era, adaptive GUIs began to emerge, which could adjust in response to user needs or environmental factors (e.g., changing themes based on time of day or user mood).

The Convergence of AI and GUI: Cross-Disciplinary Interactions

1. AI-Powered Adaptive Interfaces

The integration of AI into GUI design has created new, adaptive interfaces that can respond to a user's needs and emotional states. This convergence draws on psychology, cognitive science, and HCI to create systems that adjust their behavior based on emotional cues (e.g., facial expressions, tone of voice) or user preferences. Such systems are now used in applications ranging from personalized content recommendations to adaptive learning platforms.

- Impact on Emotional Intelligence: The intersection of AI and GUI design is particularly evident in emotion recognition systems, where AI algorithms analyze user data to detect emotional states. These interfaces then adapt their design—by changing content, layout, or tone—to improve user satisfaction and experience. This requires input from fields such as psychology (emotion theory), design (aesthetic adaptation), and AI (machine learning algorithms).

2. Voice User Interfaces (VUIs)

The integration of voice recognition AI with GUIs has given rise to Voice User Interfaces (VUIs), which allow users to interact with devices through voice commands. This convergence between AI and GUI design involves fields like linguistics, speech recognition, and HCI to improve accuracy, usability, and user satisfaction. Systems like Amazon Alexa, Google Assistant, and Apple Siri have transformed the way people interact with technology, moving beyond traditional GUI to incorporate multimodal interfaces (i.e., combining visual, auditory, and gesture-based inputs).

3. Ethical and Privacy Concerns

The combination of AI and GUI design also raises important ethical and privacy concerns, particularly when it comes to data collection and user tracking. As AI systems increasingly gather emotional or behavioral data through GUIs (e.g., monitoring facial expressions or voice tone), there is a growing need for regulations and guidelines that protect user privacy and ensure ethical AI development. This involves cross-disciplinary collaboration between AI developers, ethicists, designers, and policymakers to balance innovation with user rights.

Case Study 1: AI-Enhanced Data Visualization

In recent years, dashboards and data visualizations have become indispensable tools for businesses seeking to analyze and interpret large datasets. These tools have significantly evolved with the rise of Artificial Intelligence (AI), providing more sophisticated and interactive methods for understanding complex data. AI-enhanced data visualizations offer a deeper level of insight, streamlining data processing, presenting dynamic visual representations, and offering predictive analytics capabilities. This evolution of data visualization has transformed how businesses operate, enabling proactive decision-making and more effective strategies. In this context, the role of AI in data visualizations, its applications, challenges, and future trajectories form the cornerstone of this technological evolution.

The Role of AI in Data Visualizations and Dashboards

AI has had a profound impact on the design and functionality of data visualizations and dashboards, automating key aspects of data analysis and improving the depth of insights provided. Historically, visualizing data was a labor-intensive process that relied heavily on manual inputs and a static representation of datasets. However, with the integration of AI, the ability to process and represent data has become far more sophisticated. AI algorithms can now analyze complex datasets and automatically generate visualizations that reveal patterns, correlations, and anomalies that would have been difficult, if not impossible, to identify manually (Briland, 2012). Furthermore, AI-powered dashboards are now capable of predictive analytics, offering insights into future trends by examining historical data. This predictive capability helps businesses anticipate market shifts, consumer behavior changes, and other key variables that inform strategic decision-making (Ferrucci et al., 2013).

In addition to predictive capabilities, AI enhances user engagement with data visualizations. By enabling more interactive and dynamic visualizations, AI allows users to manipulate data in real-time, adjusting variables and exploring different perspectives. This flexibility encourages deeper understanding and more informed decision-making. Through these enhanced capabilities, AI has fundamentally shifted the role of data visualizations from passive displays of information to active, interactive tools that empower users to uncover actionable insights (Gajjar et al., 2021).

Leveraging AI in Data Visualizations and Dashboards

The integration of AI into data visualizations and dashboards has brought about several groundbreaking innovations that significantly enhance the effectiveness of data analysis. Key techniques for leveraging AI in this domain include Natural Language Generation (NLG), automated dashboard creation, predictive analytics, and personalized dashboards.

One of the most notable advancements is the use of NLG, which transforms complex datasets into easily digestible narratives. This technology allows users, even those without technical expertise, to understand key data points through simple, readable summaries. NLG is particularly valuable for generating automatic reports and insights directly from the data, making it easier for non-technical stakeholders to interpret and act on critical information (Bicocchi & D., 2020). Similarly, AI enables the automation of dashboard creation. By analyzing datasets, AI can identify the most relevant metrics and recommend the best visualization formats. Platforms like Luzmo use AI to automatically generate dashboards by detecting key data points and presenting them in the most insightful ways, reducing the manual effort needed to design dashboards and ensuring that the most pertinent information is highlighted (Gajjar et al., 2021).

Another powerful capability of AI is its ability to perform predictive analytics, which goes beyond visualizing historical and current data to forecast future trends. This predictive feature helps businesses make more informed decisions by anticipating potential outcomes and reacting proactively to emerging patterns (Ferrucci et al., 2013). Finally, AI-driven dashboards offer significant customization and personalization. By understanding the specific needs of individual users or departments, AI tailors dashboards to display the most relevant metrics based on the user's role. Whether for a support agent in an airline or an executive looking for high-level insights, this level of personalization ensures that each user receives the most pertinent data for their unique context (Bicocchi & D., 2020). Together, these

AI-driven innovations transform the way data is visualized and analyzed, making it more accessible, insightful, and actionable for users across various levels of expertise.

Automating Dashboard Creation with AI

AI is playing a crucial role in automating the entire process of dashboard creation, revolutionizing the way businesses generate, interact with, and analyze data. This innovation significantly increases the speed and accuracy of dashboard generation while enhancing user satisfaction by minimizing the need for manual intervention. Key features of AI-driven dashboard automation include voice and text interactions, adaptive interfaces, real-time updates, natural language processing (NLP), and API integration.

Voice and text interactions allow users to engage with dashboards using simple, natural language commands. Whether through voice queries or written text, users can ask questions or request specific insights, with the dashboard providing real-time responses. This feature is particularly valuable for non-technical users, as it simplifies data exploration and makes it accessible without needing deep technical expertise. Similarly, AI-powered dashboards can adapt their layout and content dynamically based on user preferences and actions. This adaptability ensures that the most relevant data is always presented in the foreground, with the interface evolving to meet the user's changing needs and preferences, enhancing overall user experience.

Real-time updates are another significant benefit of AI automation. AI ensures that dashboards remain current by automatically refreshing data in real-time, which is essential for businesses that rely on live information to make timely, informed decisions. This capability guarantees that decision-makers always have access to the latest data, reducing the risks of working with outdated information. Furthermore, by integrating natural language processing (NLP), AI enables users to query and interact with data in a conversational manner. This democratizes data access, allowing even non-technical users to ask questions and receive immediate, meaningful insights—much like a data scientist would. This feature makes data-driven decision-making more accessible across the organization (Bicocchi & D., 2020).

Finally, AI-driven dashboards can seamlessly integrate with external APIs, extending their functionality and enhancing their capabilities. For example, platforms like Luzmo leverage OpenAI's GPT-3 and GPT-4 through API connections to generate automated visualizations. This integration allows AI to pull data from various sources, process it, and create complex visual representations without requiring manual effort. By automating these processes, AI not only streamlines dashboard creation but also ensures that visualizations are always up-to-date and tailored to user needs (Gajjar et al., 2021). Through these features, AI is transforming dashboard creation, making it faster, more interactive, and accessible to a wider range of users.

Anticipated Trajectories in AI-Enhanced Data Visualization

As we look to the future, the role of AI in data visualizations and dashboards is poised for significant growth and transformation. Several key trajectories are expected to shape the evolution of this field, with advancements in automation, user engagement, and the depth of insights being at the forefront of these changes.

One of the most impactful trajectories is the **increased automation** of data visualization creation and analysis. As AI algorithms continue to advance, they will be able to handle even more complex tasks with greater efficiency. Currently, AI is already streamlining workflows by automating dashboard generation and predictive analytics. However, the future promises even more seamless automation, where AI will not only generate dashboards but will also take on the role of analyzing vast datasets and providing actionable insights without human intervention. This will significantly reduce the time and effort required to create meaningful visualizations, enabling businesses to move from raw data to decision-making much faster. In turn, this increased automation will empower organizations to make data-driven decisions with greater agility and precision. AI's ability to autonomously identify patterns, trends, and correlations in large datasets will eliminate the need for manual data wrangling and analysis, allowing businesses to focus more on strategic decision-making rather than the process of extracting insights from data.

Another anticipated shift is the **augmented engagement** between users and dashboards. As AI becomes more integrated into everyday business processes, dashboards will evolve to become more interactive and user-friendly. One of the most exciting developments will be the integration of **voice commands and gesture-based interactions** into dashboards. Rather than relying solely on clicks and manual data exploration, users will be able to interact with their dashboards in more natural, intuitive ways, such as issuing voice commands or using hand gestures to modify views or request insights. These enhancements will create a more fluid and engaging experience, making data exploration more accessible to people who may not have a background in analytics or data science. By integrating voice and gesture controls, AI-powered dashboards will foster a more inclusive and interactive environment, empowering a wider range of users to actively engage with data without requiring deep technical knowledge.

Furthermore, as AI continues to evolve, **data visualizations will become more capable of delivering richer, more nuanced insights**. Today, AI can already provide valuable insights by analyzing historical and real-time data, but as AI algorithms improve, they will be able to offer even deeper analysis and more actionable intelligence. This will be particularly important for businesses seeking to understand not only the present state of affairs but also anticipate future trends and challenges. Predictive capabilities will become more accurate, allowing organizations to make proactive decisions based on forecasts of future behavior, market conditions, or consumer actions. The integration of AI into data visualization tools will go beyond descriptive analytics (what has happened) and diagnostic analytics (why it happened) to include prescriptive analytics (what should be done) and predictive analytics (what will happen). This will enable businesses to formulate strategies that are more agile and forward-thinking, better positioning them to capitalize on emerging opportunities and mitigate potential risks.

In addition to these developments, the field of AI-enhanced data visualization will see greater personalization. As AI becomes more adept at understanding user needs and preferences, it will be able to tailor dashboards to individual users or specific roles within an organization. This level of customization will ensure that the most relevant data is always front and center, providing users with a highly contextualized and personalized experience. Whether it's an executive needing high-level summaries or a marketing team member analyzing campaign performance, AI will make it possible to present the right information in the right format at the right time. By anticipating the needs of users and adjusting accordingly, AI-powered dashboards will help users make more informed decisions with greater speed and confidence.

In summary, the future of AI in data visualizations and dashboards promises more automation, greater user engagement, and deeper insights. As AI continues to advance, it will reduce the complexity of data analysis, enhance user experiences, and enable businesses to make more informed, proactive decisions. With these evolving capabilities, AI will not only change how we interact with data but also how businesses leverage it to drive innovation and success.

Case Study 2: Real-Time Emotion Recognition for GUI Adaption

Definition

Real-time emotion recognition is the process through which a system continuously monitors and interprets the emotional state of a user as they interact with a device, application, or system. This technology uses various data inputs—such as facial expressions, voice tone, body language, and even physiological signals like heart rate or skin conductance—to infer emotions such as happiness, sadness, anger, surprise, or frustration.

Historical Context

Emotion recognition research began in the 1960s, with psychologist Paul Ekman, who identified six basic emotions—happiness, sadness, anger, fear, surprise, and disgust—that could be recognized through facial expressions. Over the decades, emotion recognition evolved alongside advances in computer vision (interpreting visual information from images or video) and natural language processing (analyzing text and speech). In the 2000s, machine learning and deep learning techniques enabled more sophisticated emotion detection, allowing systems to analyze data from multiple modalities (like voice, facial expressions, and physiological inputs) for greater accuracy. As AI and data processing capabilities advanced, emotion recognition became increasingly integrated into consumer technology, including smartphones, video games, and customer service platforms.

Introduction

Real-time emotion recognition is a critical aspect of human-computer interaction, allowing systems to detect and respond to the emotional state or mood of the user. By identifying emotions such as happiness, sadness, frustration, or anger, the system can adapt its responses to create a more personalized and satisfying experience. This is achieved through a variety of input sources, including facial expressions, vocal tones, physiological signals, and textual cues, all of which help the system recognize emotions with high accuracy (D. B., N. Bicocchi, 2020).

The integration of real-time emotion recognition into graphical user interfaces (GUIs) holds significant potential across diverse fields, such as education, customer service, and entertainment. In education, for example, emotion recognition can enable tailored feedback, keeping students engaged and motivated. If a student shows signs of boredom or frustration, the system can adjust the difficulty level of the content to reignite interest and improve the learning experience (D. Ferrucci et al., 2013). In the entertainment domain, emotion-aware systems can adjust content to match the user's mood. For instance, if a user is feeling down, the system could suggest uplifting or humorous content to improve their mood. In video games, emotion recognition could enhance gameplay by dynamically adjusting the narrative or environment based on the player's emotional responses, leading to a more immersive experience.

However, implementing real-time emotion recognition poses several challenges. A major concern is user privacy (L.C. Briland, 2012). Governments and regulatory bodies are often wary of potential data breaches, which raises concerns about the security and handling of sensitive emotional data. For emotion recognition systems to gain widespread acceptance, they must ensure the accuracy and reliability of emotion-detection algorithms (Gajjar et al., 2021). If the system misinterprets a user's emotions, it could lead to inappropriate responses that frustrate rather than assist the user. To prevent this, it is essential to verify inputs and responses through rigorous testing and validation by experts.

Emotion recognition technology relies on artificial intelligence (AI) and machine learning (ML) algorithms to identify emotional states from real-world data. Gathering and analyzing the diverse range of expressions and inputs is a complex task that requires the collaboration of experts in various fields.

Advantages of Real-Time Emotion Recognition for GUI Adaptation

1. Enhanced User Experience: By incorporating various emotional cues, GUIs can deliver more intuitive and satisfying interactions, improving overall user satisfaction.
2. Improved Accessibility: Real-time emotion recognition can assist users unfamiliar with technology. For example, icons and graphical cues could adapt based on the user’s emotional state, helping them navigate and use applications more easily.
3. Personalized Interaction: Once successfully implemented, real-time emotion recognition could make the GUI feel more like a personal assistant. For example, if a user seems sad, the system could respond with comforting content, rather than content that might exacerbate their mood. This is akin to how one might respond to a friend in distress, offering moral support instead of contributing to their frustration (L.C. Briland, 2012).
4. Increased Efficiency: Emotionally adaptive GUIs can anticipate user needs by recognizing emotional cues and adjusting the interface accordingly. This reduces friction in interactions and leads to more efficient task completion (Gajjar et al., 2021).

Future Developments

The future of real-time emotion recognition in GUI adaptation is promising, driven by advancements in artificial intelligence, machine learning, data science, the Internet of Things (IoT), and data processing.

1. Privacy Protection

To achieve widespread adoption, privacy safeguards are essential. Technologies must be developed to protect users' emotional data, addressing concerns from governments and users about data security. Ensuring user privacy will be crucial for the long-term viability of emotion recognition systems.

2. Edge Computing

Edge computing can play a key role in improving real-time emotion recognition systems. By processing data closer to the user, edge computing can reduce latency and enhance response times, making the system more responsive and suitable for a broader range of applications.

3. Regular Interface Updates

To remain relevant in a rapidly evolving technological landscape, the interfaces for emotion recognition systems must be regularly updated. Frequent updates ensure that the system stays fresh, attractive, and aligned with user expectations, contributing to a more engaging and enjoyable experience.

In conclusion, real-time emotion recognition for GUI adaptation presents a wealth of opportunities to enhance user experiences across various sectors. While challenges related to privacy, accuracy, and security must be addressed, ongoing advancements in AI, machine learning, and related fields hold promise for realizing the full potential of this technology.

Case Study 3: AI-Enchanced Customer Care Support

Introducing AI-enhanced customer care support signals a transformative shift in how businesses engage with their clients, elevating the levels of personalization and responsiveness. With the integration of Artificial Intelligence (AI) technologies, customer support operations reach new heights in both effectiveness and convenience. AI's ability to understand natural language, combined with its quick response times and 24/7 availability, empowers businesses to deliver faster, more tailored services to their customers. AI systems use natural language processing (NLP) and graphical user interface (GUI) technologies to understand and respond to customer queries, thus enhancing the overall service experience (L.C. Briland, 2012). AI not only streamlines communication but also personalizes interactions at an individual level, making it possible for businesses to recommend products, offer assistance, and provide customer support based on past interactions, purchase history, and browsing behavior. This personalized approach fosters stronger customer relationships and drives brand loyalty. Tools like chatbots, along with other AI-driven techniques, contribute to this transformation, offering businesses the opportunity to optimize customer care in various ways (Gajjar et al., 2021).

There are several ways businesses can leverage AI to improve the customer experience. One of the most significant advancements is the implementation of **shopping assistants with the right data**. These digital assistants are available around the clock to answer customer queries, providing instant responses that enhance the customer experience. The key to the success of these virtual assistants lies in the accuracy and reliability of the data they use. When these assistants have access to the most up-to-date and accurate information, they are able to provide quick, relevant, and precise responses, creating a sense of personalized and attentive service. With the ability to operate 24/7, these AI-driven tools ensure that customers receive support at any time, eliminating the limitations of traditional customer service hours and offering businesses an advantage in meeting customer expectations.

Another area where AI significantly contributes is in **accelerating repetitive tasks for customer care**. Many customer service functions involve recurring tasks, such as answering frequently asked questions (FAQs) or dealing with common customer concerns. A well-designed AI system can assist in managing these repetitive duties efficiently. For example, many businesses now feature AI-powered chatbots or self-service portals with FAQ sections on their websites to resolve common queries. These AI solutions help agents quickly understand customer issues by consolidating customer data and previous interactions, allowing for faster responses and more effective resolutions. As a result, human agents can focus on more complex or specialized inquiries, while AI handles routine tasks, increasing overall efficiency.

In addition to automating routine tasks, AI can also **connect automation with actionable insights**. By analyzing large volumes of customer data, AI systems can recommend specific actions to address customer issues. For instance, if a customer reports receiving a defective product, AI can instantly assess the situation based on available data and suggest a course of action, such as initiating a replacement order. By integrating AI into the order management systems, a customer service agent can quickly approve the proposed action with a single click, triggering the AI system to carry out the task, such as coordinating the shipment of a replacement item from the warehouse. This integration reduces the need for manual coordination, streamlining processes and making the customer support system more efficient. It also frees up agents from the burden of handling logistical tasks, allowing them to focus on higher-level customer service concerns.

AI also offers businesses an opportunity to **scale personalization** in ways that were previously challenging. Personalizing the customer experience has long been a goal for businesses, but the sheer complexity of data and the need for real-time adjustments has often made it difficult to achieve at scale. With the power of AI, businesses can now tailor content—including text, visuals, sounds, and even video—based on individual customer data. AI tools can dynamically adjust messaging across various platforms, such as emails, SMS, web interfaces, and mobile apps, to deliver highly relevant content that speaks directly to the customer's preferences and behavior. By personalizing marketing efforts in real-time, companies can create more meaningful and engaging interactions, ultimately driving conversions and fostering customer loyalty (D. Ferrucci et al., 2013; D. B., N. Bicocchi, 2020).

AI's role in **enabling employees to better serve customers** is another crucial aspect of this transformation. In brick-and-mortar retail environments, for example, employees often use AI-based tools to check stock levels and verify product availability across different store locations. If a customer is looking for an item that is out of stock, the employee can quickly check alternative locations or suggest different sizes, colors, or products. AI can even automate the process of arranging deliveries for out-of-stock items, providing the customer with an immediate solution. Such seamless integration of AI into operational workflows empowers employees to deliver better service while minimizing friction in the customer experience.

For many modern consumers, **giving them more options** for how to engage with businesses is key to enhancing the customer experience. The days of solely relying on in-store shopping are being replaced by more convenient, digital-first experiences. Many customers prefer the flexibility of ordering via voice-activated devices or browsing online at their convenience, even during late-night hours. AI makes it possible for businesses to cater to these preferences, offering customers an easy way to gather information, place orders, and get answers to simple questions through virtual assistants or chatbots. When customers have more control over how they engage with a brand, they feel valued, which strengthens their loyalty.

Incorporating **predictive analytics and forecasting** into AI-driven customer service systems is another powerful way AI can improve the customer experience. By analyzing past customer interactions and transaction data, AI can predict future demand trends, enabling businesses to better anticipate busy periods and allocate resources accordingly. For example, AI can forecast seasonal fluctuations, such as increased demand during holidays, or identify patterns that suggest a surge in customer inquiries related to a particular product or service. This allows businesses to allocate staffing resources more effectively, ensuring they are prepared to meet demand and provide timely support (L.C. Briland, 2012). Predictive analytics can also help businesses refine staffing schedules, training programs, and other operational components, ultimately improving service levels and reducing costs.

In conclusion, AI-enhanced customer care is reshaping the landscape of customer service, offering businesses the ability to provide faster, more personalized, and more efficient support. From virtual assistants to predictive analytics, AI empowers companies to meet customer expectations and address their needs in real-time. By automating repetitive tasks, connecting data insights with actionable steps, and scaling personalization, businesses can create deeper customer relationships and build loyalty. Moreover, the ability to predict demand and optimize resources helps organizations operate more effectively, reducing costs and enhancing service levels. As AI continues to evolve, businesses that embrace these tools will not only improve the customer experience but also drive revenue growth and long-term success. Ultimately, AI is becoming an indispensable tool in delivering exceptional customer service, ensuring that both businesses and their customers benefit from its capabilities.

Case Study 4: Adaptive Gaming Interface

Computer games present a unique platform for play, offering experiences that are intricately tailored to the individual player through the use of adaptive artificial intelligence (AI). This adaptability, however, needs to be carefully managed and constrained to ensure that the integrity of the game world and the player's immersive experience are maintained. As players engage with a game, they enter a temporary reality defined by its own set of rules and logic, what is commonly referred to as the "game world." This concept of play is described by Huizinga as a free, meaningful activity, enjoyed for its own sake, and distinct from the pressures of everyday life. In the game world, players can momentarily redefine themselves, experimenting with identities and behaviors in ways that are not possible in the real world. The structure of the game, including its rules and objectives, is essential to this experience. If these rules were to change too dramatically or unpredictably, players might be forced to step out of the game, thereby disrupting their sense of immersion. This could lead to a re-evaluation of the game world, diminishing the enjoyment of their fantasy game play.

The need to constrain adaptive AI in this context stems from the fact that players seek consistency and coherence within the game world, even as they interact with dynamic systems. If the game adapts too aggressively or alters the fundamental rules of play, it could undermine the player's agency and sense of control. Instead, players prefer that the game's difficulty or the challenges they face adapt to their play style and decisions, rather than changing the core structure of the game itself. One way to constrain the emergent behaviors of adaptive AI while still allowing for personalized gameplay is through the use of **formal specification** (D. Ferrucci et al., 2013). Formal specification refers to the clear, structured definition of how the game's AI should behave, which can be constructed around our understanding of how players interact with the game. By defining these interactions in advance, developers can ensure that the adaptive AI does not overstep its boundaries and disrupt the player's experience.

An example of formal specification might involve defining the structure of player actions using a framework similar to natural language syntax. In this framework, the player's actions could be viewed as "verbs" (actions the player takes) and the game world's objects as "nouns" (the elements the player interacts with). For instance, a player might choose to "attack" a monster (verb) with a sword (noun). The adaptive AI could then adjust the outcomes of these actions, such as modifying the effectiveness of the attack, but without changing the underlying structure of the interaction itself. In this way, the AI could alter the *effect* of a verb or the makeup of a noun, but the player's core experience and the rules governing the game world would remain intact. This helps to preserve the balance between adapting to the player's individual play style and maintaining a consistent, immersive world.

The primary argument presented in this framework is that a **generalized player model** is the most efficient and effective way to capture player individuality, which is crucial for the proper functioning of adaptive AI. This model would first be developed under non-adaptive circumstances, essentially creating a baseline for the player's behavior and preferences within the game. Once the game is established in its simplest form, adaptive AI can then be gradually introduced into the system, responding to the player's actions and decisions in real-time. The key to this approach is the **generalized adoption of the player profile**, which allows the AI to adjust the game's complexity and challenges in a way that feels responsive to the individual player, but without disrupting the fundamental game world (D. B., N. Bicocchi, 2020).

Over time, as the complexity of the game increases, the AI can become more sophisticated in its responses, taking into account the player's unique play style, preferences, and past behavior. The idea is to create an adaptive system that is nuanced enough to handle more intricate gameplay scenarios, while still staying within the constraints of the formal model. This progressive adaptation ensures that the game can grow alongside the player, continually offering new challenges that feel both rewarding and fair. The formal model would allow developers to test various iterations of adaptive AI, comparing simpler versions of the game with more complex ones to see how well the system adapts to the player's evolving experience. These simulations can be used to assess how different levels of AI sophistication impact the player's engagement and enjoyment of the game.

In conclusion, the design of adaptive computer games should be based on a deep understanding of player behavior and a careful balance between AI adaptability and the preservation of the game world's integrity. By using formal specification to define the boundaries of adaptive AI, developers can ensure that the game remains consistent and enjoyable, even as it becomes more responsive to the player's individual preferences. The generalized player model provides a framework for this adaptation, allowing the game to scale in complexity while staying true to the original rules and structure. As AI technology continues to evolve, adaptive games can become increasingly personalized, offering players the opportunity to immerse themselves in ever more complex and tailored experiences. Through continuous testing and refinement, developers can fine-tune the game's AI to enhance player engagement and satisfaction, creating a dynamic, interactive world that responds intelligently to each individual's play style. By building adaptive games based on real-time player feedback and testing, developers can foster a more immersive, satisfying, and enjoyable gaming experience (Gajjar et al., 2021).

Case Study 5: Interactive Financial Management Systems

Incorporating artificial intelligence (AI) functionalities into graphical user interfaces (GUIs) designed for financial administration offers a promising shift in how individuals and businesses manage their finances. These systems, which combine the power of AI with the intuitiveness of a well-designed interface, provide an accessible, user-friendly platform for overseeing various aspects of financial health. By offering dynamic tools for budgeting, investment management, goal setting, and more, these AI-driven platforms help users make informed financial decisions, optimize their financial strategies, and achieve their goals with greater efficiency.

A key feature of such systems is the Synopsis Display, which provides a comprehensive snapshot of the user's financial situation. This overview typically includes information such as account balances, spending patterns, investment performance, and upcoming financial obligations. By presenting this data in an organized and easy-to-read format, users are given immediate insight into their financial status, allowing them to take action more quickly. Furthermore, the system's Dynamic Budgeting Features enable users to set budgets for different categories such as groceries, utilities, and leisure activities. AI algorithms monitor spending behavior and suggest adjustments to the user's budget to help align their expenditures with their financial goals (L.C. Briland, 2012). This level of personalization makes financial planning more responsive and tailored to individual needs, ensuring that users stay on track with their financial objectives.

Another key functionality is AI-Driven Insights, which leverages algorithms to analyze transaction data and provide personalized financial recommendations. For example, the system might suggest switching to a lower-interest credit card to save on interest charges, refinancing a mortgage to reduce monthly payments, or adjusting investment portfolios in response to changing market conditions. These suggestions are driven by a thorough analysis of the user's financial behavior and preferences, ensuring that the recommendations are relevant and actionable. Alongside these insights, users can set and track financial objectives, such as saving for a vacation, purchasing a home, or paying down debt. The AI can monitor progress towards these goals and offer suggestions to accelerate their achievement, keeping users motivated and informed throughout the process.

Additionally, the platform enables Portfolio Management, where users can track the performance of their investments, access relevant performance metrics, and receive AI-generated recommendations for improving their investment strategy. The AI component can assess the risk levels of different assets and suggest ways to balance portfolios according to the user's risk tolerance and long-term goals. Similarly, Risk Evaluation and Mitigation is another vital feature, where AI evaluates the risks associated with different financial decisions and provides recommendations for risk management. For instance, the system might warn users about potential overdrafts, advise against taking on high-interest debt, or recommend reducing exposure to volatile investments, all based on the user's financial profile and current situation (D. Ferrucci et al., 2013).

Real-time notifications are another essential aspect of these platforms. Instant Notifications inform users of significant financial events, such as large transactions, account balances falling below a set threshold, or changes in investment performance. This feature ensures that users remain informed and can take immediate action when necessary. Furthermore, users can securely communicate with financial advisors or customer service representatives through the GUI. AI-powered **chatbots** facilitate this process by providing immediate answers to frequently asked questions, enabling users to resolve issues quickly and efficiently.

For a truly personalized experience, the GUI should offer a high degree of Tailoring and Adaptability. Users should be able to customize their dashboard to display the financial metrics most relevant to them, schedule recurring transactions, and adjust budgeting categories according to their specific needs. This flexibility ensures that the platform accommodates a wide range of users, from those managing personal finances to business owners with more complex financial requirements.

However, while the benefits of AI-powered financial management systems are substantial, there are several challenges that must be addressed to ensure their success. One of the most significant concerns is Security and Privacy Considerations. Safeguarding sensitive financial data is paramount, as breaches in security could lead to identity theft or financial loss. To mitigate this risk, robust encryption protocols, multi-factor authentication, and data obfuscation techniques should be implemented to protect user data from unauthorized access. These security measures are essential for building user trust and ensuring compliance with privacy regulations.

Another challenge lies in the Complexity of AI Algorithms. Developing and fine-tuning AI algorithms capable of accurately analyzing financial data and making reliable recommendations is a complex and time-consuming process. To overcome this challenge, continuous research and development efforts must be invested in improving the accuracy, reliability, and transparency of these algorithms (D. Ferrucci et al., 2013). This ongoing refinement will help ensure that the AI recommendations remain relevant and trustworthy, leading to better decision-making outcomes for users.

User Acceptance and Confidence also pose significant obstacles. Many users may be hesitant to rely on AI-driven recommendations, particularly if they lack an understanding of how the algorithms work. To address this issue, developers must prioritize Educational Outreach and Clarity, providing users with clear explanations of how AI algorithms generate recommendations and how they can benefit from using the system. Transparent communication and user education will help foster confidence in the technology.

Integration with Existing Frameworks presents another technical challenge. Embedding AI functionalities into existing financial systems and infrastructures can be difficult, particularly when dealing with legacy platforms or systems that are not designed to accommodate advanced AI technologies. Developers must create APIs and modular frameworks that allow seamless integration with existing tools and systems, making the transition to AI-powered solutions smoother for businesses and individuals alike.

In conclusion, the integration of AI into graphical user interfaces for financial management offers an innovative way to help individuals and businesses navigate their financial lives with greater ease and precision. By providing tailored financial insights, automated budgeting tools, and intelligent investment strategies, these platforms enable users to make informed decisions and achieve their financial goals. However, challenges such as security concerns, algorithm complexity, user trust, and regulatory compliance must be addressed to ensure the system's effectiveness and adoption. By implementing robust security protocols, continuously refining AI algorithms, educating users, and ensuring smooth integration with existing frameworks, these challenges can be overcome. Ultimately, AI-powered financial management platforms have the potential to revolutionize personal and business finance, providing users with the tools they need to make smarter financial decisions and secure their financial futures.

Case Study 6: Interactive Virtual Shopping Assistants

Interactive virtual shopping assistants represent a revolutionary innovation in the realm of online commerce, merging the power of Artificial Intelligence (AI) with the intuitive functionality of Graphical User Interface (GUI) technologies. This emerging concept is poised to reshape the digital shopping landscape by offering personalized, immersive, and highly interactive shopping experiences. By integrating AI-driven capabilities within a user-friendly GUI, these virtual assistants empower consumers to make more informed purchasing decisions while enhancing overall shopping satisfaction.

At the heart of this innovation is the virtual shopping assistant—a digital companion embedded within an online shopping platform. These assistants are designed to provide real-time, intelligent guidance and support to shoppers as they navigate through the digital marketplace. Leveraging AI algorithms, these assistants analyze a user's past purchase history, browsing behavior, and even contextual information like current trends and demographics. This deep, personalized understanding allows the assistant to deliver highly relevant product recommendations, tailoring the shopping experience to each individual consumer's needs and preferences (L.C. Briland, 2012).

The virtual shopping assistant's primary strength lies in its ability to act as a knowledgeable guide throughout the user's shopping journey. Whether helping with product selection, offering sizing advice, or addressing queries about shipping and delivery options, these assistants ensure that users can easily access the information they need. The goal is to simplify the shopping experience by offering a layer of support that not only aids in decision-making but also provides reassurance and convenience. Additionally, the real-time interaction capabilities of these assistants allow them to answer questions, suggest alternatives, or guide users through the checkout process, creating a smoother, more engaging experience than traditional e-commerce sites.

The integration of AI and GUI technologies ensures that these virtual shopping assistants evolve over time. As they engage with users and learn from their interactions, the AI algorithms improve their accuracy in making personalized recommendations, refining their understanding of individual shopping preferences. This adaptability means that the assistant becomes increasingly effective the more it is used, offering more tailored, insightful guidance as the shopper's needs change (T. Venkat Narayana Rao et al., 2020). For example, if a user consistently selects eco-friendly products, the assistant may prioritize eco-conscious recommendations or offer suggestions for sustainable alternatives when browsing.

One of the most compelling features of interactive virtual shopping assistants is the ability to offer personalized product suggestions. By analyzing various data points such as past purchases, browsing history, and even social media behavior, the AI algorithms can recommend products that align with the shopper's unique tastes and needs. This feature enhances the shopping experience by helping customers discover items they may not have found otherwise. In addition to this, certain virtual shopping assistants leverage augmented reality (AR) and virtual reality (VR) technologies to offer features like virtual try-ons. For example, a shopper can virtually try on clothes, accessories, or even visualize how furniture might look in their home before making a purchase, significantly reducing the likelihood of returns (L.C. Briland, 2012).

These interactive assistants are not limited to product recommendations alone. They also provide instantaneous support throughout the shopping experience. Whether a customer is unsure about product specifications, needs help with sizing, or is looking for specific details about a product, the assistant is there to provide timely answers. This real-time interaction ensures that customers can shop without delays or frustrations, improving their overall satisfaction. Furthermore, these assistants can integrate with multiple digital platforms, including websites, mobile apps, social media channels, and messaging platforms. This seamless integration ensures a consistent and cohesive shopping experience regardless of the device or platform the customer is using (D.B., N. Bicocchi, 2020).

The capabilities of virtual shopping assistants extend beyond individual customer interactions. These systems can play a pivotal role in intelligent inventory management. By analyzing consumer behavior, sales trends, and demand patterns, these AI-powered assistants can help retailers optimize stock levels, forecast demand, and recommend strategies for inventory replenishment. This reduces the risk of stock-outs or overstocking, ensuring that retailers can meet consumer demand efficiently (D.B., N. Bicocchi, 2020).

Another notable feature of interactive virtual shopping assistants is the ability to extract analytical insights. By analyzing shopper behavior, preferences, and transaction history, these assistants generate valuable data that retailers can use to refine their marketing strategies, tailor their product offerings, and enhance the overall customer experience. This data-driven approach allows retailers to engage with their customers on a deeper level and provide more targeted promotions and advertisements (L.C. Briland, 2012).

In addition to these features, social commerce attributes are also becoming an important aspect of virtual shopping assistants. These assistants can enable shoppers to share their purchases, reviews, and recommendations on social media, encouraging a sense of community and facilitating peer-to-peer endorsements. This social aspect helps build customer trust and fosters a more collaborative shopping environment, where users can interact with each other and share their experiences (D.B., N. Bicocchi, 2020).

In conclusion, interactive virtual shopping assistants represent a transformative development in the world of e-commerce. By combining AI with intuitive GUI systems, these assistants offer a dynamic, personalized, and immersive shopping experience that caters to the unique needs and preferences of individual consumers. They provide tailored product recommendations, real-time support, and seamless integration across platforms, while also offering features like virtual try-ons and social commerce functionalities. These assistants also enable retailers to optimize inventory management, gain valuable analytical insights, and enhance customer engagement. As AI and related technologies continue to advance, the potential for innovation in this space is limitless. Ultimately, interactive virtual shopping assistants are poised to revolutionize the online shopping experience, creating a more convenient, engaging, and personalized retail environment for customers worldwide (Gajjar et al., 2021).

Ethical Considerations

1. Bias and Discrimination

AI systems, including those embedded within GUIs, rely on data to generate outputs, make decisions, and offer recommendations. The risk of **bias** arises when these systems are trained on incomplete, unrepresentative, or flawed datasets. For instance, if a facial recognition system within a GUI has been trained predominantly on images of lighter-skinned individuals, it may be less accurate when identifying users with darker skin tones. Similarly, a virtual assistant that has been trained on biased language patterns may unintentionally perpetuate harmful stereotypes or make assumptions based on gender, age, or cultural norms.

The ethical concern here is that these biases can lead to **discriminatory outcomes** that disadvantage certain groups of people, reinforcing existing social inequalities. For example, AI-powered financial management GUIs might recommend high-interest loans or credit cards with poor terms for users from marginalized communities, based on biased data about their credit history. As such, ensuring that AI-powered GUIs are trained on diverse, balanced datasets is essential for minimizing bias and promoting **fairness**.

Ethical Mitigation Strategies:

- Implement diverse and inclusive datasets during training phases.
- Regularly audit algorithms for bias, ensuring equitable outcomes for all user groups.
- Establish checks and balances to mitigate the impact of biased decision-making and improve the fairness of AI outputs.

2. Fairness

Fairness in AI involves ensuring that the systems operate equitably for all users, regardless of background, ethnicity, gender, or socioeconomic status. The ethical principle of fairness calls for equitable access to the benefits of AI-powered systems and safeguarding individuals from being disadvantaged or unfairly treated by the technology.

For example, consider an AI-powered shopping assistant that uses user data to offer personalized product recommendations. If the assistant gives preference to luxury items or high-end brands based on a user's previous spending patterns, it may inadvertently exclude less expensive, equally viable options for users with different financial means. Such scenarios can perpetuate unfair treatment by reinforcing pre-existing consumer behavior, potentially alienating or disadvantaging users who do not fit into the system's predefined categories.

Ethical Mitigation Strategies:

- Develop AI systems that prioritize equity, providing users with options across a range of price points, features, and preferences.
- Regularly evaluate the fairness of the system's outputs, ensuring that all users have equal access to opportunities, information, and recommendations.
- Design algorithms that avoid reinforcing harmful stereotypes or assumptions.

3. Transparency

Transparency is a fundamental ethical concern in AI-powered GUIs. AI systems are often described as "black boxes" because their decision-making processes can be difficult to understand, even for developers. This lack of transparency creates a gap between the system's outputs and the reasoning behind them, leaving users in the dark about how decisions are made. Users may not know why a certain recommendation was made or how their personal data is being used to drive those recommendations.

For instance, a user interacting with a financial assistant GUI might receive advice to invest in a particular stock. Without transparency, the user may not understand why this advice was given or the underlying risk factors associated with it. Ethical AI development necessitates that users are provided with clear explanations of how AI systems work and the reasoning behind the recommendations they make.

Ethical Mitigation Strategies:

- Implement "explainable AI" (XAI) techniques to make decision-making processes more understandable for users.
- Provide users with clear and concise information about how their data is used and how recommendations are generated.
- Offer real-time feedback on AI-driven decisions, allowing users to question or challenge outcomes.

4. Accountability

With AI-powered GUIs making important decisions, the issue of accountability becomes paramount. Who is responsible when an AI system makes a mistake, provides faulty advice, or leads to harmful consequences? If a financial management tool incorrectly advises a user to make a risky investment, causing financial loss, who is to blame: the developers, the AI system itself, or the user?

Ensuring accountability in AI systems is crucial for maintaining trust in these technologies. If accountability is not clearly defined, users may feel powerless or vulnerable when interacting with AI-powered GUIs. Ethical AI deployment should prioritize assigning clear responsibility for decisions made by the system, ensuring that users have legal and practical recourse in the event of harm.

Ethical Mitigation Strategies:

- Clearly define accountability structures, identifying which parties (developers, organizations, or third-party vendors) are responsible for AI decisions.
- Provide users with easy-to-access mechanisms for filing complaints or disputes when they feel harmed by the AI system's decisions.
- Design AI systems that include built-in mechanisms for human oversight and intervention, particularly in high-stakes environments (e.g., finance, healthcare).

5. Societal Impact

The societal impact of AI-powered GUIs extends beyond individual experiences, affecting broader social, economic, and political structures. As AI continues to influence how users interact with services, businesses, and technology, it is important to consider the long-term effects on society as a whole.

One major concern is the potential for **job displacement**. As AI systems automate tasks traditionally performed by human employees—such as customer service, retail support, or financial advisory services—there could be widespread job losses in sectors where AI can perform tasks more efficiently. Another societal concern is the growing **digital divide**. As advanced AI-powered GUIs become more sophisticated, individuals who lack access to technology or the necessary skills to engage with these systems may be left behind, exacerbating inequalities in education, employment, and wealth.

Additionally, there is a risk that AI-powered systems could be used to manipulate public opinion or behavior. For example, shopping assistants, financial advisors, and even news aggregation tools can shape user preferences and decision-making processes, potentially reinforcing narrow viewpoints or consumer behaviors.

Ethical Mitigation Strategies:

- Promote public awareness and education about AI technologies to reduce the digital divide and ensure equitable access to AI-powered services.
- Foster policies that prioritize the retraining and upskilling of workers displaced by automation, ensuring a smoother transition to AI-driven economies.
- Implement regulations that prevent the misuse of AI for manipulative or exploitative purposes, such as manipulating consumer behavior or swaying political opinions.

Future Trends and Research Directions

1. Explainable AI (XAI)

One of the most pressing concerns with the widespread deployment of AI systems is their opacity. Traditional AI systems, especially deep learning models, are often described as "black boxes" because they provide outputs without clear explanations of how or why they arrived at a particular decision. This lack of transparency raises concerns about trust, accountability, and bias, particularly in sensitive domains like healthcare, finance, and law enforcement.

Explainable AI (XAI) aims to address this issue by making the decision-making process of AI systems more transparent and understandable to users, developers, and stakeholders. XAI systems are designed to offer clear, human-readable explanations of how they process input data and generate results. This is especially crucial in industries where users need to understand the rationale behind automated decisions—whether it's a loan approval, medical diagnosis, or product recommendation.

For instance, an XAI-powered financial management system might provide not only the suggestion to invest in a specific asset but also a detailed explanation of the factors driving that recommendation—such as market conditions, historical performance, or personal financial goals. By improving transparency, XAI can foster greater trust in AI-powered systems and empower users to make more informed decisions.

2. Multimodal Interfaces

Multimodal interfaces represent a major shift in how users interact with technology by combining multiple modes of input (such as voice, touch, gesture, and visual cues) to create a more intuitive and dynamic user experience. Rather than relying on a single mode of communication (e.g., typing on a keyboard or clicking a mouse), multimodal interfaces enable users to interact with systems in ways that are more natural and suited to the task at hand.

For example, a virtual shopping assistant could offer a multimodal experience where users can speak their queries, swipe through product images on a touchscreen, and even gesture to zoom in on details. This allows for more seamless and personalized interactions, as users can choose the input mode that is most comfortable or efficient in a given context.

In AI-powered GUIs, multimodal interfaces can further enhance personalization by understanding user preferences and adapting to different ways of communication. For instance, if a user prefers voice commands over typing, the interface could prioritize voice-based inputs, while still allowing touch or gesture-based interactions for tasks like navigation or detailed queries.

3. Personalized Adaptive GUIs

Personalization is one of the most sought-after features in modern software applications. As users interact with systems, personalized adaptive GUIs leverage AI and machine learning to tailor the interface to individual preferences, behaviors, and needs. Rather than presenting a static layout, these systems evolve and adapt in real time to reflect how users engage with the interface and what they value most.

A personalized adaptive GUI might adjust the layout of a dashboard based on a user's most frequently used features, prioritize certain products or services, or dynamically adjust the content based on the time of day or context. For example, in a financial management system, the interface could prioritize upcoming bill payments in the morning and display investment recommendations in the evening when the user is more likely to make decisions. This level of adaptability improves usability and creates a more efficient experience.

These systems use advanced algorithms to track user behavior, learn from interactions, and modify the interface accordingly. Machine learning models are often deployed to analyze factors such as:

- User preferences: What tools or features does the user access most frequently?
- User context: Is the user interacting with the system in a work environment or for personal use?
- Time-based patterns: Are there certain tasks the user tends to perform at specific times (e.g., checking financial data in the morning)?

As a result, personalized adaptive GUIs are particularly valuable for applications with a wide range of users or complex interfaces, such as e-commerce platforms, financial apps, and healthcare systems.

The Future of AI-Powered GUIs: Convergence of XAI, Multimodal Interfaces, and Personalization

The future of interactive AI-driven interfaces lies in the convergence of these emerging technologies. As XAI, multimodal interfaces, and personalized adaptive GUIs come together, they will transform how users interact with systems across industries.

For example, a virtual shopping assistant that leverages multimodal inputs (voice, gesture, touch) could not only offer personalized product suggestions but also explain the rationale behind each recommendation in real-time through XAI. This would combine the convenience of voice-based interaction with the transparency of explainable AI, creating an experience that is both efficient and understandable. Over time, the system would adapt to the user's preferences, learning from their behaviors to offer even more tailored suggestions.

Similarly, in the financial sector, an adaptive financial management interface could integrate multimodal inputs to support voice and touch interactions. Using XAI principles, it could explain the reasons behind budget suggestions or investment decisions, ensuring users feel confident in the system's recommendations. This combination of transparency, accessibility, and adaptability would create a new paradigm of trust and efficiency in personal finance management.

CONCLUSION

In summary, the fusion of AI and GUI advancements across diverse sectors like financial management, adaptive gaming, real-time sentiment analysis, data visualization enhancement, virtual shopping aid, and customer service presents a stimulating panorama of opportunities for both users and enterprises.

These amalgamated platforms furnish tailored experiences attuned to individual preferences and requirements. They equip users with insightful financial guidance, immersive gaming encounters, instant emotional assessment for enriched engagements, user-friendly data representation for informed decision-making, seamless virtual shopping guidance, and effective customer assistance.Nevertheless, to unlock the full potential of these platforms, several obstacles need to be addressed, including concerns about data confidentiality, the intricacy of algorithms, user confidence, system integration challenges, compliance with regulations, and the design of user interfaces.By instituting robust security protocols, refining algorithms continually, educating users, seamlessly integrating with current systems, adhering to regulatory frameworks, and prioritizing user-centric design principles, these hurdles can be surmounted(T. Venkat Narayana Rao et al.,2020).

Ultimately, interactive platforms powered by AI and GUI innovations are on the brink of reshaping various facets of human existence, offering unparalleled convenience, customization, and efficacy. As these technologies advance, they hold the potential to revolutionize our interactions with technology and society, thereby enhancing our standard of living and fostering innovation across sectors.

REFERENCES

Abeywickrama, D. B., Bicocchi, N., Mamei, M., & Zambonelli, F. (2020). The SOTA approach to engineering collective adaptive systems. *International Journal of Software Tools for Technology Transfer*, 22(4), 399–56. DOI: 10.1007/s10009-020-00554-3

Ferrucci, D., Levas, A., Bagchi, S., Gondek, D., & Mueller, E. T. (2013). Watson: Beyond jeopardy! *Artificial Intelligence*, 199, 93–105.

Gajjar, N., Sermuga Pandian, V. P., Suleri, S., & Jarke, M. (2021, April). Akin: Generating ui wireframes from ui design patterns using deep learning. In Companion Proceedings of the 26th International Conference on Intelligent User Interfaces (pp. 40-42).

Industry 4.0: Is Africa ready for digital transformation? [online] Available: https://www2.deloitte.com/content/dam/Deloitte/za/Documents/manufacturing/za-Africa-industry-4.0-report-April14.pdf.v

Mohan, V. (2008, June). D. Jeya Mala " IntelligenTester-Test Sequence Optimization framework using Multi-Agents. *Journal of Computers*.

Venkat Narayana Rao, T., & Yellu, K. R. (2016). Automatic Safety Home Bell System with Message Enabled Features, International Journal of Science. *Engineering and Computer Technology*, 6, 10.

Chapter 5
Revolutionizing Supply Chains for Optimized Demand Planning, Inventory Management, and Logistics:
An In-Depth Analysis of AI and ML Solutions in the Modern Era

Bhupinder Singh
https://orcid.org/0009-0006-4779-2553
Sharda University, India

ABSTRACT

AI-driven demand forecasting applications play a pivotal role in elevating forecast accuracy by scrutinizing historical demand and supply data. Machine learning models excel at uncovering latent patterns within historical demand data, resulting in reduced holding costs and the establishment of optimal inventory levels. These models can furnish detailed, region-specific demand insights, facilitating the customization of fulfillment processes based on region-specific requirements. The application of AI and machine learning extends across various facets of Supply Chain optimization, including demand forecasting, inventory management, and logistics automation. This technology aids in minimizing losses, cutting costs, and achieving more accurate forecasts of customer preferences. This chapter expresses the diverse aspects of AI and ML Solutions for Supply Chains for Optimized Demand Planning, Inventory Management and Logistics in the Modern Era.

DOI: 10.4018/979-8-3693-4433-0.ch005

1. INTRODUCTION

AI impact on Supply Chain operations is all-encompassing, ranging from planning to execution. Leveraging both structured and unstructured data, AI can illuminate inbound supply information, customer location profiles and more which leading to the creation of planning analytics dashboards or the drafting of Supply Chain planning documents. AI and machine learning algorithms play a pivotal role in making informed warehouse and inventory management decisions, leading to enhanced operational efficiencies and reduced costs (Lee, 2021). The advantages of incorporating AI into Supply Chain optimization are far-reaching, influencing various aspects of operations (Dash et al., 2019). From refining decision-making processes to enhancing overall efficiency in logistics and the Supply Chain, AI contributes to improved inventory management, intelligent manufacturing, dynamic logistics systems, and real-time delivery controls (Ahmad et al., 2020).

The optimal inventory levels can be determined using AI-powered tools, which analyze historical demand and supply data to steer clear of over-production and mitigate excessive inventory holding costs (Bajgoric, 2023). This approach not only liberates capital for more strategic allocations but also enhances inventory turnover and throughput rates within warehouses, distribution centers and fulfillment centers (Shen et al., 2019). These logistics networks, which comprise cargo freighters, delivery vehicles, warehouses, and distribution centers, may be optimized with the aid of artificial intelligence (AI), which is excellent at finding patterns and correlations within massive data sets (Raut et al., 2019). Tracking tangible products every time they change hands is another essential component of effective supply chain optimization. Artificial intelligence (AI) may ensure the integrity of multiparty transactions by automatically inputting, extracting, and categorizing data encoded in text files, therefore automating documentation.

Figure 1. shows the Dynamics of Introduction Split Sections (Source- Original)

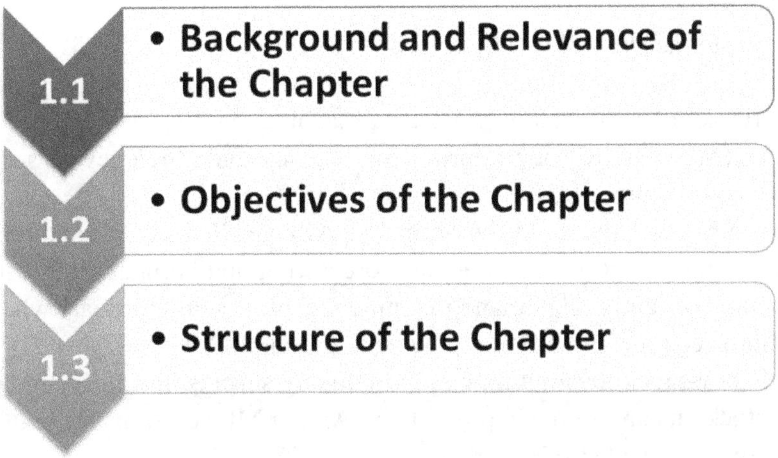

1.1 Background and Relevance of the Chapter

The more efficiently than with traditional software, businesses may use AI to improve and optimize supply chain tasks including balancing inventory levels, finding fuel-efficient delivery routes, and checking product quality (Mohiuddin Babu et al., 2022). Applications that replicate human ability to complete challenging tasks are included in artificial intelligence (AI). Among these is machine learning (ML), a kind of artificial intelligence where computers learn from vast quantities of data instead than following preprogrammed instructions (Rathore, 2019). Artificial Intelligence (AI) systems are able to outperform traditional software in a number of areas, including video feed interpretation, spoken and written language comprehension, market behavior prediction, complicated scenario decision-making, and large-scale data set discovery (Akram et al., 2022).

These features are very beneficial for supply chain workflow optimization (Goti et al., 2023). In supply chain systems, for instance, machine learning (ML) algorithms may find patterns and links in data those people or non-AI systems might overlook, resulting in more precise client demand projections and effective inventory management (Rathore, 2019). AI may also recommend other shipping routes based on traffic and weather data, lowering the chance of delays and speeding up delivery times (Riahi et al., 2021). It may keep an eye out for safety breaches and problems with quality control in workstations. As supply chain experts continue to play around with AI technology, new applications keep coming up (Casciani et al., 2022).

1.2 Objectives of the Chapter

This chapter has the following objectives to:

- scrutinize how technology related to machine learning and artificial intelligence (ML) and AI may improve the efficacy and efficiency of supply networks (Aljohani, 2023).
- determine and talk about the particular AI and ML methods and algorithms that are applied to precise demand forecasting and compare these strategies to more conventional demand planning techniques and evaluate whether one is more accurate and reliable (Pawlicka & Bal, 2022).
- study how stock level optimization, reducing surplus inventory, and preventing stockouts are all made possible by AI and ML solutions for better inventory management (Rodrigues & Pereira, 2023).
- describe how AI and ML technologies improve logistical processes, such as dynamic scheduling, predictive maintenance for transport vehicles, and route optimization and analyze the effects on supply chain agility overall, delivery times, and transportation costs (Nouinou et al., 2023).
- talk about the present restrictions and difficulties with applying AI and ML in supply chain environments, including the requirement for specific expertise, interaction with legacy systems, and problems with data quality. Examine possible future breakthroughs, new trends, and how AI and ML are changing supply chain management techniques (dos Santos et al., 2021).

Figure 2. specifies the Objectives of the Chapter (Source- Original)

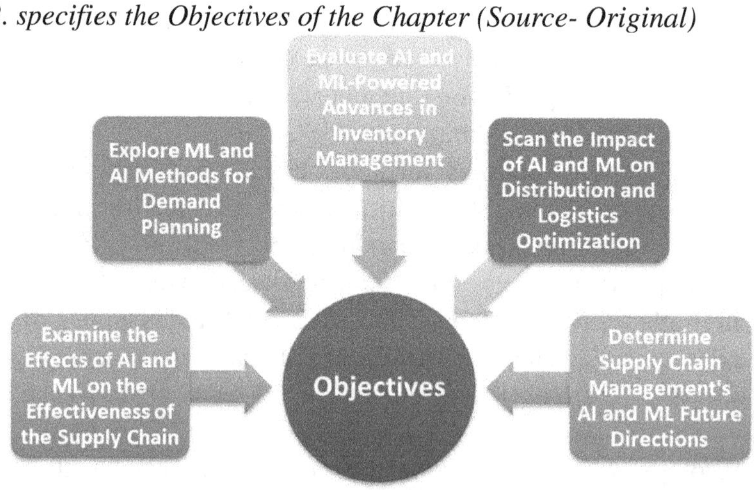

1.3 Structure of the Chapter

Revolutionizing Supply Chains for Optimized Demand Planning, Inventory Management and Logistics: An In-Depth Analysis of AI and ML Solutions in the Modern Era. Section 2 lays down the AI and ML Technologies in Supply Chain Management. Section 3 explores the Demand Planning: AI and ML-driven Demand Planning. Section 4 specifies the Inventory Management. Section 5 elaborates the Logistics and Transportation. Section 6 highlights the Challenges, Limitations and Benefits. Finally, Section 7 Conclude the Chapter with Future Scope.

Figure 3. showcasing the Flow of this Chapter (Source- Original)

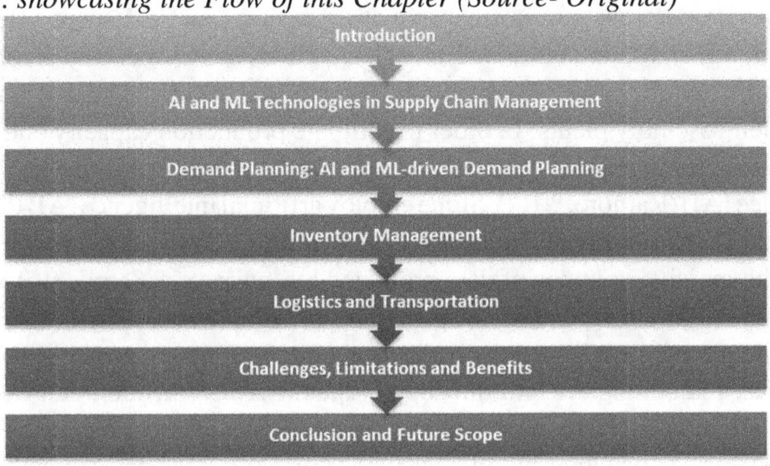

2. RESEARCH METHODOLOGY FOR THE CHAPTER

The chapter adopts a mixed methodology qualitative and quantitative. The initial stage based on a systematic literature review covering peer-reviewed journals, industry reports and case studies to provide a foundation for supply chain management from the perspective of AI and ML applications. In this review, we will point out for key trends, technologies and case studies of success in AI solutions applied to demand forecasting, inventory control and transport routes optimization. It also includes qualitative insights from expert interviews with supply chain managers, AI experts, and data analysts that provide an in-depth look at the challenges and opportunities surrounding AI/ML solutions across multiple industries. We will analyze this primary data for common factors affecting the integration of AI either succeed or fail. This study will conduct a quantitative analysis of industry case studies to look at the change in parameters like inventory metrics before and after AI, output cycle time, demand accuracy and lead times. Lastly, it involves a comparison for analysis between the various available AI models utilized in demand planning and logistics to evaluate their efficiency, cost-effectiveness with the scope of making an overall resilient supply chain.

3. AI AND ML TECHNOLOGIES IN SUPPLY CHAIN MANAGEMENT

AI technologies are being used by businesses in their supply chains to improve warehouse productivity, optimize production operations, and more (Bertola & Teunissen, 2018). Manufacturers of completed goods sometimes rely on the timely delivery of hundreds or even thousands of components sent from international partners to their assembly plants. In order to estimate production capacity and manage warehouse space depending on consumer demand, several firms employ artificial intelligence (AI) (Rathore, 2017). Some employ artificial intelligence (AI) to identify possible delays and equipment failures before they affect production (Andronie et al., 2021). The massive volumes of data produced by Internet of Things (IoT) devices and sensors across storage and transportation infrastructure are being leveraged to extract operational insights using AI (Rathore, 2023). Even with all of its potential advantages, integrating AI into the supply chain may be difficult and expensive. Robust computing systems are needed to run intelligent applications in production. These systems can be cloud-based instances or on-premises edge servers, and they must be able to receive data from integrated sensors and devices as part of an Industry 4.0 strategy. Companies usually see the greatest advantages when they train machine learning models on their own data sets, an intensive and data-dependent process.

AI is used by businesses to estimate demand, manage warehouse capacity, track inventory, optimize shipping and delivery, enhance worker safety, and guarantee the accuracy of transaction records throughout international supply chains (Liu & Lin, 2021). Artificial intelligence (AI) has the potential to greatly increase productivity and save operating expenses, but its implementation may be difficult and costly, especially when bespoke ML models need to be trained on private data. Manufacturers and logistics companies may take action to be ready for AI integration into their supply chains and to use AI's revolutionary power to manage and run their logistics networks (Weber & Schutte, 2019).

Figure 4. illuminates the Key Genesis of AI and ML Technologies in Supply Chain Management (Source- Original)

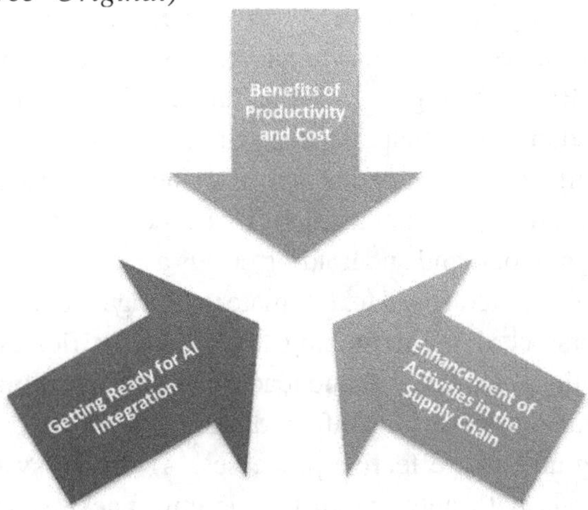

The complexity, entanglement, and expanse of today's supply chains have made it difficult for manufacturers to keep a close eye on the products and resources coming into their plants (Allal-Cherif et al., 2021). Because of AI's exceptional capacity for quick analysis of huge data sets, even the most intricate logistics networks may reveal more about their inner workings (Li et al., 2022). Machine learning-trained intelligent algorithms frequently provide important insights when analyzing enormous streams of recorded data and other logistical signals. Examples of these insights include detecting sources of variability or enhancing capacity for processes with constant and variable temporal elements that result in bottlenecks.

With AI and Machine Learning, supply chain management (SCM) is changing faster than ever before, bringing innovation and efficiency to all industries. By automating processes, improving potential forecasting, and allowing for real-time decision-making, these technologies are reinventing the way in which supply chains have historically been conducted. AI and ML help organizations to increase agility while reducing costs in the face of increasing complexity of global supply networks with a growing focus on the customer side.

Supply chain management includes several moving parts, and one of the most critical for success is demand planning. Demand forecasting was traditionally based on historical data and the art of human judgment which often resulted in inaccurate predictions and inefficiencies. AI and ML algorithms turn this process on its head, running massive datasets of information through simulations; analyzing current market conditions, consumer actions, or even external factors like the weather and economic indicators. They are used for accurate demand prediction and reduce the risk of overstocking or understocking. Companies can use predictive analytics to predict changes in the market or environment and proactively drive their strategies with greater adaptability and fortitude. To give one example: retailers can harness AI to detect trends based on the season and ensure that they are optimizing their stock accordingly. By analyzing previous patterns, ML-powered systems continually adjust their predictions so that they can accurately forecast even in overzealous markets. This not only increases operational efficiencies but also improves customer experience by maintaining product availability (Saponaro et al., 2018).

Balancing customer demand and holding cost is a key consideration in inventory management. AI and ML tech used to automate tracking inventory, forecast re-order level, minimize overstock all for optimizing these steps. Artificial systems take a close look on sales, supplier performance, and lead times so that optimal inventory levels are retained. They also give various info about the slow or dead stock, which helps in decision making and cost-effective processes. AI-driven systems also improve warehouse operations with automation for picking, packing, and replenishment. AI algorithms navigate robots and autonomous vehicles, automating warehouse activities for better accuracy and lowered labor costs. They ensure speedy and efficient order fulfillment, thus boosting operational efficiency and profitability. The other key part of the supply chain where AI and ML have a major effect is in logistics and transportation. Using AI-enabled route optimization algorithms, businesses can examine traffic data, gasoline prices and delivery timelines to calculate the best routes. It minimizes the delivery times, transportation costs and reduces environmental impact.

Machine learning improves fleet management by anticipating maintenance responsibilities, minimizing downtime and extending the lifecycle vehicles. A transparency into the shipments tracking systems provides businesses with visibility so they can monitor that progress and act accordingly in case of a delay. The other technology domains where AI is being increasingly used are for autonomous vehicles and drones especially used for last-mile delivery, which provides quicker and cheaper options.

Using AI-powered dynamic pricing models, logistics providers can increase or decrease their rates in accordance with shifts in demand in real-time to remain competitive. The integration of these technologies leads to greater visibility and control over the supply chain processes, thereby enhancing transparency amongst stakeholders and boosting customer experience. Combining of AI, ML with Internet of Things (IoT) results in high mobile supply chain ecosystem. Real Time Data from IoT DevicesIoT Devices such as Techlosses which are widely used to collect data directly from the sensor embedded-based products in a warehouse and transportation, etc. Thanks to AI and ML, you now have a data analytics engine that analyses this data, transforming it into actionable insights for real-time decision-making. Cold chain monitoring in transit – Temperature-sensitive products, like pharmaceuticals, can be checked through the entire journey to store the condition. If any odor or taste is out of the standard, action is taken immediately, which helps in reducing spoilage and maximizing quality.

Such connectivity also brings a higher level of visibility across the supply chain; businesses can track shipments, manage inventory and monitor supplier performance in real time. Focus on AI-Powered DashboardsAI-powered dashboards gives managers a bird-eye-view of operations to assess bottlenecks, optimize workflows, and react immediately to disruptions. Supply chains around the world face many risks from natural disasters to geopolitical tensions to economic uncertainties. The use of AI and ML technologies allows better management of risk, by enabling analysis on a wider array and number of data inputs to find potential disruptions, and recommend actions to mitigate that risk. By using predictive analytics models to predict supplier risks, transportation delays, and market fluctuations, businesses can create contingency plans.

Supply chain disruption during the COVID-19 pandemic pushed a lot of organizations to embrace AI-enabled solutions. They offered visibility into different suppliers, production schedules, and logistics networks and helped to reposition them for the fast-evolving environment. Predicting and mitigating disruptions makes for an agile supply chain that is consistent in unpredictability. Sustainability is gaining importance in the business landscape and AI and ML are enabling sustainable supply chains across the globe. They allow businesses to monitor and improve energy use, cut down on waste, and reduce their carbon footprint. AI-enabled apps recognize inefficiencies in transportation and production processes, recommending sustainable substitutes.

Machine learning models can, for instance, optimize packaging design to reduce the use of materials and transportation costs. AI analytics helps with ethical sourcing assurance by ensuring adherence to environmental and labor standards. Integrating AI with blockchain can help supply chain transactions be more transparent and it enables the businesses to prove accountability which will, in turn, foster trust between enterprises and consumers. Digital twin technology: AI and ML-powered digital twin tech is transforming supply chain planning and execution. A digital twin is a virtual representation of a physical supply chain system, that enables businesses to simulate scenarios, test out strategies and optimize operations without having to take any real risks. But these simulations offer wonderful glimpses into possible pitfalls and exceptional opportunities alike, helpful for mitigating risk and honing decisions. For instance, digital twins can model the effects of alterations to supplier networks, production schedules or transport routes so that firms can find best options. Using AI and ML algorithms, digital twins learn from the real-time data forever as tuned according to graphs.

While AI and the potential of ML are monumental, the adoption of those technologies remains a challenge in supply chain management. These technologies rely significantly on data quality and availability however, various organizations face challenges with incomplete or fragmented datasets. Another major challenge is maintaining data security and privacy, especially when dealing with high-sensitive customer and supplier information.

There are ethical concerns regarding the utilization of AI-driven systems which covers issues such as algorithmic bias and transparency. Stakeholders need reassurance about the fairness, lack of bias, and explainability of AI models before doing business with them. Moreover, the need to manage workforce displacement due to automation while investing in reskilling and upskilling programmes to ensure that every employee is taken care of too. The possibilities for AI and ML in supply chain management moving forward are promising. The predictive analytics will result in more accurate, leading to hyper-personalized supply chain strategies. Self-driving trucks and robotic warehouses will make their way to the big screen, bringing new definitions for logistics and inventory management as part of autonomous technology.

When some of the prices will integrate emerging technologies such as blockchain, quantum computing and edge computer for improved supply chain transparency amid security and efficiency. Sustainability would continue to be one of the driving factors, with solutions based on AI aiding in circular economy practices and therefore reducing environmental impact. Moreover, collaborative AI systems will enable supply chain professionals to make more informed decisions by combining human and machine intelligence. Demand planning, inventory optimization, logistics and risk management are some of the areas being transformed by AI and ML technologies when it comes to supply chain management. Such advancements allow organizations to drive operational efficiency, strengthen customer experience, and help sustainability. Despite appropriate hurdles and ethical concerns that want to be dealt with, the power of AI & ML in supply chains is undeniable. As these technologies develop and businesses continue to utilise them, we will uncover exponential levels of efficiency, resilience, and agility as the future of world trade evolves in an age increasingly driven by AI (Noor et al., 2022).

4. DEMAND PLANNING: AI AND ML-DRIVEN DEMAND PLANNING

AI-driven demand forecasting applications can notably enhance forecast accuracy through the analysis of historical demand and supply data and trends. Machine learning models excel at uncovering concealed patterns within historical demand data, resulting in reduced holding costs and optimal inventory levels. Moreover, these models can offer precise, region-specific demand insights, facilitating tailored fulfillment processes that align with specific regional requirements (Tsolakis et al., 2023). AI has become essential in many different industries, and supply chain companies are expected to treble their machine automation use in the next five years, according to Gartner. IoT technologies, which make use of analytics and AI concepts, are also rapidly expanding inside supply chains (Wong et al., 2023). The barriers have been broken down by globalization, which has led to strong corporate growth, especially in supply chain management and logistics, which have both profited and been greatly harmed. It is essential to remain up to date with technology changes in order to function across borders efficiently.

With guaranteeing effective transportation and prompt delivery of goods, the logistics sector is essential to supporting economies and promoting bilateral commerce. The whole supply chain management process, from locating raw materials to distributing them, is covered by the logistics industry (Sharma et al., 2021). The promise of integrating AI into logistics operations is to increase productivity and efficiency while significantly lowering operating expenses. User experience is important in supply chain management and logistics, just as it is in digital spaces. To do this, operations must be optimized using predictive analytics, process automation to reduce mistakes and delays, and digital transformation (Harale, 2021).

5. INVENTORY MANAGEMENT

AI-driven tools leverage historic demand and supply data and trends to establish optimal inventory levels, preventing over-production and reducing excessive holding costs. This approach liberates capital for more effective utilization elsewhere. Also, these tools enhance inventory turnover and throughput rates across warehouses, distribution centers (DCs), and fulfillment centers. In the fiercely competitive corporate world of today, supply chain optimization has become crucial for effective operations (Dal Forno et al., 2023). Maintaining high levels of customer satisfaction as well as cost control and profitability depend heavily on the seamless flow of goods from manufacturers to customers. The adoption of AI in supply chain management represents more than just a technological advancement; it marks a transformative shift redefining supply chain optimization and logistics with AI (Amelia et al., 2022). As demonstrated, AI enhances operational efficiency, refines demand forecasting, and facilitates warehouse automation, among other advantages. While AI greatly enhances supply chain capabilities, it functions most effectively when complemented by human expertise, ensuring strategic decision-making and addressing complex challenges remain within skilled hands. AI holds a promising future in the supply chain, offering a more agile, efficient, and responsive framework for businesses to excel in a competitive marketplace (Bu et al., 2020).

The technological advancements in artificial intelligence (AI) and machine learning (ML) have had a significant impact on supply chain management. This look at the major effects of AI and ML on supply chains in this blog, as well as how these developments boost output. With imitating human cognitive capacities in computers, artificial intelligence enables such robots to carry out activities that have historically required human intellect. Complex decision-making and problem-solving skills are part of this (Nagar et al., 2021). The important area of artificial intelligence is machine learning, which is centered on training algorithms to improve performance over time using available data. It includes a number of significant subfields, including robots, expert systems, deep learning, and natural language processing. Machine learning is essentially the application of AI concepts in real-world settings (Luce, 2018).

6. LOGISTICS AND TRANSPORTATION

Artificial Intelligence (AI) can improve supply chain processes at every level, from strategy to implementation (Khatua et al., 2021). In order to obtain insights about incoming supplies, client location profiles, and other pertinent elements, it makes use of both structured and unstructured data. Artificial Intelligence (AI) has the capability to produce supply chain planning papers and planning analytics dashboards, which may greatly enhance supply chain operations. Achieving both on-time delivery and cost reduction requires effective transportation routes and logistics. Real-time data analysis, encompassing traffic patterns and weather forecasts, is facilitated by artificial intelligence (AI) and machine learning (ML) technology. Businesses are utilizing artificial neural networks (ANNNs), which simulate the workings of the human brain, to combine cutting-edge technology like computer vision and natural language processing to automate operations, speed up decision-making, and improve consumer interactions through chatbots (Tripathi & Gupta, 2020).

These businesses may make well-informed decisions by utilizing data-driven insights, such as dynamically rerouting shipments to prevent delays and bottlenecks (Helo & Hao, 2022). This proactive strategy lowers transportation costs while also raising customer satisfaction. The key pillars of the global economy, the supply chain and logistics sector, makes sure that commodities travel smoothly across borders (Anica-Popa et al., 2021). It has several obstacles in the intricately linked and complicated marketplace of today, ranging from enhancing overall operating efficiency to managing inventory effectively. This calls for smooth coordination across multiple domains, including scheduling, transportation, and customer support. Artificial Intelligence (AI) has become a disruptive force in supply chain and logistics management, offering solutions to automate repetitive processes, optimize transportation routes, strengthen security measures, reduce costs, and enhance consumer experiences. Businesses may enhance customer happiness, boost operational efficiency, and boost profitability by utilizing AI capabilities.

Figure 5. conveys the Points on Logistics and Transportation (Source- Original)

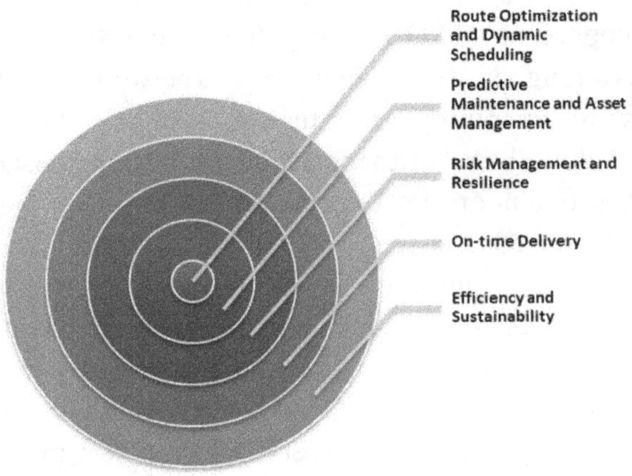

7. CHALLENGES, LIMITATIONS AND BENEFITS

The process of integrating AI into supply chain management and planning is slow. Although the technology has a great deal of promise to cut expenses and simplify procedures, it may be costly and difficult. When incorporating AI into their supply chain processes, businesses frequently run across a number of similar challenges as-

Training Expenses: The staff who will operate these novel, occasionally intimidating systems must be trained before AI can be adopted and integrated into industrial settings. This training procedure usually requires scheduling some downtime, which results in higher expenditures (Hosseinnia Shavaki et al., 2023). It deals with overcoming employee reluctance to change. To create efficient and reasonably priced training programs, supply chain partners should work with AI vendors or integrators; but it is crucial to understand that any training strategy will involve costs (Liu et al., 2020).

Initial and Continuous Cost: The expenses related to putting AI into practice go beyond just buying and setting up the required gear and software (Miroedova, 2023). Although pre-made machine learning models may be customized for a range of supply chain applications, training these models with the company's own data is frequently necessary to get the best results. Large amounts of high-quality data must be gathered, compiled, validated, transformed, and cleaned as part of this process, which can be laborious (Sharma et al., 2022). Companies run the danger of running into the "garbage in, garbage out" issue if they do not prepare their data properly. Machine learning model training is a compute-intensive activity that usually requires GPU-powered servers, which increases cloud service costs and places a significant strain on on-premises resources (Andronie et al., 2021).

Constant Management and Operation: It takes constant work to scale up and manage AI systems throughout a worldwide logistics network. Even though AI system operation requires less computing power than AI system training, stable platforms like edge servers or cloud-based virtual machines are still necessary (Sharma et al., 2020). The cloud-based solutions are lowering the cost and increasing the accessibility of AI technology. Managed data science platforms are provided by certain cloud infrastructure providers, making it easier to manage AI workflows, automate the development of machine learning models, and create them (Arunmozhi et al., 2022).

Intricate Systems: AI systems are made up of a variety of parts, including as sensors and devices that feed data in real-time, servers with GPUs for training machine learning models, edge and cloud servers for using these models in production, and apps that take action based on patterns or suggestions found (Rathore, 2017). Companies must include these components into the many links in an international supply chain. These systems need to be constantly observed, their performance adjusted, and any bugs found and fixed. Even if supply chain management may greatly benefit from AI, putting it into practice will cost a lot in terms of starting, operating, and training expenses. Also, consistent work and a strong infrastructure are needed for administering these intricate systems (Sundaram et al., 2020).

Figure 6. highlights the Challenges and Limitations (Source- Original)

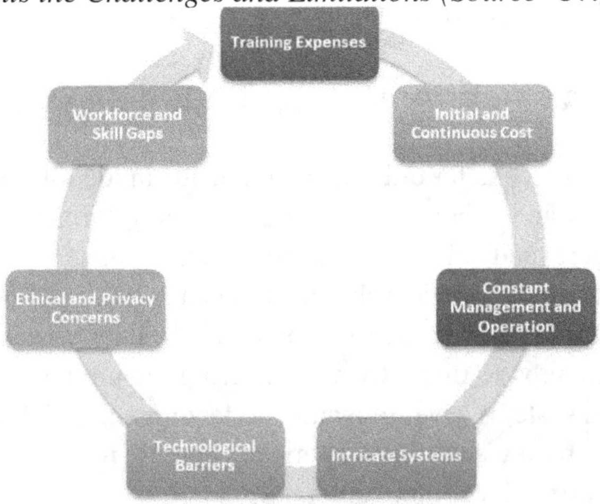

In terms of AI innovation, manufacturers have taken the lead, testing and using the technology in a variety of ways across manufacturing plants, warehouses and distribution centers, and transportation vehicles in contemporary supply chains (Gordon, 2021). This may result in a number of advantages like-

Enhanced Effectiveness of the Warehouse

AI improves warehouse productivity by making the arrangement and layout of the racks more efficient. Machine learning algorithms can recommend floor patterns that speed inventory access and minimize trip time from reception to racks to packing and shipping stations with assessing the amounts of commodities transferred through warehouse aisles (Gohil & Thakker, 2021). In order to increase fulfillment rates, these models can also schedule the best routes for employees and robots to move merchandise swiftly (Sharma, 2016). AI-enabled forecasting systems also assist producers balance inventory against carrying costs, further optimizing warehouse space, by analyzing demand signals from marketing, manufacturing lines, and point-of-sale systems (Abideen et al., 2021).

Lower Operating Expenses

Because AI can learn complicated behaviors and function in uncertain environments, it may discover and mitigate bottlenecks by doing repetitive operations like inventory monitoring, counting, and documentation more accurately and with less effort (Sima et al., 2020). Artificial intelligence (AI) may reduce the operational expenses of a complicated supply chain by identifying inefficiencies and streamlining repetitive processes (Ghoreishi & Happonen, 2021).

Reduced Waste and Errors

Artificial intelligence is far quicker than humans in identifying unusual behavior in both humans and robots. Algorithms are being trained by manufacturers, warehouse managers, and shipping firms to recognize inefficiencies in workflow, personnel mistakes, and product problems (Liu et al., 2022). AI-powered computer vision systems use data from cameras mounted in delivery trucks, manufacturing lines, and logistics hubs to inspect work, lowering the number of recalls, returns, and rework. These systems save time and cut down on material waste by identifying errors made by both machines and personnel before items are misassembled or shipped to the incorrect location (Rathore, 2023).

Enhanced Material and Worker Safety

With monitoring work settings like assembly lines, warehouses, and shipping vehicles and recognizing circumstances that endanger worker and public safety, artificial intelligence (AI) technologies may improve safety across the supply chain (Feng et al., 2022). This might entail making sure that workplace safety procedures and Occupational Safety and Health Administration (OSHA) regulations are followed, or it could entail employing computer vision to enforce the usage of personal protective equipment (PPE) (Chintalapati & Pandey, 2022).

Simulation-Based Optimisation of Operations

AI-powered simulations can help supply chain managers understand intricate, international logistics networks and suggest improvements. AI is being utilized more and more in combination with digital twins, which are visual 3D representations of real-world processes and items like assembly lines in factories or assembled commodities. Without interfering with actual operations, operations planners may replicate a variety of techniques and strategies on digital twins, such as assessing the effects of expanding capacity at different locations.

Improved Inventory Management Accuracy

Manufacturers use AI to more precisely and effectively monitor inventory levels. Demand may be estimated by AI-powered forecasting systems using inventory data from downstream customers (Kliestik et al., 2023). The system modifies the manufacturer's demand predictions in response to any decline in consumer demand (Pal & Jayarathne, 2022). Computer vision solutions, which deploy cameras on infrastructure, racks, cars, and even drones, are being used by manufacturers and supply chain managers more and more to monitor warehouse storage capacity and count items in real time (Kashem et al., 2024).

Figure 7. shares the Advantages (Source- Original)

8. ANALYSIS AND SYNTHESIS OF THE STUDY WITH IMPLICATIONS

This chapter highlights how Artificial Intelligence (AI) and Machine Learning (ML) have the capacity to revolutionize supply chains through improved demand planning, inventory management and logistics processes. Because of AI-driven predictive analytics, organizations can predict demand with unprecedented accuracy and eliminate overproduction, which means less waste. However, ML algorithms optimize inventory levels without the need of human monitoring they ensure that the right products are available at the right time, improving customer satisfaction, and reducing holding cost. Moreover, these solutions reduce cost in logistics through the automating warehouse operations, dynamic routing and real-time tracking further accelerating operational efficiencies.

Bringing together these findings, AI/ML integration emerges not simply as a technology upgrade but as an opportunity of strategic importance to modern supply chains. These tools provide actionable insights by processing extensive datasets in real-time, helping businesses to quickly adapt to market changes and minimize risks while improving resilience. As it can imagine this has deep-rooted implications catering to more agile supply chains that is flexible enough to absorb shocks during global challenges faced over recent years. Organizations using them will be able to attain sustainable practices, help create lower carbon footprints, and align with environmental objectives. In conclusion, This propounds AI/ML as instrumental for intelligent supply networks catering to Industry 5.0 and the sustainability challenges of the present-time scenario.

9. CONCLUSION

Artificial intelligence (AI)-driven supply chain management (SCM) solutions outperform conventional ones when it comes to tracking massive volumes of supplies in real-time as they move through intermediate production and distribution partners to become final goods. Improved traceability and visibility can assist manufacturers in identifying suppliers who could be breaking ethical or quality sourcing guidelines. Artificial intelligence (AI) may save time and money by increasing supply chain transparency. It can assist manufacturers in meeting the ethical, quality, and sustainability criteria that many customers and authorities demand them to keep when sourcing their components. Businesses cannot afford to do business with suppliers who breach labor, governance, or environmental laws, even if they are located abroad. Applications for supply chains powered by AI, with integrated analytics capabilities, are able to recogniz patterns that expose fraudulent or unethical sourcing practices.

10. FUTURE SCOPE AND TRENDS OF THE STUDY

The trends of the future that will transform supply chains with the help of Artificial Intelligence (AI) and Machine Learning (ML) are remarkable due to their general nature along with the potential need for transformation in global markets. Analytics will become even more predictive and prescriptive, allowing businesses to accurately predict demand patterns. Such strategies will push hyper-personalized inventory management, whereby stock would be made available at a just-in-time basis customized to regional and consumer-specific requirements.

AI/ML would also embed themselves with Internet of Things (IoT) devices to facilitate sharing of real-time information across different nodes in the supply chain, hence improving visibility and traceability. Delivery networks will be positively disrupted by autonomous logistics solutions- self-driving delivery vehicles and drones promise to overhaul last-mile delivery, making it faster and cheaper. In addition, digital twins as virtual representations of supply chain systems that can be manipulated as if they exist in the real world will help organizations to simulate and improve interactions among various processes before implementation. AI-powered solutions will be led by sustainability to cut their carbon emissions and ethical sourcing. By integrating with AI, Blockchain technology will lead trustworthy supply chain transactions among stakeholders. Workforce working with learning intelligent systems will facilitate adaptive learning making supply chain professionals leverage AI tools. Such trends foreshadow an impending future of supply chains that not only promises increased efficiency but also offers the possibility for resilience, sustainability and customer-centricity potentially transforming global commerce into a new era powered with AI.

AI-powered Supply Chain systems empower organizations to identify reputable, cost-effective suppliers, fostering leaner operations without compromising on quality, speed or service. To harness the potential of AI and machine learning for Supply Chain planning and forecasting, companies can integrate sophisticated algorithms aimed at detecting patterns and refining demand sensing. In recent years, the fragility of global supply chains has become a prominent public concern. These extensive logistics networks, essential for manufacturers worldwide, have been disrupted by transportation delays, labor stoppages, and a growing complexity and interconnectedness that amplify their persistent inefficiencies. To address these tangled networks, supply chain planners are turning to a cutting-edge technology with significant, yet largely untapped, potential. They are leveraging artificial intelligence to enhance the efficiency and resilience of supply chains as this move toward an increasingly globalized future.

REFERENCES

Abideen, A. Z., Sundram, V. P. K., Pyeman, J., Othman, A. K., & Sorooshian, S. (2021). Food supply chain transformation through technology and future research directions—A systematic review. *Logistics (Basel)*, 5(4), 83. DOI: 10.3390/logistics5040083

Ahmad, S., Miskon, S., Alabdan, R., & Tlili, I. (2020). Towards sustainable textile and apparel industry: Exploring the role of business intelligence systems in the era of industry 4.0. *Sustainability (Basel)*, 12(7), 2632. DOI: 10.3390/su12072632

Akram, S. V., Malik, P. K., Singh, R., Gehlot, A., Juyal, A., Ghafoor, K. Z., & Shrestha, S. (2022). Implementation of digitalized technologies for fashion industry 4.0: Opportunities and challenges. *Scientific Programming*, 2022, 2022. DOI: 10.1155/2022/7523246

Aljohani, A. (2023). Predictive Analytics and Machine Learning for Real-Time Supply Chain Risk Mitigation and Agility. *Sustainability (Basel)*, 15(20), 15088. DOI: 10.3390/su152015088

Allal-Cherif, O., Simon-Moya, V., & Ballester, A. C. C. (2021). Intelligent purchasing: How artificial intelligence can redefine the purchasing function. *Journal of Business Research*, 124, 69–76. DOI: 10.1016/j.jbusres.2020.11.050

Amelia, R., Hussein, A. S., & Wijayanti, R. (2022). Analysis of Factors Influencing Business Resilience: Role of Marketing Performance as Moderating Variables. *ITALIENISCH*, 12(2), 943–957.

Andronie, M., Lazaroiu, G., Iatagan, M., U ă, C., tefănescu, R., & Coco atu, M. (2021). Artificial intelligence-based decision-making algorithms, internet of things sensing networks, and deep learning-assisted smart process management in cyber-physical production systems. *Electronics (Basel)*, 10(20), 2497. DOI: 10.3390/electronics10202497

Andronie, M., Lazaroiu, G., tefanescu, R., U a, C., & Dijmarescu, I. (2021). Sustainable, smart, and sensing technologies for cyber-physical manufacturing systems: A systematic literature review. *Sustainability (Basel)*, 13(10), 5495. DOI: 10.3390/su13105495

Anica-Popa, I., Anica-Popa, L., Rădulescu, C., & Vrîncianu, M. (2021). The integration of artificial intelligence in retail: Benefits, challenges and a dedicated conceptual framework. *Amfiteatru Economic*, 23(56), 120–136. DOI: 10.24818/EA/2021/56/120

Arunmozhi, M., Venkatesh, V. G., Arisian, S., Shi, Y., & Sreedharan, V. R. (2022). Application of blockchain and smart contracts in autonomous vehicle supply chains: An experimental design. *Transportation Research Part E, Logistics and Transportation Review*, 165, 102864. DOI: 10.1016/j.tre.2022.102864

Bajgoric, N. (2023). Always-on business: integrating business continuity and business resilience. *Continuity & Resilience Review*, (ahead-of-print).

Bertola, P., & Teunissen, J. (2018). Fashion 4.0. Innovating fashion industry through digital transformation. *Research Journal of Textile and Apparel*, 22(4), 352–369. DOI: 10.1108/RJTA-03-2018-0023

Bu, L., Chen, C. H., Zhang, G., Liu, B., Dong, G., & Yuan, X. (2020). A hybrid intelligence approach for sustainable service innovation of smart and connected product: A case study. *Advanced Engineering Informatics*, 46, 101163. DOI: 10.1016/j.aei.2020.101163

Casciani, D., Chkanikova, O., & Pal, R. (2022). Exploring the nature of digital transformation in the fashion industry: opportunities for supply chains, business models, and sustainability-oriented innovations. *Sustainability: Science. Sustainability*, 18(1), 773–795. DOI: 10.1080/15487733.2022.2125640

Chintalapati, S., & Pandey, S. K. (2022). Artificial intelligence in marketing: A systematic literature review. *International Journal of Market Research*, 64(1), 38–68. DOI: 10.1177/14707853211018428

Dal Forno, A. J., Bataglini, W. V., Steffens, F., & Ulson de Souza, A. A. (2023). Industry 4.0 in textile and apparel sector: A systematic literature review. *Research Journal of Textile and Apparel*, 27(1), 95–117. DOI: 10.1108/RJTA-08-2021-0106

Dash, R., McMurtrey, M., Rebman, C., & Kar, U. K. (2019). Application of artificial intelligence in automation of supply chain management. *Journal of Strategic Innovation and Sustainability*, 14(3), 43–53.

dos Santos, C. H., Gabriel, G. T., do Amaral, J. V. S., Montevechi, J. A. B., & de Queiroz, J. A. (2021). Decision-making in a fast fashion company in the Industry 4.0 era: A Digital Twin proposal to support operational planning. *International Journal of Advanced Manufacturing Technology*, 116(5-6), 1653–1666. DOI: 10.1007/s00170-021-07543-z

Feng, Y., Lai, K. H., & Zhu, Q. (2022). Green supply chain innovation: Emergence, adoption, and challenges. *International Journal of Production Economics*, 248, 108497. DOI: 10.1016/j.ijpe.2022.108497

Ghoreishi, M., & Happonen, A. (2021, September). The case of fabric and textile industry: The emerging role of digitalization, internet-of-Things and industry 4.0 for circularity. In *Proceedings of Sixth International Congress on Information and Communication Technology: ICICT 2021,London,* Volume 3 (pp. 189-200). Singapore: Springer Singapore.

Gohil, D., & Thakker, S. V. (2021). Blockchain-integrated technologies for solving supply chain challenges. *Modern Supply Chain Research and Applications*, 3(2), 78–97. DOI: 10.1108/MSCRA-10-2020-0028

Gordon, A. (2021). Internet of things-based real-time production logistics, big data-driven decision-making processes, and industrial artificial intelligence in sustainable cyber-physical manufacturing systems. *Journal of Self-Governance and Management Economics*, 9(3), 61–73.

Goti, A., Querejeta-Lomas, L., Almeida, A., de la Puerta, J. G., & López-de-Ipiña, D. (2023). Artificial Intelligence in Business-to-Customer Fashion Retail: A Literature Review. *Mathematics*, 11(13), 2943. DOI: 10.3390/math11132943

Harale, N. (2021). *Development of the supply chain and production management system (SCPMS) for small-series fashion industry* (Doctoral dissertation, Centrale Lille Institut).

Helo, P., & Hao, Y. (2022). Artificial intelligence in operations management and supply chain management: An exploratory case study. *Production Planning and Control*, 33(16), 1573–1590. DOI: 10.1080/09537287.2021.1882690

Hosseinnia Shavaki, F., & Ebrahimi Ghahnavieh, A. (2023). Applications of deep learning into supply chain management: A systematic literature review and a framework for future research. *Artificial Intelligence Review*, 56(5), 4447–4489. DOI: 10.1007/s10462-022-10289-z PMID: 36212799

Kashem, M. A., Shamsuddoha, M., Nasir, T., & Chowdhury, A. A. (2024). Supply Chain Disruption versus Optimization: A Review on Artificial Intelligence and Blockchain. *Knowledge (Beverly Hills, Calif.)*, 3(1), 80–96.

Khatua, A., Khatua, A., Chi, X., & Cambria, E. (2021). Artificial intelligence, social media and supply chain management: The way forward. *Electronics (Basel)*, 10(19), 2348. DOI: 10.3390/electronics10192348

Kliestik, T., Nagy, M., & Valaskova, K. (2023). Global value chains and industry 4.0 in the context of lean workplaces for enhancing company performance and its comprehension via the digital readiness and expertise of workforce in the V4 nations. *Mathematics*, 11(3), 601. DOI: 10.3390/math11030601

Lee, Y. K. (2021). Transformation of the innovative and sustainable supply chain with upcoming real-time fashion systems. *Sustainability (Basel)*, 13(3), 1081. DOI: 10.3390/su13031081

Li, Q., Xue, Z., Wu, Y., & Zeng, X. (2022). The status quo and prospect of sustainable development of smart clothing. *Sustainability (Basel)*, 14(2), 990. DOI: 10.3390/su14020990

Liu, C., Feng, Y., Lin, D., Wu, L., & Guo, M. (2020). Iot based laundry services: An application of big data analytics, intelligent logistics management, and machine learning techniques. *International Journal of Production Research*, 58(17), 5113–5131. DOI: 10.1080/00207543.2019.1677961

Liu, K. S., & Lin, M. H. (2021). Performance Assessment on the Application of Artificial Intelligence to Sustainable Supply Chain Management in the Construction Material Industry. *Sustainability (Basel)*, 13(22), 12767. DOI: 10.3390/su132212767

Liu, W., Liang, Y., Lim, M. K., Long, S., & Shi, X. (2022). A theoretical framework of smart supply chain innovation for going global companies: A multi-case study from China. *International Journal of Logistics Management*, 33(3), 1090–1113. DOI: 10.1108/IJLM-10-2020-0388

Luce, L. (2018). *Artificial intelligence for fashion: How AI is revolutionizing the fashion industry*. Apress.

Miroedova, S. (2023). Thesis Study: analysis of the implementation of Artificial Intelligence in warehouses of e-commerce SMEs based on feasibility study.

Mohiuddin Babu, M., Akter, S., Rahman, M., Billah, M. M., & Hack-Polay, D. (2022). The role of artificial intelligence in shaping the future of Agile fashion industry. *Production Planning and Control*, •••, 1–15.

Nagar, D., Raghav, S., Bhardwaj, A., Kumar, R., Singh, P. L., & Sindhwani, R. (2021). Machine learning: Best way to sustain the supply chain in the era of industry 4.0. *Materials Today: Proceedings*, 47, 3676–3682. DOI: 10.1016/j.matpr.2021.01.267

Noor, A., Saeed, M. A., Ullah, T., Uddin, Ż., & Ullah Khan, R. M. W. (2022). A review of artificial intelligence applications in apparel industry. *Journal of the Textile Institute*, 113(3), 505–514. DOI: 10.1080/00405000.2021.1880088

Nouinou, H., Asadollahi-Yazdi, E., Baret, I., Nguyen, N. Q., Terzi, M., Ouazene, Y., Yalaoui, F., & Kelly, R. (2023). Decision-making in the context of Industry 4.0: Evidence from the textile and clothing industry. *Journal of Cleaner Production*, 391, 136184. DOI: 10.1016/j.jclepro.2023.136184

Pal, R., & Jayarathne, A. (2022). Digitalization in the textiles and clothing sector. In *The Digital Supply Chain* (pp. 255–271). Elsevier. DOI: 10.1016/B978-0-323-91614-1.00015-0

Pawlicka, K., & Bal, M. (2022). Sustainable Supply Chain Finances implementation model and Artificial Intelligence for innovative omnichannel logistics. *Management*, 26(1), 19–35. DOI: 10.2478/manment-2019-0082

Rathore, B. (2017). Beyond Trends: Shaping the Future of Fashion Marketing with AI, Sustainability and Machine Learning. *Eduzone: International Peer Reviewed/ Refereed Multidisciplinary Journal, 6*(2), 16-24.

Rathore, B. (2017). Exploring the Intersection of Fashion Marketing in the Metaverse: Leveraging Artificial Intelligence for Consumer Engagement and Brand Innovation. *International Journal of New Media Studies: International Peer Reviewed Scholarly Indexed Journal*, 4(2), 51–60. DOI: 10.58972/eiprmj.v4i2y17.108

Rathore, B. (2019). From Trendy to Green: Exploring AI's Role in Sustainable Fashion Marketing. *International Journal of New Media Studies: International Peer Reviewed Scholarly Indexed Journal*, 6(2), 12–22. DOI: 10.58972/eiprmj.v6i2y19.120

Rathore, B. (2019). Fashion Sustainability in the AI Era: Opportunities and Challenges in Marketing. *Eduzone: International Peer Reviewed/Refereed Multidisciplinary Journal, 8*(2), 17-24.

Rathore, B. (2023). Digital Transformation 4.0: Integration of Artificial Intelligence & Metaverse in Marketing. *Eduzone: International Peer Reviewed/Refereed Multidisciplinary Journal, 12*(1), 42-48.

Rathore, B. (2023). Integration of Artificial Intelligence& It's Practices in Apparel Industry. *ugc approved research journals in india| UGC Newly Added Journals|(I-JNMS), 10*(1), 25-37.

Raut, R. D., Mangla, S. K., Narwane, V. S., Gardas, B. B., Priyadarshinee, P., & Narkhede, B. E. (2019). Linking big data analytics and operational sustainability practices for sustainable business management. *Journal of Cleaner Production*, 224, 10–24. DOI: 10.1016/j.jclepro.2019.03.181

Riahi, Y., Saikouk, T., Gunasekaran, A., & Badraoui, I. (2021). Artificial intelligence applications in supply chain: A descriptive bibliometric analysis and future research directions. *Expert Systems with Applications*, 173, 114702. DOI: 10.1016/j.eswa.2021.114702

Rodrigues, D., & Pereira, R. (2023). How Can Artificial Intelligence Help Improve Fashion Sustainability? In *Digital Technologies and Transformation in Business, Industry and Organizations* (Vol. 2, pp. 43–61). Springer Nature Switzerland.

Saponaro, M., Le Gal, D., Gao, M., Guisiano, M., & Maniere, I. C. (2018, December). Challenges and opportunities of artificial intelligence in the fashion world. In *2018 international conference on intelligent and innovative computing applications (ICONIC)* (pp. 1-5). IEEE. DOI: 10.1109/ICONIC.2018.8601258

Sharma, P. (2016). Role of AI in Enhancing the Efficiency and Effectiveness of Shop and Delivery Propositions in Smart Cities.

Sharma, R., Kamble, S. S., Gunasekaran, A., Kumar, V., & Kumar, A. (2020). A systematic literature review on machine learning applications for sustainable agriculture supply chain performance. *Computers & Operations Research*, 119, 104926. DOI: 10.1016/j.cor.2020.104926

Sharma, R., Shishodia, A., Gunasekaran, A., Min, H., & Munim, Z. H. (2022). The role of artificial intelligence in supply chain management: Mapping the territory. *International Journal of Production Research*, 60(24), 7527–7550. DOI: 10.1080/00207543.2022.2029611

Sharma, S., Koehl, L., Bruniaux, P., Zeng, X., & Wang, Z. (2021). Development of an intelligent data-driven system to recommend personalized fashion design solutions. *Sensors (Basel)*, 21(12), 4239. DOI: 10.3390/s21124239 PMID: 34205598

Shen, B., Ding, X., Wang, Y., & Ren, S. (2019). RFID-embedded smart washing machine systems in the big data era: Value creation in fashion supply chain. *Fashion supply chain management in Asia: Concepts, models, and cases*, 99-113.

Sima, V., Gheorghe, I. G., Subic, J., & Nancu, D. (2020). Influences of the industry 4.0 revolution on the human capital development and consumer behavior: A systematic review. *Sustainability (Basel)*, 12(10), 4035. DOI: 10.3390/su12104035

Sundaram, R., Sharma, D. R., & Shakya, D. A. (2020). Digital transformation of business models: A systematic review of impact on revenue and supply chain. *International Journal of Management*, 11(5).

Tripathi, S., & Gupta, M. (2020). Transforming towards a smarter supply chain. *International Journal of Logistics Systems and Management*, 36(3), 319–342. DOI: 10.1504/IJLSM.2020.108694

Tsolakis, N., Schumacher, R., Dora, M., & Kumar, M. (2023). Artificial intelligence and blockchain implementation in supply chains: A pathway to sustainability and data monetisation? *Annals of Operations Research*, 327(1), 157–210. DOI: 10.1007/s10479-022-04785-2 PMID: 35755830

Weber, F. D., & Schütte, R. (2019). State-of-the-art and adoption of artificial intelligence in retailing. *Digital Policy. Regulation & Governance*, 21(3), 264–279. DOI: 10.1108/DPRG-09-2018-0050

Wong, C., Guo, Z. X., & Leung, S. Y. S. (2013). *Optimizing decision making in the apparel supply chain using artificial intelligence (AI): from production to retail.* Elsevier.

Chapter 6
Enhancing Supply Chain Resilience in the Fashion Apparel Industry Through Advanced Analytics: A Review

Ravishankar S. Ulle
https://orcid.org/0009-0008-1011-8738
Faculty of Management Studies, CMS Business School, Jain University, India

S. Yogananthan
https://orcid.org/0009-0007-5583-0924
Faculty of Management Studies, CMS Business School, Jain University, India

Balaji Gopalan
https://orcid.org/0000-0002-1082-5597
Faculty of Management Studies, CMS Business School, Jain University, India

Kotresh Patil
Ramaiah Institute of Management, India

ABSTRACT

The fast-paced fashion industry relies on far-flung supply chains, making it prone to disruptions. To combat this, supply chain resilience analytics steps in. It leverages data to pinpoint vulnerabilities, assess risks, and craft strategies to make fashion's supply chains more adaptable and recovery-swift in the face of surprises. This data-driven approach involves gathering and monitoring data, meticulously assessing risks, using predictive analytics to anticipate future challenges, and crafting both

DOI: 10.4018/979-8-3693-4433-0.ch006

scenario planning and contingency plans. Additionally, it optimizes supply chain networks for efficiency. By proactively identifying and mitigating risks, fashion companies can ensure smooth production, distribution, and customer satisfaction. This translates to better operational efficiency, responsiveness to customer demands, and the ability to consistently deliver high-quality products. Ultimately, supply chain resilience analytics empowers fashion companies to navigate uncertainties with greater ease and build a robust and resilient supply chain ecosystem.

INTRODUCTION

The fashion apparel industry has a rich history of evolution and adaptation, driven in part by technological advancements. In the late 19th century, the industry saw the early adoption of mass production techniques, marked by the introduction of sewing machines and standardized sizing. This laid the foundation for more efficient clothing manufacturing processes.

The late 20th century witnessed a substantial leap in technological innovation with the advent of Computer-Aided Design (CAD) and Manufacturing (CAM) technologies. Designers began using computers to create and modify patterns and designs, leading to more precise and efficient manufacturing processes. These developments marked the beginning of a digital revolution in the industry.

The fashion apparel industry is a dynamic and highly competitive sector that encompasses the design, manufacturing, distribution, and retail of clothing and accessories. It plays a crucial role in the global economy and significantly influences consumer preferences and trends. This industry is characterized by its rapid pace of change, driven by evolving fashion tastes, technological advancements, and market demands.

Significance in the Global Market

The fashion apparel industry is a major contributor to the global economy, generating substantial revenue and providing employment opportunities across the supply chain, from textile production to retail.

Fashion has a profound impact on cultural expression, reflecting societal values, trends, and individual identities. It serves as a means of communication and self-expression, influencing lifestyles and perceptions.

The industry is known for its emphasis on innovation and creativity, with designers and brands constantly striving to create unique and trend-setting products. Technological advancements, sustainable practices, and new materials contribute to ongoing innovation (Hsu, C. H., *et al.,* 2021)

Fashion is a globalized industry, with supply chains that span multiple countries. Raw materials are sourced from different regions, and manufacturing often occurs in countries with cost-effective labor (Hsu, C. H., *et al.,* 2022). This interconnected supply chain highlights the industry's reliance on efficient logistics and international trade. Consumer preferences and behaviors play a central role in shaping the fashion industry. Rapid shifts in consumer trends require agile supply chains and quick response strategies to meet market demands and remain competitive (Irfan, I., *et al.,* 2022).

The fashion industry faces increasing scrutiny for its environmental and social impact. Sustainable practices, ethical sourcing, and responsible manufacturing are becoming essential considerations for consumers and industry stakeholders.

Technology has transformed various aspects of the industry, from design and production processes to retail and marketing. E-commerce platforms, augmented reality in fitting rooms, and data analytics are examples of technology-driven advancements in the fashion sector (Ivanov, D., *et al.,* 2021).

Understanding the significance of the fashion apparel industry in the global market involves recognizing its multifaceted impact on economies, cultures, and individual lifestyles. The industry's ability to adapt to changing consumer expectations and embrace innovations will continue to shape its role in the global marketplace.

The fashion apparel industry grapples with a host of challenges and vulnerabilities within its supply chain, underscoring the intricate and interconnected nature of its global operations. One of the primary challenges is the inherent volatility in consumer demand, characterized by swift and unpredictable shifts in preferences. Short product life cycles further exacerbate this challenge, necessitating agile supply chain strategies to align production with rapidly fluctuating demand patterns. This demand volatility poses a significant hurdle for fashion companies aiming to maintain an optimal balance between inventory levels and market requirements.

The complexity of the global supply chain is another critical issue faced by the industry. With multiple suppliers, manufacturers, and distributors spread across diverse geographical locations, the fashion supply chain is highly susceptible to disruptions caused by geopolitical events, natural disasters, or political instability. The lack of transparency and visibility across the entire supply chain compounds these challenges, hindering the timely identification and resolution of potential issues.

Ethical and sustainable practices have emerged as central concerns within the fashion industry, presenting both challenges and opportunities. Growing consumer awareness has intensified the scrutiny on responsible sourcing, fair labor practices, and environmentally friendly manufacturing. Brands now navigate the intricate task of integrating ethical considerations into their supply chain management practices, adding layers of complexity to an already intricate system.

Effective inventory management remains an ongoing challenge for fashion companies. Striking a delicate balance between meeting demand and avoiding overstock or stockouts requires sophisticated forecasting and inventory optimization techniques. Excess inventory ties up valuable capital, while insufficient inventory levels can result in lost sales and reputational damage. The challenge is exacerbated by the industry's fast-paced trends and the need for quick response capabilities.

The intricate web of relationships with suppliers poses its own set of challenges. Maintaining strong ties with suppliers is critical, but issues such as communication barriers, quality control problems, and dependency on a few key suppliers add layers of vulnerability. Disruptions within the supplier network can have cascading effects, impacting the entire supply chain.

Furthermore, the fashion industry contends with the ongoing challenge of incorporating and adapting to technological advancements. While technology offers opportunities for optimization, the rapid pace of change poses implementation challenges. The adoption of new technologies, such as advanced analytics and digital platforms, demands substantial investments and a willingness to adapt to evolving industry standards (Juan, S. J., *et al.*, 2022).

In addition, the fashion industry faces risks related to counterfeiting and intellectual property infringement. Protecting designs and brands is an ongoing battle, with the potential for economic losses and damage to brand reputation. Cybersecurity threats also loom large as the industry increasingly digitizes its supply chain processes, exposing itself to potential disruptions, data breaches, and financial losses (Khan, S. A. R., *et al.*, 2023).

To address these challenges, fashion companies are embracing a holistic and strategic approach to supply chain management. Advanced analytics, digital technologies, and sustainable practices are becoming integral components of resilient supply chain strategies aimed at mitigating vulnerabilities and ensuring the industry's continued adaptability to a dynamic global market (Trihastuti, D., *et al.*, 2024).

Problem Statement

The fashion industry grapples with challenges like demand volatility, global complexities, sustainability, and intricate supplier relationships. Traditional models struggle to adapt swiftly. Global supply chains face uncertainties, demanding transparency. Consumer demands for ethics and sustainability stress the industry. Inventory management complexities persist. Supplier relationships pose challenges. On a whole, the fashion industry needs advanced analytics to tackle supply chain challenges effectively, from demand fluctuations to global complexities and sustainability goals.

Objectives of the Study

1. Explore the current supply chain challenges faced by the fashion apparel industry in its supply chain resilience, including demand volatility, global complexities, sustainability issues, and supplier relationship intricacies.
2. Assess the role of advanced analytics in addressing and mitigating the identified challenges. Examine how predictive modeling, real-time insights, and data-driven decision-making can enhance supply chain resilience in the fashion industry.
3. Investigate the current state of adoption of advanced analytics within the fashion apparel industry. Assess the extent to which companies in the sector are leveraging analytics tools and techniques to optimize supply chain operations.
4. Develop practical recommendations for fashion companies looking to adopt or enhance their use of advanced analytics in supply chain management. Provide insights into the steps, strategies, and considerations for successful implementation.

LITERATURE REVIEW

The fashion apparel supply chain is a complex and intricate network that orchestrates the entire process of bringing clothing from concept to consumer (Köksal, D., *et al.*, 2017). It is a multifaceted system involving various stages, each playing a crucial role in the creation and distribution of fashionable garments. The journey begins with the design and product development phase, where creative teams conceptualize styles, fabrics, and colors. This stage sets the foundation for the entire production process, influencing subsequent decisions in sourcing, manufacturing, and distribution.

Raw material sourcing is a pivotal stage in the supply chain, where fabrics, trims, and accessories are procured from suppliers. Given the global nature of the fashion industry, these materials often come from different parts of the world (Oksanen, L. 2023). Sustainable sourcing practices are gaining prominence in this phase, reflecting the industry's growing commitment to ethical and environmentally responsible production.

The manufacturing and production phase transforms raw materials into finished garments. This stage typically takes place in factories, often located in countries with lower production costs. The manufacturing process involves cutting, sewing, and assembling garments, with a keen focus on quality control to ensure that the final products meet the brand's standards and customer expectations.

The distribution and logistics phase is characterized by the movement of finished goods from production facilities to distribution centers. This is a complex logistical process that may involve various modes of transportation, including ships, planes, and trucks. Efficient logistics are crucial to ensuring that products reach their destination in a timely manner, considering the global nature of the fashion supply chain (Qader, G., *et al.,* 2022).

Following distribution, fashion brands engage with the wholesale and retail stages. Wholesalers may act as intermediaries, distributing products to multiple retailers (Rahman, T., *et al.,* 2022). Alternatively, some brands opt for a direct-to-retail model, managing their own stores or selling through e-commerce platforms. This stage is highly influenced by consumer behavior, trends, and market dynamics, requiring brands to stay agile and responsive to shifting demands.

The consumer stage marks the culmination of the supply chain, where individuals purchase and use the clothing. Consumer preferences and behaviors play a significant role in shaping the entire supply chain, prompting adjustments in design, production, and distribution strategies (Chowdhury, N. R., *et al.,* 2024). The feedback loop between consumers and the industry contributes to the dynamic nature of the fashion market.

Post-consumer considerations include the handling of returns and recycling. Retailers manage product returns, and sustainable practices are increasingly prioritized. Recycling and repurposing materials are integral components of responsible post-consumer practices, aligning with the industry's broader efforts toward environmental consciousness.

Several key considerations and challenges underscore the fashion apparel supply chain (Sumarliah, E., *et al*., 2021). The prevalence of fast fashion, characterized by rapid production cycles and quickly changing trends, poses challenges in managing inventory and minimizing waste. Globalization introduces complexities related to geopolitical and economic changes, influencing the movement of materials and finished products. The industry's increasing emphasis on sustainability necessitates ethical practices throughout the supply chain, from sourcing to production and recycling. Furthermore, the integration of technology, such as RFID, IoT, and data analytics, is becoming more prevalent for supply chain optimization, demand forecasting, and inventory management (Rezaei, G., *et al*., 2022).

Understanding the intricacies of the fashion apparel supply chain is essential for industry stakeholders to navigate challenges, meet consumer demands, and adapt to the evolving landscape of the global fashion market (Susitha, E. 2022). From design and sourcing to production, distribution, and post-consumer considerations, each stage plays a crucial role in shaping the industry's dynamics.

The fashion apparel supply chain, a multifaceted system, is meticulously structured to facilitate the journey of clothing from its conceptualization to the hands of consumers. Commencing with the design and product development stage, creative teams collaborate to conceptualize and sketch new styles, finalize fabric choices, and make decisions about color schemes, setting the foundation for subsequent supply chain processes (Shahadat, M. H., *et al.*, 2024).

Raw material sourcing follows, where materials such as fabrics, trims, buttons, and zippers are procured from various suppliers. This phase is characterized by the industry's increasing emphasis on sustainability, prompting the careful consideration of ethical sourcing practices and environmentally responsible material choices.

The manufacturing and production phase is a critical juncture, marking the transformation of raw materials into finished garments. Often taking place in countries with lower production costs, factories handle tasks such as cutting, sewing, and assembling garments. Quality control measures are implemented to ensure that the final products align with the brand's quality standards and design specifications.

The subsequent distribution and logistics stage involves the transportation of finished goods from manufacturing facilities to distribution centers. This intricate process requires coordination across borders, with various modes of transportation, including ships, planes, and trucks, facilitating the movement of products to regional distribution hubs.

The wholesale and retail components of the supply chain determine how products reach consumers. Fashion brands may distribute products to wholesalers who act as intermediaries, supplying multiple retailers. Alternatively, some brands opt for a direct-to-retail model, managing their own stores or utilizing e-commerce platforms. This stage is highly influenced by consumer behavior, trends, and market dynamics, necessitating brands to stay agile and responsive.

The ultimate component of the supply chain is the consumer. Consumers, through their purchasing and use of clothing, play a pivotal role in shaping the industry's dynamics (Chowdhury, M. M. H., *et al.*, 2023). Their preferences, behaviors, and adherence to current trends prompt adjustments in design, production, and distribution strategies, creating a continuous feedback loop.

Post-consumer considerations encompass the handling of product returns and sustainable practices. Retailers manage the return of unsold or unwanted items, while sustainable practices involve recycling or repurposing materials to minimize environmental impact. The industry's increasing commitment to sustainability is reflected in these practices, contributing to the broader discourse on responsible and environmentally conscious production.

The fashion supply chain, however, is not without its challenges. The industry's fast-paced production cycles, often referred to as fast fashion, present difficulties in managing inventory and minimizing waste. Globalization introduces complexities related to geopolitical and economic changes, impacting the movement of materials and finished products. The industry's focus on sustainability necessitates ethical practices throughout the supply chain, including sourcing, production, and recycling (Sarma, P. R. S., *et al.*, 2023). Furthermore, the integration of technology, such as RFID, IoT, and data analytics, is gaining prominence as tools for supply chain optimization, demand forecasting, and inventory management.

Understanding these key components and their interdependencies is essential for industry stakeholders to effectively manage the supply chain, respond to consumer demands, and adapt to the evolving dynamics of the global fashion market. This comprehensive overview underscores the intricate nature of the fashion apparel supply chain and its critical role in the broader context of the fashion industry.

The fashion apparel supply chain, a focal point of scholarly investigation, unfolds through a series of intricate stages and processes, each critical to the overall dynamic of the industry (Tao, F., *et al.*, 2018). At the genesis of this intricate system lies the design and product development stage, where creative teams meticulously conceptualize and sketch new styles, determining fabric choices and color schemes. This stage not only sets the aesthetic tone for the entire production process but also establishes the creative vision that will reverberate throughout subsequent supply chain stages.

Raw material sourcing follows suit, representing a pivotal phase marked by the procurement of fabrics, trims, buttons, and other essentials from diverse suppliers. In the academic realm, researchers delve into the complexities of this stage, investigating not only the logistics of material acquisition but also the growing emphasis on sustainability practices within the sourcing process. Ethical considerations and environmentally responsible material choices have become central focal points of inquiry, reflecting the industry's evolving standards.

The manufacturing and production phase, a linchpin in the supply chain, undergoes meticulous scrutiny from researchers (An, D.,*et al.,* 2024). Often transpiring in countries with favorable production costs, factories engage in cutting-edge processes such as cutting, sewing, and assembling garments. Scholars investigate the quality control measures implemented at this stage, exploring how they align with the brand's standards and influence the final product that reaches consumers.

Distribution and logistics represent a complex interplay of global movement, with finished goods traversing from manufacturing facilities to distribution centers. This logistical ballet, often involving ships, planes, and trucks, is a subject of scholarly examination as researchers seek to unravel the intricacies of global transportation systems, international trade dynamics, and the impact on overall supply chain efficiency.

The wholesale and retail components form a nexus where the academic lens turns toward consumer behavior, market dynamics, and the evolving strategies employed by fashion brands. Researchers delve into the implications of the wholesale and retail choices made by brands, exploring the impact on market reach, consumer accessibility, and the brand-consumer relationship. This stage becomes a microcosm of the fashion industry's adaptability to ever-shifting consumer preferences.

The culmination of the supply chain lies in the hands of consumers. This stage, often referred to as the moment of truth, becomes a focal point of research as scholars seek to unravel the intricate interplay between consumer choices, brand loyalty, and the broader trends influencing the market. Consumer behavior and feedback serve as vital indicators, shaping the subsequent cycles of design, production, and distribution.

Post-consumer considerations encapsulate the handling of returns and the emergent imperative of sustainability. Researchers scrutinize the strategies employed by retailers in managing unsold or unwanted items, examining the impact of return policies on brand reputation and consumer loyalty. Sustainable practices, including recycling and repurposing, form a growing area of investigation, with scholars contributing to the discourse on responsible post-consumer practices and their implications for the industry's environmental footprint.

In conclusion, the fashion apparel supply chain, as a subject of scholarly exploration, unveils itself through a tapestry of critical stages and processes. From the creative genesis of design to the ultimate consumer experience and post-consumer considerations, researchers dissect each facet, contributing to the evolving body of knowledge that shapes our understanding of this dynamic and complex industry.

Supply chain resilience in the fashion apparel industry has been a burgeoning area of research, reflecting the industry's heightened vulnerability to disruptions and the imperative for adaptive strategies. Scholarly works in this domain delve into multifaceted aspects, encompassing the identification of key challenges and vulnerabilities unique to the fashion supply chain, as well as the exploration of innovative approaches, including technological advancements and strategic management practices, aimed at enhancing resilience (Bevilacqua, M., *et al.,* 2020).

Researchers have systematically examined the challenges faced by the fashion apparel supply chain, recognizing the industry's susceptibility to demand volatility and rapid shifts in consumer preferences. In-depth analyses have highlighted the intricacies of managing globalized supply chains, with a focus on the impact of geopolitical events, natural disasters, and political instability. The literature underscores the need for comprehensive risk assessments to identify vulnerabilities and proactively manage disruptions that could cascade through the entire supply chain.

A significant strand of research centers on the role of technology in bolstering supply chain resilience within the fashion industry. Studies explore the adoption and integration of advanced analytics, machine learning, and artificial intelligence to enhance forecasting accuracy, optimize inventory management, and improve overall responsiveness (Chauhan, C., *et al.* 2023). The application of these technologies is seen as a transformative strategy, providing real-time insights and decision-making capabilities crucial for navigating the fast-paced and unpredictable nature of the fashion market.

Sustainability considerations within the supply chain resilience discourse have also emerged as a critical theme in recent literature (Chopra, S., & Sodhi, M. S. 2014). Researchers highlight the importance of ethical sourcing, environmentally responsible manufacturing practices, and circular economy principles. Sustainable supply chain management is posited not only as an ethical imperative but also as a strategic approach to mitigate risks associated with fluctuating consumer expectations and regulatory changes (Cohen, M., 2022).

Case studies and empirical research contribute to the literature by offering practical insights into successful implementations of supply chain resilience strategies within specific fashion companies. These real-world examples provide valuable benchmarks, allowing researchers to analyze the effectiveness of various resilience measures, identify best practices, and extract lessons learned that can inform broader industry practices.

The evolving landscape of supply chain resilience in the fashion apparel industry is also explored in terms of stakeholder collaborations and strategic partnerships (Abeysekara, N., Wang, H., & Kuruppuarachchi, D., 2019). Research emphasizes the significance of building strong relationships with suppliers, fostering transparent communication, and creating agile networks capable of adapting to unforeseen challenges. Collaborative efforts across the supply chain are identified as instrumental in building resilience, as they facilitate the sharing of information, resources, and risk mitigation strategies.

The literature on supply chain resilience within the fashion apparel industry reflects a nuanced understanding of the challenges unique to this sector and the dynamic strategies employed to enhance adaptability (Ali, I., & Gölgeci, I. 2019). From technological innovations and sustainability initiatives to collaborative stakeholder approaches, researchers contribute to the growing body of knowledge that guides industry practitioners in navigating the complexities of the modern fashion supply chain.

The resilience of the fashion apparel industry's supply chain is influenced by a multitude of factors, each contributing to the industry's ability to adapt and recover from disruptions. Researchers and industry experts have identified several key factors that significantly impact resilience, as well as successful strategies to enhance it:

Table 1. Factors Influencing Supply Chain Resilience and Corresponding Strategic Solutions in the Fashion Apparel Industry.

Factors	Strategies
Accurate demand forecasting and visibility into consumer trends are critical. Unpredictable shifts in consumer preferences can lead to excess inventory or stockouts.	- Employ advanced analytics, machine learning, and data-driven forecasting models to enhance accuracy. - Implement real-time supply chain visibility tools to respond proactively to changes in consumer behavior.
The complexity of a globalized supply chain introduces vulnerability to geopolitical events, trade disruptions, and delays in transportation.	- Diversify suppliers and adopt dual-sourcing strategies. - Regionalize production and invest in technology for transparency across the supply chain.
Growing consumer awareness and regulatory pressures demand sustainable and ethical practices, impacting sourcing, manufacturing, and overall supply chain resilience.	- Integrate sustainable sourcing and eco-friendly manufacturing processes. - Adhere to ethical labor practices and adopt circular economy principles.
The pace of technological change introduces both opportunities and challenges. Rapid adoption is crucial for staying competitive, but implementation challenges can affect resilience.	- Invest in advanced technologies like AI, machine learning, and blockchain. - Use digital platforms to enhance communication, collaboration, and responsiveness.
Strong relationships with suppliers are vital, but dependencies on a few key suppliers can create vulnerabilities.	- Build strategic partnerships and foster transparent communication. - Diversify the supplier base and adopt dual-sourcing strategies to mitigate risks.
Balancing inventory levels to meet demand while avoiding overstock or stock-outs is challenging due to the fast-paced nature of fashion trends.	- Leverage predictive analytics for demand forecasting. - Adopt agile inventory management and just-in-time inventory strategies.
Unforeseen events, such as natural disasters, geopolitical crises, or global pandemics, can severely impact the supply chain.	- Conduct scenario planning exereises and develop risk management protocols. - Implement contingency plans for effective response to disruptions.
Workforce disruptions, including shortages of skilled labor or sudden changes in employee availability, can impact the continuity of operations.	- Invest in employee training and development. - Use cross-training to build a versatile workforce and implement flexible labor practices.

By addressing these factors and implementing the corresponding strategies, the fashion apparel industry can enhance the resilience of its supply chain, enabling it to navigate challenges, adapt to dynamic market conditions, and ensure the continuous flow of products to consumers.

The literature on the application of advanced analytics in supply chain management reflects a growing recognition of its transformative potential across various industries, including the fashion apparel sector. Researchers and practitioners alike have explored the capabilities of advanced analytics in addressing challenges, optimizing operations, and enhancing decision-making within complex supply chain ecosystems.

One notable area of exploration is the use of predictive analytics for demand forecasting. Studies emphasize the significance of accurate demand forecasts in mitigating stockouts or excess inventory, both prevalent challenges in the fashion industry. Research by Liu *et al.* (2018) showcases how machine learning algorithms, integrated with historical data and external factors, can significantly improve the accuracy of demand forecasts, enabling companies to align production and inventory levels with actual market needs.

Real-time visibility and data-driven decision-making have emerged as critical themes in the literature. Scholars such as Chopra and Sodhi (2014) highlight the importance of leveraging advanced analytics for supply chain visibility, enabling organizations to monitor and respond to changes promptly. This real-time visibility, facilitated by technologies like RFID and IoT, contributes to improved risk management, allowing for proactive interventions in the face of disruptions.

The application of prescriptive analytics for inventory optimization is another area of research interest. Prescriptive analytics, as discussed by Tang *et al.* (2021), goes beyond predicting demand to recommend optimal inventory levels and distribution strategies. This approach not only aids in reducing holding costs but also enhances overall supply chain agility by aligning inventory with demand patterns.

Blockchain technology, often discussed in conjunction with advanced analytics, has garnered attention for its potential to enhance transparency and traceability in supply chains. Research by Iansiti and Lakhani (2017) explores how blockchain, when integrated with analytics, can create a more resilient and transparent supply chain, particularly relevant in industries where provenance and ethical sourcing are critical considerations (Singh, R. K., *et al.*, 2023).

The literature also addresses challenges related to supplier relationships and risk management. Studies like Vanpoucke *et al.* (2020) emphasize the role of analytics in evaluating supplier performance, identifying potential risks, and fostering collaboration. Advanced analytics can provide insights into supplier reliability, quality control, and adherence to ethical standards, contributing to the overall resilience of the supply chain (Soni, U., *et al.*, 2014).

Furthermore, the application of advanced analytics in transportation management is a subject of exploration. Researchers such as Hou,Q. *et al.,* (2020) delve into the optimization of logistics and transportation routes through analytics, leading to cost reduction, improved delivery timelines, and reduced environmental impact.

In summary, the literature on the application of advanced analytics in supply chain management reflects a multifaceted exploration of its capabilities and implications. From demand forecasting and real-time visibility to prescriptive analytics for inventory optimization and the integration of technologies like blockchain, researchers continue to contribute valuable insights (RATTI, C. 2019). The overarching theme underscores the potential of advanced analytics not only in addressing current challenges but also in transforming supply chain management practices to meet the evolving demands of modern industries.

The ethical dimensions of supply chain management are explored in conjunction with advanced analytics. Researchers investigate how analytics can be employed to monitor and ensure adherence to ethical sourcing practices, fair labor conditions, and sustainability standards throughout the supply chain (Vanpoucke, E., & Ellis, S. C. 2020).

Numerous studies emphasize the impact of advanced analytics on operational efficiency and cost reduction. Akuns *et al.* (2022) discuss how analytics-driven optimization models streamline procurement processes, reduce lead times, and minimize excess inventory. These efficiency gains contribute to overall cost reduction and improved competitiveness within the industry.

Understanding customer behavior and preferences is critical in supply chain management. Madhani, P.M. (2019) explore customer-centric analytics, focusing on the integration of customer data to optimize inventory levels, personalize demand forecasting, and improve overall customer satisfaction. This approach tailors supply chain strategies to meet evolving consumer expectations.

Within the context of humanitarian and disaster relief supply chains, researchers examine the application of advanced analytics for effective response and resource allocation. Golan, M.S, *et al.*, (2013) demonstrate how analytics-driven decision support systems optimize the distribution of aid, manage inventory levels, and enhance coordination during crisis situations.

The literature explores how advanced analytics supports sustainable practices and the transition toward a circular economy in supply chains. Walker, A. M. (2022) discuss the role of analytics in optimizing reverse logistics, recycling processes, and the circular flow of materials. This integration aligns with the increasing emphasis on environmental responsibility in supply chain management.

Collaboration across the supply chain is facilitated by advanced analytics tools. Simchi-Levi *et al.,* (2014) highlight the significance of collaborative demand planning, supported by analytics, which enables stakeholders to share information and synchronize activities. This collaborative approach enhances coordination, reduces lead times, and minimizes disruptions.

The optimization of warehouse and distribution processes through advanced analytics is a recurring theme. Attaran, M (2020) discuss how analytics-driven insights into warehouse operations, including layout design, inventory placement, and picking processes, lead to efficiency gains. Real-time analytics optimize order fulfillment, minimize bottlenecks, and enhance the overall performance of distribution networks.

Advanced analytics plays a crucial role in risk management and building supply chain resilience. Researchers explore how predictive analytics can identify potential disruptions, assess their impact, and facilitate the development of proactive mitigation strategies. Christopher, M., (2004) emphasize the need for organizations to anticipate and manage risks, especially in the face of global uncertainties.

Identification of Specific Analytics Tools and Techniques Relevant to the Fashion Apparel Industry

In the dynamic landscape of the fashion apparel industry, the application of advanced analytics tools and techniques has become imperative for optimizing operations and responding to ever-evolving market demands (Ahmad, S., *et al.*, 2020). Predictive analytics, driven by statistical algorithms and machine learning, stands out as a crucial tool for anticipating consumer preferences. Employing languages such as Python or R and platforms like Microsoft Azure Machine Learning, predictive analytics aids in demand forecasting, enabling companies to optimize inventory levels and stay ahead of shifting market trends (Choi, T. M. J. (Ed.). 2016).

Prescriptive analytics, going beyond prediction to recommend optimal actions, is particularly relevant for inventory and distribution strategies in the fashion industry. Tools such as IBM Decision Optimization or FICO Xpress Optimization Suite provide actionable insights, helping companies navigate the complex decisions surrounding inventory management and distribution. This approach contributes to a more agile and responsive supply chain.

Supply chain visibility tools, such as SAP Integrated Business Planning and Oracle SCM Cloud, offer real-time insights into the movement of goods, inventory levels, and potential disruptions. This transparency is essential for proactive decision-making, risk mitigation, and ensuring the overall efficiency of the supply chain. Integration with Radio-Frequency Identification (RFID) technology further enhances visibility by enabling accurate and real-time tracking of inventory.

The advent of the Internet of Things (IoT) introduces a paradigm shift in supply chain management, especially in monitoring conditions during transportation and optimizing warehouse operations. Platforms like Microsoft Azure IoT or AWS IoT empower the fashion industry with connected devices and sensors, facilitating data-driven decision-making and enhancing operational efficiency.

Blockchain technology, with tools like IBM Blockchain or Hyperledger Fabric, offers a decentralized and secure ledger for transparent and traceable transactions. In the fashion industry, this can be harnessed to track the authenticity of products, verify the origin of raw materials, and ensure ethical sourcing practices, aligning with the increasing importance of sustainability and ethical considerations.

Advanced Planning and Scheduling (APS) software optimizes production planning, particularly relevant in the fashion industry where rapid changes in consumer trends require agile and efficient production processes. Solutions like Preactor or SAP Advanced Planning & Optimization (APO) contribute to reducing lead times, optimizing resources, and improving overall production efficiency.

Data analytics for customer segmentation, utilizing tools like CRM software or Google Analytics, enables fashion companies to understand and segment their target audience. This information supports personalized marketing strategies, tailored product recommendations, and ultimately enhances customer satisfaction (Giri, C., *et al.*, 2019).

The integration of 3D virtual prototyping tools like Browzwear or CLO transforms the design and production processes in the fashion industry. By simulating garment designs digitally, companies can reduce reliance on physical samples, accelerate product development, and improve collaboration between design and manufacturing teams.

Sentiment analysis, powered by natural language processing, aids in understanding customer sentiments and preferences through the analysis of reviews and social media mentions. Python libraries such as NLTK or sentiment analysis APIs contribute to gauging consumer feedback, identifying trends, and shaping marketing strategies accordingly.

In the realm of augmented reality (AR) and virtual reality (VR), technologies like ARKit or Unity for VR development offer innovative solutions for the fashion industry. These tools provide opportunities for virtual try-ons, immersive shopping experiences, and interactive product displays, enhancing customer engagement and brand loyalty (Akram, S. V., *et al.*, 2022).

The collective integration of these analytics tools and techniques into the fashion apparel industry's supply chain and business operations represents a holistic and data-driven approach (Mohiuddin Babu, M., *et al.*, 2024) From demand forecasting to customer engagement and ethical sourcing, these tools empower companies to navigate the complexities of the industry, make informed decisions, and meet the evolving expectations of consumers.

Managerial Implications for the Study

The study on "Enhancing Supply Chain Resilience in the Fashion Apparel Industry through Advanced Analytics" holds significant managerial implications for companies operating in this dynamic sector. One of the key takeaways for managers is the strategic adoption of advanced analytics tools, particularly predictive and prescriptive analytics, to elevate decision-making processes across the entire supply chain (Dal Forno, A. J., *et al.*, 2023). This strategic integration aligns with broader business objectives and necessitates investment in training and skill development to ensure the proficient use of these cutting-edge technologies.

Real-time visibility within the supply chain emerges as a critical focus for managers seeking to enhance resilience. The study underscores the importance of investing in supply chain visibility tools that are seamlessly integrated with advanced analytics. These tools empower managers to monitor operations in real time, enabling proactive responses to disruptions and risks (Nouinou, H., *et al.*, 2023). The managerial action involves carefully selecting appropriate visibility solutions and establishing protocols for leveraging real-time information effectively.

Furthermore, the application of advanced analytics in demand forecasting and inventory management carries substantial managerial implications. Managers are encouraged to leverage predictive analytics for more accurate demand forecasting and prescriptive analytics for optimizing inventory levels. This entails a strategic approach to inventory management, reducing holding costs and improving overall efficiency within the supply chain (Longo, F., *et al.*, 2021).

The integration of 3D virtual prototyping tools in garment design and production processes signifies a transformative shift. Managers are advised to consider adopting these tools to reduce lead times, minimize physical samples, and foster collaboration between design and manufacturing teams. This may involve investment in suitable software and training programs to maximize the benefits of virtual prototyping.

Customer-centric strategies driven by analytics emerge as a powerful avenue for managers to enhance customer satisfaction and loyalty. Through data analytics, managers can segment customers and tailor marketing campaigns, thereby improving the overall customer experience. This customer-centric approach fosters brand loyalty and repeat business.

Incorporating IoT sensors for real-time monitoring in warehouse and transportation operations presents an opportunity for increased efficiency. Managers are encouraged to invest in IoT technologies to optimize warehouse processes and transportation efficiency. Leveraging data from IoT sensors provides insights for continuous improvement, cost reduction, and streamlined operations.

The adoption of augmented reality (AR) and virtual reality (VR) in retail operations emerges as a way to enhance the customer experience. Managers can explore applications such as virtual try-ons and immersive shopping experiences to create a unique and engaging retail environment. This may involve investments in technology infrastructure and marketing strategies to promote these innovative experiences.

Sustainability and ethical practices in the supply chain are highlighted as essential considerations. Managers are urged to prioritize these principles and use advanced analytics to monitor adherence to ethical sourcing standards (Guo, Z. X., *et al.*, 2011). Integrating sustainability metrics into supply chain performance indicators demonstrates a commitment to responsible business practices.

Recognizing the evolving nature of technology, continuous training and skill development are emphasized as a managerial imperative. Managers should invest in training programs to ensure that employees are equipped with the necessary skills to leverage advanced analytics tools effectively. Fostering a culture of innovation and adaptability positions the organization to embrace technological advancements and stay competitive in the industry.

CONCLUSION

In conclusion, the study highlights the transformative potential of advanced analytics in fortifying the resilience and competitiveness of the fashion apparel industry. From enhancing demand forecasting precision to optimizing inventory management, the adoption of predictive and prescriptive analytics emerges as a strategic imperative. Real-time visibility, facilitated by advanced analytics tools, offers a proactive approach to risk mitigation in a volatile supply chain landscape.

Blockchain technology, coupled with advanced analytics, is positioned as a robust solution for ensuring ethical sourcing and sustainability throughout the supply chain. The integration of 3D virtual prototyping streamlines design processes, reducing lead times and aligning with the industry's agility requirements. Customer-centric strategies, driven by data analytics, enhance the overall customer experience and foster brand loyalty.

In operations, the strategic deployment of IoT sensors, augmented reality, and virtual reality offers avenues for optimization and differentiation. The study underscores the dual role of advanced analytics in adherence to ethical standards and the integration of sustainability metrics, positioning these considerations as strategic differentiators.

As the industry navigates technological disruption and evolving consumer expectations, the managerial implications emphasize a cultural shift toward resilience, sustainability, and customer-centricity. The study concludes with a resounding call for proactive adaptation and the holistic embrace of advanced analytics as the linchpin of a resilient and future-ready fashion apparel industry.

REFERENCES

Abeysekara, N., Wang, H., & Kuruppuarachchi, D. (2019). Effect of supply-chain resilience on firm performance and competitive advantage: A study of the Sri Lankan apparel industry. *Business Process Management Journal*, 25(7), 1673–1695.

Ahmad, S., Miskon, S., Alabdan, R., & Tlili, I. (2020). Towards sustainable textile and apparel industry: Exploring the role of business intelligence systems in the era of industry 4.0. *Sustainability*, 12(7), 2632.

Akram, S. V., Malik, P. K., Singh, R., Gehlot, A., Juyal, A., Ghafoor, K. Z., & Shrestha, S. (2022). Implementation of digitalized technologies for fashion industry 4.0: Opportunities and challenges. *Scientific Programming*, 2022(1), 7523246.

Ali, I., & Gölgeci, I. (2019). Where is supply chain resilience research heading? A systematic and co-occurrence analysis. *International Journal of Physical Distribution & Logistics Management*, 49(8), 793–815.

An, D., Anh, D. T. L., Cam, H. L. T., Nayak, R., George, M., Cam, L. B. T., ... & Quang, H. T. (2024). Navigating global supply networks: a strategic framework for resilience in the apparel industry. *Operations Management Research*, 1-21.

Bevilacqua, M., Ciarapica, F. E., Marcucci, G., & Mazzuto, G. (2020). Fuzzy cognitive maps approach for analysing the domino effect of factors affecting supply chain resilience: A fashion industry case study. *International Journal of Production Research*, 58(20), 6370–6398.

Chauhan, C., Akram, M. U., & Chauhan, A. (2023). Mapping pathways for building resilient supply chains: A systematic literature review. *Journal of Cleaner Production*, •••, 138701.

Choi, T. M. J. (Ed.). (2016). *Information systems for the fashion and apparel industry*. Woodhead Publishing.

Chopra, S., & Sodhi, M. S. (2014). Reducing the risk of supply chain disruptions. *MIT Sloan Management Review*.

Chowdhury, M. M. H., Quaddus, M., & Chowdhury, M. (2023). Managing relational practices for performance improvement in a complex supply chain network: The mediating roles of proactive and reactive resilience in apparel industry of Bangladesh. *International Journal of Logistics Management*, 34(1), 34–59.

Chowdhury, N. R., Janan, F., Mahmud, P., Liza, S. A., & Paul, S. K. (2024). Assessing strategies to mitigate the impacts of a pandemic in apparel supply chains. *Operations Management Research*, 17(1), 38–54.

Cohen, M., Cui, S., Doetsch, S., Ernst, R., Huchzermeier, A., Kouvelis, P., & Tsay, A. A. (2022). Bespoke supply-chain resilience: The gap between theory and practice. *Journal of Operations Management*, 68(5), 515–531.

Dal Forno, A. J., Bataglini, W. V., Steffens, F., & Ulson de Souza, A. A. (2023). Industry 4.0 in textile and apparel sector: A systematic literature review. *Research Journal of Textile and Apparel*, 27(1), 95–117.

Giri, C., Jain, S., Zeng, X., & Bruniaux, P. (2019). A detailed review of artificial intelligence applied in the fashion and apparel industry. *IEEE Access : Practical Innovations, Open Solutions*, 7, 95376–95396.

Guo, Z. X., Wong, W. K., Leung, S. Y. S., & Li, M. (2011). Applications of artificial intelligence in the apparel industry: A review. *Textile Research Journal*, 81(18), 1871–1892.

Hsu, C. H., Chang, A. Y., Zhang, T. Y., Lin, W. D., & Liu, W. L. (2021). Deploying resilience enablers to mitigate risks in sustainable fashion supply chains. *Sustainability*, 13(5), 2943.

Hsu, C. H., Li, M. G., Zhang, T. Y., Chang, A. Y., Shangguan, S. Z., & Liu, W. L. (2022). Deploying big data enablers to strengthen supply chain resilience to mitigate sustainable risks based on integrated HOQ-MCDM framework. *Mathematics*, 10(8), 1233.

Irfan, I., Sumbal, M. S. U. K., Khurshid, F., & Chan, F. T. (2022). Toward a resilient supply chain model: Critical role of knowledge management and dynamic capabilities. *Industrial Management & Data Systems*, 122(5), 1153–1182.

Ivanov, D., Tang, C. S., Dolgui, A., Battini, D., & Das, A. (2021). Researchers' perspectives on Industry 4.0: Multi-disciplinary analysis and opportunities for operations management. *International Journal of Production Research*, 59(7), 2055–2078.

Juan, S. J., Li, E. Y., & Hung, W. H. (2022). An integrated model of supply chain resilience and its impact on supply chain performance under disruption. *International Journal of Logistics Management*, 33(1), 339–364.

Khan, S. A. R., Piprani, A. Z., & Yu, Z. (2023). Supply chain analytics and post-pandemic performance: Mediating role of triple-A supply chain strategies. *International Journal of Emerging Markets*, 18(6), 1330–1354.

Köksal, D., Strähle, J., Müller, M., & Freise, M. (2017). Social sustainable supply chain management in the textile and apparel industry—A literature review. *Sustainability*, 9(1), 100.

Longo, F., Padovano, A., Cimmino, B., & Pinto, P. (2021). Towards a mass customization in the fashion industry: An evolutionary decision aid model for apparel product platform design and optimization. *Computers & Industrial Engineering*, 162, 107742.

Mohiuddin Babu, M., Akter, S., Rahman, M., Billah, M. M., & Hack-Polay, D. (2024). The role of artificial intelligence in shaping the future of Agile fashion industry. *Production Planning and Control*, 35(15), 2084–2098.

Nouinou, H., Asadollahi-Yazdi, E., Baret, I., Nguyen, N. Q., Terzi, M., Ouazene, Y., & Kelly, R. (2023). Decision-making in the context of Industry 4.0: Evidence from the textile and clothing industry. *Journal of Cleaner Production*, 391, 136184.

Oksanen, L. (2023). Agile fashion retail: exploring the enablers and challenges in agile procurement and supply chain management.

Qader, G., Junaid, M., Abbas, Q., & Mubarik, M. S. (2022). Industry 4.0 enables supply chain resilience and supply chain performance. *Technological Forecasting and Social Change*, 185, 122026.

Rahman, T., Paul, S. K., Shukla, N., Agarwal, R., & Taghikhah, F. (2022). Supply chain resilience initiatives and strategies: A systematic review. *Computers & Industrial Engineering*, 170, 108317.

RATTI, C. (2019). An investigation on the adoption of blockchain technology in supply chain.

Rezaei, G., Hosseini, S. M. H., & Sana, S. S. (2022). Exploring the Relationship between Data Analytics Capability and Competitive Advantage: The Mediating Roles of Supply Chain Resilience and Organization Flexibility. *Sustainability*, 14(16), 10444.

Sarma, P. R. S., Kumar, A., Choudhary, N. A., & Mangla, S. K. (2023). Modelling resilient fashion retail supply chain strategies to mitigate the COVID-19 impact. *International Journal of Logistics Management*, 34(4), 1188–1218.

Shahadat, M. H., Chowdhury, A. Y., Jahed, M. A., Nathan, R. J., & Fekete-Farkas, M. (2024). Innovativeness, visibility, and collaboration effect on supply chain performance: Moderating role of digital supply chain integration. *Cogent Business & Management*, 11(1), 2390168.

Singh, R. K., Mishra, R., Gupta, S., & Mukherjee, A. A. (2023). Blockchain applications for secured and resilient supply chains: A systematic literature review and future research agenda. *Computers & Industrial Engineering*, 175, 108854.

Soni, U., Jain, V., & Kumar, S. (2014). Measuring supply chain resilience using a deterministic modeling approach. *Computers & Industrial Engineering*, 74, 11–25.

Sumarliah, E., Ahmad, M. N., Usmanova, K., Mousa, K., & Asad, M. (2021). Reflecting Coronavirus outbreak in the risk management of the apparel supply chain. *IEEE Engineering Management Review*, 50(1), 31–42.

Susitha, E. (2022). Strategic Choices of Digital Apparel Supply Chains to Achieve Competitive Advantage: A Literature Review.

Tao, F., Qi, Q., Liu, A., & Kusiak, A. (2018). Data-driven smart manufacturing. *Journal of Manufacturing Systems*, 48, 157–169.

Trihastuti, D., Gunawan, I., Sianto, M. E., & Sagitha, B. R. R. (2024, September). Building resilience of the green product supply chain in the apparel industry. []. *IOP Publishing*.]. *IOP Conference Series. Earth and Environmental Science*, 1388(1), 012041.

Vanpoucke, E., & Ellis, S. C. (2020). Building supply-side resilience–a behavioural view. *International Journal of Operations & Production Management*, 40(1), 11–33.

KEY TERMS AND DEFINITIONS

Advanced Analytics: The use of AI, machine learning, and data-driven methods to enhance decision-making and supply chain efficiency.

Circular Economy: A sustainable model focused on reducing waste and reusing resources through recycling and remanufacturing.

Demand Forecasting: Predicting future consumer demand using historical data and analytics to optimize production and inventory.

Scenario Planning: Preparing for various potential disruptions by creating and analyzing "what-if" scenarios to improve readiness.

Supply Chain Resilience: The ability of a supply chain to adapt, recover, and maintain operations during and after disruptions.

Sustainable Sourcing: Procuring materials in a way that minimizes environmental harm and ensures ethical labor standards.

Section 2
Key Strategies for Successful Gen AI/ML-Driven Supply Chain Transformations

Chapter 7
Mastering Change Management in AI-Powered Supply Chain Digital Transformation

Ehap Sabri
University of Texas at Dallas, USA

ABSTRACT

Transforming the supply chain using best practices and the latest digital technologies is no longer optional; it is a strategic mandate for staying relevant. However, 70% of all transformation initiatives fail. The low success rates of transformation make firms reconsider moving forward with transformation journeys. These firms have doubts about integrating digital technologies like ML and Gen AI into supply chain operations and often postpone efforts until experts address their challenges. This chapter provides the top seven challenges and explains how to address them during supply chain digital transformation programs. Additionally, it offers a practical change management framework to ensure smooth digital supply chain transformations. This framework includes eight steps (phases) needed to implement change in the organizational culture and five success factors to maintain throughout the change lifecycle. These five factors can serve as a checklist to evaluate an organization's readiness for change and its chances of a successful digital transformation.

DOI: 10.4018/979-8-3693-4433-0.ch007

INTRODUCTION

In today's complex and ever-changing business world, firms are rethinking every aspect of their supply chain performance. Groundbreaking digital technologies like generative AI and machine learning are transforming how companies handle end-to-end supply chain processes. Success now depends not just on internal operations but on effectively coordinating a global network of supply chain partners.

A firm's success is largely dependent on how effectively it can orchestrate a global network of supply chain partners to deliver goods and services that meet individual consumer needs. It's about engaging with customers efficiently through improved customer experiences. Early digital disruptors like Amazon, Uber, and Netflix have redefined traditional business models, focusing on exceptional customer experiences and engaging customers who keep coming back for more.

Digital transformation challenges traditional methods and changes the way businesses operate. One key challenge is training the workforce in new skills necessary for participating in these new ways of doing business and ensuring the changes stick.

Industries from slow-moving ones like utilities and cement to rapidly changing sectors like high-tech and retail rely on lean and agile supply chain processes for competitive advantage. Supply chains can no longer be viewed as mere back-office, transactional functions. Companies strive to drive out costs while also being agile enough to adapt to rapidly changing markets.

Transforming the supply chain using best practices and the latest digital technologies is no longer optional; it is a strategic mandate for staying relevant. It's crucial to act rapidly and launch transformation activities. However, 70% of all transformation initiatives fail. Many firms struggle to implement transformation programs and achieve the promised value or return on investment (ROI).

The low success rates of transformation programs and alarming statistics make firms reconsider moving forward with transformation journeys. These firms have doubts and questions about integrating new digital technologies like ML and Gen AI into supply chain operations and often postpone efforts until experts address their concerns. They seek to:

- Master change management and ensure user adoption
- Address the need for new skills to support processes across suppliers and partners
- Ensure continuous senior management support
- Identify comprehensive metrics and ensure continuous monitoring
- Choose the right digital technology and software provider

Relevant research and professional experience suggest that the main causes of low success rates in business transformation initiatives can be grouped into two categories: 1) lack of preparation and familiarity with the transformation lifecycle, and 2) poorly managed or neglected people-related aspects. This chapter provides the top seven challenges under each category and explains how to address these challenges during supply chain digital transformation programs. Additionally, it offers a practical change management framework to ensure smooth and successful digital supply chain transformations.

This framework includes eight steps (phases) needed to implement change in the organizational culture and five success factors to maintain throughout the change lifecycle. These five factors can serve as a checklist to evaluate an organization's readiness for change and its chances of a successful digital transformation.

In conclusion, mastering change management in AI-driven supply chain digital transformation is complex due to the advanced technology involved, cultural resistance, data dependency, and other factors. By addressing these challenges through a structured change management framework and continuous evaluation, organizations can better navigate the transformation process and achieve their desired outcomes.

Historic background on change management in the context of supply chain digital transformations is provided in the next section.

BACKGROUND

Direct Correlation between Change Management and Transformation

The complex, cross-functional nature of supply chains forces executives and managers to be more knowledgeable about the successful implementation of change. Greer and Ford (2009) conducted an extensive study on this topic and provided evidence in support of the differences between implementing non-supply chain management (NSCM) changes and supply chain management (SCM) changes, and a lower level of success was shown to be realized when implementing SCM changes than when implementing NSCM changes due to complexity. Therefore, majority of supply chain leaders are keen to transform their organizations, but they recognize that their organizations lack the knowledge and readiness to do so successfully.

Nadler and Tushman (1989) mentioned that because broader change programs are often more difficult to implement, the degree of success realized from implementing SCM changes might differ as well. Their article provides a good insight into managing large-scale planned change.

Research shows the success rate of supply chain transformation has a direct correlation to the degree of mastering change management. Ford and Greer (2005) research has indicated relationships between various change management activities and change achievement or success.

In Prosci's 2009 benchmarking study (http://www.change-management.com/tutorial-case-mod3.htm), the top trend identified by study participants was a greater recognition of the need for mastering change management. The same study showed direct correlation between struggled projects and lack of effective change management as shown in Table 1.

Table 1. Change Management Impact on Meeting Project Objectives, Staying on Schedule & Budget.

Project Criteria for success	Poor Change Management	Effective Change Management
Correlation of excellent change management to **meeting project objectives**	16%	95%
Correlation of excellent change management practice to **staying on schedule**	16%	71%
Correlation of excellent change management practice to **staying on budget**	51%	82%

Source: Prosci's 2009 Change Management Benchmarking Report

The table shows a clear correlation between effective change management practice and meeting project objectives while staying on budget and according to the schedule. For example, of the participants that had effective change management programs in place, 95% met or exceeded objectives; while only 16% - or about 1 in 6 - of those with poor change management programs met or exceeded objectives. The Prosci's benchmarking studies over the last few years suggest that mastering change management increases the success rate of organizational changes to as high as 95%.

Therefore, mastering change management is very crucial for successful supply chain transformations.

Effective Change Management Practices

Effective change management practices embrace both the inner shift in the individual's values, aspirations and behaviors and the outer shift in process, strategy, policies and systems (Karp 2005). So, effective change management practices target the organizational culture, organizational structure and recruiting, performance measurements, incentive compensations, and alignment to corporate goals and strategies.

Carolyn Aiken and Scott Keller (2009) have identified insights into four conditions required for behavioral change:

Creating a Compelling Story

What motivates senior leaders may not motivate most of the employees. Therefore, change leaders need to be able to tell change story that covers what motivates employees the most in their work. In doing so, they can unleash tremendous amount of drive. Secondly, Leaders should give opportunity for employees to write their own story. It's detected in human nature that when we choose for ourselves, we are far more committed to outcome. So, employees should be asked to suggest change rather than directly implementing change. Then this will help drive change that comes through a sense of ownership.

Role Modeling

It is a misconception that if we believe that if a leader is strong and influential then change will be successful irrespective of employees' view. Carolyn and Scott have experienced working with change program suggest that success depends less on how persuasive a few selected leaders are and more on how receptive the society is to the idea.

Reinforcing Mechanisms

Although it's difficult to establish a clear linkage between the successful change and money to be compensated, the token of appreciation for the hard work of employees boost them to be more productive.

Capacity Building

Often change management initiatives require employees to develop skills and talent needed for the desired change (new state of business). The important thing to understand here is that if employees are expected to play new role with no proper training, they often feel neglected and lose belief. So, training is crucial and should include elements related to personality types, emotional intelligence and other new process specific training.

Transformation Programs' Common Mistakes

Ramanan and Anil (2011) from Wipro Consulting Services believe that most of supply chain transformation fails because most companies tend to make common mistakes such as: Falling Into the "Leading Practices" Trap, where companies fail to understand its own supply chain situation in order to make the right choices and try to follow leading practices in market. They believe that companies will be more successful if they rethink their supply chain in a way that is driven by how it supports their business strategy and meets customer requirements. They believe that if supply chain technology are deployed without incorporating critical business requirements and process redesign then it will be simply collection of automated system with routine supply chain issues.

Use of technology as an enabler is important for effective supply chain but one needs to understand that technology can't fix the flawed supply chain design. Whenever processes are refined and new technology is implemented, organizational structure must be aligned to support these initiatives.

In the quest for growth, many companies implement change initiatives to create strong, differentiated and better customer experience. Leonard and Coltea (2013) believe that most failed transformation change initiatives didn't focus front-line managers on the exact actions they need to take to achieve the company's desired business outcomes.

In many companies, front-line employees receive dozens of high priority messages from managers, executives and change managers daily. These messages become conflicting to front line managers to know what task or metrics should focus on during a given day to deliver service. So, in this situation front line managers are unclear about work to perform which ultimately affects the productivity of the company.

Leonard and Coltea (2013) highlighted also that implementing a successful change management initiative isn't a one-time thing. Creating lasting change requires companies to evolve, and those that evolve successfully can achieve stronger financial performance.

Mastering Change Management Framework

Sabri (2019) provided detailed analysis of the most common transformation failures. He also suggested a practical and comprehensive framework to master change management addressing typical challenges and common mistakes in addition to leveraging best practices. This framework will be leveraged and enriched in this book chapter to support supply chain digital transformation.

The next section will explain the top 7 transformation challenges for supply chain transformations based on research, including the above ones, and the author's experience.

TRANSFORMATION LIFE CYCLE CHALLENGES

1) "Where" and "When" to Start

When making these kinds of drastic changes, the biggest challenges are often to know when and where to begin to translate the vision into goals, goals into strategies and strategies into process changes and projects. Very few companies have a good supply chain digital strategy. Some reasons are: 1) The lack of resources and time, 2) The lack of familiarity with the strategy development process in general, 3) The lack of knowledge of the full opportunities that digital technologies can bring to supply chain processes, and 4) The difficulty of securing a consensus since supply chain digital strategy is an integrated cross functional strategy and requires investment from resources and money standpoints.

The author has observed some companies try to take the easy route and avoid spending time on rethinking their supply chain in a way that is driven by how it supports their business strategy; meets customer needs and deploys key enablers like digital technologies.

2) Environment is no Ready

The culture of "playing it safe" is the second challenge. Firms get used to executing low-risk incremental improvements on the same business environment for an extended period, and they become resistant for big ideas of significant improvement, because they do not know how to handle transformation programs and target big results.

A specific related challenge, which is relevant to supply chain digital transformation, is the need for intensive cooperation and cross-functional collaboration among executive peers. This would force executives to get out of their comfort zones and their respective areas of responsibility and find time out of their busy daily operation schedule to envision an entirely new business.

In a consulting engagement for the author with a semiconductor company, and after conducting a risk analysis workshop with the respective managers and directors, the highest significant and probable risk for the transformation initiative came to be definite commitment from executives to follow through and provide the needed support. There were 3 previous half-baked and half-hearted transformation initiatives in the past targeting the same supply chain processes, which undermined confidence that the current program will be treated differently (Sabri, 2019). When a company has a previous record of transformation failure, lack of strong vision, no visible commitment from above, and no clear articulation why this program is different, then the result would be upsetting.

Also, McKinsey research (2009) showed that organizations that took the transformation journey for defensive reasons (to stem trouble) due to the difficult circumstances had lower success rates than the companies that took the journey for offensive reasons (like boosting growth or increasing market share). Extra care from the top is much needed when a transformation initiative is taken for defensive reasons, and more emphasis on people change management and sufficient resources is crucial.

3) Lack of Convincing "ROI"

Several companies struggled to find the best way to determine the business case including ROI (return on investment) and identify the right metrics that would capture and display the benefits in addition to defining "success" when it comes to business transformations. Therefore, they couldn't sustain the buy-in from executives.

Also, success and metrics' targets must be defined for the intermediate phases of the transformation in addition to the end state to sustain a high level of energy and focus. In one of the industry conferences, the author asked an audience of more than 80 managers to raise their hands if they are "OK" with their own performance measurement governance (metrics identification, measuring, tracking, and controlling), only 3 managers raised their hands! The widespread feeling among managers is that they are measuring too much or too little or are measuring the wrong metrics. The majority also feel that their performance measurement governance doesn't drive good behavior.

4) Inability of Selecting "the Right" Software Provider

Selecting a software provider is a hard undertaking and consumes time and internal resources. Companies is not just struggling in identifying the right software provider (partner) for digital technology, but they are still struggling with choosing the right supply chain planning technology platform. In addition, executives frequently express their concern about their companies' ability to ensure that the technology is fully utilized once deployed. Supply chain digital applications especially the planning ones require a steep learning curve for most companies.

5) New Technology is the "Silver Bullet" Perception

Some executives perceived the new technology to be the "silver bullet" to all of their business problems and forgot the fact that it is just an enabler for best practice processes and requires effective change management to be adopted.

When the transformation program is driven by a date given by IT instead of a value achieved milestone, then it is a recipe for disaster. In an attempt to meet the target date (often unrealistic); training, documentation, and change management are often neglected, resulting in something that has a short life span (people stop it after sometime) or that does not deliver the full benefit. These transformation programs might be able to "go live" from an IT standpoint but will not be well accepted or embraced by end users.

For transformation programs to work, an amalgamation has to happen between process changes, new technology capabilities, people readiness with the required new skills, and organization structure alignment changes.

6) No Clear Priorities for Day-to-Day Operations

Typically, the day-to-day operation is already at full capacity when the executives call for a transformation program. Some companies try to add transformation activities to the preexisting calendar of "run the business" meetings, but it doesn't work because short term operational issues typically come first. People in most cases are occupied more than 100% of their capacity. This affects the productivity of transformation activities since people find it difficult to prioritize their activities. Sometimes due to unavailability of the right person for transformation activity because of their preoccupancy with other day to day jobs, substitute is chosen who may not be fully aware of the desired transformation activity and hence overall productivity is affected.

Also, when companies are in the process of implementing several incremental improvement projects like six sigma or Kaizen projects, it will be a challenge to add a transformation program to the mix targeting the same functions. Companies that try to stuff too much into the organization will clog it causing employees and managers' capacity to execute to become a choke point unless the programs are prioritized and sequenced correctly.

7) Lack of Proven Transformation Methodology

Not having a proven, comprehensive and practical methodology to show the way in the transformation journey makes it impossible to address any of the above challenges. To be successful, the transformation team will require having not only knowledge and skills in organizational design and change management, but also a comprehensive methodology for planning, implementing, and sustaining the transformation changes (Sabri, 2019). There are at least three common methodology mistakes:

1. Some companies put more emphasis on IT activities compared to change management activities. They rush things and focus only on IT activities that they have to accomplish and cannot shorten.
2. The author has also witnessed another extreme, where companies spent a huge amount of time on the planning phase, little time on implementing the change, and no time on sustaining it.
3. Other companies put significant emphasis on the transformations' soft factors, such as culture, leadership, and motivation while missing out on the hard factors of change management like financial results, commitment level of executives, the resources required to execute the program, and program roadmap and duration.

The following real-life story would provide examples of some of the challenges mentioned in this section. A few years back, the author was asked to play the executive process advisory role for a global high-tech company. Their largest end-to-end supply chain transformation program was underway. The program included process improvement and technology implementation to the following processes: Sales and Operation Planning (S&OP), Demand Management, Supply Planning, Order Planning, Inventory Planning, Order Fulfillment, Logistics, and Channel Management. The author joined 18 months after the program started. In the first phase of his engagement, he spent two weeks on site conducting his own assessment and concluded that the transformation is at risk and immediate corrective action is desperately needed. Here are a few of the findings:

First, the company is taking the transformation journey for defensive reasons; they were losing market share to competition, their margin was getting smaller and smaller, and they wanted to reverse the trend. Everyone in the company was fearful for his or her job.

Secondly, the author uncovered that the employees did not understand why the business must change and their own role in making it happen, so before providing any specific recommendations, the author wanted to investigate this further to find out why there was a lack of communication and articulation of the need for change to employees. He started by asking for the business case and to his surprise the sponsor didn't have it handy. During the meeting with the finance representative on the program regarding the business case, the author discovered that the major cost saving element was "laying off" employees! This was the main reason why the company didn't want to give enough clarity to employees about the program.

Thirdly, all program tracks were working in silos with little coordination. There was no master project plan covering the overall program progress and dependency. The author had to attend the project status meetings for all tracks to have a good picture about the status of the program. It was easy to notice the mistrust that every team had regarding the other teams' ability to deliver on time. In addition, around the same time, the blame game had just started.

Fourthly, the author investigated the transformation program structure, and he found out that 9 different tracks were identified to execute the program; like program management, process, technology, data, testing, suppliers, and change management track. The role for the author was under the process track. The shocker was that appropriate expertise was identified for all tracks except for change management track, it was "TBD"! Basically, a major transformation program was underway for defensive reasons, layoff is one of the outputs of the program, the culture of the company to work in silos, the company has not done this type/scale of transformation before, and yet no one is assigned for change management!

Fifthly, there was no clear and structured transformation methodology. The transformation team took 18 months to identify the business requirements and socialize it with the IT organization. And since the duration of the first phase of the transformation program was two years; everyone was under pressure to implement, go-live, and transition in the remaining 6 months. Senior management from the business organization decided to take the IT date to "go-live" as the date they would communicate to their executives. They thought that IT will be the bottleneck and assumed that all other activities like designing the new (to-be) process, coming up with new policies, developing training manuals, conducting training sessions, defining roles and responsibilities for the new processes, defining new metrics and reports to support the new processes, and overcoming resistance issues will not be the bottleneck and will fall within the IT timeline!

Finally, there were no supply chain strategies defined. The transformation team came up with all the business requirements without considering the new strategies that they have to adopt to address their challenges and reverse the trend of losing market share.

It took this company several months and several drastic adjustments to clean up this mess and start going in the right direction. Unfortunately, several senior managers and executives lost their jobs because they were slow to react.

The challenges of supply chain transformation related to people are explained in the next section.

PEOPLE CHANGE MANAGEMENT CHALLENGES

This section will cover the top 7 people change management challenges based on the authors' experience and relevant research.

1) Executives are Slow to Come Aboard

Not having all executives on the same page early on is one of the first challenges that the change agent has to address. It is highly recommended, for this purpose, to schedule a 15 minute one-on-one meeting with all executives in the first week of the engagement. This practice is used by the author, and it was very effective in highlighting the disconnect and identifying the root cause behind it, which would make it easier to address it and bring all executives on board to support the transformation program.

Reluctant executives to support the transformation program visibly will disrupt the speed of the company's progress in planning effectively and undermine transformation significantly. Even the best planned supply chain transformation initiative would fail if top management failed to demonstrate commitment to create the sense of urgency necessary to overcome resistance to change. Executives' support is key to set proper expectations for their employees.

2) Keeping Stakeholders Engaged and Motivated

Stakeholders are the employees and managers who will be impacted by the process changes or will play a role and have an impact on the success of the transformation program. In a nutshell, the stakeholders are the people who will make the transformation happen. Disengaged stakeholders can really slow down progress and can be a reason by itself for transformation failure.

Many firms underestimate this challenge which results in catastrophic implications because no matter how sophisticated and powerful the software applications or digital technologies are and how effective best practices processes may be, in the end, it is the stakeholders who play the most significant role in the success or failure of the program. Supply chain stakeholders represent different organizations and different roles (operators, managers, planners, suppliers, customers, warehouse receivers, carriers, etc.) which add another dimension to the challenge.

3) Lack of Organizational Structure Alignment

It is necessary to look at the structural support for the change transformation program. If the foundation structure is deemed to be inadequate, restructuring becomes critical. Restructuring changes range in degree from minor adjustments to large-scale organization-wide changes that affect virtually every member of the organization.

One of the author's organizational change management engagements was to help a tire manufacturing company become a global supply chain organization and to streamline and standardize their processes. One of the deliverables was to recommend a structure for the global supply chain organization and the related roles and responsibilities. Assigning an executive vice president reporting to CEO to lead a centralized and global supply chain organization was one of the recommendations. Unfortunately, the sponsor did not have enough political clout with the CEO to make it happen before starting the design phase. This was one of main reasons that the transformation program ran into serious delays and severe change management and ownership issues.

4) Inability to Build the Right Transformation Team

Building the right transformation team is the most important change management activity in a business transformation program. In the process of building the team, senior management must be sensitive to the unique needs of the program environment.

Building the right (effective) team optimizes the efforts of the team and increases the chances of having a successful program. On the other hand, a weak team structure would undercut the efforts of hard working team members, reduce morale, and impede project success.

5) Lack of Effective Communication Plan

It's a common misconception that if people are talking to each other, it means they are communicating; communication needs to have a framework and format to be effective. Another common pitfall is that one communication plan template fits all programs or projects. While all programs or projects share the need for a communication plan, they differ in the type of information needed, frequency, and methods of communication (Sabri, Gupta, and Beitler, 2006).

Effective communication within the transformation team and between the team and other program stakeholders is essential for a smooth and successful journey.

6) Inability to Sustain On-Going Learning and Coaching

Supply Chain transformation programs require extensive and on-going training especially when it includes digital technologies and new skills and attitudes for the users of the new or improved processes. The proper allocation and commitment of resources (time, energy, and money) to conduct training and coaching to help employees in their skills acquisition is critical to the success of implementing and sustaining changes.

Although the "sustain" phase is the most difficult phase in any transformation program, there is relatively little attention by executives concerning sustaining change in organizations. While planning and implementing a change can occur relatively quickly, sustaining change involves a long period of time. Maintaining a sense of urgency and a significant level of interest is difficult over a long period of time. This phase can take months and sometime a few years. Therefore, the author typically suggests a separate budget for this phase to bring attention to it.

During this phase, the new process must be reinforced by the policies for recruiting, selecting, promoting, compensating, evaluating, and on-going training of employees. Also, acknowledging and rewarding stakeholders for new behaviors are essential to stabilize the new process and anchor the new culture.

7) Lack of Comprehensive Incentive Program

While the Communication plan addresses the "why" question by providing the "awareness" about the importance of change and the risks of not changing for the company, the incentive plan addresses the "what's in it for me" question and creates the "desire" to change. Only when managers and employees have the "awareness" of the need to change and the "desire" to support the change, then learning "how" to change can start.

Unfortunately, the lack of comprehensive incentive programs is an issue in almost every transformation program that the author has audited. In some companies, they make the incentive programs limited to managers and executives and don't include the employees. In other companies, incentive programs are in place, but not aligned to support the desired behavior and new processes. Very few companies go the extra mile to come up with an incentive program for every member of the transformation team and stakeholders who are responsible to plan and implement change.

The rule of thumb is that every stakeholder, which their processes will be impacted by the change or who will have an impact on the transformation, should be part of the incentive program. Also, the objectives of the transformation should be reflected on the stakeholders' scorecards and aligned with their incentives. Therefore, the company's human resources (HR) department should be involved early on.

COMPREHENSIVE FRAMEWORK FOR MASTERING CHANGE MANAGEMENT

Figure 1 provides a comprehensive framework for mastering change management to ensure smooth and successful digital supply chain transformation programs and address the above challenges. This framework includes 8 steps (phases) needed to implement change in the culture of the organization, and 5 success factors for companies to maintain throughout the lifecycle of change.

What follows are the required steps to be taken during the life cycle of change transformation and success factors for effective change management (as shown in Figure 1). Using these steps as systematic and comprehensive framework, executives and managers can understand what to expect and how to engage the entire organization in the process.

Figure 1. Digital Supply Chain Change Management Framework

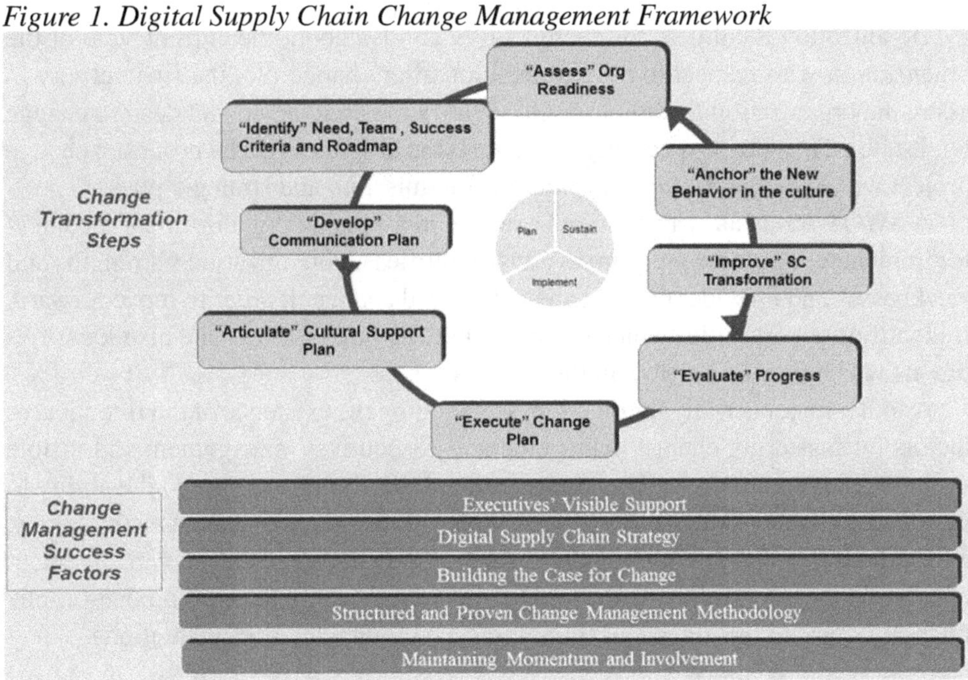

Eight Change Transformation Steps

The proposed framework proposed suggests eight steps to go thru the life cycle of change transformation effectively as shown in Figure 1 which are summarized as follows: 1) Assess, 2) Identify, 3) Develop, 4) Articulate, 5) Execute, 6) Evaluate, 7) Improve, and 8) Anchor. These steps can be also grouped under 3 phases:

- **Plan phase** which includes steps 1 to 4
- **Implement phase** which includes steps 5 & 6
- **Sustain phase** which includes steps 7 & 8

Let's understand about every step in more details:

Step # 1: "Assess" Organization Readiness

Organization Readiness for change gives an idea about the current state of the organization with respect to desired position after change. So, the first activity in assessing organizational readiness is to identify the anticipated and desired change (end state). Then the next activity is to assess the alignment of the proposed change project with the organization's current vision, mission, and strategic plan.

A SWOT Analysis is a beneficial exercise in assessing organizational readiness for implementing a new program. SWOT identifies an organization's strengths and weaknesses and may identify any areas that need change in order to move forward. It identifies opportunities which can contribute towards success and also identifies threats which may be barriers in the process.

Another major activity for this step is evaluating the existence of the five success factors for mastering change management: 1) executives' engagement and visible support, 2) commitment to develop end-to-end SC digital strategy, 3) the ability to develop a convincing business case, 4) deciding on change management methodology, and 5) the ability and previous record in maintaining the engagement & involvement of all stakeholders. This evaluation can be accomplished by scheduling one-on-one interviews, group meetings, questionnaires, and reviewing documentations.

Step # 2: "Identify" Need, Team, Success Criteria and Roadmap

Once the problem statement is defined, stakeholders are identified, scope of supply chain digital transformation is fixed and aligned with organizational goals then there is a need to articulate clearly the need for change. This activity is crucial to answer the question that everyone in the organization across all levels will have "why we need to change". It provides the "elevator pitch" or the key message that will be communicated to provide awareness. One example of a key message from a Manufacturing company is "we need to transform our supply chain to penetrate new market channels while maintaining low inventory levels and gain competitive advantage in order to increase market share profitably" (Sabri, 2019). This activity is also important to secure the buy-in from the upper management who typically ask for an explanation of how the change helps in implementing the organization's strategic plan and achieving corporate goals.

Building the right (effective) team optimizes the efforts of the team and increases the chances of having a successful program. One of the biggest challenges of building and developing a transformation team for supply chain improvement programs in today's business is that every transformation program has its own nature and resources requirements. The senior management and sponsor must be sensitive to the unique needs of the program environment. Also, the structure of the organization plays also a big role in selecting and building the transformation team. There is a need to document the required skills for every role (functional consultant, change agent, process consultant, developer, architect, program manager, project manager, etc...) based on the program charter document. This includes also determining the number of resources needed for every role. In addition, establishing a process to evaluate the performance of resources and define an incentive plan to keep them motivated is crucial (Sabri and Shaikh, 2010).

This activity should consider "why we are changing" key message to come up with the success criteria which typically provides some guidance on the expected benefits and how to measure success. A success criteria example for a company trying to improve market share by gaining competitive advantage in customer service would be 1) improve customer service level by 10%, 2) improve market share by 2% next year, 3) and maintain inventory turnover rate.

This activity is needed to identify the required process, technology and governance (KPIs, policies, roles and responsibilities. etc.) changes and finalizes the implementation timeline to achieve the expected benefits (success criteria) of the transformation program. This activity includes conducting process analysis for supply chain processes based on the transformation scope. Process analysis determines the extent of process & governance changes and identifies additional software capabilities required to support the "end state" processes. Several industry-proven process analysis methodologies can help in this exercise like six sigma, value stream mapping, benchmarking, etc.

Step # 3: "Develop" Communication Plan

Communications should have majorly two focus areas: communications about the program (why and how we are changing), and communications about the end state and solution being delivered. This includes communication with stakeholders, team members, support team members, functional group members and front-end users (both inside and outside company).

Communications about projects to stakeholders is very important for the success of supply chain transformation programs. Lack of information about the project progress to stakeholders can be threatening to the program. Regular, targeted communication enables stakeholders to be educated, prepared and confident that the project is supporting their business needs. The mode and interval of communication should be clearly defined and shared with stakeholders. Program communication should be based on facts and figures. Showing progress helps to maintain confidence among stakeholders, instill pride in program members, and continue program energy. Program communication includes setting expectations, creating awareness of desired solutions, organizational changes, concerns, and success. This communication should flow across all the stakeholders not only within the organization but also to vendors, suppliers and customers etc. Many organizations underestimate the value of this part of communication but awareness of solution to suppliers and customers helps them to prepare and understand their role and if required also help them plan their resources in advance.

Effective communication provides a clear understanding of what is taking place, motivates the team members, avoids any miscommunication between transformation team members, keeps senior executives committed, reduces the risk of conflicts, and more importantly keeps everyone informed on the progress.

The communication plan should be comprehensive enough to satisfy the information needs of all of the stakeholders. It should provide a description of what piece of information is needed, who needs it, why it is needed, when it is needed, how it is communicated, and by whom. In addition, the communication plan identifies meetings, reporting, methods and format of communications that will occur with the transformation team, program sponsor, stakeholders, partners, IT, internal and external organizations.

Step # 4: "Articulate" Cultural Support Plan

Once a communication plan is established, it's necessary to articulate a culture support plan which includes the education plan and organization structure realignment activities. Any transformation program requires culture support. Organizational culture by its very nature refuses to accept change, but over time and with education, organization structure realignment, enforcement from executives, culture does change.

Leadership development is essential if some of the individuals who will be responsible for the program have little or no leadership experience. The education plan should be tailored to help the individuals acquire these skills. Conflict resolution is one example for the soft skills that leaders need to master if transformation program is to be effectively implemented and sustained.

Training and skills acquisition for end users should be part of the education plan as well. Supply chain digital transformation programs require training, new skills and attitudes for the end users of the new or improved processes. The proper allocation and commitment of resources (time, energy, and money) to conduct training and help employees in their skills acquisition is critical to the success of changes.

On major activity of this step is to plan for organizational realignment to support the end state. The human resources department might need to update job descriptions and bonus structure to reflect the changes. This might require a pipeline of candidates with a mix of demand, supply and product expertise. Also, incentives for the company's talent should be aligned with the skill requirements for the end state.

Change leaders and agents (part of the transformation team) must anticipate resistance and be prepared to deal with various change adoption rates. It is important to focus on pioneers and early adopters first. These individuals who are a subset of the stakeholders' group are the most open to change; they are the first to embrace something new. Therefore, it is recommended to get these stakeholders on board as quickly as possible to help in changing the culture.

Step # 5: "Execute" Change Plan

Once the change plan (which includes change implementation roadmap, communication plan, education plan, and organization structure alignment changes) is approved by senior management/executives, then transformation team has the green signal to go ahead and execute the plan.

Supply chain digital transformation program typically takes two to five years, with several intermediate projects (Go-Lives) that can pay for the rest of the program. Therefore, it is recommended to develop the change plan on the idea of incremental value delivery. It is crucial to have a long-term (program) plan for success, but one should not ignore the importance of providing some quick wins (projects). Organizational stakeholders look for short-term results, and the transformation team is under pressure to present short-term wins. Short-term wins should be woven into the timetable of the program. Each project delivers a set of capabilities that have a positive impact on processes, metrics, and people and addresses a distinct business need and contributes to the success criteria.

Step # 6: "Evaluate" Progress

In transformation program, regular evaluation (health check) helps understand the current progress status and helps anticipate the future progress trend. It is critical that the transformation team understand the current progress and take key actions to avoid any unwanted delays. The prompt and proactive actions of the transformation team can save the program from going off-track. If the program is delayed and the team is not able to get back on track, then most of the time it goes off the radars of the executives' dashboard and eventually importance is lost and the program fails. Progress evaluation should be done against the schedule and expected benefits (success criteria). Since the implementation delivery strategy is to accomplish it in incremental steps (projects), the achieved value of the projects need be tracked and checked off with time.

It is acceptable for the program manager and sponsor while tracking the transformation progress toward achieving the expected benefits and reaching the new targets of the KPIs to rethink the goal and even adjust the targets either because of encountering roadblocks or because of some emerging opportunities that didn't exist earlier.

This step requires senior management's best efforts to stay engaged to build momentum for the change. Whenever executives or senior management let up before the job is done, critical momentum can be lost, and the change effort can stall.

Step # 7: "Improve" Supply Chain Transformation

Although the sustaining phase is the most difficult phase in any transformation, there is relatively little research concerning sustaining change in organizations. While planning and implementing a change can occur relatively quickly, sustaining change requires a significant amount of time. Maintaining a sense of urgency and a significant level of interest is difficult over a long period of time. This phase can take months or years.

Once a successful project improvement (short-term win) is accomplished, management must work to make it part of the organizational culture. Step # 7 helps in this aspect by encouraging the culture of continuous improvement and fine tuning the new solution (combination of new process and technology). Improvement can also be achieved by enforcing the new process through drafting policies, providing additional coaching when needed and recruiting people based on the new required skills. In addition, developing corrective actions for the root causes when performance measure targets are not achieved would achieve incremental improvement.

Step # 8: "Anchor" the New Behavior in the Culture

Acknowledging and rewarding stakeholders for adopting new "right" behaviors is essential to stabilize the improved process and anchor the new culture. Using new skills involves risk (the risk of failure) and acknowledging and rewarding those who use the new skills encourages others to do the same.

This step also involves updating performance measures (metrics) to reflect the new performance baselines. This can include developing new performance measures, modifying existing ones, adjusting targets, or establishing owners for the performance measures.

FIVE CHANGE MANAGEMENT SUCCESS FACTORS

Success Factor # 1: Executives' Visible Support

Since change is difficult and inherently unsettling, stakeholders will turn to the CEOs and executives for direction and answers. The leaders of the organization must embrace change first and then display their commitment and support. They must speak with one voice and model the desired behaviors especially since supply chain transformations require intensive cooperation and cross-functional collaboration among executive peers. This would force executives to get out of their comfort zones and their respective areas of responsibility and find time out of their busy daily operation schedule to envision an entire new business.

While there are many reasons for the failure of the transformation initiatives, lack of executive commitment is ahead of all the reasons. Many executives don't know there is a direct correlation between leadership engagement levels and the success of a transformation initiative.

Having a broad picture about change in mind, executives would need dashboards and indicators to successfully pilot an organization to desired destination. Actively executives will build planned benefits/results into their own and the leadership team's performance plans. They will initiate project-relevant communications in direct report meetings on a regular basis, visibly hold the organization's leaders accountable for the change and if required will ask frequently for their direct participation. They also engage in communication events at all levels of the organization, try to resolve resource issues or constraints, understand the implications of the change across the organization's groups and demographic groups, also monitors, identify and address organizational resistance.

Another important aspect regarding the leadership of change is to understand the level of effort required for success. The executive's role and importance continue to increase over the life of the project. Towards the end of the change cycle, efforts from transition team are maximum because of sustain phase of change cycle. Everything done up to implementation phase can fall apart if leader's proper attention and commitment is not there in last phase of change process.

Success Factor # 2: Digital Supply Chain Strategy

Very few companies have a good and documented supply chain strategy. Executives struggle with assessing the current state of the supply chain, and envisioning the new state that is required to support the vision and address current challenges, from digital technologies and processes to human resources and governance. They also struggle to decide when and where to begin and how to translate the vision into goals, goals into strategies and strategies into process changes and projects. Serious consideration should be given to following while developing strategy.

Market changes - Strategies often fail because the market conditions which were intended to be exploited change before the strategy takes hold. Reasons can be shorter product life cycle, competition with new technology, and unexpected change in financial market etc.

Uniqueness of the strategy - good strategy is one which can distinguish the company from others in ways that it makes a difference to customers. Michael Porter (1996) has written extensively and persuasively on this topic. So, leaders should take three simple steps in developing a distinctive strategy – understand the company's genuine strengths (particularly those that span multiple functions), examine the marketplace to understand what market positions are unoccupied, focus the company's strategies on bringing its variable strengths to bear in capturing those unoccupied strategic positions. Also, the strategy must consider the potential reaction to a strategy by competitive companies. To effectively anticipate the reaction of competitors over strategy, a company should have competitive intelligence capability. The study should involve understanding the competitor's market position, their competitive advantages and disadvantages, future planning, management decision trends etc.

Alignment with business models – Sometimes companies fail to align their digital supply chain strategy with the organizational goal and business models. This is a critical step which is often overlooked. Lack of research of market trend, miss connecting to customers, gap or misunderstanding of how demand would be met in the market can lead to poor business model. A basic assessment of organizational capabilities and the capability gaps created by a change in strategy is a very direct means of improving alignment.

Culture of "playing it Safe" – Companies get used to executing low-risk incremental improvements on the same business environment for an extended period, and they become close-minded for drastic improvements, because they do not know how to handle transformation programs and target big results. The scope can be overwhelming.

When companies are in the process of implementing several incremental improvement projects like Six Sigma or Kaizen projects, it will be a challenge to add a large transformation program to the mix especially when it includes new technology like digital technologies. Companies that try to stuff too much into the organization will clog it causing employees and managers' capacity to become a choke point unless the projects are prioritized and sequenced correctly.

Digital supply chain strategy ideally includes:

1) Flexible strategy as changes occurs in the global marketplace.
    a. Leveraging Gen AI and ML, companies can develop flexible strategies that adapt to changes in the global marketplace, ensuring they remain competitive and responsive to new trends and disruptions.
2) Prioritized, actionable and practical improvement plans.
    a. By using advanced AI and ML algorithms, businesses can prioritize improvement plans based on actionable insights, making them practical and effective in driving performance enhancements.
3) A three-to-five-year roadmap that guides the transformation of supply-and-demand capabilities and take planning processes to the next level
    a. The roadmap should anticipate future needs and align with long-term goals and leverage ML and Gen AI technologies
4) Linkage to one or more corporate goals like growth or customer service levels
    a. Integrating AI and ML with corporate goals such as growth and customer service levels ensure that all improvement initiatives are aligned with overarching business objectives, maximizing their impact.
5) Both large opportunities for improvement that deliver significant ROI over time, as well as "quick win" operations improvements with a fast payback,
6) Elimination to outdated roles and responsibilities, unnecessary activities, and performance metrics that no longer reflect current realities, and
7) Metrics across the supply chain to reflect the overarching digital supply chain strategy.

Success Factor # 3: Building the Case for Change

The author believes strongly, in coming years, no better core competency will help companies to compete in market other than the ability to effectively implement transformation change. With increasing pressure both external and internal, organizations will tend to undertake more projects and initiatives to remain competitive in the market. So, the ability to achieve profit and benefits will directly be tied to how effectively we manage change by engaging employees. Building the business case for change is crucial to compel leadership to give the go ahead for the transformation change program.

Developing a good business case for change is very important where every stakeholder's requirement is taken into consideration. Three steps should be followed in developing the case: First, articulate a convincing need for change based on the company's current situation and market opportunities. Here supporting details have to be strong enough to draw the attention of executives. The change case should be directly linked to the organizational goals, as this helps in grabbing the attention of stakeholders.

Second, quantify the expected operational and financial benefits, estimate cost, and calculate the return on investment (ROI). This can be a challenging step sometimes because when the case is in the initial stage one has to come up with expected financial benefit and return on investment close to actual. If the exercise is done with detailed consideration, then case becomes very convincing and can grab attention of executives based on the extent of research that went through developing the case.

Third, explain how to show progress and measure success, which metrics will be improved to achieve the expected benefits, what will be the new performance targets and deadlines, and who will be accountable. If this step is not developed well then whole change process efforts can fail. As a part of developing case equal consideration should also be given in developing performance measurement governance to track progress (Sabri, 2019).

During business case development if consideration is given to identifying the key performance measures, then while executing change program these performance indicators (measures) become more refined and can give accurate information on success.

Success Factor # 4: Structured and Proven Change Management Methodology

Ensuring a structured and proven methodology to show the way in the change transformation journey is a must. Any significant supply chain transformation program creates uncertainty and people resistance. New leaders emerge, job descriptions are changed, new skills and capabilities must be developed. Dealing with these change management issues on a reactive, case-by-case basis puts timeline, morale, and results all at risk.

A structured and formal plan for managing change—beginning with the transformation team and then engaging key stakeholders and leaders—should be developed early and executed effectively as changes move through the organization. The plan should be comprehensive to cover planning, implementing, and sustaining the transformation changes. It should also allow enough time for covering the soft factors of change management such as culture, leadership, and motivation because it takes time to change attitudes or relationships which are deeply ingrained in people as well as organization. It requires time and effort to change the culture.

In addition, the structured change plan should not miss out on the hard factors of change management like financial results, commitment level of executives, the number of resources and skills required to execute the program successfully, benchmarking and gap analysis, and program roadmap and duration which are vital for the success of the transformation program.

Success Factor # 5: Maintaining Energy and Involvement

As transformation programs progress from defining strategy and setting targets to design and implementation, they affect different organizational levels and stakeholders. Disengaged stakeholders can really slow down progress and can cause by itself for transformation failure. Setting right KPIs & tracking, performance measurement and award & recognition have the most significant impact in sustaining organizational improvement.

Right KPIs: To maintain the momentum and involvement of people in change programs, it's important to develop and measure the right KPIs. For example, as part of change initiatives a company adopts a new pricing strategy to obtain high margins. Measuring volume of sales was chosen to track the progress. But if were observe deeply we find that measuring volume encourages discounts, rebates, and warranties, all of which erode margins. So, it becomes very important to measure the right things to create the right change (Sabri, 2019).

Performance measurement and support mechanism: When an organization is going through change then management's fostering of organizational trust, respect and caring pays off. Mistakes and unwanted things will occur in the change process but at that time benefit of the doubt and continuing support to employees helps build trust. Having a structured performance system also pays off. Communicating goals and performance targets to employees upfront and let them know about the expected behavior and importance of the change with respect to employee (what's in it for them) and organization is crucial.

It is important to provide resources, key materials, training and tools to employees to achieve target performance. This proactive activity helps build positive energy among employees which signifies support of senior management in change implementation phase. Evaluating the performance of employees based on their target whether not achieved or exceeded, and providing feedback is a critical activity. Performance feedback activity should be motivating, encouraging including performance compensation to maximize the target performance. If employees are in sync and excited about the change initiatives, they will give their maximum to achieve the target.

Reward & recognition: This is closely related to above two and refers how positive attitude and work gets rewarded. It's been observed that the reward may not be exact compensation to the amount of effort put by employees but even a small token of appreciation encourages employees to such an extent that they may be able to boost their level of effort. So, highly visible incentives, such as promotion, bonuses, and recognition should be provided as reinforcements to maintain energy and sustain change.

To summarize, stakeholders should understand why change is happening, how their work will change, what is expected of them during and after the transformation program, how they will be measured, and what benefits success will bring to them personally. Transformation team leaders should be addressing all these questions explicitly and keep stakeholders involved in the process and informed to maintain momentum throughout the organization.

The key driver for this success factor is the transformation team. Building and empowering an effective transformation team is very crucial to maintaining excitement and eventually embracing change. In building the transformation team, executives must be sensitive to the unique needs of the program environment and ensure that the team is having the right skills like identifying resistance root causes and coming up with strategies to overcome resistance. The team should also try to avoid resistance in the first place by being proactive and mitigate the risk ahead of time (Sabri, 2019).

CONCLUSION

Change management in AI-driven supply chain digital transformation is more difficult than traditional supply chain transformations for several reasons:

1. **Complexity of Technology** Gen AI and ML technologies are inherently complex, requiring specialized knowledge and expertise to implement and manage. This complexity can create significant challenges in understanding and leveraging these technologies effectively, making change management more difficult.
2. **Cultural Resistance** Employees and stakeholders may resist adopting AI technologies due to fear of job displacement, lack of understanding, or skepticism about the technology's benefits.
3. **Integration with Legacy Systems** Many supply chains operate on legacy systems that may not be compatible with AI technologies. Integrating AI solutions with these existing systems can be technically challenging and resource-intensive, complicating the change management process.
4. **Skill Gaps** Implementing AI-driven transformations requires a workforce with skills in AI, data science, and advanced analytics. Addressing these skill gaps through hiring, training, and upskilling initiatives can be difficult and time-consuming.
5. **Dynamic Nature of AI** AI technologies evolve rapidly, requiring continuous learning and adaptation. This dynamic nature means that organizations must be agile and flexible, continuously updating their processes and strategies to keep pace with technological advancements.
6. **Ethical and Regulatory Concerns** The deployment of AI in supply chains raises ethical and regulatory concerns, such as data privacy, algorithmic bias, and compliance with industry standards. Navigating these concerns adds an additional layer of complexity to the change management process.

Success of AI-powered supply chain digital transformation depends majorly on mastering the change management throughout the life cycle of the change program. To be successful in the journey, the change leaders must be more knowledgeable about the change life cycle since supply chain digital transformations are complex and multifunctional in nature.

For effective change management, it is very important to have strong support from executives throughout the transformation cycle. Attacking change management with Digital Supply Chain Strategy and proven change management methodology makes transformation change cycle smooth. To sustain change management outcome, it is necessary to maintain energy and assurance of everyone's involvement.

When firms make the decision to implement supply chain digital transformation programs which typically includes process improvement, software implementation, and organizational realignment across their global operations, there is a strong influence of cultural component to this program. The changes include changes in the way work gets done every day, in individual roles and responsibilities, and in key performance indicators (KPIs).

A proven and well-defined change management framework for supply chain digital transformation can help companies overcome the culture of "this is the way we've always done it" and get employees at every level on board with the transformation plan — and achieve the expected benefits from improving supply chain performance. It will also help in accelerating the pace of change and achieve the success criteria quicker.

Every supply chain digital transformation program is unique because every firm has its own culture, industry challenges, organizational structure and skills, process maturity, and performance. However, proposed framework in this chapter is a comprehensive one that addresses all common challenges in implementing supply chain digital transformation programs and a practical one which provides executives and managers a good roadmap on what to expect and how to engage the entire organization in the process. This would ensure a successful and smooth supply chain digital transformation journey.

FUTURE TRENDS AND RESEARCH

Mastering change management is critical for the success of supply chain digital transformation. Importance of change management as separate departments within an organization is increasing. Development of structured approach and formal process is concern for many industries as still failure rate of transformation programs is high. Several initiatives around the industry are under progress to develop effective and efficient methodology on how to adopt change in organization. There is a demand to integrate change management throughout all levels of the organizational system. Leaders must link organizations goals to functional level department goals to personal level individual goals. With the advent of increase in transformation initiatives there is great demand for integration of project management methodology with change management cycle.

The author predicts more serious attention and enough allocated budget for change management track for transformation programs. This will be translated into a higher industry success rate. This will have an impact on academia in two aspects: 1) more research and case studies will be available in this area, 2) witnessing the introduction of change management as a separate MBA program in the universities.

In addition, the author predicts future research in mastering change management for AI-powered supply chain digital transformation in the following areas:

1. **Effective Communication Strategies** Investigate best practices for communicating the benefits, risks, and changes associated with AI-driven transformations to various stakeholders, ensuring clarity, transparency, and engagement.

2. **Cultural Transformation and Employee Engagement** Study the methods for fostering a culture that embraces AI and digital innovation, including strategies for increasing employee engagement, overcoming resistance, and addressing fears related to job displacement.
3. **Change Readiness Assessment Tools** Develop and validate tools for assessing an organization's readiness for AI-driven change, focusing on factors such as technological infrastructure, data quality, skill levels, and cultural preparedness.
4. **Training and Upskilling Programs** Examine the design and implementation of comprehensive training and upskilling programs that prepare the workforce for AI integration, covering technical skills, data literacy, and change management competencies.
5. **Ethical Considerations and Trust-Building** Study the ethical implications of AI in supply chain management and develop strategies for building trust among stakeholders, addressing concerns related to data privacy, algorithmic bias, and transparency.
6. **Psychological and Behavioral Aspects of Change** Investigate the psychological and behavioral aspects of change management in the context of AI adoption, understanding how employees perceive and react to AI-related changes and developing strategies to address these reactions.
7. **Integration of AI with Change Management Technologies** Explore how AI itself can be used to enhance change management processes, such as using AI-driven analytics to monitor change progress, predict resistance, and personalize change interventions for different stakeholder groups.

REFERENCES

Aiken, C., & Keller, S. (2009). The irrational side of change management. *The McKinsey Quarterly*, 2(10), 100–109.

Cynthia, B., & Keith, L. S. (2011, January–March). Organizational Change Manafgement: A Test of the Effectiveness of a Communication Plan. *Communication Research Reports*, 28(1), 62–73. DOI: 10.1080/08824096.2011.541364

Ford, M. W., & Greer, B. M. (2005). The Relationship between Management Control System Usage and Planned Change Achievement: An Exploratory Study. *Journal of Change Management*, 5(1), 29–46. DOI: 10.1080/14697010500036031

Isern, J., Meaney, M., & Wilson, S. (2009). Corporate Transformation under Pressure. *McKinsey&Company*. Retrieved from https://www.mckinsey.com/insights/organization/corporate_transformation_under_pressure

Karp, T. (2005). Unpacking the Mysteries of Change: Mental Modeling. *Journal of Change Management*, 5(1), 87–97. DOI: 10.1080/14697010500057573

Kotter, J. P. (1996). *Leading Change*. Boston Harvard Business School Press.

Leonard and Coltea. (2013).Most Change Initiatives Fail -- But They Don't Have To http://businessjournal.gallup.com

Nadler, D. A., & Tushman, M. (1989). Organizational Frame Bending: Principles for Managing Reorientation. *The Academy of Management Executive*, 3(3), 194–204.

Porter, M. (1996). What is Strategy. *Harvard Business Review*, •••, 1996. PMID: 10158475

Sabri, E. (2019). Optimization of Supply Chain Management in Contemporary Organizations: Mastering Change Management for Successful Digital Supply Chain Transformation. USA: IGI Global, 85-106.

Sabri, E., Gupta, A., & Beitler, M. (2006). *Purchase Order Management in B2B Environment: Best Practice & Technologies J.* ROSS PUBLISHING.

Sabri, E. & Shaikh, S. (2010). *Lean & Agile Value Chain Management: A Guide to the Next Level of Improvement.* USA: J. ROSS PUBLISHING Greer, B. and Ford, M. (2009). Managing Change in Supply Chains: A process Comparison. *Journal of Business Logistics, Vol. 30, No. 2* Ramanan and Anil (2011).The Top Three Reasons Supply Chain Transformations Fail *WiproConsulting Services*

Chapter 8
AI-Driven Supply Chain Segmentation: Navigating the New Business Landscape

Ehap Sabri
Ernst & Young LLP, USA

ABSTRACT

In response to the dramatic changes in the business landscape over the past few years, companies are assessing whether they have the right supply chains to support their dynamic and digital business and exploring supply chain segmentation to reduce complexity and increase profit. Today's supply chains have become increasingly complex due to globalization, outsourcing, complicated networks, logistics capacity uncertainty and volatility, and the rapid proliferation of stocking keeping units (SKUs) and product configurations. However, many companies continue to use an outdated approach to supply chain segmentation This chapter explains the concept of segmentation, its historical background, its importance for today's business, and challenges to implementation. The chapter also provides an end-to-end supply chain practical segmentation framework. Companies can utilize this to ensure a smooth and successful implementation journey leveraging digital technologies like ML and Gen AI. Several client examples will be discussed to illustrate the "fast track to success" framework.

DOI: 10.4018/979-8-3693-4433-0.ch008

INTRODUCTION

In response to the dramatic changes in the business landscape over the past few years, companies are assessing whether they have the right supply chains to support their dynamic and digital business and exploring supply chain segmentation to reduce complexity and increase profit. Today's supply chains have become increasingly complex due to globalization, outsourcing, complicated networks, logistics capacity uncertainty and volatility, and the rapid proliferation of stocking keeping units (SKUs) and product configurations. However, many manufacturers and retailers continue to use an outdated approach to supply chain segmentation, which is more of a hindrance than a help toward reducing complexity and improving margin.

It is also critical to deliver the right level of service for each product/customer/channel segment, especially as consumer behavior pushes toward more product customization and better service leading to a more compressed supply cycle. Digital technology is transforming supply chain management and driving significant innovation. Machine learning as a concept has been around for some time but has taken on a new meaning as the industry sees massive advancements in computing power and memory. In addition, change is happening faster than ever as technology trends such as IoT, virtual reality, and big data are providing countless opportunities for manufacturers and retailers across the globe.

The tightening of budgetary constraints has driven more companies to explore ways to make the supply chain more agile, customer-focused, and profit-driven (i.e., to do more with less). This is another pressure driver for the increase in supply chain segmentation popularity. Therefore, taking the journey of supply chain segmentation is no longer optional; it is a strategic mandate to stay relevant in the industry. The future belongs to companies who can profitably match their supply chains to the specific needs of their customer segments.

Generative AI (GenAI) can complement Machine Learning (ML) in supply chain segmentation by addressing some of the complexities and enhancing the capabilities of traditional ML approaches. While ML is excellent at analyzing historical data, identifying patterns and making predictions, GenAI can simulate various hypothetical scenarios, analyze unstructured data, and generate innovative solutions that traditional ML might miss.

This chapter explains the concept of segmentation, its historical background, its importance for today's business, and challenges to implementation. The chapter also provides an end-to-end supply chain practical segmentation framework. Companies can utilize this to ensure a smooth and successful implementation journey leveraging digital technologies. Several existing frameworks are relevant, but none are adequate or comprehensive by themselves. By integrating GenAI with ML, companies can develop more robust and adaptive segmentation strategies. Several client examples will be discussed to illustrate the "fast track to success" framework, highlighting how GenAI and ML together can transform supply chain segmentation and drive significant business value.

BACKGROUND

Definition for Supply Chain Segmentation Concept

Sabri (2015) defined Supply Chain segmentation as managing profitably different virtual end-to-end supply chains defined by a combination of channel/customer requirements, product characteristics, business value considerations, and differentiated supply response strategies.IT research and advisory firm Gartner (https://www.gartner.com/it-glossary/supply-chain-segmentation) describes supply chain segmentation as "Designing and operating distinctly different end-to-end value chains (from customers to suppliers) optimized by a combination of unique customer value, product attribute, manufacturing and supply capabilities, and business value considerations. In essence, supply chain segmentation is the dynamic alignment of customer channel demands and supply response capabilities optimized for net profitability across each segment."

The Segmentation Concept is Not New

The concept of supply chain segmentation is not new in literature research. It started when Fisher (1997) mentioned that the root cause of the problems troubling many supply chains is a mismatch between the type of product and the type of supply chain response. For the past 25 years supply chain literature has introduced several methods for segmentation using different criteria such as product demand volume, product demand variability, product handling, production variability, selling channel type, and end customer behavior. Authors agree that a "one size-fits-all" supply chain management is an outdated concept, yet they use very different criteria (dimensions) and profiles for supply chain design selection.

Fisher (1997) used "Product characteristics," in particular the volume of product demand and the variability of that demand, as the criteria for supply chain segmentation and created two profiles to define the product dimension: "functional" products and "innovative" products. "Functional" products, which have stable demand and long lifecycles, are necessitating an efficient supply chain model while "innovative" products, with unpredictable demand and short lifecycles, are necessitating a responsive supply chain model. Fisher drew on examples from a diverse range of consumer products, including food, fashion apparel, and automobiles, to illustrate why different supply chain designs (models) were required depending upon whether products were "functional" or "innovative."

Naylor et al. (1999) compared the lean and agile manufacturing paradigms and argued neither paradigm is better than the other. Rather, they complement one another. In addition, they developed a two-by-two matrix based on the product demand variability and production variability and assigned lean and agile supply chain models to them. For example, low variability for demand and production requires a lean supply chain model, while high variability requires an agile supply chain model. They also highlighted that the way in which an agile supply chain differentiates its products from the lean supply chain is by concentrating on the service levels at the expense of reducing costs.

Similarly, Mason-Jones et al. (2000) suggested that the best approach is to design and implement a "Leagile Supply Chain." "Lean" can be achieved by eliminating waste (non-value-added time), while "agility" usually requires technology advances. They demonstrated how the "Lean" and "Agile"' paradigms may be combined. They introduced "order winners" as a segmentation criterion and developed a two-by-two matrix that uses "order winners" criteria to determine the appropriate supply chain model. For example, if "cost" is the order winner then a "Lean" supply chain model should be selected. When service level is the order winner then an "agile" solution should be recommended.

Lovell et al. (2005) also explored supply chain segmentation by examining product characteristics but used different criteria and profiles to define it. Two profiles (high value-density products such as microchips, and low value-density products such as packaging) were introduced and assigned to two different supply chain models. Products with high value-density should be manufactured in a few centralized, large-scale plants while low value-density items require production on a decentralized basis as close to the point of consumption as possible. The authors also mentioned that product handling characteristics should be considered in the supply chain model. Lovell et al. (2005) mentioned that perishable products are very different from fragile products, which are different from hazardous goods. This will influence the type of packaging, the mode of transport, and the type of storage.

Christopher et al. (2006) argued the importance of considering "supply lead time" as another segmentation criterion. This is very relevant to the globalization trend that started at that time. The authors developed a two-by-two matrix where demand variability and supply lead time are the segmentation criteria. The authors came up with four different profiles and assigned four supply chain designs to them:

1. When the profile is unpredictable demand and short supply lead time, an agile supply chain model should be assigned to provide flexibility and responsiveness

2. When demand is predictable and supply lead time is long, a lean supply chain model should be used to reduce supply chain costs
3. When demand is predictable and supply lead time is short, a "continuous replenishment" model should be recommended
4. When demand is unpredictable and supply lead time is long, a "postponement" (leagility) model should be proposed

Christopher et al. (2006) highlighted that global sourcing and offshore manufacturing have dramatically altered the landscape of today's business and added to the importance of agility and responsiveness as competitive success factors. The challenge to today's global business is first to identify the appropriate supply chain models to meet the different needs of the different product/channel characteristics and then to manage virtual multiple supply chains.

Gattorna (2006) was the first to consider consumer behavior as a supply chain segmentation criterion and argued that segmentation criteria should go beyond just product characteristics, demand/supply attributes, and order winners. The author explained that companies should segment their customers along buying behavior lines sharing a specific value proposition and then assign the right supply chain design. The author identified four different profiles for buying behaviors segmentation criterion and recommended a specific supply chain design for each one of them:

1. "Understand Me" requires a "continuous replenishment" design that handles stable demand perfectly and allows certain degree of collaboration
2. "Be Consistent" requires a "lean" supply chain design to ensure an efficient response for fairly stable demand
3. "Respond" is often associated with innovative or new products with typical surge in demand and requires an "agile" supply chain design
4. "Surprise" is associated with unpredictable products and a "fully flexible" supply chain design

Gattorna (2006) also introduced the "dynamic alignment" concepts which allow the supplier to switch between the four supply chain models as the needs of the customer or consumer behavior change.

Christopher et al. (2009) explored more segmentation criteria and suggested five dimensions: stage of product lifecycle, delivery lead time window, volume based on Pareto classification, product form and variability of demand.

Roscoe and Parker (2013) combined Fisher's (1997) product attributes, Mason-Jones et al.'s (2000) value proposition and order winning criteria, Christopher et al.'s (2006) demand predictability and lead times, and Gattorna's (2006) behavioral segmentation and concept of dynamic alignment. The authors came up with four supply chain models for the sporting goods industry based on the combined criteria tailored for a sporting goods manufacturer:

1. Agile – Customization
2. Agile Quick – Response
3. Lean
4. Continuous Replenishment

In summary, Table 1 shows the links between segmentation criteria (dimensions), profiles, and supply chain models for the previous work done in this area.

Table 1. Summary of segmentation dimensions, profiles, and related SC model

Author(s)	Segmentation Dimensions	Profiles	Supply Chain (SC) Models
Fisher (2007)	Product	Innovative Products Functional Products	Efficient SC process Responsive SC process
Naylor, Naim, and Berry (1999)	Product & Production	High variability of products and related production High variability of products and related production	Lean SC Agile SC
Mason-Jones, Naylor, and Towill (2000)	Order Winner	Cost Service Level	Lean SC Agile SC
Lovell, Saw, and Stimson (2005)	Product	High product-value density Low product-value density	Centralized large-scale plants Decentralized close to customer plants
Christopher, Peck, and Towill (2006)	Demand and Lead Time	Unpredictable demand and short lead time Unpredictable demand and long lead time Predictable demand and long lead times Predictable demand and short lead times	Agile SC Leagile (postponement) Lean SC Lean (continuous replenishment)

continued on following page

Table 1. Continued

Author(s)	Segmentation Dimensions	Profiles	Supply Chain (SC) Models
Gattorna (2006)	Buying behavior	"Understand Me" – collaborative approach "Be Consistent" – efficient response "Demanding" – respond approach "Surprise Me" – innovative solutions	Continuous replenishment Lean SC Agile SC Fully flexible SC
Roscoe and Parker (2013) – Case Study for Sport Goods	Product Demand Channel and Order Winner/ Value Proposition	Innovative, unpredictable and Online Innovative, high quality, unstable demand and specialist stores Price sensitive, predictable and sports generalist Fit, brand, stable demand and lifestyle generalist	Agile – Customization Agile Quick – Response Lean Continuous Replenishment

Table 1 demonstrates how several existing segmentation methods may be relevant to a specific company or industry, but none are adequate by themselves for every company or across industries. The literature conceptualizes the theory of supply chain segmentation but, when it comes to reality, there are more factors in play. It is possible that pre-defined, scripted supply chain models based on certain segmentation profiles might not even be relevant to the company's customers or products (Sabri, 2023).

As previously stated, the concept of supply chain segmentation is not new. The author observed several manufacturing, fashion and retail companies which have multiple supply chain models, but most of them were developed out of necessity (reactive mode) with manual and inconsistent business practices.

Therefore, there is an urgent need for a comprehensive and practical framework for supply chain segmentation. This should not only provide best practices in profiling and identifying different supply chain models, but also provide an end-to-end approach for implementing and sustaining segmentation and successfully leveraging digital technologies.

The Benefits of Supply Chain Segmentation

Addressing Today's Business Challenges

Executives and supply chain leaders face many challenges today in every aspect of their operations and enterprise integration. The following are the top seven challenges:

1. The disruption to the supply chain which is due tactical risks like demand variability and day-to-day supply fluctuations or catastrophic events like COVID-19, war in Ukraine, Florida hurricanes, etc.
2. They need to be more customer oriented while managing the supply chain cost (bottom-line) more efficiently. Companies have long known the importance of designing offerings to serve the needs of different markets and consumers but accomplishing this can be difficult given how quickly customers' behaviors and expectations change. Also, more business-to-business (B2B) customers are expecting a business-to-consumer (B2C) experience when interacting with other businesses.
3. Information delay or latency, which creates the need for companies to design business processes that realize the information flow between business partners.
4. The increased complexity of supply chains including the need for tighter control, the growing complexity of managing information flows, SKU proliferation, and channel complexity.
5. Expensive operating cost structures, especially when companies are facing intensified competition.
6. Supporting the redesigned processes with leading-edge technology that is easy to integrate, cheap to maintain, and fast to achieve results.
7. The need to explore insourcing for certain clusters to improve responsiveness rate. More than a decade ago, many companies started moving their production operations to lower-cost countries. The industry is again on the brink of a major global shift.

To address the challenges mentioned above, companies should look for certain key enablers to implement in their operations. Supply chain segmentation is one of these key enablers. Other enablers are cross organizational collaboration, customer-centricity, visibility, process innovation, and risk management

Segmentation is Impacting the Company's Bottom Line

Any manufacturer or retailer knows, no two customers are the same. Each customer's perception of the value of a product or service and how much they are willing to pay for it is different. This is true for almost every product category available in the market from cars to snack bars.

That said, many retail and manufacturing companies are still using "one size fits all" supply chain processes: over-serving some channel/product combinations and under-serving others. For example, research into one industry showed that around 50% of a company's customer and product portfolio was unprofitable, which would require a different supply chain response to reduce cost.

Through in-depth understanding of the profit profiles of their customers, channels, and/or products, companies can tailor a more profitable supply chain strategy to each of them and thus increase the overall margin of their portfolios. It can also increase inventory turnover through optimal inventory positioning and aligning fulfillment, logistics, demand planning, manufacturing, and procurement strategies. For example, an apparel retailer can satisfy the demand for their basic products through an efficient (less costly) supply chain model and deliver their fashion products through a highly responsive supply chain model. This creates one model for standard (predictable) products and another for fashion (unpredictable) products. Each model will have different demand planning, stocking, and fulfillment policies.

In addition, supply chain segmentation would improve customer service, which would improve sales by increasing the reliability of delivering on promises and improving forecast accuracy.

FRAMEWORK FOR SUPPLY CHAIN SEGMENTATION TRANSFORMATION

Figure 1. Supply chain digital segmentation transformation framework

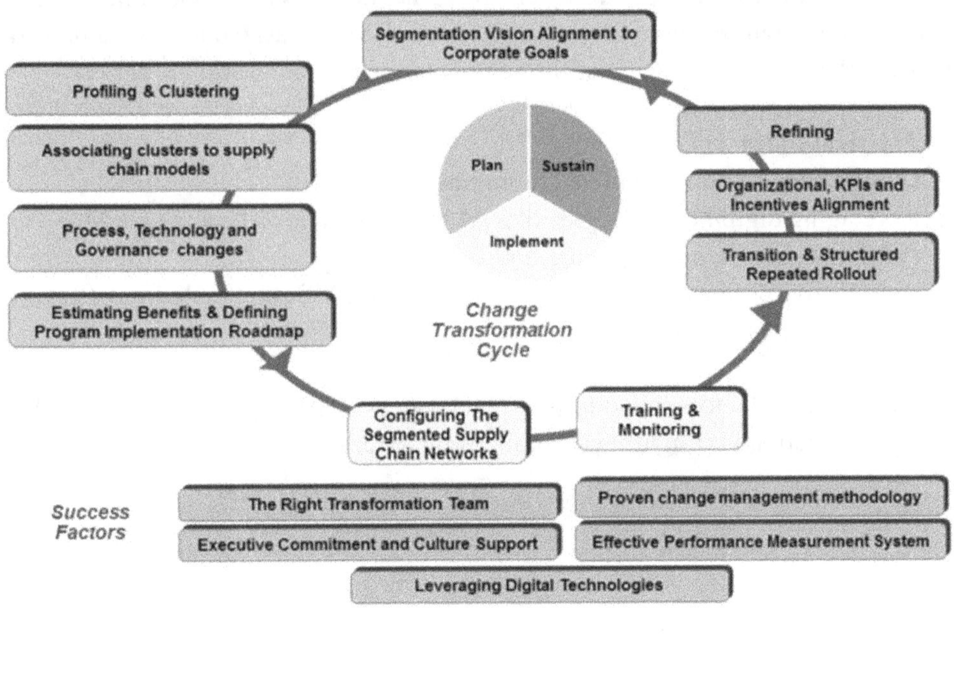

The recipe for success in managing the journey of supply chain (SC) digital segmentation transformation is mastering the change transformation cycle, leveraging digital technologies, and ensuring effective change management. Figure 1 introduces a practical and comprehensive SC segmentation transformation framework to help with implementation. This figure shows the 10-step transformation journey which typically lasts two to three years and consists of three phases: "plan" (five blue steps), "implement" (two yellow steps), and "sustain" (three green steps).

Planning starts by defining the vision and objectives and aligning them to corporate goals and needs. This is followed by profiling and clustering. Process analysis and associating clusters to supply chain models is next followed by identifying the changes in process, technology, and people required to support the new supply chain models and the new end state. The final step of the planning phase is building the business case (estimating benefits and costs) and defining the program implementation roadmap.

The "implement" phase starts by configuring the segmented supply chain networks and is followed by conducting training on the new processes and monitoring progress and adoption.

The "sustain" phase consists of three steps starting with transition and structured repeated rollout. This is followed by ensuring organizational, metrics, and incentives alignment and concluded by the "refining" step. The next planned transformation cycle can kick in after months of refining, corrective actions, and incremental improvement of the first cycle. Supply chain segmentation is not a one-time exercise or sprint; it is a journey. Five success factors are also emphasized in this framework to ensure the required support for the segmentation transformation program:

1. The right transformation teams
2. Culture support and executive commitment
3. Leveraging digital technologies like AI which includes ML and GenAI
4. Proven change management methodology
5. An effective performance measurement system (PMS) that includes data availability, metrics, and KPIs

These success factors, in addition to the discussed 10 steps, will be detailed in the coming section highlighting several best practices.

The 10-Step Supply Chain Digital Segmentation Framework

Step 1) Segmentation Vision Alignment to Corporate Goals

This step helps in establishing clearly how the supply chain segmentation transformation program is a crucial strategy to achieving corporate goals. It includes developing the vision and objectives of the segmentation transformation initiative.

The key to supply chain segmentation is finding the right balance between agility and efficiency (lean) for each product/customer/channel combination. A one-size-fits-all strategy will not allow a company to compete on a global scale in today's business. Segmentation allows companies to get the right product/service with the right value to the right customer from the right distribution center while optimizing the supply chain. Once the linkage is established and transformation program objectives are defined, communicating this to upper management and all stakeholders is important.

Step 2) Profiling and Clustering

This step determines segmentation criteria, profiling, identifying customer value propositions, and clustering.

Segmentation Criteria

Companies need to determine the segmentation criteria that will fit their needs. The author would argue against a pre-defined segmentation criteria based on general literature or a specific case study. Existing literature and case studies are an excellent starting point, but they should not be the ultimate reference. Comprehensive segmentation criteria are presented in Figure 2 under each of the segmentation dimensions. Selected criteria were underlined to highlight examples that will be detailed later in this chapter.

Figure 2. Segmentation criteria and related profiling list

AREA	Profiling
Product Characteristics	❖Product Lifecycle Stage ❖Shelf Life ❖**Functional or innovative** ❖Handling characteristics ❖Product value density ❖Supply Lead Time ❖Product Variety
Customer Characteristics	❖**Demand volume** ❖**Margin** ❖**Demand variability** ❖Large vs. Small ❖buying behavior ❖Customer Lead Time ❖Strategic Importance ❖SLAs
Channels	❖Online ❖Retailers ❖Warehouses ❖**End Consumers (B2C)** ❖**Businesses (B2B)** ❖Geography
Customer Value Proposition	❖Brand name ❖**Lead Time** ❖**Cost** ❖**Availability** ❖**Flexibility** ❖**Delivery Performance (DP)** ❖After-sales service

Profiling

Once the segmentation criteria are determined, the company needs to document a portfolio of products, customers, channels, and related profiles based on detailed analysis. This analysis is typically more extensive than the analysis most companies would have carried out previously because in this step they are trying to predict the market conditions and customer (consumer or B2B customer) behavior that will prevail in the next three to five years, rather than examining how best to compete in the present time. Such forward-looking thinking requires extensive customer research and detailed marketing analysis. The aim is to understand the company's average customer and get a solid appreciation for each existing and potential customer type. It is not just customer profiling, it is product/customer/channel profiling.

Customer Value Proposition

Companies need to identify the customer value proposition by conducting customer satisfaction surveys, and using business intelligence, market analysis reports, etc. This can also be accomplished by identifying the complexities that are present and identifying whether they are good complexities or bad complexities. Good complexities are those that improve the product or service and, most importantly, customers are willing to pay for it. Bad complexities add no value and come at a price lie increased inventory or expediting.

Figure 2 provides a list of seven typical customer value propositions listed below:

1. Brand name
2. Lead time or speed
3. Cost (price)
4. Availability
5. Flexibility
6. Delivery performance (DP)
7. After-sales service

The company can select from the list based on the previously discussed analysis. GenAI technology can be leveraged in this step as it will be discussed later.

Clustering

The key for most companies who are interested in segmentation is to identify and better align to the natural tradeoffs that exist within their business. A simple but effective way to model this is by identifying the key customer value propositions that the customers apply to the company's business offering. These value propositions have natural trade-offs between them that allow the company to develop a differentiated supply chain response.

In this activity, companies need to identify sets of clusters that best represent their business profiles and value propositions. Figure 3 provides a hypothetical example of profiling and clustering. In this example a company selected "Functional vs. Innovative" as a profile parameter for the product characteristics segmentation dimension. "Demand volume," "margin," and "demand variability" were selected under the customer characteristics dimension. In addition, B2B and B2C are the selected channels, and four customer value propositions (lead time, cost, flexibility, and delivery performance) are considered.

The next activity is to determine the clusters that best represent the selected profile parameters and value propositions. It is recommended to think big when creating this initial version and create clusters for as many profiles as possible that are relevant to the company. However, once the profile types are exhausted, it is critical to reduce them to the key few and bear in mind that each cluster probably represents a new supply chain design (model).

In the example in Figure 3, Cluster 1 represents innovative products and customers with low volume, high margin, and high demand variability (i.e., low forecast accuracy). Furthermore, this cluster represents B2C channel only. The value proposition for this cluster is reduced lead time (fast delivery), high degree of flexibility, and high delivery performance (on-time delivery). Cost is not a decision-making factor as shown in the figure.

Figure 3. Profiling and clustering approach with a retail example

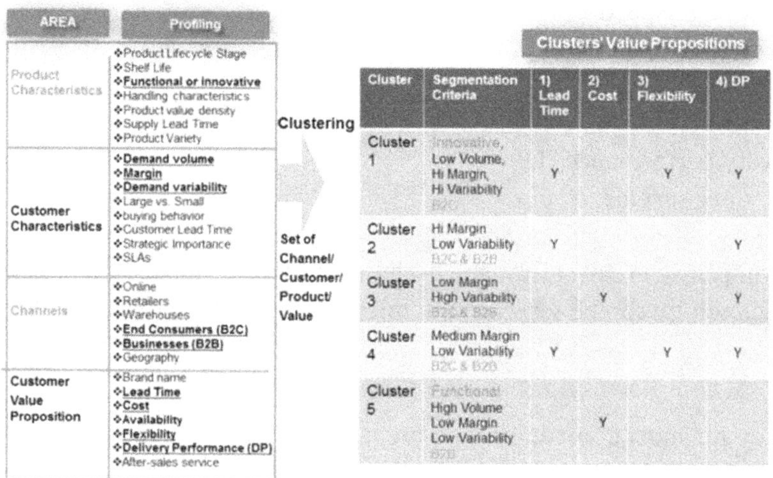

During this activity, it is often recommended to conduct a cost-to-serve analysis. The objective of this exercise is to understand which customer/product/channel combinations are winners and losers and then to structure the clusters so that some or all the losers are turned into winners. For example, a large consumer goods company, with a significant portion of business coming from major retailor, would likely have an assigned team and a set of strategies dedicated to that account. The high value of the major retailer business warrants this level of premium service. However, the cost-benefit ratio (cost to serve) would not be positive if the same strategy is applied to every mom-and-pop store that also buys the same products. The company would need a different supply chain design for those customers.

In another example, the cost to serve a customer in the US for a US company will be different than the cost to serve a customer overseas. Estimating the cost to serve across extended supply chains requires visibility into many cost data elements. These can be enabled by the digital technologies that are one of the key success factors for supply chain segmentation that will be discussed. This may require changing the replenishment model and service-level agreements for a specific customer/product combination. The author worked with a tire manufacturer to adjust its replenishment model to store products for customers (like cluster 1) in the centralized and factory distribution centers (DCs) instead of storing it closer to customers in regional DCs. This moves the inventory buffer point upstream in the supply chain, reducing overall inventory. The upstream DCs hold a larger pool of inventory, increasing the odds that downstream demand will be filled with the required product.

Step 3) Associating Clusters With Supply Chain Models

When the clusters have been finalized, the next step is to decide what needs to be done to deliver each of them top value. It is time to design the supply chain models and Step 3 is conducting process analysis and associating clusters to supply chain designs (models). The supply chain models will be driven by the unique value propositions of the clusters from the previous step. It is important to remember that the number of supply chain designs (models) should be manageable. Most literature reviews suggest two or four models. The author typically recommends the number to be based on the business requirements and the company's capabilities in managing different supply chain models.

In Figure 4, five supply chain models are selected against five clusters. Column 3 covers the value propositions which put emphasis on lead time (responsiveness), cost, flexibility, and delivery performance (reliability). Let's assume that the key processes for supply chain management are supply planning, demand planning, procurement, and order fulfillment. For every key process, key strategies will be implemented to support certain value propositions.

For example, for Cluster 1, under supply planning, postponement (keeping inventory upstream in factories or central DCs) and flexible capacity strategies are selected since one emphasis (customer value proposition) of this cluster is flexibility. In this highly innovative, product-driven, and highly variable environment with a "premium" type of customer, a "postponement" manufacturing strategy is required. Under order fulfillment, air is selected as the main transportation mode since the other emphasis is on lead time reduction. The customer is given the benefit of choice, and a fast and more flexible-focused supply chain is required to fulfill their requirements. In addition, working closer with customers when generating the forecast is a best practice strategy to control demand variability.

A multi-sourcing procurement strategy will be needed to provide flexibility in case of supply shortages for nonproprietary parts. Also, capacity contracts with key suppliers will need to have flexibility built in and delivery routes will need to be more agile and faster. As a result, the lower volumes of these innovative products will command higher prices due to higher cost and differentiated service. This should not be a customer barrier since this supply chain is designed around the customers who are willing to pay for it.

Cluster 5 targets purely cost-driven customers. The route to address "lowest-cost" emphasis is often an efficient supply chain. This supply chain uses "lean" concepts to streamline and eliminate waste from the process, implements a build to stock manufacturing supply strategy since demand variability is low for this cluster, and positions inventory closer to the customers due to high volume. In addition, advanced planning like forecasting enables high forecast accuracy which allows things to be booked much in advance and for suppliers and logistics companies to plan for optimization. Offshore manufacturing capacity and slower, cheaper routes — such as ocean — can also be used, allowing the company to reduce costs and provide the best price for the customer in this cluster.

By working with various clusters — combinations of customer types, channels, products, and value propositions — to identify their requirements and tailor their supply chain, companies can optimize their capabilities and improve the bottom line.

Figure 4. Associating clusters to supply chain models approach with an example

			Supply Chain Processes' Key Strategies			
Cluster	Supply Chain	Value Propositions	Supply Planning	Demand Planning	Procurement	Order Fulfillment
Cluster 1	Supply Chain (SC)A	1, 3, 4	• Postponement • Six Sigma to control variability • Flexible Capacity	• Customer Collaboration	• Multi Source	• Air
Cluster 2	Supply Chain B	1, 4	• Build to Stock • Stored in Regional DC	• Demand Shaping	• Buffer stock • VMI	• Cross Docks
Cluster 3	Supply Chain C	2, 4	• Build to Order • Direct Ship	• What if Analysis	• Flexible Contracts	• FTL for B2B
Cluster 4	Supply Chain D	1, 3, 4	• Stored in Centralized Warehouse • Near shore capacity	• POS Forecasting	• Bulk buys • FTL for inbound material	• Expedites
Cluster 5	Supply Chain E	2	• Inventory stored closer to customers • Lean for streamlining • offshore capacity • Build to stock	• Statistical forecasting with exception driven adjustments	• Blanket PO with locked annual QTY	• Ocean & Rail with no expedites

SC A = Responsive & Flexible Supply Chain
SC B = Responsive Supply Chain
SC C = Efficient & Reliable Supply Chain
SC D = Efficient & Flexible Supply Chain
SC E = Efficient Supply Chain

Step 4) Identifying Process, Technology and Governance Changes

The segmented supply chain strategy requires process, technology, and governance changes to demand planning, supply planning, procurement, and order fulfillment processes. In doing so, even though physical supply chain resources could remain the same, the supply chain response operates differently from one supply chain model to another and from one cluster (segment) to another.

It is important to complete a detailed, future state process map after supply chain models are approved by key stakeholders. A value stream mapping method can be leveraged to understand the cost drivers and come up with a more granular design of the future state. It is crucial to capture process, technology, and governance (organizational structure, metrics, and policies) changes and capabilities for every supply chain process that enables implementing the proposed strategies for every supply chain model in the previous step.

Companies have long struggled to deploy segmented supply chains because underlying decision support (planning) technologies have not been readily available for end-to-end supply chains. This has changed recently, which will make it easier for companies to go through the segmentation journey.

To summarize, the segmented supply chain strategy requires process, technology, and governance changes to demand planning, supply planning, procurement, and order fulfillment processes. In doing so, even though physical supply chain resources could remain the same, supply chain response operates differently from one supply chain model to another and from one cluster (segment) to another.

Figure 5 reflects an example from a real manufacturer. These are the changes that were required to support a supply chain design like Supply Chain A from Figure 4 (Responsive & Flexible Supply Chain).

Under demand planning, the manufacturer needed to implement a customer collaboration strategy which would require a process change of modifying the forecasting process to include the customer input, a technology change to enable a collaboration workbench leveraging digital technologies, and two people-related changes. The first people-related change was an organizational structure fine tuning which formed a decentralized Demand Planning Group to be closer to the customer and corresponding salesperson. The second people-related change was adding customer forecast accuracy to the set of existing metrics to establish accountability to the customer forecast.

The manufacturing company can no longer forecast demand based on past sales history alone. The segmented strategy will require market intelligence on similar products and markets along with close collaboration with marketing and sales personnel to get customers' input. The cluster (product/customer/channel) under this supply chain design (model) would need to be tracked differently to monitor market acceptance and utilize more frequent feedback cycles relative to other clusters in the company's portfolio.

Figure 5. Example for identifying process, technology and governance changes

Key Process, Technologies and Governance Changes for Supply Chain A

	Supply Planning	Demand Planning	Procurement	Order Fulfillment
Process	• Profiling Customer Lead Time • Demand prioritization	• Modifying the forecasting process to include the customer input	• Establishing a process and criteria to split the sourcing demand by the vendors	• Establishing a process for allocation
Technology	• Implementing Inventory Optimization Tool	• Enabling a collaboration workbench	• Enhancing the supplier portal to provide real time visibility for in-transit inbound material	• Supporting different modes of transportation • Enabling order promising based on allocation
Governance	• Establishing Center of excellence to supervise 6 Sigma initiatives	• Decentralized Demand Planning Group • Adding customer forecast accuracy to the set of existing metrics	• Adding supplier flexibility metric to the supplier scorecard	• Establishing a long term agreement with UPS and DHL

Under the supply planning process, demand prioritization needed to be adjusted to increase the planning priority associated with this cluster since margin was high and supply lead time was a competitive differentiator (customer value proposition). Profiling the expected lead time by customers is important to decide if a replenishment postponement strategy (such as build-to-forecast to a semi-finished stage and assemble-to-order thereafter) could be enabled for this cluster.

Under order fulfillment, a substantial emphasis was put on allocation planning and order promising sub processes. As the company strove for margin growth, finished goods supply needed to be allocated more heavily toward this cluster. The company needed to adjust its allocation policies. Additionally, higher service levels for this supply chain model required faster replenishment. This often meant smaller, more frequent shipments which raised transportation costs. Careful planning of shipments associated with this cluster, including load consolidation, mode selection, routing, and carrier selection, could significantly reduce transportation costs while ensuring high service levels. Establishing a long-term agreement with carriers was recommended to handle expedited high-value products effectively in this cluster.

Finally, under the procurement process, establishing a process and criteria to split the sourcing demand by vendors was necessary to provide flexibility and address the risk of shortage in raw material and components. Investment in technology to provide real time visibility for in-transit inbound material was required to reduce lead time variability and enable the company to react faster to delays.

Segmentation-based supply chain processes have helped this manufacturer balance value to the business against service levels required to support corporate goals for their strategic products (Cluster 1).

Step 5) Estimating Benefits and Defining the Roadmap

Cost-to-Serve Analysis

The first activity of this step is to validate "cost-to-serve" analysis against the new supply chain designs. "Cost-to-Serve" analysis is very similar to Activity Based Costing (ABC). However, it must be much more granular because in virtual supply chain there will be shared assets that necessitate allocating costs differently since each virtual supply chain (supply chain design) must be managed differently. Various resources such as power, overheads, equipment, and technology costs, must be allocated differently for each line according to usage. For example, premium freight service is used heavily for the Responsive & Flexible Supply Chain model, which requires speed in delivery (short lead time) but not used the Efficient Supply Chain. Therefore, no premium freight cost should be allocated to the Efficient Supply Chain. Currently, many companies assign all these resources to one area labeled as "overheads," but to execute the supply chain segmentation strategy effectively, they need to be separated. They also need to be analyzed more granularly to accurately estimate cost and price profitability. Based on the author's experience, getting finance involved early on during this step is crucial.

Capturing the Expected Benefits

The next activity is to estimate the benefits for every supply chain model and highlight the impact on key performance indicators' (KPIs) targets. During this phase, there is a need to: 1) identify the critical supply chain KPIs to grow the business and improve profitability, 2) capture an accurate baseline for each of these KPIs, and 3) explain how the new/updated supply chain models will impact the KPIs — positively (green color), negatively (red), or neutral (empty box) as shown in Figure 6. For example, supply chain A will get a hit from supply chain cost perspective due to the use of Air as the main transportation mode, but this strategy will improve other KPIs like order cycle time.

It is important to mention that KPIs should be the same (applicable) for all supply chain designs; it is only the targets that change. Once these KPIs (such as SCM cost, cycle time, etc.) are established, average targets across all supply chain designs must also be agreed on. These targets can be internal-based, industry-based, or competition-based. Then KPIs targets are defined for each supply chain design based on strategies that are being implemented with a goal of achieving the average targets across all of the supply chain designs. For example, the target for "Order Cycle Time" for an Efficient & Reliable Supply Chain will be lower than the average target while it is higher in Responsive Supply Chain. On the other hand, Responsive

Supply Chain is higher than the average target when it comes to supply chain cost KPI. To reiterate: positively impacting one KPI might inversely affect others.

Figure 6. Different supply chain models impact KPI targets differently

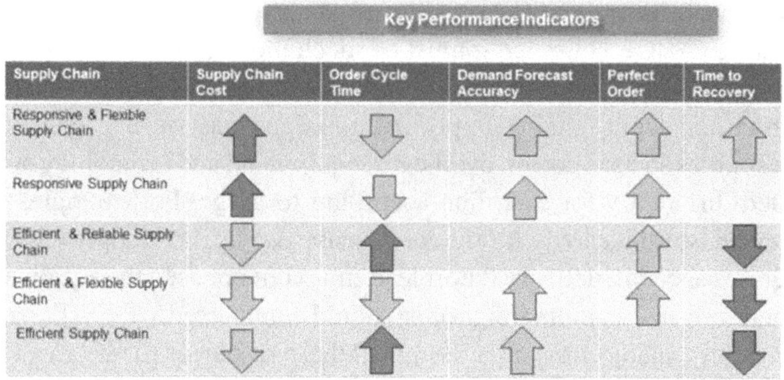

Building the Business Case

The next activity is to build the business case and significant ROI (benefits – costs) for executives to secure their buy-in on pursuing the supply chain segmentation journey.

To be able to conduct this activity successfully, the defined KPIs (as in Figure 6) should be aligned to corporate goals like increased margin, cost reduction, improvement in customer service, etc.

Building the Roadmap

The final phase of this step is to build the roadmap for the transformation program which should be broken into multiple phases (projects) with definitive outcomes for each to ensure manageable change. The idea here is to "think big," "start small," "act quick," and "win fast." No matter what your situation is, the journey to supply chain digital segmentation success is a radical ongoing overhaul of culture, process, organizational structures, technology, measurement framework, and operating models.

Senior management must approach supply chain digital segmentation as more than a single project. It must be approached as a transformation program and must become the new way of doing business.

Step 6) Configuring the Segmented Supply Chain Network

This step is the starting point for execution and implementing the supply chain digital segmentation strategy ("Implement Change" phase). It includes conducting detailed design and new process/technology deployment. As a leading practice, it is recommended to use several pilots and implementation waves to "turn on" capabilities and strategies piece by piece to reduce risk and allow enough time for stakeholders to adopt the change. Advanced supply chain planning software applications should be in place as a prerequisite to support different virtual supply chains from a planning perspective. It is important to note that although a technology investment is not necessarily a requirement for supply chain segmentation, inadequate technology frequently surfaces as a concern in the segmentation process. Also, leveraging digital technologies will make segmentation much easier and scalable.

While a company's physical supply chain assets — raw materials, factory resources, warehouses, distribution centers, retail centers, and channels — are typically the same across all supply chain designs (models), its processes and governance (organizational structure, metrics, and policies) for predicting customer demand, positioning supply, procurement, and fulfilling orders can be different. In executing these differentiated processes and enforcing governance, supply chain professionals help drive competitive advantage and profitable growth across all clusters.

After configuration is complete, a formal readiness assessment to "go live" with the new supply segmentation networks should be conducted.

It is important to reiterate that the transformation program should be broken into multiple stages with definitive outcomes for each to implement manageable change and achieve quick wins. One example would be that a company might decide to enable two supply chain models in the first stage (which might take a year) and leave the last three to the second stage. Another example is to stack the stages based on the supply chain processes like implementing the process, technology, and governances for the demand planning process in the first stage, followed by supply planning in the second stage, etc. This depends on the maturity of these processes and the size of changes. A third example would be to divide the process, technology, and governance changes into three groups: 1) "crawl," 2) "walk," and 3) "run" and then stack the stages to implement "crawl" changes first, followed by "walk" and implement the remaining changes in the third stage. Some of the stages can overlap from a timing perspective and a coordinated timeline that highlights critical stop-gate dependencies can improve the efficiency of managing these initiatives (stages).

Step 7) Training and Monitoring

A structured and comprehensive education plan — starting with the transformation team and end users and ending with engaging key stakeholders and leaders — should be developed early and executed effectively as changes move through the organization. The plan should cover planning, implementing, and sustaining the segmentation transformation. This step is critical to ensure the effectiveness of the execution.

Additionally, the education plan for end users should be tailored based on which segment they work on. For example, enabling "efficient supply chain" model requires strong knowledge in lean principles.

Monitoring is another phase of this step to ensure employee adoption to the new process of the segmented supply chain. It is important to proactively monitor the experience of the employees, suppliers, and customers to identify performance issues and provide additional training when needed to sustain positive behavior by all stakeholders, including supply chain leaders, managers, and planners.

Step 8) Transition and Structured Repeated Rollout

This step is the starting point for sustaining the new state of doing business ("Sustain Change" phase). During this step, the transformation team typically transitions to a different team (business team) to take over the transformation initiative. The transformation team is responsible for planning and implementing the process, technology, and governance changes needed to support segmented supply chain strategy. The business teams (demand planning, supply planning, procurement, and order fulfillment teams), with the help of IT customer support, would take over to lead this step and the next two steps of making the changes part of running the business environment.

During this step, a repeated rollout to other business units might occur based on the previously predefined roadmap for the segmentation transformation. Segmentation must be a living thing, with the ability to assign new products easily to existing clusters and eventually to existing supply chain designs (models).

Step 9) Organizational Structure, KPIs, and Incentives Alignments

Organizational Realignment

The first activity of this step is to ensure that organizational alignment (part of the governance changes defined earlier) is happening. The human resources department might need to update job descriptions and bonus structure to reflect the changes. This might require creating a pipeline of candidates for hiring with a mix of demand, supply and product expertise. Also, incentives for the company's talent should be aligned with the skill requirements for the new process.

Incentive Alignment

The second activity is to ensure that the KPIs and incentives are aligned so each supply chain model can drive the right business decisions and behavior effectively. This requires a clear set of goals (targets for the KPIs) and incentives to be defined earlier during Step 5. Incentives, including bonuses, should always be based on the KPIs; getting the KPIs right allows the incentives to be altered to match, which will in turn stimulate behavioral change where it is required. For example, if salespeople are to provide input in the forecasting process, they will need an incentive (such as a 20% percentage of their bonus) to ensure that this is done in a way to which the supply chain organization can respond accordingly (i.e., no overestimating or underestimating). Equally, in terms of supply, the procurement team must be incentivized to work in line with the supply chain strategy like total landed cost rather than simply focusing on lowest-cost scenarios.

Cost and Benefits Data Gathering

During Step 2, cost allocation is determined for every supply chain model. This is needed to break down the shared overhead charges that have traditionally been spread equally across all products. This is important to validate the cost to serve analysis and to estimate the cost and saving of a certain supply chain model. During this step (Step 9), the actual costs are captured and should be compared with the previous estimate. Also, the actual benefits would start to be realized and the expected business case (ROI) can be confirmed in this step.

Step 10) Refining

Fine-tuning profiles, clusters, and cost allocations are necessary as products move through their life cycles and demand shifts. Technology can be leveraged to move a product/customer/channel combination automatically from one cluster to another as the underlying attributes change. Revisiting and adjusting KPIs targets are also needed to ensure a continuous improvement culture. A cross-functional governance monthly review cadence should exist, such as a monthly meeting like Sales and Operational Planning (S&OP) review. This will also allow the company to continually align with customer value.

The transformation journey is ongoing and not a one-time exercise; it is a multiyear journey which requires multiple cycles. Each cycle might take between two and five years. Refining is the last step in the cycle during which incremental improvements and fine tuning are done. Once the success criteria, expected benefits, and KPIs targets are achieved, a new transformation cycle should be considered. This is when the company goes from Step 10 back to Step 1 to repeat the cycle to achieve additional improvements and benefits. Changes to the business model and new opportunities such as an emerging market should also trigger another transformation cycle.

The Five Success Factors for Supply Chain Segmentation

There are five key success factors required to ensure the successful implementation of supply chain segmentation as shown earlier in Figure 1.

Success Factor #1: Having the Right Transformation Team

Having the right transformation team is crucial for the supply chain segmentation journey. Special skills should be considered in selecting the transformation team such as process design and automation, lean principles knowledge, Six Sigma expertise, data analytics, systems optimization, program management, organizational influence, and communication.

Success Factor #2: Executive Commitment and Culture Support

Supply Chain segmentation is not just a business initiative, it is a change to the culture. Executive commitment and visible support are key to success. For example, executives need to enforce the culture of customer-driven and differentiation, the culture of promising what you can deliver and delivering on every promise, the culture of commitment to continuous improvement as a way of life for the organization, and the culture of praising and promoting the managers who avoid fires (being proactive) vs. promoting the fire fighters (being reactive).

Establishing a clear segmentation vision strategy enabled by digital technologies is so fundamental to a firm's future success that the CEO must inspire employees to pursue a vision of the company. However, many CEOs feel that segmentation is somewhat beyond their grasp. The CEO must step up and collaborate with the CMO, COO and CIO to jointly create a vision that the CEO can sponsor.

Establish "a differentiated supply chain response" culture, collaboration, agility, and digital innovation are second nature to employees in today's businesses. Therefore, its crucial fuel the differentiated response mindset by educating, training, and inspiring employees with roadshows and education programs,

Success Factor #3: Leveraging Digital Technologies

Technology management teams must play a pivotal role in enabling digital transformation for supply chain segmentation. CIOs must champion a business technology agenda — investments in digital technologies to define separate segments, capture KPIs, conduct cost-to-serve analysis, and collaborate with sales leveraging social media and research data to find out the value propositions for customers to win, serve, and retain them.

Let's give one use case as an example. Customers' perceptions of the value of a product or service and how much they are willing to pay for it is difficult to predict. On one end of the extreme, you have value-conscious customers who are always looking for a deal. On the other end, you have customers that will only buy premium goods and services. The other issue is that customers' behaviors and expectation change. Therefore, many firms struggle to segment their customers and markets intelligently and provide tailored products and services to those segments on an ongoing basis. Using digital technologies like GenAI and ML can be leveraged to analyze customers by collecting data from thousands or even millions of customers. Mining the collected data and combining it with external data like social media will help to keep pace with the analysis required to always identify new correlations. This will help in identifying the segmentation criteria and making it dynamic.

Also, ML will enable firms to support different supply chain strategies/responses for each segment like higher visibility, simplifications, etc. ML can support creating intelligent customer-product-channel segments and then developing supply chain strategies to deliver differentiated offerings to these segments (all while balancing the cost to serve each segment against the value that segment brings to the business).

On the other hand, GenAI can simulate future scenarios, considering unexpected events such as market disruptions or supply chain shocks, thus providing a more comprehensive predictive framework. It can offer personalized, context-aware recommendations for different segments, considering unique characteristics and needs, thus enhancing the precision and effectiveness of segmentation strategies.

Success Factor #4: Proven Change Management Methodology

Having a structured and proven methodology to show the way in the change transformation journey is a must. Any supply chain transformation program creates uncertainty and resistance. New leaders emerge, job descriptions are changed, and new skills and capabilities need to be developed. Dealing with these change management issues on a reactive, case-by-case basis puts timeline, morale, and results all at risk. A structured plan for managing change — beginning with the transformation team and then engaging key stakeholders and leaders — should be developed early and executed effectively as changes move through the organization. The plan should be comprehensive to cover planning, implementing, and sustaining the transformation changes.

For transformation programs to work, there must be convergence between the new process, new technology capabilities, people readiness with the required new skills, and organization structure alignment changes.

Success Factor #5: Effective Performance Measurement System (PMS) — Data, Metrics and KPIs

Comprehensive end-to-end measures of supply chain performance, such as total cost, inventory, forecast accuracy, and perfect order, must be established to show the trade-offs required. Supply chain performance results should be communicated to all layers. Operational and financial data will be needed at both aggregated and granular levels to analyze performance and conduct corrective actions.

The author has not come across many firms that could claim that they have mastered performance measurement across all their processes and levels. The widespread feeling among supply chain managers is that they measure too much, too little, or measure the wrong metrics. For the supply chain segmentation strategy to work, the culture of measurement should be anchored within the organization while leveraging some leading practices such as: 1) focus on a handful of key KPIs and related metrics, 2) sustain KPI tracking, 3) conduct root cause analysis on a regular basis, and 4) align incentives to achieving KPIs targets. Finally, the list of the KPIs should be comprehensive enough to include related KPIs necessary to measure achieving the customer value propositions such as delivery performance and flexibility (Sabri, 2012).

In addition, data availability/accessibility is very important. It is considered a prerequisite for supply chain segmentation because visibility to data such as customer requirements, demand, cost, materials, forecasts, product lifecycle, revenue, and margin is required to drive the right decisions regarding segmentation during planning and implementing phases.

FUTURE TRENDS

The author predicts the explosion of supply chain digital segmentation strategy implementation in the next few years. As companies redefine supply chain processes that span across suppliers and customers, there will be a need for segmentation that will result in a significant improvement in efficiency and help them achieve competitive advantage. Companies that do not come on board will realize soon that they are losing ground and customers.

The trend of mergers and acquisitions will continue to rise, and the complexity of supply chains will increase. This will intensify the need for supply chain segmentation to streamline the process of collaboration between different entities and satisfy the value propositions for customers.

The widespread use of supply chain digital segmentation strategy will lead to new options for improving business-to-business and business-to-consumer collaborations, in addition to supply chain performance, monitoring, and controlling. Intelligent performance measurement systems that can capture negative performance trends and select the correct resolutions are expected to come into widespread use in the next few years.

Segmentation criteria will be able to use structured and unstructured data (SNEW — social, news, events, and weather) and process large amounts of data. Leveraging GenAI/ML would be possible to create the segments dynamically in an automated fashion. The synergy between GenAI and ML creates a powerful combination that enhances supply chain segmentation by providing deeper insights, greater flexibility, and more innovative solutions, enabling companies to navigate the complexities of the modern business landscape effectively.

CONCLUSION

Segmentation is gaining ground in manufacturing as well as in retail and the questions around it have evolved from "what is it?" to "how can we do it?" Supply chain digital segmentation is not a one-time exercise; it is a multi-quarter journey, but it does get easier after your first venture through the 10 steps discussed as part of the proposed segmentation framework. Also, structured assessment of the five success factors should be executed early on. Segmentation must be living and ongoing, with the ability to repeat the exercise. Segmentation is a continuous journey to keep your supply chain(s) relevant to your customer(s).

Supply chain digital segmentation is not just a business initiative; it's a change in the organization's culture. Therefore, executive commitment and visible support is mandatory for success.

Technology is definitely needed for the implementation since segmentation often uncovers issues and gaps with current tools. Leveraging digital technology such as GenAI and ML makes the supply chain segmentation journey smoother and more effective. In absence of the right decision-support tools, segmentation strategies will not yield the expected benefits.

Supply chain digital segmentation strategy presents huge opportunities that are already being tapped by a few companies and supply chains who achieved significant benefits. Implementing supply chain digital segmentation strategy is key to gain competitive advantage, streamline processes, reduce waste, and eventually achieve business agility, which is significantly needed in the new age of globalization and intensive competition. The full list of the benefits is:

1. **Improved Efficiency:** By segmenting the supply chain, companies can optimize inventory levels, reduce lead times, and enhance overall operational efficiency.
2. **Cost Reduction:** Segmentation helps in identifying and eliminating inefficiencies, leading to significant cost savings in areas such as inventory management, transportation, and warehousing.
3. **Enhanced Customer Satisfaction:** Tailoring supply chain strategies to specific customer segments ensures that products are available when and where they are needed, improving on-time delivery rates and customer satisfaction.
4. **Increased Agility:** Segmentation allows companies to respond more quickly to market changes and customer demands, providing the flexibility needed to navigate the complexities of the modern business landscape.
5. **Better Collaboration:** Improved segmentation facilitates better collaboration between different entities in the supply chain, leading to more effective communication and coordination.
6. **Data-Driven Decision Making:** Leveraging advanced analytics and machine learning in segmentation provides deeper insights into supply chain performance, enabling more informed and strategic decision-making.
7. **Competitive Advantage:** Companies that effectively implement supply chain digital segmentation can achieve a competitive edge by being more responsive, efficient, and customer-focused.
8. **Sustainability:** Optimized supply chain processes contribute to sustainability efforts by reducing waste and improving resource utilization.

Disclaimer: The views reflected in this article are the views of the author(s) and do not necessarily reflect the views of Ernst & Young LLP or other members of the global EY organization.

REFERENCES

Christopher, M., Peck, H., & Towill, D. (2006). A Taxonomy for Selecting Global Supply Chain Strategies. *International Journal of Logistics Management*, 17(2), 277–287.

Christopher, M., Towill, D., Aitken, J., & Childerhouse, P. (2009). Value Chain Classification. *Journal of Manufacturing Technology Management*, 20(4), 460–474.

Fisher, M. L. (1997). What Is the Right Supply Chain for Your Product? *Harvard Business Review*, (March–April), 105–116.

Gattorna, J. (2006). *Living Supply Chains*. Pearson.

Lovell, A., Saw, R., & Stimson, J. (2005). Product Value-Density: Managing Diversity Through Supply Chain Segmentation. *International Journal of Logistics Management*, 16(1), 142–158.

Mason-Jones, R., Naylor, B., & Towill, D. (2000). Engineering the Leagile Supply Chain. *International Journal of Agile Management*, 2(1), 54–61.

Naylor, J., Naim, M., & Berry, D. (1999). Leagility: Integrating the Lean and Agile Manufacturing Paradigms in the Total Supply Chain. *International Journal of Production Economics*, 62(1–2), 107–118.

Roscoe, S., & Baker, P. (2013). Supply chain segmentation in the sporting goods industry. *International Journal of Logistics Research and Applications*, 17(2), 136–155.

Sabri, E. (2012). "Enduring Transformation: Performance measurement and governance make the difference," retrieved from https://www.apics.org/apics-for-individuals/apics-magazine-home/magazine-detail-page/2012/10/04/enduring-transformation, *APICS Magazine*.

Sabri, E. (2019). Transformation Framework for Supply Chain Segmentation in Digital Business. In *E. Sabri, Technology Optimization and Change Management for Successful Digital Supply Chains* (pp. 54–84). IGI Global.

Sabri, E. (2023). Digital Supply Chain, Disruptive Environments, and the Impact on Retailers. In *E. Sabri, How to Implement Supply Chain Digital Segmentation Successfully* (pp. 63–93). IGI Global.

Chapter 9
Realizing Value From Digital/Gen AI/ML-Driven Supply Chain Planning Transformations

Ehap Sabri
University of Texas at Dallas, USA

ABSTRACT

In today's rapidly evolving business landscape, organizations must embrace digital-driven supply chain planning transformations leveraging GEN AI/ML technologies to maintain their competitive edge. This chapter explores the potential value embedded in these transformations and provides insights into achieving and maximizing this value. It offers a proven, comprehensive performance measurement and value realization framework, illustrated by a case study and two success stories. Firms can leverage this framework to achieve value from their digital transformation efforts.

INTRODUCTION

In today's rapidly evolving business landscape, organizations must embrace digital-driven supply chain planning transformations to maintain their competitive edge. This chapter explores the potential value embedded in these transformations and provides insights into achieving and maximizing this value.

Recognizing the Need for Transformation: The chapter acknowledges the necessity for organizations to transition from traditional to digital-driven supply chain planning processes. While recognizing the need for change is crucial, implementing

DOI: 10.4018/979-8-3693-4433-0.ch009

it poses significant challenges. However, the potential benefits awaiting those who embark on this journey make it a compelling endeavor.

Unraveling the Value of Digital/Gen AI/ML-Driven Transformations: Digital technologies, including artificial intelligence (AI), machine learning (ML), and predictive analytics, bring extensive value to supply chain planning processes. These technologies enhance efficiency, agility, collaboration, and risk mitigation within the supply chain. The benefits can be grouped into the following:

1. **Efficiency Improvement**: Digital transformation optimizes resource utilization, reduces waste, and enhances overall efficiency through accurate demand prediction enabled by AI, ML, and predictive analytics.
2. **Increased Agility and optimization:** Digital supply chains empower organizations to swiftly analyze data, make informed and more accurate decisions, and foster agility in responding to market dynamics.
3. **Enhanced Collaboration**: Digital platforms facilitate real-time collaboration and transparency among supply chain stakeholders, leading to better alignment with market demands.
4. **Risk Mitigation:** Digital supply chains provide in-depth visibility, enabling organizations to identify and mitigate potential risks and disruptions through advanced analytics and preemptive strategies.

Challenges and Overcoming Obstacles: While the benefits of digital-driven supply chain planning are evident, the chapter acknowledges the challenges organizations face in fully realizing this value. Sabri (2023) highlighted that taking the initiative to transform supply chain by leveraging best practices and the latest digital technologies is no longer an option; it is a strategic mandate to stay relevant in the industry. However, the industry's reality is that 70% of all digital-driven supply chain transformation initiatives fail to achieve the expected value. This scary statistic makes firms think twice before moving forward with the transformation journey. These firms typically have questions about the best practices for integrating new digital technologies into supply chain operations. At times, they even postpone their efforts until an expert can address their concerns.

There are four key challenges that firms must overcome by implementing best practice strategies to ensure achieving the expected value.

1. **Data Quality:** Emphasizing the importance of reliable, quality data for effective algorithmic prediction and planning, and offering insights into ensuring data accuracy and consistency.

2. **Skillset Requirements:** Addressing the need for an evolved skillset to manage digitalized supply chain operations, discussing the importance of ongoing staff training and recruitment of new talent.
3. **Change Management:** Recognizing resistance to change as a significant obstacle and advocating for a structured, empathetic approach to change management to foster organizational buy-in and adoption.
4. **Performance Measurement and Value Realization Framework**: Establishing a proven framework to identify the expected value of digital transformation, monitoring it during the implementation, and ensuring its achievement is critical for the program's success.

This chapter delves into the fourth strategy, which is crucial for the success of digital/GenAI/ML supply chain transformation programs. It offers a proven, comprehensive performance measurement and value realization framework, illustrated by a case study and two success stories. Firms can leverage this framework to achieve value from their digital transformation efforts. Additionally, it outlines future research opportunities for academia and experts in this field.

This chapter aims to bridge the gap between theoretical concepts and practical implementation by providing practical insights and real-world examples. It highlights best practices and key lessons learned from leading companies, enabling other organizations to replicate these successes. Furthermore, it addresses common challenges and offers solutions to overcome them, ensuring that businesses can navigate their digital transformation journeys effectively and efficiently.

PERFORMANCE MEASUREMENT AND VALUE REALIZATION FRAMEWORK

Over the years, various performance measurement systems have been designed and studied by academics and consultants, but organizations struggle to leverage such systems effectively. Over a period of time, a disconnect between strategy and metric deployment process is introduced due to changed operational realities. To overcome these issues, a comprehensive framework to maintain alignment between the operational metrics and organizational strategies is proposed in this chapter, enabling organizations to proactively evolve performance management systems and refine operational processes as they grow.

Establishing a robust and proven performance measurement framework is essential for realizing value from digital-driven supply chain planning transformations. Maximizing value from digital-driven supply chain planning transformations requires a systematic approach. Key building blocks include:

1. **Alignment with Business Strategy:** Ensuring digital initiatives are aligned with overall business strategy and objectives. Innovation strategies should be considered during the alignment.
2. **Maturity Benchmarking and Best Practices:** Benchmarking against industry peers and adopting best practices to drive performance improvement and competitive advantage.
3. **Performance Measurement and KPIs Governance:** Defining clear, SMART objectives aligned with overall business goals and establishing comprehensive KPIs to measure progress and success.
4. **Continuous Monitoring and Improvement:** Continuously monitoring KPIs, assessing performance, and identifying areas for improvement using methodologies such as Lean Six Sigma. Fostering a culture of innovation and driving continuous improvement to stay ahead of the competition.

In conclusion, this chapter emphasizes the importance of realizing value from digital-driven supply chain transformations. By establishing a robust performance measurement framework, adopting value realization strategies, and leveraging real-world case studies, organizations can unlock the full potential of their supply chains and achieve sustainable competitive advantage in today's digitalized world. The following sections will cover the four building blocks of the framework in detail.

Alignment with Business Strategy

This section answers two questions: (a) how to align the digital transformation program to the company's strategic objectives and (b) how to maintain the linkage in a steady state.

Balanced Scorecard (BSC)

BSC, introduced by Kaplan and Norton in 1992, has been one of the most widely adopted management tools for describing, communicating, and implementing strategy. BSC retains financial metrics as the ultimate outcome measures for company success, but supplements these with metrics from three additional perspectives: customer, internal process, and learning and growth as the drivers for creating long-term shareholder value (Kaplan, 2010).

BSC has evolved from a tool for translating and communicating strategy into a strategy management framework. It helps define strategy as a collection of 'strategic objectives' and provides a comprehensive measurement framework that links operational performance improvements to customer and financial performance.

Example

Digital-driven supply chain transformation programs can be easily linked to innovative and customer satisfaction strategies like:

- Customer-Centricity: Focusing on delivering value to customers to drive revenue growth and competitive differentiation. Customer-centricity drives market share growth by creating a virtuous cycle of satisfaction, loyalty, and advocacy by continuously aligning products, services, and supply chain strategies with customer needs.
- Agility and Adaptability: Designing supply chain processes and systems with flexibility to quickly respond to market changes. Supply chain processes were designed for normal operations, not for a once-in-a-lifetime disruption. Given the extensive volatility of the industry, as experienced in the past few years by events such as the Suez Canal blockage, the COVID pandemic, semiconductor shortages followed by inflation, and targeted restrictions placed by countries like the US and its allies, how can any organization craft a recovery plan? Firms need to increase their level of agility and adaptability not just for incremental changes but also for strategic changes.

Maintaining the Linkage

When organizations change their business strategies, though not a trivial or frequent activity, the basic premise on which the BSC is designed for the organization changes. A shift or change in strategy obviously calls for a redesign of the BSC so that it remains relevant in the changed context. But how does one accommodate the changing operational realities in the BSC system? As companies gain experience in execution, fine-tune their processes, and use better technologies, the premise on which operational effectiveness and corresponding measures are defined also changes. These changes need to be accounted for in the BSC for it to remain relevant in the changed operational context. Changes in the operational contexts are more frequent but might not be incorporated in the BSC if a formal structure for defining the improved or changed measures does not exist.

Maturity Benchmarking and Best Practices

The aim of supply chain management is to optimize the supply chain and gain a competitive advantage. This is where capability maturity models provide pragmatic guidance by prescribing a road map for advancing or improving business processes. Typically, maturity models have the following components: maturity levels, key process areas (level specific), key practices (level specific), specific goals, and common features. The topmost maturity level always characterizes all managed processes as "deliberate process optimization/ improvement" (Vishwasrao, 2023).

Business processes reflect how an organization operates, while maturity models are a reflection of how organizations evolve. Reiterating a key concept, the primary purpose of the maturity model is to outline the stages of the maturation path. This includes the characteristics of each stage and the logical relationship between them. Typically, a set of measures corresponding to respective stages helps identify the current and desired levels of maturity. While most SC maturity models cover the entire supply chain, others focus on specific areas like Logistics, Sustainability, Efficient Consumer Response, and so on. With so many models to choose from, it can be a daunting task to evaluate and select the models most relevant to an organization.

Origins of Business Process Maturity Models (BPMM) can be traced to the discipline of Software Engineering in the early 1980s, which was strongly influenced by the quality management principles of the day (van Looy, 2014). 'The need for BPMMs increased due to a software crisis that started in the 1970 – 1980s. Many IT projects faced great difficulties delivering on time, on budget. and within scope. Consequently, the first maturity models for software development processes emerged. The Capability Maturity Model (initially referred to as Process Maturity Framework) developed by the Software Engineering Institute is arguably the most well-known and widely adopted maturity model. The success of this software engineering-oriented process maturity model spawned a host of similar efforts for various other business functions.

A variety of business process maturity models (BPMM) have been developed; some have been specifically designed with a Supply Chain focus. Von Looy (2014) has provided the most comprehensive review of BPMM to date. He has listed 24 maturity models, some of which have been developed in academia, while the rest by supply chain consulting firms. This survey includes the SCOR model, one of the most well-known and widely adopted supply chain business process reference models. SCOR model provides a unique framework for defining and linking performance metrics, processes, best practices, and people into a unified structure.

Van Looy (2014) also proposed an approach to strategically select the best business process maturity model for a firm by answering the following questions:

1. Which capability areas must be assessed and improved according to the organization's specific needs?
2. Must the BPMM define a roadmap per capability area, a roadmap for overall maturity, or both?
3. How much guidance must the BPMM give on your journey towards higher maturity?

4. Must the BPMM be generic (i.e., for business processes in general) or domain-specific (e.g., for business processes in supply chains or collaboration situations)?
5. Which type of data must be collected during an assessment?
6. How must information be collected during an assessment?
7. For which purpose must the BPMM be used?
8. Must evidence be explicitly given that the BPMM can assess maturity and help enhance the efficiency and effectiveness of business processes?
9. How many business processes must be assessed and improved?
10. How long must a particular assessment maximally take?
11. Must the assessment questions and corresponding level calculation be publicly available (instead of only known to the assessors)?
12. Must the BPMM explicitly recognize to include people from outside the assessed organization as respondents in the assessment?
13. How many questions must be maximally answered during an assessment?
14. Must the BPMM be free to access and use?

Identifying Current Maturity Level

The essence of any maturity assessment procedure is benchmarking, where the industry best practice and related goals form the highest level of maturity, while the current state of a process area indicates the level of maturity as defined by the model selected. First, Let us reiterate a maturity model's key components: key process areas (level specific), key practices, specific goals, and common features for a given maturity level. Qualitative or quantitative measures are necessary for each process area and the corresponding highest level of maturity indicator, i.e., the industry best-practice.

Netland and Alfnes (2008) suggest that there are five types of test procedures for identifying the current state of an organization's supply chain: a) Standard maturity self-assessment, b) Gap–analysis {as–is and to–be}, c) Counterpart triangulation, d) Third-party triangulation and e) Maturity benchmark study. Though these procedures are mentioned in the light of the SCMAT Maturity Model (see *Table 1*, Row 7), they are generic in nature and can be used with any supply chain maturity model. They define these test procedures as follows:

- *Standard Maturity Self-assessment* – 'The test is carried out by a team of company representatives either alone or with the facilitation of researchers or consultants' (Netland and Alfnes, 2008).
- *Gap Analysis* – The evaluation team (of company representatives) attempts to answer two questions for each process area on a scale of 1 to 5 on the SCMAT Maturity Scale to identify the largest improvement gaps. The first

question (as–is) is phrased as: "To which extent does our supply chain use best practice stated?" (Netland and Alfnes, 2008), whereas the second question (to–be) is phrased as: "To which extent does our supply chain aim to use the best practice stated five years from now?" (Netland and Alfnes, 2008).

- *Counterpart Triangulation* – In this procedure, the organization's upstream (vendors) and downstream (customers) supply chain partners are challenged to evaluate the organization's maturity across relevant process areas.
- *Third-party triangulation* – Similar to counterpart triangulation, third-party consultants or researchers are challenged to evaluate the organization's maturity across key process areas.

Table 1. List of Maturity Models

#	Model Name	Author / Institution
1	SC Integration Maturity Model	Aryee, Naim & Lalwani
2	SC Integration Evaluation Tool & Maturity Model	Böhme & Childerhouse
3	SC Integration Enhancement Framework (SCIEF)	Campbell & Sankaran
4	SC Management Maturity Model	McCormack et al.
5	Web-enabled SC Integration Measurement Model	McLaren
6	21st Century Logistics Framework	Michigan State University
7	SC Maturity Assessment Test (SCMAT)	Netland, Alfnes & Fauske
8	SC Management – Technology Maturity Model	Riverola
9	Logistics Scorecard (LSC)	Tokyo Institute of Technology
10	Global SC Maturity Framework	Aberdeen Group
11	SC Continuum	Accenture
12	Global Scorecard for efficient consumer response capability	CGF, Consumer Goods Forum
13	SC Management Maturity Model	CGR Management Consulting
14	SC Maturity Model	Chicago Consulting
15	SC Maturity Model	CSC, SC Management Review Magazine & Michigan State University
16	SC Maturity Monitor (SCM²)	eKNOWtion
17	SC Maturity Model	IBM
18	SC Maturity Scan	Jeroen van den Bergh Consulting & VU University Amsterdam
19	GAIA SC sustainability Maturity Model	LMI Research Institute
20	SC Compass	JDA Software
21	SC Maturity Model	PMG & PRTM
22	SCORmark Survey	SCC, Supply Chain Council & APQC
23	SC Management Maturity Model	Schoenfeldt
24	SC Integration Model	Stevens
25	SCM-CMM	Sun, Ren & Yeo

The fundamental reason for adopting maturity models is to help companies benchmark the maturity of their operations relative to industry's best practice. The SCOR model has gained increased adoption and have Akyuz & Erkan contributed to the development of performance management systems and maturity models for the following reasons:

- 'Provides a standardized way of viewing the supply chain (cross-industry standard)
- Offers a consistent 'scorecard' framework for performance development

- Emphasizes process orientation and de-emphasizes functional orientation
- Enables cross-industry benchmarks' (Akyuz & Erkan, 2010)

Performance Measurement and KPIs Governance

Organizations employ strategies and define tactics to achieve their goals with some degree of certainty. BSC is a very effective tool to translate and communicate strategy, but it does not provide a mechanism for maintaining the relevance of defined measures. The SCOR process model, on the other hand, adopts a building block approach and offers complete traceability. The SCOR–BSC framework developed by Thakkar et al. (2009) combines the salient features of a performance management framework (BSC) and a supply chain-specific process reference model (SCOR). This chapter builds upon the features of the SCOR–BSC framework by incorporating the salient features of capability maturity models to enable organizations to define operational tactics for processes at different levels of maturity and to provide guidance on improving supply chain processes while maintaining alignment with corporate goals.

The proposed tiered framework for performance measurement and KPI governance is based on design principles rooted in perspective-based models like Balanced Scorecard and the SCOR model.

It is important, however, to highlight the differences between a KPI, a metric, and a report — and to provide a collective understanding of these three terms. Key Performance Indicator (KPI) is a metric, but not all metrics are necessarily KPIs. For a metric to be considered a KPI, it should support *specific organizational goals* and strategy, be *accepted by senior management* and displayed on executive dashboards, and still *convey meaningful information* at all lower organizational levels. On the other hand, a metric is derived from a report or set of reports. So, a *Metric* must have 'a context and a target,' be based on legitimate data, and should lead to tangible action or improvement. A smart metric is characterized by: *being actionable*, having a *common interpretation*, being *transparent and simple to calculate*, and, most importantly, supported by *credible & accessible* data. Finally, *Reports* are defined as the presentation of contextual data, either in aggregated or disaggregated form.

Some Challenges in Measuring Performance Effectively

Many companies measure too much or too little—or are measuring the wrong things. Supply chain performance measurement remains a challenge for most firms for the following reasons (Sabri, 2012):

- Too many choices, which causes difficulty when identifying metrics that will yield the most information for the least investment of time and effort
- Isolated metrics are functional or departmentally oriented and not aligned with corporate strategy
- There is a need for new metrics in today's business to complement traditional metrics. Firms require metrics that can measure lean, agile environments.
- Professionals cannot understand the trade–offs and interrelation between metrics when creating a comprehensive list; for example, an increase in fill rate can be at the expense of inventory levels and cash cycle time.
- There is a lack of clear ownership of metrics and an inability to drive good behavior.
- Consistently clean data are unavailable, which results in a lack of confidence.

To address the above challenges, optimize the usage of GenAI/ML technologies, and establish the linkage to building blocks 1 and 2, a tiered framework for performance measurement and KPIs governance is proposed in Figure 1. Such a framework enables practitioners to effectively analyze the impact of improving individual processes on the overall performance of the supply chain, propagates objectives and metrics down to the operational level, and determines the success of corporate strategies. It then outlines a governance framework that effectively achieves four key objectives: 1) Identify the right KPIs, 2) Establish root–cause analysis and ownership, 3) Systematically track KPIs and metrics leveraging dashboard and scorecards, and 4) Establish governance for KPI and metrics reviews.

Figure 1. Performance Measurement, Alignment & Governance Framework

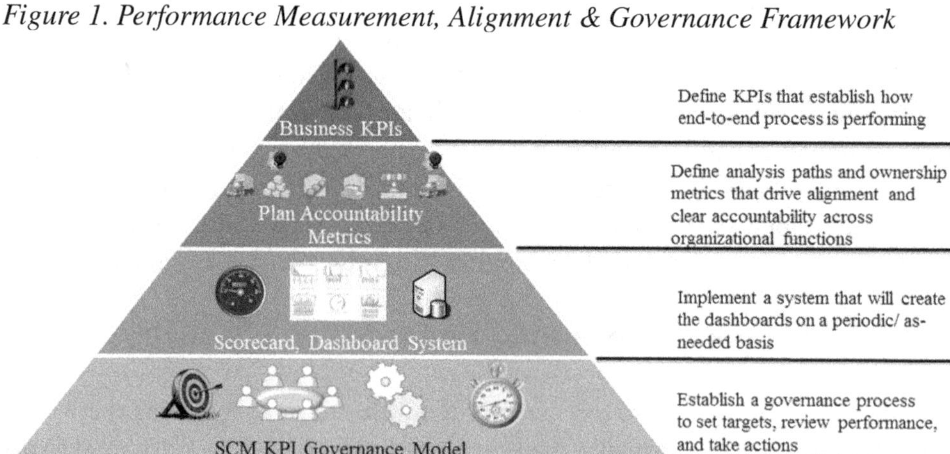

1) Identifying the Right Business KPIs

When identifying the right business KPIs, it is crucial to 1) Focus on a handful of KPIs that are most critical to the business and align them to corporate strategy and objectives and 2) Define a target performance level for every KPI based on a maturity model, benchmarking with other companies or the company's own goals.

The secondary objective is to 'establish root cause analysis and ownership.' 'The proposed KPIs need to be aligned to supply chain strategic goals and should be able to measure their successes. For example, forecast accuracy can assess the success of an effective sales and operations planning meeting mechanism. Inventory turns can measure the success of network and inventory strategy. Because it is impractical to measure every activity, identifying a reasonable number of Tier 2 metrics that have a direct linkage to KPIs (Tier 1 metrics) is necessary. With this level of granularity of investigation, ownership and corrective actions are just a consequence of the exercise. *Figure 2* provides a graphical view of how one can communicate the alignment between Strategic Goals and KPIs, and the pairing of Tier I and II metrics for root cause investigation in the event of deviation of KPI from the agreed upon or expected range.

Figure 2. Aligning KPIs to Corporate Strategic Goals

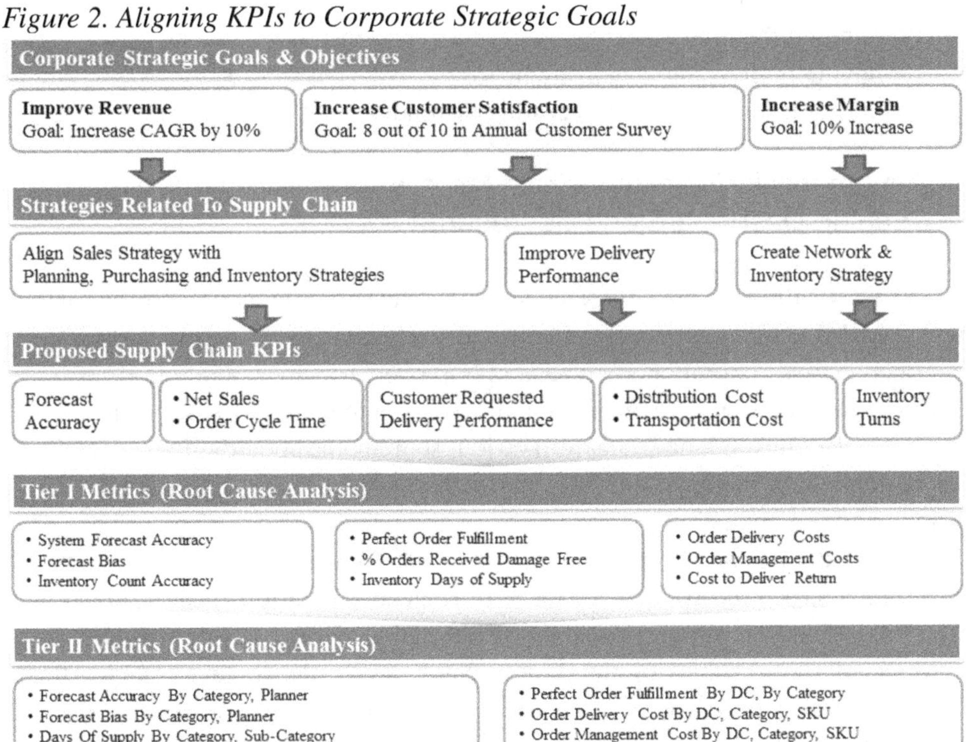

2) Identify Plan Accountability Metrics

Considering the needs identified in previous research, this comprehensive framework incorporates the SCOR performance measure into the structure of a maturity model. The 'Plan Accountability Metrics' echelon is at the crux of the metrics alignment exercise. Planning for 'accountability metrics essentially has two–stages of selection. The first stage is selecting the appropriate maturity model. All that a maturity model provides are the process areas of interest and the objectives or levels of performance expected at a particular stage of maturity. The second stage entails selecting an appropriate set of measures to ensure they provide 'coverage' for the process areas of interest. Figure 2 provides a good example of accountability metrics (Tier I and Tier II metrics) and their relationships.

It's also recommended to think about Tier III metrics as a vehicle to cascade down the root cause analysis to the individual level. For example, if forecast accuracy is low for a particular planner, looking at Tier III metrics will be an important exercise. Examples of Tier III metrics for this situation are:

1) User adoption survey results
2) Time spent in the new forecasting tool
3) # of forecast overrides
4) Fine-tuning the forecasting techniques and parameters
5) Removing outliers and cleansing history
6) Exploring leveraging ML forecasting techniques

3) Systematically Track KPIs and Metrics Leveraging Dashboard and Scorecards

Systematically tracking KPIs and metrics is crucial for the successful governance of Gen AI/ML digital transformation programs. Dashboards and scorecards provide an effective way to monitor, analyze, and improve performance in real-time. They offer a visual representation of data, making it easier to identify trends, patterns, and anomalies. By consolidating data from various sources, dashboards give stakeholders a holistic view of the supply chain's performance, facilitating informed decision-making and prompt action.

Scorecards, on the other hand, help align KPIs with strategic objectives by providing a structured framework for performance evaluation. They enable organizations to measure progress against predefined goals and ensure that all efforts are directed toward achieving the desired outcomes. In the context of Gen AI/ML digital transformation programs, scorecards can track the effectiveness of AI and ML models, the accuracy of predictive analytics, and the impact on operational efficiency. By regularly reviewing these scorecards, organizations can identify areas for improvement, adjust strategies, and optimize resource allocation to enhance overall performance.

The combination of dashboards and scorecards not only improves KPI governance but also fosters a culture of continuous improvement. These tools provide transparency and accountability, ensuring all stakeholders know their responsibilities and performance expectations. By leveraging advanced analytics and real-time data, organizations can proactively address issues, mitigate risks, and drive continuous improvement in their supply chain operations. This systematic approach to tracking and improving KPIs ensures that Gen AI/ML digital transformation programs deliver tangible value and support the organization's strategic goals.

4) Establish Governance for KPIs and Metrics Reviews

For effective governance of performance measurement, the key to success lies in the clarity of definition, interpretation, and ownership of the metrics. “A metric must be well defined so there is no dispute about it. Otherwise, managers tend to interpret it in ways that work well for them but might lead to conflict. For example, if not clearly defined, the supplier can interpret an on-time delivery performance metric as a shipping date, while the customer might assume the same metric represents a receiving date. A comprehensive set of metrics should be considered because improvement in one area is sometimes achieved at the expense of another. Also, metrics should stress results instead of activities” (Sabri, 2012).

‘Identifying what needs to be measured is just the first step; finding the right way to measure and track is the next. Measuring at regular intervals is useful for base-lining the performance prior to a major transformation program and for getting a clear picture of the impact of the change on performance. Implementing a system that creates dashboards, on a periodic or as-needed basis, to sustain KPI tracking is also highly recommended.’ *Table 2* provides a comprehensive list of parameters for tracking the KPIs and Tier I & II metrics from a governance perspective.

Table 2. Parameters for tracking metrics and KPI

Phase	Attribute	Description
Plan	Measure Name	A unique short name for the measure
	UoM	Unit of Measure
	Description	Brief description of usage and importance of the measure.
	Granularity	Identify dimensions: potential grouping
	Interpretation	Interpretation of value & its evolution; optimum & limiting values, expected (statistical) dispersion
	Example	Supply examples including units and format
	Baseline	Past or current level of performance
	Target	Derived from and aligned to corporate goals
	Metric Owner	Role accountable for achieving the target for the defined measure
Do	Computation	How are values obtained? Formula and algorithms used, data source.
	Data Source	Data repository which supplies the measure (or its components)
	Refresh Frequency	Frequency of data refresh
	Delivery Frequency	Frequency of re-calculation of the measure
	Delivery Mode	Means of consumption
	Calculation & Distribution Owner	Indicates team/ role responsible for generating and distributing the re-calculated measure.
Check	Venue	Indicates where the measure will be discussed and used for deciding on corrective action, if any.
	Audit Frequency	Scheduled frequency of review as the specified venue for oversight (?)
	Audience	Recipients and potential recipients of the measure.
	Inter-relationship	Indicate other measures which: are antagonistic to the measure, can be used to improve interpretation, are someway related to the measure.
Act	Corrective Action	Pointers to factors that may aid root cause analysis
	Timeline	Time window to act; begin at the point of problem identification
	Action Owner	Identify roles responsible & accountable for taking remedial actions, in case of deviations

Finally, to establish effective governance of performance measure reviews, establish a process to set targets—metrics without any target means no skin in the game. This can be achieved by defining the parameters in *Table 2* and establishing a process that enables systematic review of the metric collection, communication, and related corrective actions to enable (and or institute) continuous improvement. 'The highest level of maturity in establishing governance for measurement is to develop predefined corrective actions when targets are not achieved. This way, firms can achieve sustainable gains and surpass the competition. Effective performance measurement and governance are at the heart of lasting success' (Sabri, 2012).

CONTINUOUS MONITORING AND IMPROVEMENT

Continuous monitoring and improvement are vital components of effective Performance Measurement and Value Realization Framework, particularly in the context of Gen AI/ML digital transformation programs. By regularly tracking KPIs, organizations can assess performance in real-time, ensuring that all aspects of the supply chain are functioning optimally. This ongoing assessment allows companies to quickly identify and address inefficiencies, bottlenecks, and deviations from expected outcomes. Methodologies such as Lean Six Sigma play a critical role in this process, providing a structured approach to problem-solving and process improvement. Lean Six Sigma focuses on reducing waste, improving quality, and enhancing process efficiency, which aligns perfectly with the goals of digital transformation initiatives.

Implementing continuous monitoring involves leveraging dashboards and scorecards to visualize data and track progress against strategic objectives. These tools provide insights into the performance of AI and ML models, the accuracy of predictive analytics, and overall operational efficiency. By systematically analyzing this data, organizations can identify trends, uncover root causes of issues, and develop targeted improvement plans. The iterative nature of continuous improvement ensures that changes are tested, refined, and optimized over time, leading to sustained performance gains.

Fostering a culture of innovation is essential for driving continuous improvement and staying ahead of the competition. This involves encouraging a mindset where employees are empowered to seek out and implement innovative solutions. Leadership plays a crucial role in promoting this culture by supporting experimentation, rewarding creative problem-solving, and providing the necessary resources for innovation. In the context of Gen AI/ML digital transformation, this could mean exploring new AI techniques, experimenting with different ML algorithms, or adopting advanced data analytics tools.

By embedding continuous improvement and innovation into the organizational culture, companies can ensure that they achieve the expected value from the digital transformation program and that their supply chain processes remain agile and responsive to changing market conditions. This proactive approach not only enhances operational efficiency but also drives competitive advantage by enabling faster adaptation to new opportunities and challenges. Through continuous monitoring and improvement, organizations can achieve sustained success in their digital transformation efforts, delivering lasting value and positioning themselves as leaders in their industry.

Case Study: From Maturity Model to Level II Metrics Selection

Assume that a widget manufacturer who sells widgets through its own retail stores wants to align its supply chain operational metrics to its corporate goals. Management's stated goal for the company is to *increase market share by keeping its customers satisfied and adding more customers, thereby increasing revenue and improving profitability*. An external consultant has been hired to achieve metrics alignment and decides to use the proposed 'operational metrics alignment and governance framework.'

As the first step, the consultant identifies all key stakeholders and sets expectations with them regarding the outcomes, timelines, and the process to be followed (workshops) to achieve the goal of aligning operational measures to the corporate objectives. Another decision the stakeholders made using guidelines provided earlier is that the SCM–CMM model, which considers the 'Process, People and Technology triangle, across five levels of maturity,' is the most relevant maturity model for 'evolving' the company's supply chain. Next, the consultant facilitates a detailed assessment of the supply chain processes; it is determined that *most* of the processes are at Maturity Level 3. The next critical task for the stakeholders is to prepare a detailed design for developing 'accountability metrics' for all the key process areas at SCM–CMM Maturity Level 3. Doing so will help them define in detail the expectation for processes at Level 3 maturity and, over time, validate their hypothesis that their processes are indeed at Level 3 maturity.

The procedure to prepare detailed design for all the key process areas at a maturity level is as follows:

0. Select the desired maturity level as defined by the maturity model
1. Identify the defining characteristics of the maturity level and related facets
2. Select a key process area
    i) Identity facet objectives vis-à-vis maturity level
    ii) Map facet objectives (at the maturity level) to the supply chain strategies
    iii) Identify KPIs relevant to both supply chain strategies and facet objectives
3. Identify key influencing factors and related SCOR measures
4. Determine parameter values for tracking metrics (refer to *Table 2*)
5. Repeat steps 2 to 4 until all key process areas are covered
6. Begin at step 1, and repeat until all maturity levels are covered

The consultant provides more details for every step to align all stakeholders and ensure successful level II Metrics Selection:

Step 0 – Select the Desired Maturity Level

SCM–CMM maturity model is selected. The facets are People, Process, and Technology. The Maturity Levels are Ad hoc, Initial, Defined, Extended, and Networked.

Then, consultant facilities structured sessions to enable stakeholders to create the detailed design of accountability metric echelon (Tier 1 & Tier II). Facilitating these sessions will ensure collaboration and resolve potential conflicts by avoiding the selection/definition of overlapping performance measures and generate insights into the dynamics of the supply chain system as a whole.

Step 1 – Identify Characteristics and Facet Objectives for a Given Maturity Level

The SCM–CMM Level 3 objectives for each process, people, and technology facet can be described as follows.

- Process – A well-defined demand/supply balancing process that combines forecasting and planning with sourcing and manufacturing is implemented.
- People – Become more responsive to customer requests and service level
- Technology – Software programs are applied to determine where the warehousing should be located, how much space should be involved, how much inventory is required to meet demand, and how the goods should be stored and retrieved.

Once the level objectives have been identified clearly, the next step is to quantify these in terms of metrics and targets.

Step 2 – Align Facet and Organizational Objectives

Sub–Step 2a: Identify Facet Objectives vis-à-vis Maturity Level

SCM–CMM Level 3 has three key process areas: *Customer Service and Delivery*, *Advanced Planning & Scheduling (APS)* and *Network Planning*. In real life, it is advisable to consider these three key areas together for the detailed design. For the purpose of illustration, the consultant focuses on the '*Customer Service and Delivery*' process area. With respect to this particular process area, from the *People* facet perspective, the objective is to "focus on customer satisfaction and service level," from the *Process* facet perspective, the objectives would be: "Being Responsive To Customer Request," "Being Responsive To Service Levels," "Focus on Inventory needed for meeting demand," and finally "Supply & Demand Balancing." The *Tech-*

nology facet is primarily an enabler and is useful for identifying "decision support" requirements. Once the facet objectives have been listed, move to the next sub-step.

Sub–Step 2b: Map Level Objectives to Supply Chain Strategy

Before mapping the level objective identified in the previous step, one needs to know the specific supply chain strategies that help drive the corporate goals. This helps align level objectives to the supply chain strategies, which, in turn, are derived from the corporate goals themselves. The supply chain strategies relevant to the example have been briefly mentioned in *Figure 2*, but first, let's review those in the context of the corporate goals. The company's stated goal can be translated into the following objectives: a) increasing market share, b) improving customer satisfaction, c) increasing revenue, and d) improving profitability. As noted in *Figure 2*, these goals can be achieved by employing these Supply Chain strategies: i) Align sales strategy with planning, purchasing, and inventory strategies, ii) Improve delivery performance, and iii) Create network & inventory strategy.

Sub–Step 2c: Identify Relevant KPIs

The next step would be to identify the set of Key Performance Indicators (KPIs) that accurately reflect the quantification of one or more goals. Typically, company-wide KPIs would be derived from a BSC exercise. If the organization does not have a BSC or similar practice, then it is recommended that the KPI should be derived directly (as much as possible) from the measures that are relevant and acceptable to all the stakeholders. In Table *3,* the corporate objectives and corresponding supply chain strategies have been mapped to some of the Level 3 objectives. Additionally, some KPIs relevant to these supply chain strategies and level objectives have been identified; some of these would be potentially used during detailed design.

Table 3. Mapping Corporate Goals to Level Objectives

Corporate Goals	Supply Chain Strategies	Level3 Objectives	Key Performance Indicators
• Improve Revenue • Increase Customer Satisfaction • Increase Margin	• Create Network & Inventory Strategy • Align Sales Strategy with Planning, Purchasing & Inventory Strategies • Improve Delivery Performance	• Institute Supply & Demand Balancing Process • Coordinate MRP & Handling, Manufacturing & Planning • Focus on Inventory needed To Satisfy Demand • Be Responsive To Customer Requests • Be Responsive To Service Levels	• Net Sales • Forecast Accuracy • Customer Requested Delivery Performance • Order Cycle Time • Distribution Cost • Transportation Cost • Inventory Turns

Step 3 – Identify Influencing Factors and Related Measures

The most important step is identifying all possible factors that influence the process area under consideration. This is where the consultant uses an influence diagram (also called a causal loop diagram) to map the causal influence among several factors and uncover the system structure. *Figure 3* indicates one feasible way to map the influence of the factors affecting the objectives under consideration, which are represented by a measure or combination of measures. The consultant has taken a narrow view of the influencing factors and limited the investigation's scope to just one of the three key process areas at this level. In a practical setting, it is advised that practitioners take a broader view for the sake of complete coverage and to avoid missing any influencing factors.

Figure 3. Causal Loop Diagram for Level 3 Customer Service and Delivery Process Area

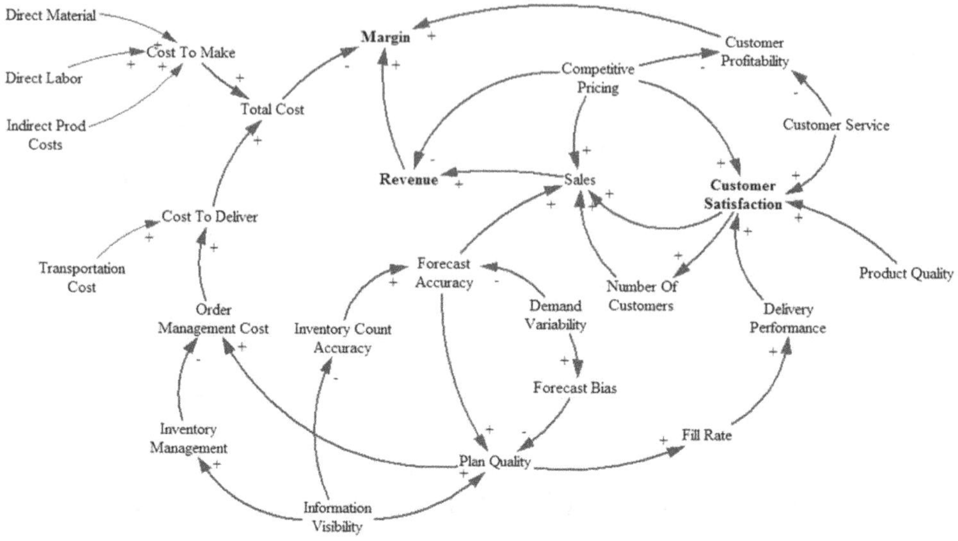

In the causal loop diagram illustrated in *Figure 3*, the consultant has identified the factors that influence three elements: Revenue, Margin, and Customer Satisfaction (which are corporate goals) from the 'Customer Service and Delivery' point of view (SCM–CMM Level 3 key process area). One will note that if the other two key process areas are considered, i.e., Network Planning and Advanced Planning & Scheduling, it will lead to additional factors being considered for mapping and influencing these three elements of the core corporate goals. Defining boundaries for identifying influencing factors is an important consideration, and generating consensus during group modeling workshops will help avoid potential adoption issues in the future.

Step 4 – Define Tier I and Tier II Metrics

One of the important outcomes of rigorous group exercise for developing CLDs would be consensus on a) the KPIs and 2) the related pairing of Tier I and Tier II measures. The consultant leverages the comprehensive list of parameters for tracking metrics as described in *Table 2,* following the PDCA format. The 'plan' parameters define how the metric will be interpreted and identify the owner. 'Do' parameters explicitly define the formula, frequency, and role responsible for calculating and maintaining the metric definition. 'Check' parameters establish the governance details like venue, frequency, and audience responsible for review of the measure.

Finally, the 'act' parameters define roles responsible for taking corrective action in case of deviations, the suggested corrective actions, and the associated timeline. While the exact mechanism for establishing a governance structure has not been defined in this chapter, the outcome of step 4 essentially prepares the groundwork for establishing the foundation for governance as part of the metrics definition phase itself. To continue with the earlier example, from the CLD in *Figure 3*, consider the KPI 'Net Sales,' the corresponding Tier I metrics would be Customer Satisfaction and Forecast Accuracy, while the Tier II metrics are shown in *Table 4*. Those interested can work through the parameters from *Table 2* to continue working on the detailed design for these metrics.

Table 4. Accountability Metrics Design Example

Stage I			Stage II	
Maturity Model	**Process Area**	**KPI**	**Tier I Metric**	**Tier II Metric**
SCM CMM	Level 3 Process Area: *Customer Service & Delivery*	Net Sales	Customer Satisfaction	• Delivery Performance • Product Quality • Customer Service
			Forecast Accuracy	• Demand Variability • Inventory Count Accuracy

Figure 4. Echelon 2 Schematic

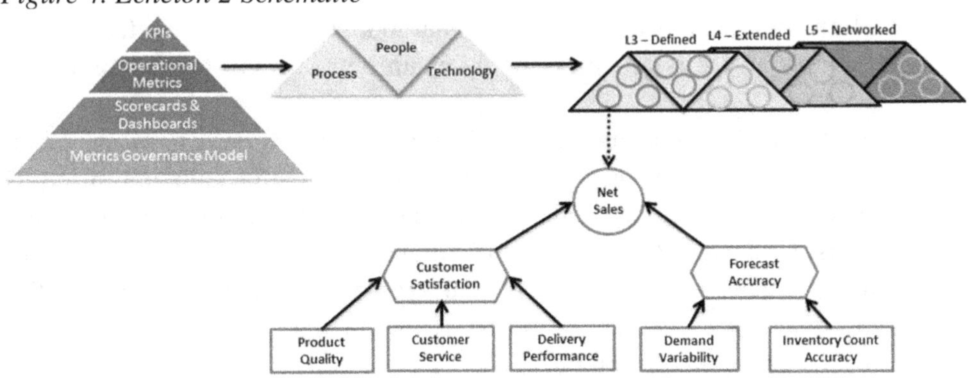

Figure 4 shows the composition of Echelon 2 vis-à-vis the maturity levels of a maturity model (in this case, Level 3 to Level 5 of the SCM-CMM) and the linkages between corresponding KPIs and Tier I and Tier II metrics. This figure shows only one KPI (Net Sales) and its corresponding Tier I and Tier II measures.

SUCCESS STORIES

Company A

- **Background:** Company A, a multinational consumer goods corporation, embarked on a digital-driven supply chain planning transformation to enhance agility and responsiveness.
- **Strategy**: Leveraging AI and ML algorithms, Company A implemented demand forecasting models to accurately predict customer demand. This enabled the company to optimize inventory levels, reduce stockouts, and improve customer satisfaction.
- **Results:** The implementation of digital-driven supply chain planning resulted in a 14% improvement in forecast accuracy, a reduction in inventory carrying costs, a 15% improvement in case fill rate, and an 8% savings in planners' productivity. Additionally, the company experienced an increase in sales revenue due to enhanced product availability.

Company B

- **Background:** Company B, a global automotive manufacturer, faced challenges managing its complex supply chain network and mitigating supply chain risks.
- **Strategy:** Utilizing advanced optimization and real-time data visualization tools, Company B enhanced visibility across its supply chain, optimized its inventory, and enabled proactive risk management and mitigation strategies.
- **Results:** Company B achieved a 10% reduction in inventory, a 75% reduction in premium freight costs, and a 30% increase in planner efficiency. The company followed the same performance measurement framework to achieve value by leveraging the author's help.

CONCLUSION AND FURTHER RESEARCH OPPORTUNITIES

This chapter presented a framework for the alignment and governance of supply chain operational metrics. Operational metrics are the leading indicators of an organization's future financial performance and are crucial to guiding changing operational dynamics and identifying opportunities for improving supply chain processes. This comprehensive framework incorporates the salient features of capability maturity models into the SCOR–BSC framework. The frameworks enable organizations to define operational tactics for processes at different levels of maturity and provide guidance on improving supply chain processes (depending on the maturity model selected) while maintaining alignment with corporate goals.

Future Research Opportunities

1. Dynamic Alignment Models:
   - o Investigate models and methodologies for maintaining continuous alignment between operational metrics and organizational strategies, particularly in rapidly changing environments.
   - o Explore the integration of real-time data analytics and AI to dynamically adjust performance measurement systems in response to operational changes.
2. Impact of Digital Transformation on Performance Measurement:
   - o Study the specific impacts of digital technologies (AI, ML, IoT) on the effectiveness and evolution of performance measurement systems.
   - o Analyze how digital transformation influences the identification and prioritization of key performance indicators (KPIs).
3. Behavioral and Cultural Factors:
   - o Research the role of organizational culture and employee behavior in the successful implementation and utilization of performance measurement systems.
   - o Identify strategies to foster a culture of continuous improvement and innovation that aligns with performance measurement objectives.
4. Case Studies on Best Practices:
   - o Conduct in-depth case studies on organizations that have successfully implemented robust performance measurement frameworks aligned with their business strategies.
   - o Identify common challenges and success factors that can inform best practices for other organizations.
5. Technological Integration and Usability:

   - Explore the integration of performance measurement systems with existing enterprise resource planning (ERP) systems and other digital platforms.
   - Assess the usability and user experience of performance measurement tools and their impact on adoption and effectiveness.
6. Longitudinal Studies on KPI Evolution:
   - Perform longitudinal studies to understand how KPIs evolve over time in response to strategic shifts and operational changes.
   - Investigate the lifecycle of KPIs and develop frameworks for their periodic review and adjustment.
7. Industry-Specific Frameworks:
   - Develop and validate industry-specific performance measurement frameworks that cater to the unique challenges and opportunities of different sectors.
   - Compare and contrast the effectiveness of these frameworks across various industries.
8. Sustainability Metrics:
   - Explore the integration of sustainability metrics into performance measurement frameworks to support corporate social responsibility (CSR) and environmental goals.
   - Investigate the impact of digital-driven supply chain planning on sustainability outcomes.

By addressing these research areas, scholars and practitioners can contribute to the development of more effective, adaptive, and comprehensive performance measurement frameworks that support digital-driven supply chain planning transformations. These insights will help organizations navigate the complexities of modern supply chains and achieve sustainable competitive advantage.

REFERENCES

Akyuz, G., & Erkan, T. (2010). Supply chain performance measurement: A literature review. *International Journal of Production Research*, 48(17), 5137–5155. DOI: 10.1080/00207540903089536

Kaplan, R. S. (2010). Conceptual Foundations of the Balanced Scorecard. Harvard Business School Accounting & Management Unit Working Paper No. 10-074. Retrieved from: https://ssrn.com/abstract=1562586

Netland, T., & Alfnes, E. (2008). A practical tool for supply chain improvement – experiences with the supply chain maturity assessment test (SCMAT). EurOMA/POMS/JOMSA Conference. Tokyo, Japan.

Sabri, E. (2012). Enduring Transformation. APICS magazine. September/October 2012, 45 – 47.

Sabri, E. H. (2023). *Digital Supply Chain, Disruptive Environments, and the Impact on Retailers: How to Master Change Management During the Supply Chain Digital Transformation Journey*. USA, IGI Global, 1-20.

Thakkar, J., Kanda, A., & Deshmukh, S. (2009). Supply chain performance measurement framework for small and medium scale enterprises. *Benchmarking*, 16(5), 702–723. DOI: 10.1108/14635770910987878

van Looy, A. (2014). *Business Process Maturity: A Comparative Study on a Sample of Business Process Maturity Models*. Spinger. DOI: 10.1007/978-3-319-04202-2

Vishwasrao, R. (2023). *Digital Supply Chain, Disruptive Environments, and the Impact on Retailers: Supply Chain Performance Measurement and Organizational Alignment in an Uncertain World:* USA, IGI Global, 36-62.

Chapter 10
Lean Digital Transformation in Health Supply Chain:
Identifying Barriers to Machine Learning and AI Applications and Strategies to Overcome

Busra Kesici
https://orcid.org/0000-0001-7107-761X
Duzce University, Turkey

Irem Duzdar
https://orcid.org/0000-0002-7642-8121
Duzce University, Turkey

ABSTRACT

One of the important sectors that need to keep up with digital transformation quickly is healthcare. Given its direct impact on human lives, it is crucial to conduct studies to improve service quality in this sector. Considering the effects of the lean management approach in the healthcare sector on digital transformation in the supply chain is the first important research question for this study. Another research question is the contribution of artificial intelligence (AI) and machine learning (ML) approaches developed in recent years to digital transformation in the healthcare sector. The necessity of digital transformation tools, including artificial intelligence and machine learning, in healthcare services and the challenges faced during their implementation were identified as criteria and a weighting analysis was conducted with the help of multi-criteria decision-making (MCDM) analysis. Step-Wise Weight

DOI: 10.4018/979-8-3693-4433-0.ch010

Assessment Ratio Analysis (SWARA) was used to determine the importance weights of the evaluation criteria. Strategies were defined with Enterprise Resource Planning (ERP) as a solution to the important weights of the challenges. The aim is to reduce costs while increasing supply chain efficiency and effectiveness by identifying practices and strategies that incorporate expert feedback from the industry.

1. INTRODUCTION

In recent years, digitalization revolutions in the sectors have paved the way for various innovations, including lean production practices. The evaluation of lean approaches in the health supply chain in terms of artificial intelligence and machine learning, which are digitalization approaches, has been an important research topic for this study. Research has been conducted on various improvements for the use of digital technologies in healthcare services. Raja et al. (2020) have summarized the existing literature on big data applications in healthcare and offered researchers a road map for future studies on this subject. Lee et al. (2015) have studied machine learning to predict patient characteristics, necessary needs, and treatment outcomes. Ankrum et al. (2019) have shortened room turnover times and increased efficiency by using robotic systems for ultraviolet disinfection processes in hospital rooms. Gunasekaran et al. (2021) have examined AI and telehealth-related digital health solutions for public health applications during the COVID-19 pandemic. It was found that a large proportion of reports explored applications of AI and big data analytics.

In healthcare processes, lean thinking practices have begun to be implemented, which is an approach that will minimize costs and maximize profit by eliminating waste and unnecessary procedures. Whether in the public or private sector, lean management principles are easy to apply across various settings, including production systems, hospitals, banks, educational institutions, non-governmental organizations, and businesses. This will boost the effectiveness of the organization (Yücenur & Ipekçi, 2021). The lean thinking approach was first introduced by Toyota in the 1950s, driven by the need to serve smaller markets with a wider range of automobiles. This approach introduced greater production flexibility in operations with as little waste and expense as possible (Moyano-Fuentes & Sacristán-Díaz, 2012). In the service sector, lean production practices have begun to be used as lean management in recent years (Bharsakade et al., 2021; Elafri et al., 2022; Nilay Yücenur et al., 2024; Perdomo-Verdecia et al., 2022). Inspired by the principles of lean manufacturing, lean practices emphasize the importance of continuous improvement, relentless focus on customer value, and ruthless prioritization of activities that contribute to organizational objectives. From the shop floor to the boardroom, lean thinking permeates every aspect of the organization, driving efficiency, productivity, and operational excellence (Kolasani, 2023).

Healthcare organizations must embrace a lean philosophy to deliver high-quality, cost-effective treatments, enabling them to achieve operational excellence and maintain a competitive edge (Bharsakade et al., 2021). Healthcare has the greatest share in the service industries in most of the countries. Healthcare systems include diverse operations required to cure peoples' physical or mental conditions based on either an illness or an injury. These operations conducted to people aim to cure an illness, keep them healthy, and rehabilitate are called curative processes (P. Kumar et al., 2018). Because of the increasing demand for healthcare, it is necessary to evaluate healthcare operations for the development of their efficiency (Baril et al., 2014). Health organizations in today's fast technical developing and cruel competitive atmosphere are forced to find out new solutions to be able to survive. Under these conditions, the searched solution may be the digital transformation to achieve these troubles in healthcare operations, increase patient experiences, and utilize the innovative tools (Kolasani, 2023).

One of these is lean thinking; the basic principle of this Japanese tool is a systematic approach for continuous development by eliminating waste times, operations and materials to process optimization and increasing the delivered value in the organization (Oliveira et al., 2017). The lean system is useful to overcome unexpected market changes in the goods production industries (Stone, 2012). The basic idea of lean thinking is to determine and remove all types of waste from the present system to increase the added value (Mustafee et al., 2013).

The aim of this study is to ensure that data is collected quickly, accurately and in real time by promoting digital transformation and the use of digital tools in order to effectively implement lean philosophy tools in hospitals and to achieve the right results. The barriers to this digital transformation in the healthcare sector are identified and weighted with MCDM techniques. In addition, the collected data are modeled appropriately with ERP strategies to support decisions to be taken in improvement processes and to demonstrate the effectiveness of digital transformation infrastructures with integrated artificial intelligence (AI) and machine learning (ML) in this process. To demonstrate this, it is intended to be a guiding study by identifying constraints and providing recommendations with evaluations.

All barriers to digital transformation have been discussed in detail by taking expert opinions and weighted with the SWARA method, the details and steps of which will be given in the following sections. In this study, MCDM analysis is adopted as it enables the simultaneous evaluation of a large number of factors.

The study makes the following important contributions to the existing literature:

i. First, the barriers to lean digital transformation in the healthcare sector are evaluated with the MCDM concept to weight the barriers to lean digital transformation in the healthcare sector with the identified SWARA methodology.
ii. A case study is explained with real-world assessments to facilitate the adoption of the lean digital transformation concept, which has been studied in recent years, and its findings are discussed in detail.
iii. The most important issues for the implementation of lean digital transformation in the healthcare supply chain and the ERP strategies required to cope with them are discussed comprehensively.

The sections of the Chapter are organized as follows. Chapter 2 presents a literature analysis of the problem addressed in this study. Chapter 3 presents the proposed methodology in detail, while Chapter 4 presents discussion and finally Chapter 5 presents conclusions and recommendations for future applications.

2. LITERATURE REVIEW

2.1 Lean Thinking in Healthcare

The lean approach in healthcare services includes the benefits of quality and lean applications in healthcare operations, such as faster and more effective patient care, reduced operational costs, increased patient satisfaction, and balancing employee workloads. Many applications that have tangible results can be listed in the Kaizen approach, which is widely used in quality processes to manage improvements in the healthcare discipline and is provided with simple arrangements. For example, motivation and training of healthcare personnel, cost and risk reduction research, encouragement for developing and implementing new ideas, informing bidders about the results of analyses made regarding their work, and respecting all kinds of offers without evaluating their impact and size (Graban, 2018). Measurable gains in patient outcomes, including greater quality, less harm from avoidable mistakes, better access, shorter wait times, and better service, are the product of successful Lean health care initiatives. Enhancing health care performance and gaining a lasting competitive edge in the global health care market are possible outcomes of implementing lean production (Kasemsap, 2016). It would be appropriate to mention some real case studies and academic studies that bring this step-by-step thinking together across the healthcare supply chain.

In the intensive care unit (ICU) at Allegheny General Hospital, Pittsburgh, USA, $0.5 million per year profit was gained and the infections decreased at 90% in 90 days after changing the intravenous line insertion procedure. Perfecting Patient Care procedures are applied to the central line depending on the root cause analyses and lean principles. The maintenance encouraged the personnel to establish preventive actions to decrease the potential mistakes of the procedures. The redesign of the process was prepared within 90 days, and within the first year, CLAB numbers decreased from 49 to 6 (10.5 to 1.2 per 1,000 central line days of use) and despite the increase deaths decreased from 19 to 1. (from 51 to 16%). Results shown that it is sustainable over a long period of time (Shannon et al., 2006). A study performed at Royal Bolton NHS Hospital, UK it is reported remarkable results with 42% reduced paper work, interdisciplinary consultation improved, and patient length stay shortened by 33%. Cash savings of £3.1 million were achieved, while the time required for important blood tests was reduced from 2 days to 2 hours and the average turnaround time in Pathology was reduced from 24 hours to 2-3 hours (Bowerman & Fillingham, 2007). Virginia Mason Medical Center (VMMC), Seattle, USA, applies general lean techniques by creating a self-developed system called Virginia Mason Production System (VMPS), which also includes Virginia Mason Hospital. VMMC employs many of lean improvement tools and techniques. In the first eight years at least 850 continuous improvement studies were done for personnel, patients and others. Implementation of several lean tools and methods gained profits in medical establishments in terms of both economic and working conditions. The Patient Safety Alert system reduced the professional liability insurance premiums by 56% because of the increase in patient safety. The lab analysis results reporting time is reduced by 85%. The application of kits containing frequently used materials increases in productivity by about 93%. Approximately 250 hours of staff is saved with reducing daily 750 miles the walking distance of nurses (Furman & Caplan, 2007). The efficiency and decreased patient waiting time has improved the application of lean principles to screening mammography workflow at Radiology Department of Medical College of Wisconsin, USA (Shah et al., 2013). The waiting time of patient reduced to 3.3 minutes from 11.1 minutes, by 70%. Total visiting time is shortened to 25.5 minutes from 33.7 minutes it means 23.4% and 40% improvement in read time of mammography screening from 4.8 to 2.9 minutes per case. At Emergency Department (ED) of Alice Ho Miu Ling Nethersole Hospital, Hong Kong, China the results of lean management applications conducted to improve the confirmation and test report waiting time is analyzed by (Chan et al., 2014). It is stated that the waiting time is shortened by 55% totally. At the Emergency Department (ED) of the Vidant Health Centres, Greenville, North Carolina, USA, a project is performed to see the highest number of blood tests and cultures required in Emergency Department, Haematology and Chemistry Lab. The decrease in the consumption of specific laboratory and expendable materials is in between 30 to 50%. The earnings in turnabout time is between 2 to 18% (Sanders & Karr, 2015). Many of the tortuous nursing problems like pharmaceutical repartition errors, infections emanating from catheters and hospital and bedsores, can be reduced by employing 5S, standardized work and A3 techniques (Ballé & Régnier, 2007).

The tools commonly employed in these studies include methodologies such as 5S, Kaizen, Value-Stream Mapping (VSM), Structured Process Redesign, Priority Admission Triage (PAT) Program, Identification of Waste, Rapid Improvement Event (RIE), Forming of Process Maps, Visual Management-Based Communication, PDCA Cycle, DMAIC Cycle (Define-Measure-Analyze-Improve-Control), the Six Sigma approach, and 3P (Production, Preparation, Process) (Baril et al., 2016; Bastian et al., 2016; Bhat et al., 2014; Curatolo et al., 2014; Dias et al., 2013; Kuo et al., 2011; Lasorsa et al., 2015; Nicholas, 2012; Yu et al., 2015) The statement reflects a conclusion derived from the literature, it understood the advantages of lean approach and introduced that many of lean methods and techniques can be used and applied for better healthcare services and focusing on the patients.

2.2 Integration of Digital Tools

With Industry 4.0, the digitalization of processes throughout the production supply chain has enabled the same developments to continue in parallel in all sectors. This situation has caused the participants of all transactions and processes in the supply chain in the health sector to start using digital transactions. It can be said of the supply chains (SCs) are under risk of different difficulties as instability, intricacy, weakness and costs. The ability of success to manage these difficulties and both informational and physical flows must be in the technological structure of SC (Abdel-Basset et al., 2018). In this way, SC evolves digitally so-called Industry 4.0 (I4.0) (Núñez-Merino et al., 2020). The aim of the SCM (supply chain management) is to obtain the highest benefit for all SC involving the end users (Lambert & Cooper, 2000). SCM is one of the basic tools suitable for various destructive applications (Haddud & Khare, 2020). The whole SC formation changes with the digitalization requirements (Garay-Rondero et al., 2019). It is necessary to evaluate the various modeling and Industry 4.0 (I4.0) concepts and factors to have a wider perspective, simultaneously information and more flexible tasks (Aqlan & Lam, 2015).

Lean 4.0, is a powerful process to raise the capabilities of Industry 4.0. which is a combination of lean production with digital applications (Liu et al., 2023). Both of the Lean Manufacturing and Industry 4.0. have similar goals, try to achieve improvements in the productivity and quality of goods and services by minimizing all wastes in manufacturing processes (Pagliosa et al., 2021). It is highlighted that the challenge of improving customer and supplier integration in lean systems (Moyano-Fuentes et al., 2019), while Rossini and Portioli (2018) emphasized the need to reduce inefficiencies in supply chains, and Allaoui et al. (2019) proposed Supply Chain Planning Systems to promote sustainability (Reyes et al., 2023). Another important problem that emerges in the healthcare sector with digitalization is the processing and security of data. Data processing in Big Data analytics is very important due to the large amount of data in the healthcare sector. This has made privacy protection and cyber security services based on big data a very critical issue in the healthcare supply chain. Solutions to cyber security problems are sought with new technologies. Blockchain is one of these technologies. The fact that blockchains are immutable, transparent and decentralized facilitates healthcare interoperability (Wang & Jones, 2019). Various case examples demonstrate the importance of data security. Two examples are the 2004 stolen of data from the Home Depot drug wholesaler, which impacted 53 million of its clients, and the 2015 theft of 80 million customers' medical records from the American insurance provider Anthem (Torre et al., 2017). It is especially important to address concerns like patient data privacy, medical device security, and healthcare system continuity. This vulnerability may be caused by unpatched or out-of-date software, weak passwords, antiquated computer systems, and accounts that have been taken from old computers (Damar et al., 2024).

Studying the I4.0 paradigm, advanced technologies are expected to increase the possibilities of enhancing business delivery by optimizing the data collection and analysis process with high accuracy and speed (Agarwal & Brem, 2015). In this scenario, companies going through a lean supply system can adopt I4.0 technologies to achieve higher performance brackets. Although there is increasing interest in weight loss with I4.0 perfecting methods, studies on the integration between the supply system and I4.0 are missing in the literature (Reyes et al., 2023). Decision-making in LSCM bindings is a challenging task due to the complexity, dynamism and uncertainty of the environment. Therefore, being able to use information management is a great advantage. Incorrect demand forecasts and insufficient sharing of parts information among chain members cause overproduction, unpaid logistics costs, increased delivery times, and substandard releases. Artificial intelligence is present in decision-making to achieve Lean goals in supply chains, and a decision-making support system proposed for LSCM employing artificial intelligence equips decision-makers with an instrument that eliminates all non-value-adding activity throughout the supply chain by making the right decisions. The system enables outsiders to improve decision-making through information management and eliminate waste such as production and stock overages, waiting options, material and unnecessary movements, thereby improving performance and productivity across the entire Lean supply chain (Liu et al., 2023). AI and ML, one of the important tools of digital tools in the health sector, are examined in depth in this study within the scope of lean digital health activities.

2.3 AI/ML Applications

AI is used in SCM in areas such as demand forecasting, inventory optimization, transportation route planning, customer segmentation, and document analysis. Demand patterns and stock levels are predicted, transportation routes are optimized and hidden patterns in data are revealed with methods such as time series analysis, machine learning, deep learning, and optimization algorithms. Communication and data analysis are facilitated with tools such as Natural Language Processing (NLP), text mining, and chatbots, while training data can be increased with techniques. These methods play a critical role in increasing efficiency, cost reduction, and customer satisfaction in supply chain processes (Nimmagadda, 2021). Concerns regarding data security and privacy of AI-based systems may exist in a supply chain that contains significant amounts of data, like the healthcare industry. Research is required to determine the extent to which AI may be applied ethically in healthcare because there are currently no common criteria for its use (Khan et al., 2023). In a study performed by (Chen et al., 2013) the Lean Production and Radio Frequency Identification techniques are implemented together, and it is observed that the effectiveness of the supply chain is improved. It is also exhibited the obtained gains by applying Lean Tools to supply chain as a whole. In a study (Manzouri et al., 2014) try to introduce the best lean techniques applicable to food enterprises with 300 questionnaires in Malaysia. They stated that the cooperative demand planning, uninterrupted development and close inventory supervision are the best procedures. For instance, in a study the practicability of Lean tools for hospitals supply chain by implementing the Kanban System has discussed (Aguila-Escobar and Garrido Veja, 2012). Employment of Markov Model is proposed by McClean et al., (2007) for improving the efficiency of patient routes in the health organizations that can be related to improvement of curing operations like Lean Principles and Six Sigma applications. In another study, it can be seen the implementation of two methodologies, Lean Methodology together with the Patient and Family Centred Care Methodology and Practice (PFCCM/P) (Aguilar-Escobar & Garrido-Vega, 2013). Some real case implications of holistic methods applied in the field of health can be found in the literature. A holistic method is introduced by (Tritos et al., 2014) that Lean SCM principles are primarily installed to healthcare operations. To grade the primacies of categories a Fuzzy Analytic Hierarchy Process (AHP) technique is employed, continuous improvement, JIT, waste elimination and enterprise integration. It is seen that for the financial and operational objectives, the Lean SCM is dominant.

AI/ML has significantly transformed supply chain management in demand forecasting, inventory management, logistics, risk management, and collaboration. Time series analysis and deep learning provide high accuracy in demand forecasting, while inventory optimization reduces inventory costs and prevents stockouts with

AI algorithms. In transportation and logistics, complex problems such as vehicle routing and load optimization are solved with AI-powered algorithms. In risk management, AI prevents disruptions by identifying potential risks from historical data and provides predictive maintenance solutions. In addition, collaboration, information sharing, and supply chain transparency are increased with technologies such as natural language processing and blockchain (Nimmagadda, 2021). There are many of troubles in the healthcare systems all over the world such as increasing illnesses, mental or physical sufficiency losses, aging, more demand for healthcare services and rising social expectations and prices (Atun, 2015).

2.4 Lean Supply Chain Management

Lean Supply Chain Management (LSCM) is an integrated set of departments or organizations to remove effectively the costs and unnecessary operations related to the stream of goods, services, finances wastes and information to satisfy the needs of individual end-users (Reyes et al., 2023). The network of suppliers generates big data and is essential in agile decision making. Especially in the healthcare supply chains the topics that require more attention in artificial intelligence approach are the automatic renewal, customer selection, smart storage, financial supply chain management and the green supply chain (Toorajipour et al., 2021). The deficiency of the healthcare systems today is the leadership. When the problems are discussed in the academic groups of AI, they cannot solve in these societies; the solution requires the contribution of citizens, patients, and clinicians under the leadership of the policy makers. The fear exaggerated that Healthcare workforce will be dismissed by AI. The true part of fear is the non-hugged opportunity cost for partially adaptation to AI (Panch et al., 2018). Some uncertainties are included in healthcare applications because of dependence to different stakeholders such as patients, citizens for meaningful practice. In conclusion, it is necessary to expedite hugging of the Machine Learning concept to provide frequent benefits in the healthcare field by the application science group (Shaw et al., 2019).

In the study of (A. Kumar et al., 2022) it is objected to define the crucial causes for achievement of transforming health supply chain to AI in a developing economy a group of twenty experts including logistics, supply chain, IT, senior managers and academicals. The AI principles are understood as improving the supply chains by employment of removing the bottlenecks, higher clearness, flexibility and shorter response periods. But there is some resistance to accepting the AI applications for the digitalization of healthcare operations, whereas it obtains many utilities to the healthcare supply chain managers (A. Kumar et al., 2022). The abilities of digitalization are hardening to raise maximum level, because of the disconnected use in the healthcare applications. This study is performed by Beaulieu and Bentahar (2021) as a roadmap to implement the new technologies to maximize the gains by employing digitalization. Companies in achieving autonomous training models and effective decision results provided functional benefits by using Artificial Intelligence (AI). There is a loss of converted data in practice and the lack of availability of developed systems on most machines limits its applications. Creating a public cloud to share definitive records of open data and models could be one way to transform AI and increase its expressiveness. The health industry was forced to re-evaluate its health benefits supply strategies because of the increasing healthcare inflation, the reports about decreasing care quality and medical faults. The solution was found in the supply chain management that was proven to be an effective strategy in all other industries for reducing costs and time spent while increasing the product quality (Ford et al., 2007).

The objectives of lean health procedures based on data technologies are various. These are reported in various healthcare research studies as using fuzzy logic to evaluate the insufficiency of healthcare supply chains, combining the task flow in emergency service lean health, machine learning and simulation techniques, or optimization of antibiotic management employing lean health and automation. As the effects of digitalization develop, especially within the framework of machine learning and artificial intelligence, it is an important conceptual framework to understand what kind of difficulties will be encountered when implementing lean activities of healthcare services. There has been a necessity for a strategic framework to be developed to overcome the resulting challenges. The rapid consolidation of healthcare institutions has created redundancy in departments, staff, and healthcare technologies within individual hospitals and practices. Enterprise resource planning (ERP), both as a concept and as a system, is a common solution to the redundancy problem in newly created organizations after a merger (Gorbenko et al., 2023). The established health system needs to develop various solution methods for the obstacles and facilitators of digital transformation by applying integrative strategies such as ERP.

Health care organizations need to renew their information technologies to use huge data bundles and innovation techniques ignoring the costs. The effective management of required data is the key to organizational success, where the manager can make data-driven decisions for competition and create value. Healthcare organizations can get the ability to use huge amounts of data and take active initiative for strategic decisions with machine learning, artificial intelligence, advanced analysis, lean thinking and Industry 4.0 techniques. It is a crucial necessity for the healthcare industry to achieve its waste reduction problem. The managerial personnel who are working different departments of healthcare institutions applying Lean 4.0, AI or Machine Learning can take the leadership tasks in this industry. Lean 4.0, ML, or AI technologies try to eliminate waste, for example, using reusable medical equipment or reducing packaging materials waste. An expected difficulty in the implementation of digitalization in the healthcare sector is the barriers to Lean 4.0.

The goal of this study is to conduct research on the current status and barriers of the relations between Digitalization, I 4.0, and Artificial Intelligence with Supply Chain Management implementation potential to the health industry that emerging lean thinking to minimize the time, money and energy lost by agile response at emergency situations. This study examines in the fields of enterprise, digitalization and data management to find a path that incite sustainable development and organizational changes by innovatively designed procedures and decisions in the health care industries. This study is performed to show that businesses in the healthcare industry can manage their strategic goals and satisfy the stakeholders with the help of agile, lean, data-driven applications in the tortuous current competitive environment. The significance of this study will provide a new horizon to SCM personnel of the health care industry and researchers in the digitalization area by reducing time, money and energy losses which is the basic area of lean production.

3. PROPOSED METHODOLOGY

After the COVID-19 process, there have been significant changes in the world to make improvements in the field of health. Because healthcare institutions encountered numerous problems and difficulties in this process. Patients want top-notch medical care, while the government and health insurance firms require the lowest possible cost. Organizations within the health system need improvement activities such as process development, waste reduction and cost reduction, just like production processes. Operational efficiency is defined as providing high-quality, error-free treatment at the lowest possible cost with quick access to care and minimal waiting times (Yaduvanshi & Sharma, 2017). Lean philosophy is different from the cost-cutting or efficiency-improving methods known in some sectors, including healthcare. This approach requires the design of a management system that can change the way healthcare services are organized and managed. This approach reduces errors and wait times, improves the quality of care for patients, creates an environment that supports staff and physicians, removes barriers so they can focus on providing care, and breaks down barriers between disconnected departmental silos, allowing facilities within the health system to work for the benefit of patients (Graban, 2018). As in all sectors, there are improvement needs in healthcare institutions. Lean digital transformation is not about solving big problems in healthcare. It is about identifying and solving some of the critical strategic barriers, including digital practices. The health sector has also started to be affected by the ever-evolving digitalization processes. The need for both digitalization and improvement of processes has revealed the need for lean digital applications.

The research subject of how the digital transformation from strategy to operations affects the Lean Production System is of interest to both academia and industry (Schumacher et al., 2020).

Machine learning and artificial intelligence are two of the most common tools of digital transformation processes in industries. These applications, which have widespread benefits for a field such as the healthcare sector that directly affects human life and should work with a zero-error policy, should be actively used in the process. Automation systems can help improve performance indicators. By applying the necessary improvement and optimization steps in processes containing inefficiency or errors, additional costs and unnecessary resource usage will be avoided (Hofmann et al., 2020).

Within the scope of this chapter, a study was conducted on the barriers of lean digital transformation applications in the health supply chain within the scope of machine learning and artificial intelligence activities to the experts in the Traditional and Complementary Medicine Application and Research Center of a university serving in Turkey and having a Faculty of Medicine. First of all, the barriers identified through a comprehensive literature review were evaluated by the experts. Then, these barriers were weighted by SWARA method. By proposing ERP strategies for the solution of the barriers obtained, results were obtained for improvements in the supply chain of the sector. The suggested approach can be shown as a flowchart, like the one in Figure 1.

Figure 1. Proposed Methodology

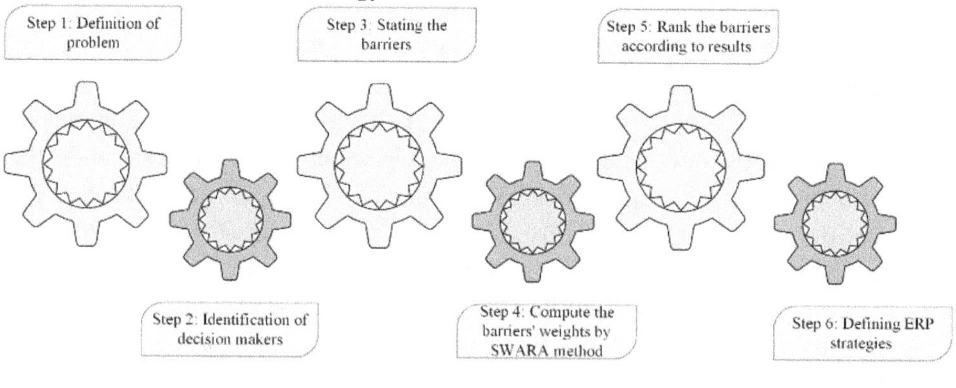

As an important step of the methodology planned in Figure 1, experts with high experience in the health sector were contacted. Table 1 shows the education and experience of these experts.

Table 1. Specific Expert Information

Expert	Experience	Education Level	Job Title
E-1	7 years	BSc	Administrative Personnel
E-2	10+ years	BSc	Doctor of Physical Therapy and Traditional Medicine
E-3	4 years	BSc	Physiotherapy and Rehabilitation Assistant Doctor
E-4	16 years	BSc	Patient Care and Health Status Monitoring Personnel
E-5	2 years	High School	Laboratory Support Personnel

After the identification of experts, the barriers in Table 2 were identified through an in-depth literature review. In total, five main categories and twenty-three sub-categories were identified.

Table 2. Main and sub-criteria definitions

No	Main barriers	Sub-barriers
1	C1: Technical (Li et al., 2023)	C11: technical maintenance (Hobeck et al., 2021)
		C12: infrastructural obstacles (Hobeck et al., 2021)
		C13: lack of standardized medical terms in the local language (Zemplényi et al., 2023)
		C14: lack of evaluation methodology (Hobeck et al., 2021)
		C15: lack of quality assessment of data entry or self-reporting (Zemplényi et al., 2023)
		C16: regulatory compliance issues in the process of managing a high volume of sensitive information (Zemplényi et al., 2023)
		C17: lack of Plan for Updating Algorithm for operations (Li et al., 2023)
2	C2: Financial (Amran et al., 2020)	C21: infrastructure costs (Hobeck et al., 2021)
		C22: lack of resources to build and maintain IT infrastructure to support AI process (Zemplényi et al., 2023)
		C23: high costs associated with securing and storing data (Zemplényi et al., 2023)
3	C3: Legal (Amran et al., 2020)	C31: legal data protection regulations (Hobeck et al., 2021)
		C32: lack of political commitment (e.g. no health digitization strategy in the country to establish relevant databases) (Zemplényi et al., 2023)
		C33: lack of access to patient-level databases due to data protection regulations (Zemplényi et al., 2023)
4	C4: Management (Amran et al., 2020)	C41: hierarchy and management resistance (Amran et al., 2020)
		C42: lack of managerial skills (Amran et al., 2020)
		C43: need for Standards Enabling Interoperability (Li et al., 2023)

continued on following page

Table 2. Continued

No	Main barriers	Sub-barriers
5	C5: Stakeholder (Li et al., 2023)	C51: deficit in responsibilities (Hobeck et al., 2021)
		C52: knowledge and competence-related appliacations (Hobeck et al., 2021)
		C53: resistance of the practitioner to changes in established practices (Hobeck et al., 2021)
		C54: lack of technical affinity or knowledge among physicians and patients (Hobeck et al., 2021)
		C55: fear of job loss on the part of the physician and technicans (Hobeck et al., 2021)
		C56: lack of appropriate skills for applying AI methods (natural language proccessing, machine learning etc.) in outcomes research (Zemplényi et al., 2023)
		C57: lack of specialized education to generate AI driven scientific evidence (Zemplényi et al., 2023)

With Artificial Intelligence (AI), the imitation of human intelligence with the help of machines, and with Machine Learning (ML), the automatic learning of machines with experience without programming, combined with improvement applications in lean processes, can provide significant improvements in the healthcare sector. The integration of all these applications into the relevant sector will bring some barriers. The adaptation of digital transformation in lean processes in the healthcare sector with strategic steps by overcoming barriers constitutes the main theme of this study. In this context, as a result of in-depth research in the literature, the barriers to Machine Learning (ML) and Artificial Intelligence (AI) for lean Digital Transformation applications in healthcare were identified. Each concept was scanned as "Lean", "Digital Transformation", "Artificial Intelligence", "Machine Learning" and "Health Sector". Barriers were identified for each concept. Five main criteria and 23 sub-criteria were categorized and defined in Table 2.

A comprehensive analysis, including a literature review and consultation with experts, identified five main barriers: Technical, Financial, Legal, Governance, and Stakeholder. A total of twenty-three sub-criteria were identified to examine these factors in more detail. The criteria and sub-criteria were evaluated by experts and weights were determined by SWARA method. Finally, considering the weights, ERP strategies were proposed to prevent barriers and improve processes in the healthcare sector. This real case study is an important roadmap to work towards lean digital transformation in the healthcare sector.

The SWARA method, which is one of the multi-criteria decision-making techniques used for criteria weighting and has been frequently used in recent years, stands for "Step-Wise Weight Assessment Ratio Analysis". SWARA method was first proposed by Keršuliene et al. (2010). It can be easily applied by decision makers (DM) because it offers an intuitive process based on the experiences and opinions of experts, proceeding step by step. It has been widely used in studies in recent years because of its user-friendly approach to weighting. In the method, the criteria to be used in the evaluation of alternatives are prioritized and ranked from important to less important. When calculating the importance weights of the remaining criteria, the ranking created by each decision maker is taken into account (Keršuliene et al., 2010).

The steps of the SWARA method can be summarized as follows:

Step 1. The opinion of experts is utilized to rank the criteria, and then their geometric means are computed in descending order of importance.

Step 2. Each criterion's relative importance is determined.

Step 3. Every criterion's coefficient is identified.

Step 4. Coefficient number is computed.

$$q_j = \begin{cases} 1 & \text{if } j = 1 \\ e_{j+1} & \text{if } j > 1 \end{cases} \tag{1}$$

Step 5. Revised significance number is evaluated.

$$S_j = \begin{cases} 1 & \text{if } j = 1 \\ \frac{S_{j-1}}{q_j} & \text{if } j > 1 \end{cases} \tag{2}$$

Step 6. The factors' weights are determined.

$$w_j = \frac{S_j}{\sum_{j=1}^{n} S_j} \tag{3}$$

The importance levels of the evaluation criteria were decided by five decision makers. Initially, each decision maker established the criteria's relative relevance. Next, it was determined which evaluation criteria the decision makers considered to be of what relative relevance. This phase included comparing each criterion to the previous criterion, beginning with the second criterion, in order to determine the relative importance of the criteria. In this step, starting from the second criterion, each criterion was compared with the previous criterion, and the comparative importance of the criteria relative to each other was determined. The coefficients of the comparative importance of the criteria were obtained with the Eq. (1). The importance vector of the criteria was determined according to Eq. (2). Then, the final importance weights of the criteria were calculated by Eq. (3). The steps were repeated for all decision-makers. The final ranking was done at the last step. The ranking of decision makers for each criterion and sub-criteria is shown in Table 3.

Table 3. The importance of the main and sub-criteria by decision-makers

Criteria	Order of priority				
	DM1	DM2	DM3	DM4	DM5
C1	3	4	1	3	2
C11	3	5	3	7	4
C12	2	3	4	1	3
C13	4	7	2	6	7
C14	7	6	7	2	6
C15	6	4	1	3	5
C16	1	2	6	4	1
C17	5	1	5	5	2
C2	4	3	2	4	3
C21	1	2	2	1	1
C22	2	1	1	2	2
C23	3	3	3	3	3
C3	1	2	5	2	1
C31	2	2	1	2	1
C32	1	1	2	1	2
C33	3	3	3	3	3
C4	2	5	4	1	4
C41	1	3	1	2	1
C42	2	1	3	1	3
C43	3	2	2	3	2
C5	5	1	3	5	5
C51	1	1	5	5	4
C52	3	2	4	4	3
C53	2	4	3	1	5
C54	5	3	2	6	6
C55	6	7	6	7	7
C56	4	5	7	3	2
C57	7	6	1	2	1

The defined operations are carried out separately for each decision maker for the main criteria and sub-criteria. Then, the criteria and sub-criteria values are obtained by taking the geometric average of the decision makers' results. Finally, general results are obtained by multiplying the local weights of the main criteria with the sub-criteria weights. In these results, the relevant criterion weights are obtained by sorting from largest to smallest.

Table 4. Weights of the main- criteria with SWARA

DM 1		DM 2		DM 3		DM 4		DM 5	
No.	**sj**	**No.**	**sj**	**No.**	**sj**	**No.**	**sj**	**No.**	**sj**
C3 LEGAL		C4 MANAGEMENT		C1 TECHNICAL		C3 LEGAL		C2 FINANCIAL	
C4 MANAGEMENT	0,6	C3 LEGAL	0,5	C2 FINANCIAL	0,7	C4 MANAGEMENT	0,5	C3 LEGAL	0,7
C1 TECHNICAL	0,5	C2 FINANCIAL	0,3	C5 STAKEHOLDER	0,3	C2 FINANCIAL	0,5	C1 TECHNICAL	0,5
C2 FINANCIAL	0,8	C5 STAKEHOLDER	0,5	C4 MANAGEMENT	0,5	C1 TECHNICAL	0,3	C4 MANAGEMENT	0,4
C5 STAKEHOLDER	0,6	C1 TECHNICAL	0,8	C3 LEGAL	0,2	C5 STAKEHOLDER	0,2	C5 STAKEHOLDER	0,2

Table 4 shows the results obtained with the evaluations made by all decision makers for each main criterion.

Table 5. Weights and Rankings of Major Challenges and Sub-criteria

RESULTS				
WEIGHTS OF MAIN CRITERIA	**WEIGHTS OF SUB-CRITERIA**	**MAIN CRITERIA * SUB-CRITERIA**	**RESULT**	**RANKING**
C1: 0,182	0,105	0,019	0,0204	14
	0,197	0,036	0,0384	10
	0,082	0,015	0,0159	18
	0,070	0,013	0,0137	20
	0,125	0,023	0,0243	13
	0,173	0,032	0,0337	11
	0,150	0,027	0,0292	12
C2: 0,215	0,394	0,085	0,0905	3
	0,374	0,081	0,0861	4
	0,214	0,046	0,0492	9
C3: 0,272	0,364	0,099	0,1060	2
	0,412	0,112	0,1200	1
	0,202	0,055	0,0589	8
C4: 0,22	0,363	0,080	0,0855	5
	0,321	0,071	0,0756	6
	0,260	0,057	0,0611	7
C5: 0,112	0,146	0,016	0,0174	15
	0,139	0,015	0,0165	17
	0,139	0,016	0,0166	16
	0,090	0,010	0,0108	21
	0,039	0,004	0,0046	23
	0,090	0,010	0,0107	22
	0,123	0,014	0,0147	19

According to the results given in the Table 5, "lack of political commitment" has been determined as the most important obstacle to lean digital transformation in the healthcare sector. "Legal data protection regulations" comes in second place. "Infrastructure costs" ranks third in the SWARA ranking. Although there is not much difference between them, "lack of resources to build and maintain IT infrastructure to support AI process" is in the fourth place, and "hierarchy and management resistance" is in the fifth place, again with a very small difference. On the other hand, according to the analysis results, "lack of technical affinity or knowledge among physicians and patients", "lack of appropriate skills for applying AI methods" and "fear of job loss on the part of the physicians and technicians" are the least important barriers. ranked twenty-one, twenty-two and twenty-third.

4. DISCUSSION

AI has a wide range of applications in supply chain management. While demand forecasting determines future trends, seasonality and demand patterns, inventory management calculates optimum stock levels and reduces costs. Transportation and route optimization allows creating dynamic and efficient routes in transportation processes. Customer segmentation allows determining customer groups based on data, while defect detection allows rapid detection of quality problems in products and processes. Document analysis extracts information from contracts, invoices and other texts, and facilitates supply chain communication with tools such as virtual assistants. In addition, the performance of artificial intelligence models is increased by enriching the training data set with data augmentation techniques (Nimmagadda, 2021). There are many methods to apply lean principles and systematizing the processes. One of these methods is ERP used for complicated procedures like pharmaceutical supply chains, and Robotic Procedure Automation (RPA) can be employed for patient appointment planning automatically. To store and sharing of patient data securely Blockchain technology and, by evaluating the patients' health problems to raise the service quality NLP can be used (Juturi, 2024; Madakam et al., 2019; Ugajin, 2023). In order to be able to carry out applications with all these lean philosophy tools in the hospital and to get accurate results, data must be collected accurately and quickly. To achieve this, digital transformation and digital tools should be used. It is essential to use an integrated AI/ML and digital transformation infrastructure to obtain results that will help decision-making by modeling these data in accordance with the decisions to be taken for the steps that need to be taken for improvement. Decision-making procedures in healthcare management generally and resource efficiency could be revolutionized by data analysis and lean healthcare (Moreno-Fergusson et al., 2021). In addition, the detection of fraud in insurance services can be a solution to problems in managing the lean health supply chain, such as cybersecurity concerns, especially involving big data, financial constraints, and problems due to workforce resistance to change.

In this study, an analysis was made to clarify this issue, considering that one of the expected difficulties in the implementation of digitalization in the healthcare sector is Lean 4.0 barriers. According to the analysis results of the evaluations made by experts, the use of ERP systems can be useful as a solution to the issues of "Infrastructure costs" and "Lack of resources to create and maintain the IT infrastructure to support the AI process", which are important obstacles to lean digital transformation in the healthcare sector. It would be useful to give examples of some of the ERP applications that can be done in this regard.

The lean philosophy, digitalization and enterprise resource planning (ERP) systems obtain some managerial benefits in healthcare industries. These administrative benefits help to manage healthcare organizations more effectively and flexibly, better control processes, and improve the quality of patient care. These may be summarized as follows.

- Standardization and continuous improvement of processes are promoted by lean philosophy and the ERP system make these processes more manageable and increases efficiency by standardizing workflows.
- ERP systems provide managers with analyses based on real-time data. This enables them to make more informed and faster decisions and strengthens strategic planning. Digitalization increases communication and collaboration between different departments where ERP systems enable teams to work more effectively by collecting all relevant information on a central platform. Lean philosophy aims to use resources effectively by reducing waste and ERP systems assist managers in planning and allocating resources so that workforce and equipment can be used more efficiently.
- ERP systems provide the required tools to track and measure an organization's performance; by using these instruments management can better monitor the level of achievement of set goals and the efficiency of processes.
- ERP systems help identify potential risks early to enable proactive measures to be taken and contribute to management's preparedness for possible problems. Digitalization enables documents and information to be stored and managed in a central location and ERP systems ensure that this information is easily accessible and securely managed.
- Lean philosophy encourages continuous training and involvement of employees whereas ERP systems support training and participation processes, enabling employees to be more effectively involved in business processes.

In light of this study, the following can be implementable digital technology proposals for the healthcare industries. In Lean Health (LH) medical treatments the "communication and sensing" topic includes five basic digital technologies big data, IoT, biomedical or digital sensors, cloud technology and remote control or monitoring. The Transportation personnel can be informed digitally, by implementing an electronic transportation Kanban system. The RFID label can be used on transportation instruments (stretchers or wheelchairs) to raise performance is another solution for patient movements in hospitals by employing digital technology applications. The electronic Kanban systems used to improve patient transportation in hospitals act as an effective barrier for example patient movement or discharging processes.

5. CONCLUSION AND FUTURE DIRECTIONS

Lean digital transformation is one of the approaches that can solve important problems in the healthcare sector, such as patient satisfaction and easy access to healthcare. By acting on lean thinking principles, industry executives can reduce patients' waiting time in queues, end care errors and reduce the cost of care by ensuring patient satisfaction.

This study aims to identify and weigh the barriers to lean digital transformation in the healthcare supply chain based on artificial intelligence and machine learning using multi-criteria decision analysis. For this purpose, firstly, the barriers to digital transformation were defined and presented as criteria, and the importance levels of these criteria were determined using the SWARA method.

According to the results obtained, "Infrastructure costs" and "Lack of resources to create and maintain the IT infrastructure to support the AI process" were found to be the two most important barriers to the digitalization of the healthcare supply chain in the digital transformation process. Infrastructure costs in a lean digital supply chain do not only cover the initial costs. They are also important in terms of sustainability and competitive advantage. Creating the right infrastructure investments affects profitability in the long term by providing cost optimization in supply chain processes.

On the other hand, the lack of resources to create and maintain the IT infrastructure that will support the artificial intelligence process requires significant infrastructure performance in the collection, analysis and storage of data. With the lack of resources, the data processing speed slows down and the performance of the digital system decreases. According to these very important barriers evaluated by experts, businesses need to develop the right strategic solutions.

At the end of this study, it is seen that sustainable data quality, technical applicability, sustainability, data stability and quality, competitiveness, government cooperation and political compatibility are important criteria. For future studies, it is recommended to develop a solution mechanism using various methods to address and overcome these barriers by thoroughly evaluating the relevant criteria.

The limitations of the study include that the application of the lean digital transformation process in the healthcare supply chain is a very new concept. As new restrictions or criteria emerge as a result of the spread of this digital transformation in the healthcare sector, the current results can be compared with detailed and in-depth analyses of new cases.

REFERENCES

Abdel-Basset, M., Manogaran, G., & Mohamed, M. (2018). Internet of Things (IoT) and its impact on supply chain: A framework for building smart, secure and efficient systems. *Future Generation Computer Systems*, 86, 614–628. DOI: 10.1016/J.FUTURE.2018.04.051

Agarwal, N., & Brem, A. (2015). Strategic business transformation through technology convergence: Implications from General Electric's industrial internet initiative. *International Journal of Technology Management*, 67(2), 196–214. DOI: 10.1504/IJTM.2015.068224

Aguilar-Escobar, V. G., & Garrido-Vega, P. (2013). Gestión Lean en logística de hospitales: Estudio de un caso. *Revista De Calidad Asistencial*, 28(1), 42–49. DOI: 10.1016/J.CALI.2012.07.001 PMID: 22980756

Allaoui, H., Guo, Y., & Sarkis, J. (2019). Decision support for collaboration planning in sustainable supply chains. *Journal of Cleaner Production*, 229, 761–774. DOI: 10.1016/J.JCLEPRO.2019.04.367

Amran, M., Daril, M., Ikbar, M., Subari, K., Mohd Amran, M. D., Januddi, F., Nuraina, S., Mohamad Ikbar, A. W., & Khairanum, S. (2020). *The Barriers in Lean Healthcare Implementation*. https://www.researchgate.net/publication/338594955

Ankrum, A. L., Neogi, S., Morckel, M. A., Wilhite, A. W., Li, Z., & Schaffzin, J. K. (2019). Reduced isolation room turnover time using Lean methodology. *Infection Control and Hospital Epidemiology*, 40(10), 1151–1156. DOI: 10.1017/ICE.2019.199 PMID: 31345277

Aqlan, F., & Lam, S. S. (2015). A fuzzy-based integrated framework for supply chain risk assessment. *International Journal of Production Economics*, 161, 54–63. DOI: 10.1016/J.IJPE.2014.11.013

Atun, R. (2015). Transitioning health systems for multimorbidity. *Lancet*, 386(9995), 721–722. DOI: 10.1016/S0140-6736(14)62254-6 PMID: 26063473

Ballé, M., & Régnier, A. (2007). Lean as a learning system in a hospital ward. *Leadership in Health Services (Bradford, England)*, 20(1), 33–41. DOI: 10.1108/17511870710721471 PMID: 20690474

Baril, C., Gascon, V., & Cartier, S. (2014). Design and analysis of an outpatient orthopaedic clinic performance with discrete event simulation and design of experiments. *Computers & Industrial Engineering*, 78, 285–298. DOI: 10.1016/J.CIE.2014.05.006

Baril, C., Gascon, V., Miller, J., & Côté, N. (2016). Use of a discrete-event simulation in a Kaizen event: A case study in healthcare. *European Journal of Operational Research*, 249(1), 327–339. DOI: 10.1016/J.EJOR.2015.08.036

Bastian, N. D., Munoz, D., & Ventura, M. (2016). A Mixed-Methods Research Framework for Healthcare Process Improvement. *Journal of Pediatric Nursing*, 31(1), e39–e51. DOI: 10.1016/J.PEDN.2015.09.003 PMID: 26453414

Beaulieu, M., & Bentahar, O. (2021). Digitalization of the healthcare supply chain: A roadmap to generate benefits and effectively support healthcare delivery. *Technological Forecasting and Social Change*, 167, 120717. DOI: 10.1016/J.TECHFORE.2021.120717

Bharsakade, R. S., Acharya, P., Ganapathy, L., & Tiwari, M. K. (2021). A lean approach to healthcare management using multi criteria decision making. *OPSEARCH*, 58(3), 610–635. DOI: 10.1007/S12597-020-00490-5/TABLES/16

Bhat, S., Gijo, E. V., & Jnanesh, N. A. (2014). Application of Lean Six Sigma methodology in the registration process of a hospital. *International Journal of Productivity and Performance Management*, 63(5), 613–643. DOI: 10.1108/IJPPM-11-2013-0191

Bowerman, J., & Fillingham, D. (2007). Can lean save lives? *Leadership in Health Services (Bradford, England)*, 20(4), 231–241. DOI: 10.1108/17511870710829346 PMID: 20698096

Chan, H., Lo, S., Lee, L., Lo, W., Yu, W., Wu, Y., Ho, S., Yeung, R., & Chan, J. (2014). Lean techniques for the improvement of patients' flow in emergency department. *World Journal of Emergency Medicine*, 5(1), 24. DOI: 10.5847/WJEM.J.ISSN.1920-8642.2014.01.004 PMID: 25215143

Chen, J. C., Cheng, C. H., Huang, P. B., Wang, K. J., Huang, C. J., & Ting, T. C. (2013). Warehouse management with lean and RFID application: A case study. *International Journal of Advanced Manufacturing Technology*, 69(1–4), 531–542. DOI: 10.1007/S00170-013-5016-8

Curatolo, N., Lamouri, S., Huet, J. C., & Rieutord, A. (2014). A critical analysis of Lean approach structuring in hospitals. *Business Process Management Journal*, 20(3), 433–454. DOI: 10.1108/BPMJ-04-2013-0051/FULL/XML

Damar, M., Özen, A., & Yılmaz, A. (2024). Cybersecurity in The Health Sector in The Reality of Artificial Intelligence, And Information Security Conceptually. *Journal of AI*, 8(1), 61–82. DOI: 10.61969/JAI.1466340 de la Torre, I., García-Zapirain, B., & López-Coronado, M. (2017). Analysis of Security in Big Data Related to Healthcare. *Journal of Digital Forensics, Security and Law, 12*(3), 5. https://doi.org/https://doi.org/10.15394/jdfsl.2017.1448

Dias, D. G., Mendes, C., & da Silva, M. M. (2013). A Method for Reengineering Healthcare Using Enterprise Ontology and Lean. *Communications in Computer and Information Science*, 415, 243–259. DOI: 10.1007/978-3-642-54105-6_16

Elafri, N., Tappert, J., Rose, B., & Yassine, M. (2022). Lean 4.0: Synergies between Lean Management tools and Industry 4.0 technologies. *IFAC-PapersOnLine*, 55(10), 2060–2066. DOI: 10.1016/J.IFACOL.2022.10.011

Ford, E. W., Ford, D. P. S., & Scanlon, E. W. (2007). Promise and Problems with Supply Chain Management Approaches to Health Care Purchasing. *Health Care Management Review*, 32(3), 192–202. http://www.lww.com/ PMID: 17666990

Furman, C., & Caplan, R. (2007). Applying the Toyota Production System: Using a patient safety alert system to reduce error. *Joint Commission Journal on Quality and Patient Safety*, 33(7), 376–386. DOI: 10.1016/S1553-7250(07)33043-2 PMID: 17711139

Garay-Rondero, C. L., Rodríguez Calvo, E. Z., & Salinas-Navarro, D. E. (2019). Experiential learning at Lean-Thinking-Learning Space. *International Journal on Interactive Design and Manufacturing*, 13(3), 1129–1144. DOI: 10.1007/S12008-019-00578-3/FIGURES/8

Gorbenko, K., Romanchuk, K., Sagliocca, F., & Mazumdar, M. (2023). A changing supply chain for a changing health care system: Barriers and facilitators of implementing enterprise resource planning. *Work (Reading, Mass.)*, 74(3), 977–990. DOI: 10.3233/WOR-210081 PMID: 36404564

Graban, M. (2018). Lean hospitals: Improving quality, patient safety, and employee engagement, third edition. *Lean Hospitals: Improving Quality, Patient Safety, and Employee Engagement, Third Edition*, 1–319. https://doi.org/ DOI: 10.4324/9781315380827/LEAN-HOSPITALS-MARK-GRABAN/ACCESSIBILITY-INFORMATION

Gunasekeran, D. V., Tseng, R. M. W. W., Tham, Y. C., & Wong, T. Y. (2021). Applications of digital health for public health responses to COVID-19: a systematic scoping review of artificial intelligence, telehealth and related technologies. In *npj Digital Medicine* (Vol. 4, Issue 1). Nature Research. https://doi.org/DOI: 10.1038/s41746-021-00412-9

Haddud, A., & Khare, A. (2020). Digitalizing supply chains potential benefits and impact on lean operations. *International Journal of Lean Six Sigma*, 11(4), 731–765. DOI: 10.1108/IJLSS-03-2019-0026/FULL/PDF

Hobeck, R., Schlieter, H., & Scheplitz, T. (2021). Overcoming diffusion barriers of digital health innovations: Conception of an assessment method. *Proceedings of the Annual Hawaii International Conference on System Sciences, 2020-January*, 3654–3663. https://doi.org/DOI: 10.24251/hicss.2021.443

Hofmann, P., Samp, C., & Urbach, N. (2020). Robotic process automation. *Electronic Markets*, 30(1), 99–106. DOI: 10.1007/S12525-019-00365-8/TABLES/1

Juturi, V. P. K. (2024). Advancing Enterprise Applications with Transformative Effects of Digital Technologies. *International Journal of Research Publication and Reviews*, 5(7). Advance online publication. DOI: 10.55248/GENGPI.5.0724.1925

Kasemsap, K. (2016). Lean thinking in global health care: Theory and applications. In *Handbook of Research on Healthcare Administration and Management*. https://doi.org/DOI: 10.4018/978-1-5225-0920-2.ch008

Khan, B., Fatima, H., Qureshi, A., Kumar, S., Hanan, A., Hussain, J., & Abdullah, S. (2023). Drawbacks of artificial intelligence and their potential solutions in the healthcare sector. *Biomedical Materials & Devices*, 1(2), 731–738.

Kolasani, S. (2023). Innovations in digital, enterprise, cloud, data transformation, and organizational change management using agile, lean, and data-driven methodologies. *International*. https://jmlai.in/

Kumar, A., Mani, V., Jain, V., Gupta, H., & Venkatesh, V. G. (2022). Managing healthcare supply chain through artificial intelligence (AI): A study of critical success factors. *Computers & Industrial Engineering*, 175, 108815. DOI: 10.1016/J.CIE.2022.108815 PMID: 36405396

Kumar, P., Bera, S., Dutta, T., & Chakraborty, S. (2018). Auxiliary flexibility in healthcare delivery system: An integrative framework and implications. *Global Journal of Flexible Systems Managment*, 19(2), 173–186. DOI: 10.1007/S40171-018-0183-Y/FIGURES/1

Kuo, A. M. H., Borycki, E., Kushniruk, A., & Lee, T. S. (2011). A healthcare Lean Six Sigma System for postanesthesia care unit workflow improvement. *Quality Management in Health Care*, 20(1), 4–14. DOI: 10.1097/QMH.0B013E3182033791 PMID: 21192203

Lambert, D. M., & Cooper, M. C. (2000). Issues in Supply Chain Management. *Industrial Marketing Management*, 29(1), 65–83. DOI: 10.1016/S0019-8501(99)00113-3

Lasorsa, I., Liuzzi, G., Calabrese, R., & Accardo, A. (2015). An innovative method for standardizing lean management approach in hospitals. *IFMBE Proceedings*, 48, 67–70. DOI: 10.1007/978-3-319-12967-9_18

Lee, E. K., Atallah, H. Y., Wright, M. D., Post, E. T., Thomas, C., Wu, D. T., & Haley, L. L. (2015). Transforming hospital emergency department workflow and patient care. *Interfaces*, 45(1), 58–82. DOI: 10.1287/inte.2014.0788

Li, L. T., Haley, L. C., Boyd, A. K., & Bernstam, E. V. (2023). Technical/Algorithm, Stakeholder, and Society (TASS) barriers to the application of artificial intelligence in medicine: A systematic review. *Journal of Biomedical Informatics*, 147. Advance online publication. DOI: 10.1016/j.jbi.2023.104531 PMID: 37884177

Liu, L., Song, W., & Liu, Y. (2023). Leveraging digital capabilities toward a circular economy: Reinforcing sustainable supply chain management with Industry 4.0 technologies. *Computers & Industrial Engineering*, 178, 109113. DOI: 10.1016/J.CIE.2023.109113

Madakam, S., Holmukhe, R. M., & Kumar Jaiswal, D. (2019). The Future Digital Work Force: Robotic Process Automation (RPA). *Journal of Information Systems and Technology Management*, 16(1), 1–17. DOI: 10.4301/S1807-1775201916001

Manzouri, M., Ab-Rahman, M. N., Zain, C. R. C. M., & Jamsari, E. A. (2014). Increasing Production and Eliminating Waste through Lean Tools and Techniques for Halal Food Companies. *Sustainability 2014, Vol. 6, Pages 9179-9204, 6*(12), 9179–9204. https://doi.org/DOI: 10.3390/SU6129179

Moreno-Fergusson, M. E., Guerrero Rueda, W. J., Ortiz Basto, G. A., Arevalo Sandoval, I. A. L., & Sanchez–Herrera, B. (2021). Analytics and Lean Health Care to Address Nurse Care Management Challenges for Inpatients in Emerging Economies. *Journal of Nursing Scholarship*, 53(6), 803–814. DOI: 10.1111/jnu.12711 PMID: 34668285

Moyano-Fuentes, J., Bruque-Cámara, S., & Maqueira-Marín, J. M. (2019). Development and validation of a lean supply chain management measurement instrument. *Production Planning and Control*, 30(1), 20–32. DOI: 10.1080/09537287.2018.1519731

Moyano-Fuentes, J., & Sacristán-Díaz, M. (2012). Learning on lean: A review of thinking and research. *International Journal of Operations & Production Management*, 32(5), 551–582. DOI: 10.1108/01443571211226498/FULL/PDF

Mustafee, N., Katsaliaki, K., Gunasekaran, A., Williams, M. D., Virtue, A., Chaussalet, T., & Kelly, J. (2013). Healthcare planning and its potential role increasing operational efficiency in the health sector: A viewpoint. *Journal of Enterprise Information Management*, 26(1–2), 8–20. DOI: 10.1108/17410391311289523/FULL/PDF

Nicholas, J. (2012). An integrated lean-methods approach to hospital facilities redesign. *Hospital Topics*, 90(2), 47–55. DOI: 10.1080/00185868.2012.679911 PMID: 22671435

Nilay Yücenur, G., Şentürk, S., & Taşpatlatanlar, E. (2024). Lean management approach in health sector: MCDM model proposal to prevention of waste. *Decision Science Letters*, 13, 427–440. DOI: 10.5267/dsl.2024.1.004

Nimmagadda, V. S. P. (2021). Artificial Intelligence for Real-Time Logistics and Transportation Optimization in Retail Supply Chains: Techniques, Models, and Applications. *Journal of Machine Learning for Healthcare Decision Support*, 1(1), 88–126. https://medlines.uk/index.php/JMLHDS/article/view/35

Núñez-Merino, M., Maqueira-Marín, J. M., Moyano-Fuentes, J., & Martínez-Jurado, P. J. (2020). Information and digital technologies of Industry 4.0 and Lean supply chain management: A systematic literature review. *International Journal of Production Research*, 58(16), 5034–5061. DOI: 10.1080/00207543.2020.1743896

Oliveira, J., Sá, J. C., & Fernandes, A. (2017). Continuous improvement through "Lean Tools": An application in a mechanical company. *Procedia Manufacturing*, 13, 1082–1089. DOI: 10.1016/J.PROMFG.2017.09.139

Pagliosa, M., Tortorella, G., & Ferreira, J. C. E. (2021). Industry 4.0 and Lean Manufacturing: A systematic literature review and future research directions. *Journal of Manufacturing Technology Management*, 32(3), 543–569. DOI: 10.1108/JMTM-12-2018-0446

Panch, T., Szolovits, P., & Atun, R. (2018). Artificial intelligence, machine learning and health systems. *Journal of Global Health*, 8(2), 020303. DOI: 10.7189/JOGH.08.020303 PMID: 30405904

Perdomo-Verdecia, V., Sacristán-Díaz, M., & Garrido-Vega, P. (2022). Lean management in hotels: Where we are and where we might go. *International Journal of Hospitality Management*, 104, 103250. DOI: 10.1016/J.IJHM.2022.103250

Raja, R., Mukherjee, I., Sarkar, B. K., & Ali, S. (2020). A Systematic Review of Healthcare Big Data. *Scientific Programming*, 2020(1), 5471849. DOI: 10.1155/2020/5471849

Reyes, J., Mula, J., & Díaz-Madroñero, M. (2023). Development of a conceptual model for lean supply chain planning in industry 4.0: Multidimensional analysis for operations management. *Production Planning and Control*, 34(12), 1209–1224. DOI: 10.1080/09537287.2021.1993373

Rossini, M., & Portioli, A. (2018). Supply chain planning: A quantitative comparison between Lean and Info-Sharing models. *Production & Manufacturing Research*, 6(1), 264–283. DOI: 10.1080/21693277.2018.1509744

Sanders, J. H., & Karr, T. (2015). Improving ED specimen TAT using Lean Six Sigma. *International Journal of Health Care Quality Assurance*, 28(5), 428–440. DOI: 10.1108/IJHCQA-10-2013-0117 PMID: 26020426

Schumacher, S., Bildstein, A., & Bauernhansl, T. (2020). The Impact of the Digital Transformation on Lean Production Systems. *Procedia CIRP*, 93, 783–788. DOI: 10.1016/J.PROCIR.2020.03.066

Shah, C. J., Sullivan, J. R., Gonyo, M. B., Wadhwa, A., & DuBois, M. S. (2013). Practice policy and quality initiatives: Using lean principles to improve screening mammography workflow. *Radiographics*, 33(5), 1505–1517. DOI: 10.1148/RG.335135017 PMID: 23813321

Shannon, R. P., Frndak, D., Grunden, N., Lloyd, J. C., Herbert, C., Patel, B., Cummins, D., Shannon, A. H., O'Neill, P. H., & Spear, S. J. (2006). Using real-time problem solving to eliminate central line infections. *Joint Commission Journal on Quality and Patient Safety*, 32(9), 479–487. DOI: 10.1016/S1553-7250(06)32063-6 PMID: 17987871

Shaw, J., Rudzicz, F., Jamieson, T., & Goldfarb, A. (2019). Artificial Intelligence and the Implementation Challenge. *J Med Internet Res 2019;21(7):E13659*Https://Www.Jmir.Org/2019/7/E13659*, 21*(7), e13659. https://doi.org/DOI: 10.2196/13659

Stone, K. B. (2012). Four decades of lean: A systematic literature review. *International Journal of Lean Six Sigma*, 3(2), 112–132. DOI: 10.1108/20401461211243702/FULL/PDF

Toorajipour, R., Sohrabpour, V., Nazarpour, A., Oghazi, P., & Fischl, M. (2021). Artificial intelligence in supply chain management: A systematic literature review. *Journal of Business Research*, 122, 502–517. DOI: 10.1016/J.JBUSRES.2020.09.009

Tritos, L., Premaratne, S., & Dotun, A. (2014). Prioritizing lean supply chain management initiatives in healthcare service operations: A Fuzzy-AHP approach. *IEEE International Conference on Industrial Engineering and Engineering Management*, 236–242. https://doi.org/DOI: 10.1109/IEEM.2013.6962410

Ugajin, A. (2023). Automation in Hospitals and Health Care. *Springer Handbooks*, (Part F674), 1209–1233. DOI: 10.1007/978-3-030-96729-1_56

Wang, L., & Jones, R. (2019). Big Data, Cybersecurity, and Challenges in Healthcare. *Conference Proceedings - IEEE SOUTHEASTCON, 2019-April*. https://doi.org/DOI: 10.1109/SOUTHEASTCON42311.2019.9020632

Yaduvanshi, D., & Sharma, A. (2017). Lean Six Sigma in Health Operations. Http://Dx.Doi.Org/10.1177/0972063417699665, *19*(2), 203–213. https://doi.org/DOI: 10.1177/0972063417699665

Yu, T., Demirli, K., & Bhuiyan, N. (2015). A general framework for lean transformation of hospitals. *IEOM 2015 - 5th International Conference on Industrial Engineering and Operations Management, Proceeding*. https://doi.org/DOI: 10.1109/IEOM.2015.7093901

Yücenur, G. N., & Ipekçi, A. (2021). SWARA/WASPAS methods for a marine current energy plant location selection problem. *Renewable Energy*, 163, 1287–1298. DOI: 10.1016/J.RENENE.2020.08.131

Zemplényi, A., Tachkov, K., Balkanyi, L., Németh, B., Petykó, Z. I., Petrova, G., Czech, M., Dawoud, D., Goettsch, W., Gutierrez Ibarluzea, I., Hren, R., Knies, S., Lorenzovici, L., Maravic, Z., Piniazhko, O., Savova, A., Manova, M., Tesar, T., Zerovnik, S., & Kaló, Z. (2023). Recommendations to overcome barriers to the use of artificial intelligence-driven evidence in health technology assessment. *Frontiers in Public Health*, 11. Advance online publication. DOI: 10.3389/fpubh.2023.1088121 PMID: 37181704

Chapter 11
Innovative Horizons: Ethical AI, Sustainability, and Economic Impacts in Supply Chain Management

Pushpender Sarao
https://orcid.org/0000-0002-2256-9113
Lovely Professional University, India

Amir Ahmad Dar
https://orcid.org/0000-0002-0379-2272
Lovely Professional University, India

S. Sindhuja
https://orcid.org/0000-0003-1472-1127
SRM Insititute of Science and Technology, India

Mehak Malhotra
Lovely Professional University, India

Akshat Jain
Lovely Professional University, India

Shruti
https://orcid.org/0000-0002-1958-0901
Lovely Professional University, India

ABSTRACT

A new era of efficiency, innovation, and sustainability in supply chain management has been brought about by the integration of Artificial Intelligence (AI) and Machine Learning (ML) technologies. Exploring the moral effects of using AI and ML in supply chains, looking at matters like data privacy, algorithmic bias, and decision-making accountability. Additionally, the critical role that AI and ML play in advancing sustainable practices in supply chains is discussed. Overall, the chapter thoroughly examines the various aspects of AI and ML in supply chains, covering everything from risk management techniques, human-machine interaction, and ethical issues to sustainability initiatives and economic effects. Organizations can leverage the full potential of AI and ML to drive innovation, sustainability, and economic prosperity in supply chain operations by addressing these crucial aspects and navigating the

DOI: 10.4018/979-8-3693-4433-0.ch011

challenges of digital transformation.

1. INTRODUCTION

Supply chain management is the coordination of several processes necessary for producing and distributing goods and services. It is essential to the success of businesses in a variety of industries. Traditional supply chain methods have undergone substantial change due to the integration of Artificial Intelligence (AI) and Machine Learning (ML) technology. While ML allows computer systems to learn from experience and enhance their performance without explicit programming, AI is computers' approximation of human intellect. The combination of these technologies presents previously unseen chances to improve supply chain management's operational effectiveness, encourage creativity, and advance sustainability (Wang et al., 2016; Ivanov et al., 2019).

Because AI and ML can maximize resource utilization and speed up processes, their application in supply chain management has gained attention. Through the utilization of intricate algorithms and predictive analytics, businesses may obtain a more profound understanding of market patterns, consumer behavior, and operational efficiency. Because of this analytical skill, the supply chain becomes much more efficient in terms of production scheduling, inventory control, and demand forecasting. AI-driven automation eliminates the need for human intervention in repetitive processes, freeing up human resources to concentrate on value-added and strategic work (Min, 2010; Choi et al., 2018).

In addition to increasing productivity, AI and ML technologies may encourage innovation and provide supply chain managers with a competitive advantage. AI systems can evaluate enormous volumes of data and spot complex patterns, which opens up new possibilities for market expansion, process improvement, and product creation. For example, supply chain analytics driven by AI may provide useful information on customer preferences, enabling companies to adjust their offerings to changing market needs. Furthermore, AI-enabled innovations like driverless cars and drones have the power to completely transform transportation and logistics, improving supply chains' adaptability and reactivity (Sanders, 2016; Monostori, 2014).

However, there are several ethical issues raised by the extensive use of AI and ML in supply chain management that need to be carefully considered. Data privacy and security are among the main problems. Customer privacy and confidentiality are in danger from the gathering and processing of enormous volumes of sensitive data. Furthermore, using AI algorithms may unintentionally reinforce pre-existing biases in the data, producing unfair or discriminating results throughout the decision-making process. Algorithmic prejudice, for instance, may lead to differences in employment or pricing policies, which might be harmful to both people and society as a whole. As a result, creating strong ethical frameworks and governance systems is crucial to guaranteeing the ethical and responsible application of ML and AI in supply chains (Lee et al., 2015; Tjahjono et al., 2017).

The application of AI and ML technologies in supply chain management can yield significant gains in productivity, creativity, and competitiveness. Large datasets can be processed thanks to these technologies, which improves operational performance and decision-making. AI has the potential to increase supply chain efficiency by streamlining manufacturing schedules, optimizing inventory levels, and providing accurate demand predictions. AI automation frees up workers to concentrate on more important responsibilities by reducing the need for human interaction in repetitive operations. This change reduces boring labor, which raises employee happiness while simultaneously increasing productivity (Baryannis et al., 2019; Wamba et al., 2017).

Moreover, supply chain procedures can be changed by the inventive powers of AI and ML. AI algorithms are capable of analyzing consumer data to spot new trends and preferences, which helps firms with market research and product creation. By using a data-driven strategy, businesses may quickly adjust to shifting market conditions and maintain their competitiveness. Furthermore, logistics may be revolutionized by integrating AI-driven technology like autonomous trucks and drones, which will make supply chains more flexible and sensitive to changes in demand (Soni et al., 2019; Agrawal et al., 2019; Dubey et al., 2017).

The ethical concerns of AI and ML in supply chain management cannot be disregarded, notwithstanding these benefits. There are serious data privacy and security issues when AI and ML systems rely on massive datasets. Retaining consumer trust requires protecting sensitive data from breaches. In addition, strict control and accountability procedures are required due to the possibility that AI algorithms can reinforce pre-existing prejudices. Algorithms with bias have the potential to treat people unfairly and worsen social injustices. It is essential to put in place governance frameworks and ethical standards that support accountability, justice, and transparency in AI and ML applications to reduce these threats (Daugherty et al., 2018; Ransbotham et al., 2017).

Improving sustainability is another benefit of supply chain management's use of AI and ML. AI may enhance resource efficiency, cut waste, and boost energy efficiency, all of which can lead to more environmentally friendly supply chain procedures. Predictive analytics, for example, may more precisely estimate demand, which minimizes overproduction and inventory waste. Additionally, AI can optimize transportation routes to reduce carbon emissions and fuel use. These environmentally friendly methods help improve supply chain operations' overall efficacy and cost-effectiveness (Hofmann et al., 2017; Wamba et al., 2015; Mishra et al., 2018).

The incorporation of AI and ML into supply chain management can greatly enhance operational effectiveness, stimulate creativity, and advance sustainability. To guarantee their responsible and equitable usage, it is crucial to address the ethical issues raised by these technologies. To protect algorithmic biases, guarantee accountability, and protect data privacy, it is imperative to establish strong ethical frameworks and governance procedures. Through the responsible use of AI and ML and the resolution of ethical dilemmas, organizations may capitalize on novel prospects for expansion and competitive advantage within the ever-changing context of contemporary supply chains (Ab Talib et al., 2015; Hazen et al., 2018).

2. LITERATURE REVIEW

Supply chain management (SCM) has seen a revolution in the application of AI and ML technologies, which have significantly improved decision-making, efficiency, and risk management. The study on the use of AI and ML in SCM is examined in this overview of the literature, with a particular emphasis on risk management strategies and human-machine interaction. It also points out gaps in the literature and research issues that need to be filled (Brynjolfsson et al., 2017).

Newly developed AI and ML techniques are effective instruments for improving supply chain risk management. With the use of these tools, it is possible to analyze huge datasets and find correlations and patterns that would be overlooked by human research alone. Disruptions brought on by outside variables like weather, unstable geopolitical situations, and changes in the economy can be anticipated by AI and ML. For example, weather conditions that could impact transport routes can be predicted using predictive analytics driven by AI, enabling businesses to take preventative action. Similar to this, ML systems can forecast possible trade interruptions by analyzing geopolitical data, allowing businesses to modify their plans as necessary (Oyewole et al., 2024; Chan et al., 2020).

The integration of AI and ML in SCM still faces obstacles despite these developments. The reliability and combination of data from many sources is one important problem that might affect how accurate prediction models are. Furthermore, even though these technologies might offer insightful information, human interpretation and action on the data are frequently necessary due to the complicated nature of supply chain networks. This emphasizes how crucial it is to create frameworks that support cooperation between humans and machines (Devenport et al., 2016).

Using the advantages of both human knowledge and machine capabilities is the idea behind human-machine collaboration. Machines are better at digesting vast amounts of data and seeing patterns; humans are better at thinking strategically and contextual decision-making. Innovation and improved decision-making in supply networks can result from human-machine collaboration. AI, for instance, can produce data-driven insights, which human managers can then utilize to make complex decisions that take larger business contexts into account (Floridi et al., 2018; Ivanov et al., 2021).

However creating training programs to provide employees the skills they need, guaranteeing uninterrupted interaction between technology and human operators, and clearly defining roles and duties are all obstacles to successful human-machine collaboration. Potential errors in AI systems must also be addressed since they may result from biased training data and produce unjust results (Ferreira et al., 2023).

The financial ramifications of supply chains including AI and ML are significant. The long-term advantages include lower labor costs, improved operational effectiveness, and the possibility of finding new revenue streams, even though the initial expenditure can be substantial. A survey claims that businesses that have integrated AI into their vendor networks have experienced notable increases in profitability and a competitive edge. These technologies do, however, also bring up ethical issues, namely about algorithmic prejudice and data privacy. AI systems must retain transparency, accountability, and justice to preserve confidence and prevent unfavorable social effects (Hallikas et al., 2021; Jain, 2023).

There are various issues and research questions raised by the incorporation of AI and ML algorithms into supply chains. How these technologies may be successfully incorporated into current supply chain systems to improve risk management is one of the most important questions. Examining the operational and technological difficulties associated with integration, such as workforce training, system compatibility, and data quality, is part of this. What frameworks might be created to maximize the collaboration between humans and machines in SCM is another crucial subject. This looks for the best ways to establish roles, make sure that communication is efficient, and make use of the complementing abilities that humans and robots have to offer (Raji et al., 2020).

The investigation is also warranted for ethical reasons. What ethical issues are raised by supply chain applications of AI and ML, and how can businesses resolve them? The necessity of ethical frameworks and norms to reduce dangers like algorithmic bias, privacy violations, and data breaches is addressed in this question. Finally, it's important to consider the financial effects of implementing AI and ML techniques in supply chains. What are the financial ramifications, and how can ROI be measured by organizations? This entails analyzing the costs and advantages of using AI and ML, taking into account possible savings, income creation, and labor dynamics effects (Abolek, 2023).

There is a lot of room for improvement in terms of productivity, security, and decision-making when AI and ML are integrated into supply chain management. These advantages do, however, come with difficulties and moral issues that need to be resolved. Future studies should concentrate on creating ethical standards for the application of AI and ML in SCM, guaranteeing data quality, and creating frameworks for human-machine collaboration. To maximize these technologies' benefits and minimize their risks, it will be imperative to address these challenges (Liu et al., 2024).

3. ETHICAL CONSIDERATIONS

The use of AI and ML in supply chain management has raised ethical questions in recent years. The ethical aspects of these technologies must be thoroughly considered as they become more and more common. The ethical implications of AI and ML in supply chains are explored in this section, with particular attention paid to concerns about algorithmic bias, data privacy, and accountability frameworks (Elkady et al., 2023; Pandey et al., 2024).

Because AI and ML technologies rely so largely on data, supply chain management systems' data security and privacy are major challenges. Confidentiality and privacy are in danger when massive amounts of sensitive data on customers, suppliers, and company operations are gathered, stored, and processed. The authenticity and confidence of supply networks can be compromised by unauthorized access or cybersecurity breaches, which can hurt people and enterprises. Consequently, protecting data privacy and making sure that all applicable regulations are followed is essential to the ethical application of AI and ML in supply chain management (Watanabe et al., 2020; Ferreira et al., 2023).

Another crucial ethical factor to take into account while utilizing AI and ML technology is algorithmic bias. Algorithms used in the supply chain for making decisions may inadvertently reinforce biases in the data, producing unfair or discriminating results. Preferential treatment or discrimination against particular suppliers or employees according to socioeconomic status, gender, or ethnicity may be the outcome of biased algorithms. These effects may run counter to the values of fairness, equality, and diversity, thus it's important to take deliberate steps to resolve ethical issues (Oliveira et al., 2019; Chen et al., 2023).

Achieving accountability in AI and ML decision-making processes is necessary to guarantee supply chains adhere to legal and societal standards. Organizations must implement comprehensive accountability frameworks to oversee, assess, and address any possible hazards linked to new technologies. To do this, explicit rules for the use of data, the construction of models, and algorithmic decision-making must be established. Transparency and supervision procedures must also be included. To promote an environment of accountability and responsibility throughout the supply chain ecosystem, stakeholders should also possess the power to contest and address instances of unethical behavior or results arising from AI and ML systems (Huang et al., 2023; Stahl, 2021).

A thorough evaluation of ethical issues is necessary before supply chain management integrates AI and ML technologies. The resolution of concerns about data privacy, algorithmic bias, and accountability mechanisms is crucial in guaranteeing that AI and ML judgments conform to ethical standards and social norms. By proactively addressing these ethical issues, supply chain management may reduce risks, build credibility, and encourage deliberate innovation. The long-term sustainability and longevity of supply chain ecosystems are supported by ethical uses of AI and ML that maintain principles like fairness, transparency, and honesty (Hagendroff, 2020; Adeyelu et al., 2024).

Several ethical issues, mostly those about confidentiality of information and algorithmic bias, have been raised by the application of AI, ML, and the Internet of Things in supply chains. Strong safeguards must be put in place to protect private data and guarantee equity in AI and ML technologies because of these worries (Floridi et al., 2018).

3.1. Data Privacy and Protection

Large volumes of data are generated and processed in supply chains by AI, ML, and IoT technologies. This data includes sensitive information about partners, customers, and business processes. Considerable privacy concerns are raised by the gathering, storing, and usage of this data. The vital significance of putting strict data protection measures in place to secure sensitive data. These precautions include access controls, data encryption, and routine audits to guarantee that information is shielded against breaches and unwanted access. It's also crucial to abide by privacy laws like the California Consumer Privacy Act (CCPA) in the US and the General Data Protection Regulation (GDPR) in Europe. These laws provide guidelines for handling data, such as getting people's express consent before collecting their information and granting them access to, the ability to edit, or the ability to have their data deleted upon request (Raji et al., 2020).

Addressing ethical concerns about data privacy also requires ensuring transparency in data management techniques. Being transparent means explaining to interested parties how their information is gathered, utilized, and safeguarded. This can be accomplished by having thorough privacy rules, frequent revisions of data protection procedures, and open ways for interested parties to voice concerns or ask questions about data privacy. Organizations may establish confidence with the people they serve and show that they are committed to using ethical data practices by being transparent (Latif et al., 2021).

3.2. Algorithmic Bias and Fairness

One major ethical concern with the application of AI and ML in supply chains is algorithmic bias. Algorithm bias can originate from several sources, such as biased implementation procedures, faulty algorithm design, or biased training data. Adverse outcomes, such as prejudice against specific groups or erroneous forecasts that have an impact on stakeholder relations and corporate operations, can result from biased algorithms. For instance, an ML algorithm trained on biassed data may persistently underestimate demand for products that are favored by particular demographic groups, resulting in stockouts and disgruntled customers (Crawford et al., 2021).

There are various tactics involved in addressing algorithmic bias. Making sure that the simulation data is reflective of the many demographics and scenarios the algorithm will face in real life is one strategy. This can be accomplished by populating the training dataset with information from many sources and demographic categories. To find and fix any prejudices that may have been accidentally introduced during development, algorithms must undergo routine audits and reviews. As part of these audits, the algorithm may be tested using various data subsets to ensure consistency and fairness (Dignum, 2023; Hoffmann, 2021).

Using fairness-aware techniques that are intended to reduce bias is another tactic. To guarantee that the results are fair to all groups, these algorithms include fairness constraints in the training phase. An algorithm that considers fairness could have a restriction that mandates a consistent level of prediction accuracy across all demographic categories. Organizations can also set moral standards that emphasize justice and equity for the development of AI and ML. Designers and data scientists can use these principles as a framework to make sure ethical issues are incorporated throughout each step of the algorithm's development process (Mittelstadt, 2019; Whittlestone et al., 2019).

To guarantee that ethical norms are upheld, the integration of AI and ML technology in supply chains also calls for constant observation and assessment. This entails keeping a close eye on how AI systems are doing and how they affect different groups of people, as well as staying receptive to criticism and adapting as needed. In this sense, establishing a governance structure for the application of AI and ML can be beneficial. Positions and duties for keeping an eye on moral behavior, frequent evaluations of AI networks, and procedures for handling moral dilemmas, as they emerge, are a few examples of what this kind of framework may entail (Zarsky, 2016).

While there are many advantages to supply chains using AI, ML, and IoT, there are also serious ethical issues to be addressed, such as algorithmic bias and data protection. Enforcing privacy laws, putting strict data protection measures into place, and keeping data management procedures transparent are all necessary to allay these worries. Furthermore, to guarantee equality and fairness in supply chain management, methods for identifying and reducing algorithmic biases must be developed and put into practice. Organizations may leverage AI and ML technology while preserving stakeholder interests and fostering trust by giving ethical issues a priority (Zou et al., 2018).

4. SUSTAINABILITY IN THE SUPPLY CHAIN

Sustainability is given top priority in modern supply chain management to lessen its negative effects on the environment while preserving profitability and efficiency. Supply chains may benefit greatly from the integration of AI and ML since it presents prospects for sustainable practices. This section looks at how waste reduction, environmental conservation, and carbon emissions reduction are some ways that AI and ML might help sustainability (Sarkis, 2013; Dubey et al., 2015; Pal, 2023).

Innovative methods for streamlining supply chain operations and reducing environmental consequences are introduced by AI and ML technologies. Organizations can detect inefficiencies and chances for improvement by analyzing large datasets through the utilization of sophisticated algorithms and predictive analytics. These technologies make it possible to create optimization algorithms that optimize transportation routes, warehouse operations, and inventory levels to reduce resource consumption and carbon emissions. Furthermore, demand forecasting is improved by machine learning algorithms, which also increase inventory control and cut down on supply chain waste (Kottala, 2021; Seuring et al., 2008).

One important method AI and ML promote sustainability in supply chains is through the application of optimization algorithms and predictive analytics to cut down on waste and carbon emissions. For instance, while AI-driven routing algorithms optimize delivery routes to minimize fuel consumption and greenhouse gas emissions, ML models estimate changes in demand to optimize inventory levels and reduce overproduction. Organizations may greatly lower their resource use and carbon footprint by utilizing these technologies, which promotes environmental sustainability on a larger scale (Negri et al., 2021; Beske et al., 2014; Beske et al., 2007).

Moreover, firms may employ innovative waste management and environmental conservation tactics thanks to AI and ML. For example, predictive maintenance models driven by machine learning may identify equipment problems early on, minimizing downtime and lowering the need for expensive repairs or replacements. Similarly to this, AI-driven QC systems find product flaws faster, which lowers the risk of product recalls and minimizes production waste. These illustrations show how resource optimization and environmental impact reduction were driven by AI and

ML may assist organizations in implementing more sustainable practices (Sanchez et al., 2020; Zhu et al., 2004).

Numerous businesses have already used AI and ML in supply chains to effectively develop sustainable initiatives. For example, the massive retail chain Walmart uses machine learning algorithms to optimize its transportation routes, which dramatically lowers fuel costs and emissions. Similarly, Amazon, an online retailer, uses AI-powered robots to optimize inventory management and reduce waste in its fulfillment centers. These case studies demonstrate the real-world advantages of incorporating AI and ML technologies into supply chain management, as well as the possibility of increased productivity and sustainability-driven innovation (Diabat et al., 2011; Zhu et al., 2013; Liu et al., 2018).

In supply chains, AI and ML provide practical ways to maximize efficiency, cut carbon emissions, minimize waste, and encourage environmental preservation. The implementation of optimization algorithms and predictive analytics can yield considerable improvements in resource efficiency and environmental performance for organizations. Additional proof of how AI and ML can spur long-term innovation and provide supply chain managers with a competitive edge comes from case studies of effective deployments (Lee et al., 2020; Sevda et al., 2024).

4.1. Real-Time Data Collection and Analysis

Real-time data gathering and analysis have greatly progressed with the application of IoT technology in supply chains, improving control and transparency over a range of processes. Important information on stock levels, equipment operation, and environmental conditions can be obtained using IoT sensors and devices. For organizations to increase operational efficiency and make well-informed decisions, this real-time data is essential. But there are drawbacks to the massive data collecting that IoT devices enable, including issues with data privacy and security (Da et al., 2014; Pundir et al., 2019).

IoT-enabled actual time gathering and analyzing of data provide previously unattainable supply chain operations visibility. IoT sensors can track machinery performance, continually track inventory levels, and measure environmental parameters like humidity and temperature. This constant data flow makes it possible to effectively manage supply chain interruptions, maintain equipment on schedule, and estimate demand with greater accuracy. Real-time inventory monitoring, for instance, helps optimize inventory levels and cut expenses by assisting in the reduction of stockouts and overstock scenarios. Comparably, keeping an eye on equipment's performance can aid in spotting possible problems before they arise, averting expensive downtime and maintenance problems (Karim et al., 2024).

4.2. Security and Privacy Concerns

There are serious security and privacy issues with the use of IoT devices in supply chains. The likelihood of cyberattacks and data breaches rises with the growth of IoT devices. These gadgets, which are frequently online, are susceptible to a range of cyber threats, such as malware, denial-of-service attacks, and hacking. Strong security protocols are essential for safeguarding private data and preserving the reliability of supply chain processes. This entails using access controls to prevent unwanted access, encrypting data transmission, and routinely patching and updating IoT devices to guard against known vulnerabilities. Furthermore, useful in detecting and reducing possible dangers are thorough cybersecurity policy development and frequent security audits (Sallam et al., 2023; Noura et al., 2019).

IoT devices offer substantial data collecting, which raises privacy problems as well. Sensitive data like customer information, employee activities, and corporate operations may be included in the data collection. Protecting sensitive information requires making sure that data privacy laws like the GDPR are followed. Before collecting personal data, organizations are required to have individuals' express agreement, to be transparent about the purpose of the collection, and to provide a way for users to access, update, or remove their data. Additionally, crucial to establishing confidence with stakeholders and proving a commitment to moral data processing are openness concerning data handling procedures (Lee et al., 2015).

4.3. Scalability and Interoperability

Two more important concerns in the deployment of IoT are scalability and interoperability. Because different IoT equipment and systems have distinct protocols for communication and data formats, integrating them might be difficult. Ensuring that all of the IoT equipment in an inventory can seamlessly share data and communicate with one another gets more difficult as the amount of devices grows. For the Internet of Things to be implemented successfully, standardized protocols must be developed and interoperability must be guaranteed across different components. Implementing standard practices to implement communication protocols, such as MQTT or CoAP, and utilizing data formats that are extensively used and interoperable with many systems are necessary to achieve this (Li et al., 2015; Minevra et al., 2015).

Integrating Internet of Things data with current SCM systems is another aspect of interoperability. It is necessary to handle, examine, and integrate the data gathered by IoT devices with other business systems, such as CRM and ERP programs. To fully reap the benefits of IoT technology, it is imperative to guarantee that these systems can exchange data and connect. In this context, middleware solutions that promote data interoperability and integration across many systems can be beneficial (Noura et al., 2019).

Overcoming these obstacles calls for an all-encompassing strategy that incorporates organizational policies and procedures in addition to technology fixes. To handle IoT technology efficiently, organizations must spend on training their staff, creating strong privacy and security policies, and cooperating with other sectors to create and implement standardized protocols. Organizations can fully utilize IoT technologies to boost productivity, optimize supply chain operations, and gain a competitive edge by tackling these obstacles (Yao et al., 2019).

5. RISK MANAGEMENT TECHNIQUES

Effective risk management is critical to the stability and sustainability of supply chain operations, particularly in the face of increasingly complex problems including natural disasters, unstable geopolitical contexts, and global pandemics. Traditional supply chain risk management strategies have been severely affected by the advent of AI and ML technologies. This section looks at how AI and ML may improve risk management plans, highlighting how they can foresee and lessen disruptions brought on by different outside variables. Massive data analysis is made possible by AI and ML technologies, which can also spot connections and patterns that people would miss. These solutions detect and mitigate hazards in the supply chain to help organizations manage risks more efficiently. They do this by utilizing robust algorithms and predictive analytics. Supply chain activities may have possible hazards and vulnerabilities identified by AI and ML systems, giving companies the ability to proactively reduce them. These algorithms do this by examining market trends, historical data, and outside variables like meteorological patterns and world events (Chopra et al., 2004; Sheffi, 2005).

One of the main benefits of AI and ML in risk management is their capacity to anticipate and lessen delays brought on by natural catastrophes or geopolitical events. AI-powered predictive analytics, for instance, can forecast weather patterns and evaluate how they can affect transportation routes and logistics networks. In a similar vein, supply chain activities may be impacted by possible interruptions or trade disputes that are detected by machine learning algorithms through the analysis of geopolitical data. Organizations may reduce the effect on their supply chains by utilizing AI and ML technologies, which offer early warnings and insights into possible disruptions. Organizations can implement prompt and efficient preventative actions thanks to these insights and notifications. Businesses may also use AI and ML to create reactive mitigation methods that improve the stability of their supply networks. Organizations may utilize AI-driven predictive analytics to find gaps and vulnerabilities in their supply chain networks rather than reacting to disruptions as they happen. Organizations may lessen the effect of interruptions on their operations by creating backup plans and strategies based on risk assessment and scenario modeling. By taking proactive steps, supply chain networks may become more adaptable and robust overall, which lowers the chance of expensive interruptions (Christopher et al., 2004; Lee et al., 2001).

The implementation of AI and ML technologies has the potential to significantly enhance supply chains by allowing companies to anticipate, evaluate, and reduce a wide variety of external risks. By utilizing sophisticated algorithms and predictive analytics, these technologies let organizations better analyze data, recognize possible dangers, and create proactive mitigation plans. Organizations may strengthen the resilience of their supply chains and guarantee continuity in the face of unanticipated obstacles and interruptions by utilizing the capabilities of AI and ML (Oger et al., 2022; Sheffi, 2005).

Because of the growing complexity of international marketplaces and technological improvements, supply chain management has undergone tremendous change in recent years. The dynamic and unpredictable nature of today's supply chain threats makes traditional risk management techniques, which mostly depend on manual procedures and historical data analysis, insufficient. Organizations may detect possible hazards and vulnerabilities in real-time and take preventive action to reduce them by utilizing AI and ML technologies, which provide a more proactive and data-driven approach to risk management (Sarkis et al., 2020; Nayak et al., 2021).

The capacity of AI and ML to analyze massive volumes of data from many sources and spot patterns and trends that can point to possible hazards is one of its main advantages in supply chain risk management. Early warning indicators of impending disruptions, like as shifts in demand, problems with suppliers' performance, or geopolitical tensions, can be identified by AI and ML algorithms through the processing of data from sensors, IoT devices, social media, and other sources. This makes it possible for organizations to foresee possible hazards and take appropriate action before they develop into serious emergencies (Govindan et al., 2014; Srivastava, 2007).

Moreover, companies may simulate numerous scenarios and evaluate the possible effects of various risk variables on their supply chain operations thanks to AI and ML technology. Organizations may find weak points in their supply chain networks and create backup plans to reduce risks by doing simulations based on historical data and predictive analytics. By taking a proactive stance, companies may reduce the negative effects of interruptions on their operations and preserve business continuity (Reuter et al., 2010; Pagell et al., 2014).

AI and ML have the potential to enhance supply chain operations and increase resilience and flexibility in addition to anticipating and reducing risks. Predictive maintenance systems that are fueled by AI, for instance, can recognize possible equipment faults before they happen, which lowers the possibility of unscheduled downtime and production delays. In a similar vein, ML algorithms can minimize the effect of interruptions on supply chain performance by optimizing transportation and inventory routes (Ivanov et al., 2009; Panigrahi et al., 2019).

Numerous case studies illustrate how AI and ML may improve supply chain resilience and reduce risks. IBM and Maersk, for instance, have optimized their supply chain operations and enhanced decision-making in response to shifting market conditions by utilizing AI-powered predictive analytics. Similarly, to improve the sustainability and robustness of their supply chains, businesses like UPS and DHL have implemented AI-driven logistics systems to optimize transportation routes and cut fuel usage (Juttner et al., 2003; Eccleston et al., 2011).

All things considered, supply chain risk management may be greatly enhanced by AI and ML technologies, which can also strengthen the sustainability and resilience of supply chain operations. Organizations may better sustain company continuity and adjust to changing market circumstances by utilizing the power of data analytics and predictive algorithms to detect and manage possible hazards in real time (Cao et al., 2011; Barhmi et al., 2023).

AI and ML will become more crucial tools for assisting businesses in navigating the difficulties and uncertainties of the contemporary business climate as supply chains continue to change and get more complicated (Nagurney, 2006).

5.1. Predictive Analytics and Risk Forecasting

Because AI and ML technology can forecast disruptions and provide actionable insights, they have completely changed risk management in SCM. Supply chain risks associated with natural disasters, geopolitical crises, and market volatility can be predicted with predictive analytics. Machine learning algorithms can anticipate possible disturbances and optimize responses by evaluating both previous data and real-time inputs. These technologies, for instance, can forecast weather patterns that can have an impact on transportation routes, allowing businesses to plan and minimize delays. Similar to this, ML systems may predict trade disruptions by analyzing geopolitical data, enabling businesses to modify their plans in advance.

However, there are several obstacles to overcome when incorporating AI-driven forecasting algorithms into current systems, especially when it comes to the quality of data and model accuracy. Data that is incomplete or inconsistent can undermine the accuracy of forecasts and decision-making procedures. To apply statistical analysis in SCM effectively, high-quality data must be ensured. Unreliable forecasts brought on by inconsistent data may lead to less-than-ideal choices and higher risks. Organizations must thus make investments in enhancing their data-gathering procedures and guaranteeing the accuracy, completeness, and timeliness of data gathered from diverse sources (Gopal et al., 2024; Ghalehkhondabi et al., 2020).

5.2. Data Quality and Integration Issues

The caliber of the data utilized for analysis has a major impact on how well AI and ML work in supply chain management. Inadequate data quality can lead to imprecise forecasts and inefficient risk mitigation techniques. Talk about the difficulties in combining data from many sources, which can result in skewed conclusions and inconsistent findings. It might be challenging to efficiently merge data from several sources, such as internal systems, logistics partners, and suppliers, because of differences in format, accuracy requirements, and other factors (Ivanov et al., 2021).

Leveraging AI and ML in SCM involves guaranteeing data consistency and building strong data integration frameworks. To enable smooth data integration, organizations must set uniform data formats and protocols. To preserve data accuracy, consistency, and quality across all sources, data governance procedures must be put into place. Additionally, combining data from several sources can be facilitated by utilizing middleware and data integration platforms, guaranteeing that models powered by AI and ML have access to complete and high-quality data (Durugbo et al., 2023; Abolek, 2023).

Organizations can use cleaning of data and pre-processing approaches to find and fix inaccuracies inconsistencies, and missing information to solve problems with the quality of their data. Maintaining data dependability and integrity can also be aided by routine validation procedures and audits. Businesses may improve the efficacy and accuracy of AI-driven forecasting techniques and get better risk management results by investing in these steps (Raji et al., 2020).

5.3. Algorithmic Bias and Fairness

One major worry with AI-driven risk management is algorithmic bias. Biases in training data can affect decision-making processes and even cause harm to stakeholders by producing unfair or discriminating results. Make the case that continual oversight and modification are necessary to remove algorithmic bias and guarantee accuracy and fairness in risk evaluations (Mišić et al., 2020; Tuncali Yaman, 2022).

There are other sources of algorithmic bias, such as human judgments ingrained in the data and past data reflecting current disparities. An ML model may perpetuate prejudices against particular regions or suppliers in its predictions, for instance, if the past information used to train the model contains such biases. This would result in the disproportionate treatment of those organizations (Chopra et al. 2004).

It's critical to put policies in place that support equality and openness in AI and ML algorithms to reduce algorithmic bias. A representative and varied set of training data that appropriately captures the intricacies and variances in the supply chain is one way to achieve this. Finding and fixing any unfair or prejudiced behaviors can be facilitated by routinely assessing and inspecting AI models for biases. Furthermore, fairness metrics can be used in model evaluation procedures to guarantee that judgments and predictions are made equally for all circumstances and groups (Tsang et al., 2019).

Multidisciplinary teams should be considered by organizations when developing and implementing AI models. These groups can offer a range of viewpoints and specialized knowledge to spot any biases and create countermeasures. AI-driven risk management solutions can be made even more equitable and inclusive by interacting with stakeholders and requesting input (Adewusi et al., 2024; Christopher et al., 2004).

6. HUMAN MACHINE COLLABORATION

A new age of human-machine collaboration has been brought about by the partnership of human intellect and creativity with the analytical powers and effectiveness of AI and ML algorithms. This is especially visible in the routine supply chain activities. This section explores the idea of human-machine collaboration in supply chains, highlighting how it may improve operational effectiveness and decision-making procedures by combining cutting-edge technology with human knowledge (Amin et al., 2024; Zhao et al., 2023).

In supply chain operations, human-machine cooperation means using the special abilities of both humans and robots to take on challenging tasks and accomplish goals for the company. Humans are superior to robots in critical thinking, problem-solving, and strategic decision-making, while machines are superior in data processing, pattern recognition, and predictive modeling. Utilizing human abilities in conjunction with AI and ML algorithms, organizations may enhance supply chain operations and stimulate innovation (Ivanov et al., 2021; Serey et al., 2023).

The idea of human-machine cooperation depends on an understanding of how people and robots complement each other's decision-making abilities. Humans can assess complicated situations and reach well-informed opinions because they possess domain knowledge, intuition, and situational awareness. On the other hand, huge data processing, pattern recognition, and insight creation are activities that AI and ML systems excel at and which people may not always be able to perform promptly. Organizations may make better-educated, data-driven choices that incorporate both human knowledge and empirical facts by combining human judgment with machine-generated insights (Baratta et al., 2023; Cazeri et al., 2022).

Structures and processes that enable smooth communication and integration between people and AI/ML algorithms are essential for effective human-machine cooperation. One strategy is to outline the tasks and roles that machines and people have in supply chain management, indicating which situations require human judgment and which might benefit from machine learning insights. Furthermore, collaborative frameworks may be used by organizations to facilitate information exchange between humans and robots, hence promoting reciprocal learning and adaptability to changing situations. This might include integrating AI/ML algorithms into current decision support systems or designing custom interfaces that make it easier for people to communicate with robots (Isaak, 2024; Yang et al., 2021).

Supply chain operations are being reshaped by the paradigm change brought about by human-machine cooperation, which leverages the complementary abilities of automation and people to promote efficiency and innovation. Organizations can optimize operations, make informed choices, and more effectively adjust to changing market situations by fusing human expertise with AI and ML technology. In the current highly digitalized supply chain environment, the idea of human-machine cooperation emphasizes how crucial it is to recognize and capitalize on the unique skills of both people and machines. In the end, this boosts competitiveness and performance (ArunKumar et al., 2024; Lee et al., 2023).

In supply chain operations, human-machine cooperation is a symbiotic connection whereby both parties cooperate to accomplish common goals. Tasks involving data analysis, pattern recognition, and predictive modeling are well-suited for machines because of their sophisticated algorithms and processing capacity. Humans, on the other hand, provide subject expertise, intuition, and critical thinking abilities that help them understand complicated situations and come to wise conclusions. Through the use of human and machine strengths, companies may open up new avenues for efficiency and innovation in their supply chains (Machuca et al., 2007; Ivanov, 2019).

The idea of human-machine cooperation is based on the understanding that neither machines nor people are fully equipped to handle the intricacies of contemporary supply chain management on their own. Instead, companies may attain the best results by combining the strengths of both human intellect and computer skills. Organizations may benefit from the efficiency and scalability of AI and ML algorithms while preserving the flexibility and creativity of human workers through the use of human-machine cooperation (Touboulic et al., 2015).

The capacity of human-machine collaboration to improve supply chain decision-making processes is one of its main benefits. Organizations may use machine-generated insights and human judgment to create better-educated, nuanced decisions that take into account a variety of viewpoints. When supply chain interruptions are predicted by AI and ML algorithms, for instance, human workers may contribute context-specific expertise and strategic vision to create efficient mitigation plans (Modgil et al., 2022).

Additionally, when humans and machines work together, organizations may develop a culture of ongoing learning and development. Organizations may improve their collective intelligence and adaptability by promoting information exchange and collaboration between humans and robots. Organizations can keep ahead of new trends and issues in the ever-changing field of supply chain management through this iterative process of learning and improvement (Akter et al., 2016).

The ability of human-machine collaboration to spur supply chain innovation is another important feature. Organizations may find new opportunities for process optimization, product creation, and market expansion by fusing human creativity with the analytical powers of AI and ML algorithms. For instance, AI-powered analytics can reveal hidden trends in customer behavior, allowing businesses to better customize their products to changing market needs (Kumar et al., 2019).

All things considered, human-machine cooperation is a revolutionary approach to supply chain management that leverages the complementary qualities of both humans and machines to promote resilience, efficiency, and creativity. Organizations may improve their competitiveness and sustainability in the global marketplace by promoting human-machine collaboration as a means of navigating the complicated modern supply chains (Wagner et al., 2008).

6.1. Enhancing Decision-Making Process

The combination of AI and ML with human judgment results in notable enhancements when included in decision-making procedures. Large-scale data processing and pattern recognition are strengths of AI and ML algorithms, which can yield insightful information based on data. Still, there are important jobs that are better left to people, such as applying strategic judgment and interpreting these findings. This synergy improves decision-making procedures, enabling businesses to address supply chain issues more skilfully. AI-driven analytics, for example, can identify patterns and anticipate possible disruptions; human decision-makers, on the other hand, can evaluate these forecasts in light of their operational and strategic goals (Brynjolfsson et al., 2017; Davenport et al., 2016).

Thus, Organizations can capitalize on the advantages of AI and human skills through effective human-machine collaboration. AI is capable of handling repetitive and data-intensive activities like demand forecasting and anomaly detection, while humans can make complicated judgments that include variables like market trends, regulatory changes, and organizational goals. This cooperative method incorporates a variety of viewpoints and areas of expertise, which not only increases decision-making efficiency but also improves decision quality (Onososen et al., 2022).

6.2. Defining Roles and Responsibilities

Roles and responsibilities must be clearly defined for human-machine collaboration to be successful. How crucial it is to create frameworks that specify which jobs are ideal for AI while other ones need human intervention. This clarity guarantees that human talents are utilized where they bring the greatest value and aid in optimizing the application of AI/ML technology. AI systems, for instance, can be employed for jobs requiring the fast and accurate processing of massive amounts of data, such as pattern recognition and data analysis. However, decision-making and strategic thinking are tasks that people might be assigned; these need judgment and contextual awareness, which AI is not entirely capable of replicating (Gümüsay et al., 2022; Kumar et al., 2024).

Determining the advantages and disadvantages of human and AI skills is necessary to establish these positions. Businesses need to evaluate which procedures are automatable and which ones need human involvement. This evaluation aids in the creation of workflows that optimize efficacy and efficiency while addressing potential obstacles such as system compatibility and integration problems (Tambe et al., 2019).

6.3. Training and Upskilling

Employee training and upskilling are critical to the workplace's use of AI and ML technology. Workers will need to acquire new skills to effectively engage with AI systems as they become more commonplace. Employees should be given the information and abilities necessary to run AI systems, understand their results, and apply them to decision-making processes through the creation of training programs (Gupta et al., 2023; Wang et al., 2023).

A significant investment in education and training is necessary to optimize the advantages of human-machine cooperation. This covers soft skills like analytical thinking, solving issues, and adaptability in addition to technical training on the usage of AI tools. Organizations may guarantee that their staff can use AI technology to improve productivity and decision-making skills by equipping workers with the appropriate skills (Ismaılova, 2024).

Organizations must think about promoting a continual learning and development culture in addition to traditional training programs. Employees may stay productive and competitive in their jobs by being encouraged to keep up with developments in AI and ML technology. Our proactive approach to skill development guarantees that staff members are equipped to successfully navigate the changing AI landscape and contribute to human-machine collaboration (Phillips et al., 2006).

7. FINANCIAL IMPLICATION

The potential for transforming operations and the huge financial consequences have generated interest in the application of AI and ML technologies in supply chain management. In addition to offering a thorough analysis of the return on investment for businesses implementing these technologies, this section explores the financial implications of integrating AI and ML into supply chains. It does this by looking at changes in labor dynamics, the emergence of new revenue streams, and improvements in competitiveness. Labor dynamics will certainly shift significantly as more companies incorporate AI and ML technology into their supply chain processes. These technologies change the duties and duties of human workers while automating repetitive jobs and simplifying procedures. Automation may replace jobs involving repetitive, manual labor, which might result in workforce reorganization and job displacement. But AI and ML also open up new doors for education and upskilling, freeing up staff members to concentrate on higher-value work like customer relationship management and strategic decision-making (Bughin et al., 2017).

Furthermore, supply chains that use AI and ML get access to new revenue streams and income streams. Businesses may more accurately and efficiently discover market trends, customer preferences, and new possibilities by utilizing data analytics and predictive modeling. This makes it possible for them to create cutting-edge goods, services, and business plans that satisfy changing consumer needs and target unexplored market niches. Supply chain optimization driven by AI may also result in cost reductions and efficiency improvements, which will improve profits and financial performance even more. To determine the financial sustainability and possible returns on investment of companies implementing AI and ML technologies in their supply chain processes, a detailed ROI study is necessary. The long-term financial effects of deploying AI and ML systems can be massive, even if the initial expenses may be high. Over time, AI and ML technologies help businesses save money and increase revenue by lowering labor expenses, increasing operational efficiency, and minimizing the cost of keeping goods on hand. Payback duration, net present value, and internal rate of return are examples of ROI measures that organizations may compute to assess the financial effect of these investments and make well-informed choices on resource allocation and strategic planning (Sotarauta, 2019).

There are a variety of financial consequences associated with implementing AI and ML into supply chains, including adjustments to labor dynamics, the creation of new revenue streams, and increased competitiveness. Automation offers chances for reskilling and upskilling as well as the potential for workforce reorganization. Additionally, through data-driven decision-making and supply chain optimization, AI and ML help businesses find new income streams and increase profitability. To assess the financial effect of these technologies and make well-informed investment decisions that support competitiveness and sustainable growth in the ever-changing business environment of today, a thorough examination of ROI measures is essential (Agrawal, 2019).

7.1. Cost-Benefit Analysis

The financial ramifications of supply chains including AI, ML, and IoT are noteworthy, encompassing big upfront costs as well as long-term gains. These innovations have the power to provide new revenue streams, improve operational efficiency, and lower expenses. Organizations must perform a comprehensive cost-benefit analysis to determine whether integrating these technologies will be financially viable (Toorajipour et al., 2021).

Combining AI, ML, and IoT might come with hefty upfront expenses. These expenses cover hiring staff, setting up the required infrastructure, and purchasing hardware and software. When IoT sensors are deployed throughout a supply chain network, for example, costs associated with buying, setting up, and verifying that the sensors operate with current systems must be paid for. In the same vein, significant investments in software licenses, data storage, and processing power are needed for AI and ML. Furthermore, the procedure of integration itself can be expensive and time-consuming, frequently requiring specialized knowledge and abilities (Coulson, 2024).

Nonetheless, there may be substantial long-term returns on these initial expenditures. Supply chain operations can be made more efficient by AI and ML through better production scheduling, inventory control, and demand forecasting. As a result of these optimizations, waste is decreased, inventory holding costs are decreased, and market responsiveness is raised. Furthermore, IoT devices enable preventative maintenance and save downtime by providing real-time data on a variety of supply chain parameters, including ambient conditions and equipment performance. Over time, these economies result in lower costs and better operational performance (Pandey et al., 2021).

IoT, AI, and ML technologies can also create new sources of income. Predictive analytics, for instance, can spot new consumer preferences and market trends, enabling businesses to create new goods and services to satisfy these needs. Through capabilities like performance analytics and remote monitoring, IoT-enabled items can also provide customers with continuing value, opening up new business prospects for businesses that operate via subscriptions. Businesses can boost growth and their competitive edge by utilizing these technologies (Domini et al., 2023).

Quantifying these possible advantages and contrasting them with the upfront and continuing expenses is a cost-benefit analysis. Organizations can use this approach to assess if the investment is justified by the financial returns. A cost-benefit analysis should take into account the size of the expenditure, the anticipated period for benefits to be realized, and any potential risks or unknowns related to implementation. Organizations can make well-informed decisions about implementing AI, ML, and IoT innovations by carefully weighing these considerations (Gillham, 2017).

7.2. Measuring Return on Investment

Assessing the financial effects of investments in AI, ML, and IoT requires measuring return on investment (ROI). Calculating the monetary benefits from these technologies using measures like the internal rate of return (IRR), payback time, and net present value (NPV). Organizations may make well-informed judgments regarding how to allocate resources and strategic planning with the aid of accurate ROI measurement.

The amount of time required for a purchase to make enough money or save enough expenses to recoup its original outlay is known as the payback period. A quicker payback time increases the project's appeal because it signals a faster return on investment. The payback period for initiatives including AI, ML, and IoT might change based on the size and intricacy of the implementation. The implementation of IoT devices for proactive upkeep, for instance, may result in a project with a quicker payback period because maintenance expenses and downtime are reduced right away (Barik, 2024).

NpV is yet another crucial indicator for assessing ROI. The distinction between the current value of money coming in and withdrawals over the course of the investment period are determined by net present value or NPV. An investment is deemed financially feasible if its expected return on investment (NPV) is positive and exceeds its cost. NPV can be used to compare the initial and continuing expenses of investments in AI, ML, and IoT with the long-term rewards, such as improved productivity and new revenue sources (Gudigantala et al., 2023).

The investment's net present value is equal to its internal rate of return, or IRR. It stands for the anticipated yearly rate of return for the investment. An investment is more profitable if its IRR is larger. Calculating the internal rate of return (IRR) can assist organizations in evaluating various investment options and ranking those having the highest prospective returns for AI, ML, and IoT initiatives. Robust analytical techniques and dependable data are necessary for accurate ROI measurement. Businesses need to rigorously monitor the expenses and returns on investments made in AI, ML, and IoT projects. Data collection on installation costs, operating money saved, and revenue enhancements are required for this. Accurately analyzing this data and determining ROI measures can be aided by advanced analytics technologies (Gudigantala et al., 2023).

When assessing ROI, organizations should take qualitative advantages into account as well as traditional financial indicators. These advantages could include higher staff engagement, better brand reputation, and higher consumer satisfaction. Even though these advantages could be more difficult to measure, they have a big influence on the total return on investments made in AI, ML, and IoT.

8. ENHANCING LOGISTICS WITH IOT, ML, AND AI: A FOCUS ON KPIS AND FINANCIAL IMPACT

In this paper, we will examine the Key Performance Indicators (KPIs) that are important for SCM and Logistics, as well as the related financial issues. Pilot studies and case studies are quite helpful in this situation since they provide useful information and real-world applications. KPIs are essential measures in logistics and SCM that aid in assessing the efficacy and efficiency of different processes. Order accuracy, delivery efficiency, turnover of stock, shipping expenses per unit, warehouse productivity, and supply network cycle time are some of these KPIs. Every one of these indicators is important for making sure supply chain activities are effective and efficient (Mostafa et al., 2020).

It is necessary to comprehend the financial ramifications of efficient SCM. Cost of goods sold (COGS), operational costs, cash-to-cash cycle time, return on assets (ROA), and gross margin return on inventory (GMROI) are important financial factors. A thorough understanding of the profitability and cost-effectiveness of supply chain activities is offered by these financial measures. Through vigilant observation of these factors, institutions can make well-informed determinations to augment their fiscal outcomes and general efficacy (Ivanov et al., 2019).

Risk management is a constant worry in logistics and supply chain management because of the sensitive and private nature of the data. AI, ML, and IoT implementation can greatly reduce these hazards. IoT devices improve supply chain visibility and real-time tracking. IoT sensors, for instance, may track the location and state of materials in materials management, minimizing loss and guaranteeing prompt replenishment. Algorithms based on machine learning can enhance inventory control, optimize routes, and forecast demand more precisely. Machine learning models are used in demand forecasting to examine past data and find trends, which results in more accurate demand estimates and improved planning (Lee et al., 2022).

Complex decision-making processes can be automated using artificial intelligence. AI systems, for example, can optimize production schedules in production planning based on capacity, availability of resources, and current demand, increasing efficiency and cutting costs. Pilot studies and case studies concentrating on certain situations like handling materials, production scheduling, sales and distribution, finance, and cost accounting will be included in the paper to demonstrate the practical benefits. There will be a case study on the application of AI-driven scheduling of production in a manufacturing plant, a pilot study showing the impact of the internet of Things sensors on inventory control and waste reduction, and examples of ML-based forecasting of demand increasing the accuracy of sales projections (Singh et al., 2024).

The article intends to demonstrate the revolutionary potential of IoT, ML, and AI in supply chain management and logistics by concentrating on these domains. These technologies address the crucial concerns of risk and secrecy in SCM by improving efficiency and accuracy while also offering substantial financial benefits. The amalgamation of these cutting-edge technologies signifies a noteworthy advancement in streamlining supply chain procedures and attaining enduring expansion (Goltsos et al., 2022).

9. PROJECT OVERVIEW AND PRACTICAL IMPLICATIONS

The objective of this project is to investigate how new technologies like AI, ML, and the IoT may be integrated with financial measurements and KPIs in SCM. The goal of the project is to illustrate the usefulness and advantages of these technologies in certain scenarios including demand forecasting, sales and distribution, manufacturing planning, materials management, finance, and cost accounting through the analysis of case studies and pilot studies (Zhou et al., 2021).

Reducing waste and improving inventory control are two major benefits of integrating IoT sensors into materials management. Electronic materials may be tracked and monitored in real-time by IoT devices, which guarantees that supplies are stored optimally and refilled as needed. As a result, the organization saves money in the long run due to increased inventory level accuracy and decreased material losses (Subhadra et al., 2024).

Production schedules can be optimized using AI-driven industrial planning systems using predictive analytics and real-time data. AI can develop effective production plans that minimize downtime and maximize resource utilization by taking into account variables like present requests, availability of assets, and production capacity. This raises overall productivity and lowers operating expenses while also increasing production efficiency (Shiyyab et al., 2023).

Through pattern recognition and analysis of historical sales data, machine learning models may greatly enhance demand forecasting. More precise demand projections lower the chance of stockouts and overstock scenarios by facilitating improved inventory management. Guaranteeing the availability of products when needed, improves customer happiness and boosts sales (Zhang et al., 2017).

Fintech and cost accounting procedures can be made more efficient by using advanced technologies like AI and ML, which automate intricate calculations and data processing. AI, for example, can offer real-time financial performance analytics, facilitating speedier decision-making and more precise financial planning. This promotes improved profit margins, cost optimization, and improved financial control (Yang et al., 2019).

More accurate forecasts based on a variety of data sources, such as market trends, seasonal fluctuations, and consumer behavior, are made possible by the incorporation of ML into demand forecasting. Better planning and resource allocation result from improved demand forecasting, which lowers inefficiencies and increases responsiveness to changes in the market (Choi et al., 2016).

There are several real-world advantages of integrating IoT, ML, and AI with SCM and logistics, such as increased productivity, lower costs, and better decision-making. Through the use of case studies and pilot studies, this project illustrates practical applications while concentrating on particular scenarios, offering insightful information about the ground-breaking possibilities of these technologies. The results underscore the significance of utilizing cutting-edge technologies to enhance supply chain operations, alleviate potential hazards, and accomplish enduring expansion in a progressively cutthroat marketplace (Chang et al., 2022; Yu et al., 2018).

10. CONCLUSION

Supply chain management is about to undergo a dramatic metamorphosis as a result of the incorporation of AI and ML technologies. These cutting-edge technologies have the power to transform operations, increase competitiveness, promote innovation, and improve operational efficiency in companies. But to ensure appropriate and sustainable deployment, ethical issues must be addressed in tandem with these exciting breakthroughs. Data privacy, algorithmic bias, accountability, and other ethical issues are major problems that demand careful consideration to reduce risks and preserve social norms and values. To encourage the responsible and accountable use of these revolutionary technologies, it is essential to establish strong ethical frameworks and governance structures.

It is impossible to exaggerate the ethical ramifications of supply chain management using AI and ML. As these technologies become more and more integrated into supply chain operations, protecting data privacy becomes a top need. Strict precautions to preserve privacy and confidentiality are required due to the gathering, storing, and use of enormous amounts of data on clients, suppliers, and business operations. Supply networks' integrity and trust are put at risk by unauthorized access and cybersecurity breaches, which are dangerous for both people and companies. Thus, protecting data privacy and abiding by applicable legal and regulatory frameworks are essential to guaranteeing the ethical use of AI and ML.

Another moral conundrum in the application of AI and ML technologies is algorithmic prejudice. In the absence of strict design and oversight, algorithms used for generating decisions may reinforce underlying biases in the data, leading to unfair or discriminating results. Preferential treatment or discrimination against specific suppliers or employees according to socioeconomic status, gender, or ethnicity might result from biased algorithms. These ramifications are incompatible with the values of justice, equality, and diversity, hence ethical problems must be addressed and minimized.

Strong accountability measures in AI and ML decision-making processes are necessary to ensure supply chains adhere to legal and societal standards. Establishing open, accountable, and monitoring processes is necessary for organizations to assess, identify, and reduce any possible dangers related to new technologies. This means defining precise policies for the use of data, building models, and making algorithmic decisions, along with supervision and transparency procedures. Furthermore, to promote an environment of accountability and responsibility throughout the supply chain ecosystem, stakeholders must have the power to question and address instances of unethical behavior or results resulting from AI and ML systems.

A crucial area for AI and ML technologies to advance significantly is supply chain sustainability. By optimizing processes, cutting waste, and promoting environmental conservation, organizations may significantly improve resource efficiency and environmental performance through the integration of these technologies. Supply chain managers may gain a competitive advantage by leveraging AI and ML to generate sustainable innovation, as demonstrated by several case studies. Moreover, the necessity of enhancing supply chain procedures emphasizes the significance of human-machine cooperation. Organizations can improve decision-making, increase productivity, and handle changing market dynamics by combining the complementary skills of people and robots. Effective communication and integration between human workers and AI/ML algorithms require collaborative frameworks and clearly defined roles and responsibilities.

The combined use of AI and ML technology signifies a revolutionary turn in supply chain management, providing unmatched prospects for inventiveness, competitiveness, and efficacy. It is impossible to ignore the ethical implications of this technological revolution, though. It is critical to address issues with algorithmic bias, data protection, and accountability to guarantee responsible and long-lasting implementation. Organizations may embrace the revolutionary potential of AI and ML technologies while respecting social norms and values by implementing strong ethical frameworks and governance systems. Furthermore, there is a great deal of potential for improving resource efficiency, environmental conservation, and supply chain sustainability through the integration of these technologies. Organizations may achieve unprecedented levels of efficiency and agility by collaborating with machines, setting themselves poised for success in the ever-changing world of contemporary supply chains.

REFERENCES

Ab Talib, M. S., Abdul Hamid, A. B., & Thoo, A. C. (2015). Critical success factors of supply chain management: A literature survey and Pareto analysis. *EuroMed Journal of Business*, 10(2), 234–263.

Abolek, A. (2023). *Work Life Balance Policies and Performance of Senior Members at University of Cape Coast* (Doctoral dissertation, University of Cape Coast).

Adewusi, A. O., Komolafe, A. M., Ejairu, E., Aderotoye, I. A., Abiona, O. O., & Oyeniran, O. C. (2024). The role of predictive analytics in optimizing supply chain resilience: A review of techniques and case studies. *International Journal of Management & Entrepreneurship Research*, 6(3), 815–837.

Adeyelu, O. O., Ugochukwu, C. E., & Shonibare, M. A. (2024). Ethical implications of AI in financial decision–making: a review with real world applications. *International Journal of Applied Research in Social Sciences*, 6(4), 608–630.

Agrawal, A., Gans, J., & Goldfarb, A. (2019). Economic policy for artificial intelligence. *Innovation Policy and the Economy*, 19(1), 139–159.

Agrawal, P., Narain, R., & Ullah, I. (2019). Analysis of barriers in implementation of digital transformation of supply chain using interpretive structural modelling approach. *Journal of Modelling in Management*, 15(1), 297–317.

Akter, S., & Wamba, S. F. (2016). Big data analytics in E-commerce: A systematic review and agenda for future research. *Electronic Markets*, 26, 173–194.

Amin, A., Bhuiyan, M. R. I., Hossain, R., Molla, C., Poli, T. A., & Milon, M. N. U. (2024). The adoption of Industry 4.0 technologies by using the technology organizational environment framework: The mediating role to manufacturing performance in a developing country. *Business Strategy & Development*, 7(2), e363.

Arunkumar, O. N., & Divya, D. (2024). A review on supply chain finance: Problem classification and future research agenda. *International Journal of Revenue Management*, 14(2), 150–202.

Baratta, A., Cimino, A., Gnoni, M. G., & Longo, F. (2023). Human Robot Collaboration in Industry 4.0: A literature review. *Procedia Computer Science*, 217, 1887–1895. PMID: 36687281

Barhmi, A., & Hajaji, O. (2023). Multidisciplinary approach to supply chain resilience: Conceptualization and scale development. *Central European Business Review, 12*(5).

Barik, T. (2024). Optimization Potential Using AI and Metaverse in Supply Chain Management: A Forward-Looking Perspective. *Business Management and Economics Engineering.*, 22, 1340–1355.

Baryannis, G., Validi, S., Dani, S., & Antoniou, G. (2019). Supply chain risk management and artificial intelligence: State of the art and future research directions. *International Journal of Production Research*, 57(7), 2179–2202.

Beske, P., Land, A., & Seuring, S. (2014). Sustainable supply chain management practices and dynamic capabilities in the food industry: A critical analysis of the literature. *International Journal of Production Economics*, 152, 131–143.

Bhagwat, R., & Sharma, M. K. (2007). Performance measurement of supply chain management: A balanced scorecard approach. *Computers & Industrial Engineering*, 53(1), 43–62.

Brynjolfsson, E., & Mcafee, A. (2017). Artificial intelligence, for real. *Harvard Business Review*, 1, 1–31.

Bughin, J., Hazan, E., & Sree Ramaswamy, P. DC, W., & Chu, M. (2017). Artificial intelligence the next digital frontier.

Cao, M., & Zhang, Q. (2011). Supply chain collaboration: Impact on collaborative advantage and firm performance. *Journal of Operations Management*, 29(3), 163–180.

Cazeri, G. T., de Santa-Eulalia, L. A., Serafim, M. P., & Anholon, R. (2022). Training for Industry 4.0: A systematic literature review and directions for future research. *Brazilian Journal of Operations & Production Management*, 19(3), 1–19.

Chan, H. L., Wei, X., Guo, S., & Leung, W. H. (2020). Corporate social responsibility (CSR) in fashion supply chains: A multi-methodological study. *Transportation Research Part E, Logistics and Transportation Review*, 142, 102063.

Chang, A., El-Rayes, N., & Shi, J. (2022). Blockchain technology for supply chain management: A comprehensive review. *FinTech*, 1(2), 191–205.

Chen, J. E., Bao, F., Li, C., & Lin, Y. (2023). The Application and Ethics of Artificial Intelligence in Blockchain: A Bibliometric-Content Analysis. *Journal of Global Information Management*, 31(7), 1–32.

Choi, T. M., Chan, H. K., & Yue, X. (2016). Recent development in big data analytics for business operations and risk management. *IEEE Transactions on Cybernetics*, 47(1), 81–92. PMID: 26766385

Choi, T. M., Wallace, S. W., & Wang, Y. (2018). Big data analytics in operations management. *Production and Operations Management*, 27(10), 1868–1883.

Chopra, S., & Sodhi, M. S. (2004). Managing risk to avoid supply-chain breakdown. *MIT Sloan Management Review*.

Christopher, M., & Lee, H. (2004). Mitigating supply chain risk through improved confidence. *International Journal of Physical Distribution & Logistics Management*, 34(5), 388–396.

Coulson-Thomas, C. (2024). Board's strategy for a future-ready business in an uncertain world.

Crawford, K., & Paglen, T. (2021). Excavating AI: The politics of images in machine learning training sets. *AI & Society*, 36(4), 1105–1116.

Da Xu, L., He, W., & Li, S. (2014). Internet of things in industries: A survey. *IEEE Transactions on Industrial Informatics*, 10(4), 2233–2243.

Daugherty, P. R., & Wilson, H. J. (2018). *Human+ machine: Reimagining work in the age of AI.* Harvard Business Press.

Davenport, T. H., & Kirby, J. (2016). *Only humans need apply: Winners and losers in the age of smart machines.* Harper Business.

Diabat, A., & Govindan, K. (2011). An analysis of the drivers affecting the implementation of green supply chain management. *Resources, Conservation and Recycling*, 55(6), 659–667.

Dignum, V. (2023, January). Responsible Artificial Intelligence---From Principles to Practice: A Keynote at TheWebConf 2022. In *ACM SIGIR Forum* (Vol. 56, No. 1, pp. 1-6). New York, NY, USA: ACM.

Domini, B., Dewi, A. S., & Cesna, G. P. (2023). Assessing the Effects of Artificial Intelligence on Startup Performance: An Analysis of Transformational Initiatives. [ITSDI]. *IAIC Transactions on Sustainable Digital Innovation*, 5(1), 24–38.

Dubey, R., Gunasekaran, A., & Ali, S. S. (2015). Exploring the relationship between leadership, operational practices, institutional pressures and environmental performance: A framework for green supply chain. *International Journal of Production Economics*, 160, 120–132.

Dubey, R., Gunasekaran, A., Childe, S. J., Papadopoulos, T., Blome, C., & Luo, Z. (2017). Antecedents of resilient supply chains: An empirical study. *IEEE Transactions on Engineering Management*, 66(1), 8–19.

Durugbo, C. M., & Al-Balushi, Z. (2023). Supply chain management in times of crisis: A systematic review. *Management Review Quarterly*, 73(3), 1179–1235.

Eccleston, C. H., & March, F. (2011). *Global environmental policy: concepts, principles, and practice*. CRC Press.

Elkady, G., & Hesham Sedky, A. (2023). Artificial Intelligence And Machine Learning For Supply Chain Resilience. *Current Integrative Engineering*, 1(1), 23–28.

Ferreira, B., & Reis, J. (2023). Artificial Intelligence in Supply Chain Management: A Systematic Literature Review and Guidelines for Future Research. In *International Joint conference on Industrial Engineering and Operations Management* (pp. 339-354). Springer.

Floridi, L., Cowls, J., Beltrametti, M., Chatila, R., Chazerand, P., Dignum, V., & Vayena, E. (2018). AI4People—an ethical framework for a good AI society: Opportunities, risks, principles, and recommendations. *Minds and Machines*, 28, 689–707. PMID: 30930541

Ghalehkhondabi, I., Ahmadi, E., & Maihami, R. (2020). An overview of big data analytics application in supply chain management published in 2010-2019. *Production*, 30, e20190140.

Gillham, J. (2017). *The economic impact of artificial intelligence on the global economy*. Price Waterhouse Coopers.

Goltsos, T. E., Syntetos, A. A., Glock, C. H., & Ioannou, G. (2022). Inventory–forecasting: Mind the gap. *European Journal of Operational Research*, 299(2), 397–419.

Gopal, P. R. C., Rana, N. P., Krishna, T. V., & Ramkumar, M. (2024). Impact of big data analytics on supply chain performance: An analysis of influencing factors. *Annals of Operations Research*, 333(2), 769–797.

Govindan, K., Kaliyan, M., Kannan, D., & Haq, A. N. (2014). Barriers analysis for green supply chain management implementation in Indian industries using analytic hierarchy process. *International Journal of Production Economics*, 147, 555–568.

Gudigantala, N., Madhavaram, S., & Bicen, P. (2023). An AI decision-making framework for business value maximization. *AI Magazine*, 44.

Gümüsay, A. A., Bohné, T., & Davenport, T. (2022). AI and the Future of Management Decision-Making. *Management and Business Review*, 1-19.

Gupta, S., Modgil, S., Lee, C. K., & Sivarajah, U. (2023). The future is yesterday: Use of AI-driven facial recognition to enhance value in the travel and tourism industry. *Information Systems Frontiers*, 25(3), 1179–1195. PMID: 35529102

Hagendorff, T. (2020). The ethics of AI ethics: An evaluation of guidelines. *Minds and Machines*, 30(1), 99–120.

Hallikas, J., Immonen, M., & Brax, S. (2021). Digitalizing procurement: The impact of data analytics on supply chain performance. *Supply Chain Management*, 26(5), 629–646.

Hazen, B. T., Skipper, J. B., Boone, C. A., & Hill, R. R. (2018). Back in business: Operations research in support of big data analytics for operations and supply chain management. *Annals of Operations Research*, 270, 201–211.

Hoffmann, A. L. (2021). Terms of inclusion: Data, discourse, violence. *New Media & Society*, 23(12), 3539–3556.

Hofmann, E., & Rüsch, M. (2017). Industry 4.0 and the current status as well as future prospects on logistics. *Computers in Industry*, 89, 23–34.

Huang, G., Ng, S. T., & Li, D. (2023). Determinants of digital twin adoption in hospital operation management. *Urban Lifeline*, 1(1), 6.

Isaak, N. (2024). A Human-Machine Collaboration Framework for the Development of Schemas. *arXiv preprint arXiv:2402.07932*.

Ismaılova, N. (2024). Explore how AI is driving sustainable economic growth and transforming business analysis worldwide. *Journal of Sustainable Development and Green Technology, 4*(2).

Ivanov, D. (2019). Disruption tails and revival policies: A simulation analysis of supply chain design and production-ordering systems in the recovery and post-disruption periods. *Computers & Industrial Engineering*, 127, 558–570.

Ivanov, D., & Dolgui, A. (2021). A digital supply chain twin for managing the disruption risks and resilience in the era of Industry 4.0. *Production Planning and Control*, 32(9), 775–788.

Ivanov, D., Dolgui, A., Das, A., & Sokolov, B. (2019). Digital supply chain twins: Managing the ripple effect, resilience, and disruption risks by data-driven optimization, simulation, and visibility. *Handbook of ripple effects in the supply chain*, 309-332.

Ivanov, D., Dolgui, A., & Sokolov, B. (2019). The impact of digital technology and Industry 4.0 on the ripple effect and supply chain risk analytics. *International Journal of Production Research*, 57(3), 829–846.

Ivanov, D., & Sokolov, B. (2009). *Adaptive supply chain management*. Springer Science & Business Media.

Jain, R. (2023). The Impact of Artificial Intelligence on Business: Opportunities and Challenges. *Available atSSRN* 4407114.

Jüttner, U., Peck, H., & Christopher, M. (2003). Supply chain risk management: outlining an agenda for future research. *International Journal of Logistics: Research and Applications, 6*(4), 197-210.

Karim, M., Rahman, M. A., Tan, S. W., Atiquzzaman, M., Pillai, P., & Alenezi, A. H. (2024). Intra-vehicular Communication Protocol for IoT Enabled Vehicle Health Monitoring System: Challenges, issues and Solutions. *IEEE Access : Practical Innovations, Open Solutions*.

Kottala, S. Y. (2021). Sustainable supply chain management practices: A review. *International Journal of Social Ecology and Sustainable Development*, 12(3), 47–65.

Kumar, B. R., Reddy, S. M., Madhuri, A., & Shireesha, M. (2024). The Role of Artificial Intelligence in Decision-Making Processes.

Kumar, R., Singh, K., & Jain, S. K. (2019). Development of a framework for agile manufacturing. *World Journal of Science. Technology and Sustainable Development*, 16(4), 161–169.

Latif, M. N. A., Aziz, N. A. A., Hussin, N. S. N., & Aziz, Z. A. (2021). Cyber security in supply chain management: A systematic review. *LogForum*, 17(1), 49–57.

Lee, E. J., Bae, J., & Kim, K. H. (2020). The effect of environmental cues on the purchase intention of sustainable products. *Journal of Business Research*, 120, 425–433.

Lee, H. L., & Whang, S. (2001). Winning the last mile of e-commerce. *MIT Sloan Management Review*.

Lee, I., & Lee, K. (2015). The Internet of Things (IoT): Applications, investments, and challenges for enterprises. *Business Horizons*, 58(4), 431–440.

Lee, I., & Mangalaraj, G. (2022). Big data analytics in supply chain management: A systematic literature review and research directions. *Big Data and Cognitive Computing, 6*(1), 17.

Lee, J., Bagheri, B., & Kao, H. A. (2015). A cyber-physical systems architecture for industry 4.0-based manufacturing systems. *Manufacturing Letters*, 3, 18–23.

Lee, K. H., Arshad, Z., Dahshan, A., Alshareef, M., Alsulami, Q. A., Bibi, A., & Javid, A. (2023). Porous aerogel structures as promising materials for photocatalysis, thermal insulation textiles, and technical applications: A review. *Catalysts*, 13(9), 1286.

Li, S., Xu, L. D., & Zhao, S. (2015). The internet of things: A survey. *Information Systems Frontiers*, 17, 243–259.

Liu, J., Feng, Y., Zhu, Q., & Sarkis, J. (2018). Green supply chain management and the circular economy: Reviewing theory for advancement of both fields. *International Journal of Physical Distribution & Logistics Management*, 48(8), 794–817.

Liu, Y., Alias, A. H. B., Haron, N. A., Bakar, N. A., & Wang, H. (2024). Exploring three pillars of construction robotics via dual-track quantitative analysis. *Automation in Construction*, 162, 105391.

Machuca, J. A., del Mar Gonzalez-Zamora, M., & Aguilar-Escobar, V. G. (2007). Service operations management research. *Journal of Operations Management*, 25(3), 585–603.

Min, H. (2010). Artificial intelligence in supply chain management: Theory and applications. *International Journal of Logistics: Research and Applications*, 13(1), 13–39.

Minerva, R., Biru, A., & Rotondi, D. (2015). Towards a definition of the Internet of Things (IoT). *IEEE Internet Initiative*, 1(1), 1–86.

Mishra, D., Gunasekaran, A., Papadopoulos, T., & Childe, S. J. (2018). Big Data and supply chain management: A review and bibliometric analysis. *Annals of Operations Research*, 270, 313–336.

Mišić, V. V., & Perakis, G. (2020). Data analytics in operations management: A review. *Manufacturing & Service Operations Management*, 22(1), 158–169.

Mittelstadt, B. (2019). Principles alone cannot guarantee ethical AI. *Nature Machine Intelligence*, 1(11), 501–507.

Modgil, S., Singh, R. K., & Hannibal, C. (2022). Artificial intelligence for supply chain resilience: Learning from Covid-19. *International Journal of Logistics Management*, 33(4), 1246–1268.

Monostori, L. (2014). Cyber-physical production systems: Roots, expectations and R&D challenges. *Procedia CIRP*, 17, 9–13.

Mostafa, N., Hamdy, W., & Elawady, H. (2020). An intelligent warehouse management system using the internet of things. *The Egyptian International Journal of Engineering Sciences and Technology, 32. Mechanical Engineering (New York, N.Y.)*, 59–65.

Nagurney, A. (2006). On the relationship between supply chain and transportation network equilibria: A supernetwork equivalence with computations. *Transportation Research Part E, Logistics and Transportation Review*, 42(4), 293–316.

Nayak, K. K., Singhal, D., & Tripathy, S. (2021). Determination of challenges and driving forces of green supply chain management in Indian manufacturing industries: A critical review. *International Journal of Logistics Systems and Management*, 40(1), 28–51.

Negri, M., Cagno, E., Colicchia, C., & Sarkis, J. (2021). Integrating sustainability and resilience in the supply chain: A systematic literature review and a research agenda. *Business Strategy and the Environment*, 30(7), 2858–2886.

Noura, M., Atiquzzaman, M., & Gaedke, M. (2019). Interoperability in internet of things: Taxonomies and open challenges. *Mobile Networks and Applications*, 24, 796–809.

Oger, R., Lauras, M., Montreuil, B., & Benaben, F. (2022). A decision support system for strategic supply chain capacity planning under uncertainty: Conceptual framework and experiment. *Enterprise Information Systems*, 16(5), 1793390.

Oliveira, T., Martins, R., Sarker, S., Thomas, M., & Popovič, A. (2019). Understanding SaaS adoption: The moderating impact of the environment context. *International Journal of Information Management*, 49, 1–12.

Onososen, A. O., & Musonda, I. (2022). Research focus for construction robotics and human-robot teams towards resilience in construction: Scientometric review. *Journal of Engineering, Design and Technology, 21*(2), 502-526.

Oyewole, A. T., Okoye, C. C., Ofodile, O. C., & Ejairu, E. (2024). Reviewing predictive analytics in supply chain management: Applications and benefits. *World Journal of Advanced Research and Reviews*, 21(3), 568–574.

Pagell, M., & Shevchenko, A. (2014). Why research in sustainable supply chain management should have no future. *The Journal of Supply Chain Management*, 50(1), 44–55.

Pal, S. (2023). Sustainability in Supply Chain Management: A Systematic Review of the Literature. *International Journal of Creative Research Thoughts*.

Pandey, B. K., Paramashivan, M. A., Kanike, U. K., Mahajan, D. A., Mahajan, R., George, A. S., & Hameed, A. S. H. (2024). Impacts of Artificial Intelligence and Machine Learning on Intelligent Supply Chains. In *AI and Machine Learning Impacts in Intelligent Supply Chain* (pp. 57–73). IGI Global.

Pandey, S., Gupta, S., & Chhajed, S. (2021). *ROI of AI: Effectiveness and Measurement. International Journal Of Engineering Research & Technology* (Vol. 10). IJERT.

Panigrahi, S. S., Bahinipati, B., & Jain, V. (2019). Sustainable supply chain management: A review of literature and implications for future research. *Management of Environmental Quality*, 30(5), 1001–1049.

Phillips-Wren, G., & Jain, L. (2006, October). Artificial intelligence for decision making. In *International Conference on Knowledge-Based and Intelligent Information and Engineering Systems* (pp. 531-536). Berlin, Heidelberg: Springer Berlin Heidelberg.

Pundir, A. K., Jagannath, J. D., & Ganapathy, L. (2019, January). Improving supply chain visibility using IoT-internet of things. In *2019 IEEE 9th annual computing and communication workshop and conference (CCWC)* (pp. 0156-0162). IEEE.

Raji, I. D., Gebru, T., Mitchell, M., Buolamwini, J., Lee, J., & Denton, E. (2020, February). Saving face: Investigating the ethical concerns of facial recognition auditing. In *Proceedings of the AAAI/ACM Conference on AI, Ethics, and Society* (pp. 145-151).

Ransbotham, S., Kiron, D., Gerbert, P., & Reeves, M. (2017). Reshaping business with artificial intelligence: Closing the gap between ambition and action. *MIT Sloan Management Review*, 59(1).

Reuter, C., Foerstl, K. A. I., Hartmann, E. V. I., & Blome, C. (2010). Sustainable global supplier management: The role of dynamic capabilities in achieving competitive advantage. *The Journal of Supply Chain Management*, 46(2), 45–63.

Sallam, K., Mohamed, M., & Mohamed, A. W. (2023). Internet of Things (IoT) in supply chain management: Challenges, opportunities, and best practices. *Sustainable Machine Intelligence Journal*, 2, 3–1.

Sánchez-Flores, R. B., Cruz-Sotelo, S. E., Ojeda-Benitez, S., & Ramírez-Barreto, M. E. (2020). Sustainable supply chain management—A literature review on emerging economies. *Sustainability*, 12(17), 6972.

Sanders, N. R. (2016). How to use big data to drive your supply chain. *California Management Review*, 58(3), 26–48.

Sarkis, J. (2013). *Green supply chain management*. Momentum Press.

Sarkis, J., Cohen, M. J., Dewick, P., & Schröder, P. (2020). A brave new world: Lessons from the COVID-19 pandemic for transitioning to sustainable supply and production. *Resources, Conservation and Recycling*, 159, 104894. PMID: 32313383

Serey, J., Alfaro, M., Fuertes, G., Vargas, M., Ternero, R., Duran, C., & Gutierrez, S. (2023). Framework for the Strategic Adoption of Industry 4.0: A Focus on Intelligent Systems. *Processes (Basel, Switzerland)*, 11(10), 2973.

Seuring, S., & Müller, M. (2008). From a literature review to a conceptual framework for sustainable supply chain management. *Journal of Cleaner Production*, 16(15), 1699–1710.

Sevda, S., & Chauhan, G. (Eds.). (2024). *Solid Waste Management*. CRC Press.

Sheffi, Y. (2005). *The resilient enterprise: overcoming vulnerability for competitive advantage*. Pearson Education India.

Shiyyab, F. S., Alzoubi, A. B., Obidat, Q. M., & Alshurafat, H. (2023). The impact of artificial intelligence disclosure on financial performance. *International Journal of Financial Studies*, 11(3), 115.

Singh, S., Madaan, G., Swapna, H. R., Kaur, P., Pandey, D., & Dadheech, P. (2024). The Role of Artificial Intelligence in Supply Chain Management. In *Utilization of AI Technology in Supply Chain Management* (pp. 26–41). IGI Global.

Soni, N., Sharma, E. K., Singh, N., & Kapoor, A. (2019). Impact of artificial intelligence on businesses: from research, innovation, market deployment to future shifts in business models. *arXiv preprint arXiv:1905.02092*.

Sotarauta, M. (2019). *Leadership for urban and regional innovation*. Sage.

Srivastava, S. K. (2007). Green supply-chain management: A state-of-the-art literature review. *International Journal of Management Reviews*, 9(1), 53–80.

Stahl, B. C. (2021). *Artificial intelligence for a better future: an ecosystem perspective on the ethics of AI and emerging digital technologies*. Springer Nature.

Stilinski, D., Frank, L., & Doris, L. (2023). Transformative Role of Artificial Intelligence in Supply Chain Management.1), 67-84.

Subhadra, P. S., Kalaivani, A., Markan, R., Kumar, R., Natarajan, S., & Rajalakshmi, M. (2024). Rise of Artificial Intelligence in Business and Industry. *Journal of Informatics Education and Research*, 4(2).

Tambe, P., Cappelli, P., & Yakubovich, V. (2019). Artificial intelligence in human resources management: Challenges and a path forward. *California Management Review*, 61(4), 15–42.

Tjahjono, B., Esplugues, C., Ares, E., & Pelaez, G. (2017). What does industry 4.0 mean to supply chain? *Procedia Manufacturing*, 13, 1175–1182.

Toorajipour, R., Sohrabpour, V., Nazarpour, A., Oghazi, P., & Fischl, M. (2021). Artificial intelligence in supply chain management: A systematic literature review. *Journal of Business Research*, 122, 502–517.

Touboulic, A., & Walker, H. (2015). Theories in sustainable supply chain management: A structured literature review. *International Journal of Physical Distribution & Logistics Management*, 45(1/2), 16–42.

Tsang, Y. P., Choy, K. L., Wu, C. H., Ho, G. T. S., & Lam, H. Y. (2019). Blockchain-driven IoT for food traceability with an integrated consensus mechanism. *IEEE Access : Practical Innovations, Open Solutions*, 7, 129000–129017.

Tuncali Yaman, T. U. T. K. U. (2022). The role of big data in logistics: Current dynamics and future prospects.

Wagner, S. M., & Bode, C. (2008). An empirical examination of supply chain performance along several dimensions of risk. *Journal of Business Logistics*, 29(1), 307–325.

Wamba, S. F., Akter, S., Edwards, A., Chopin, G., & Gnanzou, D. (2015). How 'big data'can make big impact: Findings from a systematic review and a longitudinal case study. *International Journal of Production Economics*, 165, 234–246.

Wamba, S. F., Gunasekaran, A., Akter, S., Ren, S. J. F., Dubey, R., & Childe, S. J. (2017). Big data analytics and firm performance: Effects of dynamic capabilities. *Journal of Business Research*, 70, 356–365.

Wang, G., Gunasekaran, A., Ngai, E. W., & Papadopoulos, T. (2016). Big data analytics in logistics and supply chain management: Certain investigations for research and applications. *International Journal of Production Economics*, 176, 98–110.

Wang, H., Long, Z., Chen, J., Guo, Y., & Wang, A. (2023). Collaborative decision-making in supply chain management: A review and bibliometric analysis. *Cogent Engineering*, 10(1), 2196823.

Watanabe, Y., Suda, Y., & Takeno, J. (2020). A Robot Science Approach to Simulating the Pathogenesis of Dissociative Identity Disorder. *Procedia Computer Science*, 169, 46–50.

Whittlestone, J., Nyrup, R., Alexandrova, A., & Cave, S. (2019, January). The role and limits of principles in AI ethics: Towards a focus on tensions. In *Proceedings of the 2019 AAAI/ACM Conference on AI, Ethics, and Society* (pp. 195-200).

Yang, C., Zhu, Y., & Chen, Y. (2021). A review of human–machine cooperation in the robotics domain. *IEEE Transactions on Human-Machine Systems*, 52(1), 12–25.

Yang, H., Kumara, S., Bukkapatnam, S. T., & Tsung, F. (2019). The internet of things for smart manufacturing: A review. *IISE Transactions*, 51(11), 1190–1216.

Yao, X., Zhou, J., Lin, Y., Li, Y., Yu, H., & Liu, Y. (2019). Smart manufacturing based on cyber-physical systems and beyond. *Journal of Intelligent Manufacturing*, 30, 2805–2817.

Yu, W., Chavez, R., Jacobs, M. A., & Feng, M. (2018). Data-driven supply chain capabilities and performance: A resource-based view. *Transportation Research Part E, Logistics and Transportation Review*, 114, 371–385.

Zarsky, T. Z. (2016). Incompatible: The GDPR in the age of big data. *Seton Hall Law Review*, 47, 995.

Zhang, Y., Ren, S., Liu, Y., & Si, S. (2017). A big data analytics architecture for cleaner manufacturing and maintenance processes of complex products. *Journal of Cleaner Production*, 142, 626–641.

Zhao, Y., Zhu, Z., Chen, B., Qiu, S., Huang, J., Lu, X., & Wang, F. Y. (2023). Towards parallel intelligence: An interdisciplinary solution for complex systems. *The Innovation*.

Zhou, K., Liu, T., & Zhou, L. (2021). Human-machine collaboration in the digital workplace: A human factors and ergonomics perspective. *Applied Ergonomics*, 94, 103400.

Zhu, Q., & Sarkis, J. (2004). Relationships between operational practices and performance among early adopters of green supply chain management practices in Chinese manufacturing enterprises. *Journal of Operations Management*, 22(3), 265–289.

Zhu, Q., Sarkis, J., & Lai, K. H. (2013). Institutional-based antecedents and performance outcomes of internal and external green supply chain management practices. *Journal of Purchasing and Supply Management*, 19(2), 106–117.

Zou, J., & Schiebinger, L. (2018). AI can be sexist and racist—it's time to make it fair.

Section 3
Optimizing Supply Chain Planning Processes Leveraging Gen AI/ML Technologies

Chapter 12
Leveraging AI and ML for Logistics Excellence:
Case Studies and Success Strategies

Varun Gupta
https://orcid.org/0000-0002-0714-0298
University of North Georgia, USA

ABSTRACT

This book chapter explores how Artificial Intelligence and Machine Learning (AI/ML) methods are revolutionizing logistics operations, leading to enhanced efficiency, cost savings, and customer satisfaction. Based on a review of AI/ML literature and in-depth case studies of industry leaders like Amazon, C.H. Robinson, DHL, and the Port of Rotterdam, this chapter unveils how strategic leveraging of AI/ML can provide a competitive advantage. In addition to reviewing applications in large enterprises, we also discuss the opportunities and benefits for small and medium-sized enterprises (SMEs), including practical strategies for incremental AI adoption and subscription-based tools. The chapter analyzes the key challenges and opportunities associated with AI/ML adoption, delves into ethical considerations and sustainability implications, and provides practical strategies for logistics and supply chain leaders to successfully integrate these technologies into their operations, ultimately boosting their bottom line.

DOI: 10.4018/979-8-3693-4433-0.ch012

INTRODUCTION

GenAI presents an opportunity for logistics leaders to uncover additional insights from logistics data and drive operational efficiency, KPI reporting is a challenging area for many organizations, and it is ripe for exploration with GenAI to uncover valuable findings from logistics data at a greater speed. – Carly West, Senior Director Analyst in Gartner's Supply Chain practice (Gartner.com, 2024).

Logistics refers to the intricate process of planning, implementing, and controlling the efficient and effective flow of goods, services, and related information from the point of origin to the point of consumption. The logistics industry, responsible for the intricate dance of goods across the globe, faces unprecedented challenges in our increasingly interconnected world. Globalization, the explosive growth of e-commerce, and volatile geopolitical conditions demand greater agility, efficiency, and resilience from supply chains. Traditional logistics approaches, often reliant on manual processes and limited data visibility, struggle to keep pace. This is where Artificial Intelligence and Machine Learning (AI/ML) offer transformative change to logistics stakeholders. Logistics companies can utilize the power of data analysis, predictive modeling, and intelligent automation; AI/ML empowers them to optimize their operations, anticipate disruptions, and deliver exceptional customer experiences. This chapter delves into how AI/ML transforms logistics, exploring its applications, benefits, challenges, and future potential.

Since the turn of the 21st century, technology has revolutionized the logistics industry, enabling greater efficiency, transparency, and cost-effectiveness. One of the most significant technological advancements in logistics is *digitalization*. Companies well-known for their logistics, like Amazon and DHL, have embraced digital platforms, enabling real-time tracking of shipments, streamlining operations, and enhancing customer experience. Additionally, vehicle route optimization technologies, such as those developed by FourKites and Optym, have optimized delivery routes, reducing fuel consumption and carbon emissions (Rodrigue, 2020). In a case study, the Massachusetts Institute of Technology (MIT) researchers highlighted how UPS (United Parcel Service) leveraged advanced analytics and optimization algorithms to save millions of gallons of fuel annually (Simchi-Levi et al., 1999). While AI/ML is often associated with the large-scale operations of large companies like Amazon, DHL, and UPS, small and medium-sized enterprises (SMEs) also stand to gain substantial advantages from these technologies. This chapter discusses AI/ML strategies accessible to businesses of all sizes, providing specific insights for SMEs seeking to adopt these transformative technologies.

The COVID-19 pandemic has accelerated the trend toward Digitalization within the industry and the importance of engaging customers through multiple platforms, including e-business. – André Simha, Chief Digital and Information Officer, MSC Mediterranean Shipping Company. (Leonard, 2020).

The COVID-19 pandemic, which occurred due to the spread of a novel coronavirus in late 2019 (World Health Organization, 2020), resulted in widespread and devastating logistics and supply chain disruptions for almost all types of goods across the industry. The social distancing measures had negatively impacted the operations at many logistics companies and necessitated the adoption of digital technologies. Logistics companies that had invested in digitalizing and adopting other technologies for operational efficiencies fared better than their competitors in meeting customer demand and securing the movement of goods. Many companies made immediate investment decisions for digitalization to operate in the *new normal* with social distancing and take operational decisions remotely by building or participating in digital platforms.

Modern-day movement of goods, and thereby logistics, have become increasingly complex due to globalization, volatile and uncertain global tariffs, complex supply chain networks (*VUCA* world: Volatility, Uncertainty, Complexity, and Ambiguity), rapid digitalization including online shopping and e-commerce, changes in customer demands, shorter product life cycles, and a rapid increase in the number of products. Budgetary constraints on businesses and the high levels of customer service offered by brokerage services and freight forwarders further aggravate the complexity of logistics operations. This complexity and rapid technological advancements necessitate logistics companies to invest in AI/ML as a critical strategic tool to deliver profits and gain a competitive advantage. Despite an excellent opportunity to perform better using AI solutions, many executives remain unsure where to apply AI solutions to their businesses (McKinsey, 2022).

The chapter discusses leveraging AI/ML for logistics excellence by presenting the background and the key applications. Next, the main focus of this book chapter is a discussion on how traditional logistics operations can be enhanced by AI/ML, which is conducted via specific case studies. These case studies include Amazon Logistics, C.H. Robinson – a third-party logistics (3PL) company, DHL warehousing operations, and the Port of Rotterdam for its logistics operations. Next is a discussion on the key issues, AI/ML adoption controversies, and associated problems. Following this, there is a discussion on the best practices across logistics operations. Subsequently, the chapter covers practical and proven managerial strategies for logistics companies facing technological and other disruptions, highlighting how AI/ML can help mitigate some of these challenges. This is followed by a brief discussion on future developments and other emerging areas in AI/ML applications within the logistics industry.

BACKGROUND

Definition for AI and ML in Logistics

In logistics, AI refers to the development of computer systems capable of performing tasks that typically require human intelligence, such as recognizing patterns in shipment data, making routing decisions, or predicting potential disruptions in the supply chain. ML, a subset of AI, enables computer systems to learn from data without explicit programming, constantly improving their performance in demand forecasting, inventory optimization, and fraud detection.

Key Innovative Logistics Applications of AI/ML

AI/ML technologies are transforming logistics by automating routine tasks, optimizing complex processes, and providing predictive insights. Key applications are summarized in *Table 1*.

Table 1. Innovative Logistics Applications of AI/ML

Application	Example	Benefits Over Traditional Logistics
Blockchain Technology	Secure tracking of goods throughout the supply chain	Enhanced transparency, improved traceability, reduced fraud risk
Drone Delivery	Delivering medical supplies to remote areas	Faster delivery in geographically challenging locations, reduced transportation costs
Internet of Things (IoT)	Sensors monitoring temperature and location of perishable goods	Real-time monitoring of product condition, minimized spoilage, improved quality control
Predictive Analytics	ML to anticipate demand and optimize routes	Reduced inventory costs, minimized delays, improved delivery timeframes
Route Optimization	AI-powered software planning efficient delivery routes	Reduced fuel consumption, lower emissions, faster delivery times
Warehouse Automation	Robots for picking and packing	Increased efficiency, accuracy, and safety; 24/7 operations

From *Table 1,* note the innovative logistics applications driven by intelligence, efficiency, and data. Blockchain technology promises a secure and transparent journey for goods, safeguarding against fraud and enhancing traceability across the intricate and often very complex global supply chain networks. Drone delivery has emerged as a disruptive force, particularly in remote areas or situations requiring urgent deliveries and in locations/warehouses with unfavorable or hostile work environments. This innovation cuts transportation costs, dramatically reducing delivery times, and improves work safety. IoT plays a vital role in the real-time monitoring of crucial factors like temperature and location, especially for perishable goods, ensuring superior quality control and minimizing spoilage during the storage and transportation processes.

Predictive analytics, powered by ML, helps anticipate demand and optimize delivery routes, allowing businesses to streamline inventory management, minimize delays, and ensure on-time deliveries. AI-powered route optimization designs the most efficient delivery routes, reducing fuel consumption, lowering carbon emissions, and ultimately providing faster deliveries for customers, reducing the idle time for drivers, and improving asset utilization. With robots taking over picking and packing tasks, warehouse automation promises significant improvements in efficiency, accuracy, and safety. Furthermore, it enables uninterrupted and around-the-clock operations, keeping the supply chain moving continuously.

These applications illustrate how logistics has evolved from moving goods from point A to point B to a more intelligent, adaptable, and sustainable ecosystem for global trade using AI/ML-enabled technologies.

Review of Recent Literature on Logistics Applications of AI/ML

The integration of AI/ML into logistics and supply chain management represents a paradigm shift, redefining traditional operations and offering innovative solutions to contemporary challenges. This review synthesizes recent scholarly insights into the frameworks, applications, challenges, ethical considerations, and implications for future practices in this domain.

Frameworks for AI and ML in Logistics

AI adoption in logistics has been extensively conceptualized through frameworks that emphasize automation, predictive capabilities, and real-time adaptability. Richey et al. (2023) propose a comprehensive roadmap highlighting AI's potential to enhance both upstream processes, such as supplier evaluation and inventory management, and downstream activities, including customer engagement and distribution logistics. These frameworks position AI as a tool to dynamically reconfigure supply chains, facilitate rapid decision-making, and optimize resource utilization by harnessing advanced techniques such as supervised learning, natural language processing, and generative AI models.

Extending these ideas, Pessot et al. (2023) examine how AI, as part of Industry 4.0 technologies, empowers supply chains to navigate megatrends such as sustainability demands, global disruptions, and shifting consumer expectations. Their research identifies five key capabilities supported by AI, including digital transparency, real-time data integration, and enhanced resilience to external shocks. Together, these frameworks underscore AI's role as a driver of operational excellence and strategic foresight in logistics.

Applications in Supply Chain Management

AI and ML have proven instrumental in transforming logistics operations by providing actionable insights and automating decision-making processes. Generative AI models, such as GPT-4, are increasingly utilized for supplier evaluation, allowing firms to assess performance, cost-effectiveness, and risk by analyzing vast datasets. For instance, AI can proactively identify supplier insolvencies or geopolitical disruptions, enabling businesses to adapt sourcing strategies in real-time (Treiblmaier & Rejeb, 2023). These tools enhance supply chain continuity by mitigating risks and optimizing supplier portfolios.

In inventory management, AI-powered demand forecasting tools use historical sales and market data to predict future trends with high accuracy. This enables just-in-time inventory systems, reducing storage costs and minimizing waste. ML algorithms further optimize warehouse layouts by analyzing factors such as item demand, storage capacity, and handling constraints. This integration of AI into warehouse operations facilitates efficient space utilization and streamlines order fulfillment processes (Pessot et al., 2023).

Transportation and distribution logistics also benefit from AI's capabilities. Real-time routing systems use AI-driven analytics to adjust delivery pathways based on factors such as traffic, weather conditions, and fuel efficiency. For example, dynamic AI models can suggest alternate routes to avoid delays caused by severe weather, thereby ensuring timely delivery and reducing operational costs (Dwivedi et al., 2021). Similarly, AI-powered chatbots have transformed customer engagement by providing real-time updates on order statuses, addressing grievances, and delivering personalized service experiences (Malhotra & Kharub, 2024).

Challenges in AI Integration

While AI holds immense promise for logistics, several challenges hinder its seamless integration. One of the foremost issues is data quality and availability. AI systems require vast amounts of accurate, unbiased, and representative data to function effectively. However, as Richey et al. (2023) point out, inconsistencies in data quality often result in flawed AI outputs, such as biased supplier evaluations or inaccurate demand forecasts. Addressing these challenges necessitates robust data governance frameworks, including standardized practices for data collection, processing, and validation.

Another significant barrier is the lack of technical expertise within organizations, particularly among SMEs (Abhulimen & Ejike, 2024). While larger corporations often have the resources to invest in in-house AI capabilities, SMEs typically rely on third-party solutions, which may not be fully customizable to their needs. The financial burden of deploying and maintaining AI systems further exacerbates this disparity, limiting access to advanced technologies (Sanders et al., 2019). Additionally, cybersecurity risks, including data breaches and vulnerabilities in AI algorithms, pose significant threats. For example, poorly secured AI systems can expose sensitive supply chain data to malicious actors, undermining organizational trust and operational continuity.

Ethical and Regulatory Considerations

The ethical implications of AI deployment in logistics are central to ensuring its responsible and equitable application. A critical concern is algorithmic bias, which arises when AI systems trained on incomplete or unrepresentative data perpetuate systemic inequalities. As highlighted by Budhwar et al. (2023), biases embedded in training datasets can lead to discriminatory supplier evaluations, regional disparities in resource allocation, and suboptimal decision-making processes. Developing transparent, interpretable AI models is essential to mitigate these risks and enhance trust in AI applications.

Regulatory compliance further complicates AI integration, particularly in cross-border logistics. Data privacy regulations, such as the General Data Protection Regulation (GDPR) in Europe, impose stringent requirements on data handling and AI deployment. Treiblmaier & Rejeb (2023) emphasize the need for harmonized global regulatory frameworks to enable seamless operations while safeguarding privacy and data integrity. Without consistent international standards, organizations face significant compliance challenges that hinder the scalability of AI solutions in global supply chains.

The Road Ahead for AI in Logistics

The existing literature underscores the transformative potential of AI in logistics while also highlighting areas requiring further exploration. Bias mitigation remains a critical priority. Future research should focus on developing methodologies to identify and rectify biases in AI systems, ensuring fair and equitable decision-making. Additionally, regulatory alignment across jurisdictions is essential to facilitate the global adoption of AI technologies. Studies exploring collaborative approaches to harmonize data privacy and security laws could provide valuable insights for policymakers and practitioners alike (Rejeb et al., 2021).

Sustainability is another key area of focus. AI's ability to optimize routing, reduce waste, and enhance resource efficiency positions it as a critical tool for achieving environmental and social sustainability goals. For example, generative AI systems can simulate alternative logistics scenarios to identify the most eco-friendly solutions, thereby reducing carbon footprints while maintaining operational efficiency (Dwivedi et al., 2021). Finally, integrating human expertise with AI systems remains a pressing challenge. As (Malhotra & Kharub (2024) observe, fostering collaboration between human decision-makers and AI technologies is essential to leverage AI's strengths while preserving accountability and ethical oversight.

Summary

AI and ML are redefining the logistics and supply chain landscape by enabling operational efficiencies, enhancing decision-making processes, and fostering innovation. While their applications are transformative, challenges related to data quality, technical expertise, and regulatory compliance must be addressed to unlock their full potential. By building on existing frameworks and addressing identified gaps, future research can guide organizations toward sustainable, ethical, and effective AI adoption.

MAIN FOCUS OF THE CHAPTER

As illustrated in *Figure 1*, the traditional logistics process begins with order placement, where customers submit orders through various channels. These orders are processed by verifying details and confirming with the customer. Next, inventory checks are conducted to ensure stock availability, triggering replenishment if needed. The fulfillment stage involves picking items from the warehouse and packaging and labeling for shipping. Efficient transportation planning is crucial, requiring careful consideration of routes to reduce fuel consumption and delivery times. Warehousing includes storing goods in an organized manner, managing inventory, and conducting regular audits.

Figure 1. Traditional logistics process from customer order to product delivery.

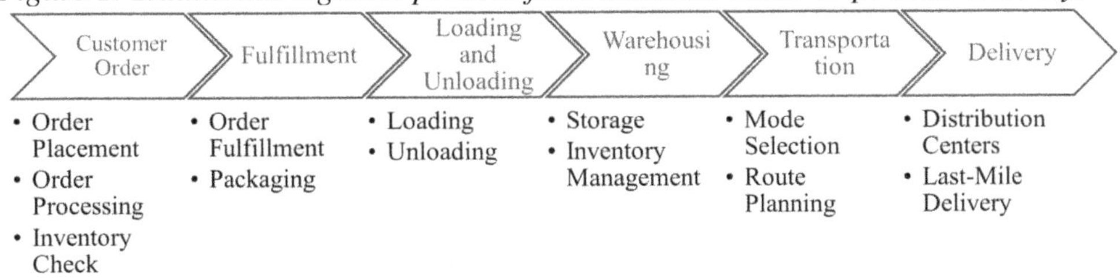

Once orders are packed, they are loaded onto delivery vehicles, which are then unloaded at distribution centers or final destinations. The last-mile delivery process ensures products reach customers promptly, with updates enhancing transparency and customer satisfaction. Upon delivery, receipts are generated, and invoices are processed to finalize the transaction. This comprehensive approach ensures a seamless flow of goods from the supplier to the end customer. Each stage of this process involves meticulous coordination and execution, highlighting the importance of effective logistics management in overcoming challenges and maintaining a competitive edge in the industry.

The traditional logistics process, while robust, is being revolutionized by AI/ML. AI-powered demand forecasting tools can analyze historical sales data, seasonality trends, and external factors like weather patterns to predict future demand more accurately than traditional methods. This allows for optimized inventory management, minimizing stockouts and reducing warehousing costs. Furthermore, AI algorithms can optimize transportation routes in real-time, considering traffic conditions, fuel efficiency, and delivery windows, leading to faster and more cost-effective delivery. In the warehouse, AI-powered robots can automate the picking and packing processes, boosting efficiency and reducing errors. This integration of AI/ML throughout the logistics process streamlines operations, reduces costs, and ultimately enhances customer satisfaction by enabling faster, more reliable delivery experiences.

Figure 2. AI/ML Integration Potential in Various Stages of the Logistics Process

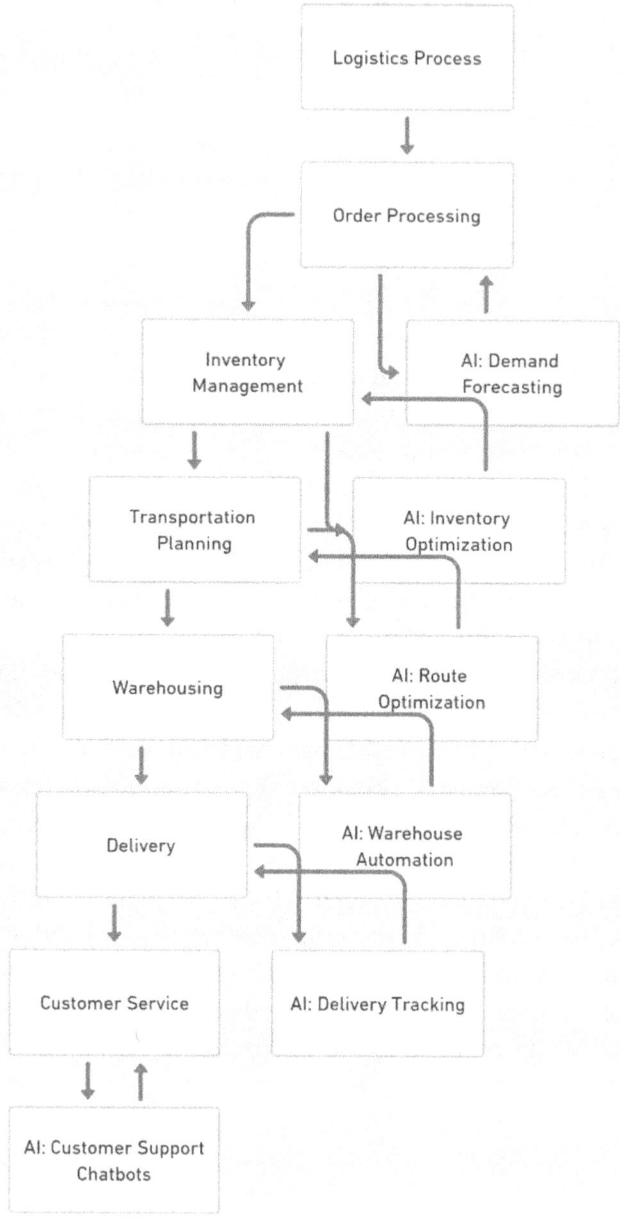

Figure 2 illustrates the key stages in a typical logistics process and highlights the areas where AI/ML can be integrated to improve efficiency and effectiveness. Each stage is connected to a specific AI/ML application that can enhance that part

of the process, providing a comprehensive view of how technology can transform logistics operations improving the process efficiency.

Order Processing: AI/ML Use - Demand Forecasting

At the initial stage of order processing, AI-driven demand forecasting plays a crucial role. By analyzing historical data, current market trends, and external factors (such as weather patterns and holidays), AI algorithms can accurately predict future demand. This enables logistics companies to manage inventory levels more effectively, ensuring that they avoid both overstock situations, which tie up capital unnecessarily, and stockouts, which can lead to missed sales opportunities and dissatisfied customers.

Inventory Management: AI/ML Use - Inventory Optimization

The next stage in the logistics process is inventory management. AI algorithms can optimize inventory levels by analyzing sales patterns, seasonality, and other relevant factors. This optimization ensures that the right amount of stock is available at the right time, reducing excess inventory and minimizing the risk of product obsolescence. AI-driven inventory management systems can dynamically adjust inventory levels in real time, responding to fluctuations in demand with greater precision than traditional methods.

Transportation Planning: AI/ML Use - Route Optimization

In the transportation planning stage, AI applications for route optimization are pivotal. AI can analyze various factors, such as traffic patterns, road conditions, and delivery schedules, to determine the most efficient routes for transportation. This reduces fuel consumption and delivery times and lowers transportation costs. By optimizing routes, AI helps logistics companies improve operational efficiency and consistently meet delivery deadlines.

Warehousing: AI/ML Use - Warehouse Automation

Within the warehousing stage, AI can significantly enhance operations through automation. AI-powered systems can automate tasks such as sorting, packing, and retrieving items. Equipped with computer vision and machine learning capabilities, these systems can improve accuracy and efficiency in warehouse operations. Automation reduces human error, increases productivity, and allows warehouses to operate around the clock, thus improving the overall throughput of logistics operations.

Product Delivery: AI/ML Use - Delivery Tracking

AI plays a vital role in the delivery stage by providing real-time tracking and delivery updates. AI systems can monitor the status of shipments, predict delivery times, and notify customers of any delays. This level of transparency improves customer satisfaction by keeping them informed and reducing uncertainty about their orders. Enhanced tracking capabilities also enable logistics companies to manage their delivery fleets better and respond promptly to any issues.

Customer Service: AI/ML Use - Customer Support Chatbots

The final stage in the logistics process involves customer service. AI-powered chatbots can handle customer inquiries and issues efficiently. These chatbots use natural language processing (NLP) to understand and respond to customer queries, providing quick and accurate responses. By automating routine customer service tasks, AI chatbots free up human agents to deal with more complex issues, improving the overall customer service experience and ensuring higher customer satisfaction.

Case Study of Amazon: AI Adoption in Logistics and Supply Chain Operations

Global e-commerce giant–Amazon faces a colossal logistical challenge: managing a worldwide network of fulfillment centers and delivering millions of packages daily. The sheer volume of operations demands high efficiency and automation to maintain competitive pricing and delivery times. Traditional approaches, while effective, could not fully address the complexities of managing inventory, optimizing routes, and predicting demand across diverse markets and seasons.

The Solution: AI/ML-Powered Logistics Transformation

To overcome these hurdles, Amazon has extensively adopted AI/ML across its logistics operations, resulting in a paradigm shift in efficiency and customer satisfaction (Amazon, 2023). Here are some key examples:

- **Predictive Analytics and Inventory Management:** Amazon uses machine learning algorithms to forecast demand, optimize inventory levels across its fulfillment centers, and minimize stockouts while reducing storage costs. This data-driven approach allows them to anticipate product trends and ensure availability, even during peak seasons like Black Friday and Christmas.

- **Route Optimization and Delivery Scheduling:** Amazon leverages AI to optimize delivery routes for its vast fleet of delivery vehicles, minimizing travel time and fuel consumption. To generate efficient delivery plans, machine learning algorithms analyze real-time traffic data, weather conditions, and delivery demands. This optimization reduces delivery costs and enhances delivery time predictability.
- **Robotics and Automation in Warehouses:** Amazon has heavily invested in robotic technology to automate tasks like picking, packing, and sorting within its fulfillment centers. These robots work alongside human employees, improving warehouse efficiency, safety, and overall throughput. This automation allows Amazon to handle higher order volumes and maintain consistent service quality even during peak periods.
- **Personalized Recommendations and Targeted Promotions:** Amazon employs AI to personalize product recommendations for customers based on their browsing history, purchase patterns, and other data points. This allows them to offer targeted promotions and improve customer engagement, increasing sales and customer satisfaction.
- **Fraud Detection and Security:** AI algorithms play a crucial role in identifying and preventing fraudulent activities within Amazon's logistics operations. Machine learning models can detect suspicious orders, track fraudulent returns, and identify patterns associated with fraud, enhancing security and protecting both the company and its customers.

Benefits and Impact

The implementation of AI/ML has yielded significant benefits for Amazon's logistics operations:

1. **Reduced Costs and Increased Efficiency:** By optimizing inventory management, routing, and warehouse operations, Amazon has achieved substantial cost savings and increased operational efficiency, allowing it to maintain competitive pricing and offer fast shipping options.
2. **Enhanced Customer Experience:** Improved delivery time predictability, personalized recommendations, and proactive fraud detection contribute to a smoother and more satisfying customer experience, building brand loyalty and driving repeat business for Amazon.
3. **Scalability and Adaptability:** AI/ML solutions are inherently scalable and adaptable, allowing Amazon to easily adjust its operations to accommodate increasing customer demands, market fluctuations, and evolving logistics landscapes.

Generative AI: The Next Frontier for Amazon Logistics

Amazon is exploring the potential of Generative AI to further enhance its logistics operations. Potential applications include:

- **Automated Customer Service:** Generative AI models could be trained to engage in natural, human-like conversations with customers, providing personalized support for inquiries related to orders, deliveries, and returns, thereby improving customer satisfaction and reducing reliance on human customer service agents.
- **Content Generation for Marketing and Product Descriptions:** Generative AI can assist in creating high-quality, engaging product descriptions, website content, and marketing materials, saving time and resources for Amazon's content creation teams.
- **Enhanced Demand Forecasting:** Generative AI models can be trained on historical data and external market factors to predict future demand with greater accuracy, allowing Amazon to optimize inventory levels and avoid stockouts while minimizing waste.
- **Personalized Delivery Experience:** Generative AI could be used to develop more customized delivery options, considering customer preferences, delivery timeframes, and special instructions, offering a more tailored and convenient delivery experience.

The implementation of Generative AI has the potential to revolutionize Amazon's logistics operations by automating tasks, enhancing customer interactions, and improving efficiency and accuracy. As Amazon continues to explore and innovate in AI, its logistics operations are poised to become even more sophisticated, agile, and customer-centric.

Case Study of C. H. Robinson: Generative AI Implementation in Email Automation

C.H. Robinson, a global third-party logistics company, recognized the need to address a long-standing barrier to automation – email-based transactions. Many shippers still preferred to request services, such as price quotes, through email rather than digital platforms, creating a bottleneck in the automation process.

The Challenge: Inefficiencies in Email-Based Transactions

Before generative AI, replying to that email request defied automation. Customers had to wait for a human just to pass along a quote from our Dynamic Pricing Engine. Now, our new technology reads the email and supplies the quote in an average 2 minutes 13 seconds. C.H. Robinson is doing this at scale, leaving our people more time to help those same customers with more complex requests. - Mark Albrecht, Vice President for Artificial Intelligence, C.H. Robinson (C.H. Robinson, 2024).

Before implementing an AI-powered solution, responding to email quote requests was a manual process requiring human intervention. On an average business day, the company received over 11,000 emails from customers and carriers requesting pricing information for truckload freight alone (C.H. Robinson, 2024). This manual approach slowed the quoting process and tied up valuable human resources that could have been better utilized for more complex tasks. Furthermore, delays in providing quotes and securing carriers could result in shippers paying premium rates in the spot market. According to research from MIT, shippers delayed in accessing the spot market could end up paying 23% to 35% extra on their shipments due to the limited availability of carriers in specific shipping lanes (C.H. Robinson, 2023).

The Solution: AI-Powered Email Automation

To address these challenges, C.H. Robinson developed a GenAI-based email transaction automation. The company's team of developers and data scientists trained a large language model (LLM) to classify incoming emails, read their contents, and replicate the steps a human would take to fulfill the customer's request. For example, when a shipper sends an email requesting a price quote, the AI-powered system can accurately identify the request, differentiate between various modes of transportation (e.g., truckload, less-than-truckload, intermodal, or air freight), and provide a quote within an average of 2 minutes and 13 seconds. This automation accelerates the quoting process and frees up C.H. Robinson's employees to focus on more complex requests and value-added tasks.

Benefits and Impact

The implementation of GenAI-powered email automation technology has yielded significant benefits for both the company and its customers:

1. **Increased Efficiency and Cost Savings**: The company streamlined its operations by automating email-based transactions, reducing the time and resources required for manual processing. This has led to increased efficiency and cost savings for the company.
2. **Faster Response Times**: Shippers can now receive price quotes and secure carriers more quickly, minimizing the risk of paying premium rates in the spot market due to delays.
3. **Improved Customer Experience**: The automated email system provides a seamless and convenient experience for shippers who prefer email for logistics transactions without sacrificing speed or cost-effectiveness.
4. **Scalability**: The AI-powered solution can handle a high volume of email requests, ensuring the company can meet the growing service demand while maintaining operational efficiency.

Case Study of DHL: AI/ML Implementation in Warehouse Operations

DHL, a global leader in logistics, used AI/ML to optimize its warehouse operations successfully.

Warehouse operations are inherently complex, involving many tasks such as receiving, sorting, storing, picking, and shipping goods. One of the primary challenges faced by DHL was the time-consuming and labor-intensive process of manually sorting and processing packages based on their labels, dimensions, and other characteristics. This manual process is prone to errors and hinders overall efficiency and productivity. Another critical challenge was effective inventory management and forecasting. With fluctuating demand patterns, varying supplier lead times, and the need to maintain optimal stock levels, accurately predicting future inventory needs was crucial to avoid overstocking or stockouts, which could have significant financial implications.

Implementation of AI/ML Solutions

DHL's team of data scientists and logistics experts collaborated to develop and implement two key initiatives (DHL, 2020) to integrate AI/ML solutions into its warehouse operations:

1. **AI-Powered Vision System for Package Sorting**: DHL deployed an AI-powered vision system in its warehouses that could automatically identify, and sort packages based on their labels, dimensions, and other characteristics. This system utilized machine learning algorithms trained on vast amounts of image

data, enabling it to recognize and classify packages with high precision accurately. This new system significantly streamlined the sorting and processing of packages, reducing the time and effort required for manual sorting. This led to improved overall efficiency and minimized the potential for human errors, ensuring accurate and timely package handling.

2. **ML-Based Predictive Analytics for Inventory Management**: DHL implemented predictive analytics to optimize inventory management and forecasting. DHL's ML models accurately predict future inventory needs by analyzing historical data on demand patterns, supplier lead times, and other relevant factors, enabling the company to maintain optimal stock levels.

DHL's proactive approach to inventory management minimized the risks of overstocking or stockouts, reducing warehousing carrying costs while ensuring product availability. Additionally, the insights provided by the ML models empowered DHL to make more informed decisions regarding inventory planning, supplier negotiations, and resource allocation.

Benefits and Impact

The implementation of AI/ML solutions in DHL's warehouse operations yielded significant benefits and operational improvements:

1. **Increased Efficiency and Productivity**: The AI-powered vision system for package sorting significantly reduced the time and effort required for manual sorting, leading to increased efficiency and productivity in DHL's warehouse operations.
2. **Labor Cost Savings**: DHL realized substantial labor cost savings by automating tasks previously performed manually, allowing for more efficient resource allocation and improved profitability.
3. **Improved Accuracy and Customer Satisfaction**: The AI-powered vision system minimized the potential for human errors in package sorting, ensuring accurate and timely package handling, and contributing to improved customer satisfaction.
4. **Optimized Inventory Management**: The ML-based predictive analytics for inventory management enabled DHL to maintain optimal stock levels, minimizing the risks of overstocking or stockouts and reducing associated costs.
5. **Competitive Advantage**: By embracing cutting-edge technologies like AI and ML, DHL positioned itself as an industry leader in innovation, attracting more business and maintaining a competitive edge in the global logistics market.

Implementation Challenges and Considerations

While the benefits of AI/ML implementation in DHL's warehouse operations were substantial, the process was not without its challenges. Some of the key considerations and issues faced during implementation included:

1. **Data Quality and Availability**: Ensuring the quality and availability of relevant data for training AI/ML models was crucial for accurate and reliable results. This requires significant data collection, cleaning, and preprocessing efforts.
2. **Integration with Existing Systems**: Integrating the AI/ML solutions with DHL's warehouse management systems (WMS) and processes required careful planning and coordination to ensure seamless operations.
3. **Change Management and Training**: Introducing new technologies warrants significant organizational change management efforts, including training personnel, adapting processes, and fostering a culture of innovation.

Despite these challenges, DHL's successful implementation of AI/ML solutions in its warehouse operations served as a compelling case study for other logistics companies seeking to leverage the power of these technologies to enhance efficiency, optimize inventory management, and maintain a competitive edge in the rapidly evolving global supply chain landscape. More recently, DHL has also used GenAI to unify around 200 career sites into a single career platform (Mearian, 2024), simplifying logistics hiring.

Case Study of Port of Rotterdam: AI/ML Implementation in Port Operations

The Port of Rotterdam, one of the largest and busiest ports in the world, has been at the forefront of leveraging cutting-edge technologies to enhance its operations and maintain its competitive edge. In recent years, the port has embraced the power of AI/ML to address some of the critical challenges it faced in managing the complex logistics operations of handling thousands of vessels and millions of containers annually (Best Practice AI, 2021).

Logistics Challenges Faced by the Port of Rotterdam

The Port of Rotterdam was challenged to accurately predict vessels' Estimated Time of Arrival (ETA). Precise ETA predictions, such as berth scheduling, labor planning, and equipment deployment, are crucial for efficient port resource allocation. However, traditional methods of ETA calculation often fell short due to the dynamic nature of maritime operations and the numerous variables involved, including weather conditions, vessel speed, and potential delays. Another significant challenge was identifying and mitigating potential bottlenecks in the supply chain. With the vast network of interconnected operations, from vessel movements to container handling and hinterland transportation, even minor disruptions could have ripple effects, leading to port congestion, vessel delays, and increased operational costs.

Implementation of Logistics AI/ML Technologies

To address these challenges, the Port of Rotterdam developed an ambitious project to leverage AI and ML technologies. The port's team of data scientists and domain experts collaborated to develop advanced algorithms and models capable of processing and analyzing vast amounts of data from various sources. For accurate ETA predictions, the port utilized historical vessel tracking data, real-time sensor information from Automatic Identification System (AIS) transponders, and other relevant data sources. This data was fed into ML models, which learned patterns and relationships, enabling them to provide more accurate ETA predictions for incoming vessels. The port employed predictive analytics powered by ML algorithms to identify potential supply chain bottlenecks. These algorithms analyzed historical data on vessel movements, container handling operations, hinterland transportation, and other relevant factors to identify patterns and potential disruptions before they occurred.

Logistics Benefits and Impact

The implementation of AI/ML technologies at the Port of Rotterdam has yielded significant benefits and operational improvements:

1. **Improved Resource Allocation**: Accurate ETA predictions enabled by AI/ML have allowed the port to optimize resource allocation, such as berth scheduling, labor planning, and equipment deployment. This increased efficiency, reduced idle time, and cost savings.
2. **Proactive Bottleneck Mitigation**: The ability to identify potential bottlenecks in advance has enabled the port to take proactive measures to mitigate disruptions and maintain smooth operations. This minimized delays, congestion, and associated costs, improving overall supply chain efficiency.
3. **Enhanced Decision-Making**: The insights provided by AI/ML models empowered port authorities and stakeholders to make more informed and data-driven decisions, leading to better strategic planning and operational optimization.

4. **Competitive Advantage**: By embracing cutting-edge technologies like AI/ML, the port positioned itself as a leader in innovation, attracting more business and maintaining its competitive edge in the global maritime industry.

Implementation Challenges and Considerations

While the benefits of AI/ML implementation at the Port of Rotterdam have been substantial, the process was not without its challenges. Some of the key considerations and issues faced during implementation included:

1. **Change Management**: Introducing new technologies often requires significant organizational change management efforts, including training personnel, adapting processes, and fostering a culture of innovation.
2. **Ethical and Privacy Concerns**: Using AI/ML technologies in logistics operations raises ethical and privacy concerns, particularly regarding handling sensitive data and potential biases in decision-making processes.
3. **Continuous Improvement**: AI/ML models require constant monitoring, evaluation, and retraining to ensure their accuracy and relevance as operational conditions and data patterns evolve.

The Port of Rotterdam's successful implementation of AI/ML technologies (Port of Rotterdam, 2024) can serve as a compelling use case for other ports and logistics organizations seeking to leverage the power of these technologies to enhance their operations, improve efficiency, and maintain a competitive edge.

AI/ML Implementation for Small and Medium-Sized Enterprises (SMEs)

SMEs represent a vital part of the global logistics ecosystem. In stark contrast to large enterprises with extensive resources, SMEs face unique challenges, including limited budgets, technical expertise, and infrastructure. However, AI/ML technologies are becoming increasingly accessible, allowing SMEs to compete effectively with larger companies by optimizing logistics operations, improving efficiency, and reducing costs. This section explores the challenges SMEs face, the strategies they can adopt for incremental AI/ML adoption, and real-life examples that highlight successful AI/ML implementations.

Adoption and Implementation Challenges for SMEs

SMEs face unique challenges in integrating AI/ML into their logistics operations that differ from large corporations. These include limited financial resources, lack of technical expertise, and the perception that AI/ML technologies are primarily suited for large-scale operations. Unlike large corporations, SMEs often lack dedicated IT departments or the capital to make substantial investments in emerging technologies. Additionally, SMEs may lack awareness of the AI/ML solutions available to them and how these solutions could be customized for their needs.

Despite these obstacles, the benefits of AI/ML for SMEs are significant. AI-driven analytics can help optimize inventory levels, reduce transportation costs, and improve demand forecasting, directly contributing to improved profitability and customer satisfaction.

Practical Strategies for AI/ML Adoption in SMEs

One of the most effective ways for SMEs to adopt AI/ML technologies is through incremental implementation. Unlike large corporations that may deploy fully integrated AI systems across their logistics operations, SMEs can start with small, manageable projects. The focus should be on affordable AI tools and subscription-based services that provide flexibility and scalability.

1. Subscription-based AI Solutions: Subscription-based AI services offer a practical entry point for SMEs into advanced logistics technology that eliminates barriers to AI adoption due to significant technology investment costs. Such services provide AI capabilities without upfront hardware and software infrastructure costs. For instance, platforms like project44 (https://www.project44.com/) offer cloud-based AI tools that help SMEs optimize inventory management, improve customer service, and streamline transportation planning. Subscription models are particularly advantageous for SMEs because they allow businesses to scale AI usage up or down depending on their current needs and budgets.
2. AI/ML-enabled Predictive Analytics: Predictive analytics, powered by ML, helps SMEs make data-driven decisions. By analyzing historical data and identifying patterns, AI can help predict future demand, enabling SMEs to optimize inventory and prevent stockouts or overstock situations. Predictive analytics tools like Demand Guru (https://help.llama.ai/release/native/demand/Home.htm), offered by Coupa (www.coupa.com), help businesses anticipate customer demand, improving service levels and reducing operational costs. For example, an SME can use AI to analyze seasonal sales data and adjust inventory accordingly, ensuring optimal stock levels during peak periods without excess.

3. AI/ML-Based Route Optimization: Route optimization is another area where AI can significantly impact SME logistics. AI-powered tools can analyze multiple data points, including traffic conditions, fuel costs, and delivery schedules, to recommend the most efficient routes for delivery. Optimized routing reduces fuel consumption and operational costs and enhances customer satisfaction by ensuring timely deliveries. Companies like Routific (https://www.routific.com) and OptimoRoute (https://optimoroute.com/) offer route optimization solutions specifically designed for small logistics operators, allowing SMEs to benefit from improved fleet efficiency without investing in custom-built software.
4. Incremental Implementation: SMEs often adopt AI and ML incrementally, starting with basic applications such as demand forecasting, route optimization, or warehouse automation before expanding into more complex systems. This cautious, step-by-step approach helps mitigate risks and control costs, which is particularly important for smaller firms with limited capital.

Real-Life Examples of AI/ML Adoption in SMEs in Logistics

1. **Tive (Boston, USA)**: A notable SME in logistics technology, Tive (https://www.tive.com) offers real-time location and condition monitoring of shipments using AI-driven predictive analytics. Their sensors and cloud-based platform allow small and medium logistics firms to monitor shipment conditions, such as temperature, humidity, and shock levels. Using AI, Tive's platform can predict potential supply chain issues, helping SMEs prevent costly delays or product spoilage. For example, a small-scale pharmaceutical company transporting temperature-sensitive products can rely on Tive's technology to avoid damages from unexpected temperature fluctuations.
2. **ShipBob (Chicago, USA)**: ShipBob (https://www.shipbob.com), an SME providing logistics and warehousing services for e-commerce businesses, uses AI algorithms to optimize warehouse management and last-mile delivery. Their AI-driven system helps small businesses minimize shipping costs and reduce delivery times. Through machine learning models, ShipBob optimizes packaging, determines the most efficient fulfillment centers to use, and ensures the fastest possible delivery routes. This enables smaller businesses to compete with larger retailers by offering faster shipping options without investing heavily in logistics infrastructure.
3. **Onfleet (San Francisco, USA)**: Onfleet (https://onfleet.com/company), a last-mile delivery software provider for SMEs, leverages machine learning algorithms to optimize delivery routes and driver dispatching. The platform integrates with SMEs' existing logistics systems, enabling more efficient fleet management. Onfleet's predictive models analyze traffic, delivery volumes,

and route patterns to ensure timely deliveries. Small delivery companies, often constrained by limited resources, benefit from these AI-enhanced optimizations that reduce fuel costs and improve customer satisfaction by providing accurate delivery times.

Comparison of AI/ML Adoption by SMEs and Larger Enterprises in Logistics

Table 2. AI/ML Adoption: SMEs vs. Larger Enterprises

Aspect	SMEs	Larger Enterprises
Resource Constraints	Limited capital for in-house AI development.	Significant resources for proprietary AI systems and large-scale investments.
	Relies on third-party vendors and pre-built AI solutions for cost efficiency.	Builds customized AI and ML platforms tailored to specific logistics needs (e.g., Amazon's autonomous warehouses).
Customization vs. Standardization	Prefers standardized, off-the-shelf AI solutions for affordability and scalability.	Develop bespoke AI solutions to align with complex, unique workflows.
	Uses tools offering general predictive analytics and optimization.	Designs proprietary algorithms (e.g., FedEx's demand forecasting models).
Scale of Operations	Focuses on localized or regional logistics improvements, such as last-mile delivery or inventory management.	Applies AI across global supply chains, optimizing multinational operations.
Scope of Operations	Limited application scope due to smaller operational reach.	Implements AI for global route optimization, warehouse management, and demand forecasting.
Risk Management	Risk-averse due to financial constraints and smaller margins.	Willing to experiment with advanced, cutting-edge AI despite uncertain outcomes.
Flexibility	Prioritizes flexible, scalable AI solutions to adapt to changing business needs.	Aims for full integration of AI into long-term logistics strategy.

Table 2 highlights how SMEs and large enterprises adopt AI/ML in logistics differently due to resource, scale, and strategy disparities. For instance, SMEs like Onfleet rely on standardized, cost-efficient platforms for last-mile delivery optimization, while large corporations such as Amazon invest in proprietary systems like autonomous warehouses. SMEs often focus on regional operations, such as optimizing local deliveries, while larger firms like FedEx implement global AI solutions for route optimization and demand forecasting. SMEs prioritize flexible, scalable solutions to manage financial risks, whereas large firms embrace experimental, cutting-edge AI to integrate into long-term logistics strategies fully.

Challenges Faced by SMEs in Adopting AI/ML in Logistics

Despite the benefits of AI and ML in logistics, SMEs face several challenges in adopting these technologies. These challenges stem from limited resources, technical expertise, and concerns about the reliability and long-term impact of AI systems on business operations.

1. Financial Constraints: The cost of implementing AI and ML technologies can be prohibitive for SMEs. While cloud-based and third-party solutions have made AI more accessible, there are still significant costs associated with integrating these technologies into existing systems. Additionally, the expense of maintaining AI models—such as updating algorithms and acquiring the necessary data—can be a burden for smaller firms that operate on tight budgets.
2. Lack of Technical Expertise: Implementing AI and ML solutions requires expertise in data science, algorithm development, and software engineering, areas where SMEs often lack in-house talent. Without skilled personnel, SMEs may struggle to customize AI tools to meet their specific logistics needs or may not fully understand how to interpret AI-generated insights, leading to suboptimal decision-making.
3. Data Limitations: AI and ML models require large datasets to function effectively, particularly for predictive analytics or optimization tasks. SMEs often do not generate the same volume of data as larger enterprises, which can limit the effectiveness of their AI models. Additionally, smaller firms may not have the infrastructure to collect, store, and analyze the necessary data.
4. Integration with Legacy Systems: Many SMEs still rely on legacy logistics systems that are not compatible with modern AI and ML technologies. Integrating new AI-driven platforms with outdated systems can be technically challenging and expensive. This issue is compounded when SMEs are required to maintain both old and new systems simultaneously during a transitional period.
5. Concerns About Reliability and Trust: SMEs are often hesitant to fully trust AI and ML systems due to concerns about the reliability of automated decision-making processes. The complexity and opacity of some AI models, particularly deep learning algorithms, can make it difficult for business owners and logistics managers to understand how decisions are being made. This "black-box" nature of AI can lead to resistance among SMEs, especially in mission-critical areas such as supply chain management and customer fulfillment.
6. Regulatory and Ethical Concerns: As AI adoption grows, SMEs must also contend with evolving regulatory and ethical frameworks governing the use of these technologies. Issues such as data privacy, algorithmic bias, and the potential displacement of human workers are particularly relevant in logistics, where AI

is increasingly being used to automate tasks traditionally performed by humans. SMEs may find it difficult to navigate these legal and ethical considerations, especially if they lack the resources to stay abreast of regulatory changes.

AI/ ML has the potential to revolutionize logistics for SMEs, offering them opportunities to optimize operations, reduce costs, and improve service delivery. While large companies continue to dominate the AI space with extensive resources and tailored solutions, SMEs are increasingly finding ways to adopt these technologies through cloud-based platforms, third-party vendors, and collaborative ecosystems. However, the road to AI adoption is not without its challenges. SMEs must overcome financial constraints, technical expertise gaps, data limitations, and concerns about reliability and integration. As AI and ML technologies continue to evolve, the logistics sector will likely see even more widespread adoption among SMEs, leveling the playing field and allowing smaller companies to compete more effectively in a rapidly changing industry.

Issues, Controversies, Problems

The solutions discussed in this chapter of the book are agnostic to the size and resources of logistics companies. Small and medium-sized enterprises (SMEs) usually lack the capital resources to implement costly but effective AI/ML strategies to sustain their operations on their own (Deloitte, 2021). Still, they can benefit from subscription-based AI solutions which are relatively inexpensive.

More recently, logistics managers are facing the challenge of incorporating their companies' ESG (Environmental, Social, and Governance) goals through sustainable AI/ML strategies (LogisticsIT.com, 2024; World Economic Forum, 2024). The increasing reliance on AI/ML raises concerns about its environmental impact. Training complex AI models requires significant computing power, leading to high energy consumption in data centers. Furthermore, AI-driven optimization, while reducing transportation costs and emissions in some areas, can inadvertently increase traffic congestion and pollution in others due to concentrated delivery routes. Implementing sustainable AI solutions can result in practices where there are only a limited number of technology providers or compatible systems, reducing flexibility and potentially amplifying the impact of any technological disruption on the logistics operation.

Another challenge with current AI/ML solutions is that they primarily focus on optimizing efficiency and cost-effectiveness. These strategies often do not factor in issues such as increased carbon footprint, resource wastage, impact on climate, and the broader implications for other industries and labor. Logistics companies must prioritize sustainability in their AI/ML strategies to mitigate these concerns. This includes exploring energy-efficient AI algorithms, optimizing data center operations, and investing in renewable energy sources. Additionally, companies can use AI to develop more sustainable transportation solutions, such as optimizing delivery routes for electric vehicles or utilizing AI-powered load optimization to reduce the number of trips required.

Optimizing routes with AI reduces fuel consumption and emissions in the short term. However, once optimized routes become the norm, any disruption in these routes due to unforeseen events (e.g., natural disasters, cyberattacks, etc.) could have a more significant impact due to the lack of alternative options. Furthermore, automation and AI-driven efficiency improvements could lead to job displacement, particularly for lower-skilled labor. While redundancy in supply chain routes and resources is generally advantageous, eliminating this redundancy once operations stabilize can result in a loss of business and jobs for suppliers and carriers.

Ethical issues and biases inherent in these technologies also pose significant challenges. AI algorithms are only as good as the data they are trained on. If this data includes biases, whether intentional or unintentional, the AI systems can perpetuate and even exacerbate these biases (Bollig et al., 2019). This can lead to unfair treatment of certain groups of workers (Ernst et al., 2018), suppliers, or regions. For example, predictive analytics used for hiring logistics staff for a company might unfairly disadvantage candidates from specific backgrounds if the historical data contains biases. Similarly, route optimization algorithms might favor routes that disadvantage certain communities, leading to uneven economic impacts.

Moreover, the use of AI in surveillance and monitoring, while beneficial for security and efficiency, raises concerns about privacy and workers' rights (Calo, 2017). The balance between leveraging AI for operational benefits and maintaining ethical standards is delicate and requires careful consideration.

However, with digitalization and improved supply chain transparency, logistics companies and their partners must better align their objectives to address these issues proactively. Enhanced collaboration and communication enabled by AI/ ML can help resolve potential environmental, labor, ethical, and operational challenges earlier, fostering a more resilient and sustainable logistics ecosystem and supply chains.

SOLUTIONS AND RECOMMENDATIONS

Integrating AI/ML into logistics operations offers numerous benefits, but successful implementation requires careful planning and execution. This section provides a framework for logistics companies to strategically adopt AI/ML, leveraging its power to optimize their processes and gain a competitive edge.

Table 3. Strategies for AI/ML Adoption in Logistics

Logistics Process	AI/ML Strategy	Strategy Description
Demand Forecasting	Time Series Analysis	Utilize historical data and seasonal patterns to predict future demand, allowing for accurate inventory planning and resource allocation.
Inventory Management	ML Models	Employ ML models to predict stockouts, optimize inventory levels across multiple locations, and minimize holding costs.
Route Optimization	Deep Learning (DL) and Reinforcement Learning (RL)	Leverage DL and RL algorithms to optimize delivery routes, considering factors like traffic, weather, and delivery deadlines, resulting in faster delivery times and lower fuel consumption.
Warehouse Management	Robotics and Computer Vision	Implement robotic systems for tasks like picking, packing, and sorting, while using computer vision for inventory tracking and anomaly detection, enhancing efficiency and accuracy.
Transportation Management	Predictive Maintenance	Utilize sensors and ML to predict equipment failures, enabling preventative maintenance and reducing downtime.
Customer Service	Chatbots and Natural Language Processing (NLP)	Deploy AI-powered chatbots to handle routine customer inquiries, provide personalized recommendations, and automate common tasks, improving customer satisfaction and freeing up human agents for more complex issues.
Fraud Detection	Anomaly Detection Algorithms	Implement ML algorithms to detect fraudulent activities like fake orders, fraudulent returns, and suspicious account behavior, enhancing security and protecting the company and its customers.

Successful AI/ML adoption requires a structured approach:

1. **Identify Key Processes:** Begin by identifying core logistics processes that can benefit from AI/ML optimization. Prioritize areas with high potential for improvement in efficiency, cost reduction, or customer satisfaction.
2. **Data Acquisition and Preparation:** Ensure access to high-quality data essential for training AI/ML models. Data should be clean, comprehensive, and relevant to the targeted process. Data preprocessing techniques like cleaning, transformation, and feature engineering are crucial for model accuracy.
3. **Model Selection and Training:** Select the appropriate AI/ML algorithms based on the specific process and available data–train models on a significant dataset to achieve high accuracy and robustness.
4. **Implementation and Monitoring:** Integrate trained AI/ML models into existing logistics systems and monitor their performance continuously. Evaluate metrics like accuracy, efficiency, and cost savings to ensure the model's effectiveness and make necessary adjustments.
5. **Continuous Improvement:** Develop a culture of continuous improvement, regularly reviewing model performance, exploring new data sources, and refining algorithms to enhance model accuracy and effectiveness.

FUTURE RESEARCH DIRECTIONS

While AI/ML applications in logistics are rapidly evolving, several areas require further research to unlock their full potential. One promising direction is the development of more sophisticated AI models capable of handling complex, dynamic environments. This involves incorporating real-time data streams, predicting unforeseen events, and adapting to changing conditions, such as weather fluctuations or unexpected disruptions in the supply chain. Further research is also needed to enhance the explainability and transparency of AI/ML models. This is crucial for building trust and understanding among logistics stakeholders, allowing for informed decision-making and mitigating potential biases within the models (Kelleher et al., 2020). Another crucial area for future research is the exploration of ethical considerations related to AI/ML in logistics. This includes addressing potential job displacement, ensuring fairness and non-discrimination in decision-making, and safeguarding privacy and data security. Addressing these concerns is essential for the responsible implementation and adoption of AI/ML across the logistics industry, contributing to a more equitable and sustainable future (Richey et al., 2023).

A critical area for future research lies in understanding and optimizing the evolving relationship between human workers and AI/ML systems in logistics. While AI excels at automating repetitive tasks and analyzing vast datasets, human expertise remains crucial for tasks requiring creativity, complex problem-solving, and adaptability to unforeseen situations (Brynjolfsson & Mitchell, 2017). Research into collaborative intelligence, where AI augments human capabilities and vice versa, will be essential for designing effective human-in-the-loop systems. This includes developing intuitive interfaces for human operators to interact with AI systems, understanding the cognitive biases humans and AI might bring to collaborative decision-making, and exploring new training programs to prepare the logistics workforce for these evolving roles.

CONCLUSIONS

This chapter has illustrated the transformative potential of AI/ML across a diverse range of logistics applications, underpinned by an extensive literature review and insights into the role of SMEs. For example, Amazon demonstrates how AI drives efficiency in demand forecasting and warehouse automation, streamlining massive e-commerce operations. Similarly, C.H. Robinson's implementation of generative AI (GenAI) showcases the optimization of traditional communication channels like email to enhance customer responsiveness. DHL's deployment of AI-powered vision systems and predictive analytics underscores the power of AI in warehouse environments, while the Port of Rotterdam exemplifies how AI can enhance resource allocation and proactively mitigate bottlenecks in complex maritime logistics.

These examples, coupled with insights from the literature, highlight that AI/ML is not a one-size-fits-all solution but rather a versatile toolkit adaptable to specific logistics challenges. For small and medium-sized enterprises (SMEs), the adoption of AI often differs significantly from large corporations, with SMEs leveraging cost-efficient cloud-based tools and third-party platforms to overcome resource constraints. This flexibility is vital for enabling smaller businesses to compete effectively despite limited budgets and technical expertise.

However, as with any powerful tool, responsible implementation is paramount. Organizations must balance the pursuit of efficiency and cost-savings with broader sustainability considerations, ethical AI practices, and the potential impact on the workforce. For instance, while AI can optimize warehouse operations, it is crucial to consider the energy consumption of these AI models and explore strategies to minimize their environmental footprint. Ethical issues, such as algorithmic bias and the transparency of decision-making processes, also demand careful attention to ensure fair and inclusive outcomes.

Looking ahead, the logistics industry must continue to explore the full potential of AI/ML while addressing the ethical, technical, and sustainability challenges these technologies present. This necessitates ongoing collaboration between industry stakeholders, technology developers, and policymakers. By embracing a holistic approach that prioritizes both innovation and responsibility, the logistics industry—whether large multinationals or SMEs—can implement AI/ML-based technologies to build a more efficient, sustainable, and ethically sound future. With a growing body of research providing actionable insights, the path forward lies in integrating AI responsibly to create equitable value across the supply chain.

REFERENCES

Abhulimen, A. O., & Ejike, O. G. (2024). Ethical considerations in AI use for SMEs and supply chains: Current challenges and future directions. *International Journal of Applied Research in Social Sciences*, 6(8), 8. Advance online publication. DOI: 10.51594/ijarss.v6i8.1391

Amazon. (2023). *Amazon.com, Inc. Annual Report (10-K)*.https://d18rn0p25nwr6d.cloudfront.net/CIK-0001018724/b22698ce-4a1c-4290-b373-531dd612a404.html

Best Practice AI. (2021). *AI Case Study | The Port of Rotterdam Authority reduces vessel waiting times by 20% with machine learning*. Best Practice AI. https://www.bestpractice.ai/ai-case-study-best-practice/the_port_of_rotterdam_authority_reduces_vessel_waiting_times_by_20%25_with_machine_learning

Bollig, B., Bouyer, P., & Reiter, F. (2019). *Identifiers in Registers—Describing Network Algorithms with Logic* (Vol. 11425, pp. 115–132). https://doi.org/DOI: 10.1007/978-3-030-17127-8_7

Brynjolfsson, E., & Mitchell, T. (2017). *What can machine learning do? Workforce implications | Science. 358*(6370), 1530–1534. https://doi.org/DOI: 10.1126/science.aap8062

Calo, R. (2017). *Artificial Intelligence Policy: A Primer and Roadmap* (SSRN Scholarly Paper 3015350). https://doi.org/DOI: 10.2139/ssrn.3015350

DHL. (2020). *DHL Group | Aug 12, 2020: Artificial Intelligence: DHL algorithm makes e-fulfillment more effective*. https://group.dhl.com/en/media-relations/press-releases/2020/artificial-intelligence-dhl-algorithm-makes-e-fulfillment-more-effective.html

Dwivedi, Y. K., Hughes, L., Ismagilova, E., Aarts, G., Coombs, C., Crick, T., Duan, Y., Dwivedi, R., Edwards, J., Eirug, A., Galanos, V., Ilavarasan, P. V., Janssen, M., Jones, P., Kar, A. K., Kizgin, H., Kronemann, B., Lal, B., Lucini, B., & Williams, M. D. (2021). Artificial Intelligence (AI): Multidisciplinary perspectives on emerging challenges, opportunities, and agenda for research, practice and policy. *International Journal of Information Management*, 57, 101994. DOI: 10.1016/j.ijinfomgt.2019.08.002

Ernst, E., Merola, R., & Samaan, D. (2018). *The economics of artificial intelligence: Implications for the future of work*.

Gartner.com. (2024). *Gartner Predicts 25% of Logistics Key Performance Indicator Reporting will be Supported by GenAI by 2028*. Gartner. https://www.gartner.com/en/newsroom/press-releases/2024-03-12-gartner-predicts-25-percent-of-logistics-key-performance-indicator-reporting-will-be-supported-by-genai-by-2028

Kelleher, J. D., Namee, B. M., & D'Arcy, A. (2020). Fundamentals of Machine Learning for Predictive Data Analytics, *second edition: Algorithms, Worked Examples, and Case Studies*. MIT Press.

Leonard, M. (2020, July 1). *MSC adds instant quotes to website*. Supply Chain Dive. https://www.supplychaindive.com/news/msc-instant-booking-quotes/580869/

Logistics, I. T. com. (2024). *The intersection of sustainability and productivity | Manufacturing & Logistics IT Magazine*. https://www.logisticsit.com/articles/2024/02/06/the-intersection-of-sustainability-and-productivity

Malhotra, G., & Kharub, M. (2024). Elevating logistics performance: Harnessing the power of artificial intelligence in e-commerce. *The International Journal of Logistics Management, ahead-of-print*(ahead-of-print). https://doi.org/DOI: 10.1108/IJLM-01-2024-0046

McKinsey. (2022). *Unlocking the promise of AI in industrials | McKinsey*. https://www.mckinsey.com/industries/automotive-and-assembly/our-insights/the-future-is-now-unlocking-the-promise-of-ai-in-industrials

Mearian, L. (2024). How DHL harnessed genAI to unify 200 career sites into a single platform. *Computerworld*. https://www.computerworld.com/article/2083870/how-dhl-harnessed-genai-to-unify-200-career-sites-into-a-single-platform.html

Pessot, E., Zangiacomi, A., Marchiori, I., & Fornasiero, R. (2023). Empowering supply chains with Industry 4.0 technologies to face megatrends. *Journal of Business Logistics*, 44(4), 609–640. DOI: 10.1111/jbl.12360

Port of Rotterdam. (2024). *Vessels participating in Nextlogic spend 20% less time in port | Port of Rotterdam*. https://www.portofrotterdam.com/en/news-and-press-releases/vessels-participating-in-nextlogic-spend-20-less-time-in-port

Rejeb, A., Rejeb, K., Simske, S., & Treiblmaier, H. (2021). Blockchain Technologies in Logistics and Supply Chain Management: A Bibliometric Review. *Logistics (Basel)*, 5(4), 4. Advance online publication. DOI: 10.3390/logistics5040072

Richey, R. G., Chowdhury, S., Davis-Sramek, B., Giannakis, M., & Dwivedi, Y. K. (2023). Artificial intelligence in logistics and supply chain management: A primer and roadmap for research. *Journal of Business Logistics*, 44(4), 532–549. DOI: 10.1111/jbl.12364

Robinson, C. H. (2023). *Put Spot Market Freight in Your Route Guide | C.H. Robinson*. https://www.chrobinson.com/en-us/resources/blog/why-you-should-put-spot-freight-in-your-route-guide/

Robinson, C. H. (2024). *New C.H. Robinson Technology Breaks a Decades-Old Barrier to Automation in the Logistics Industry*. https://investor.chrobinson.com/News-and-Events/Press-Releases/press-release-details/2024/New-C.H.-Robinson-Technology-Breaks-a-Decades-Old-Barrier-to-Automation-in-the-Logistics-Industry/default.aspx

Rodrigue, J.-P. (2020). *The Geography of Transport Systems* (5th ed.). Routledge., DOI: 10.4324/9780429346323

Sanders, N. R., Boone, T., Ganeshan, R., & Wood, J. D. (2019). Sustainable Supply Chains in the Age of AI and Digitization: Research Challenges and Opportunities. *Journal of Business Logistics*, 40(3), 229–240. DOI: 10.1111/jbl.12224

Simchi-Levi, D., Kaminsky, P., & Simchi-Levi, E. (1999). *Designing and Managing the Supply Chain: Concepts, Strategies, and Cases w/CD-ROM Package* (Book plus CD-Rom edition). McGraw-Hill/Irwin.

Treiblmaier, H., & Rejeb, A. (2023). Exploring blockchain for disaster prevention and relief: A comprehensive framework based on industry case studies. *Journal of Business Logistics*, 44(4), 550–582. DOI: 10.1111/jbl.12345

World Economic Forum. (2024, January 8). *How AI and new technologies are unlocking industry net zero*. World Economic Forum. https://www.weforum.org/agenda/2024/01/technology-ai-advancements-inclusive-future-manufacturing/

World Health Organization. (2020). *Pneumonia of unknown cause – China*. https://www.who.int/emergencies/disease-outbreak-news/item/2020-DON229

KEY TERMS AND DEFINITIONS

Artificial Intelligence (AI): The ability of machines to mimic human cognitive functions like learning and problem-solving. This ability is achieved by developing algorithms that can process information (data), identify patterns in the data, and make decisions based on that data.

Automated Container Handling: Using computerized systems and equipment to manage container movement within ports and logistics hubs increases efficiency and reduces errors.

Blockchain: A decentralized digital ledger recording transactions across numerous computers, guaranteeing security, transparency, and immutability.

Computer Vision: A subfield of AI enabling machines to interpret and analyze visual data from the environment, commonly employed in applications like image recognition and autonomous vehicles.

Cyber Security: The protection of computer systems and networks from attack by malicious agents that may result in unwanted or unauthorized information disclosure, theft of, or damage to the hardware, software, or data, as well as from the disruption or misdirection of the services provided by the computer systems.

Digitalization: The process of converting information into a digital (bits – 0,1) format, i.e., computer-readable. This allows all types of information to be stored, processed, and transmitted easily using a computer network.

GenAI (Generative AI): This type of AI focuses on creating new content, like images, text, or music. These AI models analyze vast amounts of existing data to learn patterns and then use that knowledge to create/generate an output based on the input prompt entered by a user.

Load Optimization: Maximizing vehicle capacity utilization by optimizing the distribution of goods within the vehicle.

Machine Learning (ML): The statistical process allowing machines to learn and act intelligently (make decisions using information) using historical data.

Natural Language Processing: The field of AI focuses on the interaction between computers and humans through natural language, enabling machines to understand and respond to human language.

Predictive Maintenance: The application of data analysis tools and techniques to forecast equipment failure, allowing for timely maintenance and preventing breakdowns.

Route Optimization: The process of determining the most efficient routes for transportation, resulting in reduced fuel consumption and delivery times.

Small and Medium-Sized Enterprises (SMEs): SMEs are businesses with a moderate scale of operations, typically defined by a limited workforce, lower annual revenue, or smaller market reach than large corporations. In logistics, SMEs often operate regionally, relying on scalable technologies to offset resource constraints.

Supervised Learning: Models are trained on labeled data, where the desired output is known. Examples include demand forecasting, route optimization, and inventory management.

Sustainability: Practices and strategies aim to minimize logistics operations' environmental impact, promoting eco-friendly and efficient processes.

Unsupervised Learning: Models are trained on unlabeled data, discovering patterns and relationships without explicit instructions. Applications include anomaly detection and cluster analysis for identifying potential disruptions or inefficiencies.

Chapter 13
Revolutionizing the Demand-Driven Supply Chain:
AI and Machine Learning Applications

Majda Boualam
https://orcid.org/0009-0003-5293-2520
National School of Business and Management El Jadida, Chouaib Doukkali University, Morocco

Imane Ibn El Farouk
National School of Business and Management El Jadida, Chouaib Doukkali University, Morocco

Fouad Jawab
https://orcid.org/0000-0002-0508-7278
Université Sidi Mohamed Ben Abdellah, Morocco

ABSTRACT

The application of AI in the demand-driven supply chain is changing significantly the way businesses forecast their demand and manage their inventory. In the same context of the book, which emphasizes the transformative potential of generative AI and ML in supply chains, this chapter explores how these technologies revolutionize supply chain management and presents the impacts of these technologies in DDSC.The aim of this chapter is to explore, through a literature review, how AI is transforming supply chain management by using particularly ML, and to analyze the current state of their applications in demand driven supply chain, highlighting the

DOI: 10.4018/979-8-3693-4433-0.ch013

key algorithms used, their practical implementations, and the benefits and challenges associated with their adoption. This chapter reveals that AI and ML significantly enhance forecasting accuracy, optimize inventory management, improve decision-making and operational efficiency. It also emphasizes key ML algorithms such as regression approaches and time series in predicting more accurate forecasts from historical data analysis.

INTRODUCTION

In the current global context, the classical supply chain management is being reshaped in response to customer requirements that are quickly changing and the technologies that are more and more being advanced to ensure a worldwide connection. One of the most important parts of this transformation is the Demand Driven Supply Chain (DDSC), a strategic supply chain structure that adapts to the increased market dynamics.

As businesses are adjusting their strategies following these changes, their capacity to assess various and alternative methods becomes essential for overcoming all challenges and complexities presented by the modern supply chains. Artificial Intelligence (AI) and Machine Learning (ML) application has a strong power and plays an important role in improving decision making and optimizing the balances between supply and demand, which is allowing the organizations to ideally understand and exploit market opportunities while reducing inventory and logistics costs.

The growing application of DDSC practices, driven primarily by real time visibility into demand and supply data, has significantly improved supply chain efficiency and has enabled effective demand planning (Majda & Farouk Imane, 2024). Furthermore, the implementation of AI into demand forecasting is crucial to allows businesses respond more swiftly to the changing market requirements, thereby maintaining their competitive edge (De Mattos et al., 2024). AI contributes significantly to supply chain management by improving coordination and planning and effectively aligning supply with demand, also by simulating human judgment to improve the quality of decisions in complex scenarios, so rather than replacing human roles, AI enhances the capabilities of supply chain professionals, enabling them to focus on more strategic initiatives.

In the other hand, AI delivers highly accurate demand forecasts through the use of ML algorithms to analyze massive historical sales data and market trends, while considering multiple factors like seasonal fluctuations, economic indicators, price changes and weather conditions. By processing this, supply chain organizations will be able to maintain optimal inventory levels while minimizing even completely avoiding the risks of stockouts or overstocking.

The aim of this chapter is to present the benefits of DDSC, and to explore through a literature review its interconnection with AI and ML in order to better understand how are AI and ML transforming demand forecasting in supply chains and to define what are the key ML algorithms used in supply chain management.

DDSC and its Benefits

The supply chain (SC), defined as "an interconnected network of organizations engaged in various upstream and downstream processes and activities, all contributing to the creation of value in the form of products and services for the end consumer"(Christopher & Peck, 2004), relies intensely on demand management in order to optimize this interconnection and to get to the best alignment possible between supply and demand. The customer demand, being the first input to the supply chain, should be accurately forecasted, to be able to effectively drive the production planning, optimize inventory levels, and improve sales and operations planning (S&OP) processes. By doing that, the level of collaboration between all the supply chain stakeholders will be increased, especially by managing their internal and external processes and ensuring an effective movement of physical goods, information, financial flows, and the added value to customers, by responding swiftly to market fluctuations and the continuously changing customer needs, with the final objective to improve customers satisfaction and their end to end experience.

Within this context, the concept of a "Demand Driven Supply Chain" has emerged, focusing on the ability to sense and respond to changing customer demand in real time (Carol & Chad, 2019). As per the Boston Consulting Group, DDSC is characterized as a system of coordinated technologies and processes that reacts to real time demand signals from a network of customers and suppliers, using data analytics to optimize planning and production.

The primary objectives of DDSC are to increase supply chain efficiency, reduce both lead times and the level of inventories, and improve the flow of information and goods across the supply chain (Ganji et al., 2018). DDSC aims to create a more agile network that is designed around customers being at the center and that adapts quickly to market changes and consumer's needs, by emphasizing real time responsiveness, collaboration, and synchronization across the entire supply chain.

The literature highlights that the Demand-Driven (DD) is a customer centric approach which not only improves operational effectiveness and efficiency, but also enhances customer satisfaction by ensuring that goods are available exactly when and where they are needed (Peano et al., 2017). The transition from the supply push strategy to this DD approach is important to improve supply chain responsiveness and efficiency and to allow a better alignment and balance between supply and demand, and therefore avoiding the most complicated supply issues like overstocks and stockouts (Bvuchete et al., 2020). At the core of DDSC principles is to understand that traditional supply chains, characterized by that kind of push strategies, are not adequate for addressing market's dynamics and the changing needs of modern customers, hence the importance to shift to DDSC strategies that respond to real time customer demand rather than relying only on forecasts (Bvuchete et al., 2021).

Mendes, on his part, outlines three key components of DDSC, which are crucial to ensure that it is achieved: demand management, supply management, and the integration and the incorporation of both of them (Mendes, 2011a). These three components act in synergism for the purpose of creating a supply chain that can adapt to the fluctuating market conditions and can react appropriately on a timely manner: demand management involves identifying and understanding customer needs and anticipating market's opportunities based on customer preferences, while supply management focuses on assuring that the supply chain processes including planning, manufacturing, warehousing and logistics are able to respond to those needs and can meet this demand efficiently, finally the integration of these two components is highly important for ensuring a good and quick transmission of information's flow and materials, with no interruption, across the whole supply chain, which is necessary for implementing successfully the DDSC system (Mendes, 2011b).

The implementation of demand driven supply chains represents a preeminent transformation in supply chain management fields, based primarily on real time customer demand and characterized by a specific focus on collaborative practices and the integration of advanced technologies. In the literature is highlighted the important role of collaboration and technology in achieving DDSC objectives as well as their implications for its implementation. Hence the critical need to understand those key elements and their impacts on DDSC.

Supply chain collaboration is defined as a long term partnership process where the different stakeholders of the supply chain are sharing common goals and are working closely together to achieve mutual benefits that would be unattainable if pursued undependably and individually (Cao et al., 2010), and the role of this kind of collaboration and cooperation between supply chain partners, from the supplier of the supplier to the final customer, is critical for the success of DDSC. Hilletofth (2011) underlines that effective collaboration allows for a better and quick information sharing, it also makes the different supply chain operations coordinated and integrated to each other's, which is crucial to ensure a good alignment between supply chain activities and customer demand (Hilletofth, 2011). Furthermore, Hilletofth and Eriksson (2011) identify the focus on building a strong relationship and a good cooperation between the company, its suppliers and customers, as a key success factor that is facilitating this collaboration, which should be in the entire "demand supply" chain, and that is leading to enhancing agility and responsiveness within the supply chain, and consequently increasing its success and profitability (Hilletofth

& Eriksson, 2011). This collaborative approach is applicable in multiple industries, but exceptionally is recommended for the public healthcare sector, where that kind of transformation of supply chains from "a pure push strategy" to a pull model in alignment with DDSC principles can significantly improve the healthcare outcomes and enhance the service level for patients (Bvuchete et al., 2020).

Moreover, DDSC strategies illuminate joint collaboration and planning approaches throughout the use of collaborative and integrated methods such as vendor-managed inventory (VMI), electronic kanban (e-kanban) and the collaborative planning, forecasting, and replenishment (CPFR). VMI and e-kanban are integral for their power to help on streamlining supply operations and enhancing collaboration across all organizations that are involved. CPFR is also central for DDSC by aligning all measures and strategies that will impact future activities among supply chain partners, also by well structuring their partnership process, which involves defining roles, identifying opportunities, developing work plans, setting performance metrics and ensuring that all stakeholders are connected to each other's (Majda & Farouk Imane, 2024).

With regard to technology, the literature highlights also its huge importance in facilitating the quick transfer of the real time data needed for the implementation of DDSC approach while ensuring the required level of traceability. For instance, the integration of Industry 4.0 technologies, such as the Internet of Things (IoT) and big data analytics, has a positive impact in supply chains and supports in enhancing their responsiveness and improving the visibility across their stakeholders (Pekarcıkova et al., 2019). The biggest role that is being played by these technologies in DDSC is related to real time data collection and analysis, which is the key to be able to respond quickly and successfully to demand fluctuations. Furthermore, the implementation of such advanced technologies into DDSC can lead to improved decision making and increased operational efficiency, eventually driving to the desired advantage in the current competitive environment (Ganji et al., 2018).

It is important to also note that a literature review and conceptual model have been conducted to define DDSC operations management strategies (DDSCOMSs). In this regard, several strategies were identified that specifically help to manage the balance between efficiency, responsiveness, and the capacity to develop variants and personalize customizations, including: "segmentation, legality, customization, transparency, and postponement". These five DDSCOMSs provide valuable tools for supply chain operations managers, and can each be used in a context of demand driven manufacturing industries in order to design and manage their supply chains effectively (Tiedemann, 2020).

To conclude this section, thc adoption of a demand driven approach has been essential for supply chains that are continuously trying to improve their efficiency, responsiveness, and sustainability in this modern and global context, particularly that, by generating more accurate demand forecasting based on real time data, organizations will be able to optimize their resources utilization, reduce their waste, and better manage their inventory (Mendes et al., 2016). This approach allows the improvement of: visibility, forecasting accuracy, supply and demand balance, sales levels, timely orders, customers sell-through and their satisfaction, infrastructure and fill rates, and in parallel, it also allows the reduction of: inventory levels, lost sales, warehousing and transportation costs, operations and sales planning time, stockouts, overstocking and obsolescence risks (Majda & Farouk Imane, 2024).

This section can be concluded with a case study that was elaborated by KPMG (2016) demonstrating the benefits of DDSC. The study is involving a company which through implementing a DDSC has improved the fill rates by 10%, has reduced the planning cycle time by 80%, has better aligned operations with anticipated demand and consumption at the shelf, and has moved to more systematic and fact-based global decision-making, alongside qualitative improvements mainly related to the enhanced customer satisfaction and supply chain flexibility. From a digital perspective, the integration of business intelligence technologies for predictive analytics plays a key role for real-time responsiveness, helps predicting customer needs, forecasts the needed volumes, anticipates supply chain disruptions, manages inventory levels efficiently, simulates the outcomes of potential responses to different scenarios, supports win consequence to achieve the end-to-end supply chain visibility and minimize the siloed systems. Moreover, the transition required strong managerial alignment, cultural shifts, and coordination to overcome operational barriers and fully realize the benefits of DDSC (Gampenrieder, 2016).

Overview Into the Integration of AI and ML in SCM and DDSC

Multiple technologies have been prominently presented in the literature over the years as essential tools that facilitate the manipulation of larger volumes of information, coming from diverse global sources, with maintaining a greater level of accuracy and frequency. For example, the Information Technology (IT) that has been fundamental in optimizing supply chain processes by accelerating the data collection and aggregation, also the information exchange and sharing. Furthermore, IT allows for the understanding, the interpretation and the utilization of this expanding data pool through advanced analysis and modeling, as well as by using decision support capabilities (Neubert et al., 2004). Other technologies such as radio frequency identification (RFID), sensor technology, and Electronic Product Code Information Services (EPCIS) play also an important role in processing massive data and enabling especially the "real time" information sharing and continuous access to the necessary data without any delay (Dreyer et al., 2010). This capability is key to being DDSC, allowing businesses to quickly adapt to volatile customer demand all in real time.

In the same context the emergence of AI and ML technologies that are expanding increased recognition for their ability to collect and process large amounts of data, enabling real time decision-making and more accurate predictive analytics, and allowing the optimization of supply chain operations as well as the demand forecasting and inventory management processes. The literature emphasizes that one of the most important benefits of the integration of AI and ML in supply chain management (SCM) is their predictive capabilities which allow the improvement of demand forecasting through the identification and the assessment of risks, and the anticipation of market's opportunities, in order to provide more accurate and timely forecasts, leading to more resilient and robust supply chains (Younis et al., 2022). Additionally, AI and ML proved to be such catalyzers for digital transformation in different fields of SCM by creating an added value in demand forecasting and inventory management, by optimizing logistics and transportation, by improving supplier selection and their relationship management, and also by enhancing efficiency and reducing supply costs (Singh, 2023). The particular use of AI and ML in the predictive analytics is a key element for the improvement of SCM processes, so consequently maintaining good inventory levels, ensuring the best balance between demand and supply, and therefore minimizing stockouts or overstock situations

Moreover, the application of AI and ML in the continuous improvement of supply chain processes has a strong power to ensure transparency, agility and resilience, also to improve end-to-end deliveries, which is critical in meeting customer expectations, and to create a "demand sensitive" and "customer focused" supply chain (Güler et al., 2022). Their application facilitates particularly the decision-making capabilities, drives resilience in the face of supply chain disruptions, and leads to efficiency for the entire supply chain networks (Mwangi, 2024). In addition to that, the use of AI-driven solutions has become indispensable as it improves visibility and allows a better tracking of physical and informational flows throughout the whole supply chain (Dr. Nagaraju Ellaturu & M. Rajalakshmi, 2024). This is specifically crucial for industries where customer's demand is constantly changing, in order to support companies anticipating market fluctuations and adjusting their supply operations accordingly.

In the same context of risk and disruptions management, the literature shows how AI and ML contribute to supply chain resilience, especially during the period post COVID-19 pandemic where global supply chains suffered from different vulnerabilities and faced multiple challenges, pressuring them to reevaluate their strategies in term of risk management and demand forecasting in order to remain competitive (Muhammad Firdaus Bidin, 2024). This requires process simplification, development of strategic plans, adaptability with market's complexity and dynamics through predictive analytics and autonomous systems, in the aim of maintaining operations continuity, and fostering resilience and sustainability in supply chains (Farooq & Yen, 2024). In this regard, a study has been conducted in three different types of enterprises and has demonstrated how the use of AI and ML in different business areas; notably sales, risk assessment, and supply chain management; can lead the company to the highest performance (Peng & Zhang, 2024).

The literature in term of AI and ML applications in SCM is showing a significant increase in research activity from 2018, this has been demonstrated through a bibliometric analysis done in 2023, where 338 papers and relevant publications about this field were identified. The analysis used various methodologies mainly co-authorship and citation analysis, to map the scientific trends in this growing field, and showed as results that AI and ML enhance supply chain efficiency by enabling "intelligent decision-making", reducing costs through the optimization of resources allocation, improving customer service through good inventory management and accurate demand forecasting based on real-time insights, and automating processes which increase visibility, transparency and resilience (Rana & Daultani, 2023).

Similaraly, another bibliometric literature review (BLR) has been conducted as part of the literature study carried out in this chapter, but for this one, is more about the use of AI and ML specifically in DDSC.

BLR Methodology

The objective of this BLR is to explore the dynamic intersection where DDSC meets with AI & ML imperatives. For that, a structured approach has been followed to search for documents, to select relevant articles, and analyze the collected data.

From the initial search in the international database Scopus, using DDSC, AI and ML related key terms for the fields chosen as Title, Abstract, and Key Words; 36029 results were generated, 30341 of them are in a range of years from 2014 to 2024, 2365 studies were identified in Business Management and Economics fields. After applying the open access filter, 651 studies were included in the review, that are reflecting recent advancements in AI and ML applications in DDSC. Here is the final advanced query:

TITLE-ABS-KEY ((("demand driven" OR "demand-driven" OR "DD" OR "demand driven supply chain" OR "DDSC" OR "forecasting" OR "forecasts" OR "Supply Chain" OR "SCM") AND ("Artificial Intelligence" OR "AI") AND ("Machine Learning" OR "ML" OR "Algorithm" OR "digital" OR "Digitalization" OR "blockchain" OR "industry 4.0" OR "technology" OR "tool" OR "System" OR "Systems" OR "Platform" OR "Platforms" OR "bid data" OR "model" OR "models" OR "analyse"))) AND PUBYEAR > 2013 AND PUBYEAR < 2025

AND (LIMIT-TO (SUBJAREA, "BUSI") OR LIMIT-TO (SUBJAREA, "ECON")) AND (LIMIT-TO (OA, "all"))

The final results have been extracted as a CSV file in order to conduct a bibliometric analysis of those 651 using VOSviewer, in the aim of creating a bibliometric network, constructing clusters based on co-occurrence patterns, and finally identifying the interconnections of DDSC with AI & ML.

BLR Results

The graph below shows the progression of the number of the documents published per year, with the x-axis representing the years from 2014 to 2019, and the y-axis representing the number of documents, ranging from 0 to 175. It can be observed that the number of researches gradually increases until 2018, then moves to a more significant rise after 2018, reaching the peak in 2023. This can be interpreted as a growing trend in the academic production about the impact of AI and ML in DDSC, which still has a rich potential for future exploration and development.

Figure 1. Trend over years of the published researches in AI, ML, DDSC fields

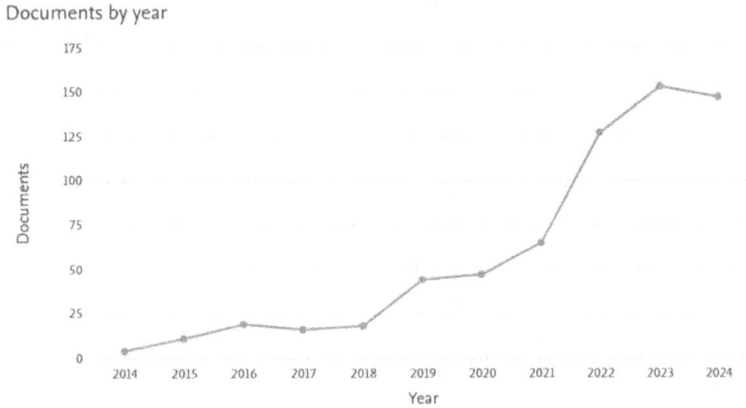

Source: retrieved from Scopus research

After conducting the bibliometric analysis using VOSviewer, a network visualization map has been created (see figure 2 below), showing the co-occurrence and the relationships between different key words related to the Forecasting in DDSC, AI and ML.

Figure 2. Visualization network for co-occurrence based on AI, ML and DDSC

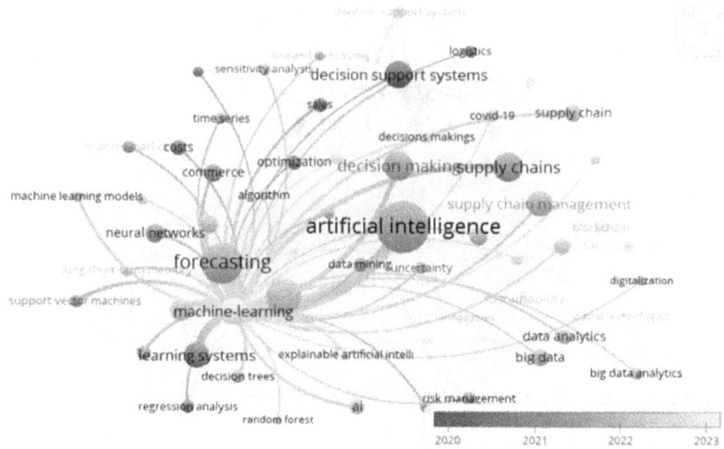

Source: authors using VOSviewer

The co-occurrence presents insights into the frequency of each individual keyword, represented by the size of each node, as well as its interaction with other pairs of keywords, visualized through the thickness level of the lines that are connecting each term to the other. This network is divided into four main clusters, represented by different colors and indicate groups of terms that are often used together, the colors vary also to show a temporal evolution over different periods, with more recent terms displayed in yellow & green and previous ones in blue & purple.

The most central and largest terms are "Artificial Intelligence", "Forecasting," "Machine Learning," and "decision support systems," which indicate that they are most frequent used concepts and are connected to various other concepts mainly "supply chains", "decision making", "big data analytics", "learning systems", "regression analysis" and "neural networks".

Below figure 3 (from VOSviewer) shows the occurrence counts of those keywords, likely representing their frequency, along with their total link strength which generally correlates with the occurrence but also reflects the importance of interrelations between those concepts in our database. From the numbers, the dominant role of "Artificial Intelligence" is remarkable, with 324 occurrences, representing 30% of the total keyword occurrences with the highest link strength (1508). "Forecasting" comes second, with 174 occurrences (16%) and a strong link strength (966), demonstrating its imperative role in predictive analytics, particularly in demand-driven supply chain management. Next is "Machine Learning" with 123 occurrences additionally to 51 as "Machine-Learning" giving a total representation of 16% as well, which reinforces its significance as a key element and facilitator of AI-driven processes. Together, these three keywords account more than 54% of the total occurrences, signaling the pivotal integration of AI and ML technologies into predictive forecasting efforts.

Other keywords like "Supply Chains" with 81 occurrences (8%) and "Supply Chain Management" with 78 occurrences (7%) reflect the context where these technologies are being applied, and supporting operationally mainly in the processes and fields of decision making, based on the occurrence of related key words "Decision Support Systems" with 63 occurrences, and "Decision-making" with 72 occurrences. Then the relatively lower frequency of "Deep Learning" with 51 occurrences and "Learning Systems" with 50 occurrences indicates their more niche applications.

These connections in both figure 2 and figure 3 indicate that AI is an interdisciplinary field that supports supply chains through Forecasting which utilizes different models from ML, and highlight how researches about AI, particularly when dichotomized with ML, put a special focus on forecasting and decision-making processes in supply chain contexts. The strong link between forecasting and supply chain management suggests that AI technologies are being actively leveraged to transform traditional supply chain practices into more data-driven and demand-responsive systems, and to improve more and more their accuracy, efficiency, and responsiveness.

Figure 3. Key words occurrences

Selected	Keyword	Occurrences	Total link strength
✓	artificial intelligence	324	1508
✓	forecasting	174	966
✓	machine learning	123	679
✓	supply chains	81	538
✓	decision making	72	493
✓	decision support systems	63	427
✓	supply chain management	78	408
✓	machine-learning	51	397
✓	learning systems	50	380
✓	deep learning	51	303

Source: authors using VOSviewer

BLR Discussion: AI Optimizing DDSC and ML Application in Demand Forecasting

Of the previously stated, the application of AI and ML plays a very important role in demand forecasting, which is integral for effective SCM, and this is what brings DDSC operational and what makes it a reality. The most significant impacts of AI and ML algorithms on DDSC is its ability to improve demand forecasting accuracy, to enhance inventory management, to optimize logistics and to lead to supply chain resilience:

Demand Forecasting. Accurate demand forecasts allow companies to balance their supply and demand, and consequently align their production and inventory strategies with actual market needs based on real-time data. By ensuring this level of accuracy through the application of AI & ML, the Bullwhip Effect, known as a common supply chain issue where a small change in costumer's demand can lead to major fluctuations in upstream orders, can be mitigated (Aamer et al., 2020; Yani & Aamer, 2023). This critical aspect represents an important role across various industries, including tourism, retail, and energy, given its direct impact on inventory management, resource planning, and strategic decision-making. ML possesses the capability to adapt efficiently to the demand swings that can be influenced by multiple factors such as seasonal variations and weather conditions, for instance, a city hotel might experience its highest demand during the holiday season, a knitwear shop would notice increased sales in autumn and winter, supermarkets confront peak times during lunch and after work hours, while a metal producer, for example, typically has regular demand throughout the year. Businesses in such cases often use meteorological forecasting services to predict these fluctuations and adjust their operations accordingly (Ivanov et al., 2021a). Over time, the methodologies employed in demand forecasting have evolved significantly, including, advanced statistical techniques, ML algorithms, as well as hybrid models in the aim of improving precision and reliability, some examples of these techniques will be discussed in detail in the subsequent sections.

Inventory Management. The real-time visibility about stock levels and supply chain dynamics enables organizations to make timely decisions regarding their replenishment strategies and their resources allocation, hence the optimization of operational efficiency (Akoh Atadoga et al., 2024; Dr. Nagaraju Ellaturu & M. Rajalakshmi, 2024). AI technologies and ML algorithms, such as the predictive analytics, help businesses anticipating customer's behavior, forecasting future trends, determining pricing strategies, and personalizing marketing campaigns in alignment with market volatility and customers preferences (Dr. Rohit Markan & M. Rajalakshmi, 2024; Muthaluri, 2024). This allows them also to optimize their inventory levels, reducing both overstocks and stockouts, which is critical for costs reductions (Krishnan & Khastgir, 2024; Muthaluri, 2024).

Logistics Optimization. AI systems can evaluate and define the most effective and efficient logistics strategies by assessing the best transportation routing to adopt, analyzing delivery schedules, and reviewing continually supplier performance. This will allow companies to not only lower transportation costs but also improve their level of responsiveness by reducing delivery times (Mohsen, 2023; Mungoli, 2023).

Optimizing the configuration of transportation networks involves several key strategies, especially the shipment consolidation which is crucial for achieving economies of scale in both distribution and transportation and consequently reducing costs through the combination of smaller shipments into larger ones, also the optimized engagement of the logistics service providers can effectively enhance the overall network performance by optimizing shipping quantities and routes (Ivanov et al., 2021b). Additionally, AI can facilitate better supplier relationship management by evaluating supplier performance level and risks, which is powerful for value creation and for making more strategic sourcing decisions (Kulkarni & Bansal, 2024). AI algorithms demonstrates a robust capability to take into consideration diverse logistics and transportation variables, including traffic conditions, weather patterns, driver availability, and vehicle capacity, in order to come up with the optimal transportation routes, and by doing this, they help rationalize delivery times, optimize fuel management, and mitigate the environmental footprint of logistics operations (Venkata, 2021). The literature outlines some important emerging trends of AI and ML in logistics, highlighting their positive impacts, starting with the predictive analytics that enhances inventory control and service quality, while the autonomous vehicles and drones can minimize labor costs and improve delivery timelines, similarly the route optimization reduces fuel use and transit times, also the warehouse automation improves operational efficiency, moreover, the predictive maintenance which prevents failures and maximizes uptime, and the smart inventory management that ensures getting the most optimal stock levels, additionally the fraud detection and prevention that defends against financial losses, also the trend of sustainable logistics which reduces environmental impact, also the digital twins creating virtual models for simulation and optimization, whereas the dynamic pricing maximizes revenue with real-time adjustments, and the trends related to blockchain that strengthen data security etc. Those, and others, are collectively transforming logistics with increased automation, transparency, traceability, and adaptability. (Rane et al., 2024). In short, the integration of AI is revolutionizing the logistics fields, especially in term of transportation by enhancing decision-making and optimizing operations based on real-time decisions, such as quickly identifying optimal carriers, also ML algorithms optimize routing through the integration of numerous variables simultaneously like traffic, delivery windows, and vehicle capacity, which consequently reduce travel time, fuel consumption, and costs. These systems can also adapt dynamically to changing conditions, ensuring timely and efficient deliveries.

Supply Chain Resilience. By providing predictive analytics, anticipating and adopting a proactive risk management, AI and ML help organizations to better prepare for uncertainties and/or to respond on a timely manner to supply chain disruptions, especially the sudden ones caused by pandemics, natural catastrophes or geopolitical events (Gupta et al., 2024; Sullivan & Wamba, 2022). This ability to quickly adapt to changing circumstances is pivotal for ensuring the continuity of operations and therefore keeping the same level of customer satisfaction in today's volatile markets (Baryannis et al., 2019; Muhammad Firdaus Bidin, 2024). This agile approach is required to be in place proactively and before competitors especially for new market requirements in the aim of financial performance and success (Amine et al., 2024; Ismail et al., 2023).

Key ML Models for Demand Forecasting

On the other hand, ML algorithms are characterized by their ability to collect and analyze vast datasets and huge amounts of historical sales data, in order to identify patterns and generate the most accurate predictions about future customers demand with better precision than traditional methods (Seyedan & Mafakheri, 2020; (Aamer et al., 2020); Nassibi et al., 2023). ML and AI algorithms improve forecasts accuracy as they are not capturing only the consumption data, but also external variables that could influence this consumption such as weather conditions, pandemics, national events or holidays for the case of food industry for example (Groene & Zakharov, 2024).

Various forecasting models utilizing ML techniques have been designed to support DDSC strategies. These models include the developed regression-based approaches, which have demonstrated effectiveness in capturing complex demand cycles (E. et al., 2010), in addition to time series analysis:

Regression-Based Approaches

The literature highlights multiple regression models, primarily Linear Regression, Ridge, Lasso, and Logistic Regression:

Linear Regression. serves as a basic tool for forecasting demand, it involves the use of regression equations to make predictions based on historical sales data (Zhang & Li, 2024), in addition to the multiple factors that are influencing customer's demand such as seasonality or promotions or economic indicators like inflation rates. This is conducted by generating forecasts through the creation of a linear relationship between the dependent variable which is market demand, and the independent variables including for example marketing spend and/or price changes. This technique assumes a linear relationship between the predicting continuous outcomes using multiple continuous or categorical predictors, where each coefficient reflects the effect of a specific predictor and is favored for its interpretability (Sainani, 2013). As an example, a retail company can use linear regression to predict future sales based on past trends, allowing for better alignment of supply and stock levels with anticipated demand. It has been proven that this tool is so effective for generating demand forecasts in a very short time and without losing much in terms of accuracy (Baltputnis et al., 2018).

Ridge Regression. helps stabilize and regularize the estimates of the coefficients, this tool is beneficial when the model is handling many correlated variables and the number of features is large, it allows the simplification of the model by invoking some "enabling hypothesis", in order to focus only on the most relevant factors (Dobriban & Wager, 2018; Shalev-Shwartz & Zhang, 2016). This allows to get interpretable models cause the fewer number of variables a model contains, the easier it is to find credible explanations (Emmert-Streib & Dehmer, 2019).

Lasso Regression. Similarly to Ridge, this technique is advantageous for businesses with several potential predictors, as it allows them to focus on the most important variables that have the biggest impact (Kadhim Abbas, 2019). In the context of sales prediction, this tool has been shown to surpass traditional methods, especially when the number of predictors is larger than the number of observations (Xu, 2024). This model is commonly applied in domains that are handling very large datasets, such as genomics and web analysis (Friedman et al., 2010).

Logistic Regression. can be employed for binary classification tasks when the dependent variable has only two values, it analyzes the relationship between a dependent variable and multiple independent ones by estimating probabilities through a logistic function (Araveeporn, 2018). This can be powerful for new product launches or for tenders' assessment, in order to predict if a product will meet a certain sales threshold or not, or whether the tender could be awarded based on historical data. By analyzing this, companies can adapt their approaches to new introductions, can guide inventory and marketing strategies, and can ensure that supply is aligned with the expected demand. In comparison to ML techniques, logistic regression generally performs similarly, although certain ML models demonstrate superior performance while combining logistic regression algorithms with others (H. Zhou et al., 2024).

In some cases, single regression model can severally adapt the demand prediction, therefore, it is important to note that hybrid models or the use of a multiple ones to forecast demand can be more effective and lead to optimal results (Y. Zhou et al., 2018). And by identifying key variables for the model, which refer to the key drivers of demand, companies can adapt their marketing and production strategies more effectively.

Time Series Analysis

When forecasting demand in a hierarchical or grouped supply chain networks, three key aspects should be addressed; selecting the appropriate model in the aim of generating base forecasts at different levels, identifying a suitable forecasting structure in alignment with the needed decision-making, and choosing the most accurate forecasting method which will allow to get the optimal results. Three methods can be approached for time series forecasting: bottom-up (BU) which generates forecasts at the lower levels and aggregates them upward through the hierarchy, top-down (TD) starts with a forecast at the top level, which is then broken down into lower-level forecasts, and finally the optimal combination (OC) (Mircetic et al., 2022).

The literature has highlighted the effectiveness of integrating time series models with ML techniques in order to improve demand forecasting capabilities. Recent studies emphasize the renewal of neural networks and their application in demand forecasting, demonstrating their ability to overcome traditional methods in multiple industrial contexts (Muñoz-Villamizar et al., 2022). In addition to that, there are other techniques such as Autoregressive Integrated Moving Average (ARIMA) and Exponential Smoothing State Space Model (ETS) that are useful for businesses operating in environments with seasonal demand patterns.

Table 1. Inputs and Outputs for ARIMA and ETS in DDSC

<table>
<tr><th>Algorithm</th><th>Inputs</th><th>Required Data Period</th><th>Outputs</th></tr>
<tr><td rowspan="2">ARIMA</td><td>Historical demand data (e.g., monthly sales figures) providing the foundation for identifying patterns</td><td rowspan="2">At least 30–50 data points (e.g., 2–4 years of monthly data)</td><td>Forecasted demand for future periods (e.g., next month's sales)</td></tr>
<tr><td>Seasonal patterns, if applicable for refinement</td><td>Confidence intervals for forecast uncertainty</td></tr>
<tr><td rowspan="2">ETS</td><td>Historical demand data</td><td rowspan="2">At least 24–36 data points (e.g., 2–3 years of monthly data)</td><td>Demand forecasts accounting for error, trend, and seasonality components</td></tr>
<tr><td>Information about trends (e.g., periodic increases in demand) which explicitly decompose the data into distinct components</td><td>Smoothed data for better trend visualization and decomposition-based analysis</td></tr>
</table>

Furthermore, the integration of deep learning models (DL), such as Long Short-Term Memory (LSTM) networks, has also been identified as good tools for generating more accurate demand forecasts by capturing complex temporal dependencies in demand data (El Filali et al., 2022; Oluwafunmi Adijat Elufioye et al., 2024). LSTM neural networks are the most appropriate for building product level demand forecasting models in a fast-moving context such as food products, also for of transportation demands assessment (Gołąbek et al., 2020; Mamede et al., 2023), and while LSTMs are generally considered better than traditional statistical and ML methods, they were slightly surpassed by linear regression and random forest approaches specifically for beverage forecasting (Gołąbek et al., 2020).

A literature review analyzed 119 papers from 2015 to 2024 about ML and DL models for demand forecasting in SCM, and provided a macro and micro level insights, highlighting various supply chain applications and the corresponding AI methods utilized to address them (Douaioui et al., 2024): for blood SCM time series forecasting are employed, while automated blood bank management relies on automated ML and forecasting techniques. Blockchain-enabled demand forecasting integrates blockchain with ML, and supply chain optimization uses evolutionary algorithms and support vector regression (SVR). In AI applications for SMEs, both ML and DL are used as key methods, while supplier selection and order allocation leverage ML and optimization models. E-healthcare SCM benefits from DL and reinforcement learning, whereas predictive analysis in SCM utilizes ML for predictive analytics. For retail demand prediction, tree-based ensembles and LSTM models are applied, and AI-based time-series forecasting for inventory incorporates and anomaly detection.

In short, the literature highlights the key areas benefiting from the application of AI & ML into DDSC are the ones that were highlighted in these previous sections, including demand forecasting, inventory management, and logistics and supply chain resilience, including multiples advantages, primarily cost reduction and customer service, which allows businesses to position themselves for success in an increasingly competitive environment. In addition to that, various ML based forecasting models have been developed based on regression approaches and time series analysis in the aim of supporting DDSC strategies through the effective processing of complex demand patterns.

Case Studies on AI Applications in SC Demand Forecasting From the Literature

This section presents a selection of case studies from various fields, demonstrating the application of some AI and ML models to enhance demand forecasting in SCM across different sectors. These case studies, presented from previous researches, highlight how diverse AI techniques have been implemented to address specific challenges, improve forecasting accuracy, and optimize operations. The analysis in the section will focus on which AI models were used, their sector-specific applications, and the key findings of each case study.

AI-Based Sales Forecasting in the Food and Beverage (F&B) Sector

The case study focuses on the implementation of AI-based sales forecasting in the food and beverage (F&B) sector, particularly targeting small and medium-sized businesses (SMBs). It aims to improve forecasts accuracy and reduce the manual effort involved in forecasting processes (Groene & Zakharov, 2024):

The methodology followed includes conducting interviews to gather the required internal data (mainly the ones related to historical sales and promotional activities), identifying convenient external data sources (like weather and regional events), performing feature engineering, and training predictive models.

The primary AI model utilized in the case study is based on a powerful ML algorithm known for its effectiveness in regression tasks, it's called extreme gradient boosting (XGBoost). The model was trained using a comprehensive dataset that included over five years of hourly sales data, which allowed the researchers to round up complex patterns in sales data and improve the accuracy of predictions compared to the traditional heuristic methods.

The findings from the case study reveal significant improvements in sales forecasting accuracy due to the use of the presented ML algorithms, specifically the achievements related to a reduction in root mean squared error (RMSE) by 22% to 33% and a reduction in mean average error (MAE) by 19% to 31% compared to manual forecasting methods. The corresponding improvement in the forecasts accuracy ranged from 6.5% to 33.3%, with the use of the AI model, especially excelling during periods where the demand was high, which is very important for effective operational planning in the F&B industry.

Another study in the food sector which evaluates the environmental impacts of "Foodforecast" ML cloud service that aims to reduce food waste in bakeries by optimizing sales forecasting (Hübner et al., 2024). This method uses a LCA "Life Cycle Assessment approach to measure both direct impacts coming from the ML model and hardware, and the indirect benefits from reduced bakery returns.

"Foodforecast" employs a pre-trained recurrent neural network (RNN) in order to assess historical sales data and get demand predictions as outputs. The ML pipeline includes data processing, model training, and deployment, with a focus on inference and data processing due to their high frequency.

After implementing "Foodforecast", the bakery reduced 30% of total returns in 2022, which led to avoid the waste of approximately 2000 tons. The study highlights the importance of considering both direct and indirect impacts of AI applications to fully understand specially their environmental implications since it this study the environmental benefits significantly outweighed the direct impacts, with global warming impacts reduced by up to 1.29 million kg CO2 in one scenario.

AI-Enhanced Inventory and Demand Forecasting in the Sector of Consumer Staples Distribution and Retail

Walmart and Amazon both used AI to optimize their inventory management and improve their customer demand predictions (Praveen Kumar et al., 2024):

The primary challenge faced by Walmart was managing an ample and diverse inventory across multiples locations. To address this, Walmart employed some ML algorithms to analyze data from various sources, including point-of-sale systems and online transactions. These models were developed and trained using historical data and seasonal trends in order to predict future demand accurately. The implementation of the AI-enhanced forecasting models at Walmart allowed for the automation of stock replenishment and distribution, and resulted in a 20% reduction in excess inventory and a 15% decrease in stockouts, enabling the company to maintain optimal inventory levels and reduce wastes, which led to significant cost savings, including reduced storage costs and minimized waste.

Amazon's case study highlights how the company relied on AI to manage its extensive inventory and meet customer expectations in terms of on time and rapid deliveries. Its approach involved collecting data based mainly on customer orders and browsing behaviors, to inform its inventory management strategies.

Amazon utilized deep learning models, including recurrent neural networks (RNNs), long short-term memory (LSTM) models, and computer vision technologies, to enhance demand forecasting and inventory management. By leveraging historical sales data and real-time customer interactions, these models optimized stock levels, improved operational efficiency, and significantly reduced forecasting errors, enhanced inventory turnover, and improved customer service level by enabling rapid responses to market demands and maintaining efficient operations across its fulfillment network.

Demand Forecasting Models in Tourism Sector

The first paper research investigates the effectiveness of combining individual tourism demand forecasting models to improve accuracy using UK inbound tourism quarterly arrival data from Q1 1993 to Q4 2007 for empirical analysis (Cang, 2014). The study explores three non-linear combination models: the standard MLP "Multi-layer Perceptron" neural network, the RBF "Radial Basis Function" neural network, and the SVR "Support Vector Regression" neural network. These models use historical data as inputs to predict future tourism demand. The SVR model, in particular, is highlighted for its ability to handle non-linear relationships between inputs and outputs, making it suitable for complex forecasting scenarios.

The empirical results from this study demonstrate that non-linear combination models outperform linear ones in forecasting accuracy, and indicates the robustness and the high performance of non-linear models in tourism demand forecasting. For example, the MLP model achieved a mean absolute percentage error (MAPE) of 4.67% for one quarter ahead forecasts in the holiday category, compared to 6.20% for the simple average linear model.

Another study discusses various AI-based techniques used in the same tourism sector with the focus on hotel demand forecasting (Wu et al., 2017). It highlights the ANN "Artificial Neural Networks" models, such as the MLP "Multi-Layer Perceptron", the RBF "Radial Basis Function", the GRNN "Generalized Regression Neural Network", and the Elman neural network, for their capability to map linear or non-linear functions without assumptions, with the mention of SVR method as well, which reduces training error using the structural risk principle.

ML and Statistical Forecasting Methods for Enhancing Pharmaceutical Sector

The study addresses the challenge of predicting pharmaceutical sales amidst using a dataset of 600,000 sales records from a single pharmacy, the research employs both traditional and advanced ML techniques. The data is categorized into eight clusters based on the Anatomical Therapeutic Chemical (ATC) Classification System, focusing on univariate time series analysis to enhance prediction accuracy (Fourkiotis & Tsadiras, 2024).

The study compares different forecasting models, starting with the traditional methods like ARIMA and exponential smoothing, and including advanced techniques such as Facebook Prophet, LSTM neural networks, and XGBoost. Each model's performance is evaluated based on its ability to predict sales accurately, with a particular intensity on capturing seasonal trends and handling complex data patterns. The XGBoost emerged as the most effective model as a result of this study, achieving the lowest MAPE values and the lowest MSE scores.

CONCLUSION

In conclusion, the literature review in this chapter underlines the great benefits of integrating AI and ML into SCM, and specially in demand forecasting, and how this is fundamentally improving the way in which businesses operate nowadays in a fast-changing market landscape, and allowing them to move beyond traditional methods and better meet market demands. Their application in DDSC is transformational through the enhancement of demand forecasting accuracy and the increase of the overall supply chain efficiency. These advanced technologies enable more agile and resilient supply chains by emerging data analysis, using predictive analytics, and leading to real-time decision-making.

The BLR was developed following a structured methodology after selecting and analyzing 651 studies focused on recent advancements in AI and ML applications in DDSC, it reveals key trends and relationships using VOSviewer co-occurrence assessment, highlighting the significant roles of AI, ML, and Forecasting in enhancing supply chain management. The analysis shows a growing academic interest in these technologies, particularly in their application to predictive analytics and decision-making processes within supply chains.

In fact, the adoption of AI and ML within DDSC has transformed significantly traditional practices by increasing forecasts accuracy, optimizing inventory management and logistics, improving responsiveness to market volatilities, enhancing supply chain efficiency, resilience and agility. AI technologies and ML algorithms facilitate advanced and mass data analytics, enabling organizations to predict and anticipate demand fluctuations, optimize inventory levels, and mitigate the risks associated with supply chain disruptions, also the ones related to overproductions and stockouts (Nguyen & Nghiem, 2023; Schroeder & Lodemann, 2021).

This chapter provides a unique contribution by offering a comprehensive literature review grounded from more than 65 bibliographic references, presenting essential definitions and concepts related to the application of AI and ML in DDSC. The inclusion of practical examples and case studies from previous researches further enriches the discussion, linking the theoretical insights with real world applications in different sectors.

Despite its strengths, the chapter has certain limitations. First, the BLR was conducted using exclusively the Scopus database (resulting in 651 studies), though the discussion and the different citations in the chapter draw from a larger array of academic sources, ensuring a balanced perspective. Second, the chapter does not encircle all ML models for demand forecasting, focusing instead on the selected algorithms mainly related to regression approaches and time series analysis, which have been deployed in order to support in generating accurate customer demand forecasts. Lastly, the presentation of AI and ML models within the context of DDSC leans more toward managerial perspectives than mathematical intricacies.

These limitations, however, do not detract from the chapter's value as a foundational reference for understanding DDSC and the integration of AI/ML in this domain. On the contrary, they highlight opportunities for future researches that might integrate the presented models with other ML mechanisms and make multiples combinations from different algorithms in order to create hybrid approaches that, each one of them, should be adapted specific industries and contexts in the aim of personalizing and improving demand forecasting activities. Future trends introduce the integration of AI with blockchain and some advancements in deep learning and reinforcement learning.

REFERENCES

Aamer, A., Eka Yani, L. P., & Alan Priyatna, I. M. (2020). Data Analytics in the Supply Chain Management: Review of Machine Learning Applications in Demand Forecasting. *Operations and Supply Chain Management: An International Journal*, 1–13. https://doi.org/DOI: 10.31387/oscm0440281

Amine, E. A., El Farouk Imane, I., Zahra, M. F., & Zineb, S. (2024). Supply Chain Maturity Models: Comparative Study Via a Systematic Review And Illustration in The Automotive Industry sector. *2024 IEEE 15th International Colloquium on Logistics and Supply Chain Management (LOGISTIQUA)*, 1–9. https://doi.org/DOI: 10.1109/LOGISTIQUA61063.2024.10571495

Araveeporn, A. (2018). A COMPARISON OF PARAMETER ESTIMATION OF LOGISTIC REGRESSION MODEL BY MAXIMUM LIKELIHOOD, RIDGE REGRESSION, MARKOV CHAIN MONTE CARLO METHODS. *Proceedings of the 35th International Academic Conference, Barcelona*. 35th International Academic Conference, Barcelona. https://doi.org/DOI: 10.20472/IAC.2018.935.004

Atadoga, A., Obi, O. C., Osasona, F., Onwusinkwue, S., Daraojimba, A. I., & Dawodu, S. O. (2024). AI in supply chain optimization: A comparative review of USA and African Trends. *International Journal of Science and Research Archive*, 11(1), 896–903. DOI: 10.30574/ijsra.2024.11.1.0156

Baltputnis, K., Petrichenko, R., & Sobolevsky, D. (2018). Heating Demand Forecasting with Multiple Regression: Model Setup and Case Study. *2018 IEEE 6th Workshop on Advances in Information, Electronic and Electrical Engineering (AIEEE)*, 1–5. https://doi.org/DOI: 10.1109/AIEEE.2018.8592144

Baryannis, G., Validi, S., Dani, S., & Antoniou, G. (2019). Supply chain risk management and artificial intelligence: State of the art and future research directions. *International Journal of Production Research*, 57(7), 2179–2202. DOI: 10.1080/00207543.2018.1530476

Bidin, M. F. (2024). Adaptive Supply Chain Risk Management Using AI Mitigating Disruptions and Enhancing Resilience in the Post-Pandemic Era. Tuijin Jishu/ Journal of Propulsion Technology, 45(02), 2655-2664.

Bvuchete, M., Grobbelaar, S. S., & Van Eeden, J. (2021). A Network Maturity Mapping Tool for Demand-Driven Supply Chain Management: A Case for the Public Healthcare Sector. *Sustainability*, 13(21), 11988. DOI: 10.3390/su132111988

Bvuchete, M., Saartjie Grobbelaar, S., & Van Eeden, J. (2020). BEST PRACTICES FOR DEMAND-DRIVEN SUPPLY CHAIN MANAGEMENT IN PUBLIC HEALTHCARE SECTOR: A SYSTEMATIC LITERATURE REVIEW. *South African Journal of Industrial Engineering*. Advance online publication. DOI: 10.7166/31-2-2006

Cang, S. (2014). A Comparative Analysis of Three Types of Tourism Demand Forecasting Models: Individual, Linear Combination and Non-linear Combination: Individual, Linear Combination and Non-linear Combination Forecasts. *International Journal of Tourism Research*, 16(6), 596–607. DOI: 10.1002/jtr.1953

Cao, M., Vonderembse, M. A., Zhang, Q., & Ragu-Nathan, T. S. (2010). Supply chain collaboration: Conceptualisation and instrument development. *International Journal of Production Research*, 48(22), 6613–6635. DOI: 10.1080/00207540903349039

Christopher, M., & Peck, H. (2004). Building the Resilient Supply Chain. *International Journal of Logistics Management*, 15(2), 1–14. DOI: 10.1108/09574090410700275

De Mattos, C. A., Correia, F. C., & Kissimoto, K. O. (2024). Artificial Intelligence Capabilities for Demand Planning Process. *Logistics (Basel)*, 8(2), 53. DOI: 10.3390/logistics8020053

Dobriban, E., & Wager, S. (2018). High-dimensional asymptotics of prediction: Ridge regression and classification. *Annals of Statistics*, 46(1). Advance online publication. DOI: 10.1214/17-AOS1549

Douaioui, K., Oucheikh, R., Benmoussa, O., & Mabrouki, C. (2024). Machine Learning and Deep Learning Models for Demand Forecasting in Supply Chain Management: A Critical Review. *Applied System Innovation*, 7(5), 93. DOI: 10.3390/asi7050093

Dreyer, H. C., Strandhagen, J. O., Romsdal, A., & Hoff, A. (2010). Principles for Real-Time, Integrated Supply Chain Control: An Example from Distribution of Pharmaceuticals. In Vallespir, B., & Alix, T. (Eds.), *Advances in Production Management Systems. New Challenges, New Approaches* (Vol. 338, pp. 187–194). Springer Berlin Heidelberg., DOI: 10.1007/978-3-642-16358-6_24

El Filali, A., Ben Lahmer, E. H., Ajouary, M. A., El Filali, S., Akantous, S., & Kasbouya, M. (2022). Machine Learning Applications in Supply Chain Management: A Deep Learning Model Using an Optimized LSTM Network for Demand Forecasting. *International Journal of Intelligent Engineering and Systems*, 15(2), 464–478. DOI: 10.22266/ijies2022.0430.42

Elufioye, O. A., Ike, C. U., Odeyemi, O., Usman, F. O., & Mhlongo, N. Z. (2024). AI-DRIVEN PREDICTIVE ANALYTICS IN AGRICULTURAL SUPPLY CHAINS: A REVIEW: ASSESSING THE BENEFITS AND CHALLENGES OF AI IN FORECASTING DEMAND AND OPTIMIZING SUPPLY IN AGRICULTURE. *Computer Science & IT Research Journal*, 5(2), 473–497. DOI: 10.51594/csitrj.v5i2.817

Emmert-Streib, F., & Dehmer, M. (2019). High-Dimensional LASSO-Based Computational Regression Models: Regularization, Shrinkage, and Selection. *Machine Learning and Knowledge Extraction*, 1(1), 359–383. DOI: 10.3390/make1010021

Farooq, M., & Yen, Y. Y. (2024). *Artificial Intelligence in Supply Chain Management: A Comprehensive Review and Framework for Resilience and Sustainability*. https://doi.org/DOI: 10.21203/rs.3.rs-3878218/v1

Fourkiotis, K. P., & Tsadiras, A. (2024). Applying Machine Learning and Statistical Forecasting Methods for Enhancing Pharmaceutical Sales Predictions. *Forecasting*, 6(1), 170–186. DOI: 10.3390/forecast6010010

Friedman, J., Hastie, T., & Tibshirani, R. (2010). Regularization Paths for Generalized Linear Models via Coordinate Descent. *Journal of Statistical Software*, 33(1). Advance online publication. DOI: 10.18637/jss.v033.i01 PMID: 20808728

Gampenrieder, E. L. (2016). *Demand-driven supply chain 2.0*.

Ganji, E. N., Coutroubis, A., & Shah, S. (2018). DCM 4.0: Integration of Industry 4.0 and Demand Chain in Global Manufacturing. *2018 IEEE International Conference on Engineering, Technology and Innovation (ICE/ITMC)*, 1–7. https://doi.org/DOI: 10.1109/ICE.2018.8436383

Gołąbek, M., Senge, R., & Neumann, R. (2020). *Demand Forecasting using Long Short-Term Memory Neural Networks* (Version 1). arXiv. https://doi.org/DOI: 10.48550/ARXIV.2008.08522

Groene, N., & Zakharov, S. (2024). Introduction of AI-based sales forecasting: How to drive digital transformation in food and beverage outlets. *Discover Artificial Intelligence*, 4(1), 1. DOI: 10.1007/s44163-023-00097-x

Güler, M., Mukul, E., & Büyüközkan, G. (2022). Assessment of Success Factors for AI Application in Supply Chain Management with Fuzzy SAW-MOORA Methods. *Proceedings of the International Conference on Industrial Engineering and Operations Management*, 2645–2652. https://doi.org/DOI: 10.46254/EU05.20220517

Gupta, S., Modgil, S., Meissonier, R., & Dwivedi, Y. K. (2024). Artificial Intelligence and Information System Resilience to Cope With Supply Chain Disruption. *IEEE Transactions on Engineering Management*, 71, 10496–10506. DOI: 10.1109/TEM.2021.3116770

Hilletofth, P. (2011). Demand-supply chain management: Industrial survival recipe for new decade. *Industrial Management & Data Systems*, 111(2), 184–211. DOI: 10.1108/02635571111115137

Hilletofth, P., & Eriksson, D. (2011). Coordinating new product development with supply chain management. *Industrial Management & Data Systems*, 111(2), 264–281. DOI: 10.1108/02635571111115173

Hübner, N., Caspers, J., Coroamă, V. C., & Finkbeiner, M. (2024). Machine-learning-based demand forecasting against food waste: Life cycle environmental impacts and benefits of a bakery case study. *Journal of Industrial Ecology*, 28(5), 1117–1131. DOI: 10.1111/jiec.13528

Ismail, M. M., Ahmed, Z., Abdel-Gawad, A. F., & Mohamed, M. (2024). Toward Supply Chain 5.0: An Integrated Multi-Criteria Decision-Making Models for Sustainable and Resilience Enterprise. Decision making: applications in management and engineering, 7(1), 160-186.

Ivanov, D., Tsipoulanidis, A., & Schönberger, J. (2021a). Demand Forecasting. In D. Ivanov, A. Tsipoulanidis, & J. Schönberger, *Global Supply Chain and Operations Management* (pp. 341–357). Springer International Publishing. https://doi.org/DOI: 10.1007/978-3-030-72331-6_11

Ivanov, D., Tsipoulanidis, A., & Schönberger, J. (2021b). Distribution and Transportation Network Design. In D. Ivanov, A. Tsipoulanidis, & J. Schönberger, *Global Supply Chain and Operations Management* (pp. 223–265). Springer International Publishing. https://doi.org/DOI: 10.1007/978-3-030-72331-6_8

Kadhim Abbas, H. (2019). Bayesian Lasso Tobit regression. *Journal of Al-Qadisiyah for Computer Science and Mathematics*, 11(2), 1–13. DOI: 10.29304/jqcm.2019.11.2.553

Kulkarni, N. D., & Bansal, S. (2024). Transforming Supply and Value Chains: The Impact of Artificial Intelligence A Review. *International Research Journal of Modernization in Engineering Technology and Science*. Advance online publication. DOI: 10.56726/IRJMETS49042

Kumar, P., Choubey, D., Amosu, O. R., & Ogunsuji, Y. M. (2024). AI-enhanced inventory and demand forecasting: Using AI to optimize inventory management and predict customer demand. *World Journal of Advanced Research and Reviews*, 23(1), 1931–1944. DOI: 10.30574/wjarr.2024.23.1.2173

Majda, B., & Farouk Imane, I. E. (2024). Demand-Driven Supply Chain Harmonizing Digitalization, Resilience, and Sustainability: Exploring the Synergy through a Bibliometric Literature Review. *2024 IEEE 15th International Colloquium on Logistics and Supply Chain Management (LOGISTIQUA)*, 1–7. https://doi.org/DOI: 10.1109/LOGISTIQUA61063.2024.10571448

Mamede, F. P., Da Silva, R. F., De Brito, I.Jr, Yoshizaki, H. T. Y., Hino, C. M., & Cugnasca, C. E. (2023). Deep Learning and Statistical Models for Forecasting Transportation Demand: A Case Study of Multiple Distribution Centers. *Logistics (Basel)*, 7(4), 86. DOI: 10.3390/logistics7040086

Mendes, P. (2011a). Key Components of Demand Driven Supply Chain. In P. Mendes, *Demand Driven Supply Chain* (pp. 39–119). Springer Berlin Heidelberg. https://doi.org/DOI: 10.1007/978-3-642-19992-9_4

Mendes, P. (2011b). Literature Review on Demand Driven Supply Chain (DDSC). In P. Mendes, *Demand Driven Supply Chain* (pp. 5–24). Springer Berlin Heidelberg. https://doi.org/DOI: 10.1007/978-3-642-19992-9_2

Mendes, P., Leal, J. E., & Thomé, A. M. T. (2016). A maturity model for demand-driven supply chains in the consumer product goods industry. *International Journal of Production Economics*, 179, 153–165. DOI: 10.1016/j.ijpe.2016.06.004

Mircetic, D., Rostami-Tabar, B., Nikolicic, S., & Maslaric, M. (2022). Forecasting hierarchical time series in supply chains: An empirical investigation. *International Journal of Production Research*, 60(8), 2514–2533. DOI: 10.1080/00207543.2021.1896817

Mohsen, B. M. (2023). Impact of Artificial Intelligence on Supply Chain Management Performance. *Journal of Service Science and Management*, 16(01), 44–58. DOI: 10.4236/jssm.2023.161004

Mungoli, N. (2023). Revolutionizing Industries: The Impact of Artificial Intelligence Technologies. *Journal of Electrical and Electronics Engineering (Oradea)*, 2(3). Advance online publication. DOI: 10.33140/JEEE.02.03.03

Muñoz-Villamizar, A., Rafavy, C. Y., & Casey, J. (2022). Machine learning and optimization-based modeling for asset management: A case study. *International Journal of Productivity and Performance Management*, 71(4), 1149–1163. DOI: 10.1108/IJPPM-05-2020-0206

Muthaluri, J. (2024). Optimizing Supply Chain Management And Marketing Strategies: AI And ML Integration For Competitive Advantage. *Educational Administration: Theory and Practice*, 8990–8997. https://doi.org/DOI: 10.53555/kuey.v30i5.4494

Mwangi, J. (2024). Analyzing the Role of Artificial Intelligence and Machine Learning in Optimizing Supply Chain Processes in Kenya. *International Journal of Supply Chain Management*, 9(1), 39–50. DOI: 10.47604/ijscm.2322

Nassibi, N., Fasihuddin, H., & Hsairi, L. (2023). Demand Forecasting Models for Food Industry by Utilizing Machine Learning Approaches. *International Journal of Advanced Computer Science and Applications*, 14(3). Advance online publication. DOI: 10.14569/IJACSA.2023.01403101

Neubert, G., Ouzrout, Y., & Bouras, A. (2004). Collaboration and integration through information technologies in supply chains. *International Journal of Technology Management*, 28(2), 259. DOI: 10.1504/IJTM.2004.005065

Nguyen, T. T. T., & Nghiem, T. L. (2023). Predicting Risks for Supply Chain Management Networks with Machine Learning Algorithm. *Journal of Trade Science*, 64–73. https://doi.org/DOI: 10.54404/JTS.2023.11.01.06

Nimmagadda, V. S. P. (2021). Artificial Intelligence for Real-Time Logistics and Transportation Optimization in Retail Supply Chains: Techniques, Models, and Applications. *Journal of Machine Learning for Healthcare Decision Support*, 1(1), 88–126.

Peano, C., Girgenti, V., Baudino, C., & Giuggioli, N. (2017). Blueberry Supply Chain in Italy: Management, Innovation and Sustainability. *Sustainability*, 9(2), 261. DOI: 10.3390/su9020261

Pekarcıkova, M., Trebuna, P., Kliment, M., & Trojan, J. (2019). Demand driven material requirements planning. Some methodical and practical comments. *Management and Production Engineering Review*. https://doi.org/DOI: 10.24425/mper.2019.129568

Peng, L., & Zhang, X. (2024). Research on the Influence of AI Application on Business Decision Making Based on Machine Learning Algorithm. *Proceedings of the 4th International Conference on Economic Management and Big Data Applications, ICEMBDA 2023, October 27–29, 2023, Tianjin, China*. Proceedings of the 4th International Conference on Economic Management and Big Data Applications, ICEMBDA 2023, October 27–29, 2023, Tianjin, China, Tianjin, People's Republic of China. https://doi.org/DOI: 10.4108/eai.27-10-2023.2341918

Rana, J., & Daultani, Y. (2023). Mapping the Role and Impact of Artificial Intelligence and Machine Learning Applications in Supply Chain Digital Transformation: A Bibliometric Analysis. *Operations Management Research*, 16(4), 1641–1666. DOI: 10.1007/s12063-022-00335-y

Rane, N. L., Desai, P., Rane, J., & Paramesha, M. (2024). Artificial intelligence, machine learning, and deep learning for sustainable and resilient supply chain and logistics management. In D. Patil (Ed), N. L. Rane (Ed), P. Desai (Ed), & J. Rane (Ed), *Trustworthy Artificial Intelligence in Industry and Society*. Deep Science Publishing. https://doi.org/DOI: 10.70593/978-81-981367-4-9_5

Sainani, K. L. (2013). Understanding Linear Regression. *PM & R*, 5(12), 1063–1068. DOI: 10.1016/j.pmrj.2013.10.002 PMID: 24140739

Sayed, H. E., Gabbar, H. A., & Miyazaki, S. (2010). Design of demand forecasting expert system for dynamic supply chains. *Expert Systems: International Journal of Knowledge Engineering and Neural Networks*.

Schroeder, M., & Lodemann, S. (2021). A Systematic Investigation of the Integration of Machine Learning into Supply Chain Risk Management. *Logistics (Basel)*, 5(3), 62. DOI: 10.3390/logistics5030062

Seyedan, M., & Mafakheri, F. (2020). Predictive big data analytics for supply chain demand forecasting: Methods, applications, and research opportunities. *Journal of Big Data*, 7(1), 53. DOI: 10.1186/s40537-020-00329-2

Shalev-Shwartz, S., & Zhang, T. (2016). Accelerated proximal stochastic dual coordinate ascent for regularized loss minimization. *Mathematical Programming*, 155(1–2), 105–145. DOI: 10.1007/s10107-014-0839-0

Singh, P. K. (2023). Digital Transformation in Supply Chain Management: Artificial Intelligence (AI) and Machine Learning (ML) as Catalysts for Value Creation. *International Journal of Supply Chain Management*, 12(6), 57–63. DOI: 10.59160/ijscm.v12i6.6216

Subhadra, P. S., Kalaivani, A., Markan, R., Kumar, R., Natarajan, S., & Rajalakshmi, M. (2024). Rise of Artificial Intelligence in Business and Industry. *Journal of Informatics Education and Research*, 4(2).

Sullivan, Y., & Wamba, S. (2022). *Artificial Intelligence, Firm Resilience to Supply Chain Disruptions, and Firm Performance. Hawaii International Conference on System Sciences*. https://doi.org/DOI: 10.24251/HICSS.2022.719

Tiedemann, F. (2020). Demand-driven supply chain operations management strategies – a literature review and conceptual model. *Production & Manufacturing Research*, 8(1), 427–485. DOI: 10.1080/21693277.2020.1856012

Vandana, M., Naveena, M., Ellaturu, N., Kumari, T. L., Bambuwala, S., & Rajalakshmi, M. Ai-Driven Solutions for Supply Chain Management. Journal of Informatics Education and Research, 4(2), 1526-4726.

Wu, D. C., Song, H., & Shen, S. (2017). New developments in tourism and hotel demand modeling and forecasting. *International Journal of Contemporary Hospitality Management*, 29(1), 507–529. DOI: 10.1108/IJCHM-05-2015-0249

Xu, M. (2024). Sales Prediction Based on Lasso Regression. *Highlights in Science. Engineering and Technology*, 88, 343–349. DOI: 10.54097/p9hyrk70

Yani, L. P. E., & Aamer, A. (2023). Demand forecasting accuracy in the pharmaceutical supply chain: A machine learning approach. *International Journal of Pharmaceutical and Healthcare Marketing*, 17(1), 1–23. DOI: 10.1108/IJPHM-05-2021-0056

Younis, H., Sundarakani, B., & Alsharairi, M. (2022). Applications of artificial intelligence and machine learning within supply chains:systematic review and future research directions. *Journal of Modelling in Management*, 17(3), 916–940. DOI: 10.1108/JM2-12-2020-0322

Zhang, W., & Li, X. (2024). A data-driven combined prediction method for the demand for intensive care unit healthcare resources in public health emergencies. *BMC Health Services Research*, 24(1), 477. DOI: 10.1186/s12913-024-10955-8 PMID: 38632553

Zhou, H., Jin, Y., Chen, G., Jin, X., Chen, J., & Wang, J. (2024). Predictive modeling of lower extreme deep vein thrombosis following radical gastrectomy for gastric cancer: Based on multiple machine learning methods. *Scientific Reports*, 14(1), 15711. DOI: 10.1038/s41598-024-66754-y PMID: 38977780

Zhou, Y., Wang, L., Zhong, R., & Tan, Y. (2018). A Markov Chain Based Demand Prediction Model for Stations in Bike Sharing Systems. *Mathematical Problems in Engineering*, 2018, 1–8. DOI: 10.1155/2018/8028714

KEY TERMS AND DEFINITIONS

DDSC: could be similar to supply chain pull approaches, it is defined as a supply chain strategy that is putting customers in the center of supply operations which are driven by real time demand signals in the aim of balancing supply and demand.

AI: set of machines and systems that are imitating human intelligence in order to support on solving problems and specially making quick decisions.

Predictive AI: consists on forecasting future demands and customers behaviors based on historical sales and real-time data.

ML: being part of AI, it allows systems to analyze massive data and to make decisions with limited intervention of human.

Regression: statistical method used in multiple statistical contexts, but in demand supply chains, it aims to predict future demand based on analyzing historical data and examining relationships between customer demand as dependent variable with the different independent ones depending on each domain and industry.

Chapter 14
Supply Chain Processes Through Artificial Intelligence and Machine Learning:
Application of Demand Planning, Reinforcement Learning, and Product Clustering

Zuber Peermohammed Shaikh
University of Pune, India

ABSTRACT

Personalization, Customization, increased transparency, sustainability, last mile tracking of shipments, etc. are some of the many features which customers are demanding, which is increasing the competition in global supply chains considerably. Additionally, the increase all product categories and the increase in product categories are also significantly to costs and risks. To meet today's supply chain challenges, businesses are embarking on digital transformation to these challenges. These chapter aims at embarking on deployment of Smart factory technologies which combine capabilities in industrial internet of things (IIoT), cloud and edge computing, robotic process automation (RPA), artificial intelligence (AI), machine learning and computer vision systems. Hence there is a huge opportunity where these technologies can potentially reinvent supply chains as customer centric, service oriented, self-learning, intelligent and agile, and, in so doing, improve customer experiences and increase margins. For organizations, providing a compelling customer experience is paramount to ensure market leadership across sectors.

DOI: 10.4018/979-8-3693-4433-0.ch014

INTRODUCTION

Supply Chain Management Processes Optimization: Leveraging artificial intelligence (AI), companies can process massive and diverse data sets from across all functions to provide better visibility within the supply chain. CSO's have consistent organizational mandates around improvement in cost, throughput, quality, safety, and revenue growth, all of these are expected to be heavily enabled by deployment of the aforementioned technologies, thereby resulting in a leaner, transparent, customer centric, agile, and connected supply chain, which is the need of the hour.

Demand Planning(DP): The business process for demand capture is implemented using a combination of simple statistical functions such as moving averages and demand numbers manually entered. DP is often done for multiple time horizons such as short-term (a month), medium-term (a quarter), and long-term (a year). The short-term demand numbers are finalized based on multiple inputs viz. statistical prediction, entered by the sales team, and/or derived from the long-term planning. Organizations often implement an approval step, where demand numbers are verified, modified, and approved by SCM managers after considering other factors such as business targets. DP also includes many other functionalities such as splitting demand entered at a higher level of hierarchy (e.g., product group) to a lower level of granularity (e.g., product grade) based on the proportions derived earlier, etc. Needless to say that as the time horizon size (time bucket) reduces (say to daily level) then forecast accuracy drops significantly. The demand numbers thus finalized are released to the next module (Supply Planning) in the desired time buckets (day, week, etc.) *(A.K.Jha et al., 2020).*

Supply Planning/Supply Optimization/Supply Network Planning(SNP): The module generates an optimal supply plan after considering current inventory levels at all storage points, inventory norms, push-pull strategies, production capacities, constraints defined, and many other design aspects in the supply chain. At its core, SNP involves generating & solving a large mathematical optimization problem using Mixed Integer Linear Programming (MILP) technique from the Operational Research (OR) tools repository. MILP is a very effective optimization technique, where variables defined can be either continuous or integer (taking binary values). Integer variables are typically used to define step functions and similar constraints. The optimization problem is generated by the SCM solution based on various configurations, master data (e.g., transportation lanes, capacity, etc.), constraints such as production capacity, and of course demand numbers. The output of the SNP module i.e., optimal supply plan is released to the next Production Planning module.

Production Planning & Scheduling: Output of SNP is used for production planning & detail scheduling based on specific constraints in the production environment (e.g., sequencing of products, other dependencies, batch processing, etc.) in addition to capacities at every step.

BACKGROUND

Literature Review: Machine Learning In Supply Chain: ML and AI for business have recently become buzzwords across different verticals. But what do they actually mean for modern supply chain management? To begin with, integrating machine learning in supply chain management can help automate a number of mundane tasks and allow the enterprises to focus on more strategic and impactful business activities. Using intelligent machine learning software, supply chain managers can optimize inventory and find most suited suppliers to keep their business running efficiently. An increasing number of businesses today are showing interest in the applications of machine learning, from its varied advantages to fully leveraging the huge amounts of data collected by warehousing, transportation systems, and industrial logistics. It can also help enterprises create an entire machine intelligence-powered supply chain model to mitigate risks, improve insights and enhance performance, all of which are extremely crucial to build a globally competitive supply chain model. A recent study by Gartner also suggests that innovative technologies like Artificial Intelligence (AI) and Machine Learning (ML) would disrupt existing supply chain operating models significantly in the future. Considered as one of the high-benefit technologies, ML techniquesenable efficient processes resulting in cost savings and increased profits. Before going into the details of how Machine Learning can revolutionise supply chain and discussing the examples of companies successfully using ML in their supply chain delivery, let's first talk a bit about Machine Learning itself. *(Bhardwaj R., 2018)*

What Is Machine Learning?: Machine learning is a subset of artificial intelligence that allows an algorithm, software or a system to learn and adjust without being specifically programmed to do so. ML typically uses data or observations to train a computer model wherein different patterns in the data (combined with actual and predicted outcomes) are analysed and used to improve how the technology functions. Machine Learning (ML) models, based on algorithms, are great at analysing trends, spotting anomalies, and deriving predictive insights within massive data sets. These powerful functionalities make it an ideal solution to address some of the main challenges of the supply chain industry.

What are the different types of machine learning?: Classical ML is often categorized by how an algorithm learns to become more accurate in its predictions. The four basic types of ML are:

- supervised learning
- unsupervised learning
- semisupervised learning
- reinforcement learning.

Machine learning vs. deep learning neural networks: Deep learning is a subfield of ML that focuses on models with multiple levels of neural networks, known as deep neural networks. These models can automatically learn and extract hierarchical features from data, making them effective for tasks such as image and speech recognition.

How does supervised machine learning work?: Supervised learning supplies algorithms with labeled training data and defines which variables the algorithm should assess for correlations. Both the input and output of the algorithm are specified. Initially, most ML algorithms used supervised learning, but unsupervised approaches are gaining popularity. Supervised learning algorithms are used for numerous tasks, including the following:

- **Binary classification.** This divides data into two categories.
- **Multiclass classification.** This chooses among more than two categories.
- **Ensemble modeling.** This combines the predictions of multiple ML models to produce a more accurate prediction.
- **Regression modeling.** This predicts continuous values based on relationships within data.

Figure 1. Machine Learning Algorithms for Supply Chain Management.

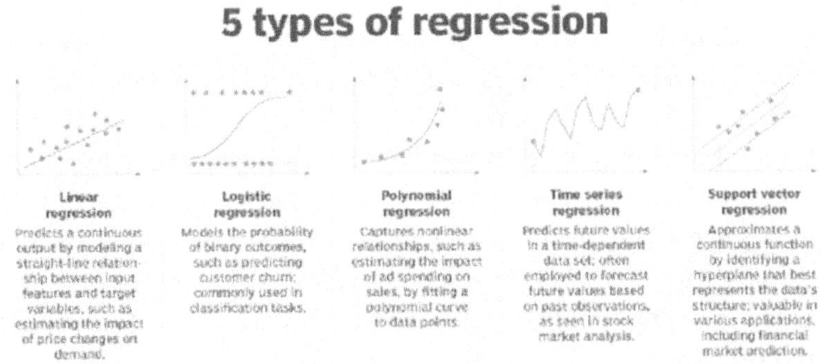

How does unsupervised machine learning work?: Unsupervised learning doesn't require labeled data. Instead, these algorithms analyze unlabeled data to identify patterns and group data points into subsets using techniques such as gradient descent. Most types of deep learning,including neural networks, are unsupervised algorithms. Unsupervised learning is effective for various tasks, including the following:

- Splitting the data set into groups based on similarity using clusteringalgorithms.
- Identifying unusual data points in a data set using anomaly detectionalgorithms.
- Discovering sets of items in a data set that frequently occur together using association rule mining.
- Decreasing the number of variables in a data set using dimensionality reduction techniques.

How does semisupervised learning work?: Semisupervised learning provides an algorithm with only a small amount of labeled training data. From this data, the algorithm learns the dimensions of the data set, which it can then apply to new, unlabeled data. Note, however, that providing too little training data can lead to overfitting, where the model simply memorizes the training data rather than truly learning the underlying patterns. Although algorithms typically perform better when they train on labeled data sets, labeling can be time-consuming and expensive. Semisupervised learning combines elements of supervised learning and unsupervised learning, striking a balance between the former's superior performance and the latter's efficiency. **Semisupervised learning can be used in the following areas, among others:**

- **Machine translation.** Algorithms can learn to translate language based on less than a full dictionary of words.

- **Fraud detection.** Algorithms can learn to identify cases of fraud with only a few positive examples.
- **Labeling data.** Algorithms trained on small data sets can learn to automatically apply data labels to larger sets. *(Bhardwaj R., 2018)*

How does reinforcement learning work?: Reinforcement learning involves programming an algorithm with a distinct goal and a set of rules to follow in achieving that goal. The algorithm seeks positive rewards for performing actions that move it closer to its goal and avoids punishments for performing actions that move it further from the goal. **Reinforcement learning is often used for tasks such as the following:**

- Helping robots learn to perform tasks in the physical world.
- Teaching bots to play video games.
- Helping enterprises plan allocation of resources.

Figure 2. Machine Learning Models for Supply Chain Management Transformation

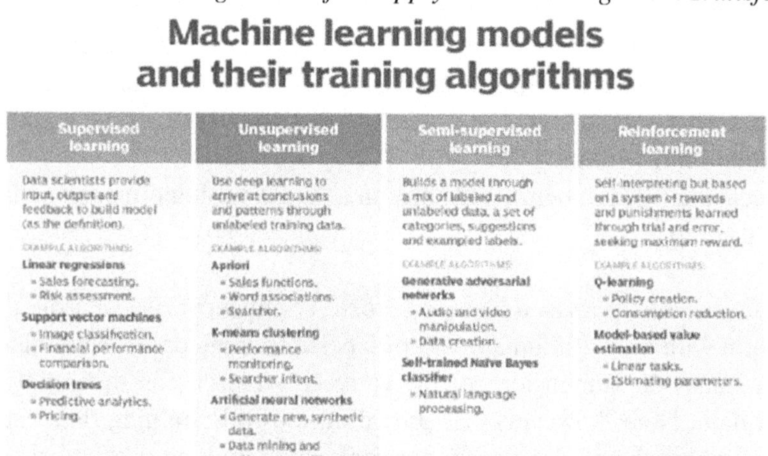

Statement of Problems

Importance of human-interpretable machine learning: Explaining the internal workings of a specific ML model can be challenging, especially when the model is complex. As machine learning evolves, the importance of explainable, transparent models will only grow, particularly in industries with heavy compliance burdens, such as banking and insurance. Developing ML models whose outcomes are understandable and explainable by human beings has become a priority due to rapid advances in and adoption of sophisticated ML techniques, such as generative AI. Researchers at AI labs such as Anthropic have made progress in understanding how generative AI models work, drawing on interpretability and explainability techniques.

Interpretable vs. explainable AI:*Interpretability* focuses on understanding an ML model's inner workings in depth, whereas *explainability* involves describing the model's decision-making in an understandable way. Interpretable ML techniques are typically used by data scientists and other ML practitioners, where explainability is more often intended to help non-experts understand machine learning models. A so-called black box model might still be explainable even if it is not interpretable, for example. (*Borodavko. B, 2021)*

Researchers could test different inputs and observe the subsequent changes in outputs, using methods such as Shapley additive explanations (SHAP) to see which factors most influence the output. In this way, researchers can arrive at a clear picture of how the model makes decisions (explainability), even if they do not fully understand the mechanics of the complex neural network inside (interpretability).

Interpretable ML techniques aim to make a model's decision-making process clearer and more transparent. Examples include decision trees, which provide a visual representation of decision paths; linear regression, which explains predictions based on weighted sums of input features; and Bayesian networks, which represent dependencies among variables in a structured and interpretable way.

Explainable AI (XAI) techniques are used after the fact to make the output of more complex ML models more comprehensible to human observers. Examples include local interpretable model-agnostic explanations (LIME), which approximate the model's behavior locally with simpler models to explain individual predictions, and SHAP values, which assign importance scores to each feature to clarify how they contribute to the model's decision *(Cardoso S., 2019).*

Focus of the Article

Machine learning applications for enterprises: Machine learning has become integral to business software. The following are some examples of how various business applications use ML:

- **Business intelligence.** BI and predictive analytics software uses ML algorithms, including linear regression and logistic regression, to identify significant data points, patterns and anomalies in large data sets. These insights help businesses make data-driven decisions, forecast trends and optimize performance. Advances in generative AI have also enabled the creation of detailed reports and dashboards that summarize complex data in easily understandable formats.

- **Customer relationship management.** Key ML applications in CRM include analyzing customer data to segment customers, predicting behaviors such as churn, making personalized recommendations, adjusting pricing, optimizing email campaigns, providing chatbot support and detecting fraud. Generative AI can also create tailored marketing content, automate responses in customer service and generate insights based on customer feedback.
- **Security and compliance.** Support vector machines can distinguish deviations in behavior from a normal baseline, which is crucial for identifying potential cyberthreats, by finding the best line or boundary for dividing data into different groups. Generative adversarial networks can create adversarial examples of malware, helping security teams train ML models that are better at distinguishing between benign and malicious software.
- **Human resource information systems.** ML models streamline hiring by filtering applications and identifying the best candidates for a position. They can also predict employee turnover, suggest professional development paths and automate interview scheduling. Generative AI can help create job descriptions and generate personalized training materials.
- **Supply chain management.** Machine learning can optimize inventory levels, streamline logistics, improve supplier selection and proactively address supply chain disruptions. Predictive analytics can forecast demand more accurately, and AI-driven simulations can model different scenarios to improve resilience.
- **Natural language processing.** NLP applications include sentiment analysis, language translation and text summarization, among others. Advances in generative AI, such as OpenAI's GPT-4 and Google's Gemini, have significantly enhanced these capabilities. Generative NLP models can produce human-like text, improve virtual assistants and enable more sophisticated language-based applications, including content creation and document summarization. (*Church E. M., 2018*).

Solutions and Recommendations

Methodology: How to choose and build the right machine learning model: Developing the right ML model to solve a problem requires diligence, experimentation and creativity. Although the process can be complex, it can be summarized into a seven-step plan for building an ML model.

Understand the business problem and define success criteria.: Convert the group's knowledge of the business problem and project objectives into a suitable ML problem definition. Consider why the project requires machine learning, the best type of algorithm for the problem, any requirements for transparency and bias reduction, and expected inputs and outputs.

Understand and identify data needs.: Determine what data is necessary to build the model and assess its readiness for model ingestion. Consider how much data is needed, how it will be split into test and training sets, and whether a pretrained ML model can be used.

Collect and prepare the data for model training.: Clean and label the data, including replacing incorrect or missing data, reducing noise and removing ambiguity. This stage can also include enhancing and augmenting data and anonymizing personal data, depending on the data set. Finally, split the data into training, test and validation sets.

Determine the model's features and train it.: Start by selecting the appropriate algorithms and techniques, including setting hyperparameters. Next, train and validate the model, then optimize it as needed by adjusting hyperparameters and weights. Depending on the business problem, algorithms might include natural language understanding capabilities, such as recurrent neural networks or transformers for natural language processing (NLP) tasks, or boosting algorithms to optimize decision tree models.

Evaluate the model's performance and establish benchmarks.: Perform confusion matrix calculations, determine business KPIs and ML metrics, measure model quality, and determine whether the model meets business goals.

Deploy the model and monitor its performance in production.: This part of the process, known as *operationalizing* the model, is typically handled collaboratively by data scientists and machine learning engineers. Continuously measure model performance, develop benchmarks for future model iterations and iterate to improve overall performance. Deployment environments can be in the cloud, at the edge or on premises.

Continuously refine and adjust the model in production.: Even after the ML model is in production and continuously monitored, the job continues. Changes in business needs, technology capabilities and real-world data can introduce new demands and requirements.

Steps for establishing ML workflows: Once the ML team is formed, it's important that everything runs smoothly. Ensure that team members can easily share knowledge and resources to establish consistent workflows and best practices. For example, implement tools for collaboration, version control and project management, such as Git and Jira. Clear and thorough documentation is also important for debugging, knowledge transfer and maintainability. For ML projects, this includes documenting data sets, model runs and code, with detailed descriptions of data sources, preprocessing steps, model architectures, hyperparameters and experiment results. A common methodology for managing ML projects is MLOps, short for*machine learning operations*: a set of practices for deploying, monitoring and maintaining ML models in production. It draws inspiration from DevOpsbut accounts for the nuances that differentiate ML from software engineering. Just as DevOps improves collaboration between software developers and IT operations, MLOps connects data scientists and ML engineers with development and operations teams. By adopting MLOps, organizations aim to improve consistency, reproducibility and collaboration in ML workflows. This involves tracking experiments, managing model versions and keeping detailed logs of data and model changes. Keeping records of model versions, data sources and parameter settings ensures that ML project teams can easily track changes and understand how different variables affect model performance. Similarly, standardized workflows and automation of repetitive tasks reduce the time and effort involved in moving models from development to production. This includes automating model training, testing and deployment. After deploying, continuous monitoring and logging ensure that models are always updated with the latest data and performing optimally. *(Darvazeh et al., 2020)*

Machine learning tools and platforms: ML development relies on a range of platforms, software frameworks, code libraries and programming languages. Here's an overview of each category and some of the top tools in that category.

Platforms: ML platforms are integrated environments that provide tools and infrastructure to support the ML model lifecycle. Key functionalities include data management; model development, training, validation and deployment; and post-deployment monitoring and management. Many platforms also include features for improving collaboration, compliance and security, as well as automated machine learning (AutoML) components that automate tasks such as model selection and parameterization. Each of the three major cloud providers offers an ML platform designed to integrate with its cloud ecosystem: Google Vertex AI, Amazon SageMaker and Microsoft Azure ML. These unified environments offer tools for model development, training and deployment, including AutoML and MLOps capabilities and support for popular frameworks such as TensorFlow and PyTorch. The choice often comes down to which platform integrates best with an organization's existing IT environment. In addition to the cloud providers' offerings, there are several third-party and open source alternatives. The following are some other popular ML platforms:

- **IBM Watson Studio.** Offers comprehensive tools for data scientists, application developers and MLOps engineers. It emphasizes AI ethics and transparency and integrates well with IBM Cloud.
- **Databricks.** A unified analytics platform well suited for big data processing. It offers collaboration features, such as collaborative notebooks, and a managed version of MLflow, a Databricks-developed open source tool for managing the ML lifecycle.
- **Snowflake.** A cloud-based data platform offering data warehousing and support for ML and data science workloads. It integrates with a wide variety of data tools and ML frameworks.
- **DataRobot.** A platform for rapid model development, deployment and management that emphasizes AutoML and MLOps. It offers an extensive prebuilt model selection and data preparation tools. (*E. Hofmann et al., 2019)*

Frameworks and libraries: ML frameworks and libraries provide the building blocks for model development: collections of functions and algorithms that ML engineers can use to design, train and deploy ML models more quickly and efficiently. In the real world, the terms *framework* and *library* are often used somewhat interchangeably. But strictly speaking, a *framework* is a comprehensive environment with high-level tools and resources for building and managing ML applications, whereas a *library* is a collection of reusable code for particular ML tasks. **The following are some of the most common ML frameworks and libraries:**

- **TensorFlow.** An open source ML framework originally developed by Google. It is widely used for deep learning, as it offers extensive support for neural networks and large-scale ML.
- **PyTorch.** An open source ML framework originally developed by Meta. It is known for its flexibility and ease of use and, like TensorFlow, is popular for deep learning models.
- **Keras.** An open source Python library that acts as an interface for building and training neural networks. It is user-friendly and is often used as a high-level API for TensorFlow and other back ends.
- **Scikit-learn.** An open source Python library for data analysis and machine learning, also known as sklearn. It is ideal for tasks such as classification, regression and clustering.

- **OpenCV.** A computer vision library that supports Python, Java and C++. It provides tools for real-time computer vision applications, including image processing, video capture and analysis.
- **NLTK.** A Python library specialized for NLP tasks. Its features include text processing libraries for classification, tokenization, stemming, tagging and parsing, among others.

FUTURE RESEARCH DIRECTIONS

Results: When deployed effectively, ML provides a competitive advantage to businesses by identifying trends and predicting outcomes with higher accuracy than conventional statistics or human intelligence. ML can benefit businesses in several ways:

Figure 3. Benefits of Machine Learning for Supply Chain Management

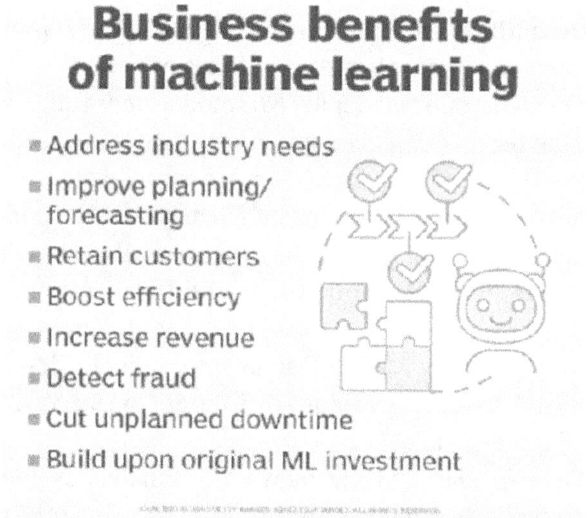

- Analyzing historical data to retain customers.
- Launching recommender systems to grow revenue.
- Improving planning and forecasting.
- Assessing patterns to detect fraud.
- Boosting efficiency and cutting costs.

But machine learning also entails a number of business challenges. First and foremost, it can be expensive. ML requires costly software, hardware and data management infrastructure, and ML projects are typically driven by data scientists and engineers who command high salaries. Another significant issue is ML bias. Algorithms trained on data sets that exclude certain populations or contain errors can lead to inaccurate models. These models can fail and, at worst, produce discriminatory outcomes. Basing core enterprise processes on biased models can cause businesses regulatory and reputational harm. (*Ferrandez S.M et.al., 2016*)

Transparency requirements can dictate ML model choice: In some industries, data scientists must use simple ML models because it's important for the business to explain how every decision was made. This need for transparency often results in a tradeoff between simplicity and accuracy. Although complex models can produce highly accurate predictions, explaining their outputs to a layperson -- or even an expert -- can be difficult. Simpler, more interpretable models are often preferred in highly regulated industries where decisions must be justified and audited. But advances in interpretability and XAI techniques are making it increasingly feasible to deploy complex models while maintaining the transparency necessary for compliance and trust.

Machine learning teams, roles and workflows: Building an ML team starts with defining the goals and scope of the ML project. Essential questions to ask include: What business problems does the ML team need to solve? What are the team's objectives? What metrics will be used to assess performance? Answering these questions is an essential part of planning a machine learning project. It helps the organization understand the project's focus (e.g., research, product development, data analysis) and the types of ML expertise required (e.g., computer vision, NLP, predictive modeling). Next, based on these considerations and budget constraints, organizations must decide what job roles will be necessary for the ML team. The project budget should include not just standard HR costs, such as salaries, benefits and onboarding, but also ML tools, infrastructure and training. While the specific composition of an ML team will vary, most enterprise ML teams will include a mix of technical and business professionals, each contributing an area of expertise to the project. (*G. Baryannis et al., 2019*)

ML team roles: An ML team typically includes some non-ML roles, such as domain experts who help interpret data and ensure relevance to the project's field, project managers who oversee the machine learning project lifecycle, product managers who plan the development of ML applications and software, and software engineers who build those applications. **In addition, several more narrowly ML-focused roles are essential for an ML team:**

- **Data scientist.** Data scientists design experiments and build models to predict outcomes and identify patterns. They collect and analyze data sets, clean and preprocess data, design model architectures, interpret model outcomes and communicate findings to business leaders and stakeholders. Data scientists need expertise in statistics, computer programming and machine learning, including popular languages like Python and R and frameworks such as PyTorch and TensorFlow.
- **Data engineer.** Data engineers are responsible for the infrastructure supporting ML projects, ensuring that data is collected, processed and stored in an accessible way. They design, build and maintain data pipelines; manage large-scale data processing systems; and create and optimize data integration processes. They need expertise in database management, data warehousing, programming languages such as SQL and Scala, and big data technologies like Hadoop and Apache Spark.
- **ML engineer.** Also known as MLOps engineers, ML engineers help bring the models developed by data scientists into production environments by using the ML pipelines maintained by data engineers. They optimize algorithms for performance; deploy and monitor ML models; maintain and scale ML infrastructure; and automate the ML lifecycle through practices such as CI/CD and data versioning. In addition to knowledge of machine learning and AI, ML engineers typically need expertise in software engineering, data architecture and cloud computing.

Programming languages: In theory, almost any programming language can be used for ML. But in practice, most programmers choose a language for an ML project based on considerations such as the availability of ML-focused code libraries, community support and versatility. Much of the time, this means Python, the most widely used language in machine learning. Python is simple and readable, making it easy for coding newcomers or developers familiar with other languages to pick up. Python also boasts a wide range of data science and ML libraries and frameworks, including TensorFlow, PyTorch, Keras, scikit-learn, pandas and NumPy. Other languages used in ML include the following:

- **R.** Known for its statistical analysis and visualization capabilities, R is widely used in academia and research. It is well suited for data manipulation, statistical modeling and graphical representation.
- **Julia.** Julia is a less well-known language designed specifically for numerical and scientific computing. It is known for its high performance, particularly when handling mathematical computations and large data sets.

- **C++.** C++ is an efficient and performant general-purpose language that is often used in production environments. It is valued for its speed and control over system resources, which make it well suited for performance-critical ML applications.
- **Scala.** The concise, general-purpose language, Scala is often used with big data frameworks such as Apache Spark. Scala combines object-oriented and functional programming paradigms, offering scalable and efficient data processing.
- **Java.** Like Scala, Java is a good fit for working with big data frameworks. It is a performant, portable and scalable general-purpose language that is commonly found in enterprise environments *(Gunasegaram A., 2004).*

Figure 4. Challenges and Pitfalls Machine Learning for Supply Chain Management.

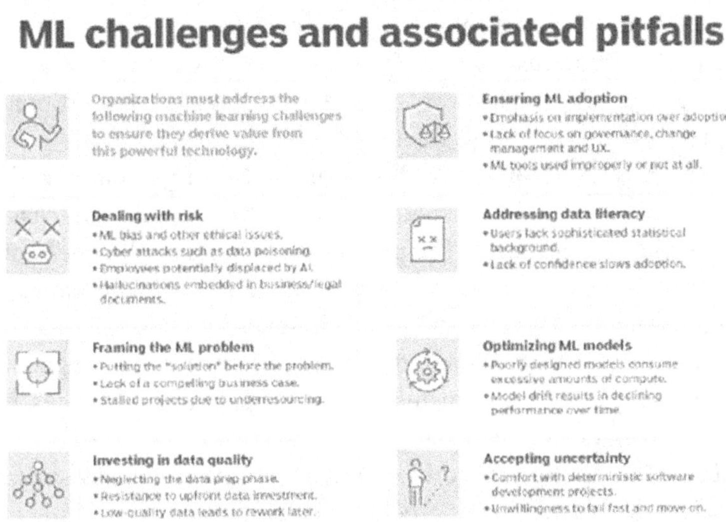

SAP Business AI built into your supply chain processes: Transform your supply chain with AI-driven insights, recommendations, and automation integrated into supply chain solutions from SAP. With SAP Business AI, you can predict events, make better informed decisions, and modernize functions from design to operate.

- Predict customer demand reliably with AI-powered demand forecasting
- Improve quality with intelligent anomaly detection and visual inspections
- Synchronize operations and maximize efficiency with predictive maintenance

- Intelligent access to information through the Joule copilot in SAP supply chain solutions

How Machine Learning Is Transforming Supply Chain Management: 9 Ways: Machine Learning is a complex yet interesting subject that can solve a number of issues across industries. Supply chain, being a heavily data reliant industry, has many applications of machine learning. Elucidated below are top 9 use cases of machine learning in supply chain management which can help drive the industry towards efficiency and optimization.

Predictive Analytics: There are several benefits of accurate demand forecasting in supply chain management, such as decreased holding costs and optimal inventory levels. Using machine learning models, companies can enjoy the benefit of predictive analytics for demand forecasting. These machine learning models are adept at identifying hidden patterns in historical demand data. Machine learning in supply chain can also be used to detect issues in the supply chain even before they disrupt the business. Having a robust supply chain forecasting system means the business is equipped with resources and intelligence to respond to emerging issues and threats. And, the effectiveness of the response increases proportionally to how fast the business can respond to problems.

Automated Quality Inspections For Robust Management: Logistics hubs usually conduct manual quality inspections to inspect containers or packages for any kind of damage during transit. The growth of artificial intelligence and machine learning have increased the scope of automating quality inspections in the supply chain lifecycle. Machine learning enabled techniques allow for automated analysis of defects in industrial equipment and to check for damages via image recognition. The benefit of these power automated quality inspections translates to reduced chances of delivering defective or faulty goods to customers. *(Herbrich, R., 2000)*

Streamlining Production Planning: Machine learning can play an instrumental role in optimising the complexity of production plans. Machine learning models and techniques can be used to train sophisticated algorithms on the already available production data in a way which helps in identification of possible areas of inefficiency and waste. Further, the use of machine learning in supply chain in creating a more adaptable environment to effectively deal with any sort of disruption is noteworthy.

Reduces Cost and Response Times:An increasing number of B2C companies are leveraging machine learning techniques to trigger automated responses and handle demand-to-supply imbalances, thus minimising the costs and improving customer experience. The ability of machine learning algorithms to analyse and learn from real-time data and historic delivery records helps supply chain managers to optimise the route for their fleet of vehicles leading to reduced driving time, cost-saving and enhanced productivity. Further, by improving connectivity with various logistics service providers and integrating freight and warehousing processes, administrative and operational costs in the supply chain can be reduced.

Warehouse Management: Efficient supply chain planning is usually synonymous with warehouse and inventory-based management. With the latest demand and supply information, machine learning can enable continuous improvement in the efforts of a company towards meeting the desired level of customer service level at the lowest cost. Machine learning in supply chain with its models, techniques and forecasting features can also solve the problem of both under or overstocking and completely transform your warehouse management for the better. Using AI and ML, you can also analyse big data sets much faster and avoid the mistakes made by humans in a typical scenario.

Reduction in Forecast Errors: Machine Learning serves as a robust analytical tool to help supply chain companies process large sets of data. Apart from processing such vast amounts of data, machine learning in supply chain also ensures that it is done with the greatest variety and variability, all thanks to telematics, IoT devices, intelligent transportation systems, and other similar powerful technologies. This enables supply chain companies to have much better insights and help them achieve accurate forecasts. A report by McKinsey also indicates that AI and ML-based implementations in supply chain can reduce forecast errors up to 50%.

Advanced Last-Mile Tracking: Last-mile delivery is a critical aspect of the entire supply chain as its efficacy can have a direct impact on multiple verticals, including customer experience and product quality. Data also suggests that the last mile delivery in supply chain constitutes 28% of all delivery costs. Machine learning in supply chain can offer great opportunities by taking into account different data points about the ways people use to enter their addresses and the total time taken to deliver the goods to specific locations. ML can also offer valuable assistance in optimising the process and providing clients with more accurate information on the shipment status.

Fraud Prevention: Machine learning algorithms are capable of both enhancing the product quality and reducing the risk of fraud by automating inspections and auditing processes followed by performing real-time analysis of results to detect anomalies or deviation from normal patterns. In addition to this, machine learning tools are also capable of preventing privileged credential abuse which is one of the primary causes of breaches across the global supply chain *(Ismail R., 2011)*.

Challenges In Logistics And Supply Chain Industry: Here are a few of the challenges faced by logistics and supply chains that Machine Learning and Artificial Intelligence-powered solutions can solve:

Inventory management: Inventory management is extremely crucial for supply chain management as it allows enterprises to deal and adjust for any unexpected shortages. No supply chain firm would want to halt their company's production while they launch a hunt to find another supplier. Similarly, they wouldn't want to overstock as that starts affecting the profits. Inventory management in supply chain is largely about striking a balance between timing the purchase orders to keep the operations going smoothly while not overstocking the items they won't need or use.

Quality and safety: With mounting pressures to deliver products on time to keep the supply chain assembly line moving, maintaining a dual check on quality as well as safety becomes a big challenge for supply chain firms. It could produce a big safety hazard to accept substandard parts not meeting the quality or safety standards. Further, environmental changes, trade disputes and economic pressures on the supply chain can easily turn into issues and risks that quickly snowball throughout the entire supply chain causing significant problems.

Problems due to scarce resources: Issues faced in logistics and supply chain due to the scarcity of resources are well known. But the implementation of AI and machine learning in the supply chain and logistics has made the understanding of various facets much easier. Algorithms predicting demand and supply after studying various factors enable early planning and stocking accordingly. Offering new insights into various aspects of the supply chain, ML has also made the management of the inventory and team members become super simple.

Inefficient supplier relationship management: A steep scarcity of supply chain professionals is yet another challenge faced by logistics firms that can make the supplier relationship management cumbersome and ineffective. Machine learning and artificial intelligence can offer useful insights into supplier data and can help supply chain companies make real-time decisions. (*K. Nayal et al., 2022)*

Why Is Machine Learning Important To Supply Chain Management?: With some of the largest and renowned firms beginning to pay attention to what machine learning can do to improve the efficiency of their supply chains, let's understand how machine learning in supply chain management addresses the problems and what are the current applications of this powerful technology in supply chain management. **There are several benefits that machine learning delivers to supply chain management including-**

- Cost efficiency due to machine learning, which systematically drives waste reduction and quality improvement
- Optimisation of product flow in the supply chain without the supply chain firms needing to hold much inventory
- Seamless supplier relationship management due to simpler, faster and proven administrative practices
- Machine learning helps derive actionable insights, allowing for quick problem solving and continual improvement.

Companies Using Machine Learning To Improve Their Supply Chain Management: Here are some of the top companies using machine learning to enhance the productivity of their supply chain management:

com – eCommerce: One of the renowned supply chain leaders in the ecommerce industry, Amazon, leverages technologically advanced and innovative systems based on artificial intelligence and machine learning such as automated warehousing and drone delivery. Amazon's robust supply chain has direct control over the main areas like packaging, order processing, delivery, customer support and reverse logistics due to heavy investments in intelligent software systems, transportation and warehousing.

Microsoft Corporation – Technology: The supply chain system of the technology giant Microsoft heavily relies on predictive insights driven by machine learning and business intelligence. The company has a massive product portfolio that generates a huge amount of data which needs to be integrated on a central level for predictive analysis and driving operational efficiencies. Machine Learning techniques have allowed the company to build a seamlessly integrated supply chain system enabling them to capture data in a real-time and analyse the same. Further, the company's robust supply chain utilises proactive and early warning systems to assist them in mitigating the risk and quick query resolution.

Alphabet Inc.– Internet Conglomerate: A well known technological giant and a highly innovative technological company, Alphabet relies on a flexible and responsive Supply Chain which can collaborate across regions in a seamless fashion. Alphabet's Supply Chain leverages machine learning, AI and robotics to become completely automated.

Procter & Gamble – Consumer Goods: The consumer goods leader, P&G, has one of the most complex supply chains with a massive product portfolio. The company excellently leverages machine learning techniques such as advanced analytics and application of data for end-to-end product flow management.

Rolls Royce – Automotive: Rolls Royce, in partnership with Google, creates autonomous ships where instead of just replacing one driver in a self-driving car, machine learning and artificial intelligence technology replaces the jobs of entire crew members. Existing ships of the company use algorithms to accurately sense what is around them in the water and accordingly classify items based on the danger they pose to the ship. ML and AI algorithms can also be used to track ship engine performance, monitor security and load and unload cargo. (*Leon S., 2017)*

Transform Supply Chain Management With Machine Learning Power: Improving the efficiency of the supply chain plays a crucial role in any enterprise. Operating their businesses within tough profit margins, any kind of process improvements can have a great impact on the bottom line profit. Innovative technologies like machine learning makes it easier to deal with challenges of volatility and forecasting demand accurately in global supply chains. Gartner predicts that at least 50% of global companies in supply chain operations would be using AI and ML related transformational technologies by 2023. This is a testament to the growing popularity of machine learning in supply chain industry. But, to be able to reap full benefits of machine learning, businesses need to plan for the future and start investing in machine learning and related technologies today to enjoy increased profitability, efficiency and better resources availability in the supply chain industry.

Discussion of Current Context of Research: Unless you work in supply chain, you might be shocked to learn about the degree of inefficiency and waste in the world due to poor inventory management. No wonder it's usually kept under wraps—or becomes controversial when exposed, as happened during the early days of Covid vaccine distribution whensignificant spoilage and waste occurred despite overwhelming demand.

Inventory challenges are not exclusive to perishable goods. Tires, for instance, can develop flat spots, dry rot, or lose their elasticity if stored for extended periods without proper care. Electronic Components like circuit boards and chips can likewise oxidize or degrade over time. And then there's the issue of obsolescence, which is especially common for electronics, apparel, appliances and automotive parts. Given these challenges, whether you're overseeing equipment spare parts, materials for manufacturing, or inventory for your distribution business, advanced inventory management strategies are more applicable and needed now than ever. Thanks to recent advances in data and AI technologies, such as RFID-based inventory tracking, AI-powered prediction and forecasting techniques, and advanced optimization algorithms, these strategies can now be implemented much more quickly and cost-effectively.

We'll explore five essential aspects of inventory optimization: Demand Forecasting, Strategic Planning, Tactical Inventory Optimization, Inventory Replenishment Planning, and Inventory Logistics & Order Fulfillment, along with some of the AI-related technologies that enable these use cases. (M. Brown, 2021)

Demand Planning & Forecasting: Anticipating Needs: Most organizations know that their demand forecasting for parts/materials and finished goods could be better. In many cases, the forecast for next year/week/month is simply the prior period's actual with an adjustment factor applied. In many cases, such as new product introductions (NPIs) without historical sales data, forecasting is more of an art than a science. Fortunately, machine learning techniques now offer better forecasting capabilities. For example, clustering techniques can forecast new items by analyzing similar products with historical data. Spare parts demand, meanwhile, hinges on historical repair data and preventative maintenance plans and schedules. A growing number of organizations are now using advanced statistical methods and machine learning algorithms to "refine their art" and help predict future demand (and maintenance) with greater accuracy. By analyzing historical data, market trends, and external factors such as seasonality and economic indicators, organizations in all industries are finding that they can, indeed, create better forecasts. With the proper integrations with your ERP and other systems that house your data, modern forecasting systems can keep the forecasts updated, reacting to market shifts in near-real time, thus giving an edge over the competition. For example, a company using advanced forecasting tools might notice a surge in demand for certain products due to a trending social media topic – ***Large Language Models (LLMs)*** can be used for this. Weekly or daily forecast systems can then incorporate the new signal and automatically propose an adjustment to the forecast. This proposal could be automatically flagged for review by the planner who can test out the impact of adjusting the production schedules or inventory levels before committing the decision to make any adjustment. Before embarking on any forecasting improvement project, it's important to be sure that any improvements in forecasting accuracy can actually be effectively utilized. That means you need systems and processes in place to be able to incorporate these improvements into your operations. (*M. Pournader et al., 2021)*

Strategic Inventory Planning: The Right Stock at the Right Place: Once you have a solid forecast, the next step is strategic planning. This involves determining where and how much of each part, material, or item should be stocked. This sounds simple but can get very complex because of the many factors that need to be considered simultaneously. Consider the problem airlines face with spare parts management. Critical parts and components must be readily available to prevent costly flight delays. However, it is not feasible or cost-effective to stock every item at every location. Questions arise: How critical is each item? What is the supplier's lead time versus what is acceptable? Can centralized stocking locations efficiently serve multiple airports? And how soon might the parts become obsolete? Although this post is focused on using AI, problems like this will continue to warrant strategic planning sessions with business stakeholders to make these decisions effectively and on an ongoing basis. By bringing together stakeholders from different parts of the business, these sessions enable comprehensive consideration of varied perspectives and requirements, leading to more informed and balanced strategic decisions. Nevertheless, AI-powered planning and scenario analysis tools effectively support these strategic meetings by providing objective, data-driven insights. Advanced planning tools and algorithms enable the simultaneous evaluation of factors such as demand patterns, supplier reliability, lead times, transportation costs, and service level requirements. This comprehensive analysis, often referred to as Multi-Echelon Inventory Optimization (when conducted across multiple locations in the supply chain from central warehouses to regional distribution centers to individual retail outlets), helps balance the need for high service levels with the goal of minimizing inventory carrying costs. (*Marr, 2016)*

Tactical Inventory Management: Planning with More Precision: Once the strategic design of your network is in place and you have a general idea of where inventory should be located, you will want to get more granular and regularly fine-tune the plan. This means shifting to a more short-term focus, like weekly – so that you can align with the most current forecast. Therefore, for tactical inventory optimization, your planning horizon typically ranges from 3 to 18 months. The goal here is the same as in strategic planning – to maintain the right inventory levels at the individual SKU level and in a way that balances holding costs, ordering costs, and stockout costs. But what's different is that it involves setting precise reorder points (ROP) and order quantities (EOQ or Economic Order Quantities) by SKU in a way that minimizes costs while still meeting service level objectives. A crucial component of this process is determining the appropriate level of safety stock. Safety stock acts as a buffer against uncertainties in demand and supply. The amount of safety stock needed is influenced by several factors, including:

- **Forecast Accuracy:** How reliable are your demand forecasts? The less accurate your forecast, the more safety stock you might need.
- **Supplier Reliability:** Do your suppliers consistently deliver on time? Variability in supplier performance can necessitate higher safety stock.
- **Replenishment Lead Times:** Is your replenishment source nearby or an ocean away? Longer lead times generally require more safety stock to mitigate the risk of stockouts.

Figure 5. Inventory Level in Supply Chain Management

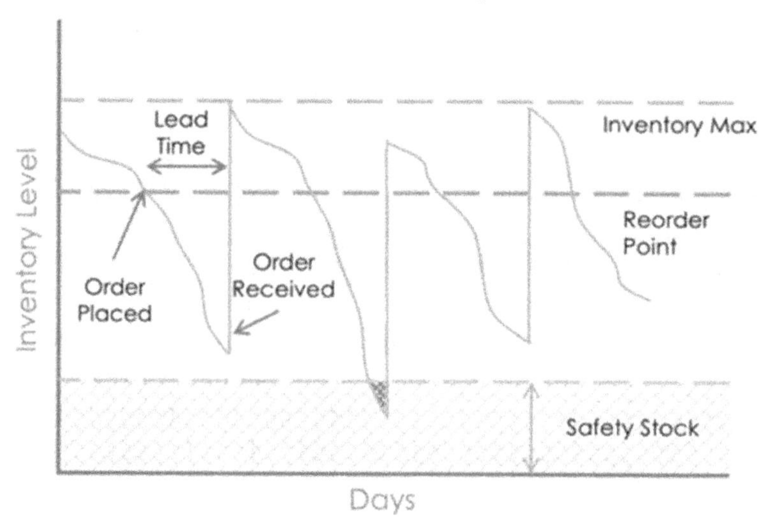

The key here, as in all inventory and spare parts planning applications, is to be as dynamic as possible so that the inventory is adjusted and therefore continually optimized based on real-time data and demand variability.

Logistics & Order Planning: Delivering Excellence: The next piece of the puzzle is logistics and order planning. This covers a broad range of strategies from improving the movement of items from receiving to delivery to customer or manufacturing line. This can include building detailed daily or weekly order schedules and logistics plans to address delivery mode selection, carrier choice, truckload optimization, efficient routing, and even packaging considerations. The primary objective is to ensure the timely and cost-effective delivery of goods while exceeding customer expectations. Advanced optimization methods often play a big role in this domain, empowering businesses to maximize transportation asset utilization, minimize costs, and streamline operations across the supply chain. **Examples of Optimization Use Cases:**

- **Transport Mode Selection:** Decision-making involves choosing the most suitable transport mode (air, sea, rail, road) based on factors like shipment urgency, cost-efficiency, and environmental impact.
- **Carrier Selection and Routing Optimization:** Optimal selection of carriers and routes using algorithms that consider factors such as delivery times, costs, and service levels, ensuring efficient distribution.
- **Packaging Optimization:** Evaluating packaging constraints and considerations such as Economic Order Quantity (EOQ) versus container capacity to determine optimal lot sizes. This may include re-evaluating packaging strategies to improve manufacturing flow and alleviate bottlenecks.
- **Warehouse Management and Slotting Optimization:** Enhancing warehouse efficiency through advanced slotting algorithms that optimize product placement based on picking patterns, product velocities, and storage constraints. This optimization reduces travel time, minimizes handling costs, and increases throughput by strategically locating high-demand items.
- **Just-in-Sequence and Just-in-Time (JIS/JIT) Delivery:** Implementing intelligent logistics systems to synchronize part deliveries with manufacturing schedules, minimizing inventory buildup on the factory floor and ensuring seamless production flow. *(P. Dauvergne, 2022)*

Case Example: An automotive manufacturer partnered with DecisionBrain to implement a custom inbound logistics planning system. The system optimized monthly truck routes for parts delivery to assembly plants, employing JIS and JIT methods to align part delivery with assembly line requirements. Through 3-D truck load optimization and smart "milk runs," the manufacturer reduced monthly planning time from 2.5 person-days to just one hour, significantly improving operational efficiency and cost-effectiveness. In summary, logistics optimization encompasses a wide range of strategies and technologies aimed at enhancing the movement of goods throughout the supply chain. By leveraging advanced algorithms and data-driven insights, businesses can achieve operational excellence, reduce costs, and deliver superior customer experiences.

Operational Execution: Inventory Replenishment & Logistics Planning: Inventory replenishment and operational execution activities are continuous processes that are executed on the most frequent basis, typically daily or weekly, to maintain optimal inventory levels and ensure a smooth flow of goods through the supply chain. It involves detailed planning to determine when, where, and how much to reorder for each SKU, taking into account granular demand forecasts, supplier lead times, and current inventory levels. Advanced algorithms and AI play a crucial role here in optimizing replenishment plans by analyzing historical data and real-time inventory levels as discussed in the prior section, but also supplier performance. This is especially important when dealing with volatile markets subject to frequent demand shifts and/or supply chain disruptions, like the sort that caused our glass beverage bottle supplier earlier to run into issues. Effective replenishment also involves close collaboration with suppliers to synchronize activities, enhance responsiveness, and reduce lead times. Automated replenishment systems, driven by AI and machine learning, use real-time data to trigger orders automatically. These systems continuously adjust reorder points and quantities based on current demand patterns, ensuring optimal inventory levels with minimal manual intervention. For example, a retailer using an automated system integrated with POS data can maintain availability of fast-selling items while managing slow-moving stock efficiently.

Emerging Innovations in Supply Chain and Inventory Management: As the landscape of inventory and supply chain management evolves, several cutting-edge techniques are emerging that promise to push the boundaries of what is possible. These advanced methods leverage the latest in artificial intelligence, machine learning, and data analytics to create unprecedented levels of efficiency and accuracy. *(Pelckmans K., 2002)*

Reinforcement Learning for Order Planning and Execution: Reinforcement learning (RL) is an area of machine learning where an agent learns to make decisions by performing actions and receiving feedback from those actions. In supply chain management, RL can be applied to optimize order planning and execution. For instance, an RL-based system can dynamically adjust order quantities and timings based on real-time data, historical patterns, and supply chain disruptions. By continuously learning and improving from the feedback received, these systems can achieve optimal inventory levels while minimizing costs and enhancing service levels.*(Surajit Bag et al., 2023)*

Large Language Models (LLMs) in Supply Chain Management: There is a growing interest in applying LLMs like GPT-4 to supply chain and inventory optimization. On the demand planning side, as already mentioned, LLMs can analyze vast amounts of textual data, such as news articles, social media posts, and market research to identify trends and predict disruptions. Beyond demand forecasting, LLMs have the potential to enhance the accessibility and value of optimization-based planning systems. For instance, an optimization-powered inventory planning system might offer a chat-like interface for users to ask questions about ways in which to achieve specific KPI objectives – perhaps by relaxing certain business constraints. This would eliminate the need for manually running and comparing various what-if scenarios, streamlining the decision-making process. On the procurement side, LLMs can analyze supplier payment terms and delivery histories to negotiate better terms or suggest alternative suppliers. Generative AI models are also being applied to contract negotiation, drafting and invoicing. (*T. H. Davenport, 2018)*

Digital Twins for Real-Time Simulation and Optimization: Digital twins are virtual replicas of physical assets, systems, or processes that enable organizations to simulate real-world scenarios in a risk-free environment. In supply chain management, digital twins serve an important role in modeling and optimizing not just inventory but the entire supply chain network. Optimization-powered systems, which combine machine learning forecasting methods with mathematical optimization models embedded into scenario-based applications, are one approach to digital twins. (*Usama awan et al., 2021)*

These systems allow for scenario testing, comparison of Key Performance Indicators (KPIs), and the simulation of different strategies. By leveraging real-time data feeds such as incoming shipment schedules, vehicle locations, and inventory levels, optimization-powered digital twins ensure forecasts remain updated and provide insights into potential bottlenecks. They enhance overall supply chain efficiency by dynamically adjusting operations based on current conditions and predictive analytics. In addition to optimization-powered systems, other types of simulation systems exist in supply chain management. These true "simulation systems" utilize different approaches, such as discrete event simulation (DES) or agent-based modeling (ABM). DES simulates the operation of complex systems as discrete events over time, allowing for the analysis of process flows, resource utilization, and system performance under various conditions. (V. *S. Narwane et al., 2021)*

ABM, on the other hand, models individual entities (agents) and their interactions within a system, providing insights into emergent behaviors and decision-making processes. Both optimization-powered digital twins and traditional simulation systems contribute to strategic decision-making by enabling organizations to experiment with different scenarios, identify potential risks, and optimize resource allocation and operational workflows. These tools are invaluable in driving continuous improvement and resilience across supply chain operations, ensuring adaptability in dynamic market environments. *(Pham D.T, 2005)*

Blockchain for Enhanced Transparency and Security: While not strictly speaking an "AI" technology, blockchain is still a relatively new and very promising "AI-adjacent" technology for addressing one of the biggest supply chain challenges today, which is transparency, traceability and security. Yet its adoption has been slower than anticipated. The promise of blockchain is that it would serve as an immutable, decentralized ledger so that every transaction and movement of an item within the supply chain would be securely recorded and verifiable, similar to the way ownership of real estate properties is recorded in public land registries, but for products traversing global supply networks. This holds significant potential to address widespread fraud and improve traceability and compliance with regulatory standards. For example in the pharmaceutical industry, blockchain can improve supply chain integrity by enabling the tracking of drugs from manufacturing through distribution. This could prevent counterfeit products from entering the market and enhance consumer safety. Similarly, in automotive and electronics sectors, where component authenticity and supply chain visibility are critical (think solar panels, batteries, communication chips, etc), blockchain can provide a trusted record of provenance as well as maintenance history. The reasons for the slow adoption of blockchain are varied and include things like complexity of aligning multiple stakeholders' systems, technology interoperability and scalability issues. Moreover, concerns about data privacy, regulatory compliance, and the high initial costs associated with implementation remain significant barriers to adoption.*(S. Modgil et al., 2022)*

AI/ML-based segmentation (clustering) of products: Generally, while implementing an SCM solution, ABC analysis of SKUs (classifying products based on their importance i.e. on sales value or volume (quantity) or the margin, etc.) is done. Such classification is used for configuring, applying, and implementing a customized strategy for every class. Such analysis makes the implementation more effective because A-class products need completely different treatment as compared to the 'C' class. For example, for 'A' class products, the organization may not allow any changes to the numbers as predicted by the model. A better approach will be segmenting SKUs using clustering (e. g. K-Means) and then applying different strategies to each segment. However, the interpretation of segments (clusters) has to be done manually by business analysts/data scientists. And same segments may be interpreted differently by different analysts. Maybe in the future, an AI-based algorithm will be available which will provide a better and more interpretable solution to the clustering problem.

Reinforcement Learning (RL) as an advisor: Reinforcement Learning (RL) is the science of decision-making. It is the third paradigm in Machine Learning (other than supervised and unsupervised learning) for learning optimal behavior in an environment to obtain the maximum reward. The optimal behavior is learned through interactions with the environment and observations of how it responds, like children exploring the world around them and understanding the actions that help them achieve a goal. RL has been extensively used for playing games like chess. Similarly, in a Supply Chain environment, the RL algorithm can observe planned & actual production movements, and production declarations, and award them appropriately. Hence RL algorithm can be used to fine-tune transactions in the supply chain. Unlike games like Chess, RL can be used as an advisor in the supply chain. However real-life applications of RL in business are still emerging hence this may appear to be at a very conceptual level and will need detailing.

Conclusion and Future Scope: Today SCM solutions are quite mature and offer a very good solution to streamline and improve the supply chains. With the adoption of the above mentioned AI/ML-based use cases, it will progress toward an automated, intelligent, and self-healing Supply Chain. Maybe SCM vendors will slowly incorporate some of them into their solutions. And supply chain planning and sourcing systems with built-in AI can help increase transparency across suppliers, and enable them to adhere to both environmental and social sustainability standards, such as paying workers fairly.

REFERENCES

Baryannis, G., Validi, S., Dani, S., & Antoniou, G. (2019). Supply chain risk management and artificial intelligence: State of the art and future research directions. *International Journal of Production Research*, 57(7), 2179–2202.

Bhardwaj, R. (2018) 'AI in Transportation – Current and Future Business Use Applications' https://www.techemergence.com/ last accessed on 28/11/2018.

Bhardwaj, R. (2018) 'Artificial Intelligence in Supply Chain Management – Current Possibilities and Applications' https://www.techemergence.com/ last accessed on 28/11/2018.

Borodavko, B., Illés, B., & Bányai, Á. (2021). Role of artificial intelligence in supply chain. *Academic Journal of Manufacturing Engineering*, 19(1), 75–79.

Browne, M. (2021). Artificial intelligence data-driven internet of things systems, real-time process monitoring, and sustainable industrial value creation in smart networked factories. *Journal of Self-Governance and Management Economics*, 9(2), 21–31.

Cardoso, S., & Martinez, L. F. (2019). Online payment strategy: How third-party internet seals of approval and payment provider reputation influence the Millennials' online transactions. *Electronic Commerce Research*, 2019(19), 189–209. DOI: 10.1007/s10660-018-9295-x

Church, E. M., & Oakley, R. L. (2018). Etsy and the long-tail: How microenterprises use hype-differentiation in online handcraft marketplaces. *Electronic Commerce Research*, 2018(18), 883–898. DOI: 10.1007/s10660-018-9300-4

Darvazeh, S. S., Vanani, I. R., & Musolu, F. M. (2020). Big data analytics and its applications in supply chain management. *New Trends in the Use of Artificial Intelligence for the Industry*, 4, 175.

Ferrandez, S. M.. (2016). Optimization of a Truck-drone in Tandem Delivery Network Using K- means and Genetic Algorithm. *Journal of Industrial Engineering and Management*, 9(2), 374–388. DOI: 10.3926/jiem.1929

Gunasegaram, A. (2004). Supply chain management: Theory and applications. *European Journal of Operational Research*, 159(2), 265–268. DOI: 10.1016/j.ejor.2003.08.015

Herbrich, R., Keilbach, M. T., Graepel, P. B.-S., & Obermayer, K. (2000). Neural networks in economics: Background, applications and new developments. *Advances in Computational Economics: Computational Techniques for Modeling Learning in Economics*, 11, 169–196. DOI: 10.1007/978-1-4615-5029-7_7

Hofmann, E., Sternberg, H., Chen, H., Pflaum, A., & Prockl, G. (2019). Supply chain management and Industry 4.0: Conducting research in the digital age. *International Journal of Physical Distribution & Logistics Management*, 49(10), 945–955.

Ismail, R., Jeffery, R., & Belle, J.-P. (2011). Using ICT as a value adding tool in South African SMEs. *Journal of African Research in Business and Technology*, 2011, 1–12. DOI: 10.5171/2011.470652

Jha, A. K., Agi, M. A., & Ngai, E. W. (2020). A note on big data analytics capability development in supply chain. *Decision Support Systems*, 138, 113382.

Leon, S. (2017) 'Integrating the Chatbot'. Retrieved from: https://www.capgemini.com, accessed on 15/09/2017.

Nayal, K., Raut, R., Priyadarshinee, P., Narkhede, B. E., Kazancoglu, Y., & Narwane, V. (2022). Exploring the role of artificial intelligence in managing agricultural supply chain risk to counter the impacts of the COVID-19 pandemic. *International Journal of Logistics Management*, 33(3), 744–772.

Chapter 15
Artificial Intelligence and Machine Learning in Optimization of Supply Chain Transformation:
Digital Operation Through Simulation

Zuber Peermohammed Shaikh
University of Pune, India

ABSTRACT

Businesses use AI to manage and optimize supply chain activities—such as monitoring product quality, balancing inventory levels, and identifying fuel-efficient delivery routes—with more efficiency than traditional software. Artificial intelligence(AI) is a general term for applications that simulate human intelligence and perform complex tasks. Its subfields include machine learning(ML), in which systems learn from consuming vast amounts of data rather than being programmed with step-by-step instructions. These learning process, AI systems can outperform traditional software in functions such as deciphering information from video feeds, interpreting spoken and written text, predicting future market behavior, making decisions in complex scenarios, and surfacing insights buried in large data sets. These kinds of capabilities are proving extremely useful in managing and optimizing workflows across almost every leg of the supply chain. These Chapters aims to Objectified the supply chain systems powered by AI/ML algorithms can discover patterns and relationships within data sets.

DOI: 10.4018/979-8-3693-4433-0.ch015

INTRODUCTION

Artificial Intelligence and Machine Learning in Optimization of Supply Chain Transformation: It is impossible to deny that digital technologies have fundamentally changed consumer behaviour, company activities and the relationships between all elements of the economy. Thus, mobile Internet has led to the "always online" mentality and the hyper-connectedness of people, companies and machines in the digital economy. Social networks accumulate a great volume of information on all of their users. Artificial intelligence provides algorithmic decision-making and automated processes management. BigData technology allows large quantities of structured and unstructured data and predictive analytics to be processed. Cloud technologies transfer complex data and knowledge to all ecosystem members. In many processes smart robots make human participation almost redundant. The augmented reality provides the opportunity to see business processes in a holistic and detailed manner. The Internet of Things makes it possible to remotely manage processes and systems, while blockchain ensures the verification of participants and transactions reliability.

Interestingly, digital technologies have both affected operations and accelerated the development and implementation of non-digital innovations, such as nanotechnologies, cognitive technologies, autonomous automobiles, genetic engineering, energy storage, 3D-printing, new manufacturing materials, new ways of oil and gas exploration and extraction and renewable energies. We can also find a definition of Supply Chain 4.0 as the application of Internet of Things, the use of advanced robotics, and the application of the advanced analytics of Big Data in supply chain management: place sensors in everything, create networks everywhere, automate anything, and analyze everything to significantly improve performance and customer satisfaction. The use of digital technologies leads to positive economic effects, such as the economy of raw materials and energy resources, due to production and consumption rationalization, as well as to the perspective of environmental rehabilitation and restoration. All this contributes to the formation of a new model of economy that is called the circular economy. This is an economy based on reconstruction, optimization and resource saving processes, facilitated by digital technologies, which achieves non-waste production and consumption, sustainable economic growth and socio-economic and environmental efficiency. The key concept of the circular economy is the development of closed loop and sustainable supply chains. AI can also analyze factors such as traffic and weather conditions to recommend alternative shipping routes, reducing the risk of unplanned delays and improving delivery times. And new use cases are constantly emerging as supply chain professionals continue to experiment with the technology, that are often imperceptible to humans or non-

AI systems, so they can more accurately forecast customer demand—which leads to more economically efficient inventory management.*(Mohsen B., 2022)*

Sustainable, or green, supply chains mean that the principles of sustainable environmental and economic growth are implemented into a traditional supply chain. The selection of suppliers, product design, manufacturing, assembly, distribution, sustainable use, consumption and disposal are subject to these requirements. Thus, the circular economy and closed loop supply chains bring companies to a new level of innovation and competitiveness, generate new revenue sources, and enable the creation of value across the entire supply chain. In a circular economy, supply chain digitalization is aimed at providing the necessary information on important elements and business processes, on bottlenecks and interruptions, as well as on options for optimizing key indicators for effective resource usage and cost reduction to achieve social, economic and environmental objectives. Digital technologies help create innovative supply chains, taking into account the product life cycle, its impact on the environment, not only in the production process, but also in use, while optimizing costs and minimizing the negative effects of production and consumption. *(McKinsey & Company, 2021)*

BACKGROUND

Literature Review of AI and ML in Optimization of Supply Chain Transformation: Machine learning has revolutionized industrial sector by helping industries optimize their day to day processes. One such segment where the technology has left its mark is supply chain optimization and management. ML in supply chain has made it possible for businesses to discover patterns and identify variables that have a significant impact on the networks' success. Supply chain optimization or even management demands that a business continually looks into data and discovers the changing patterns. This has been a manual or a semi-automated process, now it doesn't need manual intervention, all thanks to ML in supply chain. Machine learning algorithms continuously analyse supply chain data in order to find new patterns. It aids businesses in identifying opportunities that have the potential to optimize their supply chain processes. The algorithms process data using constraint-based modelling to identify a set of factors that have an impact on the supply chain with predictive accuracy. Few of the important factors that artificial intelligence in supply chain planning and machine learning helps identify include supplier quality, inventory levels, demand forecasting, procure-to-pay, product planning, transportation management and more. This study reviews various cases where Machine Learning

Techniques are being used currently and the future directions of these techniques in Supply Chain Management.

Overview of Machine Learning Algorithms: Machine learning is associated with empowering the computer programs to improve their performance at tasks through experience. Due to its complexity SC is challenging and hence its solutions can be searched in machine learning techniques. However, little has been published about the use of machine-learning techniques in the domain of SC. This section discusses several machine-learning techniques and examines applications in which they have been deployed successfully. Machine Learning Techniques have been classified into three categories and each category is powerful with regard to its own use case that can be implemented as per the requirement of industry.*(Pagoropoulos A., 2017)*

Supervised Learning: Supervised Learning is the technique where the pattern is recognized in accordance with some past data and these patterns then support the future predictions. Past data comes in pairs as input and output and predicts the future value. The idea here is to learn from the past trend provided by human operator and predict the future accordingly. These techniques are generally used in automated manufacturing like cars, trucks, chatbots, facial recognition etc. Supervised learning encapsulates various techniques such as Naïve Bayes Classifier Algorithm, regression, Logistic Regression, Support Vector Machine Algorithm, Decision Trees, Random Forests.

Reinforcement Learning: Reinforcement learning focuses on regimented learning processes, where a machine learning algorithm is provided with a set of actions (executable tasks), parameters and end values. By defining the rules, the machine learning algorithm tries to explore different options and possibilities, monitoring and evaluating each result to determine which one is optimal among them. Reinforcement learning is based on trial and error. It learns from past experiences and starts adapting its approach in response to the situation to achieve the best possible result.

Unsupervised Learning: There is no human operator to provide instructions here. The learning algorithm itself recognizes patterns and groups them accordingly. Segmenting the data into groups and performing the analysis. Under the umbrella of unsupervised learning, falls: Clustering: Clustering involves grouping sets of similar data (based on defined criteria). Its useful for segmenting data into several groups and performing analysis on each data set to find patterns.

Dimension Reduction: Dimension reduction reduces the number of variables being considered to find the exact information required.

Statement of the Problems

Artificial Neural networks: As the name suggests, the technique is inspired by the way neurons operate in our brain. Just as the neurons are connected through links in form of nodes in a brain, in a similar fashion the technique works, where the nodes (or neurons) pass signals through edges (or links) to other nodes in a highly complex network and then draw a conclusion. There are variety of neural network techniques, but most common among them is feed-forward error back-propagation, where each neuron receives an input as the weighted sum of the output of the neurons connected to it. The technique assumes that the network is described as layers of neurons called input layer, hidden layers and output layers. These layers are adjusted in the sense that output signals from the neurons are received by neurons of the following layer. The minimum number of layers can be two. One input and other output layer. This is how the signals are passed in whole network in forward direction. The complexity increases with the no. of hidden layers between input and output layer. The hidden layer increases the computational power. The training algorithm for feed forward net is error back propagation given by Rumelhart.*(Bressanelli G, 2018)*

Decision Trees & Random Forests: Decision Trees are similar to graphs in the form of trees. The decision tree consists of nodes and branches. The nodes are of two types viz. chance nodes and decision nodes. The chance nodes show what alternatives are in hand of a decision maker while with decision node the decision maker must take some decision. The branches emanating from chance nodes show various states of nature and probabilities that are associated with the chance branches while branches from decision nodes shows various alternatives in hand. There are two main types of Decision Trees viz. classification trees and regression trees. In classification tree, the variable is categorical in nature while in regression the variable is continuous in nature. Random forests are the forests of decision trees that are again used for both classification and regression tasks. They run efficiently in large databases. Forrest is the collection of decision trees and the idea behind the techniques is that due to the continuous sampling of the data that is with replacement, some trees are replaced, and some are not. The sample will have training set with growing decision trees and gives the best option in the end i.e. the tree with the lowest error rate provides the best choice.*(Salminen V, 2017)*

Support Vector Machines (SVM): Support Vector Machines (SVMs) are a novel type of universal function approximators that are based on the structural risk minimization principle from statistical learning theory as opposed to the empirical risk minimization principle on which neural networks and linear regression, to name a few, are based on. The idea of structural risk minimization is to reduce the true error on an unseen and randomly selected test example as opposed to NN and MLR, which minimize the error for the currently seen examples. Support vector machines project the data into a higher dimensional space and maximize the margins between classes or minimize the error margin for regression. Margins are ''soft'', meaning that a solution can be found even if there are contradicting examples in the training set. The problem is formulated as a convex optimization with no local minima, thus providing a unique solution as opposed to back-propagation neural networks, which may have multiple local minima and, thus cannot guarantee that the global minimum error will be achieved. A complexity parameter permits the adjustment of the number of errors versus the model complexity, and different kernels, such as the Radial Basis Function (RBF) kernel, can be used to permit non-linear mapping into the higher dimensional space.

Machine learning Adoption and Cases: Machine Learning techniques are becoming the need of the industry due to its smarter techniques to improve revenue and saving time in solving complex problems. One of the greatest uses of Machine learning in Supply Chain is prediction of the future demand of customer. According to a study by Mckinsey Global Institute, marketing and sales have had a major impact of new technologies associated with Machine Learning and Deep learning and these areas are benefitted the most. According to one of the reports by Forbes "61% of organizations picked machine learning as their company's most significant data initiative for the next year." *(Bressanelli G, 2018)*

Focus of the Article

Some vital areas of Supply Chain along with applications where Machine learning algorithms are currently in use are following:

- ML based demand and sales forecasting;
- Personalized product recommendations;
- Price and promotion recommendations to optimize mark-ups and margins;
- Inventory optimization with correct stock levels;
- Logistics planning workbench and warehouse throughput optimization;
- Building a 360° view of consumers;
- Consumer insights (sentiment analysis/preferences/social listening) using cognitive services;
- Shop-floor yield optimization;
- Predictive equipment maintenance in factories;
- Predictive lead scoring to improve lead qualification, prioritization, and acquisition Some of the case studies that are developed in the above areas are mentioned in further sub sections.

Predictive Analytics for Demand Forecasting: Retail Chain Forecast: The case is about a Retail Chain (RC) of a furniture company whose forecasts are based on buying behaviour and weather conditions. The company predicted the everyday demand for different models showcased in one of their brick and mortar stores. The models include various parameters to determine the sales pattern like, date and time of purchase, number of items purchased. By using different ML models, the firm is now able to learn the pattern of the buying behaviour and seasonality in the data. The firm observed that there is an increase in sales during the holiday season. The sales also, increase or decrease according to the weather of the day and news event i.e. there is a correlation between the two. Due to the curated weather conditions (such as temperature, rainfall levels for a city, data of mergers and acquisitions) and economic time-series data set the firm has now started to recognize the cause and effect relationship for predicting future demand.(*Gailen V., 2019)*

Best Routing Option: A company that deals in energy management, automation solutions, spanning hardware, software, and services wanted to reduce the costs involved in their existing supply chain flows for 240 manufacturing facilities around the world and 110 distribution centers and analyse potential opportunities to assimilate new business units that they had just acquired. The firm built a supply chain predictive model that could automatically create the best routing options for enormous raw materials supply chain which includes circuit breakers that are small enough to fit on a store shelf to transformers that are the size of a large room. They used Machine Learning models to feed data of enterprise supply chain data such as transportation rates and policies, data regarding product shipping routes etc. from several business units. Data engineers at first built a data extraction tool that could collect the enterprise data from all the ERP systems, verify and 'clean' the data. The customized model analyzed 200,000 transportation policy data points, 130,000 flow and routing constraints, and more than 150 initial scenarios and could identify $9.32 million (8 million Euros) in annual savings which could potentially be obtained by altering product flow in the supply chain.

AI for Warehouse Management: Automated guided vehicles (AGVs) have been operating in industrial environments since the 1950s, and until recently were largely incapable of autonomous navigation without physical path guiding mechanisms such as wires, tracks, or magnetic tapes. With incremental improvements in AI and navigation technologies such as simultaneous localization and mapping, and machine vision, AGVs can enable automated material handling across traditional manufacturing boundaries by moving between buildings. Today's AGVs have the potential of being made relatively more autonomous by integrating them with data from existing warehouse management and control systems through a connecting software layer called warehouse execution systems (WES). WES use AI to make existing logistical systems more efficient over time, and many of the top AGV players have made clear strategic decisions towards acquiring WES capabilities. We discuss some use-cases of some of the top AGV manufacturers using AI to offer WES services. A reputed firm created its own WES based on Distribution Science. Its platform can aid warehouse management operations in identifying the most-efficient picking density for warehouse robots or in optimizing the order-release workflow. The case is studied on apparel retail manufacturer to support their retail store fulfilment (replacing items in stores) by using WES. WES was used to develop a distribution center to replenish products in 3,900 retail stores. The apparel retailer needed to change their store fulfilment operations for eight individual store brands into one distribution center which meant that the distribution center need to have a high density of storage and simultaneously ensure speedy product replenishment. WES was used to optimize operational processes for the whole distribution center right from order receiving (from data in the client's ERP systems) to shipping and scheduling (with data from the WMS). The company claims that retail store replenishment system helped the retailer to accommodate up to 600,000 pieces per day replenished in their stores which was about the required demand for all replenishment of all eight brands (including peak conditions). Also, their system reduced processing costs and expanded storage capacity.*(Ghisellini P, 2016)*

Procurement with Artificial Intelligence: The most convenient way of seeing how revolutionized procurement has become is through application such as Amazon's Alexa, where after the order has been placed, the processes thereafter are in automation – from the moment procurement buyers delegating the supplier communications to virtual assistants or chatbots, to the system responding to any requests that is related to transactions, procurement, spend, payment, etc., and stretching to the decision to purchase and/or making a re-order. When invoices are submitted late, the AI system may trigger an internet search for red flags that may indicate internal problems on the supplier-end. In spend analytics, the system will be able to cross-check every single invoice that's entered, rapidly flagging-up any errors or inconsistencies, and immediately alert the appropriate people on both sides of the order, where it would usually take days if processed manually .

AI using Chatbots: A firm that has launched a chatbot, which can open conversational interfaces between human operators and sales/marketing automation services such as SAP's SalesForce. was used in the beverages industry for procurement management. Beverages manufacturer used to require employees to call help-desk operators to obtain information about their procurement needs. In most cases, that meant a forced waiting time to retrieve the information. The chatbot solution, rolled out to employees and the suppliers, reportedly was then able to provide answers to queries regarding order and shipment status, stock availability, stock prices, supplier status and contract details.

Optimization of a Truck-drone in Tandem Delivery Network: Herein, the minimal time of delivery utilizing K-means clustering to find launch locations, as well as a genetic algorithm are used to solve the truck route as a traveling salesmen problem (TSP). The optimal solution is determined by finding the minimum cost associated to the parabolic convex cost function. To evaluate the launch locations and finding the optimal min-cost, K-means algorithms are used while a generic algorithm is used to determine truck route. It is concluded that standalone systems do not provide satisfactory results as opposed to in-tandem delivery efforts.*(Ardolino M, 2017)*

SOLUTIONS AND RECOMMENDATIONS

Methodology of Current Context of Research: A Gist of Future Use-Cases Machine Learning and its core constructs are ideally suited for providing insights into improving supply chain management performance not available with previous technologies. By combining the strengths of unsupervised learning, supervised learning and reinforcement learning, machine learning is proving to be a very effective technology that continually seeks key factors that affect supply chain performance. Key functions of artificial intelligence applications that are currently beginning to be commercialized or are under research trials are compiled. Non-linear prediction methods are used to predict the behaviour of systems as in traffic congestion forecasting. Road intersections and route guidance utilise control functions of AI. Pattern recognition is useful in determining the behaviour of customer and its needs and automatic incidental detection. The use of machine Learning techniques will be continuously increasing with the advent of more advancement in Supply Chain and the coordination of entities would be even more beneficial.

With changing times, ***stiff competition and rivalry among organizations*** is on the rise. Technological advancements are happening at an exponential rate and firms are fiercely targeting growth and revenue generation. As is evident in many sectors; robotics have been adopted to achieve difficult tasks. Firms are now adopting automation in every field to pair up human and machine intelligence. Nevertheless, the evolution of AI will become more sophisticated than it already is, and this turn of events will intensify the collaboration of human & AI to an even greater heights where it could translate to something ground breaking not only in supply chain, but also in other important sectors as well.

More-precise demand forecasting: AI has become the gold standard for predicting demand based on both internal data signals, such as sales pipelines and marketing leads, and external signals, such as broader market trends, economic outlooks, and seasonal sales trends. Supply chain planners can use AI embedded in demand planning software to estimate not only demand but also the potential impact of scenarios such as economic downturns or severe weather events on demand, as well as on their own costs, production capabilities, and ability to make deliveries. *(Gunasekaran A., 2004)*

How to Prep Your Supply Chain for AI: Businesses often find it challenging and expensive to get AI fully running in production environments. They can take these steps—even before identifying a specific project, in some cases—to prepare a legacy supply chain planning and management system for a boost of intelligence.

Audit value creation: Before deciding on a specific node in their supply chain to augment with AI, manufacturers may find it useful to audit their entire logistics network to identify bottlenecks, productivity drains, and error-prone processes. These audits help business planners identify where AI and other technology investments can yield the most value.

Create a strategy and roadmap: A supply chain modernization initiative usually involves multiple problems to solve, benefits to attain, and executive leaders to appease. But most manufacturers can't afford the expense and downtime of upgrading everything at once. Before outlining specific projects, decide on priorities. Then, come up with a strategy for a far-reaching transformation that addresses the most pressing concerns in its early stages. Create a roadmap that ensures each project along the way will enable the next—and have adequate funding.

Design a solution: Having identified the specific facet of supply chain operations that will benefit most from an AI infusion, the work of designing the solution begins. Consider the types of systems needed—such as cloud-based applications, edge servers, data science platforms, and internet-connected devices and sensors—and how they will need to integrate with each other and existing IT resources. This is the point at which most companies, if they haven't already, opt to engage a systems integrator or other type of consultancy with industry expertise.

Select a vendor: Numerous technology vendors serve up supply chain solutions, and most of them claim some form of AI is built into their products. But because AI is a broad term that describes a diverse set of capabilities, there are major differences between offerings. Selecting a technology vendor is like committing to a long-term relationship—one that hopefully will endure well beyond the current project. Manufacturers, advised by their systems integrators, should carefully assess each bidder's technological capabilities, price, and support models, as well as their corporate culture, to find a fit.*(Herbrich R., 2000)*

Implementation and integration: Once a company has selected a technology vendor, it begins the process of implementation and integration. Typically, a systems integrator works closely with internal IT teams and the vendor to install systems, integrate them with existing ones, and conduct testing before deploying them into production. The implementation phase usually requires some downtime, as well as a period of employee training once it's complete. However, if cautiously scheduled and effectively executed, the switch from staging to production can be accomplished with minimal disruption.

Remember change management: Change can be disconcerting for employees who have done their job in the same way for a long time, even if it was labor-intensive and inefficient. Before implementing a new AI-enabled solution, create a strategy for preparing the organization to embrace it. The plan should involve communicating with workers about the problems or goals that motivated AI adoption, the productivity benefits the organization hopes to achieve, and the benchmarks leaders will use to evaluate the project's success.*(Pelckmans K., 2002)*

Monitor and adjust: In some ways, an AI project is never fully complete. AI is a dynamic technology that constantly improves through a feedback loop of monitoring and adjustment. And even when AI-enabled systems seem to be working well, teams should experiment with modifications and collect data that tracks the results to inform further performance refinements.

Invest in AI in Your Supply Chain with Oracle: A manufacturer's supply chain spans geographically dispersed and operationally isolated facilities—often managed by multiple independent partners—and the distribution routes connecting them. Each phase of the journey from raw material or subcomponent to finished product requires distinct technology solutions. These solutions handle functions including procurement, planning, transportation, inventory, maintenance, and analytics—and they can all benefit from AI. While these multifaceted systems do very different jobs, they cannot be siloed; data must travel alongside supplies through the entire logistics network. Oracle Fusion Cloud Supply Chain & Manufacturing (SCM) is a comprehensive suite of applications that handles and seamlessly connects each individual phase of the supply chain. These SCM applications use built-in machine learning to help improve automation, forecasts, and insights.*(Marr., 2016)*

FUTURE RESEARCH DIRECTIONS

Results of Current Context of Research: Impact of Supply Chain 4.0: Eliminating today's digital waste and adopting new technologies is a major lever to increase the operational effectiveness of supply chains. The potential impact of Supply Chain 4.0 in the next two to three years is huge – up to 30 percent lower operational costs and a reduction of 75 percent in lost sales while decreasing inventories by up to 75 percent are expected, at the same time increasing the agility of the supply chains significantly. How did we calculate these numbers? The impact numbers are based on our experience from numerous studies and quantitative calculations – the three performance indicators are highly correlated, e.g., an improved inventory profile will lead to improved service level and lower cost.

Supply chain service/lost sales.: Low customer service is either driven by a wrong promise to the customer (e.g., unrealistic lead times), a wrong inventory profile (ordered products are not available), and/or an unreliable delivery of parts. Lost sales in addition occur if the required products are not available on the shelf or in the system – customers will decide to switch to another brand. This is true for both B2C and B2B environments. By significantly improving the way we interact with the customer, by leveraging all available POS data/market intelligence, improving the forecast quality significantly (up to more than 90 percent in the relevant level, e.g., SKU), and applying methods of demand shaping in combination with demand sensing to account for systematic changes/trends, the service level will increase dramatically and with this lost sales will decrease significantly. We clearly need to keep in mind that industries like Pharma Rx, where the service level is often in the upper 90ies, will benefit less from the reduction of lost sales, but more from insights into the patient – and by providing individual service, they will be able to increase revenue.*(Leon S., 2017)*

Supply chain costs.: Driven by transportation, warehouse, and the setup of the overall network, the costs can be reduced by up to 30 percent. Roughly 50 percent of this improvement can be reached by applying advanced methods to calculate the clean sheet (bottom-up calculation of the "true" costs of the service) costs of transport and warehousing and by optimizing the network – the goal should always be to have minimal touch points and minimal kilometers driven, still meeting the required service level of the customer. In combination with smart automation and productivity improvement in warehousing, on-board units in transportation, etc., the savings potential can be achieved. The remaining 15 percent cost reduction can be reached by leveraging approaches of dynamic routing, Uberization of transport, leveraging autonomous vehicles, and – where possible – 3-D printing.

Supply chain planning.: The planning tasks such as demand planning, preparation of S&OP process, aggregated production planning, and supply planning are often time intensive and conducted mainly manually. With advanced system support, 80 to 90 percent of all planning tasks can be automated and still ensure better quality compared to tasks conducted manually. The S&OP process will move to a weekly rhythm and the decision process will be built on scenarios that can be updated in real time. This accuracy, granularity, and speed has implications for the other elements, such as service, supply chain costs, and inventory. Systems will be able to detect the exception where a planner needs to jump in to decide.*(Bhardwaj R., 2018)*

Inventory.: Inventory is used to decouple demand and supply, to buffer variability in demand and supply. By implementing new planning algorithms, the uncertainty (the standard deviation of the demand/supply or forecast error) will be reduced significantly, making safety stock unnecessary. The other important variable to drive inventory is the replenishment lead time – with more production of Lot Size 1 and fast changeover, the lead time will be reduced significantly. Also, long transport time, e.g., from Asia to the EU or the US, will be reduced due to a significant increase in local-for-local production. In addition, 3-D printing will reduce the required inventory. We believe in an overall inventory reduction of 75 percent. Capturing the value is a journey that can be started right away. Where it starts depends on the digital maturity of the current supply chain. The McKinsey digital walk-through helps companies appreciate the current digital maturity of the organization, create a sound understanding of the required levers to pull to reach the next performance level leveraging Supply Chain 4.0 tools to shape the road map for digitization, and estimate the potential impact. The diagnostic tool assesses the supply chain systematically based on six value drivers and five assessment dimensions (e.g., data, analytics). It differentiates between three archetypes of maturity levels. Supply Chain 2.0 characterizes "mainly paper-based" supply chains with a low level of digitization. Most processes are executed manually. The digital capabilities of the organization are very limited and available data is not leveraged to improve business decisions. Supply Chain 3.0 describes supply chains with "basic digital components in place." IT systems are implemented and leveraged, but digital capabilities still need to be developed. Only basic algorithms are used for planning/forecasting and only few data scientists are part of the organization to improve its digital maturity. Supply Chain 4.0 is the highest maturity level, leveraging all data available for improved, faster, and more granular support of decision making. Advanced algorithms are leveraged and a broad team of data scientists works within the organization, following a clear development path towards digital mastery.(*Pham D.T, 2005)*

Figure 1. Supply Chain Transformation Levers

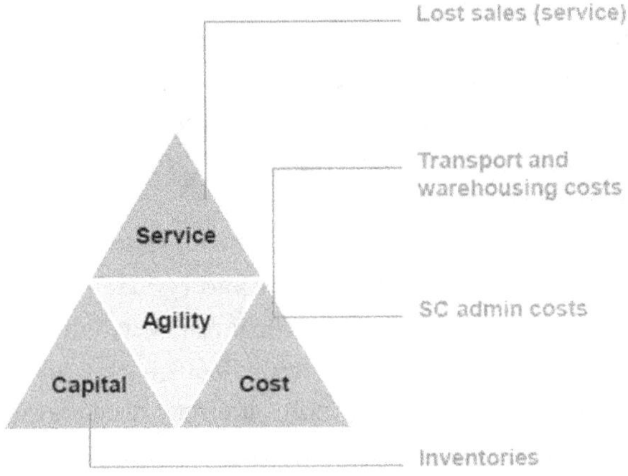

SUPPLY CHAIN AS AN ECOSYSTEM: As we can see, supply chain management conception s a continuous coordination of participants' actions in order to organize logistic processes and reduce the cost, time and risks associated with material movement across the entire supply chain. In the pre-digitalization era, the coordination of participants was carried out by a central company and was based on use of information systems (ERP, CRM, SRM, WMS etc). The most challenging obstacles for smooth interaction between supply chain elements were:

- different, often incompatible information systems of parties.
- disconnected communication and marketing channels (telephone, mail, fax, e-mail, electronic documents, personal contacts).
- lack of regular information exchange not just between separate entities but also between various departments within the same company.

Digital technologies offer efficient solutions to these issues through creating a common digital space for various supply chain participants. Among them, clients and suppliers, transport and logistic companies, wholesalers, retailers, distributors, warehouses, as well as financial and consulting firms. The continuous access of participants to actual information determines all characteristics of a supply chain. Since the last century, various attempts to build a common information space have been made. To this end, one of the first common information spaces, Single Window, was created by companies operating in the port of Felixstow (UK) in 1984. The prevalent cause of the port's inefficiency was paper document flows: the customs processing time for arriving ships in the port exceeded five days. The port stakeholders (shipping lines and agents, forwarders and brokers, customs and government authorities) invested in the development of the port community system with the electronic document flows between supply chain participants for arriving ship cargo. As the result, the time spent on the port cargo handling was reduced to six hours and the transparency and efficiency of the logistic processes was improved, which attracted new investments to the transport industry. Later, the Single Window system was implemented at many other major border checkpoints (ports and airports), and electronic document (EDI and EDIFACT) standards were registered under ISO.*(Ferrandez S.M., 2016)*

Later, such systems attracted interest from international organizations, especially those operating in the field of customs and border control. In 2008, the EU Single Window Environment for Customs program was launched, thus creating a legal framework for replacing paperwork with electronic communications at border checkpoints – an initiative which still remains an important element of international trade. In Russia, Single Window system for the Federal Customs Service have also been implemented, and by 2016 over 99% of customs declarations for imported and exported goods were submitted electronically. The country's Public Services portal is also based on the Single Window approach. Thus, evolving ecosystems are an important trend in supply chain management. The popular concept of the ecosystem was taken from biology and applied to economics and management by J. F. Moore in 1993. He defined a business ecosystem as a flexible structure consisting of people and firms interacting with each other to create and share values within the system.

An ecosystem, tapping into the participants' potential, drives new opportunities for creating new products, services and increasing customer satisfaction. An ecosystem can include supply chain participants, partner companies, consumers and even competitors. In the digital economy, the ecosystems are based on digital technologies and comprise not just companies and people but also objects and devices and thus are called digital ecosystems. Usually, ecosystems are underpinned by digital platforms.*(Li Y., 2020)*

Discussion of Current Context of Research: AI in Supply Chain: Let's consider a hypothetical American automobile manufacturer that assembles three popular models at its plant in Michigan. The tens of thousands of parts and components—such as steel, tires, spark plugs, and needles for gauges—are mainly sourced from mills and manufacturing centers in a dozen US states, as well as Canada, China, Germany, Japan, and Mexico. Some components are produced at facilities the company owns and operates, and others come from third-party distributors. Our hypothetical car company frequently receives massive deliveries, some from overseas on cargo freighters and others trucked from out of state or across North American borders. These supplies must eventually merge at the Michigan plant for final assembly into an SUV, truck, or sedan. But first, they need to be ordered, paid for, tracked, received, and stored in large warehouses with limited capacity that the company maintains in the vicinity of the plant. As if operating a supply chain this large and complex wasn't challenging enough, the car company must contend with inflation making supplies more expensive to procure and rising energy costs eating into their profit margins. Raising the prices of finished vehicles could help, but their sales leaders believe that would tank customer demand. And, in the aftermath of the pandemic, the company must satisfy new regulations that govern factory work environments, including enforcement of the use of PPE. Concerned executives ask technology consultants whether they can benefit from AI, and where in the supply chain. Their answer is yes—and almost everywhere.

For starters, ***AI can outperform the company's basic software when forecasting sales*** for each type of vehicle based on trends. It can also more accurately model how sales may be affected by scenarios such as gas price hikes or unexpected market penetration of electric vehicles. Those intelligent forecasts are a godsend to supply chain planners—they help them procure the right amount of supplies to fulfill demand without incurring additional ordering costs, overstocking their warehouses, or carrying excess inventory. The forecasts also give planners confidence to invest in opening, or save money by shuttering, various production lines and help ensure those lines are appropriately staffed.(*Yuan Y., 2018)*

Cameras connected to AI-powered visual models can monitor the car company's production lines and the distribution facilities to make sure workers follow safety and environmental protocols. Other models trained by machine learning can analyze logistics data to help optimize shipping routes, cargo loads, and warehouse operations, boosting timely deliveries. Finally, AI and decision-making models can automate repetitive processes involved not only in handling physical supplies but also in maintaining the inventory and transaction records necessary to ensure all parties in the supply chain are paid fairly and on time. It can monitor workspaces to spot poor quality control procedures and health and safety violations. Real automobile companies are improving efficiency, reducing errors, increasing accounting accuracy, and redeploying employees to better support business needs—saving them money in almost every area of their supply chain operations. Consider Mazda Motor Logistics, which uses Oracle Transportation Management to help identify the optimal carrier, route, and service level when distributing cars and car parts throughout Europe, increasing on-time deliveries.

Artificial Intelligence (AI) and Machine Learning in Supply Chain Transformation in Business Operations: Companies are employing AI systems in their supply chains to help optimize distribution routes, boost warehouse productivity, streamline factory workflows, and more. Manufacturers of finished goods often rely on hundreds, if not thousands, of components shipped from partners around the globe to arrive in their assembly facilities on a coordinated schedule. AI is proving it can find patterns and relationships buried within large data sets that help optimize these logistics networks, which span cargo freighters, delivery trucks, warehouses, and distribution centers.Supply chain optimization also requires tracking physical goods every time they switch hands. Here, AI can automate documentation with its ability to intelligently enter, extract, and classify data embedded in text files to help ensure the integrity of multiparty transactions. Some manufacturers are taking advantage of AI in forecasting, using it to predict production capacity and optimize warehouse capacity based on customer demand. Some are enlisting AI to flag potential delays and equipment malfunctions before they cause production problems. Others are using AI to derive operational insights from large streams of data that flow from proliferating Internet of Things (IoT) devices and sensors installed across their storage and transportation infrastructure. While AI offers many potential benefits to the supply chain, implementing the technology can be difficult and expensive. Running intelligent applications in production requires powerful computing systems—either on-premises edge servers or cloud-based instances—that typically need to receive data from integrated sensors and devices deployed in the field as part of an Industry 4.0 approach. Businesses typically realize the greatest benefits when they train machine learning models on their own data sets, an even more compute-intensive and data-dependent process.(*Sutrisno H., 2018)*

Supply Chain Transparency with AI: Modern supply chains have become so intricate, entangled, and expansive that manufacturers struggle to maintain end-to-end oversight of the flow of materials and goods arriving in their facilities. AI's unique ability to rapidly analyze large data sets can illuminate the inner workings of even the most complex logistics networks. When ingesting massive streams of logged data and other logistics signals, intelligent algorithms trained through machine learning often surface valuable insights, such as causes of variability or ways to improve capacity for processes with fixed and variable time elements that lead to bottlenecks. And AI-powered supply chain management (SCM) tools are better than traditional systems at tracking vast quantities of supplies in real time as they pass through intermediary manufacturing and distribution partners on the way to becoming finished products. This enhanced visibility and traceability can help manufacturers identify suppliers who are potentially violating quality or ethical sourcing practices. By upgrading supply chain transparency, AI use can create time and cost savings, which we'll describe more later. It can also help manufacturers ensure that the components they use to make their products are sourced in accordance with ethical, quality, and sustainability standards, a responsibility that regulators and many consumers expect them to fulfill. Organizations simply can't afford to work with suppliers—even those based overseas—that infringe on labor, good governance, or environmental rules, and analytics tools embedded in AI-enabled supply chain applications can identify patterns that reveal fraudulent or unethical sourcing.

Figure 2. Benefits of artificial intelligence in supply chain management.

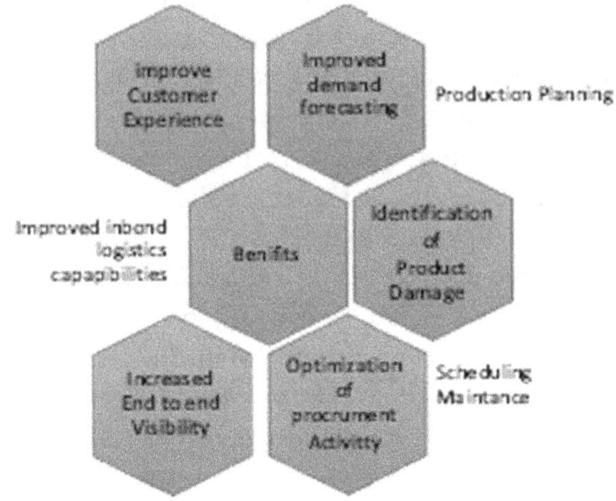

Benefits of AI in Supply Chain: Manufacturers have been at the forefront of AI innovation, experimenting with and deploying various forms of the technology across the many production facilities, storage and distribution centers, and transport vehicles in modern supply chains. This can yield a number of benefits.

Improved warehouse efficiency: AI can make warehouses more efficient by helping organize their racking and design their layouts. By evaluating the quantities of materials transported through warehouse aisles, ML models can suggest floor layouts that speed access to and the travel time of inventory—from receiving to racks to packing and shipping stations. They can also plan optimal routes for workers and robots to shuttle inventory faster, further boosting fulfillment rates. And by analyzing demand signals from marketing, production line, and point-of-sale systems, AI-enabled forecasting systems help manufacturers balance inventory against carrying costs, further optimizing warehouse capacity.

Reduced operating costs: With AI's ability to learn complex behaviors and work under unpredictable conditions, repetitive tasks, such as counting, tracking, and documenting inventory, can be completed with greater accuracy and less labor; bottlenecks are identified and mitigated. By identifying inefficiencies and learning from repetitive tasks, AI can reduce the cost of operating a complex supply chain. AI can also save manufacturers and distribution managers money by reducing the downtime of vital equipment. Intelligent systems, especially those processing data from IoT devices in smart factories, can identify malfunctions and breakdowns in their early stages or predict them before they happen, limiting disruptions and the associated financial losses.

Fewer errors and less waste: AI can usually spot anomalous behavior from both humans and machines much sooner than people can. That's why manufacturers, warehouse operators, and shipping companies are training algorithms to expose flaws in their workflows, employee errors, and product defects. Cameras installed in logistics hubs, assembly lines, and delivery vehicles feed into computer vision systems that use AI to inspect work to reduce recalls, returns, and rework. The system can catch worker and machine mistakes before products are misassembled or sent to the wrong destinations, saving time and material waste. Intelligent systems can also conduct root cause analysis, assessing large volumes of data to find correlations that explain failures and equip teams to make better fixes sooner. AI is also directly embedded in ERP systems used to manage financial transactions as goods flow through the supply chain, helping companies avoid costly billing and payment errors.

More-accurate inventory management: Manufacturers are taking advantage of AI's capabilities to manage their inventory levels with greater precision and efficiency. For example, AI-powered forecasting systems can use inventory information shared from a downstream customer to gauge that customer's demand. If the system determines that the customer's demand is decreasing, then it will adjust the manufacturer's demand forecasts accordingly. Manufacturers and supply chain managers are also increasingly deploying computer vision systems—installing cameras on supply chain infrastructure, racks, vehicles, and even drones—to tabulate goods in real time and monitor warehouse storage capacity. AI also records these workflows in inventory ledgers and automates the process of creating, updating, and extracting information from inventory documentation.

Optimized operations through simulations: Supply chain managers can run AI-powered simulations to gain more insights into the operations of complex, global logistics networks and recognize ways to improve them. They're increasingly using AI in conjunction with digital twins—graphical 3D representations of physical objects and processes, such as assembled goods or factory production lines. Operations planners can simulate various methods and approaches on digital twins—how much would output increase if they added capacity at point A versus point B?—and gauge results without disrupting real-world operations. When AI selects the models and controls the workflows, these simulations become more accurate than those run with traditional computing methods. This application of AI can help engineers and production managers assess the impacts of redesigning products, swapping out parts, or installing new machines on the factory floor. In addition to 3D digital twins, AI and ML can also help create 2D visual models of external processes so planners and operations managers can evaluate the potential impact of changing suppliers, redirecting shipping and distribution routes, or relocating storage and distribution hubs, for example.*(Glass K., 2013)*

Improved worker and material safety: AI systems can monitor work environments throughout the supply chain, such as assembly lines, storage facilities, and shipping vehicles, and flag conditions that jeopardize the safety of workers and the public. That might mean using computer vision to enforce the use of personal protective equipment (PPE) or verify that workers follow other company safety protocols and Occupational Safety and Health Administration standards. Or it could mean processing data from systems aboard vehicles such as trucks and forklifts to monitor whether drivers are operating them safely and soberly. When monitoring factory equipment, AI can help predict malfunctions and other potentially dangerous situations. And AI-powered wearable safety devices can increase protection: Consider sensor-enabled vests that connect to AI systems, analyzing warehouse workers' movements and alerting them to the risk of injury based on their posture, movements, or location in the warehouse. AI systems informed by sensors throughout distribution facilities and vehicles also help ensure that hazardous materials are properly handled and disposed of, protecting those who live and work nearby. AI can automate hazardous tasks, allowing workers to avoid situations that pose risks. For example, smart robots might use AI algorithms along with cameras and sensors to plot the most efficient route through a warehouse, then transport hazardous materials while avoiding objects in their path and relaying results to a warehouse management system. If accidents and failures occur, AI can perform root cause analysis to discover their exact causes and prevent repeats.

More-timely deliveries: Manufacturers that assemble products via complex supply chains are especially dependent on timely and well-coordinated deliveries; delayed arrival of a single component can set back an entire production schedule. AI is taking on the task of lessening these delivery holdups. Logistics companies use machine learning to train models that optimize and manage the delivery routes by which components move along the supply chain. These models can prioritize shipments based on order volumes, delivery promises, contractual deadlines, customer importance, or product availability. And they can provide all nodes in the distribution network with more-accurate estimated times of arrival, identifying shipments that, if delayed, risk creating larger problems.

Improved supply chain sustainability: By driving operational efficiencies, AI can make supply chains more sustainable and lessen their harmful environmental impact. For example, ML-trained models can help organizations reduce energy consumption by optimizing truckloads and delivery routes so trucks burn less fuel while delivering supplies. AI can also help decrease the amount of wasted product at various stages of the supply chain. Consider AI-driven production planning that analyzes past inventory levels, current demand forecasts, and real-time machine maintenance statuses to help ensure a manufacturer doesn't overproduce. AI is also used to analyze the lifecycles of finished products and deliver insights that contribute to a circular economy, where materials are reused and recycled. And supply chain planning and sourcing systems with built-in AI can help increase transparency across suppliers, and enable them to adhere to both environmental and social sustainability standards, such as paying workers fairly.

Challenges of AI in Supply Chain: Organizations use AI to optimize shipping and delivery, manage warehouse capacity, track inventory, forecast demand for specific parts and components, improve worker safety, and help ensure the integrity of transaction records throughout global supply chains. While AI can deliver massive productivity benefits to the supply chain while cutting operational costs, implementing the technology can be difficult and expensive, especially when it involves training custom-made ML models on proprietary data. Manufacturers and logistics providers can take steps to prepare their supply chains for the integration of AI systems and the way these systems can transform the management and operation of their logistics networks. Putting AI to work in planning and managing supply chains can't be done overnight. While the technology offers tremendous potential to reduce costs and simplify processes, it can sometimes be expensive and difficult to deploy. There are some common challenges companies face when infusing intelligence into their supply chain operations.

Training costs. As with any new technology, implementing AI and integrating it into production environments requires training the people who will interact with those new, sometimes intimidating systems. Training employees and overcoming their resistance to change typically requires scheduling some downtime, which comes at a cost. Prior to this downtime, partners throughout the supply chain should work with their AI vendors or integrators to develop training programs that are both constructive and affordable—though it's worth noting that any training approach will likely incur a financial cost.

Startup and operational costs. Costs of implementing AI typically go beyond procuring and integrating the hardware and software that run these systems. Machine learning algorithms don't always need to be built from scratch; there are prebuilt models available that can be tweaked to fit a multitude of supply chain use cases. To realize the greatest benefits, however, companies should train the models on their own data. Collecting, aggregating, validating, transforming, and cleaning large amounts of quality data can require a huge effort. If businesses don't properly prepare a high-quality data set, they risk a reminder of the old maxim: garbage in, garbage out. Training the ML model with this data is a compute-intensive phase that usually demands servers powered by graphics processing units (GPUs), which can cause cloud services bills to spike and monopolize on-premises resources.

Operating and managing AI systems at scale across a global logistics network isn't a one-and-done effort. While running AI systems isn't as compute-intensive as training them, it's an ongoing process that requires powerful platforms, whether edge servers or cloud-based virtual machines. However, these cloud-based solutions are making AI technology more accessible and affordable. And some cloud infrastructure vendors offer managed data science platforms that simplify the process of building ML models, automating their evolution, and managing AI workflows.

Complex systems.: AI systems have a lot of moving parts, including devices and sensors that stream real-time data, GPU-powered servers used for the initial and evolutionary training of machine learning models, edge and cloud servers that run those models in production, and applications that act on the patterns discovered or recommendations made. Organizations must integrate these elements across the many nodes of a global supply chain. They must also consistently monitor these systems and tune their performance, as well as identify and fix glitches.

Figure 3. Applications of machine learning in supply chain management.

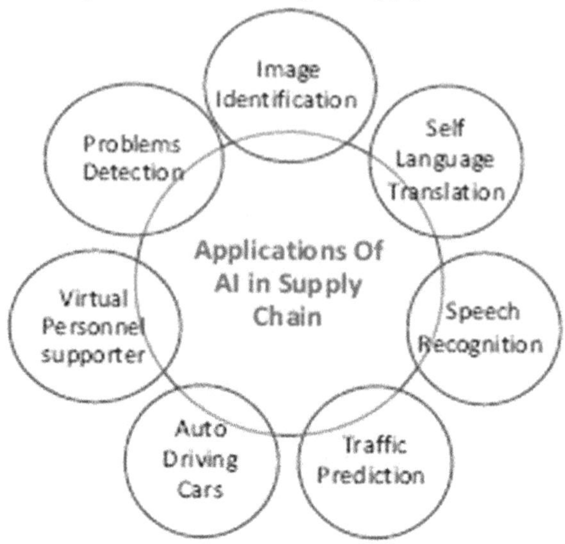

APPLICATIONS OF ARTIFICIAL INTELLIGENCE IN SUPPLY CHAIN

In maintaining a commercial enterprise successful and profitable, it is important to make certain that demanding situations and troubles inside the availability chain are addressed and solved in a short time, errors are avoided, and future possibilities are anticipated as appropriately as possible. Implementing AI and gadget getting to know algorithms inside the availability chain of your commercial enterprise proves to achieve success in the next few cases. Companies actively accumulate transportation management systems to plug freight financial savings and offer a more aggressive carrier while figuring out the effect on overall performance. Machine learning (ML) offers agencies the chance to get right of entry to the possibly insightful statistics and see the answers to the questions regarding the organization's overall performance (Figure 3).

- Do carrier stage requirements meet in terms of shipping and schedule?
- That lanes rectangular degree related to several carrier delays?
- What is the rectangular degree of the stops that cause delays to shipments?

Having all this information at hand, the organization will understand answers to conflicts most of the time as gadget getting to know promotes excessive carrier tiers and the manner of better expertise for shippers on the way to supplying consequences expeditiously.

Warehouse management: AI provides several precise stock controls that enable the call for boom and its subsequent drops. ML is utilized in warehouse optimization, assisting most of the detection of excesses and shortages of shares, saving you time.

Demand prediction: The AI to know-powered call for prediction set of rules offers several advanced calls for prognostication functions. By reading customer conduct tendencies, companies will have the ability to search for conduct and shape the customer portfolio with precision. With predictive analytics for most of the provision chain, companies' rectangular degrees are capable of controlling production and provision to the barest of shortages and excesses.

Logistics route optimization: It's crucial to have gadgets to know for direction optimization that analyses current routes for faster shipping of products. This function conjointly prevents delays in shipping and allows enhanced customer satisfaction. However, with regards to employee development, using current manufacturing data, device learning can create several appropriate environments that can obviously adapt to various circumstance changes in the future.

End-to-end visibility: AI learning algorithms play a key role in presenting stop-to-stop visibility from providers and producers to shops and clients and getting rid of the hazard of conflicts due to the fact that the era will appropriately decide inefficiencies that require a right of way response.*(Zhu L.-Y., 2014)*

CONCLUSION AND FUTURE SCOPE

Enterprises are attaining double-digit improvements in forecast error rates, demand planning productivity, cost reductions and on-time shipments through the use of machine learning today, which has revolutionized supply chain management in the process. Machine learning algorithms and the models they are based on excel at finding anomalies, patterns, and predictive insights in huge data sets. Many supply chain challenges are time, cost and resource constraintbased, which makes machine learning an ideal technology for solving them. This creates demand for the collaboration, integration and sharing of information by these entities. However, there still exists a mismatch between the real and ideal world of supply chain network. This gap persists due to the various known and unknown factors and the complex nature of Supply Chain. One of the reasons could be not knowing the real demand of the customers and thus producing more in anticipation of the demand. This study is attempted towards seeking different business applications of Machine Learning

(ML) methods in Supply Chain Optimization. The research reviews the cases where Machine Learning Techniques are being used in Supply chain optimization. Keywords: Machine Learning, Data Science, Data Analytics, Supply Chain Optimization

REFERENCES

Ardolino, M., Rapaccini, M., Saccani, N., Gaiardelli, P., Crespi, G., & Ruggeri, C. (2017). The role of digital technologies for the service transformation of industrial companies. *International Journal of Production Research*, 7543, 1–17. DOI: 10.1080/00207543.2017.1324224

Bhardwaj, R. (2018) 'AI in Transportation – Current and Future BusinessUse Applications' https://www.techemergence.com/ last accessed on 28/11/2018

Bressanelli, G., Adrodegari, F., Perona, M., & Saccani, N. (2018). Exploring How Usage Focused Business Models Enable Circular Economy through Digital Technologies. *Sustainability (Basel)*, 10(3), 639. DOI: 10.3390/su10030639

Bressanelli, G., Adrodegari, F., Perona, M., & Saccani, N. (2018). The role of digital technologies to overcome Circular Economy challenges in PSS Business Models: An exploratory case study. *Procedia CIRP*, 73, 216–221. DOI: 10.1016/j.procir.2018.03.322

Ferrandez, S. M.. (2016). Optimization of a Truck-drone in Tandem Delivery Network Using K-means and Genetic Algorithm. *Journal of Industrial Engineering and Management*, 9(2), 374–388. DOI: 10.3926/jiem.1929

Ghisellini, P., Cialani, C., & Ulgiati, S. (2016). A review on circular economy: The expected transition to a balanced interplay of environmental and economic systems. *Journal of Cleaner Production*, 114, 11–32. DOI: 10.1016/j.jclepro.2015.09.007

Gunasekaran, A. (2004). Supply chain management: Theory and applications. *European Journal of Operational Research*, 159(2), 265–268. DOI: 10.1016/j.ejor.2003.08.015

Herbrich, R., Keilbach, M. T., Graepel, P. B.-S., & Obermayer, K. (2000). Neural networks in economics: Background, applications and new developments. *Advances in Computational Economics: Computational Techniques for Modeling Learning in Economics*, 11, 169–196. DOI: 10.1007/978-1-4615-5029-7_7

Leon, S. (2017) 'Integrating the Chatbot'. Retrieved from: https://www.capgemini.com, accessed on 15/09/2017.

Li, Y., Diabat, A., & Lu, C.-C. (2020). Leagile Supplier Selection in Chinese Textile Industries: A DEMATEL Approach. *Annals of Operations Research*, 287(1), 303–322. DOI: 10.1007/s10479-019-03453-2

Vick, G. What is Reverse Logistics? URL: http://www. reverselogisticstrends. com/ reverse-logistics. php (дата обращения: 20.11. 2015).

Zage, D., Glass, K., & Colbaugh, R. (2013, June). Improving supply chain security using big data. In *2013 IEEE International Conference on Intelligence and Security Informatics* (pp. 254-259). IEEE.

ADDITIONAL READING

McKinsey & Company. (2021). Succeeding in the AI Supply-Chain Revolution. https://www.mckinsey.com/industries/metals-and-mining/our-insights/succeeding-inthe-ai-supply-chain-revolution

Mohsen, B. (2022). Role of Big Data in Supply Chain Management. [IJM]. *International Journal of Management*, 13, 24–40.

Pagoropoulos, A., Pigosso, D. C. A., & McAloone, T. C. (2017). The emergent role of digital technologies in the Circular Economy: A review. *Procedia CIRP*, 64, 19–24. DOI: 10.1016/j.procir.2017.02.047

Salminen, V., Ruohomaa, H., & Kantola, J. (2017). *Digitalization and big data supporting responsible business co-evolution. Adv. Intell. Syst. Comput* (Vol. 498). Springer., DOI: 10.1007/978-3-319-42070-7_96

Sutrisno, H. (2018). Short-Term Sales Forecast of Perishable Goods for Franchise Business. In: 2018. "Cybernetics in the next decades". Piscataway, NJ, pp. 101–105.

Yuan, Y. (2018). Research on demand forecasting of retail supply chain emergency logistics based on NRS-GA-SVM. In: 2018. Proceedings of the 30th Chinese Control and Decision Conference (2018 CCDC). Piscataway, NJ, pp. 3647–3652.

Zhu, L.-Y., Ma, Y.-Z., & Zhang, L.-Y. (2014). Ensemble model for order priority in make-to-order systems under supply chain environment. In: Lan, H., ed. 2014. *International Conference on Management Science & Engineering (ICMSE)*, Piscataway, NJ, pp. 321–328. DOI: 10.1109/ICMSE.2014.6930247

Chapter 16
Revolutionizing Supply Chain Forecasting With Generative AI and Machine Learning

James Kanyepe
https://orcid.org/0000-0002-6871-8831
University of Botswana, Botswana

Rudolph Boy
University of Botswana, Botswana

Munyaradzi Chibaro
University of Botswana, Botswana

Thuso Mphela
University of Botswana, Botswana

Katlego Tlhakanelo
https://orcid.org/0009-0007-1013-292X
University of Botswana, Botswana

ABSTRACT

This chapter examines the paradigm shift in supply chain forecasting brought about by generative AI and machine learning technologies. Through real-world examples and case studies, the proposed chapter explores how these technologies enhance forecast accuracy, streamline operations, and drive cost efficiency. The study employed systematic analysis of the literature, drawing upon prominent academic databases such as Google Scholar, Scopus, Web of Science, and IEEE

DOI: 10.4018/979-8-3693-4433-0.ch016

Xplore. Academic publications, reports, and related materials were obtained via comprehensive keyword searches to serve as primary sources of data, with a focus on English-language literature to ensure consistency and accessibility. Through the synthesis of data extracted from selected studies, this chapter provides a structured overview of the literature, discussing implications for theory, practice, and future research in supply chain forecasting.

1. INTRODUCTION

Supply chain management is a complex, fluid and dynamic field that plays a crucial role in the success of businesses across various industries. In the modern era, supply chain management requires accurate demand forecasting, efficient allocation of resources and optimized capacity planning, amongst other pertinent variables (Tadayonrad & Ndiaye, 2023). However, traditional forecasting methods used by most organizations often struggle to cope with the increasing complexity and volatility of modern supply chains ecosystems and structures (Aljohani, 2023). This is due to rapidly changing consumer preferences, global economic fluctuations, and unexpected disruptions. In light of these challenges, the advent of generative artificial intelligence (AI) and machine learning (ML) technologies has offered new possibilities for transforming supply chain forecasting (Yandrapalli, 2023).

Generative AI and machine learning algorithms can analyze vast amounts of data, identify patterns, and generate predictive models with unprecedented accuracy and speed (Alwahedi et al., 2024). Unlike traditional forecasting methods, which rely on historical data and predefined rules, generative AI and machine learning have the flexibility to adapt to changing conditions in real time, making them well suited and adaptive for dynamic and unpredictable supply chain environments. Despite the potential benefits of generative AI and machine learning, their adoption in supply chain forecasting is still in its early stages (Jackson et al., 2024). Many businesses are still reliant on outdated forecasting methods, resulting in suboptimal inventory levels, inefficient resource utilization, and missed opportunities for cost savings and revenue growth (Fildes, Ma & Kolassa, 2022).

This chapter aims to explore the transformative impact of generative AI and machine learning on supply chain forecasting. By examining real-world case studies, analyzing the latest advancements in AI technology, and identifying best practices for implementation, this chapter seeks to provide insights into how businesses can leverage generative AI and machine learning to improve forecast accuracy, streamline resource allocation, and optimize capacity planning.

2. BACKGROUND TO THE STUDY

The rapidly evolving landscape of supply chain management is increasingly influenced by technological advancements, with generative artificial intelligence (AI) and machine learning (ML) emerging as pivotal forces in transforming forecasting practices (Eyo-Udo, 2024) owing to the influence of the Fourth Industrial Revolution matrixes. Traditionally, supply chain forecasting has relied on conventional statistical methods and heuristics that, while useful, often fall short in addressing the complexities of modern supply chains (Barbosa-Povoa & Pinto, 2020). Several scholars have reported that traditional methods frequently struggle with the dynamic and volatile nature of demand, supply variability, and the complex relationships among numerous influencing factors.

Babai et al. (2022) reported that the growth in global supply chains presents intricacies and interconnectedness, which requires more sophisticated forecasting tools. Generative AI and machine learning offer innovative approaches that promise to address the limitations posed by traditional forecasting methods by providing more accurate, adaptive, and actionable forecasting capabilities. For example, generative AI, through techniques such as generative adversarial networks (GANs) and variational autoencoders (VAEs), excels in modeling complex data distributions and generating synthetic data that reflect real-world scenarios (Goyal & Mahmoud, 2024). This capability allows organizations to simulate various demand and supply conditions, thus improving their ability to anticipate and plan for uncertainties (Khlie et al. (2024)). On the other hand, machine learning leverages vast amounts of historical data to identify patterns, trends, and anomalies that can enhance predictive accuracy (Bharadiya, 2023).

Despite the promising advancements in generative AI and machine learning, significant research gaps remain in understanding their full scope and impact on supply chain forecasting (Jackson, et al. 2024). One critical gap is the limited empirical evidence on the practical application of these technologies across diverse supply chain contexts. While theoretical models and pilot studies highlight their potential, comprehensive case studies and real-world evaluations that demonstrate how generative AI and machine learning perform in various industry settings and supply chain scenarios are lacking (Li et al., 2024). This gap impedes the ability to generalize findings and develop best practices for implementation.

Research on the challenges involved in integrating these technologies with existing forecasting systems and workflows is lacking. The shift from traditional forecasting methods to advanced AI-driven approaches presents complexities related to data integration, model calibration, and system compatibility (Muthukalyani, 2023). Although generative AI and machine learning have improved forecast accuracy, their impact on other aspects of forecasting, such as interpretability and decision-making support, has not been fully explored. Addressing these research gaps will contribute to a more comprehensive understanding of how generative AI and machine learning can revolutionize supply chain forecasting and offer valuable insights for practitioners.

3. RESEARCH OBJECTIVES

a) To examine traditional supply chain forecasting methods
b) To examine the current challenges in supply chain forecasting.
c) To explore the ability of generative AI and machine learning to increase the accuracy and efficiency of supply chain forecasting.

4. METHODOLOGY

This chapter adopted a systematic analysis of the literature as a methodological research entry point aimed at exploring the paradigm shift in supply chain forecasting caused by generative AI and machine learning technologies. Academic databases, including Google Scholar, Scopus, Web of Science, and IEEE Xplore, served as primary sources for gathering relevant literature which will be subjected to critical analytical desktop review and analysis. A comprehensive set of keywords related to the supply chain, supply chain forecasting, demand forecasting, artificial intelligence, generative artificial intelligence and machine learning were used, and searches were conducted to retrieve academic publications, reports, and related materials. The methodology is shown in Figure 1.

Figure 1. Methodology

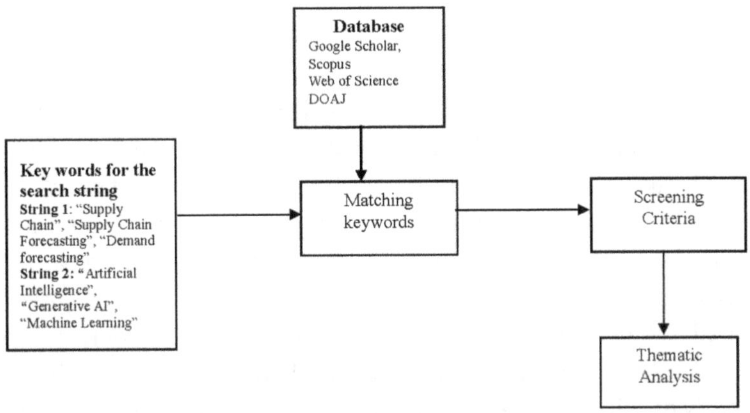

Source: Author (2024)

To ensure the relevance and quality of the sources, only peer-reviewed articles published in English were included. The selection process involved reviewing abstracts to assess their relevance to the research objectives, followed by a detailed reading of full texts to verify their contribution to the topic. Studies were evaluated based on their findings, methodologies, and alignment with the chapter's focus on supply chain forecasting using AI and ML. This step helped narrow down the most pertinent sources, ensuring a comprehensive overview of the literature. Thematic analysis was applied to the selected literature to identify key themes and patterns. This process included coding significant sections of the data, grouping them by shared characteristics, and synthesizing these groups to draw overarching insights. The analysis emphasized how generative AI and machine learning enhance forecast accuracy, streamline operations, and influence decision-making processes. This approach facilitated the extraction of valuable information on practical applications, theoretical implications, and potential research directions.

By providing a detailed account of the research process—including database searches, keyword strategies, and thematic analysis—this chapter offers a clearer, more transparent view of how the literature review was conducted, enhancing the reliability and validity of the findings.

5. LITERATURE REVIEW

5.1 Supply Chain Forecasting

Supply chain forecasting is the process which entails, *inter alia*, predicting future demand, supply, and trends within the supply chain to make informed decisions (Seyedan & Mafakheri, 2020). It involves analyzing historical data, market trends, and other variables to estimate future requirements for goods, materials, and resources. Central to supply chain forecasting is demand forecasting, which involves predicting customer demand for products or services with a high degree of accuracy (Babai et al., 2022). According to Jeyaraman et al. (2024), demand forecasting plays a crucial role in optimizing production schedules, managing inventory, and ensuring timely distribution. Additionally, supply chain forecasting involves supply forecasting, which predicts the availability of materials, components, and finished goods from suppliers (Seyedan & Mafakheri, 2020). Accurate supply forecasting allows companies to synchronize their procurement and production processes, which reduces the risk of supply chain disruptions and enhances overall efficiency (Tarigan, Siagian & Jie, 2021).

Supply chain forecasting also encompasses capacity and complex facility of forecasting, which involves estimating the production capacity required to meet anticipated demand (Seyedan & Mafakheri, 2020). Capacity forecasting includes planning for the necessary labor, machinery, and production schedules to ensure that manufacturing processes can accommodate fluctuations in demand without compromising efficiency. Tadayonrad and Ndiaye (2023) asserted that supply chain forecasting also involves lead time forecasting, which encompasses the analysis of procurement, manufacturing, transportation, and order fulfillment lead times. Accurate lead time forecasts are essential for maintaining appropriate inventory levels, scheduling production, and fulfilling customer orders on time.

5.2 Generative AI

According to Goodfellow et al. (2020), generative artificial intelligence (GAI) refers to artificial intelligence systems with the ability to create text, images, or other forms of media through generative models. Zhang, Zhu and Su (2023) posited that generative models acquire an understanding of patterns and structures within their training data, subsequently generating novel data with similar characteristics. GAIs include various types, such as generative adversarial networks (GANs), transformer-based models (TRMs), variational autoencoders (VAEs), and diffusion models (DMs) (Bandi et al., 2024).

A generative adversarial network (GAN) is a genus of machine learning frameworks and a prominent framework for approaching generative AI. The novel aspect of this generative adversarial network setup is that it does not depend upon heavily annotated training data (Saxena & Cao, 2021). On the other hand, transformers use both self-attention and multihead attention mechanisms to learn the dependencies between the objects regardless of the distance between them and to learn the different relationships and patterns between the inputs (de Santana Correia & Colombini, 2022). VAEs consist of an encoder and a decoder where the purpose of an encoder is to encode the given input in a lower dimension called latent space, and the decoder decodes the latent output of the encoder into its original input shape (Notin et al., 2021).

5.3 Machine Learning

Machine learning is a subset of artificial intelligence (AI) that critically focuses on enabling computers to learn from data and improve their performance over time without being explicitly programmed for every task (Taye, 2023). It can also be defined as the study of computer algorithms that improve automatically through experience and the use of data (DhallD., Kau & Juneja,2020). ML algorithms build a model based on sample data, known as "training data," to make predictions or decisions without being explicitly programmed to perform the task Sarker, I. H. (2021). Machine learning systems use algorithms and statistical models to identify patterns, make decisions, and predict outcomes on the basis of input data (Ofori, Maina & Gitonga, 2020). The activities carried out by computers via an algorithm have no error margin and follow a series of stages. Unlike commands intended to produce an output from an input, there are circumstances when computers make choices on the basis of existing sample data. In these scenarios, computers, like people, may make mistakes during the decision-making process. Machine learning is the process of allowing computers to learn from analyzing data and experience in the same way that a human brain does (Lv et al., Z2020). The major target of machine learning is to develop models that can upskill themselves to ameliorate them, recognize complicated patterns, and discover solutions to different advanced issues via past data (Jaiswal, Gupta & Tiwari, 2023).

5.4 Traditional Supply Chain Forecasting Methods

Traditional supply chain forecasting methods have been foundational and crisp in helping businesses predict demand, manage inventory, and plan for future supply chain activities. Various methods have been suggested in the literature, including time series analysis, trend analysis, qualitative methods, and naive and causal models.

5.4.1 Time Series Analysis

Time series analysis analyses historical data to identify patterns, trends, seasonal variations, and cycles (Zakhidov, 2024). Time series analysis includes techniques such as moving averages and exponential smoothing. Moving Averages is a simple method where the forecast is based on the average of past data points over a specific period. This helps smooth out fluctuations and highlights underlying trends (Rabbani et al., 2021). On the other hand, exponential smoothing is a weighted averaging method where more recent data points are given more weight in the forecast. Compared with moving averages, this technique adapts more quickly to changes in demand patterns (Cieżak & Kutyłowska, 2023).

5.4.2 Causal Models

Causal models, also conceived as econometric models, incorporate external variables (such as economic indicators, marketing activities, pricing changes, and consumer behavior) that are believed to influence demand (Abolghasemi et al., 2020). Forecasts can be performed through regression analysis where the relationship between demand and one or more independent variables is quantified.

5.4.3 Qualitative Methods

Qualitative forecasting methods rely mostly on expert judgment, market research, and experience rather than purely on historical data (Zellner et al., 2021). These methods are particularly useful when historical data are limited, such as when a new product is launched or when it enters a new market. Qualitative methods also include the Delphi method and market surveys. The Delphi method is a structured communication technique that gathers forecasts from a panel of experts. The experts provide their predictions anonymously, and the results are aggregated and shared with the group for further refinement in multiple rounds until a consensus is reached (Ismail & Taliep, 2023). On the other hand, market surveys involve directly gathering information from customers or sales teams about expected future demand (Seyedan & Mafakheri, 2020). This method is valuable for capturing insights into market trends and customer intentions that may not yet be reflected in historical data (Ren, Chan & Siqin, 2020).

5.4.4 Naive Forecasting

Naive forecasting is a method where the forecast for a future period is set to be the same as the last observed value or is based on a basic rule, such as the assumption that demand will grow at a constant rate (Borucka, 2023). This method requires minimal computation and is often used as a benchmark to evaluate the performance of more complex forecasting models (Gonçalves et al., 2021).

5.4.5 Trend Analysis

Trend analysis involves identifying and extrapolating long-term trends in historical data (Calleja-Sanz et al., 2020). This method assumes that historical trends will continue, making it useful for forecasting in stable environments where the underlying conditions are not expected to change significantly (Grinin, Grinin & Korotayev, 2021).

5.4.6 Seasonal Decomposition

Seasonal decomposition involves breaking historical data into their seasonal components, trend components, and residuals (random fluctuations) (Stefenon et al., 2023), and businesses can better understand how seasonal factors influence demand and adjust their forecasts accordingly by isolating seasonal and trend components. This method is particularly valuable for industries with strong seasonal demand patterns, such as retail or agriculture (Borucka, 2023).

5.4.7 Judgmental Forecasting

Judgmental forecasting is based on the intuition and experience of individuals within the organization, such as managers, sales teams, or industry experts (Goodwin & Fildes, R2022). This method is often used in conjunction with quantitative methods to adjust forecasts on the basis of qualitative insights, such as expected market shifts or upcoming events.

5.5 Challenges in Supply Chain Forecasting

Demand volatility remains one of the most pressing challenges besetting supply chain forecasting. The rapid pace of change in consumer preferences, driven by factors such as technological advancements, cultural shifts, and social media influence, creates significant unpredictability (Suherlan & Okombo, 2023). For example, a product can suddenly surge in popularity due to a viral trend, leading to unexpected spikes in demand that traditional forecasting methods may struggle to anticipate (Chase, 2021). Moreover, macroeconomic factors, such as inflation rates and changes in disposable income, can also cause fluctuations in demand, further complicating the forecasting process (Araujo & Gaglianone, 2023). The COVID-19 pandemic exemplified the extreme nature of demand volatility, where certain products experienced unprecedented demand, whereas others experienced sharp declines (Amankwah-Amoah, Khan & Wood, 2021). To mitigate the impact of demand volatility, companies are increasingly turning to advanced technologies such as generative AI and machine learning (Recio-Román, Recio-Menéndez & Román-González, 2024). These technologies offer the potential to analyze vast datasets in real time, capturing subtle shifts in consumer behavior that might be missed by conventional methods. Despite the promise of AI-driven forecasting, the unpredictable nature of demand means that companies must also build flexibility and resilience in their supply chains to respond swiftly to unexpected changes (Modgil, Singh & Hannibal, 2022).

Data quality and availability are crucial for accurate supply chain forecasting, but they present significant challenges (Seyedan & Mafakheri, 2020). Forecasting models depend on historical data to predict future trends. However, if the data are incomplete, outdated, or inaccurate, the predictions are likely flawed (Wang et al., 2023). In many instances, supply chain data are scattered across multiple systems and stakeholders, making it challenging to consolidate and ensure consistency. Furthermore, data entry errors and inconsistencies in data formats can further diminish data quality, resulting in unreliable forecasts (Aldoseri, Al-Khalifa & Hamouda, 2023). The lack of real-time data availability also poses a challenge, as forecasts based on old data fail to capture current market conditions (Bechtsis et al., 2022). To improve data quality, it is important to standardize data collection processes across the supply chain and implement strong data governance practices. Additionally, advanced analytics tools powered by AI can assist in cleaning and enriching data, thereby reducing the impact of inaccuracies (Aldoseri et al., 2023).

The increasing complexity of global supply chains adds another layer of difficulty to accurate forecasting (Brintrup et al., 2020). Supply chains today often span multiple countries and involve numerous suppliers, each with its own processes, lead times, and risks (Baldwin & Freeman, 2022). This complexity makes it challenging to maintain visibility across the entire supply chain, leading to potential blind spots in forecasting. For example, disruptions at a second- or third-tier supplier may go unnoticed until they significantly impact the supply chain, at which point it may be too late to adjust the forecast (Azadegan & Dooley, 2021). Managing complex supply chains requires advanced forecasting models that can account for the multitude of variables at play (Feizabadi, 2022). Machine learning algorithms can help identify patterns and correlations that may not be immediately apparent, enabling more proactive management of the supply chain (Pasupuleti et al., 2024). Lead time variability presents a significant challenge in forecasting for the supply chain. Fluctuations in the time it takes for suppliers to deliver goods can result in inconsistent inventory levels (Alnahhal, Ahrens & Salah, 2021). Unpredictable lead times can cause companies to either overestimate or underestimate the amount of stock needed, leading to either excess inventory or stockouts (Kanyepe et al., 2023).

To ameliorate lead time variability, closer collaboration with suppliers is necessary to understand the factors contributing to lead time fluctuations and to develop strategies for minimizing them (Dominguez et al., 2020). Companies can also benefit from implementing buffer inventories or safety stock to cushion against variability, although this approach must be carefully balanced to avoid excessive inventory costs (Choi et al., 2023). Utilizing advanced forecasting tools that incorporate real-time data from suppliers can also help adjust forecasts dynamically as lead times change (Seyedan & Mafakheri, 2020). However, these solutions are not foolproof and must be complemented by broader supply chain strategies aimed at improving supplier reliability and responsiveness.

Integrating and adopting new forecasting technologies with existing supply chain systems is a significant challenge, often leading to compatibility issues and resistance to change (Sobb, Turnbull, & Moustafa, 2020). Legacy systems, which many companies still rely on, may not be designed to handle the data processing requirements of advanced AI and machine learning tools (Devan, Shanmugam & Tomar, 2021). This creates difficulties in leveraging the full potential of these technologies, as they may not seamlessly integrate with existing enterprise resource planning (ERP) systems, warehouse management systems (WMSs), or other supply chain software. Additionally, the process of integrating new technologies often requires substantial time and financial investment, which can be a barrier for companies with limited resources (Indrawati, 2020). Beyond these technical challenges, there is also the issue of organizational resistance to the adoption of new technologies. Employees accustomed to traditional forecasting methods may be hesitant to embrace AI-driven solutions, fearing that these tools could render their roles obsolete or require them to acquire new skills (Păvăloaia & Necula, 2023).

External factors such as geopolitical events, regulatory changes, and environmental conditions introduce significant uncertainty into supply chain forecasting (Odulaja et al., 2023). Geopolitical events, including trade wars, sanctions, and political instability, can disrupt supply chains by causing delays, increasing costs, or even cutting off access to critical suppliers or markets (Bednarski et al., 2024). For example, the imposition of tariffs can lead to sudden shifts in supply chain strategies, requiring companies to adapt their forecasts quickly to account for new cost structures. Similarly, regulatory changes, such as new environmental regulations or labor laws, can impact the availability and cost of goods, further complicating the forecasting process (Niaz & Nwagwu, 2023). Environmental factors, including natural disasters and climate change, also pose a substantial risk to supply chain stability (Ojo, 2024). Events such as hurricanes, floods, and wildfires can disrupt transportation networks, damage infrastructure, and delay production, making it difficult to predict supply chain performance accurately (Kanike, 2023). To manage these external risks, companies must incorporate scenario planning into their forecasting models, considering a range of potential disruptions and their impacts (Ivanov & Dolgui, 2021).

Traditional supply chain forecasting methods often have limited predictive capabilities, particularly in regard to accounting for nonlinear relationships and complex interdependencies within the supply chain (Feizabadi, 2022). These methods typically rely on historical data and linear models, which may not capture the full range of variables influencing supply chain performance. For example, traditional models may struggle to predict the impact of a sudden change in consumer behavior or a new technological innovation on supply chain dynamics (Chase, 2021). This limitation results in forecasts that may be accurate under stable conditions but fall short in the face of volatility and complexity. To address these limitations, companies are increasingly exploring advanced analytics and AI-driven forecasting models that can analyze large datasets and uncover hidden patterns and correlations (Essien, 2023). Machine learning algorithms, for example, can learn from past data and continuously refine their predictions as new data become available, offering more accurate and dynamic forecasts (Lazzeri, 2020). However, these advanced models require substantial computational power and expertise to be implemented effectively, and there is always a risk of overfitting or relying too heavily on complex models that may not fully align with the realities of the supply chain.

Human error is an inherent challenge adversely impacting supply chain forecasting, particularly when manual processes and subjective judgments are involved (Caiado et al., 2021). Forecasting often requires input from various stakeholders, such as sales teams, inventory managers, and procurement officers, each of whom may introduce biases and assumptions to the process. For example, sales teams might provide overly optimistic forecasts on the basis of expected sales growth, whereas inventory managers may be more conservative, leading to discrepancies in the final forecast. These subjective inputs can introduce errors and inconsistencies, reducing the overall accuracy of the forecast. Minimizing human error requires a more systematic and data-driven approach to forecasting (Bousdekis et al., 2021). By leveraging AI and machine learning, companies can reduce their reliance on human judgment and instead base forecasts on objective data analysis (Campbell et al., 2020). However, while automation can mitigate some aspects of human error, it is not a panacea. It is important to maintain a level of human oversight to ensure that automated forecasts align with business objectives and real-world conditions.

5.6 The Capabilities of Generative AI and Machine Learning to Enhance the Accuracy of Supply Chain Forecasting

Generative AI and machine learning excel at recognizing complex patterns in large datasets, which traditional statistical methods might overlook (Farahani et al., 2023). These technologies can analyze historical data, market trends, customer behavior, and external factors (such as economic indicators) to identify correlations and causations that influence supply chain dynamics. By detecting these patterns, AI and ML models can produce more accurate forecasts, even in volatile and complex environments (Ganesh & Kalpana, 2022). One of the most significant capabilities of generative AI and ML is their ability to process vast amounts of data in real time (Ooi et al., 2023). This means that supply chain forecasts can be continuously updated as new information becomes available, such as changes in demand, supply disruptions, or shifts in market conditions (Syntetos et al., 2016). This real-time adaptability allows companies to make proactive decisions, reducing the risk of stockouts or excess inventory and optimizing resource allocation.

Generative AI can create a wide range of potential scenarios on the basis of different variables, allowing companies to simulate various supply chain outcomes (Jackson et al., 2024). For example, AI-driven models can generate forecasts under different economic conditions, supply disruptions, or changes in consumer behavior. This capability enables businesses to prepare for multiple eventualities and develop contingency plans, enhancing the resilience of their supply chains (Ambulkar et al., 2022). Machine learning models can automate decision-making processes by continuously learning from new data and refining their predictions. This reduces the need for manual intervention in forecasting, leading to faster and more consistent decision-making (Gil et al., 2021). For example, ML algorithms can automatically adjust inventory levels or reorder points on the basis of real-time demand forecasts, optimizing the supply chain without requiring constant human oversight (Tuli, Mohammed & Sachani, 2024).

Generative AI and machine learning can also incorporate unstructured data sources, such as social media, news articles, and weather reports, into forecasting models (Veluru, 2024). This broadens the scope of data inputs beyond traditional structured data (such as sales records), providing a more holistic view of factors that could impact the supply chain. By analyzing these diverse data sources, AI-driven models can identify early warning signals and trends that might influence future demand or supply chain disruptions (Johnson & Girard, 2024). On the other hand, human-generated forecasts can be prone to bias and error, particularly when they are based on subjective judgment or limited data (Abeliuk et al., 2020). Machine learning models mitigate this risk by relying on data-driven analysis rather than human intuition. By enhancing the accuracy of supply chain forecasts, generative AI and machine learning contribute to cost optimization (Gayam, Yellu & Thuniki, 2021). More accurate forecasts reduce the likelihood of overproduction, excess inventory, and emergency restocking, all of which incur additional costs (Jauhar et al., 2024).

Furthermore, AI and ML can facilitate better collaboration across the supply chain by providing a single source of truth for all stakeholders (Gurzawska, 2020). Real-time forecasting data can be shared with suppliers, manufacturers, and distributors, improving visibility and coordination across the supply chain (Modgil, Singh & Hannibal, 2022). This collaborative approach helps align production and logistics with actual demand, reducing inefficiencies and improving overall supply chain performance.

6. RESULTS AND DISCUSSION

Traditional Supply Chain Forecasting Methods

While traditional supply chain forecasting methods have been effective and plausible for many years, they have several limitations, especially in today's dynamic and complex supply chain. Traditional supply chain forecasting methods often depend heavily on historical data to predict future trends (Ren, Chan & Siqin, 2020). This reliance can be problematic when historical data do not accurately represent current or future conditions. For instance, a retailer that uses historical sales data to forecast demand may struggle if consumer preferences shift dramatically or if a new competitor enters the market. In addition, traditional forecasting methods can be inflexible and slow to adapt to changes. These methods often assume that patterns from the past will continue unchanged into the future, which can be problematic in dynamic environments (Orang et al., 2023). For example, during the COVID-19 pandemic, many traditional forecasting models have failed to account for rapid changes in consumer behavior and supply chain disruptions, leading to significant mismatches between supply and demand.

Challenges in Supply Chain Forecasting

Many traditional forecasting methods use models that oversimplify complex supply chains. These models may fail to account for the intricate interactions between different elements of the supply chain or the impact of external factors (Friday et al., 2023). For example, a basic moving average model might not capture the effects of a global supply chain disruption, such as a natural disaster affecting raw material availability. Additionally, traditional forecasting methods often provide forecasts at an aggregated level, which may not be useful for detailed operational planning (Nikolopoulos, 2021). For example, a monthly forecast of overall demand might not provide the detailed insights needed for managing inventory at individual store locations. This lack of granularity can result in mismatches between supply and demand at specific locations, leading to stockouts in some stores, whereas other locations face excess inventory. Traditional forecasting methods often prioritize quantitative data, potentially neglecting qualitative insights (Seyedan & Mafakheri, 2020). For example, a company might rely solely on sales data and ignore market research or consumer feedback that indicates a changing trend or emerging preference. This overreliance on quantitative data can lead to forecasts that do not align with actual market dynamics, resulting in misaligned inventory levels and missed opportunities (Rehmani et al., 2021).

Generative AI and Machine Learning in Supply Chain Forecasting

Generative AI (GAI) and machine learning (ML) offer transformative advantages for supply chain forecasting by addressing the limitations of traditional statistical models. One of the primary merits of the GAI and ML methods is their ability to handle complex, multidimensional datasets that encompass not only historical sales data but also external factors such as social media trends, weather patterns, and macroeconomic indicators (Bao et al., 2024). By integrating a wide variety of data sources, ML models can detect patterns and relationships that are difficult to identify through conventional methods, leading to more accurate and robust demand forecasting. Moreover, ML algorithms can continuously improve over time as new data become available, allowing for adaptive and real-time forecasting, a key requirement in fast-changing market environments (Garinian et al., 2021).

Another significant advantage of the GAI and ML methods is their capacity to simulate and predict supply chain disruptions. Generative models, such as generative adversarial networks (GANs), can be used to create synthetic scenarios, help organizations explore "what-if" situations and assess the impact of unforeseen events such as supplier delays, natural disasters, or geopolitical instability (Georginova, 2023). This proactive approach enables companies to design resilient supply chains by identifying vulnerabilities before disruptions occur, improving both operational continuity and decision-making processes. By generating alternative futures, the GAI supports better risk management and strategic planning, providing a significant advantage over traditional forecasting techniques that rely solely on historical data (Majumder & Dey, 2024).

Furthermore, GAI and ML enhance scalability and flexibility in supply chain operations. Traditional forecasting models often require manual adjustments and may not scale well when applied to large, global supply chains with complex product lines (Seyedan & Mafakheri, 2020). In contrast, ML-driven models can be easily deployed across different levels of the supply chain, from local distribution centers to global networks, and can automatically adjust to changing business conditions (Tuli et al., 2024). Additionally, GAI models provide a mechanism for personalized forecasting, tailoring predictions to specific regions, customer segments, or product categories (Akhtar et al., 2024). This level of granularity enables businesses to optimize inventory management, reduce costs, and improve service levels, thereby driving efficiency and responsiveness throughout the supply chain.

7. MANAGERIAL IMPLICATIONS

The integration of generative AI (GAI) and machine learning (ML) in supply chain forecasting has significant managerial implications that can revolutionize decision-making processes and enhance operational efficiency. One key implication is the ability to make more data-driven, predictive decisions. With AI-powered models, managers can move away from reactive decision-making on the basis of historical trends to proactive planning on the basis of real-time data and predictive analytics. This shift enables more accurate demand forecasting, which reduces stockouts, overproduction, and inventory costs. Managers can now better align production schedules, optimize procurement processes, and respond swiftly to changes in market conditions, ultimately enhancing customer satisfaction and supply chain resilience.

Another major implication is the enhanced ability to manage supply chain risk. The GAI allows managers to simulate multiple future scenarios and explore the impacts of potential disruptions, such as supplier failures, natural disasters, or unexpected shifts in demand. This capability fosters a more robust risk management strategy, enabling managers to develop contingency plans and ensuring business continuity in the face of uncertainty. By adopting AI-based forecasting, managers can also improve supplier collaboration and transparency across the supply chain, further mitigating risks and fostering stronger partnerships. This proactive approach to risk management leads to more stable and resilient supply chain networks.

Finally, the scalability and customization provided by the GAI and ML models allow managers to apply forecasting tools across diverse regions, product lines, and market conditions. The adaptability of these AI models enables managers to handle large-scale operations without significant manual intervention, improving operational flexibility and responsiveness. Moreover, managers can customize forecasts for specific customer segments or geographic markets, improving service levels and targeting inventory strategies more effectively. This scalability not only improves supply chain efficiency but also supports growth initiatives and market expansion efforts by providing managers with actionable insights tailored to their specific operational needs.

8. IMPLICATIONS TO FUTURE RESEARCH

Looking ahead, several promising avenues for future research in the application of AI and machine learning in supply chain forecasting exist. One key area is investigating how these technologies can be leveraged to better manage supply chain disruptions, such as those resulting from geopolitical events, natural disasters, or pandemics. Exploring adaptive AI-driven models that simulate multiple disruption scenarios and assist companies in creating robust contingency plans could be transformative. Additionally, future studies could examine how AI and ML can support smaller businesses in overcoming resource limitations, enhancing forecast accuracy, and achieving cost efficiencies. Research in this area could reveal tailored solutions and strategies that democratise the advantages of AI, enabling even smaller supply chains to become more resilient and competitive.

9. CONCLUSION

Traditional supply chain forecasting methods have several limitations. They rely heavily on historical data to predict future trends, are slow to adapt to changes, and often oversimplify complex supply chains. They also tend to provide forecasts at an aggregated level. However, generative AI (GAI) and machine learning (ML) can revolutionize supply chain forecasting by addressing these limitations. GAI and ML can handle complex, multidimensional datasets that include not only historical sales data but also external factors such as social media trends, weather patterns, and macroeconomic indicators. Additionally, GAI and ML enhance scalability and flexibility in supply chain operations.

REFERENCES

Abeliuk, A., Benjamin, D. M., Morstatter, F., & Galstyan, A. (2020). Quantifying machine influence over human forecasters. *Scientific Reports*, 10(1), 15940. PMID: 32994447

Abolghasemi, M., Beh, E., Tarr, G., & Gerlach, R. (2020). Demand forecasting in supply chain: The impact of demand volatility in the presence of promotion. *Computers & Industrial Engineering*, 142, 106380.

Akhtar, P., Ghouri, A. M., Ashraf, A., Lim, J. J., Khan, N. R., & Ma, S. (2024). Smart product platforming powered by AI and Generative AI: Personalization for the circular economy. *International Journal of Production Economics*, 273, 109283.

Aldoseri, A., Al-Khalifa, K. N., & Hamouda, A. M. (2023). Re-thinking data strategy and integration for artificial intelligence: Concepts, opportunities, and challenges. *Applied Sciences (Basel, Switzerland)*, 13(12), 7082.

Aljohani, A. (2023). Predictive analytics and machine learning for real-time supply chain risk mitigation and agility. *Sustainability*, 15(20), 15088.

Alnahhal, M., Ahrens, D., & Salah, B. (2021). Dynamic lead-time forecasting using machine learning in a make-to-order supply chain. *Applied Sciences (Basel, Switzerland)*, 11(21), 10105.

Alwahedi, F., Aldhaheri, A., Ferrag, M. A., Battah, A., & Tihanyi, N. (2024). Machine learning techniques for IoT security: Current research and future vision with generative AI and large language models. *Internet of Things and Cyber-Physical Systems*.

Amankwah-Amoah, J., Khan, Z., & Wood, G. (2021). COVID-19 and business failures: The paradoxes of experience, scale, and scope for theory and practice. *European Management Journal*, 39(2), 179–184. PMID: 38620607

Ambulkar, S., Ramaswami, S., Blackhurst, J., & Johnny Rungtusanatham, M. (2022). Supply chain disruption risk: An unintended consequence of product innovation. *International Journal of Production Research*, 60(24), 7194–7213.

Araujo, G. S., & Gaglianone, W. P. (2023). Machine learning methods for inflation forecasting in Brazil: New contenders versus classical models. *Latin American Journal of Central Banking*, 4(2), 100087.

Azadegan, A., & Dooley, K. (2021). A typology of supply network resilience strategies: Complex collaborations in a complex world. *The Journal of Supply Chain Management*, 57(1), 17–26.

Babai, M. Z., Boylan, J. E., & Rostami-Tabar, B. (2022). Demand forecasting in supply chains: A review of aggregation and hierarchical approaches. *International Journal of Production Research*, 60(1), 324–348.

Baldwin, R., & Freeman, R. (2022). Risks and global supply chains: What we know and what we need to know. *Annual Review of Economics*, 14(1), 153–180.

Bandi, A., Adapa, P. V. S. R., & Kuchi, Y. E. V. P. K. (2023). The power of generative ai: A review of requirements, models, input–output formats, evaluation metrics, and challenges. *Future Internet*, 15(8), 260.

Bao, W., Cao, Y., Yang, Y., Che, H., Huang, J., & Wen, S. (2024). Data-driven stock forecasting models based on neural networks: A review. *Information Fusion*, •••, 102616.

Barbosa-Povoa, A. P., & Pinto, J. M. (2020). Process supply chains: Perspectives from academia and industry. *Computers & Chemical Engineering*, 132, 106606.

Bechtsis, D., Tsolakis, N., Iakovou, E., & Vlachos, D. (2022). Data-driven secure, resilient and sustainable supply chains: Gaps, opportunities, and a new generalised data sharing and data monetisation framework. *International Journal of Production Research*, 60(14), 4397–4417.

Bednarski, L., Roscoe, S., Blome, C., & Schleper, M. C. (2024). Geopolitical disruptions in global supply chains: A state-of-the-art literature review. *Production Planning and Control*, •••, 1–27.

Bharadiya, J. P. (2023). Machine learning and AI in business intelligence: Trends and opportunities. [IJC]. *International Journal of Computer*, 48(1), 123–134.

Borucka, A. (2023). Seasonal methods of demand forecasting in the supply chain as support for the company's sustainable growth. *Sustainability*, 15(9), 7399.

Bousdekis, A., Lepenioti, K., Apostolou, D., & Mentzas, G. (2021). A review of data-driven decision-making methods for industry 4.0 maintenance applications. *Electronics (Basel)*, 10(7), 828.

Brintrup, A., Pak, J., Ratiney, D., Pearce, T., Wichmann, P., Woodall, P., & McFarlane, D. (2020). Supply chain data analytics for predicting supplier disruptions: A case study in complex asset manufacturing. *International Journal of Production Research*, 58(11), 3330–3341.

Caiado, R. G. G., Scavarda, L. F., Gavião, L. O., Ivson, P., de Mattos Nascimento, D. L., & Garza-Reyes, J. A. (2021). A fuzzy rule-based industry 4.0 maturity model for operations and supply chain management. *International Journal of Production Economics*, 231, 107883.

Calleja-Sanz, G., Olivella-Nadal, J., & Solé-Parellada, F. (2020). Technology forecasting: Recent trends and new methods. *Research methodology in management and industrial engineering*, 45-69.

Campbell, C., Sands, S., Ferraro, C., Tsao, H. Y. J., & Mavrommatis, A. (2020). From data to action: How marketers can leverage AI. *Business Horizons*, 63(2), 227–243.

Chase, C. W. (2021). *Consumption-based Forecasting and Planning: Predicting Changing Demand Patterns in the New Digital Economy*. John Wiley & Sons.

Choi, T. Y., Netland, T. H., Sanders, N., Sodhi, M. S., & Wagner, S. M. (2023). Just-in-time for supply chains in turbulent times. *Production and Operations Management*, 32(7), 2331–2340.

Cieżak, W., & Kutyłowska, M. (2023). Application of exponential smoothing method to forecasting daily water consumption in rural areas. *Archives of Civil Engineering*, 69(3).

de Santana Correia, A., & Colombini, E. L. (2022). Attention, please! A survey of neural attention models in deep learning. *Artificial Intelligence Review*, 55(8), 6037–6124.

Devan, M., Shanmugam, L., & Tomar, M. (2021). AI-Powered Data Migration Strategies for Cloud Environments: Techniques, Frameworks, and Real-World Applications. *Australian Journal of Machine Learning Research & Applications*, 1(2), 79–111.

Dhall, D., Kaur, R., & Juneja, M. (2020). Machine learning: a review of the algorithms and its applications. *Proceedings of ICRIC 2019: Recent innovations in computing*, 47-63.

Dominguez, R., Cannella, S., Ponte, B., & Framinan, J. M. (2020). On the dynamics of closed-loop supply chains under remanufacturing lead time variability. *Omega*, 97, 102106.

Essien, A. (2023). AI-Driven Innovation: Leveraging Big Data Analytics for Innovation. In *Innovation Analytics: Tools for Competitive Advantage* (pp. 119-137).

Eyo-Udo, N. (2024). Leveraging artificial intelligence for enhanced supply chain optimization. *Open Access Research Journal of Multidisciplinary Studies, 7*(2), 001-015.

Farahani, M. A., McCormick, M. R., Gianinny, R., Hudacheck, F., Harik, R., Liu, Z., & Wuest, T. (2023). Time-series pattern recognition in Smart Manufacturing Systems: A literature review and ontology. *Journal of Manufacturing Systems*, 69, 208–241.

Feizabadi, J. (2022). Machine learning demand forecasting and supply chain performance. *International Journal of Logistics Research and Applications*, 25(2), 119–142.

Fildes, R., Ma, S., & Kolassa, S. (2022). Retail forecasting: Research and practice. *International Journal of Forecasting*, 38(4), 1283–1318. PMID: 36217499

Friday, D., Ryan, S., Melnyk, S. A., & Proulx, D. (2023). Supply chain deep uncertainties and risks: the 'new normal. In *Supply Chain Risk and Disruption Management: Latest Tools, Techniques and Management Approaches* (pp. 51–72). Springer Nature Singapore.

Ganesh, A. D., & Kalpana, P. (2022). Future of artificial intelligence and its influence on supply chain risk management–A systematic review. *Computers & Industrial Engineering*, 169, 108206.

Garinian, E. O. M., Fierro, T. E. S., Saucedo, J. A. M., & Aguilar, R. R. (2021, October). Machine Learning Applications for Demand Driven in Supply Chain: Literature Review. In *The International Conference on Artificial Intelligence and Applied Mathematics in Engineering* (pp. 763-772). Cham: Springer International Publishing.

Gayam, S. R., Yellu, R. R., & Thuniki, P. (2021). Optimizing supply chain management through artificial Intelligence: Techniques for predictive maintenance, demand forecasting, and inventory optimization. *Journal of AI-Assisted Scientific Discovery*, 1(1), 129–144.

Georginova, T. (2023). Tools to Reduce Vulnerability from Hybrid Threats. In *Ix Scientific-Professional Conference Security and Crisis Management-Theory And Practice (SeCMan)* (pp. 144-151). Regional Association for Security and Crisis Management-RASEC S4 GLOSEC Global Security.

Gil, Y., Garijo, D., Khider, D., Knoblock, C. A., Ratnakar, V., Osorio, M., & Shu, L. (2021). Artificial intelligence for modeling complex systems: Taming the complexity of expert models to improve decision making. *ACM Transactions on Interactive Intelligent Systems*, 11(2), 1–49.

Gonçalves, J. N., Cortez, P., Carvalho, M. S., & Frazao, N. M. (2021). A multivariate approach for multi-step demand forecasting in assembly industries: Empirical evidence from an automotive supply chain. *Decision Support Systems*, 142, 113452.

Goodfellow, I., Pouget-Abadie, J., Mirza, M., Xu, B., Warde-Farley, D., Ozair, S., & Bengio, Y. (2020). Generative adversarial networks. *Communications of the ACM*, 63(11), 139–144.

Goodwin, P., & Fildes, R. (2022). Forecasting with judgment. In *The Palgrave Handbook of Operations Research* (pp. 541–572). Springer International Publishing.

Goyal, M., & Mahmoud, Q. H. (2024). A Systematic Review of Synthetic Data Generation Techniques Using Generative AI. *Electronics (Basel)*, 13(17), 3509.

Grinin, L., Grinin, A., & Korotayev, A. (2021). Global trends and forecasts of the 21st century. *World Futures*, 77(5), 335–370.

Gurzawska, A. (2020). Towards responsible and sustainable supply chains–innovation, multi-stakeholder approach and governance. *Philosophy of Management*, 19(3), 267–295.

Indrawati, H. (2020). Barriers to technological innovations of SMEs: How to solve them? *International Journal of Innovation Science*, 12(5), 545–564.

Ismail, G., & Taliep, N. (2023). The Delphi Method. In *Handbook of Social Sciences and Global Public Health* (pp. 1–19). Springer International Publishing.

Ivanov, D., & Dolgui, A. (2021). A digital supply chain twin for managing the disruption risks and resilience in the era of Industry 4.0. *Production Planning and Control*, 32(9), 775–788.

Jackson, I., Ivanov, D., Dolgui, A., & Namdar, J. (2024). Generative artificial intelligence in supply chain and operations management: A capability-based framework for analysis and implementation. *International Journal of Production Research*, •••, 1–26.

Jaiswal, R., Gupta, S., & Tiwari, A. K. (2023). Dissecting the compensation conundrum: A machine learning-based prognostication of key determinants in a complex labor market. *Management Decision*, 61(8), 2322–2353.

Jauhar, S. K., Jani, S. M., Kamble, S. S., Pratap, S., Belhadi, A., & Gupta, S. (2024). How to use no-code artificial intelligence to predict and minimize the inventory distortions for resilient supply chains. *International Journal of Production Research*, 62(15), 5510–5534.

Jeyaraman, J., Krishnamoorthy, G., Konidena, B. K., & Sistla, S. M. K. (2024). Machine Learning for Demand Forecasting in Manufacturing. *International Journal for Multidisciplinary Research*, 6(1), 1–115.

Johnson, M., & Girard, G. (2024). Empirical Analysis of AI-Driven Systems for Identifying Supply Chain Risks and Strengthening Resilience. *Journal of Environmental Science and Technology*, 3(1), 858–867.

Kanike, U. K. (2023). Factors disrupting supply chain management in manufacturing industries. *Journal of Supply Chain Management Science*, 4(1-2), 1–24.

Kanyepe, , JZizhou, , BAlphaneta, , MChifamba, , N. (2023). Lead-time management, information sharing and performance of the motor industry in Zimbabwe. *European Journal of Management Studies, 28*(3), 229-246. https://doi.org/10.1108/EJMS-06-2023-0044

Khlie, K., Benmamoun, Z., Fethallah, W., & Jebbor, I. (2024). Leveraging variational autoencoders and recurrent neural networks for demand forecasting in supply chain management: A case study. *Journal of Infrastructure. Policy and Development*, 8(8), 6639.

Lazzeri, F. (2020). *Machine learning for time series forecasting with Python*. John Wiley & Sons.

Li, L., Liu, Y., Jin, Y., Cheng, T. E., & Zhang, Q. (2024). Generative AI-enabled supply chain management: A coordination theory perspective. *International Journal of Production Economics*, •••, 109388.

Lv, Z., Qiao, L., Wang, Q., & Piccialli, F. (2020). Advanced machine-learning methods for brain-computer interfacing. *IEEE/ACM Transactions on Computational Biology and Bioinformatics*, 18(5), 1688–1698. PMID: 32750892

Majumder, S., & Dey, N. (2024). Industry 4.0 Challenges and Risks. In *A Notion of Enterprise Risk Management: Enhancing Strategies and Wellbeing Programs* (pp. 81-107). Emerald Publishing Limited.

Modgil, S., Singh, R. K., & Hannibal, C. (2022). Artificial intelligence for supply chain resilience: Learning from Covid-19. *International Journal of Logistics Management*, 33(4), 1246–1268.

Niaz, M., & Nwagwu, U. (2023). Managing Healthcare Product Demand Effectively in The Post-Covid-19 Environment: Navigating Demand Variability and Forecasting Complexities. [AJEMB]. *American Journal of Economic and Management Business*, 2(8), 316–330.

Nikolopoulos, K. (2021). We need to talk about intermittent demand forecasting. *European Journal of Operational Research*, 291(2), 549–559.

Notin, P., Hernández-Lobato, J. M., & Gal, Y. (2021). Improving black-box optimization in VAE latent space using decoder uncertainty. *Advances in Neural Information Processing Systems*, 34, 802–814.

Odulaja, B. A., Oke, T. T., Eleogu, T., Abdul, A. A., & Daraojimba, H. O. (2023). Resilience in the face of uncertainty: A review on the impact of supply chain volatility amid ongoing geopolitical disruptions. *International Journal of Applied Research in Social Sciences*, 5(10), 463–486.

Ofori, F., Maina, E., & Gitonga, R. (2020). Using machine learning algorithms to predict students' performance and improve learning outcome: A literature based review. *Journal of Information Technology*, 4(1), 33–55.

Ojo, B. (2024). Resilience and sustainability of supply chains in the face of natural disasters and climate change. *International Journal of Science and Research Archive*, 12(1), 2996–3007.

Ooi, K. B., Tan, G. W. H., Al-Emran, M., Al-Sharafi, M. A., Capatina, A., Chakraborty, A., & Wong, L. W. (2023). The potential of generative artificial intelligence across disciplines: Perspectives and future directions. *Journal of Computer Information Systems*, •••, 1–32.

Orang, O., de Lima e Silva, P. C., & Guimarães, F. G. (2023). Time series forecasting using fuzzy cognitive maps: A survey. *Artificial Intelligence Review*, 56(8), 7733–7794.

Pasupuleti, V., Thuraka, B., Kodete, C. S., & Malisetty, S. (2024). Enhancing supply chain agility and sustainability through machine learning: Optimization techniques for logistics and inventory management. *Logistics (Basel)*, 8(3), 73.

Patel, S., Patel, U., Nanavati, J., & Patel, A. (2024, February). Analyzing Generative Models for Realistic Data Augmentation across Modalities and Applications. In *2024 11th International Conference on Computing for Sustainable Global Development (INDIACom)* (pp. 1601-1606). IEEE.

Păvăloaia, V. D., & Necula, S. C. (2023). Artificial intelligence as a disruptive technology—A systematic literature review. *Electronics (Basel)*, 12(5), 1102.

Rabbani, M. B. A., Musarat, M. A., Alaloul, W. S., Rabbani, M. S., Maqsoom, A., Ayub, S., & Altaf, M. (2021). A comparison between seasonal autoregressive integrated moving average (SARIMA) and exponential smoothing (ES) based on time series model for forecasting road accidents. *Arabian Journal for Science and Engineering*, 46(11), 11113–11138.

Recio-Román, A., Recio-Menéndez, M., & Román-González, M. V. (2024). The Future of Retail: Harnessing Generative AI for Disruptive Innovation and Sector Transformation. In *Reshaping Marketing Science in Wholesaling and Retailing* (pp. 309–333). IGI Global.

Rehmani, K., Naseem, A., Ahmad, Y., Mirza, M. Z., & Syed, T. H. (2021). Development of a hybrid framework for inventory leanness in Technical Services Organizations. *PLoS One*, 16(2), e0247144. PMID: 33606793

Ren, S., Chan, H. L., & Siqin, T. (2020). Demand forecasting in retail operations for fashionable products: Methods, practices, and real case study. *Annals of Operations Research*, 291, 761–777.

Sarker, I. H. (2021). Machine learning: Algorithms, real-world applications and research directions. *SN Computer Science*, 2(3), 160. PMID: 33778771

Saxena, D., & Cao, J. (2021). Generative adversarial networks (GANs) challenges, solutions, and future directions. *ACM Computing Surveys*, 54(3), 1–42.

Seyedan, M., & Mafakheri, F. (2020). Predictive big data analytics for supply chain demand forecasting: Methods, applications, and research opportunities. *Journal of Big Data*, 7(1), 53.

Sobb, T., Turnbull, B., & Moustafa, N. (2020). Supply chain 4.0: A survey of cyber security challenges, solutions and future directions. *Electronics (Basel)*, 9(11), 1864.

Stefenon, S. F., Seman, L. O., Mariani, V. C., & Coelho, L. D. S. (2023). Aggregating prophet and seasonal trend decomposition for time series forecasting of Italian electricity spot prices. *Energies*, 16(3), 1371.

Suherlan, S., & Okombo, M. O. (2023). Technological innovation in marketing and its effect on consumer behaviour. [TACIT]. *Technology and Society Perspectives*, 1(2), 94–103.

Syntetos, A. A., Babai, Z., Boylan, J. E., Kolassa, S., & Nikolopoulos, K. (2016). Supply chain forecasting: Theory, practice, their gap and the future. *European Journal of Operational Research*, 252(1), 1–26.

Tadayonrad, Y., & Ndiaye, A. B. (2023). A new key performance indicator model for demand forecasting in inventory management considering supply chain reliability and seasonality. *Supply Chain Analytics*, 3, 100026.

Tarigan, Z. J. H., Siagian, H., & Jie, F. (2021). Impact of internal integration, supply chain partnership, supply chain agility, and supply chain resilience on sustainable advantage. *Sustainability*, 13(10), 5460.

Taye, M. M. (2023). Understanding of machine learning with deep learning: Architectures, workflow, applications and future directions. *Computers*, 12(5), 91.

Tuli, F. A., Mohammed, M. A., & Sachani, D. K. (2024). Supply Chain Optimization: Machine Learning Applications in Inventory Management for E-Commerce. *Global Disclosure of Economics and Business*, 13(1), 1–20.

Veluru, C. S. (2024). Investigating the Impact of Artificial Intelligence and Generative AI in E-Commerce and Supply Chain: A Comprehensive. *European Journal of Advances in Engineering and Technology*, 11(4), 131–143.

Wang, X., Hyndman, R. J., Li, F., & Kang, Y. (2023). Forecast combinations: An over 50-year review. *International Journal of Forecasting*, 39(4), 1518–1547.

Yandrapalli, V. (2023). Revolutionizing supply chains using power of generative ai. *International Journal of Research Publication and Reviews*, 4(12), 1556–1562.

Zakhidov, G. (2024). Economic indicators: Tools for analyzing market trends and predicting future performance. *International Multidisciplinary Journal of Universal Scientific Prospectives*, 2(3), 23–29.

Zellner, M., Abbas, A. E., Budescu, D. V., & Galstyan, A. (2021). A survey of human judgement and quantitative forecasting methods. *Royal Society Open Science*, 8(2), 201187. PMID: 33972849

Zhang, B., Zhu, J., & Su, H. (2023). Toward the third generation artificial intelligence. *Science China. Information Sciences*, 66(2), 121101.

Chapter 17
Leveraging Artificial Intelligence and Machine Learning for Closed-Loop Integrated Business Planning

Salim Shaikh
Blue Yonder Inc., USA

Abdullah Shaikh
Lean and Agile, USA

ABSTRACT

Modern supply chains have become increasingly complex due to factors such as mergers, acquisitions, the rise of omnichannel strategies, and market volatility. To effectively serve this diverse customer base and manage various products, markets, and channels profitably, businesses need a closed-loop Integrated Business Planning process wherein diverse internal and external stakeholders—such as sales, marketing, development, operations, sourcing, finance, transportation, warehousing and trading partners—collaborate inside a formalized structure to formulate a cohesive corporate strategy. A closed-loop IBP process can integrate social, news, events, and weather (SNEW) data, demand sensing, and advancements in artificial intelligence (AI) and machine learning (ML). This approach enables companies to gather real-time signals from digital sources, allowing for agile, automated, responsive, and flexible decision-making. By leveraging AI and ML for predictive and prescriptive analytics, organizations can quickly adjust their plans through a continuously adaptive, self-learning IBP process.

DOI: 10.4018/979-8-3693-4433-0.ch017

INTRODUCTION

The supply chains of the 21st century are getting increasingly complex due to a rise in mergers, acquisitions, omni-channel conflicts, direct-to-consumer channels, rapid product configuration proliferation, diminishing product lifecycles, and market volatility. The globalized culture of "Buy anywhere, make anywhere, and sell anywhere" offers advantages: the ability to procure superior raw materials globally, manufacture products in the most economical locations, and distribute products to customers worldwide. However, globalization is associated with some adverse outcomes, such as heightened susceptibility to natural disasters, labor disputes, inflation, tariffs, geopolitical tensions, and trade restrictions. For numerous years, lean manufacturing has been a crucial element in the continuous endeavor to improve the efficiency of supply chain operations.

For decades, the lean strategy—rooted in the 40-year-old Toyota Production System and focused on eliminating waste, reducing costs, and achieving operational excellence—has been instrumental in enhancing supply chain efficiencies. By optimizing traditional supply chains to be as lean as possible, companies were able to deliver goods quickly and economically while minimizing inventory levels, improving operational performance, lowering the cost of goods sold, and maximizing asset utilization. However, the lean approach was initially based on assumptions of stable demand and uninterrupted supply, leading to smooth production and just-in-time deliveries. In today's volatile, uncertain, complex, and ambiguous (VUCA) environment, these assumptions no longer hold true due to unpredictable demand and supply fluctuations

Recent events such as Brexit, tariffs, changes in the North American Free Trade Agreement, and the COVID-19 pandemic have revealed that many supply chains were overly lean and fragile, and thus, lacked the robustness and resilience needed to handle severe disruptions. Simply being lean is no longer viable, as these disruptions have exposed the weaknesses of overly optimized networks in terms of impact, severity, and duration of disruption. At the same time, adding buffer inventory, building excess capacity, or increasing labor to enhance resilience is not sustainable in an environment of shrinking margins and intense competition, where profitability remains crucial.

This requires creating a supply chain that is simultaneously lean, resilient, agile, and responsive, while making sure that it can meet customer demand: proactively identifying issues, remaining robust and resilient in the face of disruptions, responding quickly to market changes, and maintaining efficiency to improve productivity and reduce costs.

The companies that will emerge strongest are those that successfully balance lean principles with resilience in their supply chains. It is not about choosing between being lean or resilient, but rather about shifting the balance, enhancing resiliency while maintaining efficiency.

Moreover, customers increasingly want a personalized and consistent experience across all touchpoints, encompassing retail, mobile, and internet platforms. Organizations require an integrated business planning (IBP) process capable of operating with speed, agility, responsiveness, and flexibility. Utilizing machine learning and artificial intelligence for predictive and prescriptive analytics, thereby facilitating rapid realignment of plans through a continuous closed-loop replanning process. Artificial intelligence and machine learning assist organizations in comprehending the patterns inside data, enabling them to utilize these insights to transform and innovate an organization's demand planning, master planning, inventory planning, transportation management, warehouse management, and IBP processes for competitive advantage. Prescriptive and predictive analytics provide proactive automation and enhancement of future recommendations by utilizing and evaluating the effectiveness of planners' prior activities. Furthermore, enterprises must possess exceptional management capabilities to prioritize their responses to existing and anticipated disruptions according to their severity and impact, while also conducting real-time what-if scenario analyses using insights to better comprehend the associated trade-offs. Real-time collaboration with trading partners will significantly aid firms in addressing exceptions and implementing decisions throughout the supply chain and extended network. Consequently, allowing the IBP process to evaluate previously executed supply chain strategies and data to discern the elements that lead to unsuccessful supply chain operations. This information enables the forecasting of prospective supply chain challenges and allows for the proactive implementation of solutions. This will allow firms to make decisions more rapidly and effectively, leading to enhanced consumer experiences and a substantial competitive advantage in the marketplace.

BACKGROUND

What is Closed-Loop Integrated Business Planning?

IBP entails a closed-loop continuous process wherein diverse internal and external stakeholders—such as sales, marketing, development, operations, sourcing, finance, transportation, warehousing and trading partners—collaborate inside a formalized structure to formulate a cohesive corporate strategy. This strategy harmonizes the perspectives of all functional areas while ensuring alignment with the strategic business plan. The volume, velocity, and frequency of data have significantly increased due to the integration of internet of things (IoT) and big data into supply chains. It is increasingly essential for businesses to visualize, analyze, and respond to information throughout the supply chain in real-time. Companies ought to derive insights from their past experiences to enhance their ability to detect and respond to supply chain threats and opportunities. A closed-loop IBP process can assimilate real-time signals from the digital edge, including social, news, events, and weather (SNEW) data, competitor promotions, as well as data from physical assets such as smartphones, sensors, radars, and satellites. This closed-loop IBP offers predictive visibility to detect or anticipate disruptions prior to their occurrence and utilizes prescriptive analytics to address unpredictability through risk mitigation strategies. If a corporation lacks agility and cannot adapt to supply chain interruptions or fluctuating market conditions, demand will surpass supply, leading to diminished customer service, heightened expediting charges, and higher overtime expenses. Conversely, an excess of supply relative to demand will lead to surplus stocks, product obsolescence, and a decline in prices and sales. Consequently, it is imperative for a company to exert control over and adeptly handle the effects of variability.

Historically, organizations addressed issues arising from siloed planning by allocating additional inventory, capacity, and planners. In the current landscape of diminishing profit margins and fierce competition, where profitability is paramount, this method will no longer be viable. Sabri and Shaikh (2010) articulated the guiding principles of Lean and Agile Value Chain Management (LAVCM) in their book "Lean & Agile Value Chain Management (LAVCM): A Guide to the Next Level of Improvement." Closed-loop IBP leverages these foundational principles and augments them by incorporating real-time signals to deliver predictive visibility through artificial intelligence (AI) and machine learning (ML), enabling the anticipation of disruptions prior to their occurrence. Subsequently, it employs prescriptive analytics to address unpredictability via risk mitigation strategies. Consequently, closed-loop IBP serves as a transformative differentiator that drives growth in revenue and market share.

PRINCIPLES OF CLOSED-LOOP INTEGRATED BUSINESS PLANNING

Principle 1: Prioritize client success. This principle emphasizes the alignment and synchronization of the organization's efforts to meet the client's requirements. This entails shifting from an emphasis on products or channels to prioritizing the primary objective of supply chains: fulfilling customer demand, comprehending the evolving requirements of customers across various markets, enhancing visibility into fluctuating customer demand, and integrating digital data signals into your IBP process to respond more adeptly to the changing needs of customers.

Principle 2: Establish a mutually beneficial and trustworthy environment for all stakeholders. The second guiding principle is to create a reliable environment that serves the interests of all stakeholders. Based on the author's own experience, typically, only a minor fraction of stakeholders concur that their current key performance indicators (KPIs) are fostering the desired behaviors. This is because many organizations utilize measurements that inevitably portray the organization and its personnel in a favorable light. This mostly results from the correlation between the bonuses and promotions of various stakeholders and the outcomes assessed by "feel good" performance indicators. In sales, a prevalent practice termed "sandbagging" involves a sales executive presenting a reduced forecast at the year's end, coinciding with the finalization of the subsequent year's quota, followed by an immediate increase in the forecast at the beginning of the new year to ensure adequate supply to fulfill the quota. IBP is an interdisciplinary technique that drives enterprises to transcend localized, segmented performance indicators. This entails selecting appropriate metrics that pertain to controllable and significant facets of organizational performance, essential for the enterprise's success, while fostering a culture and value system that promotes the integration of metrics into the organization's core structure.

Principle 3: Eradicate waste and minimize non-value-added operations. This idea promotes operational efficiency and lean practices in enterprises by eradicating superfluous tasks, hence reallocating resources to value-added endeavors such as collaboration and the development of hypothetical scenarios for risk reduction. By utilizing technology and standardizing processes, stakeholders can allocate more time to addressing real-world issues, transforming IBP into an executive decision-making process rather than a futile exercise of merely aggregating data from various sources for reporting purposes. This contrasts with the conventional approach, which merely involves aggregating data from many sources and treating it as a reporting task. Technological advancements have reached a stage where machine learning can be employed to automate outcome storage and institutionalize resolution workflows to address widespread and enduring issues.

Principle 4: Institutionalize ongoing enhancement. Establishing a disciplined, systematic, and a repeatable IBP process on a consistent cadence that incentivizes continuous improvement and management by exception, is essential for embedding it into the organization's core identity.

Principle 5: Integrate planning with execution. This approach emphasizes a unified "one-number" strategy that the entire organization endeavors to attain through ongoing closed-loop, vertical integration of strategic, tactical, and operational planning. This integration connects the closed-loop IBP process to annual budgets and everyday sales and operations execution (S&OE) operations. In recent decades, markets have exhibited increased volatility, and supply networks have become more susceptible to risk. The demand for more agility in business is a direct response to the volatility of the global economy.

Machine learning and artificial intelligence technology can be employed to enhance automation and agility, while also mitigating risk through swift prescriptive and predictive what-if scenario analyses. Moreover, companies can enhance their flexibility, agility, and responsiveness by establishing appropriate capacity and inventory buffers and employing multi-sourcing strategies to mitigate the impacts of uncertainty

MATURITY LEVELS

Levels of Maturity

A recent survey on IBP practices was conducted across various industries, encompassing discrete manufacturing (high-tech, semiconductor, automotive, industrial, metals, diversified manufacturing, and aerospace and defense) and process manufacturing (chemical, consumer packaged goods, pharmaceuticals, and food and beverage). Several key findings from the survey indicated that over fifty percent of organizations continued to employ spreadsheet-based technology to manage their IBP processes. Excel-based spreadsheets are effective for data presentation; nevertheless, they lack the capability to handle what-if scenarios, data aggregation, and analysis across many plans. The respondents identified several significant challenges in their current IBP processes, including insufficient technology for comprehensive visibility and transparency, the inability to perform what-if scenario analyses for trade-off exploration or risk mitigation strategy formulation, difficulties in linking plans from various stakeholders, and a lack of executive sponsorship. The respondents said that a significant problem in their present IBP processes is the absence of executive sponsorship. Almost ninety percent of participants recognized attaining effective cross-functional team alignment as a major challenge for their firms. Additional significant functional requirements identified include process orchestration via calendars, plan visibility across diverse stakeholders, and the ability to aggregate and disaggregate data across several hierarchical levels.

Although most firms engage in IBP to some extent, they fail to achieve the maximum potential benefits since they are either functioning at Level 1 or, at best, at Level 2 on the process maturity scale. At the onset of the year, these enterprises often prepare budgets for their anticipated revenue and profit levels. Nonetheless, at a certain juncture within the year, a divergence emerges between these budgets and the actual revenue and profit levels. The predominant inquiry is, “Can we adhere to the budget? How will we compensate for the shortfall?" There remains optimism and assurance that the corporation will realign and bridge the deficit prior to that juncture. Eventually, both reality and anxiety emerge, prompting the inquiry, "How can we reduce expenses to align with our budget?"

Enhancing the existing IBP process and advancing to greater levels of maturity is not a singular occurrence; instead, it is a prolonged endeavor that must be executed over an extended duration. The maturity level of the IBP process inside the organization is often assessed in its current state, revealing any existing deficiencies. Following thorough analysis and evaluation, a strategic improvement plan is established to guide the company through a systematic progression towards advanced phases of "to-be" process maturity, ultimately achieving Level 4, the pinnacle of IBP process maturity and excellence. Organizations seeking to enhance their IBP maturity might utilize the maturity model as a framework to facilitate their progression.

Level 1: Siloed Sales and Operations Planning

At the Siloed S&OP level, the supply chain lacks digital capabilities, hence precluding any enhancement of its end-to-end or functional performance. The situation is marked by several stakeholders functioning in isolation, focused on addressing immediate priorities, engaging in continual crisis management, and reacting impulsively to problems without designated leadership. Each department possesses distinct ad hoc manual processes and individual interpretations of the plan, with choices being made as independent functional units. This leads to numerous actions that do not contribute value, contradicting Principle 3 of the organization (Eliminate waste and decrease non-value-added activities). The sole plan implemented is a quarterly financial review. The S&OP process is beset by challenges due to its reliance on an "over the wall" strategy for communication across the many stages of the S&OP process. Furthermore, there is an absence of consistency in business processes across the organization, resulting in each department employing its own methodology for task completion. This contravenes Principle 4 as it engenders superfluous duplication of effort and results in duplicate tasks. No KPIs have been created at any level, including the departmental level, resulting in a lack of ownership of the strategy, which often culminates in a culture of blaming and finger-pointing.

Level 2: Functional Sales and Operations Planning

Functional S&OP is defined by isolated digital capabilities and a lack of a unified end-to-end supply chain perspective. The prioritization of departmental operating efficiency, objectives, and goals ultimately supersedes customer desires, thus contradicting Principle 1 (Prioritize customer success). The supply chain remains fragmented, resulting in a lack of shared digital demand signals that may facilitate a cohesive supply response. This inhibits the establishment of a coordinated supply response. Analogous to the preceding point, supply signals are not uniformly disseminated across the various functions of the supply chain, leading to a deficiency in end-to-end supply chain visibility. In several instances, enterprises may excel in strategizing their sales, operations, and finances; nonetheless, the challenge is in the disconnection of these planning processes. The final outcome is an abundance of plans categorized into distinct functional domains, each possessing its own narrow performance metrics. This leads to competitive behavior and indecision, where the winner is often the individual who asserts themselves the most. This level emphasizes on short-term objectives, lacking any correlation with the organization's overarching business plan. Rather than focusing on future planning and sustaining long-term perspective, most time and effort is devoted to analyzing previous performance. The distribution of data across many systems has resulted in considerable discrepancies between the aggregate and detailed plans. This violates Principle 3, as it results in an excessive allocation of time to aggregating data from many systems and generating substantive reports, rather than analyzing the data.Despite the organization's considerable efforts and achievement in attaining a demand-supply equilibrium, there is a possibility that it may fail to meet its market goals as outlined in its business plan.

Furthermore, firms functioning at Level 2 employ technology in a limited capacity. Typically, technology consolidates S&OP data from ERP feeds into Excel; however, it lacks the ability to compare various what-if scenarios.

Level 3: Digital Integrated Business Planning

The integration of digital capabilities throughout the supply chain is a hallmark of digital IBP. For example, demand can be detected by demand signals from users' mobile devices, and this information is subsequently disseminated across the supply chain. Furthermore, to effectively respond to or influence demand profitably, it is essential to evaluate cost-service trade-offs along the supply chain. It encompasses a systematic IBP process directed by senior management that transcends departmental barriers and fosters cross-functional alignment in alignment with Principle 1 (Prioritize customer success). This level emphasizes long-term considerations and financial reconciliation throughout all demand and supply activities. Furthermore, there exist documented cross-functional KPIs that fit with the organization's objectives, thereby fulfilling the criteria of Principle 2 - Establish a mutually beneficial and trustworthy environment for all parties. To facilitate the IBP process, firms at Level 3 have proficiently utilized technology to implement dashboards, alerts, exceptions, action items, calendars, and what-if scenarios for swift financial impact analysis. Employing technology to automate procedures aligns with Principle 3 by allowing them to eliminate waste and minimize fruitless exercises. Organizations encountering volatile economic and market conditions find that this IBP maturity level lacks predictive visibility, machine learning, artificial intelligence, automation, flexibility, and responsiveness to adjust plans across the extended enterprise, in response to unforeseen disruptions related to personnel, materials, capacity, or demand, thereby affecting even the most efficient supply chains.

A recent poll of supply chain executives suggested that more than sixty percent of respondents attributed significant interruptions to abrupt market shifts, while over seventy percent identified supply-side concerns as the principal driver of these disruptions. Companies must possess the ability to swiftly collect and understand demand and supply fluctuations, followed by the capacity to promptly evaluate the comprehensive impact of those changes across the whole supply chain.

Level 4: Closed-Loop Integrated Business Planning with Artificial Intelligence and Machine Learning

IBP with artificial intelligence and machine learning represents the pinnacle of process maturity, utilizing the five guiding principles to align and synchronize the entire organization to fulfill client requirements, hence reinforcing Principle 1. The supply chain engages with customers, suppliers, and trading partners to perceive, influence, and react to demand using digital capabilities. At this peak level of maturity, the closed-loop IBP process serves as a crucial link between strategic business planning, tactical planning, and sales and operations execution, underscoring Principle 5 and establishing a closed-loop continuous strategy deployment mechanism. This contrasts with the conventional approach of merely balancing demand, supply, and inventory.

Executive management directs the process and delineates duties and responsibilities clearly and succinctly. There are comprehensive cross-functional and cross-organizational KPIs designed for both internal and external collaboration. These KPIs are intended to incentivize individuals to pursue actions that match with corporate objectives, rather than those that are shortsighted and contradictory to departmental goals, thereby adhering to Principle 2. An individual process owner is accountable and responsible, with metrics embedded in the organization's basis. A goal performance level has been specified for each statistic. This individual meticulously monitors performance relative to the objective, and upon detecting any discrepancy, promptly analyzes the root reason for the divergence and proactively devises a remedy to realign progress. The primary emphasis centers around anticipating future product launches, market trends, competition, and new market opportunities, rather than exclusively reviewing historical budget deviations. Senior management acknowledges and praises managers who utilize significant metrics effectively, conveying this recognition throughout all organizational levels and business facets.

Advancements in technology have significantly improved the ability to swiftly adjust forecasts with actionable insights. For example, when sales and marketing teams plan a new promotion to boost demand, IBP can generate a demand scenario that quickly evaluates supply chain constraints and competing demands. This guided analysis enables better decision-making, optimizing the product mix and timing of the promotion. The outcome is real-time decision-making that enhances revenue, profitability, customer satisfaction, and cost savings by reducing inventory and waste throughout the supply chain. Organizations can further boost team performance and increase productivity through embedded generative AI insights, recommendations, and process automation.

Employing segmentation, grounded in factors such as risk, margins, criticality, revenue, volume, lead times, and life cycle stage, enables the organization to prioritize and allocate resources to essential customers and products, while also informing decisions related to product portfolio management and market entry and exit strategies. The "peanut butter spread" method is avoided in favor of utilizing segmentation. Unsupervised machine learning may be employed in the future to extract insights from unstructured data and autonomously generate clusters that reveal significant patterns within the data. The ability to autonomously segment data utilizing numerous features, rather than merely one or two, constitutes one of the most important use cases of machine learning. This facilitates automation and eradicates several non-value-added operations (consistent with Principle 3), hence liberating stakeholders' time for more value-added endeavors like exception management, collaboration with customers, suppliers, and scenario analysis. The automation and eradication of repetitive operations are facilitated by the extensive application of advanced technologies, including machine learning and artificial intelligence. This approach facilitates faster decision-making by targeting specific areas of the supply network, eliminating the need for unnecessary analysis of the entire system. It improves planner efficiency by prioritizing the most critical and recurring issues, rather than focusing on less important ones.

The closed-loop IBP process can assimilate real-time digital signals from external sources, including CPI, inflation, GDP, interest rates, fuel prices, IHS data, SNEW data, competitor promotions, smartphones, sensors, radars, satellites, and others, to deliver predictive visibility that detects disruptions prior to their occurrence. Furthermore, it can then utilize a prescriptive analysis of this data to alleviate the associated risks.

Machine learning algorithms will analyze this data to understand how the specified parameters interrelate to create a significant probability of supply chain failure. In the near future, this self-learning supply chain will notify a planner that the simultaneous occurrence of specific occurrences signifies a forthcoming risk in the supply chain. In such instances, the machine will either avert failure by repositioning the inventory to a different area or notify the planner to respond to the issue.

Furthermore, social sentiment data from Twitter, Facebook, Instagram, and Google searches is utilized to integrate unstructured data into ideation, new product development, demand sensing, marketing, and crowdsourcing. This facilitates enhanced customer insights, which can subsequently be utilized to recalibrate strategies and respond with agility to customer input. Machine learning can facilitate the comprehension of the underlying patterns in the data, as well as the relationships among such patterns. If an event transpires today, a subsequent event will occur in the future. In the near future, supply networks will be governed by deep learning algorithms. They will examine various combinations of parameters, identify which factors predict service failures, and develop cost-effective risk mitigation solutions to prevent such failures.

Machine learning can be employed to automate the proactive resolution of challenges by evaluating the efficacy of prior outcomes. The ability to schedule and coordinate the process guarantees adherence to procedures and the consistency of procedural steps, instilling structure and discipline within the process. Furthermore, AI/ML technology is employed to produce audit trails of conducted meetings, and summarize meetings together with action items, their assignments, and current statuses. To guarantee transparency and accountability, all assumptions, risks, and opportunities related to the different resolution possibilities have been meticulously documented and monitored. This top-down, middle-out, and bottom-up reconciliation allows diverse stakeholders to contribute inputs at various tiers of the adaptable hierarchy, while concurrently guaranteeing alignment with the broader corporate plan. Closed-loop IBP is an exception-driven S&OP approach that enhances stakeholder efficiency (Principle 3). It enables stakeholders to prioritize exceptions and proactively identify, assess, and rectify discrepancies, emphasizing the plan-do-check-act paradigm for ongoing enhancement. Digital process playbooks and their corresponding lever libraries are now integrally incorporated into the organization's culture. For example, if a discrepancy arises between predicted revenues and actual revenues, the digital process playbook would identify the root causes, which may include competitor actions, macroeconomic trends, or an inappropriate product mix. Considering the discovered root cause, potential resolution strategies may encompass initiating a promotion, introducing a new product, enhancing customer collaboration, augmenting forecast accuracy to optimize product mix, or adjusting pricing. Automation of these pre-defined scenarios, derived from playbooks, enables planners to allocate more time to analyzing the scenarios and selecting the one that most effectively aligns with corporate objectives of maximizing revenue, enhancing margins, minimizing costs, or capturing market share.

Gen AI IBP assistant enhances decision-making by leveraging data to complement human intuition, enabling faster and more informed choices. Users can interact with the assistant using everyday language, and it retrieves data from all relevant and authorized sources. The assistant then presents insights in an easy-to-understand format and suggests next steps, eliminating the need for manual data wrangling, switching between different software, or relying on technical teams to build the framework or views. It also ensures enhanced data security and quality assurance, controlling access based on user roles, permissions, and the supply chain context. Additionally, prompt engineering guarantees the most accurate and relevant insights, responses, and recommendations.

A car manufacturer in an industry characterized by demand fluctuations and extended product lead times has initiated a transformation of its comprehensive supply chain planning processes and technologies to enhance its responsiveness to market changes. This was executed to guarantee that the organization could fulfill the requirements of its consumers. The organization has successfully transitioned from Level 1 (Siloed S&OP) to Level 3 (Digital IBP) and has a roadmap to progress to Level 4 - IBP with artificial intelligence and machine learning. Initially, the organization embarked on digital transformation with proprietary S&OP technologies that significantly constrained its scalability and integration potential, hindering its capacity to sustain a dynamic business environment. Furthermore, it employed a sequential planning method among sales, marketing, supply chain, and manufacturing, resulting in considerable manual ad hoc interventions and inefficient operations. This contravened Principle 3, which asserts that planning should not occur in a sequential manner.

The enterprise has successfully re-engineered its comprehensive planning procedures and tools following its transition to Level 3 (Digital IBP), allowing for more prompt responses to market fluctuations. The organization has enhanced the precision of its forecasts, decreased the time required for planning, and minimized the effort and errors related to the planning process. Technology is being utilized to synchronize supply, demand, and capacity across strategic, tactical, and operational levels, facilitating a continuous and collaborative best-practice process. Technology has been employed to enable quick reaction demand realization simulations and capacity expansion simulations to assess their effects on operational and financial plans. This guarantees that the entire firm can respond swiftly to changing market conditions and undertake suitable actions when required, such as augmenting or reducing capacity.

CONCLUSION

Businesses today adopt a mindset popularized by Amazon, wherein customers expect to receive their products within hours or days in lieu of weeks or months. Customers want swift and rapid responses to their inquiries. A critical differentiator for a company's survival and success is its capacity to foresee and adeptly respond to client wants. Customers anticipate a greater variety of alternatives, increased options, complete product availability, and 24/7 support. A single missing delivery constitutes a performance failure. Businesses must consistently enhance their ability to identify and respond effectively to threats and opportunities. Consequently, IBP has become essential for attaining strategic goals. Big data is seeing exponential expansion in volume, variety, frequency, and pace. This expansion has provided businesses with an unprecedented opportunity to obtain a deeper understanding of their customers. Companies can utilize real-time digital data signals to anticipate disruptions before they occur, subsequently employing prescriptive analytics to manage the associated risks through IBP. This ongoing closed-loop approach unites many internal and external stakeholders formally and systematically. The stakeholders comprise sales, marketing, development, operations, sourcing, finance, and trading partners. A closed-loop IBP process involves sharing demand and supply plans with key stakeholders across the organization. Demand and supply plans spanning long-, medium-, and short-term horizons, can be communicated to Yard Management Systems (YMS), Warehouse Management Systems (WMS), and Transportation Management Systems (TMS). This enhances planning for parts, labor, space, yard management, warehouse storage, handling, and transportation capacity. Additionally, these plans can factor in labor and transportation constraints to create executable supply plans, improving plan adherence, reducing expedited shipping and labor costs, and maximizing on-time, in-full (OTIF) deliveries and employee productivity. Consequently, the corporation may formulate a cohesive strategy that harmonizes the perspectives of various functional areas while assuring alignment with the overarching strategic business plan.

The subsequent five fundamental principles are integrated and augmented by closed-loop IBP: prioritize customer needs, foster a collaborative and trustworthy atmosphere among all stakeholders, eliminate non-value-adding activities, institutionalize a culture of continuous improvement, and complete the cycle of closed-loop planning and execution. The assessment of business processes in their current state is the initial step towards achieving closed-loop IBP. This assessment must delineate the interaction between the organization's processes and technology, as well as highlight the company's current position on the IBP maturity scale. Uncertainty and variability will continue to increase; however, they can be mitigated through responsiveness and agility by exploring diverse "what-if" scenarios (i.e., adjusting critical variables such as volumes, capacity, mix, and price, assessing their effects on bottom-line costs and top-line revenues, and formulating contingency plans). Process playbooks enable a company to analyze and assess various potential strategies, facilitating the development of a cohesive plan that incorporates the perspectives of all functional areas while aligning with the overarching corporate strategy. Process orchestration and playbooks ensure consistent global process compliance and repeatability, even when stakeholders and participants are distributed across various geographies and time zones providing stability and reliability in the most volatile and competitive business environments.

The advancement of artificial intelligence and machine learning enables businesses to forecast events, discern trends and anomalies, analyze correlations among patterns and variables, comprehend the implications of various response strategies, and offer recommendations. Companies now possess enhanced decision support due to their capacity to examine outcomes, including consumer insights and historical behavior, modifying supply parameter settings accordingly. Responses to internal and external perturbations are coordinated across the supply chain rather than being controlled within individual business units. This supersedes the conventional management methodology. Furthermore, the ability to detect fluctuations in demand and supply through data analysis, and subsequently integrate that knowledge into an organization's planning processes, facilitates a more effective alignment with the specific needs of its client base. This allows a business to make decisions more swiftly, efficiently, and profitably, while simultaneously reducing costs and waste throughout the supply chain. Companies can now bypass traditional frameworks and advance directly to predictive and cognitive models that diminish variability and decrease risk, provided their supply chains are supported by digital technology.

Organizations can enhance their IBP capabilities by using real-time simulations of influencing factors in machine learning (ML) models, which draw from a comprehensive list of industry and market-specific variables. By simulating demand drivers in real-time, they can make faster, more informed decisions with actionable insights that improve explainability. Leveraging a blend of statistical methods, AI, and ML algorithms allows organizations to generate highly accurate demand forecasts.

For example, the global automotive industry is undergoing a significant transformation as manufacturers and consumers transition from internal combustion engine (ICE) vehicles to electric vehicles (EVs). While this shift offers substantial environmental benefits, it also introduces challenges and complexities for automotive integrated business planning (IBP) teams. Striking the right product mix across EVs, ICEs, and hybrids—across various regions and channels—is difficult. Additionally, modern consumers increasingly demand personalized products, a trend that will likely continue as smart features, electric powertrains, and hybrid models evolve and multiply.

Automakers face difficulties in predicting which vehicle configurations will match market demand, leading to potential overproduction and the accumulation of unsold inventory. This results in profit-eroding discounts and missed sales opportunities when consumer preferences vary significantly across global markets. OEMs that can accurately predict customer needs and adjust their supply chains accordingly will remain competitive and profitable.

One Japanese automotive OEM is using AI and ML to process large volumes of near real-time demand data, while also incorporating economic indicators such as the Consumer Price Index (CPI), inflation rates, gross domestic product (GDP), interest rates, fuel prices, dealer inventory, competitor pricing, and more. This approach enables them to create highly accurate, granular demand forecasts at the Model Trim Option Color (MTOC) level. These forecasts are dynamic and adapt to market shifts as conditions evolve.

This AI-driven solution helps manage the complexity of demand across all models, channels, and regions, ensuring that the right product is available in the right place at the right time. It simplifies the complex product mix seen in today's global automotive market. Furthermore, the ideal solution would not only utilize advanced AI and data science but also integrate machine learning, cloud computing, and predictive analytics to significantly reduce the time between planning and decision-making from days to mere minutes. By running hundreds of what-if simulations quickly, this powerful solution can predict the impact of real-world demand drivers and autonomously provide optimal recommendations. This enables a new level of decision-making speed, responsiveness, and agility.

Consequently, to thrive in the contemporary global marketplace, marked by heightened market volatility and uncertainty, abbreviated product lifecycles, omnichannel fulfillment, direct-to-consumer channels, and same-day delivery, closed-loop IBP will likely become the most significant facilitator of enterprise excellence. Closed-loop IBP can minimize waste and enhance efficiency while offering flexibility, reactivity, and risk management in reaction to evolving business situations. Initiating a journey towards this form of maturity can positively influence various facets of an organization, yielding advantages such as enhanced forecast precision, optimized asset utilization, augmented supply chain transparency, elevated on-time delivery rates, improved profit margins, decreased expenditures, increased profitability, expedited response times, accelerated time to market, and heightened shareholder value.

REFERENCES

Sabri, E., & Shaikh, S. (2010). *Lean & Agile Value Chain Management (LAVCM): A Guide to the Next Level of Improvement. J.* Ross Publishing.

ADDITIONAL READING

Sabri, E., & Shaikh, S. (2010). *Lean & Agile Value Chain Management (LAVCM): A Guide to the Next Level of Improvement. J.* Ross Publishing.

Shaikh, S., Sabri, E., & Esturi, S. (2017). Making the journey to a multimodal, segmented supply chain. Retrieved from (http://www.supplychainquarterly.com/topics/Strategy/20170626-making-the-journey-to-a-multimodal-segmented-supply-chain/)

Thomas, H. (2018). *Davenport, Rajeev Ronanki*. Artificial Intelligence for the Real World.

KEY TERMS AND DEFINITIONS

Agile: Refers to the methodology that enhances adaptability and reactivity.

Change Management: Involves overseeing individuals, teams, and organizations as they transition from the existing AS-IS state to a prospective TO-BE state.

Closed-Loop Integrated Business Planning: Encompasses a closed-loop, continuous process wherein various internal and external stakeholders—including sales, marketing, development, operations, sourcing, finance, and trading partners—collaborate within a formalized structure to formulate a cohesive corporate strategy. This strategy reconciles the perspectives of all functional areas while ensuring alignment with the overarching strategic business plan. A Closed-Loop Integrated Business Planning process can assimilate real-time signals from the digital edge, including SNEW data and competitor promotions, as well as from physical assets such as smartphones, sensors, radars, and satellites. It offers predictive visibility to detect or anticipate disruptions prior to their occurrence and utilizes prescriptive analytics to navigate unpredictability through risk mitigation strategies.

Lean: Is a methodology focused on the eradication of waste and the enhancement of operational efficiency.

Machine Learning: Is a domain of artificial intelligence that employs statistical methods to discern patterns within data, build correlations among those patterns, and "learn" from data without explicit programming.

Risk Management: Is the process of conducting what-if analyses to facilitate risk mitigation methods aimed at minimizing the impact of adverse events.

Segmentation: Is the process of categorizing the portfolio (product, market, channel, etc.) into clusters based on attributes such as risk, margins, criticality, revenue, volume, lead times, and life cycle stage. This enables the organization to allocate greater emphasis and resources to key customers and products, facilitating decisions regarding product portfolio management and market entry or exit, thereby allowing for differentiated service treatment for specific groups.

SNEW: The capacity to assimilate real-time digital signals from external sources, including SNEW (social, news, events, and weather data), can enhance predictive visibility to anticipate events or disruptions, hence facilitating improved and expedited decision-making.

Chapter 18
Data-Driven Supply Chain Revolution:
Metamorphosize Through Science

Kshitij Mathur
https://orcid.org/0009-0006-4940-3910
Independent Researcher, UK

Satyam Sinha
https://orcid.org/0000-0002-0682-652X
Independent Researcher, India

ABSTRACT

In an era where data is the new oil, supply chains are undergoing a fundamental transformation. The chapter " Data-Driven Supply Chain Revolution: Metamorphosize through Science" aims to provide a deep understanding of the synergy between AI/ML and supply chain management. This chapter will explore the strategies, technologies, and best practices necessary for organizations to harness generative AI and ML for Supply Chain Innovation projects. This chapter starts with the reference of the five core SCM processes of the SCOR model and then elaborates how gen AI and ML solution can address the key challenges in each area. Applying these solutions to Forecasting, Inventory Optimization, Production Planning and Logistics have been shared in detail. An approach to adopt the solution in an organization is explained. Key challenges faced to implement the solution and efficient Change Management approach will be defined.

INTRODUCTION TO AI IN SUPPLY CHAINS

"In God we trust. All others must bring Data." – Dr. W. Edwards Deming

DOI: 10.4018/979-8-3693-4433-0.ch018

The great management guru Peter Drucker once implied (Peter F. Drucker, 1975), "What gets measured gets improved". The secret sauce for Supply Chain transformation is to identify the fundamental block of data, measure it correctly and then extract meaning out of it, to take a vital decision. In an era where data is the new gold, Supply chains are undergoing monumental evolution.

Unlocking the full potential of data-driven insights is the goal of business success. Artificial Intelligence (AI) (including Generative) and Machine Learning (ML), along with Deep Learning Analytics and Cognitive Science, serve as crucial tools in shedding light on the unknown and quantifying the value of benefits. Ensuring that an organization delivers products and services of the right quality, quantity, timing, location, and cost requires both resilience and agility, driven by data & appropriate insights. It is imperative for organizations to integrate business decisions with data and insights effectively.

The main objective of a supply chain is to efficiently and effectively oversee the movement of goods, information, and finances from suppliers to customers with objectives on Customer Satisfaction, Cost Efficiency, Optimisation of resources, Risk management, etc. however, they often get limited due to Complexity in terms of aligning & coordinating global supply chain, Lack of visibility which makes it difficult to track products, manage inventory, and respond to disruptions (Coyle et al., 12th edition, 2024). Other challenges that supply chain faces is with high cost due to transportation, storage, labor, and compliance requirements. Or vulnerability to various disruptions, such as natural disasters, political instability, and supplier failures, which can halt operations.

In the context of generative AI, machine learning (ML), and data science, supply chain models are evolving to become more data-driven, predictive, and adaptive. The models consume historical data and ML algorithms to forecast demand, optimize inventory levels, and predict potential disruptions. Accuracy improvement has many benefits viz; better placement of products, reduce SLOB (slow & obsolete) inventories. Optimization algorithms can transform route planning, warehouse management, and production scheduling bottleneck constraints.

Data science, powered by AI and machine learning, is fundamentally transforming supply chains, ushering in a new era of efficiency, agility, and innovation. Traditionally, supply chains have relied on linear processes, manual oversight, and historical data to drive decision-making. However, the integration of advanced data science techniques has revolutionized how supply chains operate, allowing companies to optimize every aspect of their operations.

One of the most significant impacts of data science is the ability to harness vast amounts of data to make more informed decisions. Machine learning algorithms analyse historical data, real-time inputs, and external factors to predict demand, optimize inventory levels, and streamline logistics. This predictive capability reduces waste, lowers costs, and ensures that products are available when and where they are needed, enhancing overall efficiency.

In today's rapidly evolving business landscape, the integration of AI and ML with supply chain management is essential for companies striving to remain competitive and agile. The torch bearers of the AI story are making huge investments in the fields of AI, both in the solutioning as well as the core hardware like GPU chips. The general market is backing the investment as it is evident by the soaring stock prices of companies who have decided to invest in the AI/ML solution. The leaders of Supply Chain in an organization should be ready to embrace the new AI/ML based solution so that the overall KPIs of the SCM shows progress and the stakeholders get a solid return on investment.

Furthermore, AI-driven analytics provide supply chains with unprecedented agility. By continuously monitoring and analysing data, these systems can quickly identify disruptions or shifts in demand, enabling companies to respond in real-time. This agility is crucial in today's fast-paced, globalized market, where unexpected changes can have significant consequences. With AI and machine learning, supply chains can adapt to new challenges, such as sudden changes in consumer behaviour or disruptions in supply lines, more swiftly and effectively than ever before.

Despite these advancements, the integration of data science into supply chains is not without challenges. Issues such as data quality, privacy concerns, and the need for significant investment in technology and expertise must be carefully managed. However, the benefits far outweigh the challenges, and companies that successfully integrate AI and machine learning into their supply chains are gaining a competitive edge in the marketplace.

In an era where data is the new oil, supply chains are undergoing a fundamental transformation. The chapter" Data-Driven Supply Chain Revolution: Metamorphosize through Science" aims to provide a deep understanding of the synergy between AI/ML and supply chain management. This chapter will explore the strategies, technologies, and best practices necessary for organizations to harness generative AI and ML for Supply Chain Innovation projects. This chapter starts with the reference of the five core SCM processes of the SCOR model and then elaborates how gen AI and ML solution can address the key challenges in each area. Applying these solutions to Forecasting, Inventory Optimization, Production Planning and Logistics have been shared in detail. An approach to adopt the solution in an organization is explained. Key challenges faced to implement the solution and efficient Change Management approach will be defined.

Supply Chain Models

Supply chain models are frameworks or strategies that businesses use to manage the flow of goods, information, and resources from suppliers to customers. These models help companies optimize their operations, reduce costs, and improve efficiency. (Sunil & Peter 2000 ; Martin Christopher, 2000 ; Caro et al., 2015 ; David et al., 2000). Here are some common supply chain models:

1) Continuous Flow Model:

The Continuous Flow supply chain model is a strategy designed for industries with stable and predictable demand. This model emphasizes efficiency, consistency, and smooth operation, making it ideal for sectors where demand remains relatively constant, such as food and beverage, pharmaceuticals, or household goods. The primary goal of the Continuous Flow model is to maintain a steady, uninterrupted flow of products through the supply chain, from raw material procurement to final delivery to the customer.

2) Agile Model:

The Agile supply chain model is a strategic approach designed to thrive in environments characterized by uncertainty, variability, and rapidly changing customer demands. Unlike more traditional supply chain models, which focus on efficiency and cost reduction, the Agile model emphasizes flexibility, responsiveness, and the ability to adapt quickly to changes in the market. This model is particularly well-suited for industries with volatile demand, short product life cycles, and high levels of customization, such as fashion, electronics, and technology.

3) Fast Chain Model:

The Fast Chain supply chain model is a dynamic and responsive approach designed to address the needs of industries with short product life cycles and rapidly changing consumer preferences. This model prioritizes speed and efficiency, enabling companies to bring new products to market quickly and stay ahead of competitors. It is particularly relevant for sectors such as fashion, consumer electronics, and other industries where trends shift frequently, and product innovation is key to maintaining market relevance.

4) Flexible Model:

The Flexible supply chain model is a strategic approach designed to manage and adapt to fluctuating demand, diverse customer requirements, and varying market conditions. This model is characterized by its ability to adjust processes, resources, and strategies in response to changes, making it particularly useful for industries where demand is unpredictable or where products and services need to be tailored to specific customer needs. The Flexible model blends elements of efficiency and responsiveness, aiming to balance stability with adaptability.

5) Custom-Configured Model:

The Custom-Configured supply chain model is designed to address the complexities of industries where products are highly customized or require specific configurations to meet unique customer requirements. Unlike standard supply chain models, which focus on mass production and efficiency, the Custom-Configured model emphasizes flexibility, personalization, and the ability to tailor products to individual specifications. This approach is particularly relevant in sectors such as automotive, aerospace, and high-end electronics, where customization and specific configurations play a critical role in meeting customer expectations.

6) Efficient Chain Model:

The Efficient Chain supply chain model is a strategic approach that emphasizes cost reduction, high-volume production, and streamlined operations. This model is particularly suited for industries where competition is driven primarily by price and where the goal is to achieve the lowest possible costs while maintaining acceptable quality levels. The Efficient Chain model focuses on optimizing each aspect of the supply chain to reduce waste, improve operational efficiency, and maximize economies of scale.

7) Demand-Driven Model:

A Demand-Driven Supply Chain is an operational strategy that focuses on responding to actual customer demand rather than relying solely on forecasts. The model leverages real time data, advance statistical techniques with agile operations on a collaborative platform. By aligning production closely with actual demand, businesses can ensure product availability while minimizing stockouts or overstock situations. The ability to respond swiftly to market changes gives companies a competitive edge, enabling them to capitalize on new opportunities faster than their rivals.

SCOR Model

The Supply Chain Operations Reference (SCOR) model is a comprehensive framework used to evaluate and improve supply chain performance. Developed by the Supply Chain Council (SCC), the SCOR model integrates business processes, metrics, best practices, and technology into a unified structure. It provides organizations with the tools necessary to address, improve, and communicate supply chain management practices within and between all interested parties. (Peter & Robert, 2003; Rolf, 2007)

Key Components of the SCOR Model

1) Plan

It focuses on balancing supply and demand to meet business goals effectively. It encompasses activities such as demand forecasting, inventory planning, and capacity management. By integrating financial objectives with supply chain strategies, the "Plan" phase ensures that resources are optimally allocated to meet customer needs while minimizing costs. Key metrics like forecast accuracy, inventory turns, and capacity utilization are used to measure performance and guide continuous improvement efforts. This strategic alignment enables organizations to anticipate market changes, mitigate risks, and enhance overall operational efficiency.

2) Source

This model will define the procurement of goods and services required for production. This phase involves selecting suppliers, managing vendor relationships, and acquiring necessary materials or services efficiently. Activities include supplier selection, procurement processes, and performance management to ensure high-quality inputs at optimal costs. Key metrics such as supplier lead time, procurement cost per order, and supplier defect rates are used to evaluate sourcing effectiveness. By optimizing these activities, organizations can reduce costs, improve supply chain reliability, and maintain strong supplier partnerships that contribute to overall operational success.

3) Make

It's the transformation of raw materials into finished products through efficient manufacturing processes. This phase includes activities such as production scheduling, manufacturing operations, and quality control to ensure that products meet specified requirements and are produced cost-effectively. Key metrics like manufacturing cycle time, yield rates, and production costs are utilized to measure performance and identify areas for improvement. By optimizing these processes, organizations can achieve higher efficiency, better product quality, and reduced production costs, thereby enhancing overall supply chain performance and customer satisfaction.

4) Deliver

It ensures that the finished products are delivered to customers efficiently and effectively. This phase encompasses activities such as order management, warehousing, and transportation management. Key metrics like on-time delivery rate, order fulfilment cycle time, and shipping costs are used to gauge performance. By optimizing these activities, organizations can enhance customer satisfaction through timely deliveries while minimizing logistics costs. Effective delivery processes also ensure accurate order fulfilment and efficient inventory management, contributing to overall operational success and a competitive edge in the marketplace.

THE EVOLUTION OF DATA-DRIVEN SUPPLY CHAIN:

Historical Perspective

The use of data in supply chains has undergone significant transformation over the decades, evolving from rudimentary record-keeping to sophisticated, real-time analytics. In the early stages of industrialization, supply chain management relied heavily on manual processes and basic data entry methods. Paper-based systems were used for tracking inventory levels, order processing, and shipment details. This approach was labour-intensive and prone to errors, making it difficult to achieve high levels of efficiency and accuracy. (Puneeta et al.,2023)

The Advent of Computerization

The introduction of computers in the mid-20th century marked a pivotal shift in supply chain management. Early computer systems enabled companies to digitize records and automate routine tasks such as inventory management and order processing. Enterprise Resource Planning (ERP) systems emerged in the 1990s, integrating various business functions into a single platform. These systems provided better visibility into operations and facilitated more accurate demand forecasting through historical sales data analysis.

Rise of Advanced Analytics

With the advent of the internet and advancements in data storage technologies in the early 2000s, supply chains began to leverage more complex forms of data analytics. Companies started using predictive analytics to forecast demand more accurately, optimize inventory levels, and improve supplier relationships. Real-time data collection became possible with Radio Frequency Identification (RFID) technology and Internet of Things (IoT) devices, providing granular insights into every aspect of the supply chain.

Big Data and Machine Learning

In recent years, big data analytics and machine learning have revolutionized supply chain management (Nada & John 2019). These technologies enable organizations to analyse vast amounts of structured and unstructured data from multiple sources—such as social media trends, weather patterns, and economic indicators—to make more informed decisions. Machine learning algorithms can identify patterns that humans might miss, allowing for predictive maintenance of equipment, dynamic pricing strategies, and enhanced risk management.

BENEFITS OF AI

The Role Today

Today's data-driven supply chains are characterized by their agility, resilience, and customer-centricity. Advanced analytics platforms provide end-to-end visibility across the entire supply chain network. Real-time tracking systems ensure that any disruptions are quickly identified and mitigated. Moreover, artificial intelligence (AI) is increasingly being used for automated decision-making processes that further enhance efficiency.

The role of data in supply chains has evolved dramatically from basic record-keeping to an integral component driving strategic decision-making. Technological advancements have enabled organizations to harness the power of real-time analytics for improved operational efficiency, risk management, and customer satisfaction. As technology continues to advance—bringing innovations like blockchain for secure transactions or quantum computing for even faster data processing—the future holds immense potential for further enhancing the capabilities of data-driven supply chains.

Harnessing Generative AI and ML for Supply Chain Innovation

As per the Supply Chain Operations Reference (SCOR) model, the supply chain processes are interconnected and must function harmoniously to achieve the supply chain's goals. However, these sub-functions often operate independently in different sectors such as Hi-Tech, Retail, CPG, Manufacturing, Healthcare, etc. Each sub-function focuses on optimizing its local Key Performance Indicators (KPIs) and fails to align with the overall objectives of the organization. This siloed approach hinders the efficiency and effectiveness of the supply chain.

Gen AI/ML Have the Potential to Address Key Challenges in the Plan Function in Several Ways

Demand Forecasting Accuracy: Gen AI/ML algorithms can analyse historical sales data, market trends, and external factors to improve demand forecasting accuracy. By identifying patterns and correlations in large datasets, these algorithms can generate more accurate forecasts, reducing forecasting errors and improving inventory planning.

Inventory Optimization: Gen AI/ML can optimize inventory levels by dynamically adjusting stock levels based on real-time demand signals, lead times, and supply chain constraints. These algorithms can help minimize excess inventory while ensuring product availability, leading to lower carrying costs and reduced stockouts.

Supply Chain Visibility: By leveraging advanced analytics and real-time data integration, Gen AI/ML can enhance supply chain visibility. These algorithms can analyse data from multiple sources, including suppliers, manufacturers, and logistics providers, to provide real-time insights into inventory levels, order status, and production schedules.

Production Scheduling: Gen AI/ML algorithms can optimize production schedules by considering factors such as equipment availability, labour constraints, and production capacity. These algorithms can generate optimal production plans that balance demand requirements with resource constraints, minimizing bottlenecks and maximizing throughput.

Risk Management: Gen AI/ML can improve risk management by analysing historical data and identifying potential risk factors. These algorithms can predict and mitigate supply chain disruptions, such as supplier failures or natural disasters, by providing early warnings and recommending proactive risk mitigation strategies.

Integration and Collaboration: Gen AI/ML can facilitate integration and collaboration across supply chain partners by providing a centralized platform for data sharing and communication. These algorithms can automate routine tasks, streamline processes, and enable real-time collaboration, leading to improved efficiency and responsiveness across the supply chain.

Gen AI/ML Offer Solutions to Key Challenges in the Make Function in the Following Ways

Production Efficiency: Gen AI/ML algorithms can optimize production processes by analysing historical production data, equipment performance, and maintenance records. By identifying inefficiencies and bottlenecks, these algorithms can suggest improvements to enhance production efficiency and reduce downtime.

Quality Control: Gen AI/ML can improve quality control by analysing data from sensors, cameras, and other sources to detect defects and anomalies in real time. These algorithms can identify patterns indicative of quality issues and trigger alerts or automatic adjustments to maintain product quality standards.

Predictive Maintenance: Gen AI/ML algorithms can predict equipment failures and maintenance needs by analysing sensor data, historical maintenance records, and environmental factors. By predicting when equipment is likely to fail, these algorithms can schedule preventive maintenance activities to minimize downtime and extend equipment lifespan.

Supply Chain Integration: Gen AI/ML can facilitate integration between the Make function and other supply chain processes by providing real-time visibility and data sharing capabilities. These algorithms can analyse production data in conjunction with demand forecasts, inventory levels, and supplier performance metrics to optimize production scheduling and resource allocation.

Product Customization: Gen AI/ML can enable mass customization by analysing customer preferences, market trends, and production capabilities to generate personalized product configurations. These algorithms can optimize production processes to accommodate varying customer demands while minimizing costs and lead times.

Sustainability and Environmental Impact: Gen AI/ML can help reduce the environmental impact of production processes by optimizing resource usage, minimizing waste, and identifying opportunities for energy efficiency improvements. These algorithms can analyse production data to identify areas for optimization and recommend sustainable practices to reduce carbon emissions (Scope 1/2/3) and minimize environmental footprint.

Computer Vision to identify defects: Computer vision technology can be utilized in discrete manufacturing to identify defects in products during the production process. By employing advanced algorithms and image processing techniques, computer vision systems can analyse images of manufactured parts or products to detect any abnormalities or deviations from quality standards.

Gen AI/ML Can Address Key Challenges in the Deliver and Return Functions in the Following Ways

Logistics Optimization: Gen AI/ML algorithms can optimize delivery routes, transportation modes, and warehouse operations to improve efficiency and reduce costs. By analysing historical data, traffic patterns, and customer preferences, these algorithms can identify the most cost-effective and timely delivery options.

Real-Time Tracking and Visibility: Gen AI/ML can provide real-time tracking and visibility into shipment status, inventory levels, and order fulfilment. By analysing sensor data, RFID tags, and other sources of information, these algorithms can provide timely updates and alerts to customers and supply chain partners.

Return Management: Gen AI/ML can improve return management processes by analysing customer feedback, product reviews, and return patterns to identify the root causes of returns and reduce return rates. These algorithms can recommend preventive measures, such as product improvements or better packaging, to minimize returns and improve customer satisfaction.

Fraud Detection: Gen AI/ML can detect fraudulent activities in the delivery and return process, such as theft, counterfeiting, or false claims. By analysing transaction data, customer behaviour, and historical patterns, these algorithms can identify suspicious activities and trigger alerts for further investigation.

CHALLENGES OF USING AI

Challenges for Gen AI/ML in Supply Chain

Data Quality and Availability: Gen AI/ML algorithms require large volumes of high-quality data for training and validation. However, supply chain data often suffers from inconsistencies, inaccuracies, and incompleteness, making it challenging to obtain reliable insights.

Data Integration and Compatibility: Supply chain data is typically fragmented across multiple systems and sources, including ERP, CRM, WMS, and IoT devices. Integrating and harmonizing these disparate data sets to feed into Gen AI/ML models can be complex and time-consuming.

Scalability and Performance: Gen AI/ML models need to handle large-scale, real-time data streams from across the supply chain. Ensuring the scalability and performance of these models to process and analyse data in a timely manner can be challenging, particularly as data volumes continue to grow.

Interpretability: Gen AI/ML models often operate as "black boxes," making it difficult for users to understand how they arrive at their predictions or recommendations. Enhancing the interpretability and explanation of these models is crucial for gaining trust and acceptance among supply chain stakeholders.

Overfitting, Bias and Hallucination: Gen AI/ML models may suffer from overfitting, where they perform well on training data but fail to generalize to unseen data. Additionally, biases inherent in the data used to train the models can lead to biased predictions or recommendations, perpetuating existing inequalities or inefficiencies in the supply chain.

Change Management and Adoption: Implementing Gen AI/ML technologies requires organizational change and buy-in from stakeholders at all levels. Resistance to change, lack of awareness or understanding, and cultural barriers can hinder the adoption and successful deployment of these technologies in the supply chain.

Security and Privacy Concerns: Gen AI/ML applications in the supply chain raise security and privacy concerns related to the handling and sharing of sensitive data. Ensuring data confidentiality, integrity, and compliance with regulatory requirements is essential to mitigate these risks.

High costs of implementing AI: Implementing AI solutions often demands significant financial investment in infrastructure such as acquisition of advanced software, cloud storage and computing resources. Companies need to hire skilled professionals such as data scientists, machine learning engineers and IT specialists to develop and maintain these systems which increases the budget. For smaller companies or those with limited financial resources these expenses can be overwhelming potentially delaying or even preventing the adoption of AI altogether.

Change Management: Employees may fear that automation and machine learning systems will replace their roles leading to job insecurity during introduction of AI into the workplace. This fear can result in a lack of cooperation, low morale or even active pushback against AI initiatives. Even though the job losses are not a concern they may feel overwhelmed by the prospect of learning and adapting to new technologies particularly if they lack prior experience with advanced systems. Employees who have been following traditional processes for years may struggle to adapt to AI-driven workflows or feel intimidated by the advanced technologies. They may view AI as overly complex or alien creating a sense of insecurity and reluctance to engage with the systems. This hesitation can slow down the integration of AI causing inefficiencies and delays in achieving the desired results which poses a significant barrier to fully realizing the potential of AI in an organization

The Danger of Over-Reliance on AI and ML Insights

While the benefits of AI and ML in the supply chain are undeniable, there is a growing risk that companies may over-rely on these systems, treating their insights as infallible and acting on them without human validation. This blind dependence can lead to flawed decisions for several reasons:

Data Quality Issues: AI and ML models are only as good as the data they are trained on. If the underlying data is incomplete, outdated, or biased, the insights generated by these systems will be flawed. For example, a demand forecasting model trained on historical sales data may fail to account for sudden market shifts or unforeseen events like natural disasters or global pandemics, leading to incorrect predictions.

Complexity of Real-World Scenarios: The real world is often more complex than the data models can capture. (Puneeta et al.,2023). AI and ML algorithms excel at recognizing patterns and making predictions based on past data, but they struggle with unprecedented events or nuanced decision-making scenarios that require judgment, creativity, or ethical considerations. In situations where variables are rapidly changing or where human values play a key role, relying purely on machine-generated insights can result in suboptimal or even harmful outcomes.

Lack of Contextual Understanding: AI lacks the ability to fully understand the broader business context or industry-specific nuances that humans can interpret based on experience. A machine learning model may recommend switching suppliers based on cost efficiency, but human expertise is needed to evaluate factors like long-term relationships, supplier reliability, or potential quality issues that the model may not have considered.

Overconfidence in Automation: Over-reliance on AI can create a false sense of security, leading to a diminished role for human judgment. Supply chain managers may overlook potential issues, trusting that the algorithms have accounted for every possible scenario. This overconfidence in automated systems can exacerbate the impact of AI failures, especially in high-stakes environments where errors can lead to significant operational disruptions or financial losses.

CONSTITUENTS OF AI

What are the Key Components of a Data-Driven Supply Chain

The foundation block to enable a strong data driven strategy starts with Data. For a Supply chain system from Plan to Deliver, various stages, processes, physical machines, IT systems generate various kinds of Data. This goldmine can be exploited by aid of Artificial Intelligence/Machine Learning analytics to provide the best-in-class solution. It is important to secure the system, applications, data and insights from vulnerabilities of the world. Therefore, Cyber security plays a vital role.

Figure 1. Data mines available to AI learning

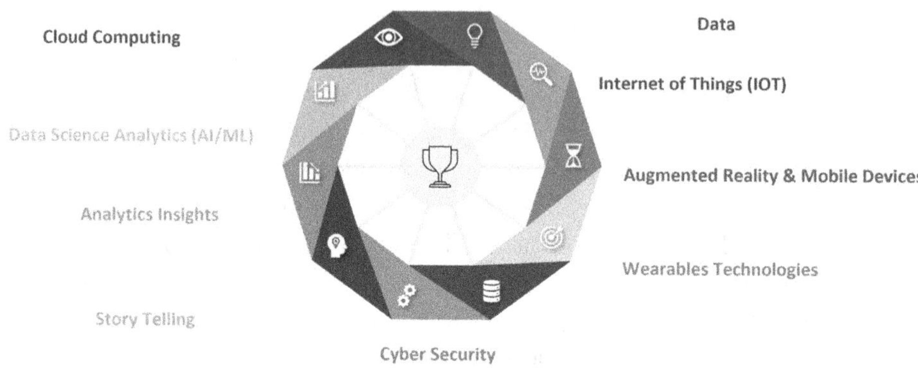

Data is found in both Structural & Un-structural form. Collection of information which can be presented in the form of matrices with column & rows are called as Structural data. Video, Audio, Images are the form of Unstructured data.

Devices viz; RFID (Radio Frequency Identifier), GPS tracker, temperature sensors are kinds of Internet of Things (IOT). These devices generate structured & unstructured data sets, which can be beneficial to safe driving, fleet monitoring, vehicle health.

Augmented Reality supplements the surrounding by including a digital layer to the real environment through a digital solution. It generates unstructured dataset. Consider a situation where an operator in Warehouse wants to collect data from labels. The operator can use AR specific glasses to read that data. On the contrary, an environment is curated for simulation in the digital landscape is termed as Virtual Reality.

Data is stored either on Premise or on cloud.

The next step post data collection is to evaluate the meaning of it to solve core business challenges of Supply chain. That's where Statistics, Data Science, Artificial Intelligence comes handy.

Data Science/Machine Learning Algorithm Tree

During World War 2 at Bletchley Park, Milton Keynes, UK, Alan Turing built a machine to perform computation exercises to break the configurational setting of Enigma machine. The machine was capable to execute instructions on the available information to derive the string of desired outputs. It's an initial machine which leveraged algorithms to achieve the results. Turing machine is considered the ideal model of a computer to leverage Statistical & Mathematical algorithms.

Machine learning algorithms are a subset of artificial intelligence, that enable systems to learn from data and improve their performance over time without being explicitly programmed. (Vadim, 2024; Peter, 2012; Pedro, 2015). In supply chain management, ML algorithms analyse vast amounts of data to identify patterns, make predictions, and optimize processes. There are different categorisations of Machine Learning algorithm, each for specific purpose.

Figure 2. Machine Learning Algorithms

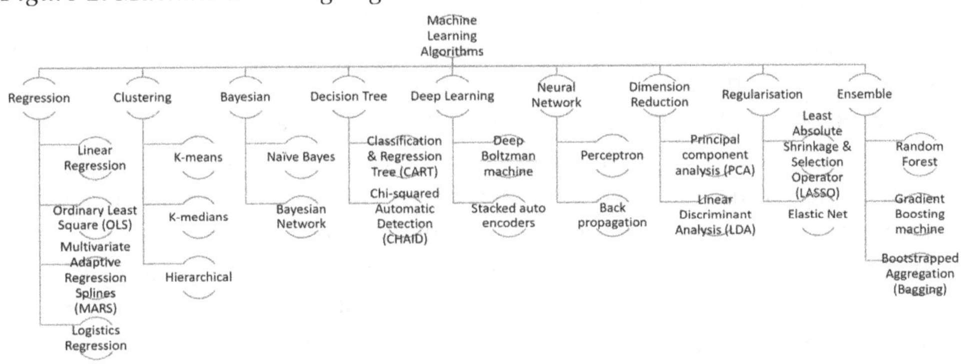

Regression algorithms are used to predict continuous numerical values based on input data. The objective is to identify a relationship between input (independent) variables (features) and target (dependent). It is high importance in the use cases to predict future demand based on historical sales/volume/seasonality/marketing efforts/ economic indicators pattern. This helps businesses optimize inventory levels, reduce overstock or stockouts, and adjust production schedules to meet anticipated demand.

Clustering is a type of machine learning algorithm used for grouping similar data points into clusters based on their features. It is an unsupervised learning method, meaning it works without predefined labels, and is commonly applied in various supply chain tasks. For example, in demand segmentation, clustering algorithms can group customers or products with similar purchasing patterns, allowing for more targeted inventory management and marketing strategies. In logistics, clustering helps in optimizing delivery routes by grouping nearby locations, reducing transportation costs and improving efficiency. Using algorithms like k-means clustering, the analyst can group customers based on similarities in purchasing behaviour, location, or order frequency. The algorithm can analyse customer data and identify distinct clusters, such as high-frequency buyers, seasonal purchasers, or price-sensitive customers. By clustering customers into these segments, supply chain managers can tailor inventory levels, optimize delivery routes, and personalize marketing strategies for each group.

Bayesian machine learning algorithms in supply chain management is risk assessment and decision-making under uncertainty. Bayesian networks can be used to model complex dependencies and probabilities across different supply chain factors, such as supplier reliability, transportation delays, and fluctuating demand. For instance, a company could apply Bayesian inference to update the probability of a supplier delivering late based on past performance, current market conditions, or geopolitical risks. This allows businesses to dynamically adjust inventory levels, choose alternative suppliers, or reroute shipments based on real-time risk assessments. By continuously updating predictions as new data becomes available, Bayesian algorithms help make more informed, probabilistic decisions, reducing supply chain disruptions.

Decision tree algorithm used for both classification and regression tasks, it models decisions and their possible consequences as a tree-like structure of choices. At each "node" of the tree, a question or condition about the data is posed, leading to different branches that represent possible outcomes or decisions. This process continues until a final decision or prediction is made at the "leaf" nodes. Decision trees are highly interpretable, as each branch represents a clear decision path based on specific input variables, making them useful for understanding how decisions are made from data. They can be applied to inventory management, supplier selection, and demand forecasting. For example, a decision tree can help optimize inventory restocking decisions by analysing variables such as demand patterns, lead times, and holding costs. Based on these inputs, the decision tree can recommend whether to reorder a product, how much stock to hold, or when to expect shortages. Similarly, decision trees can evaluate potential supplier risks by considering factors like pricing, reliability, and delivery times, aiding in supplier selection or diversification strategies.

Deep learning utilizes neural networks with multiple layers to analyse complex datasets. Unlike traditional machine learning algorithms that require feature extraction by humans, deep learning models can automatically discover representations needed for classification or prediction tasks from raw data. This capability makes deep learning particularly powerful for handling large volumes of unstructured data like images and text. They can be used for advanced applications such as image recognition for quality control, natural language processing for customer service automation, and predictive maintenance by analysing sensor data from machinery. Their application has revolutionized supply chain by enhancing efficiency, reducing costs, and improving decision-making processes. Predictive analytics powered by these technologies enables more accurate demand forecasting, helping companies maintain optimal inventory levels and reduce stockouts or overstock situations. In logistics, machine learning algorithms optimize routing plans to minimize delivery times and fuel consumption. Deep learning applications further extend capabilities; for instance, computer vision systems inspect products on production lines for defects in real-time, while advanced NLP models analyse customer feedback to improve service quality.

Inspired by the human brain's structure, neural networks consist of interconnected nodes or "neurons" that work together to process information. They have ability to model complex patterns and relationships within data. At its core, a neural network consists of an input layer, one or more hidden layers, and an output layer. Each layer comprises neurons that are connected by weighted edges. The weights adjust as the network learns from data during training, enabling it to make accurate predictions or classifications. Activation functions introduce non-linearity into the model, allowing it to capture intricate patterns in the data. The training process involves feeding input data through the network while adjusting weights based on errors between predicted and actual outcomes. Techniques such as backpropagation optimize these weights iteratively by minimizing a loss function. This iterative learning enables neural networks to generalize from training data to unseen scenarios effectively. Neural networks play a crucial role in predictive maintenance—a proactive approach to equipment upkeep that minimizes downtime and extends machinery life. Sensor data from manufacturing equipment or transportation vehicles are used upon which neural networks applied to predict potential failures before occurrence. These models identify patterns of wear & tear or breakdowns, allowing for timely interventions that prevent costly disruptions in production or logistics operations. Inventory optimization is another use case where neural networks has an edge, consuming various data sources such as sales history, supplier lead times, production schedules, and external factors like weather conditions or economic indicators—neural networks can provide real-time insights into optimal inventory levels across multiple locations. Generative Adversarial Networks (GANs) are a class of neural networks used for generating realistic scenarios based on existing data distributions. GANs can simulate various "what-if" scenarios—such as changes in demand patterns due to market shifts or disruptions caused by natural disasters to prepare proactive contingency plans. Another class is where agents learn optimal actions through trial-and-error interactions with an environment. It is termed as Reinforcement learning, which has huge application in Route Planning by dynamic adaptation of routing strategies based on real-time traffic conditions. These algorithms also optimize picking paths within warehouses by continuously improving upon previous experiences.

With the abundance of data pointers due to scaled storage & compute set up. It's too difficult to separate right set of data pointers from the noise to arrive at the most appropriate desired outcome. Dimensionality reduction algorithms offer a solution by simplifying datasets without losing critical information. It has techniques which reduces the number of input variables or features in a dataset while retaining its essential characteristics. The primary goals are to simplify models, enhance computational efficiency, and mitigate issues like overfitting. Principal Component Analysis (PCA) transforms original variables into a new set of uncorrelated variables called principal components. These components capture the maximum variance in the data, making it easier to identify underlying patterns. t-Distributed Stochastic Neighbour Embedding (t-SNE) is a non-linear technique particularly effective for visualizing high-dimensional data in lower dimensions (e.g., 2D or 3D). It preserves local structure while revealing clusters or groupings within the data. Linear Discriminant Analysis (LDA) is used for both dimensionality reduction and classification tasks by maximizing class separability. It projects data onto a lower-dimensional space where classes are most distinguishable. Autoencoders are neural network-based models that learn efficient coding for input data through unsupervised learning. They compress data into a lower-dimensional representation before reconstructing it back to its original form. Accurate demand forecasting is crucial for optimizing inventory levels and meeting customer expectations. It can be influenced by numerous factors such as market trends, seasonal variations, promotions, and economic indicators, resulting in high-dimensional datasets. PCA can reduce dimensionality to focus on key factors driving demand fluctuations while discarding irrelevant noise. Hidden patterns or anomalies affecting future demand predictions can be identified by visualizing historical sales data using t-SNE. Inventory management requires balancing stock levels across multiple locations based on various influencing factors. LDA can be used to better classify products based on their turnover rates or demand variability to facilitate targeted inventory strategies for the specific product categories. Autoencoders help compress multi-location inventory datasets into lower dimensions—allowing real-time monitoring & optimization decisions without compromising accuracy.

Regularization is a technique used to prevent overfitting, improve model generalization, and enhance predictive performance. It involves adding a penalty term to the loss function, which constrains the model's complexity by discouraging overly complex or large coefficients. It aims to strike a balance between fitting the training data well and maintaining simplicity to generalize better on unseen data. Overfitting occurs when a model captures noise or random fluctuations in the training data rather than underlying patterns, leading to poor performance on new data. Regularization addresses this issue by introducing additional constraints that penalize excessive complexity. L1 regularization (Lasso) adds the absolute values of coefficients as a penalty term to the loss function. It can drive some coefficients to zero, effectively performing feature selection by eliminating less important variables. L2 Regularization (Ridge) adds the squared values of coefficients as a penalty term. Unlike L1, it does not eliminate features but shrinks their values, reducing variance without necessarily setting them to zero. Elastic Net combines both L1 and L2 penalties, offering a balanced approach that leverages the strengths of both techniques. It is particularly useful when dealing with highly correlated features. Dropout is commonly used in neural networks where randomly selected neurons are ignored during training iterations. This prevents co-adaptation among neurons and enhances model robustness. Every supply chain practitioner wish to have resilient robust supply chains amidst uncertainties and disruptions such as natural disasters, geopolitical events, pandemics and identify risks to mitigate them. Lasso/Ridge/Elastic Net combined approaches enable comprehensive risk assessments integrating diverse risk-related parameters providing holistic views enabling proactive contingency planning minimizing potential adverse impacts safeguarding continuity operations. It has emerged indispensable tools via transforming traditional supply chain practices into highly efficient systems which are capable to handle complexities which are inherent in today's globalized and interconnected marketplaces. From enhancing demand forecasting accuracy to optimizing inventories and evaluating supplier performances by facilitating real-time decision-making to have robust risk management strategies and innovative applications. Advanced techniques can be leveraged for better efficiencies to drive sustainable growth in the competitive world.

Ensemble algorithms combine multiple machine learning models to achieve better predictive or prescriptive performance than any single model. The combined effort of the model improves the power of system. Ensemble methods are meta-algorithms that combine several base models to produce one optimal predictive model. The primary objective is to reduce errors by leveraging the strengths of different models while mitigating their weaknesses. Bagging (Bootstrap Aggregating) algorithm involves training multiple versions of a model on different subsets of the training data and then averaging their predictions, example is Random Forests. Boosting sequentially applies weak learners to re-weighted versions of the data, focusing more on instances that previous models misclassified. Gradient Boosting Machines (GBM), AdaBoost are the examples. Stacking involves training a meta-model to combine the predictions of several base models. Examples to include, leveraging logistic regression as a meta-model over decision trees, SVMs. Voting combines predictions from multiple models through majority voting or weighted averaging, such as combining predictions from logistic regression, decision trees, and neural networks. High-quality standards should be followed throughout the production processes which necessitates continuous monitoring and detecting potential defects much in advance. Ensembles models facilitate real-time defect detection and diverse anomaly detection mechanisms, examples include but not limited to combining convolutional neural networks (CNNs) with support vector machines (SVMs) to identify defects during assembly line inspection.

Tech Architecture for the Implementation

Figure 3. Tech Landscape

To successfully implement a data-driven supply chain, it's advised to adopt a robust technology architecture that incorporates scalable computation, efficient data storage, powerful machine learning frameworks, and intuitive visual tools. (Raman, 2023; Katherine et al., 2022; Emmanuel, 2020). In the above architecture design, data is generated from multiple systems/sources which is moved to a central location at nucleus where it's stored. Multi-layer data cleanup process is formalised at the nucleus to arrive at the meaningful data sets. Varied machine learning algorithms are applied at computation phase to generate Predictive & Prescriptive results via insights/dashboards.

The cornerstone of a data-driven supply chain is efficient and scalable data storage architecture. With data flowing from multiple sources like IoT devices, ERP systems, and customer interactions, it is essential to centralize and store this information in a manner that supports both real-time and batch processing. Cloud-based solutions such as Amazon S3, Azure Data Lake, and Google Cloud Storage offer scalable and cost-effective storage for vast amounts of structured and unstructured data. These platforms can store everything from raw sensor data to customer purchase histories, providing a unified repository for all supply chain data. Structured data are stored in cloud-based data warehouses such as Amazon Redshift, Azure Synapse Analytics, and Google BigQuery. They support high-performance querying and analytics to conduct historical analysis, track KPIs, and report on supply chain metrics in near real-time. By integrating both data lakes and warehouses, we can manage raw, unprocessed data alongside refined, ready-to-use data for analytics and machine learning. Tools like Apache Kafka, AWS Glue, or Azure Data Factory are key components for the data pipelines. These systems automate the extraction, transformation, and loading (ETL) processes, ensuring that data is consistently prepared and ready for machine learning models or business intelligence systems.

Complex calculations performed using algorithms and data analytics has a dependency on flexible computational architecture. The system should be flexible enough to manage the demand of high computation and balance it in real time with batch processing executions. It is supplied by elasticity provided by the cloud platforms. Services like AWS Lambda, Google Cloud Functions, and Azure Functions allow to process data in real-time without needing to manage physical servers. For example, real-time shipment tracking can leverage these serverless architectures to process incoming IoT data and immediately notify users of potential delays. Tools such as Apache Spark and Databricks offer distributed computing capabilities, allowing companies to process massive datasets quickly. Databricks, which integrates seamlessly with platforms like AWS, GCP, and Azure, provides an environment where businesses can run machine learning algorithms, build data pipelines, and conduct large-scale data analysis in a collaborative, cloud-native manner. With the ability to process petabytes of data, these platforms enable real-time insights and rapid decision-making across the supply chain. Machine learning services like Amazon SageMaker, Azure Machine Learning, and Google AI Platform offer managed infrastructure to train, deploy, and manage machine learning models. These platforms provide scalable environments for running complex ML algorithms, enabling companies to perform demand forecasting, inventory optimization, and predictive maintenance on a large scale. They simplify the development process by offering built-in tools for model training, hyperparameter tuning, and deployment.

Main component of data-driven supply chain is the skillset to extract insights from data through machine learning algorithms. Python provides the flexibility to leverage algorithms, libraries and tools to derive meaningful values from the dataset. It is widely used for data science and machine learning applications due to its agility and simplicity. Libraries such as TensorFlow, PyTorch, scikit-learn, and XGBoost offer pre-built algorithms for tasks like demand forecasting, supply chain optimization, and anomaly detection. Python's extensive support for data manipulation (via Pandas), visualization (via Matplotlib and Seaborn), and deep learning makes it ideal for implementing machine learning models that can analyze complex supply chain data. After building machine learning models, the next step involves training and deploying them in production. Cloud platforms like AWS, Azure, and GCP provide managed services that simplify this process. For instance, Amazon SageMaker or Azure ML supports end-to-end workflows for training models on large datasets and deploying them for real-time inference in production environments. This is critical for applications like real-time demand forecasting, where predictions need to be made rapidly based on up-to-date data. To make machine learning more accessible, platforms offer AutoML services, such as Google AutoML and Azure AutoML, which automatically build and optimize machine learning models without needing deep expertise. This is particularly useful in supply chain applications where teams may not have dedicated data scientists but still need to leverage machine learning for decision-making.

Once machine learning models and advanced analytics processes are in place, it is critical to present these insights in an accessible format. Visual tools that offer real-time dashboards and interactive reports are essential for driving data-driven decision-making across the supply chain. Platforms like Tableau, Power BI, and Google Data Studio provide powerful visualization capabilities, allowing supply chain managers to create real-time dashboards that monitor inventory levels, transportation metrics, and supplier performance. These tools connect seamlessly with cloud data sources and machine learning outputs, offering rich, interactive visuals that translate complex data into actionable insights. Customized dashboards can be developed using Python frameworks such as Dash and Plotly. These enable supply chain analyst to build tailored dashboards and visualization tools that integrate directly with machine learning models. This is particularly valuable for supply chain teams that need to monitor specific KPIs or access real-time forecasts, route optimization suggestions, and risk alerts.

The use of cloud platforms like Azure, Google Cloud Platform (GCP), and Amazon Web Services (AWS) is critical to the scalability and flexibility of the data-driven supply chain. These platforms provide a range of services that support data storage, machine learning, computation, and visualization. Microsoft Azure provides a comprehensive ecosystem for supply chain solutions, including Azure Synapse Analytics for big data processing, Azure Machine Learning for model training, and Power BI for visualization. It also offers strong integration with Microsoft ERP and CRM systems, making it a popular choice for businesses already embedded in the Microsoft ecosystem. Google Cloud Platform (GCP) is known for its advanced AI capabilities, including Google AI Platform and BigQuery for large-scale data processing and machine learning. GCP's AutoML features enable easy deployment of machine learning models, while tools like Google Data Studio offer seamless data visualization options. Its strength lies in its ease of use and powerful AI-driven services. Amazon Web Services (AWS) is one of the most versatile cloud platforms, offering a wide range of services like Amazon SageMaker for machine learning, Redshift for data warehousing, and Kinesis for real-time data processing. AWS's vast toolset is ideal for managing highly scalable and complex supply chains that require significant customization and advanced features.

Modus Operandi or Framework for Adoption of Gen AI/ML in SCM

Business Context & Assessment: Conduct a comprehensive assessment of the organization's supply chain processes, challenges, and opportunities. Identify areas where Gen AI/ML can add value and reduce risk of the organisation.

Data Collection and Preparation: Gather relevant data from internal and external sources, including historical sales data, inventory records, supplier performance metrics, and market trends. Cleanse, preprocess, and format the data to ensure accuracy and consistency for analysis.

Technology Evaluation: Evaluate available Gen AI/ML technologies and solutions to determine the most suitable options for the organization's needs and objectives. Consider factors such as scalability, interoperability, ease of integration, and cost-effectiveness.

Pilot Testing: Conduct pilot tests or proof-of-concept projects to validate the feasibility and effectiveness of Gen AI/ML applications in specific supply chain processes. Define clear success criteria and metrics to measure the impact of the pilot projects on key performance indicators (KPIs).

Model Development and Training: Develop and train Gen AI/ML models using the collected data to address specific supply chain challenges. Choose appropriate algorithms, techniques, and frameworks based on the nature of the data and the desired outcomes. A trial for Fitment of Algorithm should be followed.

Model selection follows the below stepwise process.

- Gen AI/ML Foundation: A rich data fabric layer that helps to prepare and govern high quality data for AI that can be trusted.
- Augmented Gen AI/ML: A full range of AI driven Business Intelligence (BI) capabilities including Large Language Models (LLM) for Natural Language processing to enable proactive Analytics solutions.
- Self-service Gen AI/ML: An environment to create unlimited AI/ML experiments through a simple yet powerful experiences.

Integration and Deployment: Integrate Gen AI/ML models into existing SCM systems and workflows. Ensure seamless communication and interoperability between Gen AI/ML applications and other supply chain technologies and platforms.

Monitoring and Optimization: Continuously monitor the performance of Gen AI/ML models and algorithms to ensure accuracy, reliability, and effectiveness. Regularly update and refine the models based on new data and insights to optimize their performance over time.

Change Management and Training: Provide training and support to supply chain professionals and stakeholders to familiarize them with Gen AI/ML technologies and processes. Foster a culture of innovation and continuous improvement to encourage adoption and utilization of Gen AI/ML capabilities.

Evaluation and Iteration: Regularly evaluate the impact of Gen AI/ML adoption on supply chain performance, efficiency, and outcomes. Identify areas for improvement and optimization and iterate on the implementation strategy to maximize the value of Gen AI/ML in SCM.

The Human Element: Combining AI/ML With Expertise

To mitigate the risks of over-reliance on AI and ML, supply chain practitioners must maintain a balance between leveraging the power of these technologies and applying human judgment. Here are key strategies for integrating AI with human expertise.

Human-in-the-Loop Systems: One approach is to implement human-in-the-loop (HITL) systems, where AI generates insights, but human decision-makers review, validate, and adjust those insights before taking action. For example, in demand forecasting, AI can provide baseline predictions, but supply chain managers can review those forecasts in light of market knowledge, emerging trends, or one-time events that the model may not have captured.

Contextualizing AI Insights: While AI can highlight patterns and recommend actions, human experts must interpret these findings within the larger business context. Humans bring the ability to assess broader market conditions, company goals, and customer preferences, ensuring that AI-driven decisions align with strategic objectives.

Continuous Monitoring and Model Updating: AI and ML models should not be static. They need continuous monitoring and updating to remain effective. Human experts play a crucial role in identifying when models are underperforming, assessing when data quality issues arise, and determining when new factors need to be incorporated into the models. Regular audits and updates ensure that AI systems evolve as business needs and external conditions change.

Collaboration between Data Scientists and Business Leaders: Effective AI implementation in the supply chain requires close collaboration between data scientists who build the algorithms and business leaders who understand the operational needs. Data scientists can fine-tune models based on feedback from supply chain managers, ensuring that AI insights are not only accurate but also actionable and relevant to specific business challenges.

Scenario Planning and Simulations: AI can be used to run what-if simulations, generating various scenarios based on different inputs. While these simulations offer valuable insights into possible future outcomes, it is the human decision-makers who must weigh the trade-offs, assess risks, and choose the most appropriate course of action. Scenario planning with human oversight ensures that supply chain decisions are well-rounded and consider multiple perspectives.

EXAMPLES OF AI IN ACTION

Case Study: Safety Stock (Inventories) Estimation in CPG Industries Using AI/ML Model

For any Consumer-Packaged Goods (CPG) industries there are 2 kinds of Inventories viz: Cycle Stock and Safety Stock. Cycle Stock is used on a regular basis for their Production of Finished (or Semi-finished) goods. Safety Stock is leveraged during unforeseen events or uncertainty. This case study guides users in terms of balancing Safety Stocks estimation using 3 different kinds of approaches. The first is to Calculate Safety Stocks based on Industry proven Key Performance Indicators KPIs (e.g., Days Coverage and Service Level) and later mentions Prediction of Safety Stocks. Multiple models are simulated for Prediction. But optimal results are obtained from Extreme Gradient Boosting Algorithm. The final model is ensembled for both Calculated and Predicted parts, based on varied weights. This Safety Stock estimated provided better results for the Organization as compared to the initial frequent Stock Out scenarios.

Manufacturing organization's Finances are directly associated with their Production and Sale of Finished (or Semi-finished) goods. In Supply Chain, Product moves from Supplier to Consumer and Money travels vice versa. Hence to be successful, the organization need to streamline their Products in Markets at the optimal rate. Therefore, it is very important for any Integrated Supply Chain unit to efficiently manage their Production of the goods.

In order to produce a single Product (SKU), various sub-assemblies/components or raw materials are used. This is called Bill of Material. Organizations invest in Procuring/Holding/Transport/etc. of sub- assemblies/components or raw materials under the constraints of Financial Budgets. Therefore, they want to Optimize their Inventories.

Generally, there are 2 kinds of Inventories viz: Cycle Stock and Safety Stock. Cycle Stock is used on a regular basis for Production of Finished (or Semi-finished) goods. Safety Stock is leveraged during unforeseen events or uncertainty.

This case study presents a methodology for Safety Stock Estimation of the individual items used in production of the finished goods. The approach is divided into 2 sub parts. The first part is to Calculate Safety Stock using Days Coverage and Service Level metric. Minimum units of Safety Stocks are to be maintained so that there is no stock out situation till new replenishments arrives within their Lead Time. The second part highlights the Predicting of Safety Stocks under similar conditions. Simulations is performed using various Machine Learning Algorithms. The best result is obtained using the Extreme Gradient Boosting Algorithm. An ensemble model is formed for both the parts with differentiative weights to arrive at an optimal estimation of Safety Stocks at every individual (leaf level Bill of Material) items., incorporating the applicable criteria that follow.

Safety Stock Calculation: Using Day's Coverage

Model Formulation

Let 'Coverage' (Day's Coverage) > 0 represents the period when the Plant can run without stock out and considering arrival lead time of the item. It is calculated as below.

$$\text{Coverage} = (\text{OH} + \text{MP}) / \text{D} \qquad (1)$$

Where,

OH = On Hands Inventory
MP = Make Plan for that period
D = Demand for that period
Coverage = Day's Supply Available

As per defined KPI, Coverage is calculated for different combinations of Suppliers-Categories-etc.

Also, the Average Demand is calculated for that period. Safety Stock is Calculated based on the below conditions.

When Coverage $\leq$ Comp_LT

Safety Stock

$$= ((Comp\_LT - Coverage) \times Avg\_Demand)) \quad (2)$$

When Coverage > Comp_LT

$$Safety\ Stock = (Avg\_Demand) \quad (3)$$

Where,

Comp_LT = Component Lead Time

Avg_Demand = Mean Demand

Results:

It has been observed that for a few cases, Coverage is not sufficient as compared to Component Lead Time.

Reference to Table 1, it is inferred that only 20% of the cases have sufficient Coverage for Stocks.

Table 1. Safety Stock Calculation based on Coverage

Supplier	Supplier Status	Category	Comp	Comp_LT	Critical	Period	OH	Making plan	Demand	Coverage
Supplier 1	Key	Cat 1	2302	20	No	01-01-2017	147967	0	634834	0.23
Supplier 1	Key	Cat 1	2302	20	No	01-02-2017	1546684	2672884	1590050	2.65
Supplier 1	Key	Cat 1	2302	20	No	01-03-2017	782801	0	763883	1.02
Supplier 1	Key	Cat 1	2302	20	No	01-04-2017	1383806	711698	170195	12.31
Supplier 1	Key	Cat 1	2302	20	No	01-05-2017	569525	0	435885	1.31
Supplier 2	Key	Cat 1	2302	10	Yes	01-06-2017	842303	0	472229	1.78
Supplier 2	Key	Cat 1	2302	10	Yes	01-07-2017	1460461	1296354	405418	6.8
Supplier 2	Key	Cat 1	2302	10	Yes	01-08-2017	1314532	162044	307973	4.79
Supplier 2	Key	Cat 1	2302	10	Yes	01-09-2017	449189	472133	136040	6.77
Supplier 2	Key	Cat 1	2302	10	Yes	01-10-2017	273394	0	84230.3	3.25
Supplier 3	Key	Cat 1	2302	10	Yes	01-11-2017	842303	0	275681.5	3.06
Supplier 3	Key	Cat 1	2302	10	Yes	01-12-2017	1460461	1296354	147657.6	18.67
Supplier 3	Key	Cat 1	2302	10	Yes	01-01-2018	1314532	162044	92132.2	16.03
Supplier 3	Key	Cat 1	2302	10	Yes	01-02-2018	449189	472133	27339.4	33.7
Supplier 3	Key	Cat 1	2302	10	Yes	01-03-2018	273394	0	146168	1.87

Reference to Table. 2, Safety Stocks are calculated considering difference between Coverage and Component Lead Time. It also displays Safety Stock defined by Business team (SS_BusinessDef). It is interesting to note that Business defined Safety Stock is much lesser as compared to minimum requirement.

Table 2. Safety Stock Calculation based Using Coverage

Avg_Demand	SS_BusinessDef	SS_Calculation
379314.4	12768	7497877.46
379314.4	12768	6579688.9
379314.4	12768	7197579.66
379314.4	12768	2916028.34
379314.4	12768	7090677.84
379314.4	12768	3116570.44
379314.4	12768	1213831.72
379314.4	12768	1974521.78
379314.4	12768	1224262.04
379314.4	12768	2561968.51
379314.4	12768	2634206.4
379314.4	12768	379314.4
379314.4	12768	379314.4
379314.4	12768	379314.4
379314.4	12768	3083670.78

Safety Stock Calculation – using Level of Service (Confidence Intervals):

Model Formulation:

Another methodology to define Safety Stocks is by using Confidence Intervals (CI)..

From a set of sample data, the estimated range of values being calculated, followed by a confidence interval being formed. This is likely to include a population parameter which is unknown. The general notation for the parameter in question is θ, this is parameter is the population mean μ, that is estimated through the sample mean $\bar{x}$.

The level CI of a confidence interval gives the probability that the interval produced by the method employed includes the true value of the parameter θ.

Let us define critical variables for computation of Safety Stocks as per the table below.

Reference to Table. 3, we will calculate the combined standard deviation of Lead Time and Demand by using the expression below.

$$Sc = \sqrt{((t * Sd2) + (d2 * St2))} \qquad (4)$$

Desired Service Level (CI) will vary as per the choice of Business from 80% to 99%. Service Factor (k) will be determined based on CI, as per the table below. Please note, it is calculated based on Z Scores from Normal Distribution (Lisa, 2011).

Table 3. Critical variables declaration

Particulars	Indicator
Safety Stock	SS
Service Factor	k
Combined standard deviation of lead time and demand	Sc
Average Replenishment Lead Time	t
Standard Deviation of Demand	Sd
Average Demand	d
Standard Deviation of Replenishment Cycle	St
Desired Service Level (Confidence Level)	CI

The last step is to calculate Safety stock in conjunction with Service Factor (k) as per below expression.

$$SS = (k * Sc) \quad (5)$$

Reference to Table.4, for this paper Confidence Interval is assumed at 90%. Hence, Service Factor (k) taken under consideration is 1.64 for computation of Safety Stocks.

Table 4. Service factor (k) determination based on CI

Level of Significance	Confidence Interval%	Service Factor (k)
0.80	80.00	1.282
0.85	85.00	1.44
0.90	90.00	1.645
0.95	95.00	1.96
0.99	99.00	2.576
0.995	99.50	2.807
0.999	99.90	3.291

Results:

As per equation (4), it is interesting to observe for Combined Standard deviation of Demand and Lead Time. An important point to be noted is that even the calculation of Safety Stocks using 90% Confidence Interval is much higher than the Business defined level. It clearly shows the benefit of Scientific methodology being applied for Safety Stock estimation.

However, Mean Safety Stock Calculation using Level of Significance varies as against the methodology of using Day's Coverage differ by 16%.

Reference to Table. 5 in conjunction to Table.1 and Table.2, Safety Stock Estimation can be compared from both computation methodology.

Table 5. Safety Stock Calculation Based Using Service Levels

Avg_Demand	Std_Demand	Avg_Comp_LT	Std_Comp_LT	Comb_Std_LT_Dem	SS_BusinessDef	SS_Calc	SS_Calc_CI
379314.4	383994.64	13.33	4.71	2272299.58	12768	7497877.46	3737932.81
379314.4	383994.64	13.33	4.71	2272299.58	12768	6579688.9	3737932.81
379314.4	383994.64	13.33	4.71	2272299.58	12768	7197579.66	3737932.81
379314.4	383994.64	13.33	4.71	2272299.58	12768	2916028.34	3737932.81
379314.4	383994.64	13.33	4.71	2272299.58	12768	7090677.84	3737932.81
379314.4	383994.64	13.33	4.71	2272299.58	12768	3116570.44	3737932.81
379314.4	383994.64	13.33	4.71	2272299.58	12768	1213831.72	3737932.81
379314.4	383994.64	13.33	4.71	2272299.58	12768	1974521.78	3737932.81
379314.4	383994.64	13.33	4.71	2272299.58	12768	1224262.04	3737932.81
379314.4	383994.64	13.33	4.71	2272299.58	12768	2561968.51	3737932.81
379314.4	383994.64	13.33	4.71	2272299.58	12768	2634206.4	3737932.81
379314.4	383994.64	13.33	4.71	2272299.58	12768	379314.4	3737932.81
379314.4	383994.64	13.33	4.71	2272299.58	12768	379314.4	3737932.81
379314.4	383994.64	13.33	4.71	2272299.58	12768	379314.4	3737932.81
379314.4	383994.64	13.33	4.71	2272299.58	12768	3083670.78	3737932.81

Safety Stock Prediction

Model Formulation

A numerical feature matrix as input is required for many statistical learning algorithms. The feature engineering is needed to encode the different categories into a suitable feature vector for categorical variables are present in the data. One simple and widely used encoding method i.e. hot encoding method [1,3,6,10,32, 29,30]. For example, the 3-dimensional feature vectors: [1, 0, 0], [0,1, 0], [0, 0, 1] represents a variable categorically. A variable having as categories female, male, other can be encoded respectively. In the resulting vector space, each category is orthogonal and equidistant to the others, which agrees with classical intuitions about nominal categorical variables.

As a pre activity for Data harmonization, one hot encoding is performed. Features are differentiated for Categorical compared to Continuous. Leveraging the technique supports building Predictive models in terms of numbers rather than of string values.

Input data is transformed in prescribed format using One hot encoding technique to arrive in ready data set for Prediction problem.

Post data stabilization phase, Prediction model is built using XgBoost Algorithm.

Extreme Gradient Boosting (XgBoost) initiated as a research project by (Tian-qi Chen, 2016), is an optimized distributed gradient boosting Tree Algorithm. It implements machine learning algorithms under the Gradient Boosting framework.

(Cheng Li, 2014) considering exposition of gradient boosting, like other boosting methods, Gradient Boosting combines weak "learners" into a single strong learner in an iterative fashion.

It is easiest to explain in the least-squares regression setting, where the goal is to "teach" a model F to predict values of the form $\hat{y}$=F(x) by minimizing the mean squared error where i indexes over some training set of size n of actual values of the output variable y.

Indexes over some training set of size n of actual values of y.

At each stage m, $1 \leq m \leq M$, of gradient boosting, it may be assumed that there is some imperfect model Fm (at the outset, a very weak model that just predicts the mean y in the training set could be used). The gradient boosting algorithm improves on F_m by constructing a new model that adds an estimator h to provide a better model:

$$F_{m+1}(x) = F_m(x) + h(x) \qquad (6)$$

To find h, the gradient boosting solution starts with the observation that a perfect h would imply.

$$F_{m+1}(x) = F_m(x) + h(x) = y \qquad (7)$$

$$h(x) = y - F_m(x) \qquad (8)$$

Therefore, gradient boosting will fit h to the residual y - F_m (x). As in other boosting variants, each F_{m+1} attempts to correct the errors of its predecessor F_m. A generalization of this idea to loss functions other than squared error, and to classification and ranking problems, follows from the observation that residuals.

y - F (x) for a given model are the negative gradients (with respect to F (x)) of the squared error loss function 1 (y F (x))^2. So, gradient boosting is a gradient descent algorithm, and generalizing it entails "plugging in" a different loss and its gradient.

Set (x_i, y_i) is a sample training set, where x_i = Rn is the input space (with multiple features), and y_i is the output value. The goal is to find an approximation F^(x) to a function F (x) that minimizes the expected value of some specified loss function L(y, F (x)).

$$F\hat{} = \arg\min Ex,y[L(y, F(x))] \qquad (9)$$

The gradient boosting method assumes a real-valued y and seeks an approximation F^(x) in the form of a weighted sum of functions hi(x) from some class , called base (or weak) learners.

$$\widehat{F}(x) = \sum_{i=1}^{M} \gamma_i h_i(x) + const \qquad (10)$$

In accordance with the empirical risk minimization principle, the method tries to find an approximation F^(x) that minimizes the average value of the loss function on the training set, i.e., minimizes the empirical risk. It does so by starting with a model, consisting of a constant function F0(x), and incrementally expands it in a greedy fashion.

$$F_0(x) = \arg\min_{\gamma} \sum_{i=1}^{n} L(\gamma_i, \gamma) \tag{11}$$

$$F_m(x) = F_{m-1}(x) + \arg\min_{h_m \in H} \left[\sum_{i=1}^{n} L(y_i, F_{m-1}(x_i) + h_m(x_i)) \right] \tag{12}$$

where hm ϵ is a base learner function.

Choosing the best function h at each step for an arbitrary loss function L is a computationally infeasible optimization problem in general. Therefore, we restrict our approach to a simplified version of the problem. The idea is to apply the steepest descent step to this minimization problem. If we considered the continuous case, i.e. where is the set of arbitrary differentiable functions on R, we would update the model in accordance with the following equations.

$$F_m(x) = F_{m-1}(x) - \gamma_m \sum \nabla_{F_{m-1}} L(y_i, F_{m-1}(x_i)) \tag{13}$$

$$\gamma_m = \arg\min_{\gamma} \sum_{i=1}^{n} L\left(y_i, F_{m-1}(x_i) - \gamma \nabla_{F_{m-1}} L(y_i, F_{m-1}(x_i))\right) \tag{14}$$

where the derivatives are taken with respect to the functions Fi for i ϵ {1, .., m }. In the discrete case however, i.e. when the set is finite, we choose the candidate function h closest to the gradient of L for which the coefficient γ may then be calculated with the aid of line search on the above equations.

This approach is a heuristic and therefore doesn't yield an exact solution to the given problem, but rather an approximation.

In pseudocode, the generic gradient boosting method is best described in (Friedman, 1999; Hastie et al., 2009).

Input: training set {(xi, yi)}n, a differentiable loss function L(y, F (x)), number of iterations M

Algorithm:

Step 1) Initialize model with a constant value.

$$F_0(x) = \arg\min_{\gamma} \sum_{i=1}^{n} L(y_i, \gamma) \tag{15}$$

Step 2) For m = 1 to M, Compute so-called pseudo-residuals

$$\gamma_{im} = -\left[\frac{\partial L(y_i, F(x_i))}{\partial F(x_i)}\right]_{F(x)=F_{m-1}(x)} \tag{16}$$

Fit a base learner (e.g. tree) $h_m(x)$ to pseudo-residuals, i.e. train it using the training set $\{(x_i, r_{im})\}^{n}_{i=1}$

Compute multiplier γ_m by solving the following one- dimensional optimization problem.

$$\gamma_m = \arg\min_{\gamma} \sum_{i=1}^{n} L(y_i, F_{m-1}(x_i) + \gamma h_m(x_i)) \tag{17}$$

Update the model.

$$F_m(x) = F_{m-1}(x) + \gamma_m h_m(x) \tag{18}$$

Table 6. Safety Stock Estimation, Prediction and Actuals

Period	SS_BusinessDef	SS_Calc	SS_Calc_CI	SS_Pred	Safety_Stocks
01-01-2017	12768	7497877.46	3737932.81	2235488.628	5581326.498
01-02-2017	12768	6579688.9	3737932.81	1975335.201	4975726.94
01-03-2017	12768	7197579.66	3737932.81	2150404.251	5379946.594
01-04-2017	12768	2916028.34	3737932.81	937298.0436	3076418.549
01-05-2017	12768	7090677.84	3737932.81	2120115.402	5308996.651
01-06-2017	12768	3116570.44	3737932.81	994118.3038	3143663.385
01-07-2017	12768	1213831.72	3737932.81	455008.9995	2894991.299
01-08-2017	12768	1974521.78	3737932.81	670537.8523	2870205.335
01-09-2017	12768	1224262.04	3737932.81	457964.2584	2893031.401
01-10-2017	12768	2561968.51	3737932.81	836981.0905	2975579.597
01-11-2017	12768	2634206.4	3737932.81	857448.4922	2994140.725
01-12-2017	12768	379314.4	3737932.81	218562.4267	3266700.3
01-01-2018	12768	379314.4	3737932.81	218562.4267	3266700.3
01-02-2018	12768	379314.4	3737932.81	218562.4267	3266700.3
01-03-2018	12768	3083670.78	3737932.81	984796.7354	3132172.418

Step 3) Output F_m (x)

Results:

Table 6. represents the forecast outcome for Safety stocks. Leveraging all the models, a final ensemble model is developed for Safety Stocks. This model performs Weighted Average Computation to arrive at the outcome.

Figure 4. Graphical Representation of Safety Stock Comparison

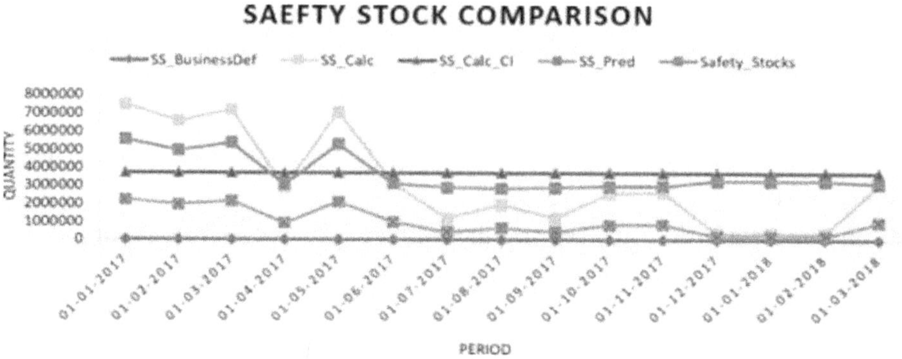

Reference to Fig. 1, based on consolidated model of Safety Stocks, Integrated Supply Chain team can leverage this model in contrast to their existing models. It has been observed that with dynamic calculation using both methodologies and forecasts, Stock out situations can be averted.

Software and Hardware

The routines were implemented in Python programming language, using various Machine Learning modules viz; SVM, Scikit-learn, etc. Computer specifications used to execute the algorithm and generate the learning models were comparable to industry standards. Once constructed, each optimized model performs the prediction quickly, promptly allowing the analysis and parameter testing in the design cycles.

Conclusion for Case Study

Integrated Supply Chain team mostly suffers from Stock out scenarios of Materials (Raw/Semi-finished/Finished). From the above experiment, the ensembled model of Heuristic and Prediction provides a better result as compared to the existing process.

FUTURE TRENDS

Tomorrow's Digital Supply Chain

The future of the Digital Supply Chain involves continued advancements in technology, data analytics, and automation to further enhance efficiency, agility, and resilience across supply chain operations. Tomorrow's Digital Supply Chain is characterized by several key trends. (Amit et al., 2020; Bart & Dmitry, 2022; Stephen & Yingli, 2022; Sengun & Steven, 2024)

Integration of Emerging Technologies: Tomorrow's Digital Supply Chain will leverage emerging technologies such as Gen Artificial Intelligence (AI), Machine Learning (ML), Internet of Things (IoT), Blockchain, and Robotics to enable real-time visibility, predictive analytics, and autonomous decision-making.

Predictive and Prescriptive Analytics: Advanced data analytics capabilities will enable organizations to predict demand fluctuations, anticipate supply chain disruptions, and prescribe optimal actions to mitigate risks and capitalize on opportunities.

End-to-End Visibility: Enhanced connectivity and data sharing among supply chain partners will enable end-to-end visibility across the entire supply chain, from raw material sourcing to final product delivery. This visibility will enable faster response times, better inventory management, and improved customer service.

Supply Chain Digitization: Paper-based processes will be replaced by digital workflows and electronic documentation, streamlining communication, collaboration, and transaction processing among supply chain stakeholders.

Sustainability and Circular Economy: Tomorrow's Digital Supply Chain will prioritize sustainability and environmental responsibility, with organizations adopting circular economy principles to minimize waste, reduce carbon emissions, and optimize resource usage.

Agile and Adaptive Operations: Agile supply chain strategies and flexible operating models will enable organizations to quickly respond to changing market dynamics, customer preferences, and regulatory requirements.

Supply Chain Resilience: Building resilience into the supply chain will be a top priority, with organizations diversifying sourcing strategies, increasing inventory buffers, and implementing risk mitigation measures to withstand disruptions such as natural disasters, geopolitical instability, and pandemics.

Customer-Centricity: Tomorrow's Digital Supply Chain will focus on delivering personalized experiences and tailored solutions to meet the evolving needs and expectations of customers. Customer-centricity will drive innovation and differentiation in supply chain strategies and processes.

CONCLUSION

The advent of data-driven technologies in blend with AI has profoundly transformed the supply chain landscape while creating a revolution that empowers businesses to operate with unprecedented efficiency, agility, and precision. This metamorphosis driven by advancements in data science/ artificial intelligence (AI) and machine learning (ML) marks a paradigm shift in how supply chains are managed and optimized. The essence of the data-driven supply chain lies in leveraging vast amounts of data to predict trends, manage risks and optimize operations in real time. By utilizing predictive analytics, the business can forecast demand with greater accuracy and reducing waste while ensuring timely delivery of goods. Similarly, AI-powered tools streamline processes such as inventory management, route optimization, and supplier collaboration driving down costs while enhancing service levels. This revolution extends beyond operational improvements to foster strategic advantages. Companies that embrace a data-driven approach gain deeper insights into consumer behaviour enabling the customization of products and services to meet evolving customer needs.

However, the journey toward a data-driven supply chain is not without challenges. The need for robust data infrastructure, skilled personnel, and secure data-sharing frameworks is paramount. Organizations must also address issues of data privacy and ethical considerations ensuring that the adoption of these technologies aligns with regulatory standards and societal values.

In summary, the data-driven supply chain represents a metamorphosis powered by science and technology. It offers unparalleled opportunities for innovation, efficiency, and sustainability. Businesses that harness this revolution stand to gain a significant competitive edge, ensuring resilience and growth in an increasingly complex global market. As we look to the future, the fusion of data science with supply chain management will continue to redefine the industry shaping a smarter more connected world.

"Data-Driven Supply Chain Revolution: Metamorphosize through Science" will be an essential resource for anyone looking to navigate the complexities of integrating AI/ML based solutions in their digital supply chain solution. By offering a holistic perspective on digital transformation in the supply chain, this chapter will equip its readers with the knowledge and tools they need to adopt AI/ML solution in their Supply Chain journey.

REFERENCES

Al-Khedhairi, A., & Tadj, L. (2007). Optimal control of a production inventory system with Weibull distributed deterioration. *Applied Mathematical Sciences*, 1(35), 1703–1714.

Bolstorff, P., & Rosenbaum, R. G. (2007). Supply chain excellence: a handbook for dramatic improvement using the SCOR model. AMACOM/American Management Association.

Caro, F., & Martínez-de-Albéniz, V. (2015). Fast Fashion: Business Model Overview and Research Opportunities. In Agrawal, N., & Smith, S. (Eds.), *Retail Supply Chain Management. International Series in Operations Research & Management Science* (Vol. 223). Springer., DOI: 10.1007/978-1-4899-7562-1_9

Cerda, P., Varoquaux, G., & Kégl, B. (2018). Similarity encoding for learning with dirty categorical variables. *Machine Learning*, 107(8), 1477–1494.

Chand, M., Jain, V., & Ajmera, P. (Eds.). (2023). *Data-Driven technologies and artificial intelligence in supply chain: Tools and Techniques*. CRC Press.

Chen, T. (2016). XGBoost: A Scalable Tree Boosting System. DOI: 10.1145/2939672.2939785

Cheng, L. (2014). A gentle introduction to gradient boosting.

Chopra, S., & Meindl, P. (2001). Strategy, planning, and operation. *Supply Chain Management*, 15(5), 71–85.

Domingos, P. (2015). *The Master Algorithm*. How the Quest for the Ultimate Learning Machine Will Remake Our World.

Drucker, P. (2012). *The practice of management*. Routledge.

Flach, P. (2012). *Machine learning: the art and science of algorithms that make sense of data*. Cambridge university press.

Friedman, J. H. (February 1999). "Greedy Function Approximation: A Gradient Boosting Machine

Hastie, T., Tibshirani, R., & Friedman, J. H. (2009). *"10. Boosting and Additive Trees". The Elements of Statistical Learning* (2nd ed.). Springer. DOI: 10.1007/978-0-387-84858-7

MacCarthy, B. L., & Ivanov, D. (Eds.). (2022). *The digital supply chain*. Elsevier.

Pettit, S., & Wang, Y. (2022). *Cardiff University Press*. Digital Supply Chain Transformation, Emerging Technologies for Sustainable Growth.

Poluha, R. G. (2007). Application of the SCOR model in supply chain management. Cambria Press.

Potdar, K., Pardawala, T., & Pai, C. (2017). A Comparative Study of Categorical Variable Encoding Techniques for Neural Network Classifiers. *International Journal of Computer Applications*, 175(4), 7–9. DOI: 10.5120/ijca2017915495

Compilation of References

Aamer, A., Eka Yani, L. P., & Alan Priyatna, I. M. (2020). Data Analytics in the Supply Chain Management: Review of Machine Learning Applications in Demand Forecasting. *Operations and Supply Chain Management: An International Journal*, 1–13. https://doi.org/DOI: 10.31387/oscm0440281

Ab Talib, M. S., Abdul Hamid, A. B., & Thoo, A. C. (2015). Critical success factors of supply chain management: A literature survey and Pareto analysis. *EuroMed Journal of Business*, 10(2), 234–263.

Abdel-Basset, M., Manogaran, G., & Mohamed, M. (2018). Internet of Things (IoT) and its impact on supply chain: A framework for building smart, secure and efficient systems. *Future Generation Computer Systems*, 86, 614–628. DOI: 10.1016/J.FUTURE.2018.04.051

Abeliuk, A., Benjamin, D. M., Morstatter, F., & Galstyan, A. (2020). Quantifying machine influence over human forecasters. *Scientific Reports*, 10(1), 15940. PMID: 32994447

Abeysekara, N., Wang, H., & Kuruppuarachchi, D. (2019). Effect of supply-chain resilience on firm performance and competitive advantage: A study of the Sri Lankan apparel industry. *Business Process Management Journal*, 25(7), 1673–1695.

Abeywickrama, D. B., Bicocchi, N., Mamei, M., & Zambonelli, F. (2020). The SOTA approach to engineering collective adaptive systems. *International Journal of Software Tools for Technology Transfer*, 22(4), 399–56. DOI: 10.1007/s10009-020-00554-3

Abhulimen, A. O., & Ejike, O. G. (2024). Ethical considerations in AI use for SMEs and supply chains: Current challenges and future directions. *International Journal of Applied Research in Social Sciences*, 6(8), 8. Advance online publication. DOI: 10.51594/ijarss.v6i8.1391

Abideen, A. Z., Sundram, V. P. K., Pyeman, J., Othman, A. K., & Sorooshian, S. (2021). Food supply chain transformation through technology and future research directions—A systematic review. *Logistics (Basel)*, 5(4), 83. DOI: 10.3390/logistics5040083

Abolek, A. (2023). *Work Life Balance Policies and Performance of Senior Members at University of Cape Coast* (Doctoral dissertation, University of Cape Coast).

Abolghasemi, M., Beh, E., Tarr, G., & Gerlach, R. (2020). Demand forecasting in supply chain: The impact of demand volatility in the presence of promotion. *Computers & Industrial Engineering*, 142, 106380.

Adewusi, A. O., Komolafe, A. M., Ejairu, E., Aderotoye, I. A., Abiona, O. O., & Oyeniran, O. C. (2024). The role of predictive analytics in optimizing supply chain resilience: A review of techniques and case studies. *International Journal of Management & Entrepreneurship Research*, 6(3), 815–837.

Adeyelu, O. O., Ugochukwu, C. E., & Shonibare, M. A. (2024). Ethical implications of AI in financial decision–making: a review with real world applications. *International Journal of Applied Research in Social Sciences*, 6(4), 608–630.

Agarwal, N., & Brem, A. (2015). Strategic business transformation through technology convergence: Implications from General Electric's industrial internet initiative. *International Journal of Technology Management*, 67(2), 196–214. DOI: 10.1504/IJTM.2015.068224

Ageron, B., Bentahar, O., & Gunasekaran, A. (2020, July). Digital supply chain: Challenges and future directions. In Supply chain forum [). Taylor & Francis.]. *International Journal (Toronto, Ont.)*, 21(3), 133–138.

Agrawal, A., Gans, J., & Goldfarb, A. (2019). Economic policy for artificial intelligence. *Innovation Policy and the Economy*, 19(1), 139–159.

Agrawal, P., Narain, R., & Ullah, I. (2019). Analysis of barriers in implementation of digital transformation of supply chain using interpretive structural modelling approach. *Journal of Modelling in Management*, 15(1), 297–317.

Aguilar-Escobar, V. G., & Garrido-Vega, P. (2013). Gestión Lean en logística de hospitales: Estudio de un caso. *Revista De Calidad Asistencial*, 28(1), 42–49. DOI: 10.1016/J.CALI.2012.07.001 PMID: 22980756

Ahmad, S., Miskon, S., Alabdan, R., & Tlili, I. (2020). Towards sustainable textile and apparel industry: Exploring the role of business intelligence systems in the era of industry 4.0. *Sustainability (Basel)*, 12(7), 2632. DOI: 10.3390/su12072632

Ahmad, S., Miskon, S., Alabdan, R., & Tlili, I. (2020). Towards sustainable textile and apparel industry: Exploring the role of business intelligence systems in the era of industry 4.0. *Sustainability*, 12(7), 2632.

Aiken, C., & Keller, S. (2009). The irrational side of change management. *The McKinsey Quarterly*, 2(10), 100–109.

Akhtar, P., Ghouri, A. M., Ashraf, A., Lim, J. J., Khan, N. R., & Ma, S. (2024). Smart product platforming powered by AI and Generative AI: Personalization for the circular economy. *International Journal of Production Economics*, 273, 109283.

Akram, S. V., Malik, P. K., Singh, R., Gehlot, A., Juyal, A., Ghafoor, K. Z., & Shrestha, S. (2022). Implementation of digitalized technologies for fashion industry 4.0: Opportunities and challenges. *Scientific Programming*, 2022, 2022. DOI: 10.1155/2022/7523246

Akter, S., & Wamba, S. F. (2016). Big data analytics in E-commerce: A systematic review and agenda for future research. *Electronic Markets*, 26, 173–194.

Akyuz, G., & Erkan, T. (2010). Supply chain performance measurement: A literature review. *International Journal of Production Research*, 48(17), 5137–5155. DOI: 10.1080/00207540903089536

Aldoseri, A., Al-Khalifa, K. N., & Hamouda, A. M. (2023). Re-thinking data strategy and integration for artificial intelligence: Concepts, opportunities, and challenges. *Applied Sciences (Basel, Switzerland)*, 13(12), 7082.

Ali, I., & Gölgeci, I. (2019). Where is supply chain resilience research heading? A systematic and co-occurrence analysis. *International Journal of Physical Distribution & Logistics Management*, 49(8), 793–815.

Aljohani, A. (2023). Predictive Analytics and Machine Learning for Real-Time Supply Chain Risk Mitigation and Agility. *Sustainability (Basel)*, 15(20), 15088. DOI: 10.3390/su152015088

Aljohani, A. (2023). Predictive analytics and machine learning for real-time supply chain risk mitigation and agility. *Sustainability*, 15(20), 15088.

Al-Khedhairi, A., & Tadj, L. (2007). Optimal control of a production inventory system with Weibull distributed deterioration. *Applied Mathematical Sciences*, 1(35), 1703–1714.

Allal-Cherif, O., Simon-Moya, V., & Ballester, A. C. C. (2021). Intelligent purchasing: How artificial intelligence can redefine the purchasing function. *Journal of Business Research*, 124, 69–76. DOI: 10.1016/j.jbusres.2020.11.050

Allaoui, H., Guo, Y., & Sarkis, J. (2019). Decision support for collaboration planning in sustainable supply chains. *Journal of Cleaner Production*, 229, 761–774. DOI: 10.1016/J.JCLEPRO.2019.04.367

Alnahhal, M., Ahrens, D., & Salah, B. (2021). Dynamic lead-time forecasting using machine learning in a make-to-order supply chain. *Applied Sciences (Basel, Switzerland)*, 11(21), 10105.

Alwahedi, F., Aldhaheri, A., Ferrag, M. A., Battah, A., & Tihanyi, N. (2024). Machine learning techniques for IoT security: Current research and future vision with generative AI and large language models. *Internet of Things and Cyber-Physical Systems*.

Amankwah-Amoah, J., Khan, Z., & Wood, G. (2021). COVID-19 and business failures: The paradoxes of experience, scale, and scope for theory and practice. *European Management Journal*, 39(2), 179–184. PMID: 38620607

Amazon. (2023). *Amazon.com, Inc. Annual Report (10-K)*.https://d18rn0p25nwr6d.cloudfront.net/CIK-0001018724/b22698ce-4a1c-4290-b373-531dd612a404.html

Ambulkar, S., Ramaswami, S., Blackhurst, J., & Johnny Rungtusanatham, M. (2022). Supply chain disruption risk: An unintended consequence of product innovation. *International Journal of Production Research*, 60(24), 7194–7213.

Amelia, R., Hussein, A. S., & Wijayanti, R. (2022). Analysis of Factors Influencing Business Resilience: Role of Marketing Performance as Moderating Variables. *ITALIENISCH*, 12(2), 943–957.

Amin, A., Bhuiyan, M. R. I., Hossain, R., Molla, C., Poli, T. A., & Milon, M. N. U. (2024). The adoption of Industry 4.0 technologies by using the technology organizational environment framework: The mediating role to manufacturing performance in a developing country. *Business Strategy & Development*, 7(2), e363.

Amine, E. A., El Farouk Imane, I., Zahra, M. F., & Zineb, S. (2024). Supply Chain Maturity Models: Comparative Study Via a Systematic Review And Illustration in The Automotive Industry sector. *2024 IEEE 15th International Colloquium on Logistics and Supply Chain Management (LOGISTIQUA)*, 1–9. https://doi.org/DOI: 10.1109/LOGISTIQUA61063.2024.10571495

Amran, M., Daril, M., Ikbar, M., Subari, K., Mohd Amran, M. D., Januddi, F., Nuraina, S., Mohamad Ikbar, A. W., & Khairanum, S. (2020). *The Barriers in Lean Healthcare Implementation*. https://www.researchgate.net/publication/338594955

An, D., Anh, D. T. L., Cam, H. L. T., Nayak, R., George, M., Cam, L. B. T., ... & Quang, H. T. (2024). Navigating global supply networks: a strategic framework for resilience in the apparel industry. *Operations Management Research*, 1-21.

Andronie, M., Lazaroiu, G., Iatagan, M., U ă, C., tefănescu, R., & Coco atu, M. (2021). Artificial intelligence-based decision-making algorithms, internet of things sensing networks, and deep learning-assisted smart process management in cyber-physical production systems. *Electronics (Basel)*, 10(20), 2497. DOI: 10.3390/electronics10202497

Andronie, M., Lazaroiu, G., tefanescu, R., U a, C., & Dijmarescu, I. (2021). Sustainable, smart, and sensing technologies for cyber-physical manufacturing systems: A systematic literature review. *Sustainability (Basel)*, 13(10), 5495. DOI: 10.3390/su13105495

Anica-Popa, I., Anica-Popa, L., Rădulescu, C., & Vrîncianu, M. (2021). The integration of artificial intelligence in retail: Benefits, challenges and a dedicated conceptual framework. *Amfiteatru Economic*, 23(56), 120–136. DOI: 10.24818/EA/2021/56/120

Ankrum, A. L., Neogi, S., Morckel, M. A., Wilhite, A. W., Li, Z., & Schaffzin, J. K. (2019). Reduced isolation room turnover time using Lean methodology. *Infection Control and Hospital Epidemiology*, 40(10), 1151–1156. DOI: 10.1017/ICE.2019.199 PMID: 31345277

Aqlan, F., & Lam, S. S. (2015). A fuzzy-based integrated framework for supply chain risk assessment. *International Journal of Production Economics*, 161, 54–63. DOI: 10.1016/J.IJPE.2014.11.013

Araujo, G. S., & Gaglianone, W. P. (2023). Machine learning methods for inflation forecasting in Brazil: New contenders versus classical models. *Latin American Journal of Central Banking*, 4(2), 100087.

Araveeporn, A. (2018). A COMPARISON OF PARAMETER ESTIMATION OF LOGISTIC REGRESSION MODEL BY MAXIMUM LIKELIHOOD, RIDGE REGRESSION, MARKOV CHAIN MONTE CARLO METHODS. *Proceedings of the 35th International Academic Conference, Barcelona*. 35th International Academic Conference, Barcelona. https://doi.org/DOI: 10.20472/IAC.2018.935.004

Ardolino, M., Rapaccini, M., Saccani, N., Gaiardelli, P., Crespi, G., & Ruggeri, C. (2017). The role of digital technologies for the service transformation of industrial companies. *International Journal of Production Research*, 7543, 1–17. DOI: 10.1080/00207543.2017.1324224

Arunkumar, O. N., & Divya, D. (2024). A review on supply chain finance: Problem classification and future research agenda. *International Journal of Revenue Management*, 14(2), 150–202.

Arunmozhi, M., Venkatesh, V. G., Arisian, S., Shi, Y., & Sreedharan, V. R. (2022). Application of blockchain and smart contracts in autonomous vehicle supply chains: An experimental design. *Transportation Research Part E, Logistics and Transportation Review*, 165, 102864. DOI: 10.1016/j.tre.2022.102864

Atadoga, A., Obi, O. C., Osasona, F., Onwusinkwue, S., Daraojimba, A. I., & Dawodu, S. O. (2024). AI in supply chain optimization: A comparative review of USA and African Trends. *International Journal of Science and Research Archive*, 11(1), 896–903. DOI: 10.30574/ijsra.2024.11.1.0156

Atun, R. (2015). Transitioning health systems for multimorbidity. *Lancet*, 386(9995), 721–722. DOI: 10.1016/S0140-6736(14)62254-6 PMID: 26063473

Azadegan, A., & Dooley, K. (2021). A typology of supply network resilience strategies: Complex collaborations in a complex world. *The Journal of Supply Chain Management*, 57(1), 17–26.

Babai, M. Z., Boylan, J. E., & Rostami-Tabar, B. (2022). Demand forecasting in supply chains: A review of aggregation and hierarchical approaches. *International Journal of Production Research*, 60(1), 324–348.

Bajgoric, N. (2023). Always-on business: integrating business continuity and business resilience. *Continuity & Resilience Review*, (ahead-of-print).

Baldwin, R., & Freeman, R. (2022). Risks and global supply chains: What we know and what we need to know. *Annual Review of Economics*, 14(1), 153–180.

Ballé, M., & Régnier, A. (2007). Lean as a learning system in a hospital ward. *Leadership in Health Services (Bradford, England)*, 20(1), 33–41. DOI: 10.1108/17511870710721471 PMID: 20690474

Baltputnis, K., Petrichenko, R., & Sobolevsky, D. (2018). Heating Demand Forecasting with Multiple Regression: Model Setup and Case Study. *2018 IEEE 6th Workshop on Advances in Information, Electronic and Electrical Engineering (AIEEE)*, 1–5. https://doi.org/DOI: 10.1109/AIEEE.2018.8592144

Bandi, A., Adapa, P. V. S. R., & Kuchi, Y. E. V. P. K. (2023). The power of generative ai: A review of requirements, models, input–output formats, evaluation metrics, and challenges. *Future Internet*, 15(8), 260.

Bao, W., Cao, Y., Yang, Y., Che, H., Huang, J., & Wen, S. (2024). Data-driven stock forecasting models based on neural networks: A review. *Information Fusion*, •••, 102616.

Baratta, A., Cimino, A., Gnoni, M. G., & Longo, F. (2023). Human Robot Collaboration in Industry 4.0: A literature review. *Procedia Computer Science*, 217, 1887–1895. PMID: 36687281

Barbosa-Povoa, A. P., & Pinto, J. M. (2020). Process supply chains: Perspectives from academia and industry. *Computers & Chemical Engineering*, 132, 106606.

Bardhan, P. (2003). *International Trade Growth and Development: Essays*. Wiley-Backwell. DOI: 10.1002/9780470752777

Barhmi, A., & Hajaji, O. (2023). Multidisciplinary approach to supply chain resilience: Conceptualization and scale development. *Central European Business Review, 12*(5).

Barik, T. (2024). Optimization Potential Using AI and Metaverse in Supply Chain Management: A Forward-Looking Perspective. *Business Management and Economics Engineering.*, 22, 1340–1355.

Baril, C., Gascon, V., & Cartier, S. (2014). Design and analysis of an outpatient orthopaedic clinic performance with discrete event simulation and design of experiments. *Computers & Industrial Engineering*, 78, 285–298. DOI: 10.1016/J.CIE.2014.05.006

Baril, C., Gascon, V., Miller, J., & Côté, N. (2016). Use of a discrete-event simulation in a Kaizen event: A case study in healthcare. *European Journal of Operational Research*, 249(1), 327–339. DOI: 10.1016/J.EJOR.2015.08.036

Baryannis, G., Validi, S., Dani, S., & Antoniou, G. (2019). Supply chain risk management and artificial intelligence: State of the art and future research directions. *International Journal of Production Research*, 57(7), 2179–2202.

Bastian, N. D., Munoz, D., & Ventura, M. (2016). A Mixed-Methods Research Framework for Healthcare Process Improvement. *Journal of Pediatric Nursing*, 31(1), e39–e51. DOI: 10.1016/J.PEDN.2015.09.003 PMID: 26453414

Beaulieu, M., & Bentahar, O. (2021). Digitalization of the healthcare supply chain: A roadmap to generate benefits and effectively support healthcare delivery. *Technological Forecasting and Social Change*, 167, 120717. DOI: 10.1016/J.TECHFORE.2021.120717

Bechtsis, D., Tsolakis, N., Iakovou, E., & Vlachos, D. (2022). Data-driven secure, resilient and sustainable supply chains: Gaps, opportunities, and a new generalised data sharing and data monetisation framework. *International Journal of Production Research*, 60(14), 4397–4417.

Bednarski, L., Roscoe, S., Blome, C., & Schleper, M. C. (2024). Geopolitical disruptions in global supply chains: A state-of-the-art literature review. *Production Planning and Control*, •••, 1–27.

Bengesi, S., El-Sayed, H., Sarker, M. K., Houkpati, Y., Irungu, J., & Oladunni, T. (2024). Advancements in Generative AI: A Comprehensive Review of GANs, GPT, Autoencoders, Diffusion Model, and Transformers. *IEEE Access : Practical Innovations, Open Solutions*.

Berger, P. (2024). New disruptions geopolitics hang over 2024 supply chains. The Wall Street Journal.

Bertola, P., & Teunissen, J. (2018). Fashion 4.0. Innovating fashion industry through digital transformation. *Research Journal of Textile and Apparel*, 22(4), 352–369. DOI: 10.1108/RJTA-03-2018-0023

Beske, P., Land, A., & Seuring, S. (2014). Sustainable supply chain management practices and dynamic capabilities in the food industry: A critical analysis of the literature. *International Journal of Production Economics*, 152, 131–143.

Best Practice AI. (2021). *AI Case Study | The Port of Rotterdam Authority reduces vessel waiting times by 20% with machine learning*. Best Practice AI. https://www.bestpractice.ai/ai-case-study-best-practice/the_port_of_rotterdam_authority_reduces_vessel_waiting_times_by_20%25_with_machine_learning

Bevilacqua, M., Ciarapica, F. E., Marcucci, G., & Mazzuto, G. (2020). Fuzzy cognitive maps approach for analysing the domino effect of factors affecting supply chain resilience: A fashion industry case study. *International Journal of Production Research*, 58(20), 6370–6398.

Bhagwat, R., & Sharma, M. K. (2007). Performance measurement of supply chain management: A balanced scorecard approach. *Computers & Industrial Engineering*, 53(1), 43–62.

Bharadiya, J. P. (2023). Machine learning and AI in business intelligence: Trends and opportunities. [IJC]. *International Journal of Computer*, 48(1), 123–134.

Bhardwaj, R. (2018) 'AI in Transportation – Current and Future Business Use Applications' https://www.techemergence.com/ last accessed on 28/11/2018.

Bhardwaj, R. (2018) 'AI in Transportation – Current and Future BusinessUse Applications' https://www.techemergence.com/ last accessed on 28/11/2018

Bhardwaj, R. (2018) 'Artificial Intelligence in Supply Chain Management – Current Possibilities and Applications' https://www.techemergence.com/ last accessed on 28/11/2018.

Bharsakade, R. S., Acharya, P., Ganapathy, L., & Tiwari, M. K. (2021). A lean approach to healthcare management using multi criteria decision making. *OPSEARCH*, 58(3), 610–635. DOI: 10.1007/S12597-020-00490-5/TABLES/16

Bhat, S., Gijo, E. V., & Jnanesh, N. A. (2014). Application of Lean Six Sigma methodology in the registration process of a hospital. *International Journal of Productivity and Performance Management*, 63(5), 613–643. DOI: 10.1108/IJPPM-11-2013-0191

Bidin, M. F. (2024). Adaptive Supply Chain Risk Management Using AI Mitigating Disruptions and Enhancing Resilience in the Post-Pandemic Era. Tuijin Jishu/ Journal of Propulsion Technology, 45(02), 2655-2664.

Blue Yonder Inc. (2020). The autonomous supply chain: seven steps to get there. https://blueyonder.com/ knowledge-center/collateral/7-steps-to-an-autonomous-supply-chain-white-paper

Blue Yonder Inc. (2023). The Next Evolution of Technology Innovations Transforming Supply Chain Planning. https://blog.blueyonder.com/the-next-evolution-of-technology-innovations-transforming-supply-chain-planning/

Bollig, B., Bouyer, P., & Reiter, F. (2019). *Identifiers in Registers—Describing Network Algorithms with Logic* (Vol. 11425, pp. 115–132). https://doi.org/DOI: 10.1007/978-3-030-17127-8_7

Bolstorff, P., & Rosenbaum, R. G. (2007). Supply chain excellence: a handbook for dramatic improvement using the SCOR model. AMACOM/American Management Association.

Borodavko, B., Illés, B., & Bányai, Á. (2021). Role of artificial intelligence in supply chain. *Academic Journal of Manufacturing Engineering*, 19(1), 75–79.

Borucka, A. (2023). Seasonal methods of demand forecasting in the supply chain as support for the company's sustainable growth. *Sustainability*, 15(9), 7399.

Bousdekis, A., Lepenioti, K., Apostolou, D., & Mentzas, G. (2021). A review of data-driven decision-making methods for industry 4.0 maintenance applications. *Electronics (Basel)*, 10(7), 828.

Bowerman, J., & Fillingham, D. (2007). Can lean save lives? *Leadership in Health Services (Bradford, England)*, 20(4), 231–241. DOI: 10.1108/17511870710829346 PMID: 20698096

Bressanelli, G., Adrodegari, F., Perona, M., & Saccani, N. (2018). Exploring How Usage Focused Business Models Enable Circular Economy through Digital Technologies. *Sustainability (Basel)*, 10(3), 639. DOI: 10.3390/su10030639

Bressanelli, G., Adrodegari, F., Perona, M., & Saccani, N. (2018). The role of digital technologies to overcome Circular Economy challenges in PSS Business Models: An exploratory case study. *Procedia CIRP*, 73, 216–221. DOI: 10.1016/j.procir.2018.03.322

Brintrup, A., Pak, J., Ratiney, D., Pearce, T., Wichmann, P., Woodall, P., & McFarlane, D. (2020). Supply chain data analytics for predicting supplier disruptions: A case study in complex asset manufacturing. *International Journal of Production Research*, 58(11), 3330–3341.

Browne, M. (2021). Artificial intelligence data-driven internet of things systems, real-time process monitoring, and sustainable industrial value creation in smart networked factories. *Journal of Self-Governance and Management Economics*, 9(2), 21–31.

Brynjolfsson, E., & Mitchell, T. (2017). *What can machine learning do? Workforce implications | Science. 358*(6370), 1530–1534. https://doi.org/DOI: 10.1126/science.aap8062

Brynjolfsson, E., & Mcafee, A. (2017). Artificial intelligence, for real. *Harvard Business Review*, 1, 1–31.

Bughin, J., Hazan, E., & Sree Ramaswamy, P. DC, W., & Chu, M. (2017). Artificial intelligence the next digital frontier.

Bu, L., Chen, C. H., Zhang, G., Liu, B., Dong, G., & Yuan, X. (2020). A hybrid intelligence approach for sustainable service innovation of smart and connected product: A case study. *Advanced Engineering Informatics*, 46, 101163. DOI: 10.1016/j.aei.2020.101163

Bvuchete, M., Grobbelaar, S. S., & Van Eeden, J. (2021). A Network Maturity Mapping Tool for Demand-Driven Supply Chain Management: A Case for the Public Healthcare Sector. *Sustainability*, 13(21), 11988. DOI: 10.3390/su132111988

Bvuchete, M., Saartjie Grobbelaar, S., & Van Eeden, J. (2020). BEST PRACTICES FOR DEMAND-DRIVEN SUPPLY CHAIN MANAGEMENT IN PUBLIC HEALTHCARE SECTOR: A SYSTEMATIC LITERATURE REVIEW. *South African Journal of Industrial Engineering*. Advance online publication. DOI: 10.7166/31-2-2006

Caiado, R. G. G., Scavarda, L. F., Gavião, L. O., Ivson, P., de Mattos Nascimento, D. L., & Garza-Reyes, J. A. (2021). A fuzzy rule-based industry 4.0 maturity model for operations and supply chain management. *International Journal of Production Economics*, 231, 107883.

Calleja-Sanz, G., Olivella-Nadal, J., & Solé-Parellada, F. (2020). Technology forecasting: Recent trends and new methods. *Research methodology in management and industrial engineering*, 45-69.

Calo, R. (2017). *Artificial Intelligence Policy: A Primer and Roadmap* (SSRN Scholarly Paper 3015350). https://doi.org/DOI: 10.2139/ssrn.3015350

Campbell, C., Sands, S., Ferraro, C., Tsao, H. Y. J., & Mavrommatis, A. (2020). From data to action: How marketers can leverage AI. *Business Horizons*, 63(2), 227–243.

Cang, S. (2014). A Comparative Analysis of Three Types of Tourism Demand Forecasting Models: Individual, Linear Combination and Non-linear Combination: Individual, Linear Combination and Non-linear Combination Forecasts. *International Journal of Tourism Research*, 16(6), 596–607. DOI: 10.1002/jtr.1953

Cao, M., Vonderembse, M. A., Zhang, Q., & Ragu-Nathan, T. S. (2010). Supply chain collaboration: Conceptualisation and instrument development. *International Journal of Production Research*, 48(22), 6613–6635. DOI: 10.1080/00207540903349039

Cao, M., & Zhang, Q. (2011). Supply chain collaboration: Impact on collaborative advantage and firm performance. *Journal of Operations Management*, 29(3), 163–180.

Cardoso, S., & Martinez, L. F. (2019). Online payment strategy: How third-party internet seals of approval and payment provider reputation influence the Millennials' online transactions. *Electronic Commerce Research*, 2019(19), 189–209. DOI: 10.1007/s10660-018-9295-x

Caro, F., & Martínez-de-Albéniz, V. (2015). Fast Fashion: Business Model Overview and Research Opportunities. In Agrawal, N., & Smith, S. (Eds.), *Retail Supply Chain Management. International Series in Operations Research & Management Science* (Vol. 223). Springer., DOI: 10.1007/978-1-4899-7562-1_9

Casciani, D., Chkanikova, O., & Pal, R. (2022). Exploring the nature of digital transformation in the fashion industry: opportunities for supply chains, business models, and sustainability-oriented innovations. *Sustainability: Science. Sustainability*, 18(1), 773–795. DOI: 10.1080/15487733.2022.2125640

Cazeri, G. T., de Santa-Eulalia, L. A., Serafim, M. P., & Anholon, R. (2022). Training for Industry 4.0: A systematic literature review and directions for future research. *Brazilian Journal of Operations & Production Management*, 19(3), 1–19.

Cerda, P., Varoquaux, G., & Kégl, B. (2018). Similarity encoding for learning with dirty categorical variables. *Machine Learning*, 107(8), 1477–1494.

Chand, M., Jain, V., & Ajmera, P. (Eds.). (2023). *Data-Driven technologies and artificial intelligence in supply chain: Tools and Techniques*. CRC Press.

Chang, A., El-Rayes, N., & Shi, J. (2022). Blockchain technology for supply chain management: A comprehensive review. *FinTech*, 1(2), 191–205.

Chan, H. L., Wei, X., Guo, S., & Leung, W. H. (2020). Corporate social responsibility (CSR) in fashion supply chains: A multi-methodological study. *Transportation Research Part E, Logistics and Transportation Review*, 142, 102063.

Chan, H., Lo, S., Lee, L., Lo, W., Yu, W., Wu, Y., Ho, S., Yeung, R., & Chan, J. (2014). Lean techniques for the improvement of patients' flow in emergency department. *World Journal of Emergency Medicine*, 5(1), 24. DOI: 10.5847/WJEM.J.ISSN.1920-8642.2014.01.004 PMID: 25215143

Chase, C. W. (2021). *Consumption-based Forecasting and Planning: Predicting Changing Demand Patterns in the New Digital Economy*. John Wiley & Sons.

Chauhan, C., Akram, M. U., & Chauhan, A. (2023). Mapping pathways for building resilient supply chains: A systematic literature review. *Journal of Cleaner Production*, •••, 138701.

Cheng, L. (2014). A gentle introduction to gradient boosting.

Chen, J. C., Cheng, C. H., Huang, P. B., Wang, K. J., Huang, C. J., & Ting, T. C. (2013). Warehouse management with lean and RFID application: A case study. *International Journal of Advanced Manufacturing Technology*, 69(1–4), 531–542. DOI: 10.1007/S00170-013-5016-8

Chen, J. E., Bao, F., Li, C., & Lin, Y. (2023). The Application and Ethics of Artificial Intelligence in Blockchain: A Bibliometric-Content Analysis. *Journal of Global Information Management*, 31(7), 1–32.

Chen, T. (2016). XGBoost: A Scalable Tree Boosting System. DOI: 10.1145/2939672.2939785

Chintalapati, S., & Pandey, S. K. (2022). Artificial intelligence in marketing: A systematic literature review. *International Journal of Market Research*, 64(1), 38–68. DOI: 10.1177/14707853211018428

Choi, T. M. J. (Ed.). (2016). *Information systems for the fashion and apparel industry*. Woodhead Publishing.

Choi, T. M., Chan, H. K., & Yue, X. (2016). Recent development in big data analytics for business operations and risk management. *IEEE Transactions on Cybernetics*, 47(1), 81–92. PMID: 26766385

Choi, T. M., Wallace, S. W., & Wang, Y. (2018). Big data analytics in operations management. *Production and Operations Management*, 27(10), 1868–1883.

Choi, T. Y., Netland, T. H., Sanders, N., Sodhi, M. S., & Wagner, S. M. (2023). Just-in-time for supply chains in turbulent times. *Production and Operations Management*, 32(7), 2331–2340.

Chopra, S., & Meindl, P. (2001). Strategy, planning, and operation. *Supply Chain Management*, 15(5), 71–85.

Chopra, S., & Sodhi, M. S. (2004). Managing risk to avoid supply-chain breakdown. *MIT Sloan Management Review*.

Chopra, S., & Sodhi, M. S. (2014). Reducing the risk of supply chain disruptions. *MIT Sloan Management Review*.

Chowdhury, M. M. H., Quaddus, M., & Chowdhury, M. (2023). Managing relational practices for performance improvement in a complex supply chain network: The mediating roles of proactive and reactive resilience in apparel industry of Bangladesh. *International Journal of Logistics Management*, 34(1), 34–59.

Chowdhury, N. R., Janan, F., Mahmud, P., Liza, S. A., & Paul, S. K. (2024). Assessing strategies to mitigate the impacts of a pandemic in apparel supply chains. *Operations Management Research*, 17(1), 38–54.

Christopher, M., & Lee, H. (2004). Mitigating supply chain risk through improved confidence. *International Journal of Physical Distribution & Logistics Management*, 34(5), 388–396.

Christopher, M., & Peck, H. (2004). Building the Resilient Supply Chain. *International Journal of Logistics Management*, 15(2), 1–14. DOI: 10.1108/09574090410700275

Christopher, M., Peck, H., & Towill, D. (2006). A Taxonomy for Selecting Global Supply Chain Strategies. *International Journal of Logistics Management*, 17(2), 277–287.

Christopher, M., Towill, D., Aitken, J., & Childerhouse, P. (2009). Value Chain Classification. *Journal of Manufacturing Technology Management*, 20(4), 460–474.

Church, E. M., & Oakley, R. L. (2018). Etsy and the long-tail: How microenterprises use hype-differentiation in online handcraft marketplaces. *Electronic Commerce Research*, 2018(18), 883–898. DOI: 10.1007/s10660-018-9300-4

Cieżak, W., & Kutyłowska, M. (2023). Application of exponential smoothing method to forecasting daily water consumption in rural areas. *Archives of Civil Engineering*, 69(3).

Cohen, M., Cui, S., Doetsch, S., Ernst, R., Huchzermeier, A., Kouvelis, P., & Tsay, A. A. (2022). Bespoke supply-chain resilience: The gap between theory and practice. *Journal of Operations Management*, 68(5), 515–531.

Coulson-Thomas, C. (2024). Board's strategy for a future-ready business in an uncertain world.

Crawford, K., & Paglen, T. (2021). Excavating AI: The politics of images in machine learning training sets. *AI & Society*, 36(4), 1105–1116.

Curatolo, N., Lamouri, S., Huet, J. C., & Rieutord, A. (2014). A critical analysis of Lean approach structuring in hospitals. *Business Process Management Journal*, 20(3), 433–454. DOI: 10.1108/BPMJ-04-2013-0051/FULL/XML

Cynthia, B., & Keith, L. S. (2011, January–March). Organizational Change Manafgement: A Test of the Effectiveness of a Communication Plan. *Communication Research Reports*, 28(1), 62–73. DOI: 10.1080/08824096.2011.541364

Da Xu, L., He, W., & Li, S. (2014). Internet of things in industries: A survey. *IEEE Transactions on Industrial Informatics*, 10(4), 2233–2243.

Dal Forno, A. J., Bataglini, W. V., Steffens, F., & Ulson de Souza, A. A. (2023). Industry 4.0 in textile and apparel sector: A systematic literature review. *Research Journal of Textile and Apparel*, 27(1), 95–117. DOI: 10.1108/RJTA-08-2021-0106

Damar, M., Özen, A., & Yılmaz, A. (2024). Cybersecurity in The Health Sector in The Reality of Artificial Intelligence, And Information Security Conceptually. *Journal of AI*, 8(1), 61–82. DOI: 10.61969/JAI.1466340

Darvazeh, S. S., Vanani, I. R., & Musolu, F. M. (2020). Big data analytics and its applications in supply chain management. *New Trends in the Use of Artificial Intelligence for the Industry*, 4, 175.

Dash, R., McMurtrey, M., Rebman, C., & Kar, U. K. (2019). Application of artificial intelligence in automation of supply chain management. *Journal of Strategic Innovation and Sustainability*, 14(3), 43–53.

Daugherty, P. R., & Wilson, H. J. (2018). *Human+ machine: Reimagining work in the age of AI*. Harvard Business Press.

Davenport, T. H., & Kirby, J. (2016). *Only humans need apply: Winners and losers in the age of smart machines*. Harper Business.

de la Torre, I., García-Zapirain, B., & López-Coronado, M. (2017). Analysis of Security in Big Data Related to Healthcare. *Journal of Digital Forensics, Security and Law, 12*(3), 5. https://doi.org/https://doi.org/10.15394/jdfsl.2017.1448

De Mattos, C. A., Correia, F. C., & Kissimoto, K. O. (2024). Artificial Intelligence Capabilities for Demand Planning Process. *Logistics (Basel)*, 8(2), 53. DOI: 10.3390/logistics8020053

de Santana Correia, A., & Colombini, E. L. (2022). Attention, please! A survey of neural attention models in deep learning. *Artificial Intelligence Review*, 55(8), 6037–6124.

Deloitte. (2023). *How Generative AI will transform Sourcing and Procurement Operations.*

Devan, M., Shanmugam, L., & Tomar, M. (2021). AI-Powered Data Migration Strategies for Cloud Environments: Techniques, Frameworks, and Real-World Applications. *Australian Journal of Machine Learning Research & Applications*, 1(2), 79–111.

Dhall, D., Kaur, R., & Juneja, M. (2020). Machine learning: a review of the algorithms and its applications. *Proceedings of ICRIC 2019: Recent innovations in computing*, 47-63.

DHL. (2020). *DHL Group | Aug 12, 2020: Artificial Intelligence: DHL algorithm makes e-fulfillment more effective.* https://group.dhl.com/en/media-relations/press-releases/2020/artificial-intelligence-dhl-algorithm-makes-e-fulfillment-more-effective.html

Diabat, A., & Govindan, K. (2011). An analysis of the drivers affecting the implementation of green supply chain management. *Resources, Conservation and Recycling*, 55(6), 659–667.

Dias, D. G., Mendes, C., & da Silva, M. M. (2013). A Method for Reengineering Healthcare Using Enterprise Ontology and Lean. *Communications in Computer and Information Science*, 415, 243–259. DOI: 10.1007/978-3-642-54105-6_16

Dignum, V. (2023, January). Responsible Artificial Intelligence---From Principles to Practice: A Keynote at TheWebConf 2022. In *ACM SIGIR Forum* (Vol. 56, No. 1, pp. 1-6). New York, NY, USA: ACM.

Dobriban, E., & Wager, S. (2018). High-dimensional asymptotics of prediction: Ridge regression and classification. *Annals of Statistics*, 46(1). Advance online publication. DOI: 10.1214/17-AOS1549

Domingos, P. (2015). *The Master Algorithm*. How the Quest for the Ultimate Learning Machine Will Remake Our World.

Dominguez, R., Cannella, S., Ponte, B., & Framinan, J. M. (2020). On the dynamics of closed-loop supply chains under remanufacturing lead time variability. *Omega*, 97, 102106.

Domini, B., Dewi, A. S., & Cesna, G. P. (2023). Assessing the Effects of Artificial Intelligence on Startup Performance: An Analysis of Transformational Initiatives. [ITSDI]. *IAIC Transactions on Sustainable Digital Innovation*, 5(1), 24–38.

dos Santos, C. H., Gabriel, G. T., do Amaral, J. V. S., Montevechi, J. A. B., & de Queiroz, J. A. (2021). Decision-making in a fast fashion company in the Industry 4.0 era: A Digital Twin proposal to support operational planning. *International Journal of Advanced Manufacturing Technology*, 116(5-6), 1653–1666. DOI: 10.1007/s00170-021-07543-z

Douaioui, K., Oucheikh, R., Benmoussa, O., & Mabrouki, C. (2024). Machine Learning and Deep Learning Models for Demand Forecasting in Supply Chain Management: A Critical Review. *Applied System Innovation*, 7(5), 93. DOI: 10.3390/asi7050093

Dreyer, H. C., Strandhagen, J. O., Romsdal, A., & Hoff, A. (2010). Principles for Real-Time, Integrated Supply Chain Control: An Example from Distribution of Pharmaceuticals. In Vallespir, B., & Alix, T. (Eds.), *Advances in Production Management Systems. New Challenges, New Approaches* (Vol. 338, pp. 187–194). Springer Berlin Heidelberg., DOI: 10.1007/978-3-642-16358-6_24

Drucker, P. (2012). *The practice of management*. Routledge.

Dubey, R., Gunasekaran, A., & Ali, S. S. (2015). Exploring the relationship between leadership, operational practices, institutional pressures and environmental performance: A framework for green supply chain. *International Journal of Production Economics*, 160, 120–132.

Dubey, R., Gunasekaran, A., Childe, S. J., Papadopoulos, T., Blome, C., & Luo, Z. (2017). Antecedents of resilient supply chains: An empirical study. *IEEE Transactions on Engineering Management*, 66(1), 8–19.

Durugbo, C. M., & Al-Balushi, Z. (2023). Supply chain management in times of crisis: A systematic review. *Management Review Quarterly*, 73(3), 1179–1235.

Dwivedi, Y. K., Hughes, L., Ismagilova, E., Aarts, G., Coombs, C., Crick, T., Duan, Y., Dwivedi, R., Edwards, J., Eirug, A., Galanos, V., Ilavarasan, P. V., Janssen, M., Jones, P., Kar, A. K., Kizgin, H., Kronemann, B., Lal, B., Lucini, B., & Williams, M. D. (2021). Artificial Intelligence (AI): Multidisciplinary perspectives on emerging challenges, opportunities, and agenda for research, practice and policy. *International Journal of Information Management*, 57, 101994. DOI: 10.1016/j.ijinfomgt.2019.08.002

Dzinkowski, R. (2024). "The Latest Supply Chain Crisis," Global Finance, https://gfmag.com/economics-policy-regulation/houthis-gaza-supply-chain-crisis,

Eccleston, C. H., & March, F. (2011). *Global environmental policy: concepts, principles, and practice*. CRC Press.

El Filali, A., Ben Lahmer, E. H., Ajouary, M. A., El Filali, S., Akantous, S., & Kasbouya, M. (2022). Machine Learning Applications in Supply Chain Management: A Deep Learning Model Using an Optimized LSTM Network for Demand Forecasting. *International Journal of Intelligent Engineering and Systems*, 15(2), 464–478. DOI: 10.22266/ijies2022.0430.42

Elafri, N., Tappert, J., Rose, B., & Yassine, M. (2022). Lean 4.0: Synergies between Lean Management tools and Industry 4.0 technologies. *IFAC-PapersOnLine*, 55(10), 2060–2066. DOI: 10.1016/J.IFACOL.2022.10.011

Elkady, G., & Hesham Sedky, A. (2023). Artificial Intelligence And Machine Learning For Supply Chain Resilience. *Current Integrative Engineering*, 1(1), 23–28.

Elufioye, O. A., Ike, C. U., Odeyemi, O., Usman, F. O., & Mhlongo, N. Z. (2024). AI-DRIVEN PREDICTIVE ANALYTICS IN AGRICULTURAL SUPPLY CHAINS: A REVIEW: ASSESSING THE BENEFITS AND CHALLENGES OF AI IN FORECASTING DEMAND AND OPTIMIZING SUPPLY IN AGRICULTURE. *Computer Science & IT Research Journal*, 5(2), 473–497. DOI: 10.51594/csitrj.v5i2.817

Emmert-Streib, F., & Dehmer, M. (2019). High-Dimensional LASSO-Based Computational Regression Models: Regularization, Shrinkage, and Selection. *Machine Learning and Knowledge Extraction*, 1(1), 359–383. DOI: 10.3390/make1010021

Ernst, E., Merola, R., & Samaan, D. (2018). *The economics of artificial intelligence: Implications for the future of work.*

Essien, A. (2023). AI-Driven Innovation: Leveraging Big Data Analytics for Innovation. In *Innovation Analytics: Tools for Competitive Advantage* (pp. 119-137).

Eyo-Udo, N. (2024). Leveraging artificial intelligence for enhanced supply chain optimization. *Open Access Research Journal of Multidisciplinary Studies, 7*(2), 001-015.

Farahani, M. A., McCormick, M. R., Gianinny, R., Hudacheck, F., Harik, R., Liu, Z., & Wuest, T. (2023). Time-series pattern recognition in Smart Manufacturing Systems: A literature review and ontology. *Journal of Manufacturing Systems*, 69, 208–241.

Farooq, M., & Yen, Y. Y. (2024). *Artificial Intelligence in Supply Chain Management: A Comprehensive Review and Framework for Resilience and Sustainability.* https://doi.org/DOI: 10.21203/rs.3.rs-3878218/v1

Feizabadi, J. (2022). Machine learning demand forecasting and supply chain performance. *International Journal of Logistics Research and Applications*, 25(2), 119–142.

Feng, Y., Lai, K. H., & Zhu, Q. (2022). Green supply chain innovation: Emergence, adoption, and challenges. *International Journal of Production Economics*, 248, 108497. DOI: 10.1016/j.ijpe.2022.108497

Ferrandez, S. M.. (2016). Optimization of a Truck-drone in Tandem Delivery Network Using K- means and Genetic Algorithm. *Journal of Industrial Engineering and Management*, 9(2), 374–388. DOI: 10.3926/jiem.1929

Ferreira, B., & Reis, J. (2023). Artificial Intelligence in Supply Chain Management: A Systematic Literature Review and Guidelines for Future Research. In *International Joint conference on Industrial Engineering and Operations Management* (pp. 339-354). Springer.

Ferrucci, D., Levas, A., Bagchi, S., Gondek, D., & Mueller, E. T. (2013). Watson: Beyond jeopardy! *Artificial Intelligence*, 199, 93–105.

Fildes, R., Ma, S., & Kolassa, S. (2022). Retail forecasting: Research and practice. *International Journal of Forecasting*, 38(4), 1283–1318. PMID: 36217499

Fisher, M. L. (1997). What Is the Right Supply Chain for Your Product? *Harvard Business Review*, (March–April), 105–116.

Flach, P. (2012). *Machine learning: the art and science of algorithms that make sense of data.* Cambridge university press.

Floridi, L., Cowls, J., Beltrametti, M., Chatila, R., Chazerand, P., Dignum, V., & Vayena, E. (2018). AI4People—an ethical framework for a good AI society: Opportunities, risks, principles, and recommendations. *Minds and Machines*, 28, 689–707. PMID: 30930541

Ford, E. W., Ford, D. P. S., & Scanlon, E. W. (2007). Promise and Problems with Supply Chain Management Approaches to Health Care Purchasing. *Health Care Management Review*, 32(3), 192–202. http://www.lww.com/ PMID: 17666990

Ford, M. W., & Greer, B. M. (2005). The Relationship between Management Control System Usage and Planned Change Achievement: An Exploratory Study. *Journal of Change Management*, 5(1), 29–46. DOI: 10.1080/14697010500036031

Fourkiotis, K. P., & Tsadiras, A. (2024). Applying Machine Learning and Statistical Forecasting Methods for Enhancing Pharmaceutical Sales Predictions. *Forecasting*, 6(1), 170–186. DOI: 10.3390/forecast6010010

Friday, D., Ryan, S., Melnyk, S. A., & Proulx, D. (2023). Supply chain deep uncertainties and risks: the 'new normal. In *Supply Chain Risk and Disruption Management: Latest Tools, Techniques and Management Approaches* (pp. 51–72). Springer Nature Singapore.

Friedman, J. H. (February 1999). "Greedy Function Approximation: A Gradient Boosting Machine

Friedman, J., Hastie, T., & Tibshirani, R. (2010). Regularization Paths for Generalized Linear Models via Coordinate Descent. *Journal of Statistical Software*, 33(1). Advance online publication. DOI: 10.18637/jss.v033.i01 PMID: 20808728

Furman, C., & Caplan, R. (2007). Applying the Toyota Production System: Using a patient safety alert system to reduce error. *Joint Commission Journal on Quality and Patient Safety*, 33(7), 376–386. DOI: 10.1016/S1553-7250(07)33043-2 PMID: 17711139

Gajjar, N., Sermuga Pandian, V. P., Suleri, S., & Jarke, M. (2021, April). Akin: Generating ui wireframes from ui design patterns using deep learning. In Companion Proceedings of the 26th International Conference on Intelligent User Interfaces (pp. 40-42).

Gampenrieder, E. L. (2016). *Demand-driven supply chain 2.0.*

Ganesh, A. D., & Kalpana, P. (2022). Future of artificial intelligence and its influence on supply chain risk management–A systematic review. *Computers & Industrial Engineering*, 169, 108206.

Ganji, E. N., Coutroubis, A., & Shah, S. (2018). DCM 4.0: Integration of Industry 4.0 and Demand Chain in Global Manufacturing. *2018 IEEE International Conference on Engineering, Technology and Innovation (ICE/ITMC)*, 1–7. https://doi.org/DOI: 10.1109/ICE.2018.8436383

Garay-Rondero, C. L., Rodríguez Calvo, E. Z., & Salinas-Navarro, D. E. (2019). Experiential learning at Lean-Thinking-Learning Space. *International Journal on Interactive Design and Manufacturing*, 13(3), 1129–1144. DOI: 10.1007/S12008-019-00578-3/FIGURES/8

Garinian, E. O. M., Fierro, T. E. S., Saucedo, J. A. M., & Aguilar, R. R. (2021, October). Machine Learning Applications for Demand Driven in Supply Chain: Literature Review. In *The International Conference on Artificial Intelligence and Applied Mathematics in Engineering* (pp. 763-772). Cham: Springer International Publishing.

Gartner.com. (2024). *Gartner Predicts 25% of Logistics Key Performance Indicator Reporting will be Supported by GenAI by 2028*. Gartner. https://www.gartner.com/en/newsroom/press-releases/2024-03-12-gartner-predicts-25-percent-of-logistics-key-performance-indicator-reporting-will-be-supported-by-genai-by-2028

Gattorna, J. (2006). *Living Supply Chains*. Pearson.

Gayam, S. R., Yellu, R. R., & Thuniki, P. (2021). Optimizing supply chain management through artificial Intelligence: Techniques for predictive maintenance, demand forecasting, and inventory optimization. *Journal of AI-Assisted Scientific Discovery*, 1(1), 129–144.

Georginova, T. (2023). Tools to Reduce Vulnerability from Hybrid Threats. In *Ix Scientific-Professional Conference Security and Crisis Management-Theory And Practice (SeCMan)* (pp. 144-151). Regional Association for Security and Crisis Management-RASEC S4 GLOSEC Global Security.

Ghalehkhondabi, I., Ahmadi, E., & Maihami, R. (2020). An overview of big data analytics application in supply chain management published in 2010-2019. *Production*, 30, e20190140.

Ghisellini, P., Cialani, C., & Ulgiati, S. (2016). A review on circular economy: The expected transition to a balanced interplay of environmental and economic systems. *Journal of Cleaner Production*, 114, 11–32. DOI: 10.1016/j.jclepro.2015.09.007

Ghoreishi, M., & Happonen, A. (2021, September). The case of fabric and textile industry: The emerging role of digitalization, internet-of-Things and industry 4.0 for circularity. In *Proceedings of Sixth International Congress on Information and Communication Technology: ICICT 2021,London,* Volume 3 (pp. 189-200). Singapore: Springer Singapore.

Gill, S. K., & Kaur, R. (2023). ChapGPT: Vision and challenges.

Gillham, J. (2017). *The economic impact of artificial intelligence on the global economy*. Price Waterhouse Coopers.

Gil, Y., Garijo, D., Khider, D., Knoblock, C. A., Ratnakar, V., Osorio, M., & Shu, L. (2021). Artificial intelligence for modeling complex systems: Taming the complexity of expert models to improve decision making. *ACM Transactions on Interactive Intelligent Systems*, 11(2), 1–49.

Giri, C., Jain, S., Zeng, X., & Bruniaux, P. (2019). A detailed review of artificial intelligence applied in the fashion and apparel industry. *IEEE Access : Practical Innovations, Open Solutions*, 7, 95376–95396.

Gohil, D., & Thakker, S. V. (2021). Blockchain-integrated technologies for solving supply chain challenges. *Modern Supply Chain Research and Applications*, 3(2), 78–97. DOI: 10.1108/MSCRA-10-2020-0028

Gołąbek, M., Senge, R., & Neumann, R. (2020). *Demand Forecasting using Long Short-Term Memory Neural Networks* (Version 1). arXiv. https://doi.org/DOI: 10.48550/ARXIV.2008.08522

Goltsos, T. E., Syntetos, A. A., Glock, C. H., & Ioannou, G. (2022). Inventory–forecasting: Mind the gap. *European Journal of Operational Research*, 299(2), 397–419.

Gonçalves, J. N., Cortez, P., Carvalho, M. S., & Frazao, N. M. (2021). A multivariate approach for multi-step demand forecasting in assembly industries: Empirical evidence from an automotive supply chain. *Decision Support Systems*, 142, 113452.

Goodfellow, I., Pouget-Abadie, J., Mirza, M., Xu, B., Warde-Farley, D., Ozair, S., & Bengio, Y. (2020). Generative adversarial networks. *Communications of the ACM*, 63(11), 139–144.

Goodwin, P., & Fildes, R. (2022). Forecasting with judgment. In *The Palgrave Handbook of Operations Research* (pp. 541–572). Springer International Publishing.

Gopal, P. R. C., Rana, N. P., Krishna, T. V., & Ramkumar, M. (2024). Impact of big data analytics on supply chain performance: An analysis of influencing factors. *Annals of Operations Research*, 333(2), 769–797.

Gorbenko, K., Romanchuk, K., Sagliocca, F., & Mazumdar, M. (2023). A changing supply chain for a changing health care system: Barriers and facilitators of implementing enterprise resource planning. *Work (Reading, Mass.)*, 74(3), 977–990. DOI: 10.3233/WOR-210081 PMID: 36404564

Gordon, A. (2021). Internet of things-based real-time production logistics, big data-driven decision-making processes, and industrial artificial intelligence in sustainable cyber-physical manufacturing systems. *Journal of Self-Governance and Management Economics*, 9(3), 61–73.

Goti, A., Querejeta-Lomas, L., Almeida, A., de la Puerta, J. G., & López-de-Ipiña, D. (2023). Artificial Intelligence in Business-to-Customer Fashion Retail: A Literature Review. *Mathematics*, 11(13), 2943. DOI: 10.3390/math11132943

Govindan, K., Kaliyan, M., Kannan, D., & Haq, A. N. (2014). Barriers analysis for green supply chain management implementation in Indian industries using analytic hierarchy process. *International Journal of Production Economics*, 147, 555–568.

Goyal, M., & Mahmoud, Q. H. (2024). A Systematic Review of Synthetic Data Generation Techniques Using Generative AI. *Electronics (Basel)*, 13(17), 3509.

Graban, M. (2018). Lean hospitals: Improving quality, patient safety, and employee engagement, third edition. *Lean Hospitals: Improving Quality, Patient Safety, and Employee Engagement, Third Edition*, 1–319. https://doi.org/ DOI: 10.4324/9781315380827/LEAN-HOSPITALS-MARK-GRABAN/ACCESSIBILITY-INFORMATION

Grinin, L., Grinin, A., & Korotayev, A. (2021). Global trends and forecasts of the 21st century. *World Futures*, 77(5), 335–370.

Groene, N., & Zakharov, S. (2024). Introduction of AI-based sales forecasting: How to drive digital transformation in food and beverage outlets. *Discover Artificial Intelligence*, 4(1), 1. DOI: 10.1007/s44163-023-00097-x

Gudigantala, N., Madhavaram, S., & Bicen, P. (2023). An AI decision-making framework for business value maximization. *AI Magazine*, 44.

Güler, M., Mukul, E., & Büyüközkan, G. (2022). Assessment of Success Factors for AI Application in Supply Chain Management with Fuzzy SAW-MOORA Methods. *Proceedings of the International Conference on Industrial Engineering and Operations Management*, 2645–2652. https://doi.org/DOI: 10.46254/EU05.20220517

Gümüsay, A. A., Bohné, T., & Davenport, T. (2022). AI and the Future of Management Decision-Making. *Management and Business Review*, 1-19.

Gunasegaram, A. (2004). Supply chain management: Theory and applications. *European Journal of Operational Research*, 159(2), 265–268. DOI: 10.1016/j.ejor.2003.08.015

Gunasekeran, D. V., Tseng, R. M. W. W., Tham, Y. C., & Wong, T. Y. (2021). Applications of digital health for public health responses to COVID-19: a systematic scoping review of artificial intelligence, telehealth and related technologies. In *npj Digital Medicine* (Vol. 4, Issue 1). Nature Research. https://doi.org/DOI: 10.1038/s41746-021-00412-9

Guo, Z. X., Wong, W. K., Leung, S. Y. S., & Li, M. (2011). Applications of artificial intelligence in the apparel industry: A review. *Textile Research Journal*, 81(18), 1871–1892.

Gupta, S., Modgil, S., Lee, C. K., & Sivarajah, U. (2023). The future is yesterday: Use of AI-driven facial recognition to enhance value in the travel and tourism industry. *Information Systems Frontiers*, 25(3), 1179–1195. PMID: 35529102

Gupta, S., Modgil, S., Meissonier, R., & Dwivedi, Y. K. (2024). Artificial Intelligence and Information System Resilience to Cope With Supply Chain Disruption. *IEEE Transactions on Engineering Management*, 71, 10496–10506. DOI: 10.1109/TEM.2021.3116770

Gurzawska, A. (2020). Towards responsible and sustainable supply chains–innovation, multi-stakeholder approach and governance. *Philosophy of Management*, 19(3), 267–295.

Haddud, A., & Khare, A. (2020). Digitalizing supply chains potential benefits and impact on lean operations. *International Journal of Lean Six Sigma*, 11(4), 731–765. DOI: 10.1108/IJLSS-03-2019-0026/FULL/PDF

Hagendorff, T. (2020). The ethics of AI ethics: An evaluation of guidelines. *Minds and Machines*, 30(1), 99–120.

Hallikas, J., Immonen, M., & Brax, S. (2021). Digitalizing procurement: The impact of data analytics on supply chain performance. *Supply Chain Management*, 26(5), 629–646.

Hamilton, E. (2023). The global supply chain consequences of the Russia-Ukraine war. University of Florida News, 21.

Harale, N. (2021). *Development of the supply chain and production management system (SCPMS) for small-series fashion industry* (Doctoral dissertation, Centrale Lille Institut).

Harlin, T., Rova, G. B., Singla, A., Sokolov, O., & Sukharevsky, A. (2023). Exploring opportunities in the generative AI value chain.

Hastie, T., Tibshirani, R., & Friedman, J. H. (2009). *"10. Boosting and Additive Trees". The Elements of Statistical Learning* (2nd ed.). Springer. DOI: 10.1007/978-0-387-84858-7

Hazen, B. T., Skipper, J. B., Boone, C. A., & Hill, R. R. (2018). Back in business: Operations research in support of big data analytics for operations and supply chain management. *Annals of Operations Research*, 270, 201–211.

Helo, P., & Hao, Y. (2022). Artificial intelligence in operations management and supply chain management: An exploratory case study. *Production Planning and Control*, 33(16), 1573–1590. DOI: 10.1080/09537287.2021.1882690

Herbrich, R., Keilbach, M. T., Graepel, P. B.-S., & Obermayer, K. (2000). Neural networks in economics: Background, applications and new developments. *Advances in Computational Economics: Computational Techniques for Modeling Learning in Economics*, 11, 169–196. DOI: 10.1007/978-1-4615-5029-7_7

Hilletofth, P. (2011). Demand-supply chain management: Industrial survival recipe for new decade. *Industrial Management & Data Systems*, 111(2), 184–211. DOI: 10.1108/02635571111115137

Hilletofth, P., & Eriksson, D. (2011). Coordinating new product development with supply chain management. *Industrial Management & Data Systems*, 111(2), 264–281. DOI: 10.1108/02635571111115173

Hobeck, R., Schlieter, H., & Scheplitz, T. (2021). Overcoming diffusion barriers of digital health innovations: Conception of an assessment method. *Proceedings of the Annual Hawaii International Conference on System Sciences, 2020-January*, 3654–3663. https://doi.org/DOI: 10.24251/hicss.2021.443

Hoffmann, A. L. (2021). Terms of inclusion: Data, discourse, violence. *New Media & Society*, 23(12), 3539–3556.

Hofmann, E., & Rüsch, M. (2017). Industry 4.0 and the current status as well as future prospects on logistics. *Computers in Industry*, 89, 23–34.

Hofmann, E., Sternberg, H., Chen, H., Pflaum, A., & Prockl, G. (2019). Supply chain management and Industry 4.0: Conducting research in the digital age. *International Journal of Physical Distribution & Logistics Management*, 49(10), 945–955.

Hofmann, P., Samp, C., & Urbach, N. (2020). Robotic process automation. *Electronic Markets*, 30(1), 99–106. DOI: 10.1007/S12525-019-00365-8/TABLES/1

Hosseinnia Shavaki, F., & Ebrahimi Ghahnavieh, A. (2023). Applications of deep learning into supply chain management: A systematic literature review and a framework for future research. *Artificial Intelligence Review*, 56(5), 4447–4489. DOI: 10.1007/s10462-022-10289-z PMID: 36212799

Hsu, C. H., Chang, A. Y., Zhang, T. Y., Lin, W. D., & Liu, W. L. (2021). Deploying resilience enablers to mitigate risks in sustainable fashion supply chains. *Sustainability*, 13(5), 2943.

Hsu, C. H., Li, M. G., Zhang, T. Y., Chang, A. Y., Shangguan, S. Z., & Liu, W. L. (2022). Deploying big data enablers to strengthen supply chain resilience to mitigate sustainable risks based on integrated HOQ-MCDM framework. *Mathematics*, 10(8), 1233.

Huang, G., Ng, S. T., & Li, D. (2023). Determinants of digital twin adoption in hospital operation management. *Urban Lifeline*, 1(1), 6.

Hübner, N., Caspers, J., Coroamă, V. C., & Finkbeiner, M. (2024). Machine-learning-based demand forecasting against food waste: Life cycle environmental impacts and benefits of a bakery case study. *Journal of Industrial Ecology*, 28(5), 1117–1131. DOI: 10.1111/jiec.13528

Hyunjin, C. (2020). A study on application of generative design system in manufacturing process. [). IOP Publishing.]. *IOP Conference Series. Materials Science and Engineering*, 727(1), 012011.

Indrawati, H. (2020). Barriers to technological innovations of SMEs: How to solve them? *International Journal of Innovation Science*, 12(5), 545–564.

Industry 4.0: Is Africa ready for digital transformation? [online] Available: https://www2.deloitte.com/content/dam/Deloitte/za/Documents/manufacturing/za-Africa-industry-4.0-report-April14.pdf.v

Irfan, I., Sumbal, M. S. U. K., Khurshid, F., & Chan, F. T. (2022). Toward a resilient supply chain model: Critical role of knowledge management and dynamic capabilities. *Industrial Management & Data Systems*, 122(5), 1153–1182.

Isaak, N. (2024). A Human-Machine Collaboration Framework for the Development of Schemas. *arXiv preprint arXiv:2402.07932*.

Isern, J., Meaney, M., & Wilson, S. (2009). Corporate Transformation under Pressure. *McKinsey&Company*. Retrieved from https://www.mckinsey.com/insights/organization/corporate_transformation_under_pressure

Ismail, M. M., Ahmed, Z., Abdel-Gawad, A. F., & Mohamed, M. (2024). Toward Supply Chain 5.0: An Integrated Multi-Criteria Decision-Making Models for Sustainable and Resilience Enterprise. Decision making: applications in management and engineering, 7(1), 160-186.

Ismail, G., & Taliep, N. (2023). The Delphi Method. In *Handbook of Social Sciences and Global Public Health* (pp. 1–19). Springer International Publishing.

Ismaılova, N. (2024). Explore how AI is driving sustainable economic growth and transforming business analysis worldwide. *Journal of Sustainable Development and Green Technology, 4*(2).

Ismail, R., Jeffery, R., & Belle, J.-P. (2011). Using ICT as a value adding tool in South African SMEs. *Journal of African Research in Business and Technology*, 2011, 1–12. DOI: 10.5171/2011.470652

Ivanov, D., & Sokolov, B. (2009). *Adaptive supply chain management*. Springer Science & Business Media.

Ivanov, D., Dolgui, A., Das, A., & Sokolov, B. (2019). Digital supply chain twins: Managing the ripple effect, resilience, and disruption risks by data-driven optimization, simulation, and visibility. *Handbook of ripple effects in the supply chain*, 309-332.

Ivanov, D., Tsipoulanidis, A., & Schönberger, J. (2021a). Demand Forecasting. In D. Ivanov, A. Tsipoulanidis, & J. Schönberger, *Global Supply Chain and Operations Management* (pp. 341–357). Springer International Publishing. https://doi.org/DOI: 10.1007/978-3-030-72331-6_11

Ivanov, D., Tsipoulanidis, A., & Schönberger, J. (2021b). Distribution and Transportation Network Design. In D. Ivanov, A. Tsipoulanidis, & J. Schönberger, *Global Supply Chain and Operations Management* (pp. 223–265). Springer International Publishing. https://doi.org/DOI: 10.1007/978-3-030-72331-6_8

Ivanov, D. (2019). Disruption tails and revival policies: A simulation analysis of supply chain design and production-ordering systems in the recovery and post-disruption periods. *Computers & Industrial Engineering*, 127, 558–570.

Ivanov, D., & Dolgui, A. (2021). A digital supply chain twin for managing the disruption risks and resilience in the era of Industry 4.0. *Production Planning and Control*, 32(9), 775–788.

Ivanov, D., Dolgui, A., & Sokolov, B. (2019). The impact of digital technology and Industry 4.0 on the ripple effect and supply chain risk analytics. *International Journal of Production Research*, 57(3), 829–846.

Ivanov, D., Tang, C. S., Dolgui, A., Battini, D., & Das, A. (2021). Researchers' perspectives on Industry 4.0: Multi-disciplinary analysis and opportunities for operations management. *International Journal of Production Research*, 59(7), 2055–2078.

Jackson, I., Ivanov, D., Dolgui, A., & Namdar, J. (2024). Generative artificial intelligence in supply chain and operations management: A capability-based framework for analysis and implementation. *International Journal of Production Research*, •••, 1–26.

Jain, R. (2023). The Impact of Artificial Intelligence on Business: Opportunities and Challenges. *Available atSSRN* 4407114.

Jaiswal, R., Gupta, S., & Tiwari, A. K. (2023). Dissecting the compensation conundrum: A machine learning-based prognostication of key determinants in a complex labor market. *Management Decision*, 61(8), 2322–2353.

Jauhar, S. K., Jani, S. M., Kamble, S. S., Pratap, S., Belhadi, A., & Gupta, S. (2024). How to use no-code artificial intelligence to predict and minimize the inventory distortions for resilient supply chains. *International Journal of Production Research*, 62(15), 5510–5534.

Jeyaraman, J., Krishnamoorthy, G., Konidena, B. K., & Sistla, S. M. K. (2024). Machine Learning for Demand Forecasting in Manufacturing. *International Journal for Multidisciplinary Research*, 6(1), 1–115.

Jha, A. K., Agi, M. A., & Ngai, E. W. (2020). A note on big data analytics capability development in supply chain. *Decision Support Systems*, 138, 113382.

Johnson, M., & Girard, G. (2024). Empirical Analysis of AI-Driven Systems for Identifying Supply Chain Risks and Strengthening Resilience. *Journal of Environmental Science and Technology*, 3(1), 858–867.

Juan, S. J., Li, E. Y., & Hung, W. H. (2022). An integrated model of supply chain resilience and its impact on supply chain performance under disruption. *International Journal of Logistics Management*, 33(1), 339–364.

Jüttner, U., Peck, H., & Christopher, M. (2003). Supply chain risk management: outlining an agenda for future research. *International Journal of Logistics: Research and Applications, 6*(4), 197-210.

Juturi, V. P. K. (2024). Advancing Enterprise Applications with Transformative Effects of Digital Technologies. *International Journal of Research Publication and Reviews*, 5(7). Advance online publication. DOI: 10.55248/GENGPI.5.0724.1925

Kadhim Abbas, H. (2019). Bayesian Lasso Tobit regression. *Journal of Al-Qadisiyah for Computer Science and Mathematics*, 11(2), 1–13. DOI: 10.29304/jqcm.2019.11.2.553

Kanike, U. K. (2023). Factors disrupting supply chain management in manufacturing industries. *Journal of Supply Chain Management Science*, 4(1-2), 1–24.

Kanyepe, , JZizhou, , BAlphaneta, , MChifamba, , N. (2023). Lead-time management, information sharing and performance of the motor industry in Zimbabwe. *European Journal of Management Studies, 28*(3), 229-246. https://doi.org/10.1108/EJMS-06-2023-0044

Kaplan, R. S. (2010). Conceptual Foundations of the Balanced Scorecard. Harvard Business School Accounting & Management Unit Working Paper No. 10-074. Retrieved from: https://ssrn.com/abstract=1562586

Karim, M., Rahman, M. A., Tan, S. W., Atiquzzaman, M., Pillai, P., & Alenezi, A. H. (2024). Intra-vehicular Communication Protocol for IoT Enabled Vehicle Health Monitoring System: Challenges, issues and Solutions. *IEEE Access : Practical Innovations, Open Solutions*.

Karp, T. (2005). Unpacking the Mysteries of Change: Mental Modeling. *Journal of Change Management*, 5(1), 87–97. DOI: 10.1080/14697010500057573

Kasemsap, K. (2016). Lean thinking in global health care: Theory and applications. In *Handbook of Research on Healthcare Administration and Management*. https://doi.org/DOI: 10.4018/978-1-5225-0920-2.ch008

Kashem, M. A., Shamsuddoha, M., Nasir, T., & Chowdhury, A. A. (2024). Supply Chain Disruption versus Optimization: A Review on Artificial Intelligence and Blockchain. *Knowledge (Beverly Hills, Calif.)*, 3(1), 80–96.

Kelleher, J. D., Namee, B. M., & D'Arcy, A. (2020). Fundamentals of Machine Learning for Predictive Data Analytics, *second edition: Algorithms, Worked Examples, and Case Studies*. MIT Press.

Keown, D. (2024). "Exscientia Launches AWS AI-powered Platform to Advance Drug Discovery," *Exscientia.com*, https://investors.exscientia.ai/press-releases/press-release-details/2024/Exscientia-Launches-AWS-AI-powered-Platform-to-Advance-Drug-Discovery/default.aspx.

Khan, B., Fatima, H., Qureshi, A., Kumar, S., Hanan, A., Hussain, J., & Abdullah, S. (2023). Drawbacks of artificial intelligence and their potential solutions in the healthcare sector. *Biomedical Materials & Devices*, 1(2), 731–738.

Khan, S. A. R., Piprani, A. Z., & Yu, Z. (2023). Supply chain analytics and post-pandemic performance: Mediating role of triple-A supply chain strategies. *International Journal of Emerging Markets*, 18(6), 1330–1354.

Khatua, A., Khatua, A., Chi, X., & Cambria, E. (2021). Artificial intelligence, social media and supply chain management: The way forward. *Electronics (Basel)*, 10(19), 2348. DOI: 10.3390/electronics10192348

Khlie, K., Benmamoun, Z., Fethallah, W., & Jebbor, I. (2024). Leveraging variational autoencoders and recurrent neural networks for demand forecasting in supply chain management: A case study. *Journal of Infrastructure. Policy and Development*, 8(8), 6639.

Kliestik, T., Nagy, M., & Valaskova, K. (2023). Global value chains and industry 4.0 in the context of lean workplaces for enhancing company performance and its comprehension via the digital readiness and expertise of workforce in the V4 nations. *Mathematics*, 11(3), 601. DOI: 10.3390/math11030601

Köksal, D., Strähle, J., Müller, M., & Freise, M. (2017). Social sustainable supply chain management in the textile and apparel industry—A literature review. *Sustainability*, 9(1), 100.

Kolasani, S. (2023). Innovations in digital, enterprise, cloud, data transformation, and organizational change management using agile, lean, and data-driven methodologies. *International*. https://jmlai.in/

Kottala, S. Y. (2021). Sustainable supply chain management practices: A review. *International Journal of Social Ecology and Sustainable Development*, 12(3), 47–65.

Kotter, J. P. (1996). *Leading Change*. Boston Harvard Business School Press.

Kulkarni, N. D., & Bansal, S. (2024). Transforming Supply and Value Chains: The Impact of Artificial Intelligence A Review. *International Research Journal of Modernization in Engineering Technology and Science*. Advance online publication. DOI: 10.56726/IRJMETS49042

Kumar, B. R., Reddy, S. M., Madhuri, A., & Shireesha, M. (2024). The Role of Artificial Intelligence in Decision-Making Processes.

Kumar, A., Mani, V., Jain, V., Gupta, H., & Venkatesh, V. G. (2022). Managing healthcare supply chain through artificial intelligence (AI): A study of critical success factors. *Computers & Industrial Engineering*, 175, 108815. DOI: 10.1016/J.CIE.2022.108815 PMID: 36405396

Kumar, P., Bera, S., Dutta, T., & Chakraborty, S. (2018). Auxiliary flexibility in healthcare delivery system: An integrative framework and implications. *Global Journal of Flexible Systems Managment*, 19(2), 173–186. DOI: 10.1007/S40171-018-0183-Y/FIGURES/1

Kumar, P., Choubey, D., Amosu, O. R., & Ogunsuji, Y. M. (2024). AI-enhanced inventory and demand forecasting: Using AI to optimize inventory management and predict customer demand. *World Journal of Advanced Research and Reviews*, 23(1), 1931–1944. DOI: 10.30574/wjarr.2024.23.1.2173

Kumar, R., Singh, K., & Jain, S. K. (2019). Development of a framework for agile manufacturing. *World Journal of Science. Technology and Sustainable Development*, 16(4), 161–169.

Kuo, A. M. H., Borycki, E., Kushniruk, A., & Lee, T. S. (2011). A healthcare Lean Six Sigma System for postanesthesia care unit workflow improvement. *Quality Management in Health Care*, 20(1), 4–14. DOI: 10.1097/QMH.0B013E3182033791 PMID: 21192203

Kurkina, I. (2023). "Leveraging of Cloud Computing in Supply Chain Management," *Academy Smart*, academysmart.com/insights/ leveraging-of-cloud-computing-in-supply-chain-management.

Lambert, D. M., & Cooper, M. C. (2000). Issues in Supply Chain Management. *Industrial Marketing Management*, 29(1), 65–83. DOI: 10.1016/S0019-8501(99)00113-3

Lasorsa, I., Liuzzi, G., Calabrese, R., & Accardo, A. (2015). An innovative method for standardizing lean management approach in hospitals. *IFMBE Proceedings*, 48, 67–70. DOI: 10.1007/978-3-319-12967-9_18

Latif, M. N. A., Aziz, N. A. A., Hussin, N. S. N., & Aziz, Z. A. (2021). Cyber security in supply chain management: A systematic review. *LogForum*, 17(1), 49–57.

Lazzeri, F. (2020). *Machine learning for time series forecasting with Python*. John Wiley & Sons.

Lee, I., & Mangalaraj, G. (2022). Big data analytics in supply chain management: A systematic literature review and research directions. *Big Data and Cognitive Computing, 6*(1), 17.

Lee, E. J., Bae, J., & Kim, K. H. (2020). The effect of environmental cues on the purchase intention of sustainable products. *Journal of Business Research*, 120, 425–433.

Lee, E. K., Atallah, H. Y., Wright, M. D., Post, E. T., Thomas, C., Wu, D. T., & Haley, L. L. (2015). Transforming hospital emergency department workflow and patient care. *Interfaces*, 45(1), 58–82. DOI: 10.1287/inte.2014.0788

Lee, H. L., & Whang, S. (2001). Winning the last mile of e-commerce. *MIT Sloan Management Review*.

Lee, I., & Lee, K. (2015). The Internet of Things (IoT): Applications, investments, and challenges for enterprises. *Business Horizons*, 58(4), 431–440.

Lee, J., Bagheri, B., & Kao, H. A. (2015). A cyber-physical systems architecture for industry 4.0-based manufacturing systems. *Manufacturing Letters*, 3, 18–23.

Lee, K. H., Arshad, Z., Dahshan, A., Alshareef, M., Alsulami, Q. A., Bibi, A., & Javid, A. (2023). Porous aerogel structures as promising materials for photocatalysis, thermal insulation textiles, and technical applications: A review. *Catalysts*, 13(9), 1286.

Lee, Y. K. (2021). Transformation of the innovative and sustainable supply chain with upcoming real-time fashion systems. *Sustainability (Basel)*, 13(3), 1081. DOI: 10.3390/su13031081

Leon, S. (2017) 'Integrating the Chatbot'. Retrieved from: https://www.capgemini.com, accessed on 15/09/2017.

Leonard and Coltea. (2013).Most Change Initiatives Fail -- But They Don't Have To http://businessjournal.gallup.com

Leonard, M. (2020, July 1). *MSC adds instant quotes to website*. Supply Chain Dive. https://www.supplychaindive.com/news/msc-instant-booking-quotes/580869/

Li, L. T., Haley, L. C., Boyd, A. K., & Bernstam, E. V. (2023). Technical/Algorithm, Stakeholder, and Society (TASS) barriers to the application of artificial intelligence in medicine: A systematic review. *Journal of Biomedical Informatics*, 147. Advance online publication. DOI: 10.1016/j.jbi.2023.104531 PMID: 37884177

Li, L., Liu, Y., Jin, Y., Cheng, T. E., & Zhang, Q. (2024). Generative AI-enabled supply chain management: A coordination theory perspective. *International Journal of Production Economics*, •••, 109388.

Li, Q., Xue, Z., Wu, Y., & Zeng, X. (2022). The status quo and prospect of sustainable development of smart clothing. *Sustainability (Basel)*, 14(2), 990. DOI: 10.3390/su14020990

Li, S., Xu, L. D., & Zhao, S. (2015). The internet of things: A survey. *Information Systems Frontiers*, 17, 243–259.

Liu, C., Feng, Y., Lin, D., Wu, L., & Guo, M. (2020). Iot based laundry services: An application of big data analytics, intelligent logistics management, and machine learning techniques. *International Journal of Production Research*, 58(17), 5113–5131. DOI: 10.1080/00207543.2019.1677961

Liu, J., Feng, Y., Zhu, Q., & Sarkis, J. (2018). Green supply chain management and the circular economy: Reviewing theory for advancement of both fields. *International Journal of Physical Distribution & Logistics Management*, 48(8), 794–817.

Liu, K. S., & Lin, M. H. (2021). Performance Assessment on the Application of Artificial Intelligence to Sustainable Supply Chain Management in the Construction Material Industry. *Sustainability (Basel)*, 13(22), 12767. DOI: 10.3390/su132212767

Liu, L., Song, W., & Liu, Y. (2023). Leveraging digital capabilities toward a circular economy: Reinforcing sustainable supply chain management with Industry 4.0 technologies. *Computers & Industrial Engineering*, 178, 109113. DOI: 10.1016/J.CIE.2023.109113

Liu, W., Liang, Y., Lim, M. K., Long, S., & Shi, X. (2022). A theoretical framework of smart supply chain innovation for going global companies: A multi-case study from China. *International Journal of Logistics Management*, 33(3), 1090–1113. DOI: 10.1108/IJLM-10-2020-0388

Liu, Y., Alias, A. H. B., Haron, N. A., Bakar, N. A., & Wang, H. (2024). Exploring three pillars of construction robotics via dual-track quantitative analysis. *Automation in Construction*, 162, 105391.

Li, Y., Diabat, A., & Lu, C.-C. (2020). Leagile Supplier Selection in Chinese Textile Industries: A DEMATEL Approach. *Annals of Operations Research*, 287(1), 303–322. DOI: 10.1007/s10479-019-03453-2

Logistics, I. T. com. (2024). *The intersection of sustainability and productivity | Manufacturing & Logistics IT Magazine*. https://www.logisticsit.com/articles/2024/02/06/the-intersection-of-sustainability-and-productivity

Longo, F., Padovano, A., Cimmino, B., & Pinto, P. (2021). Towards a mass customization in the fashion industry: An evolutionary decision aid model for apparel product platform design and optimization. *Computers & Industrial Engineering*, 162, 107742.

Lovell, A., Saw, R., & Stimson, J. (2005). Product Value-Density: Managing Diversity Through Supply Chain Segmentation. *International Journal of Logistics Management*, 16(1), 142–158.

Luce, L. (2018). *Artificial intelligence for fashion: How AI is revolutionizing the fashion industry*. Apress.

Lv, Z., Qiao, L., Wang, Q., & Piccialli, F. (2020). Advanced machine-learning methods for brain-computer interfacing. *IEEE/ACM Transactions on Computational Biology and Bioinformatics*, 18(5), 1688–1698. PMID: 32750892

MacCarthy, B. L., & Ivanov, D. (Eds.). (2022). *The digital supply chain*. Elsevier.

Machuca, J. A., del Mar Gonzalez-Zamora, M., & Aguilar-Escobar, V. G. (2007). Service operations management research. *Journal of Operations Management*, 25(3), 585–603.

Madakam, S., Holmukhe, R. M., & Kumar Jaiswal, D. (2019). The Future Digital Work Force: Robotic Process Automation (RPA). *Journal of Information Systems and Technology Management*, 16(1), 1–17. DOI: 10.4301/S1807-1775201916001

Majda, B., & Farouk Imane, I. E. (2024). Demand-Driven Supply Chain Harmonizing Digitalization, Resilience, and Sustainability: Exploring the Synergy through a Bibliometric Literature Review. *2024 IEEE 15th International Colloquium on Logistics and Supply Chain Management (LOGISTIQUA)*, 1–7. https://doi.org/DOI: 10.1109/LOGISTIQUA61063.2024.10571448

Majumder, S., & Dey, N. (2024). Industry 4.0 Challenges and Risks. In *A Notion of Enterprise Risk Management: Enhancing Strategies and Wellbeing Programs* (pp. 81-107). Emerald Publishing Limited.

Malhotra, G., & Kharub, M. (2024). Elevating logistics performance: Harnessing the power of artificial intelligence in e-commerce. *The International Journal of Logistics Management, ahead-of-print*(ahead-of-print). https://doi.org/DOI: 10.1108/IJLM-01-2024-0046

Mamede, F. P., Da Silva, R. F., De Brito, I.Jr, Yoshizaki, H. T. Y., Hino, C. M., & Cugnasca, C. E. (2023). Deep Learning and Statistical Models for Forecasting Transportation Demand: A Case Study of Multiple Distribution Centers. *Logistics (Basel)*, 7(4), 86. DOI: 10.3390/logistics7040086

Manzouri, M., Ab-Rahman, M. N., Zain, C. R. C. M., & Jamsari, E. A. (2014). Increasing Production and Eliminating Waste through Lean Tools and Techniques for Halal Food Companies. *Sustainability 2014, Vol. 6, Pages 9179-9204, 6*(12), 9179–9204. https://doi.org/DOI: 10.3390/SU6129179

Mason-Jones, R., Naylor, B., & Towill, D. (2000). Engineering the Leagile Supply Chain. *International Journal of Agile Management*, 2(1), 54–61.

McKesson Health Systems Editorial Team. "Challenges Affecting Supply Chain to Continue Beyond Pandemic," McKesson, https://www.mckesson.com/pharmacy-management/health-systems/prescribed-perspectives/challenges-affecting-supply-chain-to-continue-beyond-pandemic, 2022

McKinsey & Company. (2020). Launching the journey to autonomous supply chain planning. Kuntze, C., Lal, S., & Seibert, K. https://www.mckinsey.com/capabilities/operations/our-insights/launching-the-journey-to-autonomous-supply-chain-planning

McKinsey (2023). What is generative AI?

McKinsey. (2022). *Unlocking the promise of AI in industrials | McKinsey*. https://www.mckinsey.com/industries/automotive-and-assembly/our-insights/the-future-is-now-unlocking-the-promise-of-ai-in-industrials

Mearian, L. (2024). How DHL harnessed genAI to unify 200 career sites into a single platform. *Computerworld*. https://www.computerworld.com/article/2083870/how-dhl-harnessed-genai-to-unify-200-career-sites-into-a-single-platform.html

Mendes, P. (2011a). Key Components of Demand Driven Supply Chain. In P. Mendes, *Demand Driven Supply Chain* (pp. 39–119). Springer Berlin Heidelberg. https://doi.org/DOI: 10.1007/978-3-642-19992-9_4

Mendes, P. (2011b). Literature Review on Demand Driven Supply Chain (DDSC). In P. Mendes, *Demand Driven Supply Chain* (pp. 5–24). Springer Berlin Heidelberg. https://doi.org/DOI: 10.1007/978-3-642-19992-9_2

Mendes, P., Leal, J. E., & Thomé, A. M. T. (2016). A maturity model for demand-driven supply chains in the consumer product goods industry. *International Journal of Production Economics*, 179, 153–165. DOI: 10.1016/j.ijpe.2016.06.004

Microsoft Inc. (2024). Optimize supply chain resiliency by integrating diverse AI-powered solutions. Raval, R. https://www.microsoft.com/en-us/industry/blog/manufacturing-and-mobility/2024/08/29/optimize-supply-chain-resiliency-by-integrating-diverse-ai-powered-solutions/

Minerva, R., Biru, A., & Rotondi, D. (2015). Towards a definition of the Internet of Things (IoT). *IEEE Internet Initiative*, 1(1), 1–86.

Min, H. (2010). Artificial intelligence in supply chain management: Theory and applications. *International Journal of Logistics: Research and Applications*, 13(1), 13–39.

Mircetic, D., Rostami-Tabar, B., Nikolicic, S., & Maslaric, M. (2022). Forecasting hierarchical time series in supply chains: An empirical investigation. *International Journal of Production Research*, 60(8), 2514–2533. DOI: 10.1080/00207543.2021.1896817

Miroedova, S. (2023). Thesis Study: analysis of the implementation of Artificial Intelligence in warehouses of e-commerce SMEs based on feasibility study.

Mishra, D., Gunasekaran, A., Papadopoulos, T., & Childe, S. J. (2018). Big Data and supply chain management: A review and bibliometric analysis. *Annals of Operations Research*, 270, 313–336.

Mišić, V. V., & Perakis, G. (2020). Data analytics in operations management: A review. *Manufacturing & Service Operations Management*, 22(1), 158–169.

Mittelstadt, B. (2019). Principles alone cannot guarantee ethical AI. *Nature Machine Intelligence*, 1(11), 501–507.

Modgil, S., Singh, R. K., & Hannibal, C. (2022). Artificial intelligence for supply chain resilience: Learning from Covid-19. *International Journal of Logistics Management*, 33(4), 1246–1268.

Mohan, V. (2008, June). D. Jeya Mala " IntelligenTester-Test Sequence Optimization framework using Multi-Agents. *Journal of Computers*.

Mohiuddin Babu, M., Akter, S., Rahman, M., Billah, M. M., & Hack-Polay, D. (2022). The role of artificial intelligence in shaping the future of Agile fashion industry. *Production Planning and Control*, •••, 1–15.

Mohsen, B. M. (2023). Impact of Artificial Intelligence on Supply Chain Management Performance. *Journal of Service Science and Management*, 16(01), 44–58. DOI: 10.4236/jssm.2023.161004

Monostori, L. (2014). Cyber-physical production systems: Roots, expectations and R&D challenges. *Procedia CIRP*, 17, 9–13.

Moreno-Fergusson, M. E., Guerrero Rueda, W. J., Ortiz Basto, G. A., Arevalo Sandoval, I. A. L., & Sanchez–Herrera, B. (2021). Analytics and Lean Health Care to Address Nurse Care Management Challenges for Inpatients in Emerging Economies. *Journal of Nursing Scholarship*, 53(6), 803–814. DOI: 10.1111/jnu.12711 PMID: 34668285

Mostafa, N., Hamdy, W., & Elawady, H. (2020). An intelligent warehouse management system using the internet of things. *The Egyptian International Journal of Engineering Sciences and Technology, 32. Mechanical Engineering (New York, N.Y.)*, 59–65.

Moyano-Fuentes, J., Bruque-Cámara, S., & Maqueira-Marín, J. M. (2019). Development and validation of a lean supply chain management measurement instrument. *Production Planning and Control*, 30(1), 20–32. DOI: 10.1080/09537287.2018.1519731

Moyano-Fuentes, J., & Sacristán-Díaz, M. (2012). Learning on lean: A review of thinking and research. *International Journal of Operations & Production Management*, 32(5), 551–582. DOI: 10.1108/01443571211226498/FULL/PDF

Mungoli, N. (2023). Revolutionizing Industries: The Impact of Artificial Intelligence Technologies. *Journal of Electrical and Electronics Engineering (Oradea)*, 2(3). Advance online publication. DOI: 10.33140/JEEE.02.03.03

Muñoz-Villamizar, A., Rafavy, C. Y., & Casey, J. (2022). Machine learning and optimization-based modeling for asset management: A case study. *International Journal of Productivity and Performance Management*, 71(4), 1149–1163. DOI: 10.1108/IJPPM-05-2020-0206

Mustafee, N., Katsaliaki, K., Gunasekaran, A., Williams, M. D., Virtue, A., Chaussalet, T., & Kelly, J. (2013). Healthcare planning and its potential role increasing operational efficiency in the health sector: A viewpoint. *Journal of Enterprise Information Management*, 26(1–2), 8–20. DOI: 10.1108/17410391311289523/FULL/PDF

Muthaluri, J. (2024). Optimizing Supply Chain Management And Marketing Strategies: AI And ML Integration For Competitive Advantage. *Educational Administration: Theory and Practice*, 8990–8997. https://doi.org/DOI: 10.53555/kuey.v30i5.4494

Mwangi, J. (2024). Analyzing the Role of Artificial Intelligence and Machine Learning in Optimizing Supply Chain Processes in Kenya. *International Journal of Supply Chain Management*, 9(1), 39–50. DOI: 10.47604/ijscm.2322

Nadler, D. A., & Tushman, M. (1989). Organizational Frame Bending: Principles for Managing Reorientation. *The Academy of Management Executive*, 3(3), 194–204.

Nagar, D., Raghav, S., Bhardwaj, A., Kumar, R., Singh, P. L., & Sindhwani, R. (2021). Machine learning: Best way to sustain the supply chain in the era of industry 4.0. *Materials Today: Proceedings*, 47, 3676–3682. DOI: 10.1016/j.matpr.2021.01.267

Nagurney, A. (2006). On the relationship between supply chain and transportation network equilibria: A supernetwork equivalence with computations. *Transportation Research Part E, Logistics and Transportation Review*, 42(4), 293–316.

Nassibi, N., Fasihuddin, H., & Hsairi, L. (2023). Demand Forecasting Models for Food Industry by Utilizing Machine Learning Approaches. *International Journal of Advanced Computer Science and Applications*, 14(3). Advance online publication. DOI: 10.14569/IJACSA.2023.01403101

Nayak, K. K., Singhal, D., & Tripathy, S. (2021). Determination of challenges and driving forces of green supply chain management in Indian manufacturing industries: A critical review. *International Journal of Logistics Systems and Management*, 40(1), 28–51.

Nayal, K., Raut, R., Priyadarshinee, P., Narkhede, B. E., Kazancoglu, Y., & Narwane, V. (2022). Exploring the role of artificial intelligence in managing agricultural supply chain risk to counter the impacts of the COVID-19 pandemic. *International Journal of Logistics Management*, 33(3), 744–772.

Naylor, J., Naim, M., & Berry, D. (1999). Leagility: Integrating the Lean and Agile Manufacturing Paradigms in the Total Supply Chain. *International Journal of Production Economics*, 62(1–2), 107–118.

Negri, M., Cagno, E., Colicchia, C., & Sarkis, J. (2021). Integrating sustainability and resilience in the supply chain: A systematic literature review and a research agenda. *Business Strategy and the Environment*, 30(7), 2858–2886.

Netland, T., & Alfnes, E. (2008). A practical tool for supply chain improvement – experiences with the supply chain maturity assessment test (SCMAT). EurOMA/POMS/JOMSA Conference. Tokyo, Japan.

Neubert, G., Ouzrout, Y., & Bouras, A. (2004). Collaboration and integration through information technologies in supply chains. *International Journal of Technology Management*, 28(2), 259. DOI: 10.1504/IJTM.2004.005065

Nguyen, T. T. T., & Nghiem, T. L. (2023). Predicting Risks for Supply Chain Management Networks with Machine Learning Algorithm. *Journal of Trade Science*, 64–73. https://doi.org/DOI: 10.54404/JTS.2023.11.01.06

Niaz, M., & Nwagwu, U. (2023). Managing Healthcare Product Demand Effectively in The Post-Covid-19 Environment: Navigating Demand Variability and Forecasting Complexities. [AJEMB]. *American Journal of Economic and Management Business*, 2(8), 316–330.

Nicholas, J. (2012). An integrated lean-methods approach to hospital facilities redesign. *Hospital Topics*, 90(2), 47–55. DOI: 10.1080/00185868.2012.679911 PMID: 22671435

Nikolopoulos, K. (2021). We need to talk about intermittent demand forecasting. *European Journal of Operational Research*, 291(2), 549–559.

Nilay Yücenur, G., Şentürk, S., & Taşpatlatanlar, E. (2024). Lean management approach in health sector: MCDM model proposal to prevention of waste. *Decision Science Letters*, 13, 427–440. DOI: 10.5267/dsl.2024.1.004

Nimmagadda, V. S. P. (2021). Artificial Intelligence for Real-Time Logistics and Transportation Optimization in Retail Supply Chains: Techniques, Models, and Applications. *Journal of Machine Learning for Healthcare Decision Support*, 1(1), 88–126. https://medlines.uk/index.php/JMLHDS/article/view/35

Noor, A., Saeed, M. A., Ullah, T., Uddin, Z., & Ullah Khan, R. M. W. (2022). A review of artificial intelligence applications in apparel industry. *Journal of the Textile Institute*, 113(3), 505–514. DOI: 10.1080/00405000.2021.1880088

Noorden, C., Stokel, W., & Van, R. (2023). The Promise and Peril of generative AI.

Notin, P., Hernández-Lobato, J. M., & Gal, Y. (2021). Improving black-box optimization in VAE latent space using decoder uncertainty. *Advances in Neural Information Processing Systems*, 34, 802–814.

Nouinou, H., Asadollahi-Yazdi, E., Baret, I., Nguyen, N. Q., Terzi, M., Ouazene, Y., Yalaoui, F., & Kelly, R. (2023). Decision-making in the context of Industry 4.0: Evidence from the textile and clothing industry. *Journal of Cleaner Production*, 391, 136184. DOI: 10.1016/j.jclepro.2023.136184

Noura, M., Atiquzzaman, M., & Gaedke, M. (2019). Interoperability in internet of things: Taxonomies and open challenges. *Mobile Networks and Applications*, 24, 796–809.

Núñez-Merino, M., Maqueira-Marín, J. M., Moyano-Fuentes, J., & Martínez-Jurado, P. J. (2020). Information and digital technologies of Industry 4.0 and Lean supply chain management: A systematic literature review. *International Journal of Production Research*, 58(16), 5034–5061. DOI: 10.1080/00207543.2020.1743896

O'Toole, J. (2011). "Thailand floods stall automakers," *CNNMoney*, www.money.cnn.com/2011/10/28/news/international/ thailand_floods_automakers/index.htm.

Odulaja, B. A., Oke, T. T., Eleogu, T., Abdul, A. A., & Daraojimba, H. O. (2023). Resilience in the face of uncertainty: A review on the impact of supply chain volatility amid ongoing geopolitical disruptions. *International Journal of Applied Research in Social Sciences*, 5(10), 463–486.

Ofori, F., Maina, E., & Gitonga, R. (2020). Using machine learning algorithms to predict students' performance and improve learning outcome: A literature based review. *Journal of Information Technology*, 4(1), 33–55.

Oger, R., Lauras, M., Montreuil, B., & Benaben, F. (2022). A decision support system for strategic supply chain capacity planning under uncertainty: Conceptual framework and experiment. *Enterprise Information Systems*, 16(5), 1793390.

Ojo, B. (2024). Resilience and sustainability of supply chains in the face of natural disasters and climate change. *International Journal of Science and Research Archive*, 12(1), 2996–3007.

Oksanen, L. (2023). Agile fashion retail: exploring the enablers and challenges in agile procurement and supply chain management.

Oliveira, J., Sá, J. C., & Fernandes, A. (2017). Continuous improvement through "Lean Tools": An application in a mechanical company. *Procedia Manufacturing*, 13, 1082–1089. DOI: 10.1016/J.PROMFG.2017.09.139

Oliveira, T., Martins, R., Sarker, S., Thomas, M., & Popovič, A. (2019). Understanding SaaS adoption: The moderating impact of the environment context. *International Journal of Information Management*, 49, 1–12.

Onososen, A. O., & Musonda, I. (2022). Research focus for construction robotics and human-robot teams towards resilience in construction: Scientometric review. *Journal of Engineering, Design and Technology, 21*(2), 502-526.

Ooi, K. B., Tan, G. W. H., Al-Emran, M., Al-Sharafi, M. A., Capatina, A., Chakraborty, A., & Wong, L. W. (2023). The potential of generative artificial intelligence across disciplines: Perspectives and future directions. *Journal of Computer Information Systems*, •••, 1–32.

Orang, O., de Lima e Silva, P. C., & Guimarães, F. G. (2023). Time series forecasting using fuzzy cognitive maps: A survey. *Artificial Intelligence Review*, 56(8), 7733–7794.

Oyewole, A. T., Okoye, C. C., Ofodile, O. C., & Ejairu, E. (2024). Reviewing predictive analytics in supply chain management: Applications and benefits. *World Journal of Advanced Research and Reviews*, 21(3), 568–574.

Pagell, M., & Shevchenko, A. (2014). Why research in sustainable supply chain management should have no future. *The Journal of Supply Chain Management*, 50(1), 44–55.

Pagliosa, M., Tortorella, G., & Ferreira, J. C. E. (2021). Industry 4.0 and Lean Manufacturing: A systematic literature review and future research directions. *Journal of Manufacturing Technology Management*, 32(3), 543–569. DOI: 10.1108/JMTM-12-2018-0446

Pal, K. (2018). "A Big Data Framework for Decision Making in Supply Chain", In M. V Kumar, G. D. Putnik, J. Javakrishna, V. M. Pillai, L. Varela (Edited); IGI Publication, September 2018, USA, Chapter 1, IGI Global Publication, Hershey PA, USA.

Pal, K. (2020). "Information Sharing for Manufacturing Supply Chain Management Based on Blockchain Technology", in Dr Idongesit Williams (Eds.), Cross-Industry Use of Blockchain Technology and Opportunities for the Future, Chapter 1, May, IGI Global Publication, Hershey PA, USA. DOI: 10.4018/978-1-7998-3632-2.ch001

Pal, K., & Ul-Haque, A. (2000). "Internet of Things and Blockchain Technology in Apparel Manufacturing Supply Chain Data Management", In the proceeding of 11th International Conference on Ambient Systems, Networks and Technologies (ANT-2020), Procedia Computer Science, pp. 450- 457, April 6-9, Warsaw, Poland.

Pal, S. (2023). Sustainability in Supply Chain Management: A Systematic Review of the Literature. *International Journal of Creative Research Thoughts*.

Pal, K. (2017). Supply Chain Coordination Based on Web Services. In Chan, H. K., Subramanian, N., & Abdulrahman, M. D. (Eds.), *Supply Chain Management in the Big Data Era* (pp. 137–171). IGI Global Publication. DOI: 10.4018/978-1-5225-0956-1.ch009

Pal, K., & Karakostas, B. (2014). A Multi Agent-Based Service Framework for Supply Chain Management, In the proceeding of International Conference on Ambient Systems, Networks and Technology. *Procedia Computer Science*, 32, 53–60. DOI: 10.1016/j.procs.2014.05.397

Pal, R., & Jayarathne, A. (2022). Digitalization in the textiles and clothing sector. In *The Digital Supply Chain* (pp. 255–271). Elsevier. DOI: 10.1016/B978-0-323-91614-1.00015-0

Panch, T., Szolovits, P., & Atun, R. (2018). Artificial intelligence, machine learning and health systems. *Journal of Global Health*, 8(2), 020303. DOI: 10.7189/JOGH.08.020303 PMID: 30405904

Pandey, B. K., Paramashivan, M. A., Kanike, U. K., Mahajan, D. A., Mahajan, R., George, A. S., & Hameed, A. S. H. (2024). Impacts of Artificial Intelligence and Machine Learning on Intelligent Supply Chains. In *AI and Machine Learning Impacts in Intelligent Supply Chain* (pp. 57–73). IGI Global.

Pandey, S., Gupta, S., & Chhajed, S. (2021). *ROI of AI: Effectiveness and Measurement. International Journal Of Engineering Research & Technology* (Vol. 10). IJERT.

Panigrahi, S. S., Bahinipati, B., & Jain, V. (2019). Sustainable supply chain management: A review of literature and implications for future research. *Management of Environmental Quality*, 30(5), 1001–1049.

Pasupuleti, V., Thuraka, B., Kodete, C. S., & Malisetty, S. (2024). Enhancing supply chain agility and sustainability through machine learning: Optimization techniques for logistics and inventory management. *Logistics (Basel)*, 8(3), 73.

Patel, S., Patel, U., Nanavati, J., & Patel, A. (2024, February). Analyzing Generative Models for Realistic Data Augmentation across Modalities and Applications. In *2024 11th International Conference on Computing for Sustainable Global Development (INDIACom)* (pp. 1601-1606). IEEE.

Păvăloaia, V. D., & Necula, S. C. (2023). Artificial intelligence as a disruptive technology—A systematic literature review. *Electronics (Basel)*, 12(5), 1102.

Pawlicka, K., & Bal, M. (2022). Sustainable Supply Chain Finances implementation model and Artificial Intelligence for innovative omnichannel logistics. *Management*, 26(1), 19–35. DOI: 10.2478/manment-2019-0082

Peano, C., Girgenti, V., Baudino, C., & Giuggioli, N. (2017). Blueberry Supply Chain in Italy: Management, Innovation and Sustainability. *Sustainability*, 9(2), 261. DOI: 10.3390/su9020261

Pekarcıkova, M., Trebuna, P., Kliment, M., & Trojan, J. (2019). Demand driven material requirements planning. Some methodical and practical comments. *Management and Production Engineering Review*. https://doi.org/DOI: 10.24425/mper.2019.129568

Peng, L., & Zhang, X. (2024). Research on the Influence of AI Application on Business Decision Making Based on Machine Learning Algorithm. *Proceedings of the 4th International Conference on Economic Management and Big Data Applications, ICEMBDA 2023, October 27–29, 2023, Tianjin, China*. Proceedings of the 4th International Conference on Economic Management and Big Data Applications, ICEMBDA 2023, October 27–29, 2023, Tianjin, China, Tianjin, People's Republic of China. https://doi.org/DOI: 10.4108/eai.27-10-2023.2341918

Perdomo-Verdecia, V., Sacristán-Díaz, M., & Garrido-Vega, P. (2022). Lean management in hotels: Where we are and where we might go. *International Journal of Hospitality Management*, 104, 103250. DOI: 10.1016/J.IJHM.2022.103250

Pessot, E., Zangiacomi, A., Marchiori, I., & Fornasiero, R. (2023). Empowering supply chains with Industry 4.0 technologies to face megatrends. *Journal ofBusiness Logistics*, 44(4), 609–640. DOI: 10.1111/jbl.12360

Pettit, S., & Wang, Y. (2022). *Cardiff University Press*. Digital Supply Chain Transformation, Emerging Technologies for Sustainable Growth.

Phillips-Wren, G., & Jain, L. (2006, October). Artificial intelligence for decision making. In *International Conference on Knowledge-Based and Intelligent Information and Engineering Systems* (pp. 531-536). Berlin, Heidelberg: Springer Berlin Heidelberg.

Poluha, R. G. (2007). Application of the SCOR model in supply chain management. Cambria Press.

Port of Rotterdam. (2024). *Vessels participating in Nextlogic spend 20% less time in port | Port of Rotterdam*. https://www.portofrotterdam.com/en/news-and-press-releases/vessels-participating-in-nextlogic-spend-20-less-time-in-port

Porter, M. (1996). What is Strategy. *Harvard Business Review*, •••, 1996. PMID: 10158475

Potdar, K., Pardawala, T., & Pai, C. (2017). A Comparative Study of Categorical Variable Encoding Techniques for Neural Network Classifiers. *International Journal of Computer Applications*, 175(4), 7–9. DOI: 10.5120/ijca2017915495

Pundir, A. K., Jagannath, J. D., & Ganapathy, L. (2019, January). Improving supply chain visibility using IoT-internet of things. In *2019 IEEE 9th annual computing and communication workshop and conference (CCWC)* (pp. 0156-0162). IEEE.

Qader, G., Junaid, M., Abbas, Q., & Mubarik, M. S. (2022). Industry 4.0 enables supply chain resilience and supply chain performance. *Technological Forecasting and Social Change*, 185, 122026.

Rabbani, M. B. A., Musarat, M. A., Alaloul, W. S., Rabbani, M. S., Maqsoom, A., Ayub, S., & Altaf, M. (2021). A comparison between seasonal autoregressive integrated moving average (SARIMA) and exponential smoothing (ES) based on time series model for forecasting road accidents. *Arabian Journal for Science and Engineering*, 46(11), 11113–11138.

Rahman, T., Paul, S. K., Shukla, N., Agarwal, R., & Taghikhah, F. (2022). Supply chain resilience initiatives and strategies: A systematic review. *Computers & Industrial Engineering*, 170, 108317.

Raja, R., Mukherjee, I., Sarkar, B. K., & Ali, S. (2020). A Systematic Review of Healthcare Big Data. *Scientific Programming*, 2020(1), 5471849. DOI: 10.1155/2020/5471849

Raji, I. D., Gebru, T., Mitchell, M., Buolamwini, J., Lee, J., & Denton, E. (2020, February). Saving face: Investigating the ethical concerns of facial recognition auditing. In *Proceedings of the AAAI/ACM Conference on AI, Ethics, and Society* (pp. 145-151).

Rana, J., & Daultani, Y. (2023). Mapping the Role and Impact of Artificial Intelligence and Machine Learning Applications in Supply Chain Digital Transformation: A Bibliometric Analysis. *Operations Management Research*, 16(4), 1641–1666. DOI: 10.1007/s12063-022-00335-y

Rane, N. L., Desai, P., Rane, J., & Paramesha, M. (2024). Artificial intelligence, machine learning, and deep learning for sustainable and resilient supply chain and logistics management. In D. Patil (Ed), N. L. Rane (Ed), P. Desai (Ed), & J. Rane (Ed), *Trustworthy Artificial Intelligence in Industry and Society*. Deep Science Publishing. https://doi.org/DOI: 10.70593/978-81-981367-4-9_5

Ransbotham, S., Kiron, D., Gerbert, P., & Reeves, M. (2017). Reshaping business with artificial intelligence: Closing the gap between ambition and action. *MIT Sloan Management Review*, 59(1).

Rathore, B. (2017). Beyond Trends: Shaping the Future of Fashion Marketing with AI, Sustainability and Machine Learning. *Eduzone: International Peer Reviewed/ Refereed Multidisciplinary Journal, 6*(2), 16-24.

Rathore, B. (2019). Fashion Sustainability in the AI Era: Opportunities and Challenges in Marketing. *Eduzone: International Peer Reviewed/Refereed Multidisciplinary Journal, 8*(2), 17-24.

Rathore, B. (2023). Digital Transformation 4.0: Integration of Artificial Intelligence & Metaverse in Marketing. *Eduzone: International Peer Reviewed/Refereed Multidisciplinary Journal, 12*(1), 42-48.

Rathore, B. (2023). Integration of Artificial Intelligence& It's Practices in Apparel Industry. *ugc approved research journals in india| UGC Newly Added Journals|(I-JNMS), 10*(1), 25-37.

Rathore, B. (2017). Exploring the Intersection of Fashion Marketing in the Metaverse: Leveraging Artificial Intelligence for Consumer Engagement and Brand Innovation. *International Journal of New Media Studies: International Peer Reviewed Scholarly Indexed Journal*, 4(2), 51–60. DOI: 10.58972/eiprmj.v4i2y17.108

Rathore, B. (2019). From Trendy to Green: Exploring AI's Role in Sustainable Fashion Marketing. *International Journal of New Media Studies: International Peer Reviewed Scholarly Indexed Journal*, 6(2), 12–22. DOI: 10.58972/eiprmj.v6i2y19.120

RATTI, C. (2019). An investigation on the adoption of blockchain technology in supply chain.

Raut, R. D., Mangla, S. K., Narwane, V. S., Gardas, B. B., Priyadarshinee, P., & Narkhede, B. E. (2019). Linking big data analytics and operational sustainability practices for sustainable business management. *Journal of Cleaner Production*, 224, 10–24. DOI: 10.1016/j.jclepro.2019.03.181

Recio-Román, A., Recio-Menéndez, M., & Román-González, M. V. (2024). The Future of Retail: Harnessing Generative AI for Disruptive Innovation and Sector Transformation. In *Reshaping Marketing Science in Wholesaling and Retailing* (pp. 309–333). IGI Global.

Rehmani, K., Naseem, A., Ahmad, Y., Mirza, M. Z., & Syed, T. H. (2021). Development of a hybrid framework for inventory leanness in Technical Services Organizations. *PLoS One*, 16(2), e0247144. PMID: 33606793

Rejeb, A., Rejeb, K., Simske, S., & Treiblmaier, H. (2021). Blockchain Technologies in Logistics and Supply Chain Management: A Bibliometric Review. *Logistics (Basel)*, 5(4), 4. Advance online publication. DOI: 10.3390/logistics5040072

Ren, S., Chan, H. L., & Siqin, T. (2020). Demand forecasting in retail operations for fashionable products: Methods, practices, and real case study. *Annals of Operations Research*, 291, 761–777.

Reuter, C., Foerstl, K. A. I., Hartmann, E. V. I., & Blome, C. (2010). Sustainable global supplier management: The role of dynamic capabilities in achieving competitive advantage. *The Journal of Supply Chain Management*, 46(2), 45–63.

Reyes, J., Mula, J., & Díaz-Madroñero, M. (2023). Development of a conceptual model for lean supply chain planning in industry 4.0: Multidimensional analysis for operations management. *Production Planning and Control*, 34(12), 1209–1224. DOI: 10.1080/09537287.2021.1993373

Rezaei, G., Hosseini, S. M. H., & Sana, S. S. (2022). Exploring the Relationship between Data Analytics Capability and Competitive Advantage: The Mediating Roles of Supply Chain Resilience and Organization Flexibility. *Sustainability*, 14(16), 10444.

Riahi, Y., Saikouk, T., Gunasekaran, A., & Badraoui, I. (2021). Artificial intelligence applications in supply chain: A descriptive bibliometric analysis and future research directions. *Expert Systems with Applications*, 173, 114702. DOI: 10.1016/j.eswa.2021.114702

Richey, R. G., Chowdhury, S., Davis-Sramek, B., Giannakis, M., & Dwivedi, Y. K. (2023). Artificial intelligence in logistics and supply chain management: A primer and roadmap for research. *Journal of Business Logistics*, 44(4), 532–549. DOI: 10.1111/jbl.12364

Robinson, C. H. (2023). *Put Spot Market Freight in Your Route Guide | C.H. Robinson*. https://www.chrobinson.com/en-us/resources/blog/why-you-should-put-spot-freight-in-your-route-guide/

Robinson, C. H. (2024). *New C.H. Robinson Technology Breaks a Decades-Old Barrier to Automation in the Logistics Industry*. https://investor.chrobinson.com/News-and-Events/Press-Releases/press-release-details/2024/New-C.H.-Robinson-Technology-Breaks-a-Decades-Old-Barrier-to-Automation-in-the-Logistics-Industry/default.aspx

Rodrigue, J.-P. (2020). *The Geography of Transport Systems* (5th ed.). Routledge., DOI: 10.4324/9780429346323

Rodrigues, D., & Pereira, R. (2023). How Can Artificial Intelligence Help Improve Fashion Sustainability? In *Digital Technologies and Transformation in Business, Industry and Organizations* (Vol. 2, pp. 43–61). Springer Nature Switzerland.

Roscoe, S., & Baker, P. (2013). Supply chain segmentation in the sporting goods industry. *International Journal of Logistics Research and Applications*, 17(2), 136–155.

Rossini, M., & Portioli, A. (2018). Supply chain planning: A quantitative comparison between Lean and Info-Sharing models. *Production & Manufacturing Research*, 6(1), 264–283. DOI: 10.1080/21693277.2018.1509744

Sabri, E. & Shaikh, S. (2010). *Lean & Agile Value Chain Management: A Guide to the Next Level of Improvement.* USA: J. ROSS PUBLISHING Greer, B. and Ford, M. (2009). Managing Change in Supply Chains: A process Comparison. *Journal of Business Logistics, Vol. 30, No. 2* Ramanan and Anil (2011).The Top Three Reasons Supply Chain Transformations Fail *WiproConsulting Services*

Sabri, E. (2012). "Enduring Transformation: Performance measurement and governance make the difference," retrieved from https://www.apics.org/apics-for -individuals/apics-magazine-home/magazine-detail-page/2012/10/04/enduring -transformation, *APICS Magazine*.

Sabri, E. (2012). Enduring Transformation. APICS magazine. September/October 2012, 45 – 47.

Sabri, E. (2019). Optimization of Supply Chain Management in Contemporary Organizations: Mastering Change Management for Successful Digital Supply Chain Transformation. USA: IGI Global, 85-106.

Sabri, E. H. (2023). *Digital Supply Chain, Disruptive Environments, and the Impact on Retailers: How to Master Change Management During the Supply Chain Digital Transformation Journey*. USA, IGI Global, 1-20.

Sabri, E. (2019). Transformation Framework for Supply Chain Segmentation in Digital Business. In *E. Sabri, Technology Optimization and Change Management for Successful Digital Supply Chains* (pp. 54–84). IGI Global.

Sabri, E. (2023). Digital Supply Chain, Disruptive Environments, and the Impact on Retailers. In *E. Sabri, How to Implement Supply Chain Digital Segmentation Successfully* (pp. 63–93). IGI Global.

Sabri, E., Gupta, A., & Beitler, M. (2006). *Purchase Order Management in B2B Environment: Best Practice & Technologies J.* ROSS PUBLISHING.

Sabri, E., & Shaikh, S. (2010). *Lean & Agile Value Chain Management (LAVCM): A Guide to the Next Level of Improvement. J.* Ross Publishing.

Sainani, K. L. (2013). Understanding Linear Regression. *PM & R*, 5(12), 1063–1068. DOI: 10.1016/j.pmrj.2013.10.002 PMID: 24140739

Sallam, K., Mohamed, M., & Mohamed, A. W. (2023). Internet of Things (IoT) in supply chain management: Challenges, opportunities, and best practices. *Sustainable Machine Intelligence Journal*, 2, 3–1.

Sánchez-Flores, R. B., Cruz-Sotelo, S. E., Ojeda-Benitez, S., & Ramírez-Barreto, M. E. (2020). Sustainable supply chain management—A literature review on emerging economies. *Sustainability*, 12(17), 6972.

Sanders, J. H., & Karr, T. (2015). Improving ED specimen TAT using Lean Six Sigma. *International Journal of Health Care Quality Assurance*, 28(5), 428–440. DOI: 10.1108/IJHCQA-10-2013-0117 PMID: 26020426

Sanders, N. R. (2016). How to use big data to drive your supply chain. *California Management Review*, 58(3), 26–48.

Sanders, N. R., Boone, T., Ganeshan, R., & Wood, J. D. (2019). Sustainable Supply Chains in the Age of AI and Digitization: Research Challenges and Opportunities. *Journal of Business Logistics*, 40(3), 229–240. DOI: 10.1111/jbl.12224

Saponaro, M., Le Gal, D., Gao, M., Guisiano, M., & Maniere, I. C. (2018, December). Challenges and opportunities of artificial intelligence in the fashion world. In *2018 international conference on intelligent and innovative computing applications (ICONIC)* (pp. 1-5). IEEE. DOI: 10.1109/ICONIC.2018.8601258

Sarker, I. H. (2021). Machine learning: Algorithms, real-world applications and research directions. *SN Computer Science*, 2(3), 160. PMID: 33778771

Sarkis, J. (2013). *Green supply chain management*. Momentum Press.

Sarkis, J., Cohen, M. J., Dewick, P., & Schröder, P. (2020). A brave new world: Lessons from the COVID-19 pandemic for transitioning to sustainable supply and production. *Resources, Conservation and Recycling*, 159, 104894. PMID: 32313383

Sarma, P. R. S., Kumar, A., Choudhary, N. A., & Mangla, S. K. (2023). Modelling resilient fashion retail supply chain strategies to mitigate the COVID-19 impact. *International Journal of Logistics Management*, 34(4), 1188–1218.

Saxena, D., & Cao, J. (2021). Generative adversarial networks (GANs) challenges, solutions, and future directions. *ACM Computing Surveys*, 54(3), 1–42.

Sayed, H. E., Gabbar, H. A., & Miyazaki, S. (2010). Design of demand forecasting expert system for dynamic supply chains. *Expert Systems: International Journal of Knowledge Engineering and Neural Networks*.

Schroeder, M., & Lodemann, S. (2021). A Systematic Investigation of the Integration of Machine Learning into Supply Chain Risk Management. *Logistics (Basel)*, 5(3), 62. DOI: 10.3390/logistics5030062

Schumacher, S., Bildstein, A., & Bauernhansl, T. (2020). The Impact of the Digital Transformation on Lean Production Systems. *Procedia CIRP*, 93, 783–788. DOI: 10.1016/J.PROCIR.2020.03.066

Segal, E. (2024). "Most Surveyed Companies Are Vulnerable To Another Supply Chain Crisis," Forbes, https://www.forbes.com/sites/edwardsegal/2024/01/28/most-surveyed-companies-are-vulnerable-to-another-supply-chain-crisis,

Serey, J., Alfaro, M., Fuertes, G., Vargas, M., Ternero, R., Duran, C., & Gutierrez, S. (2023). Framework for the Strategic Adoption of Industry 4.0: A Focus on Intelligent Systems. *Processes (Basel, Switzerland)*, 11(10), 2973.

Seuring, S., & Müller, M. (2008). From a literature review to a conceptual framework for sustainable supply chain management. *Journal of Cleaner Production*, 16(15), 1699–1710.

Sevda, S., & Chauhan, G. (Eds.). (2024). *Solid Waste Management*. CRC Press.

Seyedan, M., & Mafakheri, F. (2020). Predictive big data analytics for supply chain demand forecasting: Methods, applications, and research opportunities. *Journal of Big Data*, 7(1), 53. DOI: 10.1186/s40537-020-00329-2

Shahadat, M. H., Chowdhury, A. Y., Jahed, M. A., Nathan, R. J., & Fekete-Farkas, M. (2024). Innovativeness, visibility, and collaboration effect on supply chain performance: Moderating role of digital supply chain integration. *Cogent Business & Management*, 11(1), 2390168.

Shah, C. J., Sullivan, J. R., Gonyo, M. B., Wadhwa, A., & DuBois, M. S. (2013). Practice policy and quality initiatives: Using lean principles to improve screening mammography workflow. *Radiographics*, 33(5), 1505–1517. DOI: 10.1148/RG.335135017 PMID: 23813321

Shalev-Shwartz, S., & Zhang, T. (2016). Accelerated proximal stochastic dual coordinate ascent for regularized loss minimization. *Mathematical Programming*, 155(1–2), 105–145. DOI: 10.1007/s10107-014-0839-0

Shannon, R. P., Frndak, D., Grunden, N., Lloyd, J. C., Herbert, C., Patel, B., Cummins, D., Shannon, A. H., O'Neill, P. H., & Spear, S. J. (2006). Using real-time problem solving to eliminate central line infections. *Joint Commission Journal on Quality and Patient Safety*, 32(9), 479–487. DOI: 10.1016/S1553-7250(06)32063-6 PMID: 17987871

Sharma, P. (2016). Role of AI in Enhancing the Efficiency and Effectiveness of Shop and Delivery Propositions in Smart Cities.

Sharma, R., Kamble, S. S., Gunasekaran, A., Kumar, V., & Kumar, A. (2020). A systematic literature review on machine learning applications for sustainable agriculture supply chain performance. *Computers & Operations Research*, 119, 104926. DOI: 10.1016/j.cor.2020.104926

Sharma, R., Shishodia, A., Gunasekaran, A., Min, H., & Munim, Z. H. (2022). The role of artificial intelligence in supply chain management: Mapping the territory. *International Journal of Production Research*, 60(24), 7527–7550. DOI: 10.1080/00207543.2022.2029611

Sharma, S., Koehl, L., Bruniaux, P., Zeng, X., & Wang, Z. (2021). Development of an intelligent data-driven system to recommend personalized fashion design solutions. *Sensors (Basel)*, 21(12), 4239. DOI: 10.3390/s21124239 PMID: 34205598

Shaw, J., Rudzicz, F., Jamieson, T., & Goldfarb, A. (2019). Artificial Intelligence and the Implementation Challenge. *J Med Internet Res 2019;21(7):E13659*Https://Www.Jmir.Org/2019/7/E13659, *21*(7), e13659. https://doi.org/DOI: 10.2196/13659

Sheffi, Y. (2005). *The resilient enterprise: overcoming vulnerability for competitive advantage*. Pearson Education India.

Shen, B., Ding, X., Wang, Y., & Ren, S. (2019). RFID-embedded smart washing machine systems in the big data era: Value creation in fashion supply chain. *Fashion supply chain management in Asia: Concepts, models, and cases*, 99-113.

Shiyyab, F. S., Alzoubi, A. B., Obidat, Q. M., & Alshurafat, H. (2023). The impact of artificial intelligence disclosure on financial performance. *International Journal of Financial Studies*, 11(3), 115.

Siemens (2024). https://www.siemens.com/global/en/products/services/gbs/our-insights/newsroom/generative-ai.html

Sima, V., Gheorghe, I. G., Subic, J., & Nancu, D. (2020). Influences of the industry 4.0 revolution on the human capital development and consumer behavior: A systematic review. *Sustainability (Basel)*, 12(10), 4035. DOI: 10.3390/su12104035

Simchi-Levi, D., Kaminsky, P., & Simchi-Levi, E. (1999). *Designing and Managing the Supply Chain: Concepts, Strategies, and Cases w/CD-ROM Package* (Book plus CD-Rom edition). McGraw-Hill/Irwin.

Singh, P. K. (2023). Digital Transformation in Supply Chain Management: Artificial Intelligence (AI) and Machine Learning (ML) as Catalysts for Value Creation. *International Journal of Supply Chain Management*, 12(6), 57–63. DOI: 10.59160/ijscm.v12i6.6216

Singh, R. K., Mishra, R., Gupta, S., & Mukherjee, A. A. (2023). Blockchain applications for secured and resilient supply chains: A systematic literature review and future research agenda. *Computers & Industrial Engineering*, 175, 108854.

Singh, S., Madaan, G., Swapna, H. R., Kaur, P., Pandey, D., & Dadheech, P. (2024). The Role of Artificial Intelligence in Supply Chain Management. In *Utilization of AI Technology in Supply Chain Management* (pp. 26–41). IGI Global.

Sobb, T., Turnbull, B., & Moustafa, N. (2020). Supply chain 4.0: A survey of cyber security challenges, solutions and future directions. *Electronics (Basel)*, 9(11), 1864.

Soni, N., Sharma, E. K., Singh, N., & Kapoor, A. (2019). Impact of artificial intelligence on businesses: from research, innovation, market deployment to future shifts in business models. *arXiv preprint arXiv:1905.02092*.

Soni, U., Jain, V., & Kumar, S. (2014). Measuring supply chain resilience using a deterministic modeling approach. *Computers & Industrial Engineering*, 74, 11–25.

Sotarauta, M. (2019). *Leadership for urban and regional innovation*. Sage.

Srivastava, S. K. (2007). Green supply-chain management: A state-of-the-art literature review. *International Journal of Management Reviews*, 9(1), 53–80.

Stahl, B. C. (2021). *Artificial intelligence for a better future: an ecosystem perspective on the ethics of AI and emerging digital technologies*. Springer Nature.

Stefenon, S. F., Seman, L. O., Mariani, V. C., & Coelho, L. D. S. (2023). Aggregating prophet and seasonal trend decomposition for time series forecasting of Italian electricity spot prices. *Energies*, 16(3), 1371.

Steinberg, G., ... (2024). "How will GenAI prompt a step change toward autonomous supply chains?" EY, www.ey.com/en_gl/insights/consulting/how-will-genai-prompt-a-step-change-toward-autonomous-supply-chains.

Stiglitz, J. (2017). *Globalization and its Discontents Revisited: Anti-Globalization in the Era of Trump*. Penguin.

Stilinski, D., Frank, L., & Doris, L. (2023). Transformative Role of Artificial Intelligence in Supply Chain Management.1), 67-84.

Stone, K. B. (2012). Four decades of lean: A systematic literature review. *International Journal of Lean Six Sigma*, 3(2), 112–132. DOI: 10.1108/20401461211243702/FULL/PDF

Stöppler, D. (2024). "For increased usability and efficiency: myDHLi meets GenAI," *DHL.com*, www.group.dhl.com/en/media-relations/press-releases/2024/for-increased-usability-and-efficiency-mydhli-meets-genai.html.

Subhadra, P. S., Kalaivani, A., Markan, R., Kumar, R., Natarajan, S., & Rajalakshmi, M. (2024). Rise of Artificial Intelligence in Business and Industry. *Journal of Informatics Education and Research*, 4(2).

Suherlan, S., & Okombo, M. O. (2023). Technological innovation in marketing and its effect on consumer behaviour. [TACIT]. *Technology and Society Perspectives*, 1(2), 94–103.

Sullivan, Y., & Wamba, S. (2022). *Artificial Intelligence, Firm Resilience to Supply Chain Disruptions, and Firm Performance. Hawaii International Conference on System Sciences*. https://doi.org/DOI: 10.24251/HICSS.2022.719

Sumarliah, E., Ahmad, M. N., Usmanova, K., Mousa, K., & Asad, M. (2021). Reflecting Coronavirus outbreak in the risk management of the apparel supply chain. *IEEE Engineering Management Review*, 50(1), 31–42.

Sundaram, R., Sharma, D. R., & Shakya, D. A. (2020). Digital transformation of business models: A systematic review of impact on revenue and supply chain. *International Journal of Management*, 11(5).

Susitha, E. (2022). Strategic Choices of Digital Apparel Supply Chains to Achieve Competitive Advantage: A Literature Review.

Syntetos, A. A., Babai, Z., Boylan, J. E., Kolassa, S., & Nikolopoulos, K. (2016). Supply chain forecasting: Theory, practice, their gap and the future. *European Journal of Operational Research*, 252(1), 1–26.

Tadayonrad, Y., & Ndiaye, A. B. (2023). A new key performance indicator model for demand forecasting in inventory management considering supply chain reliability and seasonality. *Supply Chain Analytics*, 3, 100026.

Tambe, P., Cappelli, P., & Yakubovich, V. (2019). Artificial intelligence in human resources management: Challenges and a path forward. *California Management Review*, 61(4), 15–42.

Tao, F., Qi, Q., Liu, A., & Kusiak, A. (2018). Data-driven smart manufacturing. *Journal of Manufacturing Systems*, 48, 157–169.

Tarigan, Z. J. H., Siagian, H., & Jie, F. (2021). Impact of internal integration, supply chain partnership, supply chain agility, and supply chain resilience on sustainable advantage. *Sustainability*, 13(10), 5460.

Taye, M. M. (2023). Understanding of machine learning with deep learning: Architectures, workflow, applications and future directions. *Computers*, 12(5), 91.

Tett, G. (2023). "How rising conflict is reshuffling global supply chains," Financial Times, https://www.ft.com/content/98766d3f-65ad-41c0-84cc-9b6e2757a17c,

Thakkar, J., Kanda, A., & Deshmukh, S. (2009). Supply chain performance measurement framework for small and medium scale enterprises. *Benchmarking*, 16(5), 702–723. DOI: 10.1108/14635770910987878

Thyattchristopher (2024). https://digitaltechnologysolutions.tech.blog/2024/03/16.

Tiedemann, F. (2020). Demand-driven supply chain operations management strategies – a literature review and conceptual model. *Production & Manufacturing Research*, 8(1), 427–485. DOI: 10.1080/21693277.2020.1856012

Tjahjono, B., Esplugues, C., Ares, E., & Pelaez, G. (2017). What does industry 4.0 mean to supply chain? *Procedia Manufacturing*, 13, 1175–1182.

Toorajipour, R., Sohrabpour, V., Nazarpour, A., Oghazi, P., & Fischl, M. (2021). Artificial intelligence in supply chain management: A systematic literature review. *Journal of Business Research*, 122, 502–517. DOI: 10.1016/J.JBUSRES.2020.09.009

Touboulic, A., & Walker, H. (2015). Theories in sustainable supply chain management: A structured literature review. *International Journal of Physical Distribution & Logistics Management*, 45(1/2), 16–42.

Treiblmaier, H., & Rejeb, A. (2023). Exploring blockchain for disaster prevention and relief: A comprehensive framework based on industry case studies. *Journal of Business Logistics*, 44(4), 550–582. DOI: 10.1111/jbl.12345

Trihastuti, D., Gunawan, I., Sianto, M. E., & Sagitha, B. R. R. (2024, September). Building resilience of the green product supply chain in the apparel industry. []. *IOP Publishing*.]. *IOP Conference Series. Earth and Environmental Science*, 1388(1), 012041.

Tripathi, S., & Gupta, M. (2020). Transforming towards a smarter supply chain. *International Journal of Logistics Systems and Management*, 36(3), 319–342. DOI: 10.1504/IJLSM.2020.108694

Tritos, L., Premaratne, S., & Dotun, A. (2014). Prioritizing lean supply chain management initiatives in healthcare service operations: A Fuzzy-AHP approach. *IEEE International Conference on Industrial Engineering and Engineering Management*, 236–242. https://doi.org/DOI: 10.1109/IEEM.2013.6962410

Tsang, Y. P., Choy, K. L., Wu, C. H., Ho, G. T. S., & Lam, H. Y. (2019). Blockchain-driven IoT for food traceability with an integrated consensus mechanism. *IEEE Access : Practical Innovations, Open Solutions*, 7, 129000–129017.

Tsolakis, N., Schumacher, R., Dora, M., & Kumar, M. (2023). Artificial intelligence and blockchain implementation in supply chains: A pathway to sustainability and data monetisation? *Annals of Operations Research*, 327(1), 157–210. DOI: 10.1007/s10479-022-04785-2 PMID: 35755830

Tuli, F. A., Mohammed, M. A., & Sachani, D. K. (2024). Supply Chain Optimization: Machine Learning Applications in Inventory Management for E-Commerce. *Global Disclosure of Economics and Business*, 13(1), 1–20.

Tuncali Yaman, T. U. T. K. U. (2022). The role of big data in logistics: Current dynamics and future prospects.

Ugajin, A. (2023). Automation in Hospitals and Health Care. *Springer Handbooks*, (Part F674), 1209–1233. DOI: 10.1007/978-3-030-96729-1_56

Van Hoek, R., DeWitt, M., Lacity, M., & Johnson, T. (2022). "How Walmart Automated Supplier Negotiations," *HBR.org*, www.hbr.org/2022/11/how-walmart-automated-supplier-negotiations.

van Looy, A. (2014). *Business Process Maturity: A Comparative Study on a Sample of Business Process Maturity Models*. Spinger. DOI: 10.1007/978-3-319-04202-2

Vandana, M., Naveena, M., Ellaturu, N., Kumari, T. L., Bambuwala, S., & Rajalakshmi, M. Ai-Driven Solutions for Supply Chain Management. Journal of Informatics Education and Research, 4(2), 1526-4726.

Vanpoucke, E., & Ellis, S. C. (2020). Building supply-side resilience–a behavioural view. *International Journal of Operations & Production Management*, 40(1), 11–33.

Veluru, C. S. (2024). Investigating the Impact of Artificial Intelligence and Generative AI in E-Commerce and Supply Chain: A Comprehensive. *European Journal of Advances in Engineering and Technology*, 11(4), 131–143.

Venkat Narayana Rao, T., & Yellu, K. R. (2016). Automatic Safety Home Bell System with Message Enabled Features, International Journal of Science. *Engineering and Computer Technology*, 6, 10.

Vick, G. What is Reverse Logistics? URL: http://www. reverselogisticstrends. com/reverse-logistics. php (дата обращения: 20.11. 2015).

Vishwasrao, R. (2023). *Digital Supply Chain, Disruptive Environments, and the Impact on Retailers: Supply Chain Performance Measurement and Organizational Alignment in an Uncertain World:* USA, IGI Global, 36-62.

Wagner, S. M., & Bode, C. (2008). An empirical examination of supply chain performance along several dimensions of risk. *Journal of Business Logistics*, 29(1), 307–325.

Wamba, S. F., Akter, S., Edwards, A., Chopin, G., & Gnanzou, D. (2015). How 'big data'can make big impact: Findings from a systematic review and a longitudinal case study. *International Journal of Production Economics*, 165, 234–246.

Wamba, S. F., Gunasekaran, A., Akter, S., Ren, S. J. F., Dubey, R., & Childe, S. J. (2017). Big data analytics and firm performance: Effects of dynamic capabilities. *Journal of Business Research*, 70, 356–365.

Wang, G., Gunasekaran, A., Ngai, E. W., & Papadopoulos, T. (2016). Big data analytics in logistics and supply chain management: Certain investigations for research and applications. *International Journal of Production Economics*, 176, 98–110.

Wang, H., Long, Z., Chen, J., Guo, Y., & Wang, A. (2023). Collaborative decision-making in supply chain management: A review and bibliometric analysis. *Cogent Engineering*, 10(1), 2196823.

Wang, L., & Jones, R. (2019). Big Data, Cybersecurity, and Challenges in Healthcare. *Conference Proceedings - IEEE SOUTHEASTCON, 2019-April*. https://doi .org/DOI: 10.1109/SOUTHEASTCON42311.2019.9020632

Wang, X., Hyndman, R. J., Li, F., & Kang, Y. (2023). Forecast combinations: An over 50-year review. *International Journal of Forecasting*, 39(4), 1518–1547.

Watanabe, Y., Suda, Y., & Takeno, J. (2020). A Robot Science Approach to Simulating the Pathogenesis of Dissociative Identity Disorder. *Procedia Computer Science*, 169, 46–50.

Weber, F. D., & Schütte, R. (2019). State-of-the-art and adoption of artificial intelligence in retailing. *Digital Policy. Regulation & Governance*, 21(3), 264–279. DOI: 10.1108/DPRG-09-2018-0050

Whittlestone, J., Nyrup, R., Alexandrova, A., & Cave, S. (2019, January). The role and limits of principles in AI ethics: Towards a focus on tensions. In *Proceedings of the 2019 AAAI/ACM Conference on AI, Ethics, and Society* (pp. 195-200).

Wong, C., Guo, Z. X., & Leung, S. Y. S. (2013). *Optimizing decision making in the apparel supply chain using artificial intelligence (AI): from production to retail.* Elsevier.

World Economic Forum. (2024, January 8). *How AI and new technologies are unlocking industry net zero*. World Economic Forum. https://www.weforum.org/agenda/2024/01/technology-ai-advancements-inclusive-future-manufacturing/

World Health Organization. (2020). *Pneumonia of unknown cause – China*. https://www.who.int/emergencies/disease-outbreak-news/item/2020-DON229

Wu, D. C., Song, H., & Shen, S. (2017). New developments in tourism and hotel demand modeling and forecasting. *International Journal of Contemporary Hospitality Management*, 29(1), 507–529. DOI: 10.1108/IJCHM-05-2015-0249

Xu, L., Mak, S., Proselkov, Y., & Brintrup, A. (2024). Towards Autonomous Supply Chains: Definition, Characteristics, Conceptual Framework, and Autonomy Levels. *Journal of Industrial Information Integration*.

Xu, M. (2024). Sales Prediction Based on Lasso Regression. *Highlights in Science. Engineering and Technology*, 88, 343–349. DOI: 10.54097/p9hyrk70

Yaduvanshi, D., & Sharma, A. (2017). Lean Six Sigma in Health Operations. Http://Dx.Doi.Org/10.1177/0972063417699665*, 19*(2), 203–213. https://doi.org/DOI: 10.1177/0972063417699665

Yandrapalli, V. (2023). Revolutionizing supply chains using power of generative ai. *International Journal of Research Publication and Reviews*, 4(12), 1556–1562.

Yang, C., Zhu, Y., & Chen, Y. (2021). A review of human–machine cooperation in the robotics domain. *IEEE Transactions on Human-Machine Systems*, 52(1), 12–25.

Yang, H., Kumara, S., Bukkapatnam, S. T., & Tsung, F. (2019). The internet of things for smart manufacturing: A review. *IISE Transactions*, 51(11), 1190–1216.

Yang, J., Wang, Y., Miao, Q., Wang, F. Y., Zhao, A., Deng, J. L., & Liubo, V. L. (2023). Steps towards Industry 5.0 [parallel industries with cyber-physical-social intelligence]. *Building (London)*, •••, 6S.

Yani, L. P. E., & Aamer, A. (2023). Demand forecasting accuracy in the pharmaceutical supply chain: A machine learning approach. *International Journal of Pharmaceutical and Healthcare Marketing*, 17(1), 1–23. DOI: 10.1108/IJPHM-05-2021-0056

Yao, X., Zhou, J., Lin, Y., Li, Y., Yu, H., & Liu, Y. (2019). Smart manufacturing based on cyber-physical systems and beyond. *Journal of Intelligent Manufacturing*, 30, 2805–2817.

Younis, H., Sundarakani, B., & Alsharairi, M. (2022). Applications of artificial intelligence and machine learning within supply chains:systematic review and future research directions. *Journal of Modelling in Management*, 17(3), 916–940. DOI: 10.1108/JM2-12-2020-0322

Yu, T., Demirli, K., & Bhuiyan, N. (2015). A general framework for lean transformation of hospitals. *IEOM 2015 - 5th International Conference on Industrial Engineering and Operations Management, Proceeding*. https://doi.org/DOI: 10.1109/IEOM.2015.7093901

Yücenur, G. N., & Ipekçi, A. (2021). SWARA/WASPAS methods for a marine current energy plant location selection problem. *Renewable Energy*, 163, 1287–1298. DOI: 10.1016/J.RENENE.2020.08.131

Yu, W., Chavez, R., Jacobs, M. A., & Feng, M. (2018). Data-driven supply chain capabilities and performance: A resource-based view. *Transportation Research Part E, Logistics and Transportation Review*, 114, 371–385.

Zage, D., Glass, K., & Colbaugh, R. (2013, June). Improving supply chain security using big data. In *2013 IEEE International Conference on Intelligence and Security Informatics* (pp. 254-259). IEEE.

Zakhidov, G. (2024). Economic indicators: Tools for analyzing market trends and predicting future performance. *International Multidisciplinary Journal of Universal Scientific Prospectives*, 2(3), 23–29.

Zarsky, T. Z. (2016). Incompatible: The GDPR in the age of big data. *Seton Hall Law Review*, 47, 995.

Zellner, M., Abbas, A. E., Budescu, D. V., & Galstyan, A. (2021). A survey of human judgement and quantitative forecasting methods. *Royal Society Open Science*, 8(2), 201187. PMID: 33972849

Zemplényi, A., Tachkov, K., Balkanyi, L., Németh, B., Petykó, Z. I., Petrova, G., Czech, M., Dawoud, D., Goettsch, W., Gutierrez Ibarluzea, I., Hren, R., Knies, S., Lorenzovici, L., Maravic, Z., Piniazhko, O., Savova, A., Manova, M., Tesar, T., Zerovnik, S., & Kaló, Z. (2023). Recommendations to overcome barriers to the use of artificial intelligence-driven evidence in health technology assessment. *Frontiers in Public Health*, 11. Advance online publication. DOI: 10.3389/fpubh.2023.1088121 PMID: 37181704

Zhang, B., Zhu, J., & Su, H. (2023). Toward the third generation artificial intelligence. *Science China. Information Sciences*, 66(2), 121101.

Zhang, W., & Li, X. (2024). A data-driven combined prediction method for the demand for intensive care unit healthcare resources in public health emergencies. *BMC Health Services Research*, 24(1), 477. DOI: 10.1186/s12913-024-10955-8 PMID: 38632553

Zhang, Y., Ren, S., Liu, Y., & Si, S. (2017). A big data analytics architecture for cleaner manufacturing and maintenance processes of complex products. *Journal of Cleaner Production*, 142, 626–641.

Zhao, Y., Zhu, Z., Chen, B., Qiu, S., Huang, J., Lu, X., & Wang, F. Y. (2023). Towards parallel intelligence: An interdisciplinary solution for complex systems. *The Innovation*.

Zhou, H., Jin, Y., Chen, G., Jin, X., Chen, J., & Wang, J. (2024). Predictive modeling of lower extreme deep vein thrombosis following radical gastrectomy for gastric cancer: Based on multiple machine learning methods. *Scientific Reports*, 14(1), 15711. DOI: 10.1038/s41598-024-66754-y PMID: 38977780

Zhou, K., Liu, T., & Zhou, L. (2021). Human-machine collaboration in the digital workplace: A human factors and ergonomics perspective. *Applied Ergonomics*, 94, 103400.

Zhou, Y., Wang, L., Zhong, R., & Tan, Y. (2018). A Markov Chain Based Demand Prediction Model for Stations in Bike Sharing Systems. *Mathematical Problems in Engineering*, 2018, 1–8. DOI: 10.1155/2018/8028714

Zhu, Q., & Sarkis, J. (2004). Relationships between operational practices and performance among early adopters of green supply chain management practices in Chinese manufacturing enterprises. *Journal of Operations Management*, 22(3), 265–289.

Zhu, Q., Sarkis, J., & Lai, K. H. (2013). Institutional-based antecedents and performance outcomes of internal and external green supply chain management practices. *Journal of Purchasing and Supply Management*, 19(2), 106–117.

Zou, J., & Schiebinger, L. (2018). AI can be sexist and racist—it's time to make it fair.

About the Contributors

Ehap Sabri is the supply chain planning practice leader, business professor, and author with 25+ years of industry experience sought after for his expertise in strategy development and supply chain management. Dr. Sabri played a variety of advisory roles and provided management consulting services for several companies across different industries to develop and implement best practice strategies and processes, thereby deriving value and significant cost reductions. Ehap provides subject matter expertise for executives & managers seeking strategic approaches for success in end-to-end process transformation, digital technology enablement, change management, education, organizational structure, and performance measurement. Dr. Ehap Sabri has a doctorate in Industrial Engineering from the University of Cincinnati in Ohio. He is also a Certified Fellow in Production and Inventory Management (CFPIM) by APICS and has Lean Six Sigma Master Black Belt in process improvement. He is a professor at the University of Texas at Dallas for the MBA Programs and has published 5 books in supply chain management. He also serves as the board president for non-profit public charter school. He currently resides in Irving, TX with his wife and two daughters.

***

Amir Ahmad Dar is the Faculty in the Department of Mathematics at Lovely Professional University Punjab. The area of interest: Financial mathematics, financial economics, statistics and business mathematics.

Irem Duzdar received her M.Sc. degree in Industrial Engineering from Istanbul Commerce University in 2006 and her Ph.D. degree in Industrial Engineering from Marmara University in 2015. She worked as a young researcher under the 6th Framework Programme of the European Union at Istanbul Commerce University. She then served as a lecturer in the Industrial Engineering departments of various foundation universities in Istanbul for 7 years. Since 2015, she has been a faculty member in the Department of Industrial Engineering at Düzce University. In 2023, she was awarded the title of Associate Professor in the field of Quantitative Decision Methods by the Interuniversity Council. Her primary research areas include efficiency in industrial applications and energy, quality improvement, data mining, and decision-making methods.

Balaji Gopalan is an Assistant Professor working with the Department of Decision Sciences at CMS B School, Bangalore (India). His area of specialization includes production and operations management, logistics and supply chain management and value co-creation.

Varun Gupta is an associate professor of logistics and analytics in the management department at the Mike Cottrell College of Business, the University of North Georgia. He currently directs the logistics lab and the logistics and supply chain curriculum. He has over 10 years of experience working on academic-industry partnership projects in analytics, logistics, and supply chain management. His research on supply chain risk management and pricing has been published in top journals in the field of operations and supply chain management. He has a Ph.D. in Operations Management, an M.S. in Supply Chain Management, and an MBA from the University of Texas at Dallas. His hometown is New Delhi, India

Fouad Jawab is a professor at the Higher School of Technology of the Sidi Mohamed Ben Abdellah University in Fez, Morocco. He is responsible for the research team "Industrial Management and Logistics" (MILOG), vice-director of the "Industrial Technologies and Services" (IST) laboratory and former director of the laboratory "International Management, Decision Techniques and Logistics" (MIDLOG). He has directed the Department of Science and Management Techniques (STG) as well as the University Diploma of Technology (DUT) "Logistics and Transport Management (GLT)" and currently directs the Professional License "LOGISTICS.

Busra Kesici She completed his undergraduate education at Çankaya University, Department of Industrial Engineering as an honor student. She received her master's and doctorate degrees from Düzce University, Institute of Social Sciences, Department of Business Administration. Dr. Kesici worked as a lecturer at Düzce University Vocational School of Social Sciences, Department of Management and Organization between 2018 - 2023. As of 2023, he has been working at Düzce University, Faculty of Engineering, Department of Industrial Engineering. After completing his undergraduate education, he worked as a quality system manager in an international automotive supply industry company for five years. His main research interests are production management, quality management and supply chain management.

Kshitij Mathur is a Senior Manager based in the UK, leads Data Science portfolio for Supply Chain at a Fortune 500 CPG organisation. He has over 17 years of Supply Chain industry wide experience with blend in Data Science/Artificial Intelligence, spread over CPG/Retail/Manufacturing/Semi-Conductor/Hi-Tech/ Pharma & Healthcare. He has rich experience in Digital Transformation, Supply Chain Strategy & Execution. He is alma mater from Indian Institute of Science, Bangalore; Indian Institute of Management, Bangalore; Indian Statistical Institute, Bangalore.

Kamalendu Pal is associated with the Department of Computer Science, School of Science and Technology at City, University of London. He has a diverse academic background, having received a BSc (Hons) degree in Physics from Calcutta University, India, followed by a Postgraduate Diploma in Computer Science from Pune, India. He has also worked as a research assistant for the government of India's two research and development organizations under the Council of Scientific and Industrial Research (CSIR). Later, Kamalendu graduated with his MSc in Software Systems Technology from the University of Sheffield, a Postgraduate Diploma in Artificial Intelligence from Kingston University, an MPhil in Computer Science from University College London, an MBA from the University of Hull, and a diploma in Higher Education teaching practice from City, University of London, United Kingdom. Kamalendu is an accomplished researcher, having published over a hundred-twenty international research articles (including book chapters) in the scientific community. His research papers have been published in prestigious journals such as the ACM SIGMIS Database, Expert Systems with Applications, Decision Support Systems, and international conferences. His research interests include various fields of computer science - such as knowledge-based systems, decision support systems, teaching and learning practices, blockchain technology, software engineering, service-oriented computing, sensor network simulation, and supply chain management. Kamalendu is also on the editorial board of an international computer science journal. He is a member of the British Computer Society, the Institution of Engineering and Technology, and the IEEE Computer Society.

Yogananthan S is an Assistant Professor working with the Department of Decision Sciences at CMS Business School, Bangalore (India). His areas of specialization include production and operations management, logistics and supply chain management, Sustainability, and value co-creation.

Ravishankar S Ulle is an Assistant Professor working with the Department of Decision Sciences at CMS Business School, Bangalore (India). His areas of specialization include production and operations management, logistics and supply chain management, Sustainability, and value co-creation.

Pushpender Sarao is a Professor in School of Computer Science & Engineering, Lovely Professional University, Phagwara, Punjab, India. He is BE, M.Tech, Ph.D in Computer Science and Engineering. He is author of five books in computer science, wireless networks. He is a member of IEEE, ACM, ICSES, RES, and IAENG, and life member of ISTE, CSI and IEI. He got published more than 82 research papers in national and international reputed journals. Also he shared his research experience in more than 24 national and international conferences. He attended several FDP and seminars/workshops in engineering institutions and state universities. He is member of editorial board for 25 national and international journals. His main research work focuses on routing protocols in wireless mesh networks, mobile ad-hoc network. He has 14 years of teaching experience and 10 years of industrial experience.

Salim Shaikh (CPIM, CSCP) is Corporate Vice President at Blue Yonder and leads the Global Industry Strategy for Automotive and Aerospace & Defense. With over 27 years of experience in Presales Consulting, Services Consulting, Education Services, Solutions Strategy, and Industry Strategy, Salim has been instrumental in driving supply chain innovation and delivering business value to customers across industry verticals. Before joining Blue Yonder, he worked in the automotive industry and is recognized as a thought leader, speaker, and author. He has published over thirty works, including co-authoring four books on supply chain digital transformations, and was named a "Pro to Know" by Supply & Demand Chain Executive magazine in 2016. Salim holds an M.S. in Industrial Engineering from Purdue University and an MBA from the University of Texas at Dallas. He resides in Dallas with his wife and three children and enjoys yoga, cricket, and tennis in his free time.

Shruti is working as an assistant professor in lovely professional university. My research areas are network security and deep learning. I am pursuing Ph.d from NIT jalandhar.

Bhupinder Singh working as Professor at Sharda University, India. Also, Honorary Professor in University of South Wales UK and Santo Tomas University Tunja, Colombia. His areas of publications as Smart Healthcare, Medicines, fuzzy logics, artificial intelligence, robotics, machine learning, deep learning, federated learning, IoT, PV Glasses, metaverse and many more. He has 3 books, 139 paper publications, 163 paper presentations in international/national conferences and seminars, participated in more than 40 workshops/FDP's/QIP's, 25 courses from international universities of repute, organized more than 59 events with international and national academicians and industry people's, editor-in-chief and co-editor in journals, developed new courses. He has given talks at international universities, resource person in international conferences such as in Nanyang Technological University Singapore, Tashkent State University of Law Uzbekistan; KIMEP University Kazakhstan, All'ah meh Tabatabi University Iran, the Iranian Association of International Criminal law, Iran and Hague Center for International Law and Investment, The Netherlands, Northumbria University Newcastle UK,

Satyam Sinha is a seasoned Supply Chain professional with a short entrepreneurial stint in the recruitment industry. He has over 17 years of SCM experience in consulting, solution implementation and enhancement for key SCM processes across different geographies and industries. He was involved in end-to-end implementation of Blue Yonder (JDA/i2) solution for global customers. He is experienced in leading Digital Transformation initiatives and setting up Supply Chain Capability centers in large organizations. He is also an advisor in emerging startups. He has published a book on the experience of his startup failure. The name of the book is My First Attempt to Failure and it is available on Amazon.

K. Vignesh graduated in the 1st year of BTech from SNIST Hyderabad. I am enthusiastic about researching, especially about AI.

Index

A

B

C

D

T

U

V

W

www.ingramcontent.com/pod-product-compliance
Lightning Source LLC
LaVergne TN
LVHW080354011026
849161LV00009B/2305
9798369344330